THE POPULATION
OF THE SOVIET UNION:
History and Prospects

By Frank Lorimer

LEAGUE OF NATIONS, GENEVA, 1946

Series of League of Nations Publications

II. ECONOMIC AND FINANCIAL
1946. II. A. 3.

PRINTED IN THE UNITED STATES OF AMERICA
BY PRINCETON UNIVERSITY PRESS, PRINCETON, N.J.
7/46/3500

CONTENTS

CONTENTS

TABLES

[v]

CONTENTS

[vii]

CONTENTS

CONTENTS
FIGURES

[ix]

PLATES

PREFACE

THIS volume by Dr. Frank Lorimer on *The Population of the Soviet Union* constitutes one of a series of demographic studies which Princeton University's Office of Population Research, under the direction of Professor Frank W. Notestein, is preparing for the League of Nations. The other volumes in this series are: *The Future Population of Europe and the Soviet Union,* which was published in 1944, *The Economic Demography of Eastern and Southern Europe,* published in 1945, and *Europe's Population: The Interwar Years,* the manuscript of which is at the moment of writing nearly completed.

Dr. Frank Lorimer gives us a picture in this volume of much more than the demographic characteristics of the U.S.S.R. at the present day, or before the outbreak of what we can now fortunately call the late war. He is concerned at once with the dynamics of population growth and with the ethnic and economic background and economic evolution of the vast area with which he deals. Thus, in the first two chapters and a part of the third, he traces the growth of the Russian population from the early eighteenth to the end of the nineteenth century—the rise of the Russian nation and the economic structure of the Russian Empire. In later chapters he deals with the ethnic composition of the Soviet population, with the great economic and social changes which have taken place under the Soviets, with the trends of the Soviet population, especially during the period 1926 to 1939, and, in so far as the information permits, with the changes caused by the recent years of warfare. As he suggests in his Preface, the census of 1926 forms, as it were, the pivot of his whole analysis. That census provides the only comprehensive account of the people of the Soviet Union, because publication of the full returns from the census of 1939 was prevented by the war. Furthermore, the position in time of that census between the only two other complete enumerations in Russia makes it possible to analyze population changes during the preceding and succeeding intervals, 1897-1926, and 1926-1939.

In handling the material available to him, Dr. Lorimer has shown throughout a rare combination of ingenuity, judgment and care. The publication of his analysis and description, as a valuable contribution to the very important subject with which he deals, should not, however, be taken to identify the League of Nations with all the views contained in it.

As Dr. Lorimer mentions in his Preface, the United States Department of State has been good enough to allow us to reproduce maps planned in its Office of Geography and Cartography.

Our thanks are thus due to the United States Department of State, to the President of Princeton University for the arrangement under which this volume was published, to the Director of the Office of Population Research, and to Dr. Frank Lorimer himself, the author of this volume.

A. LOVEDAY
Director of the Economic, Financial
and Transit Department

League of Nations
September 1945

AUTHOR'S PREFACE

THE student of the population of the Union of Soviet Socialist Republics has at his disposal a large body of demographic and related material, but on many critical points material is wholly lacking or fragmentary. The First All-Union Census, December 17, 1926, provided one of the most complete accounts ever presented of the population of any country. This gives a substantial basis for the study of later trends. The summary data from the Census of January 17, 1939, provide a second reliable bench mark, but the publication of the complete returns from this census was interrupted by war. Fairly complete vital statistics are available for the years immediately preceding and following the 1926 census. However, the publication of vital statistics was discontinued shortly thereafter, except for summary or selected data for certain years. The author has therefore been forced to resort to devious and often doubtful interpolations and inferences in treating population changes in the years intervening between 1926 and 1939, and in estimating recent trends.

The study of the population of the Russian plain in ancient times and the history of population trends in the Russian Empire provide an important background for the investigation of population changes in the Soviet Union. There is an extensive literature on this subject, but a paucity of objective, comprehensive data. Only one complete census was ever taken in the Russian Empire, in 1897. Vital statistics and migration data are wholly lacking or without value prior to the middle of the nineteenth century, and they never attained a high degree of accuracy. As one recedes in time from 1897, the earlier material becomes extremely sketchy. Again, between 1897 and 1926, the orderly sequence of population changes, as well as the collection and publication of statistics, was interrupted by war and revolution. Information on economic and social conditions in both the Imperial and Soviet periods, required for the interpretation of population changes, is abundant but at many points incomplete or ambiguous.

The major characteristics and trends of the Soviet population, nevertheless, emerge with considerable clarity from various items of information considered in their mutual relations. The broad outlines of the account have greater validity than many of its constituent items.

It may be hoped that the victory of the Soviet Union and its allies in the Second World War and the new international relations established by the United Nations will make possible more complete presentation of demographic and related data on the Soviet Union. In that case, errors that undoubtedly infect the present account can be corrected and the facts can be set in more perfect perspective. There is also sound basis for the expectation that in coming decades the development of the Soviet population will follow lines of more regular pattern and sequence than during the last few decades, thus making possible more accurate analysis of trends and prospects. In the meantime, the results of this investigation are presented as an imperfect account of population trends that have large significance for the whole world.

———

This is one of a series of studies undertaken for the Economic, Financial and Transit Department of the League of Nations by the Office of Population Research, Princeton University, under the direction of Professor Frank W. Notestein. The counsel of Professor Notestein and his associates has afforded constant stimulus and encouragement. Specific contributions by various members of the Princeton staff are cited in the text. The text was checked and edited with extraordinary care and skill by Dr. Louise Kennedy Kiser. The graphs were prepared by Daphne Notestein.

The author is deeply indebted to his colleague, Dr. Myron Kantorovitz Gordon. The undertaking required the collaboration of a person with statistical experience and with high standards of scholarship who was also familiar with the Russian language. The author was peculiarly fortunate in obtaining the aid of a friend with these particular qualifications. Among other services, Dr. Gordon accepted primary responsibility for the preparation of the Bibliography. Valuable counsel and aid were received from various specialists on Russian and Soviet affairs, especially from Dr. Sergius Yakobson, Research Fellow of the Library of Congress. The work was also facilitated by the cooperation of Mr. N. R. Rodionoff of the Slavic Division of the Library of Congress. Mrs. Helen Erskine and Mrs. Rose Ettinger contributed much to the progress of the research, and Miss Dorothy Whitfield to the final preparation of the manuscript.

The maps were planned by Dr. Clarence Odell and Mr. Lawrence H. Hoffman in the Office of Geography and Cartography, United States Department of State, and drawn by the American Geographical Society. The Department of State assumes no responsibility for the data on which these maps are based.

The author wishes to express his appreciation, and that of the Office of Population Research, to the Carnegie Corporation of New York and the Milbank Memorial Fund for the financial support that made this study possible—to the Carnegie Corporation for substantial grants made to Princeton University specifically in support of the cooperative project of the Office and the League of which this study is one result; and to the Milbank Memorial Fund for special assistance of this project, as well as for the regular support it has given the Office since its inception. It is to be understood, of course, that neither foundation is author, owner, publisher, or proprietor of this report or is to be understood as approving by virtue of its grants any of the statements made or views expressed in it. In all matters of fact or interpretation the author alone is responsible.

FRANK LORIMER

Office of Population Research
Princeton University
September 1945

CHAPTER I

THE POPULATION OF THE RUSSIAN PLAIN TO THE END OF THE NINETEENTH CENTURY

1. Russia as a New Continent

RUSSIA is a new country, like the Americas and Australia. A few centuries ago its population possessed only a fraction of the natural resources that now sustain its economic life. The expansion southward into the black soil region during the seventeenth, eighteenth, and nineteenth centuries did not immediately bring about any marked change in the economic and social life of the Russian people. Mother Russia continued to nurture her children in ancient institutions, but her increasing population was supported on a land base which was larger and richer than that to which their forebears had been restricted. Meanwhile, the virgin resources of Asiatic Russia were slowly and partially appropriated. Here the best soils awaited the utilization of modern techniques to overcome the barrier of distance and the limitations of low rainfall and frost. Finally, within the last twenty-five years, exploration of the fuel and mineral resources of sparsely inhabited regions has suddenly opened up new vistas of opportunity.

A comparison of the Soviet Union with North America shows a surprising similarity in area and population. The land area within the January-1939 borders of the U.S.S.R. (21,176,-000 square kilometers or 8,176,000 square miles) is practically equal to that of Central and North America, excluding the Caribbean Islands and Greenland. The population of the Soviet Union at the beginning of 1939 (170,467,000 persons) was equal to 100.5 percent of the population of Central and North America (same area).[1] Both of these land masses have great and diverse natural resources. The coal resources of the Soviet Union are not equal to those of North America but the deposits of either area are ample to support great industrial progress for many centuries. Both areas have great water power potentials, petroleum, forests, and mineral resources. The Soviet Union has a great belt of unusually rich soils, but North America's abundant rainfall and higher proportion of land in the Temperate Zone raises its capacity for agricultural production above that of the Soviet territory. Granted equal efficiency in the utilization of their resources, North America could presumably support a somewhat larger population at a given income level than the Soviet Union, but the capacities of these two continents are not widely divergent. Each of these great land masses, with wealth and diversity of natural resources, was preserved through historical circumstances from accumulating populations of such density as those of Europe and Asia today.

There were, of course, no barriers between the Russian plain and the more densely populated regions of the Old World, such as the oceans separating America from Europe and Asia. But a peculiar combination of geographical and cultural factors operated with similar effect to inhibit the growth of population in Russia until a few centuries ago. Incidentally, the ocean barrier was only one of the factors responsible for the relatively small number of people in North America at the time of Columbus. It is significant that the population of the American forests, prairies, and great plains was very sparse at that time in comparison with the population of Mexico, Central America, and the northern Andes. Cultural factors, interacting with geographical conditions through many centuries, have determined the distribution of population in different parts of the world, with results that greatly influence the relative opportunities of

---

[1] Data from *Statistical Year-Book of the League of Nations, 1939/40*, Table 2. Areas of inland waters in Canada, United States, and Nicaragua have been subtracted from totals as given in the *Year-Book*.

people in different lands today. The factors that inhibited population growth in Russia, America, and Australia in ancient times have left these continents in a peculiarly favorable position today.

A little more than two hundred years ago, at the death of Peter the Great in 1725, there were only about 20 million people in European Russia. We refer here to an area, arbitrarily defined for estimating population changes, that covers 4,800,000 square kilometers, including all the European part of the late Russian Empire except Congress Poland, the Duchy of Finland, and the provinces of Estland, Kurland, Lifland, and Bessarabia. There were slightly over 4 persons per square kilometer, or about 11 persons per square mile, in the whole area. If we exclude the sparsely settled northern and eastern districts (1,565,000 square kilometers, with 1,270,000 persons), the estimated average density in the rest of European Russia was still only about 6 persons per square kilometer. Non-Russian Europe had at this time an average density of about 20 persons per square kilometer.[2] Russia had already acquired control of Siberia, but only about two percent of the Russian subjects of Peter the Great lived beyond the Urals. It is impossible to estimate the indigenous population of Asiatic Russia at this time. One must, of course, take into account the densely populated but restricted districts in the Transcaucasus and Central Asia, which were later included within the Russian Empire. Even so, at the beginning of the eighteenth century there was on the average less than 1 person per square kilometer in the Asiatic portion of the later Russian Empire (land area: 16,400,000 square kilometers). This whole expanse, with considerable resources for agriculture in spite of climatic limitations and with tremendous fuel and mineral resources, remained almost vacant.

2. Geographical and Cultural Factors in the Demographic History of Russia

Several authors have reported guesses about the number of people in Russia or parts of Russia in ancient times.[3] Such quantitative formulations have slight factual basis and contribute little to the understanding of historical developments. We shall, therefore, disregard all quantitative statements about the Russian population prior to the eighteenth century. Instead, we shall merely give a summary account of geographical, cultural, and historical conditions that determined the growth and distribution of population in the Russian plain during ancient and mediaeval times to the reign of Peter the Great. From that time on, we shall attempt to provide numerical estimates of the population trend.

In ancient times the movements of people were not appreciably affected by anything below the top soil on the surface of the earth. Great portions of the Russian plain were therefore cut off, as regards their power to attract many inhabitants, by two great arcs. One of these arcs is roughly indicated by the line above which spring wheat cannot be grown without resort to special techniques (see Plate I). This line, beginning north of Leningrad, runs east and south to the middle Urals; it runs nearly due east across Siberia to a point about 300 miles from Lake Baykal, then dips sharply to the southeast across Lake Baykal to the mountains that cross the border between Siberia and Mongolia; finally it runs northeast to the Pacific above the Amur River valley except at its northern outlet to the Okhotsk Sea. More than half of the U.S.S.R. territory lies within this northern arc. The converse arc around the semi-desert zone is indicated by the line where the balance of moisture in May, June, and July is only 0.5—using an index of rainfall in relation to temperature, since the latter in large measure determines evaporation. This cuts off a portion of European Russia near the Caspian Sea, and most of the

[2] Area: 5,200,000 square kilometers. The estimated population of Europe, including European Russia, in 1724 as indicated by interpolation between the estimates for the years 1650 and 1750 by Carr-Saunders, following Willcox, is 128,000,000. (See Carr-Saunders, Title 44, p. 42.)

[3] For example, Urlanis, Title 340.

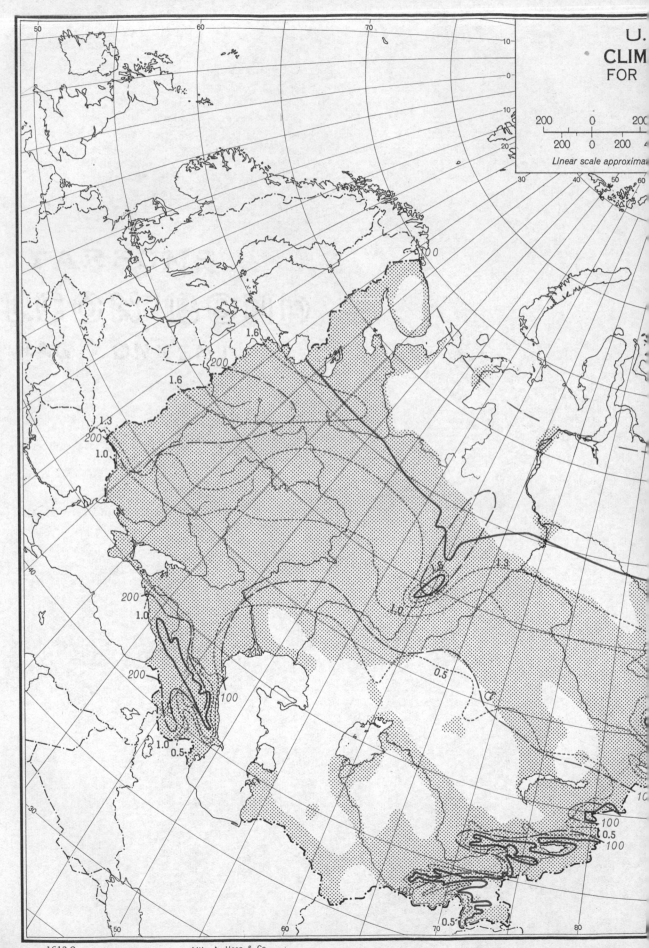

200   0   200

200   0   200

Linear scale approxima

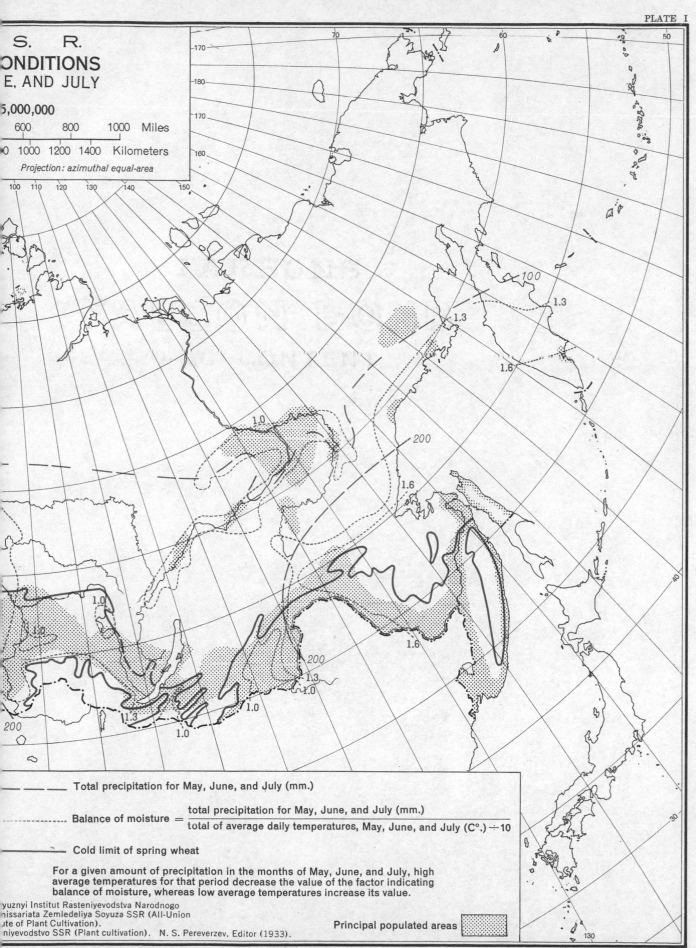

PLATE I

S. R.
ONDITIONS
E, AND JULY

5,000,000

| | | | | Miles |
| 600 | 800 | 1000 | | Miles |

0 1000 1200 1400 Kilometers

Projection: azimuthal equal-area

—— —— —— Total precipitation for May, June, and July (mm.)

.... Balance of moisture = $\dfrac{\text{total precipitation for May, June, and July (mm.)}}{\text{total of average daily temperatures, May, June, and July (C°.)} \div 10}$

———— —— Cold limit of spring wheat

For a given amount of precipitation in the months of May, June, and July, high average temperatures for that period decrease the value of the factor indicating balance of moisture, whereas low average temperatures increase its value.

yuznyi Institut Rasteniyevodstva Narodnogo
missariata Zemledeliya Soyuza SSR (All-Union
ute of Plant Cultivation).
niyevodstvo SSR (Plant cultivation). N. S. Pereverzev. Editor (1933).

Principal populated areas

Prepared by Department of State, Division
of Geography and Cartography
Drawn by American Geographical Society

Asiatic steppe region. The mountains to the east and south of this arid zone and the rivers flowing from these mountains to the Aral Sea supply the moisture that sustains life in Central Asia. The space between these arcs is very broad in the west, from Lake Ladoga to the Black Sea; it narrows to a corridor that is only about 400 miles wide in the vicinity of the southern Urals, but widens out again in western Siberia.

These climatic zones determine the patterns of vegetation and animal life. The treeless tundra lies along the Arctic Ocean. South of the tundra, the Russian plain is divided into forest and steppe zones (see Plate II). The northern part of the steppe (*step'*) is the rich feather-grass prairie zone.[4] These black soil prairies cover a wide region in the south-central part of European Russia, including a large part of the Ukraine, but are more restricted in Siberia. North of the prairies are the hardwood forests of western and central Russia and the swampy, coniferous forests (*taiga*) of northern Russia and Siberia. To the south the prairies give way to dry grasslands and, in Asia, to semi-deserts and deserts. The steppes extend from the rivers that flow around the Carpathian Mountains into the Black Sea eastward to the mountains of Central Asia. They cover the southern portion of the Ukraine, the region of the Don, the middle and lower Volga districts, the North Caucasus, and then fan out beyond the Caspian into the Asiatic steppes, which are more than a thousand miles wide.

The north-central portion of the Eurasian land mass remained under the last glacial ice cap long after it had receded from western Europe. Great areas here are still occupied by swampy forests or frozen tundra. The hard, dry soils in the southern portion of the Russian plain, like those of the North American plain and the Argentine, were not adapted to the support of a large population dependent on neolithic techniques. These physical conditions account for the sparsity of population in the Russian plain in very ancient times but they do not, in themselves, account for the persistence of this situation through the mediaeval period. The black soil zone of southern Russia remained largely unoccupied long after the plough culture, which was essential for its effective exploitation, was well developed in other parts of Europe and Asia.

There was only one important center of ancient civilization within the Russian plain. This was the region of ancient Turkic civilization known to the Greeks as Bactria and in recent times as Russian Turkestan or Central Asia. This region today comprises four Soviet republics: Uzbekistan, Tadzhikistan, Turkmenia, and Kirgizia. There are loose, rich soils in the valley floors of the mountains which form the southern and eastern borders of this region. Fertile strips within the desert are watered by the Syr Darya and the Amu Darya and their tributaries, which rise in the Tien Shan mountains to the east and flow westward into the Aral Sea.[5] The natural oases in this region were enlarged, even before the time of Alexander the Great, by primitive irrigation systems. The ancient cities of Central Asia served as trading centers and fortresses for the agrarian population, and as markets for the exchange of goods brought by caravan from China and from Babylonia, Persia, and Byzantium. After the eighth century they became centers for the diffusion of Mohammedan culture. This restricted region was incapable of supporting a large population or stimulating an extensive civilization in the surrounding regions. It was isolated to the south by a mountain wall (the Hindu Kush), to the west and north by deserts and dry grasslands, and to the east by mountains (the Tien Shan, the Altay, and the Soyan), and beyond these mountains by the deserts of Chinese Turkestan and Mongolia.

Georgia in the Transcaucasus (outside the Russian plain) was also a center of ancient civili-

---

[4] The land referred to here as "black soil prairies" is a part of the steppe zone. It is treated here as a distinct zone because of its special importance in the economic and cultural history of the Russian people.

[5] The breathings used in the transliteration of Russian names in maps, tables, and bibliography are ordinarily omitted in the text unless required for identification.

zation; but this region was likewise restricted and isolated by mountain barriers. There were scattered Greek settlements on the shores of the Black Sea. One nation, the Khazars, formed originally by people from the steppes but influenced by Greek and Jewish culture and at times supported by Byzantium, maintained an outpost of civilization on the Caspian from the fifth to the twelfth century. But none of these isolated centers of civilization along the southern margin of the Russian plain supplied an adequate base for its effective conquest and occupation.

Mountain pastures and valleys in the ranges that fringe the plain supported even smaller aggregations of population in ancient times. The ranges referred to here are the Caucasus and the Little Caucasus (Armenia); the Iranian plateau; the mountains of Central Asia; the mountains and plateaus of eastern Siberia; and, in the center of the plain, the Urals. The pastoral peoples nourished in these mountain districts constantly overflowed their narrow confines and forced migrant tribes into the plain. Conversely, remnants of nations that migrated across the plain settled in the mountain districts. This process led to the formation of many different ethnic types to the south and east of the broad forest zone.[6]

The nomad population of the steppes was necessarily sparse, and its composition was constantly changed by wars and migrations. But the nomad tribes were knit by strong social bonds into powerful political units. They were able to move swiftly across the plain to conduct predatory raids and, if necessary, to organize vast military migrations. The walled cities of Central Asia remained secure against them except in cases of the most powerful invasions, and the strong nation of the Khazars in the Caspian region, established during the seventh century, successfully beat off the nomads until it finally succumbed in the twelfth century. With these exceptions, the nomad warriors prevented any permanent settlements in the southern part of the Russian plain until a few centuries ago.

The forest zone of northern Russia and Siberia is continuous with that of western Europe; but the movement of people east and west through the forests required passage from one river system to another and was partially blocked in the west by the Pripet Marshes and in the center by the low Ural Mountains, which mark the conventional boundary between Europe and Asia. The population of the forest zone was dependent on hunting and fishing and the collection of forest products, gradually supplemented by apiculture, herding, and agriculture.

In the eighth century, the forest villagers in the central portion of the Russian plain, both east and west of the Urals, were mainly Finnic, although the eastward movement of Slavic tribes around the Pripet Marshes had been in progress for several centuries. The Slavs gradually achieved dominance in the forests of European Russia, pushing back or absorbing the Finns but leaving large isolated Finnic blocks in the north, in the Volga-Kama region, and in Siberia. The entrance of the Slavic tribes introduced some new cultural patterns, but it did not radically change the status of the population in the forest zone. The Slavs in the Russian plain gradually formed three main linguistic groups: Great Russians, in the central districts; Little Russians, or Ukrainians, in the southwest; and Belorussians (White Russians) north of the

[6] Among these distinct nationalities in the southern and eastern parts of the old Russian Empire are the Osetins, Kabardians, Circassians, Chechens, Lesgi, and other peoples of the Caucasus region; Georgians; Armenians; Iranians; Turks from the Altay and Ural regions; and the Mongolians, Manchus, and other indigenous nationalities of northeastern Asia.

The Turkic peoples, having become dominant in the steppes, are the most widely dispersed. They include the Uzbeks, Turkmen, and Kirgiz of Central Asia; the Kazakhs of the Asiatic steppe region; the Bashkirs in the vicinity of the southern Urals; the Yakuts in the Lena valley of eastern Siberia; the Tatars in western Siberia, the upper Volga, the North Caucasus, and the Crimea; and the Azers, who entered the Transcaucasus by way of Iran. The Iranians are represented by the Tadzhiks of Central Asia and by several of the many small nations in the Caucasus. The Mongolians are represented within the present Soviet Union principally by the Buryats in the vicinity of Lake Baykal and by the Kalmyks on the western shore of the Caspian Sea. The Tungusi and some of the other nationalities of eastern Siberia are related to the Manchus.

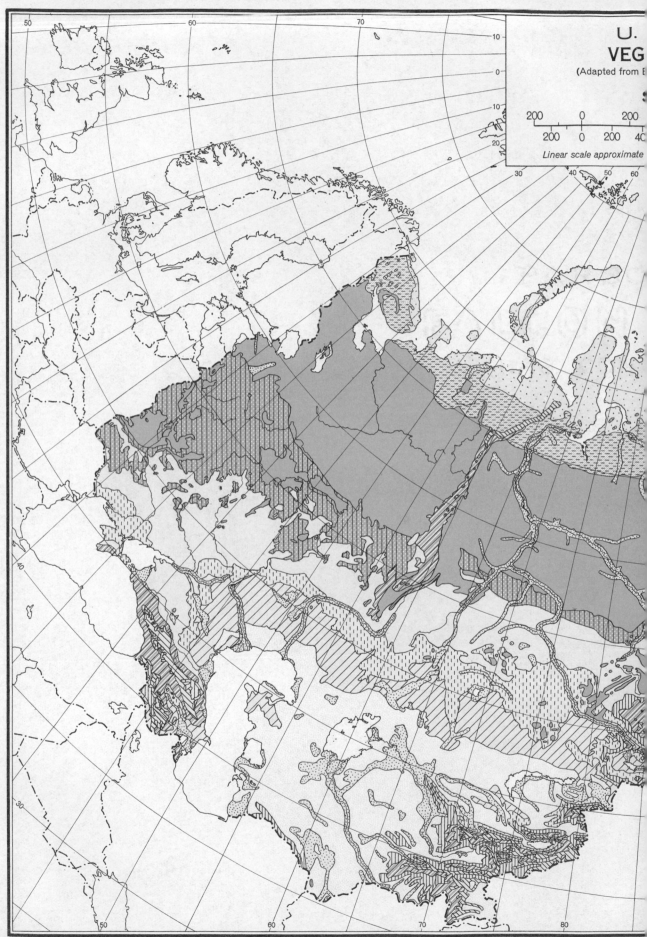

50   60   70   10

0

10

20

30   40   50   60

40

30

50   60   70   80

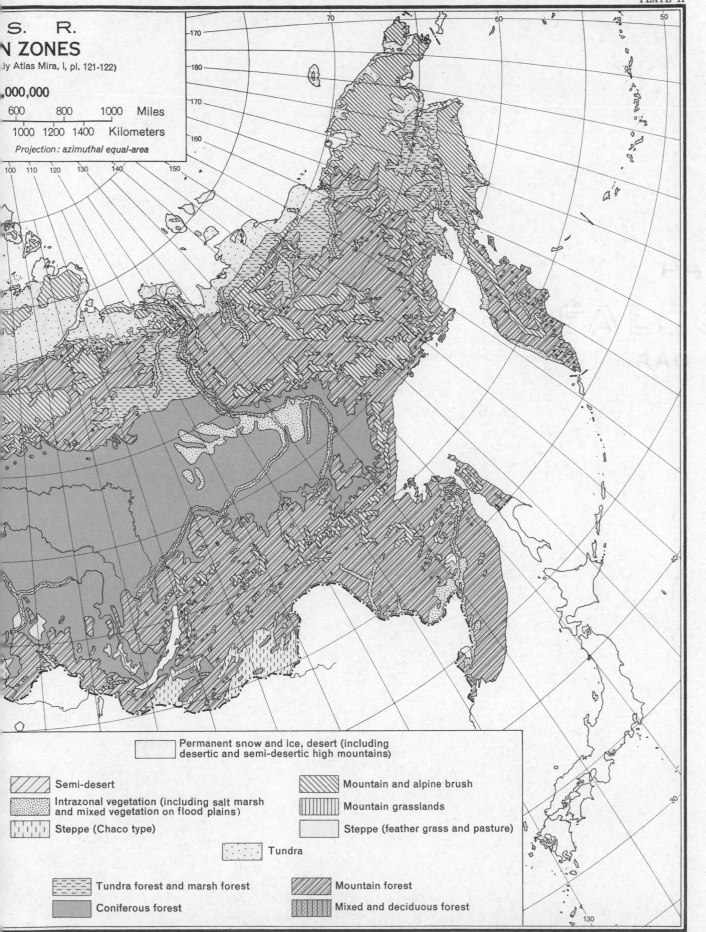

PLATE II

S. R.

N ZONES

iy Atlas Mira, I, pl. 121-122)

,000,000

| 600 | | 800 | | 1000 | Miles |
| 1000 | 1200 | 1400 | | Kilometers |

Projection: azimuthal equal-area

Permanent snow and ice, desert (including
desertic and semi-desertic high mountains)

Semi-desert

Intrazonal vegetation (including salt marsh
and mixed vegetation on flood plains)

Steppe (Chaco type)

Tundra

Tundra forest and marsh forest

Coniferous forest

Mountain and alpine brush

Mountain grasslands

Steppe (feather grass and pasture)

Mountain forest

Mixed and deciduous forest

Prepared by Department of State, Division
of Geography and Cartography
Drawn by American Geographical Society

Pripet Marshes, between the Poles and Lithuanians to the west and north and the Great Russians to the east. Archaeological research has shown that in some areas, as in Kiev, the Slavic settlements were built on the foundations of older towns and may have inherited more advanced cultural institutions and trade associations than did the settlements in the deeper forest regions.

Meanwhile, the fertile prairies of south-central Russia, with a rainfall of about twenty inches per year, remained largely unoccupied. This region, which was the richest potential resource of an agrarian economy, was a kind of no-man's land, deadlocked between the antagonistic cultures of the forest and the steppe. This deadlock was eventually broken (1) by the gradual increase of population in the forest zone, (2) by improved military techniques, and (3) by the concentration of political power around trading centers in the forest zone. The driving force in all these changes was the stimulus of commerce with southern, western, and northern Europe.

3. Rise of the Russian Nation

Novgorod (at Lake Ilmen, on the trade route from the Baltic into central Russia) and Kiev (on the Dnepr River, the principal highway between Byzantium and the Baltic) became the most important centers of mediaeval Russia. Kiev gained the ascendancy. Vladimir, Grand Prince of Kiev, became the first Christian ruler in Russia near the end of the tenth century. At that time the power of Kiev, on the margin between the forest zone and the prairies, reached north toward the Baltic, but Kiev did not exercise effective control in the south over the lower Dnepr as it passed through the steppes to the Black Sea. The Khazars had for a time checked the power of the nomads in southern Russia and thus indirectly contributed to the rise of Kiev. After the fall of the Khazars, Kiev was severely harassed by nomad bands, especially the Pechenegs and Polovtsi of the neighboring steppes. The power of Kiev declined during the twelfth century and many of its inhabitants moved north into the deeper, less exposed forests of Poland, Lithuania, and Russia. A Tatar army delivered the *coup de grâce* in 1240, destroying the city and scattering its inhabitants.

The Tatar invasion of Europe in the early thirteenth century marked the climax of a long series of military migrations across southern Russia that began in prehistoric times and continued through the first millennium of the Christian era, including the movements of the Scythians and Sarmathians across the steppes, the Bulgars from the Volga valley, the Goths from the northwest, and the Huns and Avars from Central Asia. These migrations and raids had repeatedly interrupted the development of stable communities and the growth of the population. They left, as residue, many small nations in isolated and protected places, especially in the vicinity of the Caucasus Mountains at the gateway between Europe and Asia.

The whole territory later embraced by the Russian Empire was first united in a single suzerainty, along with southeastern Europe, Persia, and China, under Ghengis Khan and the small company of Mongols from eastern Asia who dominated Eurasia in the thirteenth century. This remarkable feat was accomplished through a skillful manipulation of the leaders and forces of other nations, principally the Turkic tribes of the Asiatic steppes. The vast, loose structure of the Great Khan's empire provided a pattern that facilitated and influenced the later formation of the Russian Empire. The Tatars, largely Turkic in origin and Mohammedan in religion but organized as "hordes" by the Mongols, were thus established on the Volga, in the Crimea, in the North Caucasus, in Siberia, and in Central Asia. The unity of the Tatar realm persisted in theory for some time, but in reality it disappeared at the death of Ghengis Khan. His successors, the Khans of the several hordes and their officers, the Emirs, dominated the Russian scene for several centuries from Samarkand in Central Asia, Sarai-Batu at the mouth of the

Volga (the present site of Astrakhan), Kazan (the present capital of the Tatar Soviet Socialist Republic on the Volga), Sarai-Berke on the Don (near the present site of Stalingrad), and other centers. The Nogays in the North Caucasus and the Krym (Crimean) Tatars, who became the allies of the Porte in Turko-Russian wars, remained powerful until near the end of the eighteenth century. Their conquest during the reign of Catherine the Great opened "New Russia," the Black Sea steppe districts, to occupation by the Russian population. The last of the Khanates within the present territory of the Soviet Union disappeared when the Emir of Bukhara fled with his harem in 1920.

The people in the more obscure towns of the central forest region enjoyed an advantage during the period of Tatar ascendancy. The Grand Dukes of Moscow rose to power as collectors of revenue with the protection of the Tatar Khans. One of the Grand Dukes achieved sufficient status in the early fourteenth century to effect a marital alliance with Uzbek, Khan of the White Horde. Toward the end of the fourteenth century, the Grand Duke Dimitri rebelled, but Moscow was promptly burned and the Tatar yoke was re-established for another century. Ivan (III) the Great successfully refused the payment of tribute in 1480 and brought various cities, including Novgorod, into the expanding Moscow realm. But this realm was limited by stronger nations in Poland and Sweden and by the Tatar power which remained unbroken on the Volga, in the North Caucasus, and in the Black Sea region. Ivan (IV) the Dread conquered Kazan and Astrakhan and part of the North Caucasus in the middle of the sixteenth century. Moscow then became the dominant power in the Russian plain.

The period between the reigns of Ivan the Dread and Peter the Great, from the middle of the sixteenth to the beginning of the eighteenth century, was characterized by an expansion of Russian population—northward along the route to Arkhangelsk, eastward into Siberia for the collection of furs and other forest products, and southward into the northern districts of the black soil zone. This period was marked by great internal conflicts and by frequent wars with Turkey and the Tatars and with Poland and Sweden.

The expansion of the Russian population during and after the sixteenth century was facilitated by the formation of pioneer bands (free-booters, *kosaki*, or Cossacks) on the edge of the steppes in the southern "border" (*ukrain*) of the Muscovite and Polish realms. These bands, which at first were independent of any national authority, were recruited from free workers, escaped serfs, and adventurers from various nations who joined in expeditions to hunt game and honey in the steppes. A rigid military discipline was established under the leadership of elected hetmen. This type of organization became firmly established in the region "beyond the falls" (*Zaparozhye*) of the Dnepr, and from there spread to pioneer groups in the upper Don region and other districts. For a time these bands served different monarchs as mercenaries but eventually they were absorbed by the Moscow government as a privileged farmer-warrior class, who guarded and cultivated the frontier, protected the Tsar, and provided strong military reserves. Thus the Cossacks became the pioneers of Russian expansion into the Ukraine, the Caucasus, Siberia, and Central Asia. The first Russian expedition into Siberia was led by the hetman Yermak in 1581 in the interest of the house of Stroganov, a family of traders; and a Cossack outpost was established among the Yakuts in 1632. A few years later Russian military expeditions reached the Pacific—before Russia gained access to either the Baltic or the Black Sea.

A pictorial map, reproduced here from an official report on Asiatic Russia in the late Imperial period, portrays the Russian scene at the time of Ivan the Dread as drawn by a contemporary English cartographer. The author has used the space in "Corelia" (Karelia), north of the Gulf of Finland, to display the Imperial canopy—in the style of the Great Khan's golden

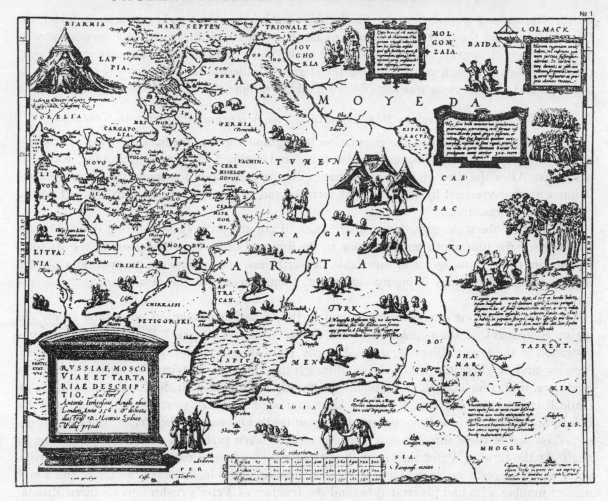

FIGURE I. A Description of Russia, Moscovia, and Tartaria [By Antony Jenkinson. London, 1562. From *Aziatskaya Rossiya*, Vol. IV, Atlas, Title 415]

tent—of Ivan Vasilyevich, Great Sovereign of Russia, Prince of Moskva, *et cetera*. Most of the Russian towns are located between Smolensk on a tributary of the "Neper" (Dnepr) and "Cazane" (Kazan) in the country of the "Ceremis" (Volga Tatars), or to the north and west of a line between Smolensk and Kazan; many are clustered in the center near Moscow. (The cities mentioned here are marked by squares, not shown in the original.) The ancient cities of Central Asia are also shown, far to the east and south. Between these two clusters of settled communities, Tatars peacefully pitch their tents or lead their camels across the Asiatic steppes. Other Tatar tribes, represented by charging warriors, are shown north of the Black Sea (the region here designated as "Crimea") and north of the Caspian. The legend in the lower right-hand corner notes the distance from Central Asia to "Casgar" (Kashgar) on the Chinese border as thirty days, and to "Camboda" as three months. Other legends describe the strange customs of the Kirgiz and other dwellers in these outer regions, with the notation that they "speak their own language."

The costly but successful wars of Peter the Great in the first quarter of the eighteenth century established the security of the Russian Empire in the west and laid the basis for its rapid expansion to the south and east. Peter's reign may, therefore, be regarded as the culmination

[7]

of the transitional period between the initial consolidation of the Moscow state under the Grand Dukes and the final establishment of the Russian Empire as a major European power. Russian power, however, was not established in the Black Sea and Caucasus regions until near the end of the eighteenth century during the reign of Catherine II. The conquest of the Transcaucasus and Central Asia was not effected until the middle of the nineteenth century.

4. Growth of the Russian Population in the Eighteenth and Nineteenth Centuries

It is probable that the Russian population throughout the late mediaeval period alternately grew through natural increase in peaceful times and declined in periods of famine, war, and pestilence. After the time of Peter the Great in the early eighteenth century, the Russian population was characterized by rapid natural increase and gradual expansion into a broad realm, rich in natural resources.

Information about the growth and distribution of population in Russia during the eighteenth and most of the nineteenth century, prior to the first and only complete census of the Russian Empire in 1897, is meager and unreliable. Nevertheless, the available data provide a picture that in its broad outlines is highly significant, though many of the details are certainly erroneous.

We shall center our attention on changes in the "Russian population" that now forms the major component of the population of the Soviet Union. The term "Russian" is sometimes restricted to the Great Russians, derived chiefly from the inhabitants of the Grand Duchy of Moscow and neighboring principalities, although it was not so restricted in ancient usage. As used here, it also includes the Ukrainians (culturally associated with the former inhabitants of Little Russia east of the Dnepr and the Moscow-Polish "border" west of the Dnepr) and the Belorussians (i.e., White Russians, in the region north and east of the Pripet Marshes). Persons classified in these three groups made up seventy-seven percent of the Soviet population in 1926. At the time of Peter the Great the parent stocks of these nationalities lived in Europe north of the steppe zone, except a few hundred thousand who had crossed the Urals and a still smaller number who had penetrated beyond the frontier of Peter's realm into southern Russia. Most of the ancestors of the present Ukrainians and Belorussians lived outside the jurisdiction of Peter the Great in districts that at one time had been part of Lithuania but were then within the Kingdom of Poland or the disputed southern "border."

The European area covered by the 1724 census is referred to here as "Peter's realm," although his authority extended beyond this area into a border region to the south and into Siberia.[7] The core of Peter's realm was formed by the central district around Moscow, a western district in the direction of Smolensk, and a northwestern district in the direction of St. Petersburg. His realm also included large but sparsely settled districts to the north in the direction of Arkhangelsk and to the east between Moscow and the Urals. To the south it included a district designated here as the "Old South," because it was already well settled in Peter's time, although it had been a wilderness two centuries earlier.

The "land base" of the Russian population in the early eighteenth century is defined as "Peter's realm" *plus* Lithuania and Belorussia to the west and a border region to the south which corresponds roughly to the northern part of the present Ukrainian Republic. The latter region, with areas farther to the south (along the Black Sea, the North Caucasus, and the lower Volga—areas not yet occupied by Russian forces), are referred to here as the "New South."

During the next two centuries the Russian population spread out from this land base into

---

[7] The areas included in Peter's realm are defined and described in detail in Appendix I.

the newly acquired parts of the New South and into Asiatic Russia. Other ethnic groups (Karelians, Estonians, and other Finnic peoples in the northwest; Tatar, Finnic, and Chuvash groups to the east in the Volga-Ural region; Lithuanians, Jews, Germans, and others) shared the land base occupied chiefly by Russians, Ukrainians, and Belorussians. The history of these groups is bound up with that of the Russians. Together they formed a "demographic pool" that rose through natural increase and sent forth streams of migrants into southern Russia and Siberia. We shall refer to this pool and its streams as the "Russian population," although it included non-Russian elements. The non-Russian colonies in southern Russia that preserved distinct languages and traditions were recruited in large part from outside the territory defined here as the land base of the Russian population. The expanding *Russian population* is therefore defined for purposes of population analysis as the *total* population of the original land base at any time from 1724 to 1897, *plus* Russians, Ukrainians, and Belorussians in districts to the south and east.

In order to simplify the treatment we omit certain areas in the European part of the Russian Empire that were chiefly occupied by non-Russian nationalities, had a fairly distinct demographic history, and were not included in the original territory of the U.S.S.R., namely, the Grand Duchy of Finland, the Vistula provinces (Congress Poland), Bessarabia, Estland, Kurland, and Lifland. We also omit, in Asia, the semi-autonomous Khanates of Khiva and Bukhara, which had a negligible number of Russian citizens in 1897.

Estimates of the Russian population, as defined above, for the years 1724, 1859, and 1897 are summarized in Table 1, and the growth of the Russian population is presented graphically in Figure 2. More detailed estimates and a description of the procedures followed are given in Appendix I. This derivation involves many dubious adjustments. At this point we need only call attention to its main features and their limitations.

(1) The Russian population as here defined was not, of course, wholly unaffected by migration. These effects varied at different times. They may or may not cancel out in their net effect on population growth from 1724 to 1897. During the eighteenth and nineteenth centuries considerable numbers of Jews, Poles, Lithuanians, Finns, Germans, Bulgarians, and others moved into Russia proper. Such migrants and their descendants are excluded from our estimate only if they settled in southern or Asiatic Russia *and* retained a non-Russian language. In the late nineteenth century these eastward movements were outweighed by the westward movements to Bessarabia, western Europe, and the Americas, but these movements were not large prior to the last decade of the nineteenth century.

(2) The estimates for 1897, based on the first and only real census of the Russian Empire, have the highest validity, but even these figures are not infallible.

(3) The estimates of total population in the regions within Peter's realm in 1724 are developed from the data of the "census" of males in taxable classes, referred to in Russian literature as the "first revision," not taking into account early enumerations of households or the suppressed census of 1710. The estimates for the Lithuanian, Belorussian, and Ukrainian regions at this time reflect subjective judgments concerning relative densities in the light of historical information about contemporary conditions. The estimates for 1859 are, with some modifications, official estimates based on the results of the "tenth revision."

(4) The estimates of non-Russian population in southern Russia in 1724 and in 1859 are based on broad assumptions and are subject to great error. These assumptions do not affect the totals for 1859, which are based on semi-official estimates, but rather the figures for the "Russian population" in these districts, which are obtained by subtraction of the estimated

[9]

non-Russian population from the reported totals. The estimates for southern Russia (outside Peter's realm) in 1724 have no value, except as giving a rough indication of the actual situation.

The estimates presented here show that the central and northern parts of European Russia, which supported only about one-third (32.5 percent) of the Russian population at the end of

TABLE I

Growth and Distribution of the Russian Population, 1724-1897[1]

Region	Land Area[2] Sq. Km. (In thousands)	Russian Population[3]					
		1724		1859		1897	
		Number (In thousands)	Percent	Number (In thousands)	Percent	Number (In thousands)	Percent
Total	21,197	17,900[4]	100	58,629[5]	100	94,331[6]	100
European Part	4,800	17,500	98	55,205	94	87,384	92.6
Center, West, Northwest	617	6,690	37.4	11,542	20	15,741	16.7
Lithuania-Belorussia .	303	3,300	18.4	5,399	9	10,063	10.7
Northeast, East	1,565	1,270	7	3,500	6	4,886	5.2
	2,485	11,260	63	20,441	35	30,690	32.5
Old South	869	4,640	26	20,233	34.5	28,173	29.9
New South	1,446	1,600[4]	9	14,531[5]	24.8	28,521	30.2
	2,315	6,240	35	34,764	59	56,694	60.1
Asiatic Part	16,397	400	2	3,424	6	6,947	7.4

[1] Summary of Appendix I, Table A 2. Percentages for 1724 and 1859 have not been carried beyond the decimal point (except in a few cases where totals are affected) because these estimates have a wide margin of error.

[2] Area of the Russian Empire at the time of the 1897 census, *minus* the Duchy of Finland, Congress Poland, and the provinces of Estland, Lifland, Kurland, and Bessarabia, and the Khanates of Khiva and Bukhara (see Appendix Tables A 2 and A 3).

[3] The *Russian population* includes: (1) All classes within the original land base—this is the European part of the area covered by the "census" under Peter the Great in 1724, plus adjacent Lithuanian and Belorussian districts (outside Peter's realm), plus northern Ukrainian districts subject to Peter's authority but not covered by the census; and (2) Russians, Ukrainians, and Belorussians in other areas.

[4] The estimated number of non-Russians in southern districts of European Russia not subject to Peter's authority in 1724 was about 2 million. These have not been included in this table showing the Russian population.

[5] The estimated number of non-Russians in the same southern districts in 1859 was 3,019,000 persons. These have not been included in the Russian population.

[6] This figure does not include 13,724,000 persons in various parts of the Russian Empire (exclusive of Finland, Khiva, and Bukhara), and 17,585,000 non-Russians in southern and Asiatic parts of the total area. The total population of the Russian Empire according to the 1897 census was 125,640,000.

the nineteenth century, had contained nearly two-thirds (63 percent) of its parent population in the early eighteenth century. The great expansion during the 135 years from 1724 to 1859 was the movement from the forest zone of central and northern Russia into the black soil and steppe zones of southern Russia. The area referred to here as the New South had only an estimated 1.6 million Russians (mostly in the Ukraine region) in 1724; but it had a Russian population of 14.5 million persons in 1859. The percentage of the total Russian population located in this area rose from about 9 percent to 25 percent during the interval. The percentage of the total Russian population to be found in the Old South (northern black soil districts, already well occupied by the time of Peter the Great) also increased, but at a slower rate, from 26 percent in 1724 to 34.5 percent in 1859. Southern Russia (Old South and New South, combined) had been mostly wilderness in the sixteenth century; it held about 6 million Russians, plus some 2 million non-Russians, in 1724; but in 1859 it supported about 35 million Russians, or 59 percent of the total Russian population. Meanwhile, the number of Russians living east of the Urals increased from about 400 thousand in 1724, or 2 percent of the total, to 3.4 mil-

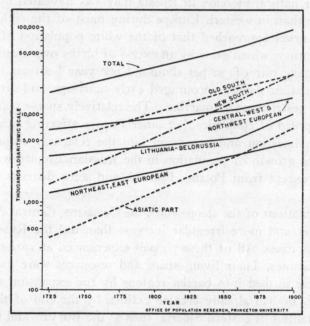

FIGURE 2. Growth of the Russian Population by Regions, 1724-1897 [Table 1]

lion in 1859, or 6 percent of the total. Thus the land base of the Russian people was extended as their number increased.

The Russian population was less mobile from 1859 to 1897 than it had been during the preceding three centuries. By the middle of the nineteenth century most of the best farming land in southern Russia, except in some parts of the North Caucasus, was already occupied; and the movement eastward to Siberia and the Asiatic steppes did not draw large numbers until near the close of the nineteenth century. The proportion of the total Russian population in the New South increased from 25 percent in 1859 to 30 percent in 1897. But the proportion in the Old South, where there was now a sense of population pressure, decreased during the same interval from 34.5 percent to 30 percent, so that the proportion of the total Russian population in these two areas, combined, remained about constant. Asiatic Russia's share of the total Russian population increased gradually during this interval from 5.8 percent in 1859 to 7.4 percent in 1897.

According to our estimates, the total Russian population increased from 17,900,000 persons in 1724 to 58,629,000 in 1859 and to 94,331,000 in 1897. The average rates of increase per year (geometric) indicated by these figures are 9 per thousand during the earlier period and 13 per thousand during the later period. These rates are higher than the average rates of increase indicated for the continent of Europe as a whole by Carr-Saunders' estimates. The latter run as follows: 1770-1800, 6.8 per thousand; 1800-1850, 7.1 per thousand; 1850-1900, 8.2 per thousand; the corresponding figure for the first decade of the twentieth century is 11.1 per thousand.[8] Early vital statistics for England and Sweden show very low apparent rates of natural increase at the beginning of the eighteenth century, rising to slightly over 10 per thousand in England and slightly under 10 per thousand in Sweden around 1800, owing to an irregular but general decline in the death rates.[9] The gap between the birth rate and the death rate in these countries then widened somewhat to give higher rates of natural increase until near the end of the nineteenth century; thereafter, in both England and Sweden the rapid drop in the birth rate began to narrow the gap.

The average rate of natural increase in Russia may (as indicated by our estimates) have been somewhat higher than in western Europe during most of the eighteenth and nineteenth centuries; it certainly never approached that of the white population of the United States in the early nineteenth century, which grew by an excess of births over deaths, apart from migration, at the extraordinary rate of 30 per thousand per year between 1800 and 1840.[10] The feudal structure of Russian society encouraged early marriage and large families, although serfdom entailed some restrictions on marriage. The relatively sparse population in many areas tended to retard the spread of epidemics, but other factors affecting health were unfavorable. In any case, owing to isolation and expansion into the relatively empty spaces of southern Russia and Siberia, the growth of population in the Russian Empire was not appreciably affected by emigration, except from Poland, Finland, and some districts in Belorussia and the Ukraine.

The indigenous populations of the steppe zone, the Caucasus, Central Asia, and Siberia must have had a much lower and more irregular increase than did the Russian population—with actual decrease in some cases. All of these peoples experienced at various times the ordeal of conquest by Russian armies. Their living space and resources were narrowed. Some of the smaller tribes that were pushed into barren regions by the expansion of larger nationalities were becoming extinct, or had already become extinct, by the end of the nineteenth century. Even the larger nationalities of eastern Siberia, such as the Buryats and the Yakuts, for whom it is possible to compare the data of the 1897 and the 1926 censuses, show very low rates of increase at this time.

5. Population Densities in the Russian Empire, 1897

Table 2 presents the number of persons per square kilometer in the various parts of European Russia for which population estimates have been prepared for 1724, 1859, and 1897. The figures do not refer merely to the "Russian population" treated in the preceding section, but show estimated density of total population. The area referred to here is defined in Table 1.

The *total* population in the European area treated here, 4,800 thousand square kilometers, increased 4.7 fold according to our estimates, or from 19.5 million in 1724 to 92 million persons in 1897.[11] But the density of population in western, central, and southern Russia, excluding the sparsely settled northern and eastern districts, was only 27 persons per square kilometer in 1897. This is less than the density of population in the center, around Moscow, in 1724, and on the whole the natural resources of this larger area tended to be superior to those of its historical center.

The land base of the Russian population was enlarged somewhat between the early sixteenth and the early eighteenth century, and population growth in the troublous times before Peter the Great was certainly slow and irregular. This land base, as we have seen, was then greatly

---

[8] Carr-Saunders, Title 44, pp. 21-22.   [9] *Ibid.*, pp. 60-69 (charts and text).

[10] Calculation based on estimates by Warren S. Thompson and P. K. Whelpton, *Population Trends in the United States* (New York: McGraw-Hill, 1933), pp. 5 and 303.

[11] See Appendix I, Table A 2.

expanded between 1724 and 1859. The conclusion of the Russian historian Kluchevsky seems amply justified and conservative. Basing his opinion largely on documents relating to the social conditions of Russian life, he concluded: "It would appear that the peasantry of the sixteenth century enjoyed the use [per capita] of no more arable land—even if of no less—than was assigned to their distant descendants by the Polozhenie of February 19, 1861 [Edict of Emancipation]."[12] Apparently, the growth of population in Russia did not exceed the expansion of its

TABLE 2

Estimated Population Densities in European Russia:
1724, 1859, 1897[1]

Region	Total Population per Square Kilometer		
	1724	1859	1897
Center, Northwest, West	11	19	26
Center	30	—	46
Northwest	5	—	18
West , ...	8	—	30
Lithuania-Belorussia	11	18	33
North, East	1	2	3
North	0.6	—	2
East	2	—	10
Old South	5	23	32
Southwest	11	—	50
South	4	—	38
Southeast	5	—	26
New South	2	12	23
Ukraine (Northern)	5	—	55
Black Sea Region	1	—	32
Don Region	1	—	16
North Caucasus	4	—	17
Volga Steppe	2	—	10
Total (4,800,000 sq. kilometers) .	4	12	19
Total, *except* North and East (3,235,000 sq. kilometers) .	6	17	27

[1] Based on Appendix I, Table A 2.

land base until the last half century of the Empire. By that time the immense, largely undeveloped resources of Asiatic Russia were beginning to attract new settlers, although the utilization of these resources was severely hampered by the economic and social structure of the Empire. The situation of Russia with respect to population growth in relation to resources was, therefore, quite different even at the end of the nineteenth century from that of other parts of Europe and eastern and southern Asia. Russia, in contrast to these lands, remained a "new" continent.

The average densities of population in the various political divisions of the Russian Empire according to the 1897 census are shown on the accompanying map. (See Plate III.) It is sig-

[12] Kluchevsky, Title 131, Vol. 2, p. 213.

nificant that not a single province among the fifty provinces of European Russia proper had so high a density as the Vistula provinces (Congress Poland) as a whole: 74 persons per square kilometer. Only three provinces were in the same class in this respect: Moscow, 73 persons; Podolsk, 72 persons; and Kiev, 70 persons. Only two other provinces had more than 50 persons per square kilometer: Poltava with 56 and Kursk with 51. All of these Russian provinces except Moscow are in the black soil prairie zone, which forms the central portion of the Ukraine and south-central Russia. By 1897, the distribution of population in European Russia had become well adjusted to its natural resources for agrarian economy.

The relatively low density of population in European Russia as a whole must be attributed chiefly to the historical circumstances that shaped the growth and distribution of its population. The extremely low density of population in many parts of the Russian Empire, especially in Siberia and the Asiatic steppe regions, was due primarily to the natural limitations of these sections for the support of agriculture at a low technological level. It was also due to the isolation and insecurity of scattered regions where natural conditions were favorable for the development of agriculture. The fact that many of these sparsely populated districts possessed great mineral and fuel resources had, of course, no influence on the distribution of population so long as economic, cultural, and political conditions prevented their effective exploitation.

In spite of its natural advantages, Russia remained a culturally retarded and poverty-stricken nation. Eventually its plight gave rise to an acute sense of population pressure and "land hunger." This was due more to retarded social development and inefficiency than to lack of adequate resources for the support of its population, even with primary dependence on agriculture. At the beginning of the twentieth century Russia was commonly regarded as an overpopulated country. In reality, it was the land of greatest opportunity in the eastern hemisphere.

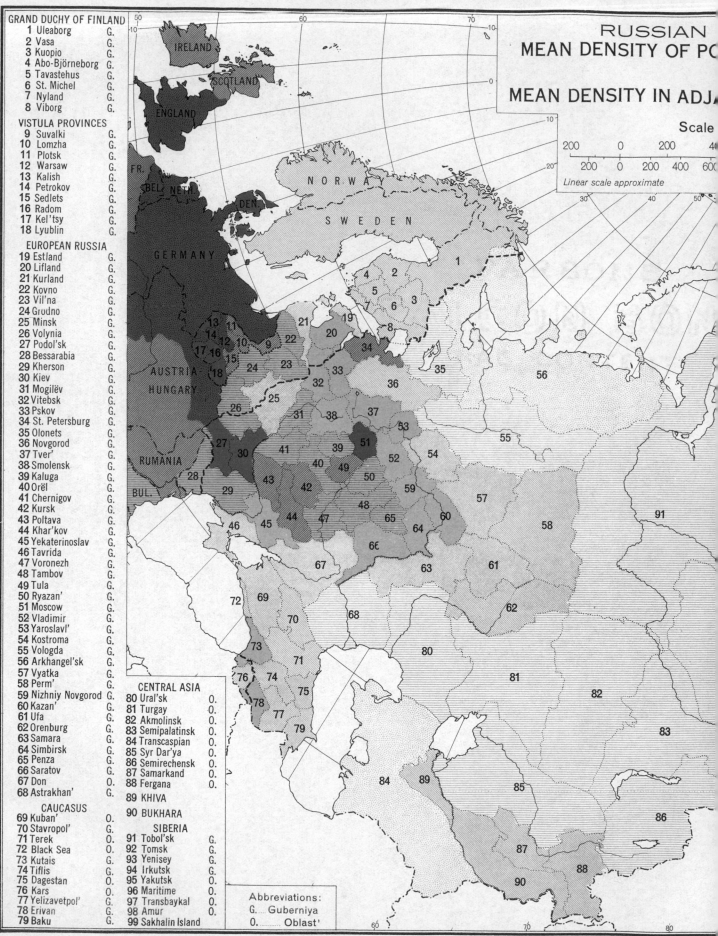

RUSSIAN
MEAN DENSITY OF PO

MEAN DENSITY IN ADJA

Scale

Linear scale approximate

GRAND DUCHY OF FINLAND
1 Uleaborg G.
2 Vasa G.
3 Kuopio G.
4 Abo-Björneborg G.
5 Tavastehus G.
6 St. Michel G.
7 Nyland G.
8 Viborg G.

VISTULA PROVINCES
9 Suvalki G.
10 Lomzha G.
11 Plotsk G.
12 Warsaw G.
13 Kalish G.
14 Petrokov G.
15 Sedlets G.
16 Radom G.
17 Kel'tsy G.
18 Lyublin G.

EUROPEAN RUSSIA
19 Estland G.
20 Lifland G.
21 Kurland G.
22 Kovno G.
23 Vil'na G.
24 Grodno G.
25 Minsk G.
26 Volynia G.
27 Podol'sk G.
28 Bessarabia G.
29 Kherson G.
30 Kiev G.
31 Mogilëv G.
32 Vitebsk G.
33 Pskov G.
34 St. Petersburg G.
35 Olonets G.
36 Novgorod G.
37 Tver' G.
38 Smolensk G.
39 Kaluga G.
40 Orël G.
41 Chernigov G.
42 Kursk G.
43 Poltava G.
44 Khar'kov G.
45 Yekaterinoslav G.
46 Tavrida G.
47 Voronezh G.
48 Tambov G.
49 Tula G.
50 Ryazan' G.
51 Moscow G.
52 Vladimir G.
53 Yaroslavl' G.
54 Kostroma G.
55 Vologda G.
56 Arkhangel'sk G.
57 Vyatka G.
58 Perm' G.
59 Nizhniy Novgorod G.
60 Kazan' G.
61 Ufa G.
62 Orenburg G.
63 Samara G.
64 Simbirsk G.
65 Penza G.
66 Saratov G.
67 Don O.
68 Astrakhan' G.

CAUCASUS
69 Kuban' O.
70 Stavropol' G.
71 Terek O.
72 Black Sea O.
73 Kutais G.
74 Tiflis G.
75 Dagestan O.
76 Kars O.
77 Yelizavetpol' G.
78 Erivan G.
79 Baku G.

CENTRAL ASIA
80 Ural'sk O.
81 Turgay O.
82 Akmolinsk O.
83 Semipalatinsk O.
84 Transcaspian O.
85 Syr Dar'ya O.
86 Semirechensk O.
87 Samarkand O.
88 Fergana O.
89 KHIVA
90 BUKHARA

SIBERIA
91 Tobol'sk G.
92 Tomsk G.
93 Yenisey G.
94 Irkutsk G.
95 Yakutsk O.
96 Maritime O.
97 Transbaykal O.
98 Amur O.
99 Sakhalin Island

Abbreviations:
G..... Guberniya
O......... Oblast'

1615-G

Lith. A. Hoen & Co., Inc.

PLATE III

E 1897
ON BY PROVINCES

UROPEAN NATIONS

800   1000 Miles
200   1400 Kilometers
ojection: azimuthal equal-area

96

95

93

99

96

98

94

97

POPULATION PER SQUARE-KILOMETER

| 1 | 5 | 15 | 25 | 35 | 45 | 60 | 80 |

Boundary, international, 1897   —·—·—·—   Boundary, Vistula Provinces   ············
Boundary, U.S.S.R., January 17, 1939,   —————   Boundary, provincial   ··········
(where differing from 1897 boundary)

Prepared by Department of State, Division
of Geography and Cartography
Drawn by American Geographical Society

CHAPTER II

ECONOMIC STRUCTURE OF THE RUSSIAN EMPIRE

RUSSIAN economy remained predominantly agrarian through the nineteenth and the first three decades of the twentieth century—the term "agrarian" implying a primary reliance on agriculture at the pre-scientific and pre-mechanical level. Industrial development was slow and irregular, beset by social and political upheavals.

The economic organization of the Empire was violently disrupted during the years of war, revolution, and civil war. The year 1921 brought a new catastrophe—famine and the further spread of epidemics. But the same year marked the inauguration of the Soviet's "New Economic Policy," characterized by the encouragement of private enterprise and foreign concessions as well as the more orderly development of public activities. The constitutional structure of the Union of Soviet Socialist Republics was formed in December, 1922. By December, 1926, the time of the First All-Union Census, the distribution of productive forces was fairly similar to that prevailing in the late prewar period. It is estimated that in 1913 there were 11,250,000 workers and employees of all sorts within the 1926 area of the Soviet Union— about 8 per 100 persons in the whole population. Among these employees and workers an estimated 2,885,000 were engaged in industry and mining, and 691,000 in railway transportation; the remainder were employed in trade, service, railway, river and road transportation, rural industries, crafts, agriculture, and forestry.[1] In 1926, the number of persons reported as employed personnel was 9,583,000, or 6.5 per 100 total population. Industrial employment in 1926 was nearly the same as—but probably somewhat lower than—that in the same area in 1913. According to the 1926 census, only 15 percent of the entire population of the Soviet Union were supported by industry, transportation, and trade. It is apparent that the roots of industry and commerce in the Russian economy were still shallow at the end of the Imperial regime.

1. The Agrarian Background

At the beginning of the nineteenth century Russian agriculture was dependent on the labor of serfs who were legally bound to the estates of private landlords, the Church, or the Tsar. The obligations of the serfs entailed, in addition to the Imperial taxation, the payment to the landlord of a fixed share of the products (*obrok*) or labor services (*barshchina*), the latter being in theory limited to three days' service per week. The barshchina system was prevalent in Belorussia, the Ukraine, and southern Russia. A large proportion of the serfs in the north and in Siberia were attached to the Imperial or Crown lands. Russian agriculture at this time was characterized by a high degree of local self-sufficiency, as shown by wide variation in the price of staple foodstuffs in different markets. For example, if the average price of rye in Kiev in the years 1797 to 1803 is taken as 100, the price in other markets ran as follows: Astrakhan, 200; Moscow, 270; St. Petersburg, 291.[2] Nearly half a million persons, including serfs and exiles and a few free laborers, were used in mining and metallurgy in the Urals or in the gold and silver mines in Siberia. There were less than a hundred thousand workers in processing industries of all sorts in the Russian Empire at this time.[3] Russian economy in the early nineteenth century may, therefore, be described as almost wholly dependent on extractive industries, chiefly subsistence agriculture organized on a feudal basis at a low level of effi-

---

[1] *Narodnoye Khozyaystvo SSSR, 1932,* Title 407, pp. xxii-xxiii.
[2] Pavlovsky, Title 231, pp. 24-26.   [3] Lyashchenko, Title 182, p. 438.

[15]

ciency. These conditions persisted as the basis of Russian economy during the following decades, but they underwent progressive modification before the Revolution and the era of the Soviets.

The serfs were legally emancipated in 1861 by a series of Imperial edicts applicable to different regions, and were allotted part of the estates on which they had worked. The landlords were compensated by bonds issued by the government. The government, in turn, assessed the peasants for redemption payments on these allotments over a period of forty-nine years. The landlords were allowed, as an alternative, to provide lands on a rental basis but most of them accepted the allotment plan, and this was made universal by a later edict. Landlords were also given the option of transferring to the peasants an amount of land equal to one-fifth the prescribed allotment as a free grant. In parts of southern Russia where land values were rising rapidly, many landlords accepted this option, but this was rarely the case elsewhere. Except in Little Russia, the Ukraine, and Belorussia, the allotments were made to the *mir* (peasant community), and the mir was held responsible for redemption payments and taxes. In northern and central Russia the number of persons in each peasant family was taken into account in fixing the allotments, and provision was made for periodic redistribution of strips within the mir. In Little Russia, east of the middle Dnepr, there was a combination of communal and individual holdings. In the Ukraine and Belorussia there was no statutory prescription regarding the size of the allotments, and this was determined in relation to previous usage, according to the land inventory of 1858. Common holdings were arranged only by local agreement in the Ukraine and were not established in Belorussia. In areas where the barshchina system was in force, the allotments tended to be smaller than in other areas. In parts of the black soil region only about one-fifth of the land of the nobles was allotted to the peasants. In northern Russia the landlords tended to transfer only crop lands and to retain the meadows. The allotments to serfs on Imperial and Crown lands were generally larger than to serfs on private estates.[4]

Altogether, the land allotted to the peasants in European Russia (forty-nine provinces, exclusive of the Don and North Caucasus regions and part of Bessarabia) amounted to about 123 million hectares in 1861—an average of 2.5 hectares per person, assuming an emancipated serf population of about 50 million persons, including dependents.[5] By 1905 the peasant lands within the same geographical limits, including both the allotments and lands subsequently purchased, totaled about 176 million hectares, an increase of over 40 percent. The peasant population in these districts had increased meanwhile by about 68 percent, or 56 percent if we exclude the peasants who had given up rural residence and were registered in towns and cities.[6] These figures do not suggest high population density according to European standards, if agriculture were efficiently developed within a balanced economy. As it was, the redemption dues plus taxes often exceeded the productive capacity of the peasant lands.

The peasants, even after emancipation, could not move to new localities with much greater freedom than before. Siberia, which had been frequently sought as a refuge by escaped serfs, was still legally closed to former serfs; this ban remained in effect for two decades after the emancipation. In the greater part of Russia, especially in the older districts of central Russia, the peasants were bound by their obligations to the mir; by an unauthorized movement they forfeited without compensation their only claim to property. The redistribution of population continued as in the past through organized colonies, relocation of peasants on new lands of the nobility, and unauthorized movements.

The peasants were able to supplement their crop income by seasonal employment in forests

---

[4] For a more complete description of the situation, see, among others: Pavlovsky, Title 231.
[5] Robinson, Title 276, p. 291.   [6] *Ibid.*

or towns or on other farms, in varying degrees in different areas. According to local investigations such supplemental employment supplied one-fourth of the income of the peasant families in one forest district and one-eighth of the income of the families in one steppe district.[7] Traditional handcrafts and small shop industries yielded an important part of these supplemental earnings, and furnished full-time employment to other families in the same class.

The agricultural measures introduced by Stolypin, beginning in 1906, were designed to change Russian agriculture from a feudal to a capitalistic basis. These measures included cancellation of the redemption payments, four years in advance of the original forty-nine year limit, and the dissolution of the mir, thus enabling peasants to dispose of their lands. Other measures were taken to promote the consolidation of larger holdings. The government provided grants to farmers for the purchase of farm machinery, and thus stimulated the manufacture and importation of improved agricultural equipment. It also sponsored an extensive land settlement program, directed principally to the development of Siberian agriculture. The large private holdings in southern Russia and the growth of the grain export trade through the Black Sea ports had given agriculture in these newer districts a more commercial character than elsewhere in the Empire, and the introduction of agricultural machinery proceeded much more rapidly here.

The trends of sown land and the productivity of agriculture in European Russia in relation to the rural population are shown in Table 3 and Figure 3. The analysis begins with the year 1883, since prior to that time the necessary data are too unreliable to warrant a study of trends.[8] The basic data used in our analysis are subject to error, but they give an approximate index of the trend of agricultural productivity per capita of rural population in European Russia during the three decades prior to the First World War.

The estimated average population in the rural districts of European Russia rises from 68,900,000 persons in the period 1883-1887 to 99,300,000 persons in the period 1910-1914. During the interval between these periods, the sown land per 100 persons in the rural population decreased from 95 hectares to 80 hectares. But, whereas there was a decrease of 23 percent in the sown area per capita of rural population in the non-black soil zone, there was a corresponding decrease of only 13 percent in the black soil zone because of the more rapid extension of cultivated land in southern Russia. Meanwhile, the average productivity per unit of sown land had risen in both zones. The proportion of the total rural population of European Russia living in the black soil and steppe zone rose from 64 percent around 1885 to 66 percent around 1912. The net result of these changes is an apparent increase of about 13 percent in the per capita productivity of agriculture in European Russia during the quarter century preceding the First World War. This may be considered a slow advance but at least it indicates an apparent trend toward improvement rather than deterioration. It is also possible that increase in supplementary sources of income offset the apparent absence of any gain in productivity per capita in the non-black soil zone.

2. Mining and Industry

The trend of industrial development in Russia gives a similar picture of positive but slow advance, lagging far behind the advances in western Europe. Industrial statistics for the Rus-

---

[7] *Ibid.*, p. 246.

[8] The agricultural data are taken from Obukhov (Title 223), and grouped by periods selected so as to minimize fluctuations. The population data for the same groups of provinces are taken from Zaytsev, Title 374, who gives estimates of total population by provinces, with preliminary estimates of rural-urban distribution. The preliminary estimates of urban population are apparently too low, and Zaytsev corrects the figure for the total urban population of European Russia. We have applied this correction factor to the total urban populations of the black soil and non-black soil zones and subtracted the "corrected" urban figures from totals to give estimated rural populations.

TABLE 3

Trend of Sown Land and Grain Production Related to Rural Population
in European Russia (50 Provinces), 1883-1914[1]

Population, Land Use, Production, and Date	Total Rural Population	Black Soil	Non-Black Soil
Estimated Rural Population in Thousands (Period Averages)			
1883-1887	68,876.8	43,940.9	24,935.9
1888-1893	74,774.9	48,106.5	26,668.4
1894-1898	80,184.5	51,697.7	28,486.8
1899-1903	86,172.8	56,083.4	30,089.4
1904-1909	93,269.7	61,350.5	31,919.2
1910-1914	99,312.0	65,621.9	33,690.0
Hectares of Sown Land per 100 Persons in the Rural Population			
1883-1887	94.7	103.6	79.3
1888-1893	89.4	98.7	73.7
1894-1898	83.8	91.5	70.0
1899-1903	84.6	93.9	67.6
1904-1909	82.2	91.9	63.1
1910-1914	80.1	89.8	60.7
Production of Bread Grains: Kilograms per Hectare			
1883-1887	554	547	567
1888-1893	545	525	587
1894-1898	646	637	668
1899-1903	681	686	668
1904-1909	681	679	690
1910-1914	740	746	724
Production of Bread Grains: Kilograms Per Capita of Rural Population			
1883-1887	524	566	450
1888-1893	487	518	432
1894-1898	542	582	467
1899-1903	577	645	451
1904-1909	560	624	435
1910-1914	592	670	440
Index of Production of Bread Grains Per Capita of Rural Population (1883-1887 = 100)			
1883-1887	100	100	100
1888-1893	93	92	96
1894-1898	103	103	104
1899-1903	110	114	100
1904-1909	107	110	97
1910-1914	113	118	98

[1] Data on sown area and production of bread grains are from Obukhov, Title 223, pp. 56-58. Data on rural population are from Zaytsev, Title 374, pp. 64-65, with adjustments (see Footnote 8, page 17). See Appendix II for absolute figures on sown area and production and for list of provinces in black soil and non-black soil zones. "Black soil zone" here includes the steppe region of European Russia.

sian Empire are, as might be expected, quite imperfect and frequently confusing; but their general trend is fairly apparent.

The number of workers in mining and metallurgy dropped at first, after the emancipation of the serfs, to about 200,000 persons in 1865.[9] Twenty years later, in 1885, the number of workers in mining and metallurgy as reported by the Department of Mines was 349,000. The iron resources of the Ukraine were just beginning to be exploited at this time, and coal mining in southern Russia was also beginning to assume real importance. Mining in the Ural region reached a peak during the period of large railway construction near the end of the nineteenth century. With the greater development of the Ukraine, the Ural region then passed into eclipse, until the metal resources of the Urals were linked with the coal resources of eastern Siberia

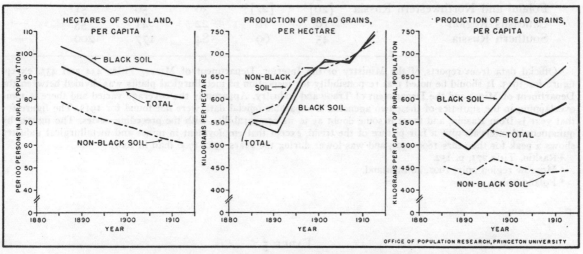

FIGURE 3. Trend of Sown Land and Grain Production Related to Rural Population in European Russia, 1883-1914 [Table 3]

and Kazakhstan in the Soviet production program. The number of workers in the petroleum industry, centered in Baku, rose rapidly near the end of the nineteenth century to 50,000 workers in 1907, but declined somewhat thereafter. The development of metallurgy in the Ukraine and that of the petroleum industry in the Transcaucasus were financed chiefly with foreign capital and stimulated by foreign enterprise. The smaller manganese mines of the Transcaucasus were developed with Russian capital. The trend of employment in mining and metallurgy from 1885 to 1907, as given in reports by the Department of Mines, is presented in Table 4, and the distribution of such workers by type of product in 1913 is shown in Table 5.

Linen, hemp, and woolen industries were among those first developed in the Russian Empire. These were located chiefly in northern Russia, Belorussia, and Poland. A cotton cloth industry, using English yarns at first, grew up around Moscow and Vladimir. The first cotton spinning mill in Russia, using English machinery, was opened in 1808. In 1842, after England removed the ban on the export of textile machinery, the cotton industry grew rapidly.[10] This led, in turn, to the increased production of native cotton and the introduction of new varieties in Turkestan; but there was no development of cotton processing industries, except ginning, in Asiatic Russia. On the eve of the First World War, textile manufacturing still occupied 40 percent of all industrial workers in the Russian Empire (see Table 6).

[9] Rashin, Title 271, pp. 46-47, 108, 112-113.
[10] Russian Empire, Ministry of Finance, *The Industries of Russia*, Title 437.

TABLE 4

Number of Workers in Mining and Metallurgy: Russian Empire, 1885-1907, 1913[1]
(Numbers in Thousands)

Region	1885	1890	1895	1900	1907	1913
Russian Empire	349	436	498	715	656	648[2]
Including:						
Ural Region	189	232	232	272	232	—
Siberia	47	49	57	58	58	—
Central Russia	25	30	50	75	—[3]	—
Poland and Northwestern Russia	[20][4]	[22][4]	36	50	51	—
Caucasus Region	10	18	22	41	55	—
Southern Russia	45	69	84	177	200	—

[1] Official data from reports of the Ministry of the Interior, Department of Mines, Titles 434 and 435, except figure for 1913. It should be noted that responsibility for inspection of metallurgical plants was divided between the Department of Mines and the Department of Trade and Industry. Apparently the coverage varied and there is some overlapping in the statistics of these two agencies. Comparable official data were not found for 1913. The figure for that year is from Rashin, and there is some doubt as to its comparability with the preceding series. The figures by quinquennial intervals give a fair picture of the trend, except that employment in mines and metallurgical industry shows a peak for the years 1899-1901, and was lower during the years 1902-1906 than in 1907.

[2] Rashin, Title 271, p. 152.

[3] Moscow region only, 1907, 40 thousand.

[4] Poland only.

TABLE 5

Workers in Mining and Metallurgy: Russian Empire, 1913[1]

Distribution by Industry	Number (In thousands)
Total	647.7
Extraction of Fuels	325.0
Coal	224.5
Oil	44.5
Peat	56.0
Extraction of Minerals	171.8
Gold and Platinum	88.6
Iron	49.6
Manganese	6.2
Asbestos	7.2
Salt	19.0
Metallurgy	150.9
Ferrous	139.5
Non-ferrous	11.4

[1] Rashin, Title 271, p. 152.

TABLE 6

Workers by Industry: Russian Empire, 1913[1]

Industry	Number (In thousands)
All Industries	2,282.0
Textiles	918.2
Cotton	566.1
Wool	166.6
Silk	34.7
Linen	104.5
Miscellaneous	46.3
All Other	1,363.8
Paper and Print	107.7
Wood	132.1
Metals	385.6
Mineral Products	215.6
Animal Products	55.7
Foodstuffs	369.0
Chemicals	90.5
Other	7.6

[1] Rashin, Title 271, p. 140.

The estimated growth in the total number of industrial workers in factories relative to the growth of population in the Russian Empire is shown in Figure 4. (See also Table 7 and notes.) The proportion of the Russian population actively occupied in manufacturing and mechanical industries on the eve of World War I, though twice as high as in 1860, was still extremely low, with less than 2 industrial workers per 100 persons in the total population. At about this time in the United States there were 11.6 gainfully occupied persons in manufacturing and mechanical industries per 100 total population, and the corresponding proportion in 1820 had been about 3.6 percent.[11] However, the proportion of factory operatives reported in the population of Japan in 1900 was only 0.96 percent, rising to 1.46 percent in 1910—before the industrial boom in that country during World War I and subsequent years.[12] The percentage increase in the ratio of industrial workers to total population in the Russian Empire from 1900 to 1913 was apparently similar to that in the United States from 1820 to 1830, but definitely below the relative increase in the proportion of factory operatives in the Japanese population from 1900 to 1910. The figures for various countries and times cited here are not strictly comparable, and the data for the Russian Empire are particularly dubious; but they serve to indicate the retarded status of industry in Imperial Russia, even in the late prewar period.

Russian industry remained largely concentrated in a few areas, often on the basis of tradition or, as in the case of St. Petersburg, because of contacts with western Europe. Two districts, Moscow and Vladimir, claimed over one-third of all the industrial workers in Russia in

[11] U.S. Bureau of the Census. *Thirteenth Census of the United States: 1910.* Vol. I, p. 30, and Vol. IV, p. 40. Also, P. K. Whelpton, "Occupational Groups in the United States, 1820-1920," *Journal of the American Statistical Association* 31:335-343, September, 1926.

[12] Ryoichi Ishii, *Population Pressure and Economic Life in Japan* (London: P. S. King and Son, 1937), pp. 59, 227.

TABLE 7

Trend in Number of Industrial Workers Related to Total Population in the Russian Empire,
1815-1913[1]

Year	Estimated Population	Number of Industrial Workers[2]	Industrial Workers as Percent of Total Population
1815	42,510,200	173,000	0.4
1825	52,285,100	210,000	0.4
1835	60,185,300	288,000	0.48
1860	74,120,100	565,000	0.76
1900	131,710,000	1,692,000	1.28
1913	161,723,000	2,282,000	1.41

[1] Exclusive of Finland, Khiva, and Bukhara. Population estimates from Volkov, Title 352, p. 8 (using estimates by Zaytsev, Title 374, since 1897). Figures on workers from Rashin, Title 271, pp. 40-41, 160.

[2] The figures on industrial workers are based chiefly on factory inspection statistics, which were incomplete in coverage but which overlapped with statistics on employment in mines (see Table 4, Note 1). If the figure for workers in mining and metallurgy in 1913 (Table 4) is added to the figure given here for 1913, the gross sum (2,930,000) is 1.8 percent of the estimated total population. In December, 1926, according to the First All-Union Census, wage workers, salaried personnel, and entrepreneurs in manufacturing and mining in the U.S.S.R. were 1.9 percent of the total population (see Table 37). If equally complete and accurate statistics were available for the Russian Empire in 1913, the proportion of the total population shown as active personnel in manufacturing and mining would probably have been very close to the corresponding percentage for the U.S.S.R., December, 1926.

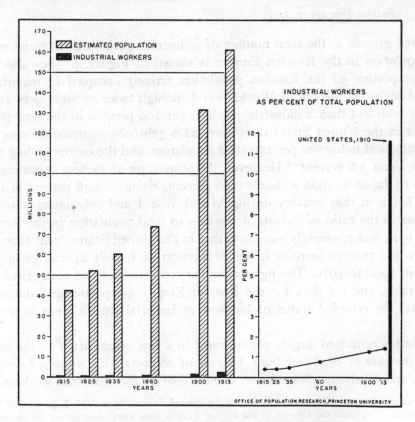

FIGURE 4. Trend in Number of Industrial Workers Related to Total
Population in the Russian Empire, 1815-1913 [Table 7]

the early nineteenth century and still held more than one-fourth of all industrial workers in 1913. After the middle of the nineteenth century the development of metal industries in St. Petersburg and later in the Ukraine assumed increased importance. These new centers of mechanical industry developed skilled workers, but neither center equaled Moscow in the total number of industrial employees prior to the First World War. As late as 1913, 6 provinces in central and northern Russia had 43 percent of all industrial workers in the Russian Empire and 4 provinces of the Ukraine had 10 percent (Table 8).

TABLE 8

Workers in Manufacturing in the Russian Empire and in Selected Provinces, 1815-1913[1]
(Numbers in Thousands)

Province	1815	1825	1835	1860	1900	1913
Russian Empire	173	210	288	565	1,692	2,282
In Central and Northern Russia:						
Moscow	31.9	45.0	66.8	107.3	286.8	384.1
Vladimir	28.1	35.5	66.0	87.1	158.2	208.9
St. Petersburg	5	6	6	33	165	218
Kostroma	—	—	—	—	59.9	93.2
Tver'	—	—	—	—	33.7	44.1
Yaroslavl'	—	—	—	—	33.6	39.2
In Southern Russia:						
Kiev	1.6	3.2	2.6	32.1	63.0	77.9
Khar'kov	2.7	0.9	3.0	12.1	38.2	53.2
Kherson	—	—	—	—	30.9	50.4
Yekaterinoslav	—	—	—	—	28.4	39.3
In Urals:						
Perm'	—	—	—	—	19	24

[1] Rashin, Title 271, pp. 40-41, 162. Corresponding data for all provinces for all years are not given in this source. See also Table 4, Note 1.

There were only about 21 thousand industrial workers in Central Asia and the Asiatic steppe region (not including Khiva and Bukhara) in 1914, i.e., about 0.2 industrial workers per 100 population.[13] Over one-third of these workers were engaged in cotton ginning; about one-tenth worked in the ancient silk industry (mostly small shops with two or three workers); less than one-tenth were in the petroleum industry; the remainder were engaged in miscellaneous small industries. This region, which included over 7 percent of the population of the Russian Empire, had less than 1 percent of its industrial workers. Moreover, the relatively few Russians living here supplied a fifth of all industrial workers and three-fourths of the skilled workers. The total number of industrial workers reported for Siberia a few years earlier (1908) was 37 thousand, or about 0.4 industrial workers per 100 population.[14] There was little industrial development in the Caucasus region (either in the North Caucasus or in the Transcaucasus), except the mining of petroleum, manganese, and copper in the Transcaucasus, which, at its peak in 1907, gave employment to 55 thousand workers. (See Table 4.)

[13] Lyashchenko, Title 182, p. 513.
[14] *Ibid.*, p. 496.

3. Transportation

The first railway of any importance in Russia was the line from St. Petersburg to Moscow, constructed in the 1840's. Lines were then developed between Warsaw and Moscow via Smolensk, and between Moscow and Yekaterinoslav and Theodosia via Kursk and Kharkov. The latter was extended to Odessa about 1860, and was supplemented about the same time by lines to Novocherkassk in the North Caucasus and to Saratov in southeastern Russia. A comparison of the extension of railways in European Russia, the United States, and western Europe from 1850 to 1880 is given in Table 9. Railway construction had barely begun in European Russia

TABLE 9
Length of Railways in European Russia and Other Areas, 1850 and 1880[1]

Area	Kilometers	
	1850	1880
European Russia (including Poland and Finland)	1,040	23,400
United States	14,500	150,700
Western Europe	22,900	145,100

[1] Oppengeim, Title 229, p. 76.

in 1850 and it was still comparatively slight in 1880. Moreover, even within European Russia the western parts were much more adequately serviced by railways than were the eastern areas.

There were no railways in Asiatic Russia until the last quarter of the nineteenth century. The Trans-Siberian railway was not begun until 1891; 1,400 kilometers of this line were in operation by 1896, and 1,900 additional kilometers were put into operation during the next three years.[15] The line from the Caspian into Central Asia and that from Baku to Batum across the Transcaucasus were opened in the 1880's. The line from European Russia across the Asiatic steppes to Tashkent was completed in the last decade of the nineteenth century. A summation of railway construction in various periods to 1916 brings the total to 81,000 kilometers in European Russia (plus the Transcaucasus and including Poland and Finland) and 16,000 kilometers in Siberia and Central Asia—with a total of 93,000 kilometers in operation in 1917.[16] Thus, only one-sixth of the railway construction of the Russian Empire was laid in Asiatic Russia (excluding the Transcaucasus), although the latter embraced nearly three-fourths of the total area. According to Mikhailov there were only 58,500 kilometers of railway within the present territory of the Soviet Union in 1913.[17]

Inland water transportation has played an important part in the development of Russian territory. But travel across Siberia required the use of portages and followed indirect routes through the branches of rivers flowing north into the Arctic. The Asiatic steppes, for the most part, have no rivers; those from Central Asia do not reach the Caspian. Moreover, the railway system was not well integrated with river transportation. Russian roads are notoriously bad. Inadequate transportation was, therefore, an important link in the chain of conditions that retarded economic progress and the redistribution of population in Russia.

4. Colonization and the Economy of Outlying Regions

For a long time interest in the development of Asiatic Russia was limited to the exploitation of easily available resources, such as furs, fish, and precious metals. The earliest Russian

[15] Mertons, Title 191, p. 280.   [16] Oppengeim, Title 229, pp. 107-108.   [17] Mikhailov, Title 194, p. 60.

settlers in Siberia were traders and military adventurers, many of whom intermarried with the indigenous population. Political interest in the extension of the bounds of the Russian Empire in Asia and the northern Pacific changed from time to time, as is evidenced by negotiations with China over the Amur and Ussuri regions in the third quarter of the nineteenth century and the sale of Alaska to the United States in 1867. The assignment of criminals to work in Siberian mines began in the eighteenth century; nearly a million criminals, political exiles, and their followers had crossed to Siberia before the end of the century. The director of prisons estimated that in 1896 there were about 300,000 exiles, prisoners, and their followers in Siberia, including escaped convicts. About 50,000 persons were sent to Siberia in the year following the revolution of 1905.[18] The main elements in the Russian occupation of Siberia, however, were Cossack settlements, individual adventurers, and agricultural colonies located on the Imperial domain.

In the latter half of the nineteenth century, the gradual occupation of the remaining virgin lands in southern Russia gave an impetus to the extension of agricultural settlements into the northern part of the Asiatic steppes, western Siberia, and finally eastern Siberia, Central Asia, and the Far East. The Russian government, however, did not take a strong interest in the promotion of colonization in Siberia until the last decade of the nineteenth century, the era of the construction of the Trans-Siberian and Tashkent railways. Legal restrictions on individual migration to Siberia were first removed in 1904.

The extent of sown land cultivated by Russians in Siberia, the Far East, the Asiatic steppes, and Turkestan increased from about 8 million hectares in 1905 to about 12 million hectares in 1911.[19] Of all land in Asiatic Russia (exclusive of the Transcaucasus) cultivated by Russian migrants or their descendants in 1911, 44 percent was in western Siberia, 10 percent in eastern Siberia, 9 in the Far East, 17 in the steppe region, and 19 percent in Turkestan, mostly in the eastern or northern districts. At the same time only 2.6 million hectares were cultivated by the indigenous Asiatic population, whereof 60 percent was in Turkestan, 30 percent in the steppe region, and only 10 percent in all Siberia, including Far Eastern districts.[20] Wheat constituted the principal crop in western Siberia at the time, accounting for 50 percent of the sown land; nearly three-fourths of the wheat crop was exported to other regions. Wheat and fodder crops were developed by Russian settlers in Turkestan, whereas most of the cotton was cultivated by the indigenous population.

Turkestan was not brought under final subjection to the Russian Empire until 1880, although parts had been conquered during the preceding decade. The settlement of Russian colonists in this region was resented by the native population. Owing to initial disorders, colonization was suspended for fifteen years. Thereafter the settlement of Russians in Turkestan progressed slowly until shortly before the First World War, when an ambitious program was initiated for the establishment of Russian communities in the eastern part of Russian Turkestan. In the course of the war there were serious disorders in this region, involving expulsion of Russian colonists and resistance to conscription. These events caused an absolute decrease of population during the war years in some parts of Asiatic Russia.

Emigration to Asiatic Russia rose rapidly with the building of the Trans-Siberian and Tashkent railways, but after reaching a peak in 1907 it remained at a lower level during the rest of the prewar period. The estimated number of permanent migrants settling in Asiatic

[18] Great Britain, Foreign Office, Title 90. The number of "exiles and prisoners" reported as "settling in Asiatic Russia," 1901-1910, is given by Obolensky-Ossinsky as only 25,000, but this may include adjustment for returned exiles (see Table 10).

[19] Lyashchenko, Title 182, p. 492.

[20] *Ibid.*

Russia in successive periods from the beginning of the nineteenth century to the outbreak of World War I is shown in Figure 5 and Table 10.

TABLE 10

Russian Migrants Reported as Settling in Asiatic Russia, 1801-1914[1]

(Numbers in Thousands)

Period	Total Number[2]			Annual Average[2]		
	Peasants	Exiles and Prisoners	Total	Peasants	Exiles and Prisoners	Total
1801-1850	125	250	375	3	5	8
1851-1860	91	100	191	9	10	19
1861-1870	114	140	254	11	14	25
1871-1880	68	180	248	7	18	25
1881-1890	279	140	419	28	14	42
1891-1900	1,078	130	1,208	108	13	121
1901-1910	2,257	25	2,282	226	3	229
1911-1914	696	27	723	174	6	180

[1] Obolensky-Ossinsky, Title 221, p. 556. (Cf. Russian text, Title 220, p. 84.) Apparent error in original text for total, 1891-1900, corrected to agree with sum of items and with corresponding yearly averages.

[2] Illegal migrants in period prior to abolition of serfdom not included except in 1801-1850. Figures for "Prisoners and Exiles" are incomplete. The estimated total number of unreported migrants and those omitted from Table 10 during the nineteenth century was "not more than 700 thousand." *Ibid.*

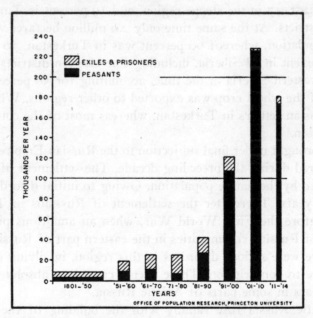

FIGURE 5. Russian Migrants Reported as Settling in Asiatic Russia, 1801-1914 [Table 10]

From 1897 to 1911, during the peak period of the eastward migration, there was a gross increase of 3,600,000 persons in the population of Siberia, according to official estimates—including both growth through migration and excess of births over deaths. During the same period there were estimated gross increases of 1,368,000 persons in the Asiatic steppe region, and 1,212,000 persons in Russian Turkestan, exclusive of Khiva and Bukhara. However, there were only about 400,000 Russians in Turkestan in 1911, in contrast to 1,500,000 in the Asiatic steppe region and 8,000,000 in Siberia. Russians formed 85 percent of the total population of Siberia at this time and were predominant in all major administrative districts, except Yakutia and Kamchatka. They formed 40 percent of the population of the steppe region, but were predominant only in the north-central area (Akmolinsk District). They formed 6 percent of the population of Turkestan, with the highest proportion (17 percent) in Semirechensk, which corresponds roughly to the present Soviet republic of Kirgiz. (See Table 11.)

TABLE 11

Population Change in Asiatic Russia, 1897-1911; Proportion of Russians, by Province, 1911[1]

Division and Guberniya or Oblast'	Total Population			Russian Population, 1911	
	Number (In thousands)		Percent Increase 1897-1911[2]	Number (In thousands)	Percent of Total Population[2]
	1897	1911			
Siberia	5,760	9,366	63	7,996	85
Tobol'sk	1,434	1,975	38	1,828	93
Tomsk	1,928	3,674	91	3,463	94
Yenisey	570	966	69	875	91
Irkutsk	515	750	46	588	78
Transbaykal	672	869	29	591	68
Yakutsk	269	277	3	18	7
Amur	120	286	140	242	85
Maritime	189	524	177	380	73
Kamchatka	35	36	4	4	12
Sakhalin	28	9	—69	6	63
Steppe Region and Turkestan	7,747	10,327	33	1,950	19
Ural'sk	645	804	25	298	37
Turgay	453	713	57	235	33
Akmolinsk	683	1,444	112	835	58
Semipalatinsk	685	874	28	175	20
Transcaspian	382	472	24	42	11
Syr Dar'ya	1,478	1,817	23	103	6
Samarkand	860	960	12	23	2
Fergana	1,572	2,042	30	34	2
Semirechensk	988	1,202	22	204	17
Subtotals					
Asiatic Steppes[3]	2,466	3,834	56	1,544	40
Turkestan	5,281	6,493	23	407	6

[1] *Aziatskaya Rossiya*, Title 415, Vol. I, pp. 82 ff. Data given here do not include Transcaucasus.

[2] Percentages have been calculated from absolute figures, wherever available, in this and following tables; these differ slightly from percentages indicated by rounded figures (in thousands) shown in tables. The same explanation of discrepancies applies to totals and subtotals.

[3] Ural'sk, Turgay, Akmolinsk, and Semipalatinsk districts.

5. Relations between Population, Resources, and Economic Structure

The fundamental principle controlling the development of Asiatic Russia during the Imperial period was a development *in extenso*—the expansion of an agrarian economy into lands that were thinly settled, and the exploitation of easily available resources. As we have already noted, the sense of population pressure, or "land hunger," in European Russia was due to the character of the Russian economy rather than to the absolute relation of population to natural resources.[21] A fundamental solution through technological advance and the development of a balanced, integrated economy in the whole Empire seemed impossible or at least remote. Since vertical expansion was thus apparently blocked, this pressure found partial relief in a horizontal expansion into new areas.

The central agricultural belt between Siberia and the steppe region generally has less rainfall than the corresponding region in European Russia. The agricultural resources of Asiatic Russia, although undoubtedly very great, require the application of advanced agricultural techniques. Moreover, prior to the late nineteenth century, the lack of transportation facilities prevented the effective development of commercial agriculture beyond the Urals. Although legal obstacles hindered the movement of Russians to Siberia during the eighteenth and nineteenth centuries, it is clear that the main inhibiting factors were the natural limitations of the territory, including distance, and the retarded development of industry, capital, transportation, and technology in the Russian Empire.

As industrial activity was heightened in western Europe, Russia slowly emerged from a locally self-sufficient feudal economy and developed many of the characteristics of a colonial economy. Russian economy became heavily dependent on foreign capital, about ninety percent of the mining industry in Russia being financed by foreign investments.[22] In the late prewar years, although the flow of foreign investments continued, the interest on previous investments exceeded the increments of foreign capital, so that the value of imports was held below the value of exports at this time.[23] The prices of most foodstuffs, which bulked large in Russian exports, were about one-third lower in Russia than in England, Germany, or France but the prices of most manufactured goods were very much higher.[24] Above all, the whole Russian economy remained predominantly agrarian at a low technical level.

The conditions of the Russian economy as a whole fixed the level on which the economic integration of the various parts of the Empire was worked out. The outlying regions, therefore, might be characterized as the colonial appendages of a nation whose economic relations to the outside world also had many of the characteristics of a colonial economy.

The economic situation of the Empire was not by any means wholly static. The indices of industrial production, industrial employment, development of transportation, and probably, as we have seen, productivity per agricultural worker, all showed upward trends. But the potentialities of Russian natural resources for a highly productive modern economy remained largely unrealized and the lags in organization and technology were painfully apparent.

[21] Chapter I, particularly Section 5.
[23] *Encyclopedia Britannica*, fourteenth edition: Russia.
[22] Lyashchenko, Title 182, p. 598.
[24] Robinson, Title 276, pp. 245-246.

CHAPTER III

POPULATION CHANGES DURING WORLD WAR I, REVOLUTION, AND CIVIL WAR

1. General Description

THE Union of Soviet Socialist Republics was formed by act of the First All-Union Congress of Soviets, December 30, 1922. It was extended within the next two years to embrace the central Asiatic territory of the former Russian Empire, including two vassal territories, the Khanate of Khiva and the Emirate of Bukhara; it then covered a land area of 21,176,000 square kilometers (8,176,000 square miles).[1] The same territory had a population of about 106,080,000 persons at the time of the Imperial census of February 9, 1897[2] (assuming a population of 2,175,000 in Khiva and Bukhara, not covered by the census).[3] Its enumerated population on December 17, 1926, was 147,027,915 persons. An increase of about 41 million persons, or 38.6 percent, in slightly less than thirty years, in spite of the catastrophic events of the period 1914-1922, is evidence of the rapid growth characteristic of the Russian population in the prewar years and in the years immediately preceding the first Soviet census.

The Russian demographer Volkov, who has made the most exhaustive study of population changes during this period, estimates that World War I and the Revolution and the subsequent civil wars, foreign intervention, famine, and epidemics caused a deficit of 30 million persons in population within the U.S.S.R. area.[4] Two independent estimates described below are somewhat lower, but have a similar order of magnitude.

Volkov estimated the population change within the area of the U.S.S.R. year by year. If we compare his estimated figures[5] for January 1 of each year, 1915-1923, with the "expected" increase each year at the estimated rate observed in the prewar period, we obtain estimates of the *relative* gain or loss each year—ignoring the compounding of such gains or losses as they affect changes in other years (see Table 12 and graphic representation in Figure 6). The total deficit thus indicated for these years (ignoring cumulative effects) is 28.5 million. Only 31 percent of this loss is attributed to the years of the World War, 1915-1917. The remainder, a deficit of 19,651,000 persons, is assigned to the years 1918-1923. Moreover, the greatest loss apparently did not occur in 1922, the year of most acute famine, but in 1920 (see Figure 6). This suggests that the most deadly forces in Russia during these terrible years were the lice that carried typhus, and other bearers of infectious diseases.

A summary of estimated population changes from 1897 to 1923 in various major divisions of the U.S.S.R., according to Volkov, is shown in Figure 7. According to his estimates there was an increase of 34.7 percent in the population of the U.S.S.R. area (minus Khiva and Bukhara) from 1897 to 1914. Somewhat similar proportional increases are credited to the Transcaucasus (33 percent) and to Turkestan (35 percent). Although absolute increases in other areas were, of course, less than in European Russia, larger proportional increases during

---

[1] See Appendix I, Table A 4.　　　　　　　　[2] Old calendar: January 28, 1897.

[3] Estimates of population in the U.S.S.R. area, 1897, vary somewhat. The figure given here is that from Volkov, Title 352, p. 33, plus the estimated population of Khiva and Bukhara. The corresponding figure obtained from the compilation of "population study areas" is 106,070,000. (See Section 7 of Chapter X, especially Table 67, and also Appendix I, Tables A 2 and A 3.)

[4] Volkov, Title 352, p. 262. His figure of 30,200,000 refers to the differences between "observed" and "expected" population in 1930. However, the population of the Khiva and Bukhara areas is included in the "observed" population but omitted in calculating the "expected" population.

[5] Plus estimated figures for the population of Khiva and Bukhara, on the arbitrary assumption of constant increase, 1897-1926.

TABLE 12

Population Estimates for U.S.S.R. Area, 1914-1927, according to Volkov—with Annual Increment or Decrement Relative to Expected Increase at Prewar Rate

(Numbers in Thousands)

Year	Population at Beginning of Year[1]	Expected Increase at Constant Rate (.01662)[2]	Estimated Actual Increase (+) or Decrease (—)	Increment (+) or Decrement (—) Relative to Expected Increase (C)—(B)
	(A)	(B)	(C)	(D)
1914	142,389	2,367	+2,693	+ 326
1915	145,082	2,411	— 310	—2,721
1916	144,772	2,406	+ 229	—2,177
1917	145,001	2,410	—1,551	—3,961
1918	143,450	2,384	—1,185	—3,569
1919	142,265	2,364	—2,590	—4,954
1920	139,675	2,321	—2,799	—5,120
1921	136,876	2,275	— 368	—2,643
1922	136,508	2,269	— 406	—2,675
1923	136,102	2,262	+1,572	— 690
1924	137,674	2,288	+2,945	+ 657
1925	140,619	2,337	+3,141	+ 804
1926	143,760	2,389	+3,368	+ 979
1927	147,128	—	—	—
Sum of Decrements, 1915-1917				— 8,859
Sum of Decrements, 1918-1923				—19,651
Sum of Decrements, 1915-1923				—28,510

[1] Volkov, Title 352, p. 209. Estimated population of Khiva and Bukhara, 1914 (2,475,900), and constant yearly increment (17,700) added to give continuity, 1914-1924. Volkov's figures for 1925, 1926, and 1927 include Khiva and Bukhara.

[2] Our estimate, see text, p. 36.

the prewar period are indicated for the North Caucasus and Don region (52 percent), for the Asiatic steppe region (60 percent), and for Siberia and the Far East (74 percent); the estimated increase in the European area outside the North Caucasus and Don region was 29.5 percent.

Population growth was checked sharply in all areas during the war years but absolute decreases from 1914 to 1918 are indicated only for the North Caucasus (—8 percent) and for Turkestan (—17 percent). The large absolute loss in Turkestan (1.23 million persons) is attributed to the rebellion of the Kirgiz and other indigenous groups against conscription for military labor in 1916 and to related disorders involving mass executions, the movement of nomads across the Russian borders to Chinese Turkestan and Afghanistan, and the return of many Russian colonists. Although the population in the European part of the U.S.S.R. (apart from the North Caucasus and Don region) grew slightly during the war years, there was, according to Volkov, an absolute decrease of nearly 7 million persons (—7 percent) in the years from 1918 to 1923. There was, moreover, a decrease of over 2 million persons (—22 percent) in the North Caucasus and Don area during the same period—giving an estimated decrease of

9 million persons in the European part of the U.S.S.R. Siberia, in these years, had a small increase, estimated as less than 1 million persons. The return of the Kirgiz, driven back from Chinese Turkestan, plus drought refugees from the Volga and Asiatic steppe regions brought an increase of somewhat over 1 million persons to Russian Turkestan. The population of the Transcaucasus decreased from 1918 to 1923 by less than one-half million (—6 percent), and that of the Asiatic steppe region apparently remained stationary from 1914 to 1923. Accord-

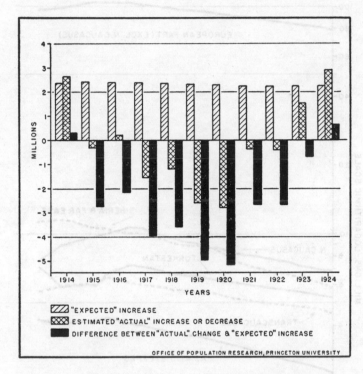

FIGURE 6. Population Change according to Volkov, Relative to Expected Increase Each Year: U.S.S.R. Area, 1914-1924 [Table 12]

ing to Volkov, there was an absolute decrease of over 7 million persons within the U.S.S.R. area from January 1, 1918, to January 1, 1923.

The urban population increased during the war years, 1914 to 1918, but declined sharply in absolute number and in proportion to the total population from 1918 to 1921. During these years industry was disorganized; also, many peasants hastily returned to their villages to occupy the expropriated estates of the nobility. During the famine years there was an increase of population in many cities, owing to the influx of refugees from the stricken countryside in the Volga region. Thereafter, there was a constant and rapid increase of urban population.[6]

According to the census of 1897, there were only 12,969,000 persons in places then classified as urban within the U.S.S.R. area.[7] The urban population was really somewhat larger because many communities avoided incorporation in order to escape increased taxation. Places in the U.S.S.R. that were classified in 1926 as urban had 15,955,000 inhabitants in 1897, representing

[6] Statements based on treatment by Volkov, Title 352. However, his estimated absolute figures on urban population were not corrected for changes in legal status of communities, and are, therefore, not reproduced here.

[7] Compiled from census data, plus hypothetical figure of 129,000 for urban population of Khiva and Bukhara in 1897.

15.0 percent of the total population.[8] There was an appreciable increase of urban population within the territory later organized as the Soviet Union during the next seventeen years. The estimated number of persons living in urban places (1926 list) rose to 24,888,000 by January 1, 1914.[9] This figure is about 17.5 percent of the estimated total population at that time. The

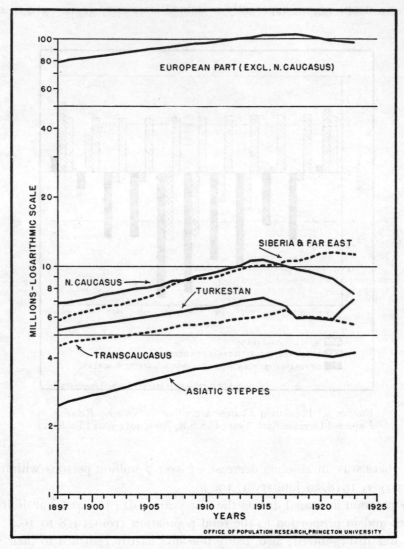

FIGURE 7. Population of the U.S.S.R.: By Division of Territory, 1897-1923
[Data from Volkov, Title 352]

urban population was then about 4 million greater than it would have been if the cities had merely increased at the same rate as the whole population. The proportion of the Soviet population living in cities on December 17, 1926 (17.9 percent), was only slightly higher than the

---

[8] Estimate of population in Soviet list of cities from *Socialist Reconstruction in the USSR*, Title 408, p. 397, plus same hypothetical figure for cities of Khiva and Bukhara. This proportion of 15.0 is slightly less than the corresponding figure for the United States in 1850 (on the basis of criteria that are probably somewhat less inclusive).

[9] *Ibid.*, Title 408, p. 397, with addition of estimate for cities of Khiva and Bukhara, assuming same rate of increase as in other urban places. The total population of the U.S.S.R. area, including Khiva and Bukhara, in 1914 was 142,389,000, according to Volkov.

estimated proportion in 1914—after the influx to cities during the World War, the later exodus during the revolutionary period, and the return movement after the civil wars. The absolute number of persons living in urban places according to the 1926 census was 26,314,114.

The population of Moscow is reported to have fallen from 1,852,000 in 1917 to 1,120,000 persons in 1920; but it rose to 2,029,000 persons in 1926. The population of Leningrad dropped from 2,300,000 in 1917 to 740,000 in 1920 and rose, somewhat more slowly, to 1,690,000 in 1926.[10] These changes reflect great movements in and out of these cities, and also rapid variations in fertility and mortality. The reported birth rate per 1,000 population in Moscow fell from 31 in 1914 to 20 in 1917, 15 in 1918, and 17 in 1919. It rose to the prewar level in 1921 and fluctuated around this level during the next four years. Meanwhile, the apparent death rate per 1,000 population in Moscow rose from 23 in 1914 to 30 in 1918, 45 in 1919, and 36 in 1920. It then dropped below the prewar level in 1923 and later years.[11] In Leningrad the apparent death rates in 1918, 1919, and 1920 were 47, 77, and 51, respectively, per 1,000 population—in contrast to earlier and later rates of 22 in 1914 and 16 in 1923.[12] Such figures illustrate the violence of population changes in Russia at this time.

2. Estimate of the Prewar Population Trend

The critical point in estimating the demographic effects of the war and subsequent disorders concerns the population at the outbreak of the war (seventeen years after the last census) and the "normal" rate of growth during the late prewar years. Volkov's estimate of the population in the European part of the U.S.S.R. area in 1914 is based chiefly on a critical treatment of local registration data by Zaytsev. His estimate for 1914 is far below that obtained by the former Central Statistical Committee through mere compilation of local registration data, but it is possible that this figure is still somewhat too high. Any exaggeration of the figure for 1914 raises the estimated rate of increase from 1897 to 1914, and thus causes a still greater exaggeration in the "expected" population for 1926. In view of imperfections and duplications in the local registers, we shall rely primarily on estimates of natural increase and net migration, though these are also subject to error.

The birth and death rates and the rate of natural increase (excess of births over deaths) in European Russia were all considerably lower in the western provinces that were largely lost by the Soviet Union than in the part remaining under the U.S.S.R. This is not surprising in view of the higher literacy of the people in the western provinces and their closer cultural contacts with western Europe. The estimated rates for the period 1899-1913 are presented in Table 13 and Figure 8.[13]

The rate of natural increase shows a tendency during this period toward a gradual decline in the area lost by the U.S.S.R. (represented by 11 provinces) but it remained fairly constant within the European part of the U.S.S.R. area. The change in the three-year average rates from the beginning to the end of the period is shown in Table 14.

In view of the difficulty of determining migration by region, we have used an indirect procedure in estimating the net population growth within the U.S.S.R. area from 1897 to 1914. We estimated the natural increase in all European Russia (including the North Caucasus) on

---

[10] Prokopovich, Title 260, p. 20.   [11] *Ibid.*, p. 21.   [12] *Ibid.*, p. 26.

[13] The necessary data for the years 1897 to 1898 were not located. In obtaining the "expected" population in 1914 it is assumed that the average rates of natural increase observed for the period 1899-1913 also prevailed during the two preceding years. It should be noted that the areas to which these rates are applied have only approximate, not complete, correspondence to the areas used in their derivation. The North Caucasus is included in the Soviet area to which these rates are applied. The U.S.S.R. also includes parts of some of the 11 provinces selected as representing the area lost by the U.S.S.R.

TABLE 13

Estimated Births, Deaths, and Natural Increase per 1,000 Population in 11 European Provinces Lost in Whole or in Part to the U.S.S.R.;[1] and in 39 European Provinces Remaining within the U.S.S.R., 1899-1913[2]

Year	11 Provinces			39 Provinces		
	Births	Deaths	Natural Increase	Births	Deaths	Natural Increase
1899	41.1	25.2	15.9	50.7	33.4	17.3
1900	40.3	24.4	15.9	51.0	32.3	18.7
1901	39.5	24.7	14.8	49.6	33.6	16.0
1902	41.0	23.4	17.6	50.6	33.1	17.5
1903	37.8	24.4	13.4	50.2	31.1	19.1
1904	38.6	23.7	14.9	50.6	31.1	19.5
1905	35.1	25.0	10.1	47.0	33.2	13.8
1906	36.4	21.7	14.7	49.3	31.6	17.7
1907	36.5	20.5	16.0	49.5	30.2	19.3
1908	34.4	20.6	13.8	47.3	30.2	17.1
1909	35.6	21.3	14.3	47.3	31.6	15.7
1910	34.6	23.0	11.6	48.1	33.3	14.8
1911	33.8	20.9	12.9	47.9	29.2	18.7
1912	34.4	19.3	15.1	46.6	28.7	17.9
1913	32.8	20.3	12.5	48.3	30.9	17.4

[1] Exclusive of St. Petersburg and Arkhangel'sk provinces, in which the territory transferred was a negligible fraction of the total.

[2] Number of births and deaths, by provinces, from *Statisticheskiy Yezhegodnik Rossii*, gg. 1904-1916, Title 397. Estimated population for 50 provinces from Zaytsev (see Volkov, Title 352, p. 26), assuming constant change in proportion between 11 and 39 provinces, 1897-1914, with 1914 figures from Zaytsev, Title 374, pp. 60, 92.

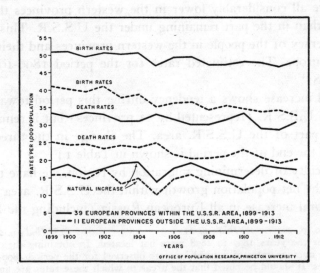

FIGURE 8. Births, Deaths, and Natural Increase in European Russia. Estimated Rates: (1) Outside, (2) Within the U.S.S.R. Area, 1899-1913 [Table 13]

TABLE 14

Births, Deaths, and Natural Increase per 1,000 Population: European Provinces, 1899-1901 and 1911-1913[1]

Area	Births		Deaths		Natural Increase	
	1899-1901	1911-1913	1899-1901	1911-1913	1899-1901	1911-1913
11 Provinces (representing separated areas)	40.3	33.7	24.8	20.2	15.5	13.5
39 Provinces (representing Soviet area)	50.4	47.6	33.1	29.6	17.3	18.0

[1] Based on Table 13.

the basis of the reported vital statistics, and subtracted the estimated net out-migration from this whole area to other countries and to Asiatic Russia. We then distributed this derived actual population, 1914, between non-Soviet and Soviet territory in proportion to Volkov's estimates. These figures and related estimates are given in Table 15.

TABLE 15

Estimated Population of European Russia, 1897-1914
(Numbers in Thousands)

Population, Natural Increase, and Migration	European Area Not in U.S.S.R.	European Part of U.S.S.R.	All European Russia
Population, 1/1/1897[1]	11,882.0	85,915.4	97,797
Estimated annual rate of natural increase per thousand[2]	14.23	17.36	—
Population expected if there had been no migration, 1/1/1914	15,108	115,118	130,226
Estimated net migration to foreign countries[3]	—470	—875	—1,345
Estimated net migration to Asiatic Russia, 1897-1914[4]	—	—	—3,556
Estimated total net migration	—	—	—4,901
Estimated population (adjusted for migration), 1/1/1914	—	—	125,325
Estimates by Volkov, 1/1/1914[1]	14,748	112,819	127,567
Estimated population, 1/1/1914	14,489[5]	110,836[5]	125,325
Estimated natural increase	3,226	29,203	32,429
Estimated total net migration	—619	—4,282	—4,901
Net migration to Asiatic Russia and foreign countries as percent of natural increase	19.2	14.7	15.1

[1] Volkov, Title 352, p. 26 (column 2); p. 33.
[2] Table 13.
[3] Distribution between divisions obtained by applying distribution of ethnic groups according to 1897 census to estimated net number of migrants in each ethnic group. (See Appendix III.)
[4] Estimate by Obolensky-Ossinsky, Title 221, p. 556.
[5] Estimated total (125,325 thousand) divided between non-Soviet and Soviet areas in proportion to division in preceding line.

The percentage of natural increase lost through migration of all types during the period 1897 to 1914 was apparently greater in the western districts acquired by other nations (19 percent) than within the Soviet part of European Russia (15 percent). Moreover, our figures indicate that more than two-thirds of the permanent migrants from the non-Soviet area of European Russia went to foreign countries, whereas nearly four-fifths of those from the Soviet area settled in Siberia or Central Asia. Incidentally, emigration from Russia to foreign countries was very small until near the end of the nineteenth century. According to Obolensky-Ossinsky, the net outflow from the Russian Empire, mostly from Polish, Lithuanian, or Finnish areas, from 1828 to 1890 was only 1,162,000 persons. The estimated net outflow from 1890 to 1915 was nearly three times as large, i.e., 3,348,000.[14]

The estimate of the population in the European part of the U.S.S.R. area in 1914 obtained in this way is 110,836,000, or 1,983,000 below the corresponding estimate by Volkov. Our estimate is not necessarily more accurate, but we shall use this more conservative figure. Combining this figure for the European part of the Soviet area with official estimates for the Asiatic part[15] gives 140,405,000 as the estimated total population in the territory of the Soviet Union, January 1, 1914 (see Table 16). The average annual rate of increase thus indicated

TABLE 16

Estimated Population in U.S.S.R. Territory, 1897-1914[1]

(Numbers in Thousands)

Area	1897	1914	Percent Increase 1897-1914
Total	106,080	140,405	32.4
European Part	85,915	110,836	29.0
Siberia and Far East	5,750	10,001	73.9
Asiatic Steppes	2,466	3,956	60.4
Turkestan	5,281	7,148	35.4
Khiva and Bukhara[2]	2,175	2,475	13.8
Transcaucasus	4,493	5,989	33.3

[1] All figures except those for European Part and for Khiva and Bukhara are the official estimates, cited by Volkov, Title 352.

[2] The estimates for Khiva and Bukhara are based on examination of maps and census data for 1926, with arbitrary assumption of equal increments, 1897-1926, to give a period increase proportional to that of other populations in areas of four Central Asiatic republics. Compare estimate of 2,600,000 population in Khiva and Bukhara, 1913, in *Narodnoye Khozyaystvo SSSR, 1932*, Title 407, p. xxii.

for the period 1897 to 1914 is 16.62 per 1,000 population. About 875,000 persons had emigrated from the U.S.S.R. territory to foreign countries between 1897 and 1914. The average rate of *natural increase* from 1897 to 1914 was, therefore, somewhat higher, i.e., about 17.15 per thousand per year.

3. Estimated Loss in Wars, Revolution, and Famine

The population trend in the U.S.S.R. area from 1897 to 1914, as estimated above, and the growth from the beginning of 1914 to the end of 1926 to be expected from a continuation of

[14] Obolensky-Ossinsky, Title 221, p. 523.

[15] Estimates based on Russian registration data are apparently more reliable for migrant-receiving areas than for areas of net out-migration. The figures for Asiatic Russia check reasonably well with data on migration and hypothetical estimates of natural increase.

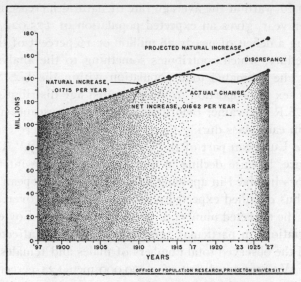

FIGURE 9. Estimated Trend in Population, U.S.S.R. Area, 1897-1914, with Projection to 1927 and "Actual" Change, 1914-1927 (Degrees of Shading Show Relative Reliability of Population Estimates) [Table 17]

the prewar rate of natural increase (starting at the "actual" 1914 level) are shown in Figure 9. The diagram also shows the actual population in the same area at the end of 1926. The solid line between the actual 1914 and 1926 levels is based on Volkov's estimates of year-by-year changes, adjusted by equal absolute increments to give the net change indicated by our figure for 1914 and the census figure for 1926. It gives an approximate picture of "actual change" during this period. The discrepancy between the "expected growth" and the "actual change" gives an indication of loss due to catastrophic events. The relatively small effect of continued normal migration from the U.S.S.R. area during these years is ignored here, but will be taken into account below as a factor in the total loss during this period.

The magnitude of the estimated loss is shown numerically in Table 17. Projecting the esti-

TABLE 17

Estimated Deficit in Population of the U.S.S.R., 1926, Attributed to Effects of War and Postwar Conditions (Method A)

(Numbers in Thousands)

Condition	Expected Dec. 17, 1926	Observed Dec. 17, 1926	Difference Exp. — Obs.	Deficit as Percent of Expected
Estimated Population January 1, 1914: 140,405				
(1) At estimated rate of growth, 1897-1914 (.01662 per annum)	173,884	147,028	26,856	15
(2) At estimated rate of natural increase, 1897-1914 (.01715 per annum)	175,022	147,028	27,994	16

mated 1914 population forward at the average rate of natural increase in the preceding period, 17.15 per thousand per year, gives an expected population of 175,022,000 at the time of the 1926 census—indicating a deficit of nearly 28 million or 16 percent of the expected population.

An alternative procedure, which contributes something to the analysis of this deficit, was developed as follows. The estimated total population within the U.S.S.R. area in 1897 was distributed by age and sex in proportion to the computed age distribution of the population in the area of the R.S.F.S.R., Ukraine, Belorussia, and the Transcaucasus.[16] The expected proportions of survivors in each class during the next thirty years were estimated on the basis of life-table values for the European part of the U.S.S.R., 1896-1897.[17] This would appear to be a conservative procedure, because decline in mortality during the interval might be expected to overbalance the errors involved in applying values for the European part of the area to the total population. We thus obtained expected persons aged 30 and over, February 9, 1927, and treated these results as the expected number at the time of the first Soviet census, December 17, 1926. We ignored variations in particular age classes (seriously affected by errors in age reporting) but compared the observed total numbers of males and females aged 30 and over with the expected numbers. We found a deficit of 7,290,000 men (24 percent of the expected male population aged 30 and over) and 4,772,000 women (15 percent of the expected female population aged 30 and over), i.e., a total deficit of about 12 million persons among those who were already living at the time of the Imperial census.

In order to estimate the deficit in younger age groups, we noted that 15.24 percent of the 1897 population in Soviet territory (population used in the previous experiment) were children. Under normal conditions this proportion presumably would have remained fairly constant for several decades, with a slow decline in the birth rate being offset by gradual improvement in infant mortality. On this assumption, by extrapolating the expected population (as in Method A) to December 17, 1926, in selected years, we derived the expected number of children under 5 years of age at five-year intervals preceding the Soviet census. We then estimated the proportions of such children expected to be living at various ages at the time of the census, using averages of survival ratios for the European part of the U.S.S.R. in 1896-1897 and in 1926-1927, weighted in proportion to the distances of the mid-point of the exposure period from January 1, 1927, and from January 1, 1897, respectively.[18] The estimated deficits in various age classes indicated by this procedure are shown in Table 18. The low figure obtained for the deficit in the age class 15-19 years is presumably spurious, owing to errors in age reporting in 1926 which fictitiously increased the number in this age group,[19] but apart from this peculiar deviation the pattern presented is reasonable. The peak deficit occurs, as we should expect, in the age class 5-9 years, born in the most disastrous period, 1917-1921. There is an estimated deficit of 6,700,000 persons in this group, or 31 percent. The apparent deficit in all classes under 30 years of age is 17,565,000 persons. Adding this to the previous total loss of persons aged 30 years and over gives an apparent deficit of 29,627,000. The estimated net emigration during the years 1897 to 1914 must be deducted from this total, and allowance must be made for the natural increase of the emigrant population (assumed to have been absent during fifty percent of the prewar period). After making these adjustments, the estimated deficit is 28,-314,000, or 16 percent of the expected population. The fact that this estimate differs by only 320,000 (about 1 percent) from that obtained by Method A must be regarded as sheer coinci-

[16] Census of 1926, Title 391, Vol. 17, Table 14. Persons of known age and sex in each five-year class, as here reported, were multiplied by 1.048 to give estimated distribution for total U.S.S.R. area, giving a total of 106,062,000 persons.

[17] Novosel'skiy and Payevskiy, Title 417, Table 55.   [18] See Appendix III.

[19] See discussion of sex ratios in this Chapter, p. 42.

dence. Both procedures are subject to large errors. One is justified only in concluding that the actual deficit was somewhere in the vicinity of 28 million persons, and probably not less than 25 million or over 30 million.

4. Factors Underlying the Population Deficit

Estimates of international migration across the borders of Soviet territory between 1914 and 1926 are very divergent. Von Rimscha, relying largely on statistics of refugees registered with the American Red Cross, arrived at a total of 2,935,000.[20] This estimate is generally re-

TABLE 18

Estimated Deficit in Population of the U.S.S.R., 1926, Attributed to Effects of War and Postwar Conditions (Method B)[1]

(Numbers in Thousands)

Approximate Birth Years	Age at Census Dec. 17, 1926	Expected Population	Observed Population	Difference Exp. — Obs.	Deficit as Percent of Expected
1897-1901	25-29	13,770	12,045	1,725	13
1902-1906	20-24	15,620	13,822	1,798	12
1907-1911	15-19	17,609	16,986	623	4
1912-1916	10-14	19,630	17,101	2,529	13
1917-1921	5-9	21,988	15,279	6,709	31
1922-1926	0-4	26,517	22,336	4,181	16
	0-29	115,134	97,569	17,565	15
Males, 30 and Over		30,431	23,141[2]	7,290	24
Females, 30 and Over		31,090	26,318[2]	4,772	15
Both Sexes, 30 and Over		61,521	49,459	12,062	20
Total, All Ages		176,655	147,028	29,627	17
Correction:					
Emigrants, 1897-1914		—875	—	—	—
Natural Increase of Emigrants		—438	—	—	—
Total, Corrected		175,342	147,028	28,314	16

[1] For survival values, see Appendix III. For description of other items, see text.
[2] Adjusted by distribution of persons of unknown age. Actual census data for persons 30 years and over are: males, 23,126,798; females, 26,302,159.

garded as too high. Simpson places the total number of refugees from Soviet territory at less than 1,000,000 (with 718,000 unassimilated refugees in Europe and the Near East and 145,-000 in the Far East, January 1, 1922); but his figure takes account only of persons formally registered as refugees, with Nansen passports.[21] Kulischer estimates the number of refugees as about 1,500,000 and, adding repatriated aliens and other migrants, he considers the total net emigration from Soviet territory during this period to be about 2,000,000 persons.[22] Most of

20 Rimscha, Title 274, pp. 50-51.
21 Simpson, Title 299, pp. 80-82, 559-561.
22 Eugene Kulischer, Letter.

the indigenous population who fled from Central Asia across the borders of the Empire either perished or eventually returned to Soviet territory, so that their number need not be taken into account in this calculation.

Subtracting the net number of migrants (2 million) from the total deficit as previously estimated leaves a deficit of 26 million persons due to excess mortality and reduced fertility. In the total deficit previously obtained (Method B) before correction for emigration prior to or after the war (gross figure: 29,627,000), 16,208,000 fell within age classes born before 1912 and 13,419,000 among those born in later years. Deducting the children represented in the allowance for "expected natural increase" of prewar emigrants would bring the latter figure down to a little below 13 million. A large part of this loss must be attributed to child mortality during the period of civil disorders and famine, so that the total loss due to reduction in births must have been less than 10 million. Our estimates, therefore, indicate that there were more than 16 million deaths above the expected number. This measures in terms of extinguished lives the approximate magnitude of the cost of war and revolution in Russia, including their indirect effects on health, during a period of about ten years.

Deaths among Russian forces during World War I are estimated as somewhere in the vicinity of 2,000,000 (see Table 19). Also some 2,300,000 were returned from the front

TABLE 19

Estimates of Number of Deaths in Russian Military Forces, 1914-1917
(Numbers in Thousands)

Cause	Golovine[1]	Kohn[2]
Total	1,860	Over 1,662
Reported as killed	626	665
Killed but not reported	674	—
Killed; reported as "missing"	—	"Over 200"
Died from wounds	350	318
Died from disease, exposure, etc.	140	130
Died in enemy prisons	70	285
Other deaths, including Caucasian front not covered in previous figures	—	64

[1] Golovine, Title 86, p. 103.   [2] Kohn, Title 133, pp. 137 ff.

because of wounds or illness,[23] and over 700,000 were returned from enemy prisons because of illness.[24] Many of those who apparently recovered undoubtedly had a shortened life.

There may have been some increase in deaths among the civilian population, especially in urban centers, during the years of World War I. Kohn concludes that this was the case. Any such increase did not, at least, rise to large proportions. However, food shortages, the crowding of refugees from war areas chiefly into cities near the front, overcrowded and unsanitary hospitals, prison camps, and the general disorganization of war were weakening resistance to disease and preparing foci for the rapid spread of a series of epidemics. The most serious epidemics reached a peak around 1920. The number of deaths from four major types of epidemics in the European area, estimated from data on reported cases and fatality rates, is shown in Table 20. Typhus alone during four years, 1919-1922, caused more than 2 million deaths.

[23] Lubny-Gertsyk, Title 180, p. 22.
[24] Volkov, Title 352, p. 63. Altogether about 5 million Russians were captured on various fronts, 1914-1917.

TABLE 20

Estimated Number of Deaths from Typhus, Typhoid, Dysentery, and Cholera in the European Part of the U.S.S.R., 1914-1923[1]

Year	Typhus	Typhoid	Dysentery	Cholera	Total: Four Causes
Total	2,286,440	674,230	238,210	127,710	3,326,590
1914	17,960	62,190	22,920	510	103,580
1915	15,350	49,950	19,170	8,430	92,900
1916	23,600	50,480	15,070	1,140	90,290
1917	19,210	39,290	14,800	510	73,810
1918	46,590	35,920	6,720	20,480	109,710
1919	764,010	88,820	18,740	2,280	873,850
1920	834,060	136,090	41,670	4,220	1,016,040
1921	178,710	114,700	48,720	77,380	419,510
1922	322,440	70,450	33,070	12,250	438,210
1923	64,510	26,340	17,330	510	108,690

[1] Volkov, Title 352, p. 190.

The great famine in the Volga region came in 1921, with its effects reaching a peak in 1922. There were also serious famines in other parts of the U.S.S.R., including the forest districts of western Siberia. The principal scenes of conflict in the period of counter-revolution and foreign intervention, 1918-1922, were the Baltic region, the Polish border, the Ukraine, the North Caucasus and the Crimea, the Transcaucasus, Siberia, and Central Asia. Order was generally restored by the time of the formal organization of the Soviet Union at the end of 1922, but disorders in Central Asia continued over a much longer period. The magnitude of the several items in the enormous population loss to Russia during these years is shown in Figure 10, according to the estimates presented above. These estimates give merely an approximate quantitative expression of terrific changes that cannot be accurately measured.

5. Effects of War Losses on the Soviet Population

The catastrophes of the war and postwar years left their scars on the initial population of the Soviet Union in broken families, homeless children, and debilitated individuals. One of the

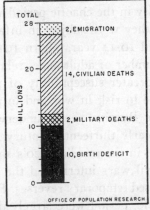

FIGURE 10. Factors in Estimated Population Loss: U.S.S.R. Area, 1914-1926

[41]

outstanding effects was the relatively low proportion of males in the adult population enumerated in the 1926 census. In the "expected" population (Method B) for 1926, there were 98 males per 100 females at ages 30 years and over. Actually, the 1926 census showed only 23,126,798 males and 26,302,159 females aged 30 and over, giving a sex ratio of only 88 males per 100 females in the mature adult population. As might be expected, children under 15 years of age were about equally divided between boys and girls, with a slight excess of males. A deficit of males appeared at all later ages.

According to the census, the exact sex ratios by five-year age classes to age 30 were as follows:

Ages	Males per 100 Females
0-4	101.4
5-9	100.4
10-14	102.3
15-19	92.0
20-24	94.5
25-29	83.9
30 and over	87.9

The sex ratio in the class 15-19 years is erratic, in relation to other classes in this series. The figures here are apparently distorted by a fictitious crowding of girls into this most marriageable class in reporting the ages of those slightly younger or those older than 15-19 years, or by some fictitious reporting of the ages of boys, with reference to conditions of work or military service. We also noted above that the total number in this class seems high in relation to the expected number; this evidence lends added weight to the hypothesis that the number of girls is appreciably exaggerated. Incidentally, the data by single years (see Appendix VI, Table A 17) indicate a peculiar concentration on age 12, the number of such boys being 36 percent and that of girls 31 percent above the mean of those aged 11 and 13. The population, by sex, in successive five-year age classes is shown in Figure 11. The diagram reveals other minor erratic variations, chiefly owing to gross exaggeration of the numbers at rounded ages, e.g., 40, 50, and 60 years. However, the diagram also shows great variations that are not fictitious.

The conspicuous shortage in the age class 5-9 (children born during the years 1917-1921) shows the effects of depleted fertility in the chaotic period when these children were born, and the heightened mortality to which they were subject in infancy and early childhood. The next older five-year cohort, children aged 10-14 years (born 1912-1916), also shows severe reduction. The consistent deficit in the number of adult males relative to the number of adult females must be attributed in part to the greater susceptibility of males to many infectious diseases, as well as to their greater exposure to risk in war and in precarious occupations.

During the years 1915-1923 the Russian people underwent the most cataclysmic changes since the Mongol invasion in the early thirteenth century. Nevertheless, as we shall see, the basic patterns of population change in the middle 1920's show much continuity with those of the prewar period. Foreign and civil wars interrupted the growth of the Russian population and its expansion eastward, and caused temporary reverses. But the trends of births, deaths, and internal migration in the early Soviet period were largely dominated by forces that were previously operative. New social forces and economic planning then introduced radically new trends, but these represented new interests or new reactions to chronic conditions. They did not stem, to any great extent, from the preceding catastrophes, except, of course, in so far as the war provided the occasion and set the stage for the Revolution.

The events of the decade preceding the formation of the U.S.S.R. can never be repeated in the same pattern. The Soviet Union today has been engaged in a war which, in its military proportions, was far more terrific than the First World War. The effects of this new catastrophe on the Russian population may, however, be more limited than those of the previous war with its sequelae of famine and epidemics. The setback in the growth of the Soviet population, will, of

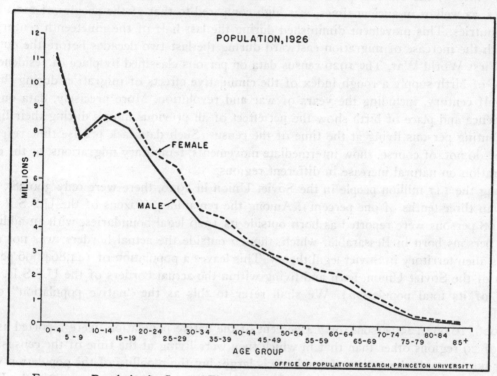

FIGURE 11. Population by Sex and Five-Year Age Classes: U.S.S.R., 1926 [Table A 17]

course, be great; but the net population deficit is likely to be less than that incurred during the years 1914-1922.

The consideration of major factors in the Russian population deficit during the years of international and civil war carries some important implications not only for the Soviet Union but for other areas as well. It shows how easily a devastating war can give rise to a series of disorders, famine, and disease that may exact a greater toll in human lives than war itself. It remains to be seen to what extent the facilities of contemporary science and agencies for the administration of health and economic affairs will modify these dire consequences in the immediate future.

CHAPTER IV

RESIDENCE OF THE SOVIET POPULATION, 1926, IN RELATION TO PLACE OF BIRTH

1. Data of the 1926 Census Relating to Migration

THE mobility of the Russian population in the seventeenth, eighteenth, and early nineteenth centuries, as well as in ancient times, was high compared to that of the peoples of most European countries. This movement diminished during the last half of the nineteenth century, but rose with the increase of migration eastward during the last two decades before the outbreak of the First World War. The 1926 census data on persons classified by place of residence and by place of birth supply a rough index of the cumulative effects of migration during the previous half century, including the years of war and revolution. More precisely, data on place of residence and place of birth show the net effect of all previous moves during their lives in redistributing persons living at the time of the census. Such data lack precise time reference, and they do not, of course, show intermediate movements, temporary migrations, or the effects of migration on natural increase in different regions.

Among the 147 million people in the Soviet Union in 1926, there were only 390,385 aliens (less than three-tenths of one percent). Among the remainder, citizens of the U.S.S.R., only 1,703,168 persons were reported as born outside its 1926 legal boundaries, with an additional 69,666 persons born in Bessarabia, which, though outside the actual borders, was not recognized as alien territory in Soviet legal theory. This leaves a population of 144,864,696 persons, citizens of the Soviet Union, born and living within the actual borders of the U.S.S.R. (98.5 percent of its total population). We shall refer to this as the "native population" of the U.S.S.R.

In 1926, 10,692,125 persons, or 7.4 percent of the native population, were reported as born in one of 29 regions other than that in which they were living at the time of the census.[1] The number born outside the region of residence is large; but the mobility of the population within the U.S.S.R. area during the previous half century was lower than it was within the United States during a comparable period. Whereas 7.4 percent of the native Soviet persons in 1926 were living in one of 29 regions other than the region of birth, 15.4 percent of all native persons in the United States in 1930 were living in one of 9 geographical divisions other than that in which they were born, and 23.4 percent were living in one of the 48 states (plus the District of Columbia) other than that in which they were born.

2. Definition of Census Regions

The 1926 census presents summary and analytical data by "regions," and, in the case of some of the larger regions, by "subregions." Such regions were established for planning and administrative purposes, and were frequently revised. Those used in the presentation of the 1926 census data are referred to here as "census regions." The boundaries of these regions coincide with the boundaries of political divisions, but in most cases they include several political divisions (see Plate IV). There were nineteen regions within the largest constituent republic, the Russian Soviet Federated Socialist Republic. The Transcaucasian Soviet Federated Socialist Republic, which was a political entity at this time, was sometimes recognized as one region, sometimes divided among its three constituent republics. In the cross-tabulation of census data on migra-

[1] The birthplace by region of 183,934 persons reported as born in the U.S.S.R. was given as "unknown."

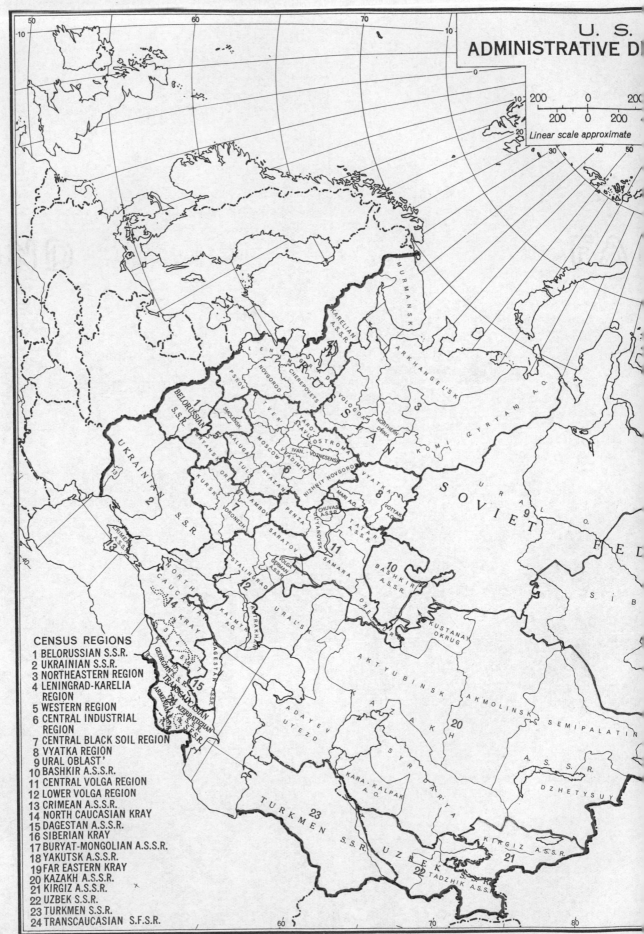

U. S.
ADMINISTRATIVE DI

200   0   200
200   0   200
Linear scale approximate

CENSUS REGIONS
1 BELORUSSIAN S.S.R.
2 UKRAINIAN S.S.R.
3 NORTHEASTERN REGION
4 LENINGRAD-KARELIA
  REGION
5 WESTERN REGION
6 CENTRAL INDUSTRIAL
  REGION
7 CENTRAL BLACK SOIL REGION
8 VYATKA REGION
9 URAL OBLAST'
10 BASHKIR A.S.S.R.
11 CENTRAL VOLGA REGION
12 LOWER VOLGA REGION
13 CRIMEAN A.S.S.R.
14 NORTH CAUCASIAN KRAY
15 DAGESTAN A.S.S.R.
16 SIBERIAN KRAY
17 BURYAT-MONGOLIAN A.S.S.R.
18 YAKUTSK A.S.S.R.
19 FAR EASTERN KRAY
20 KAZAKH A.S.S.R.
21 KIRGIZ A.S.S.R.
22 UZBEK S.S.R.
23 TURKMEN S.S.R.
24 TRANSCAUCASIAN S.F.S.R.

1616-G   Lith. A. Hoen & Co., Inc.

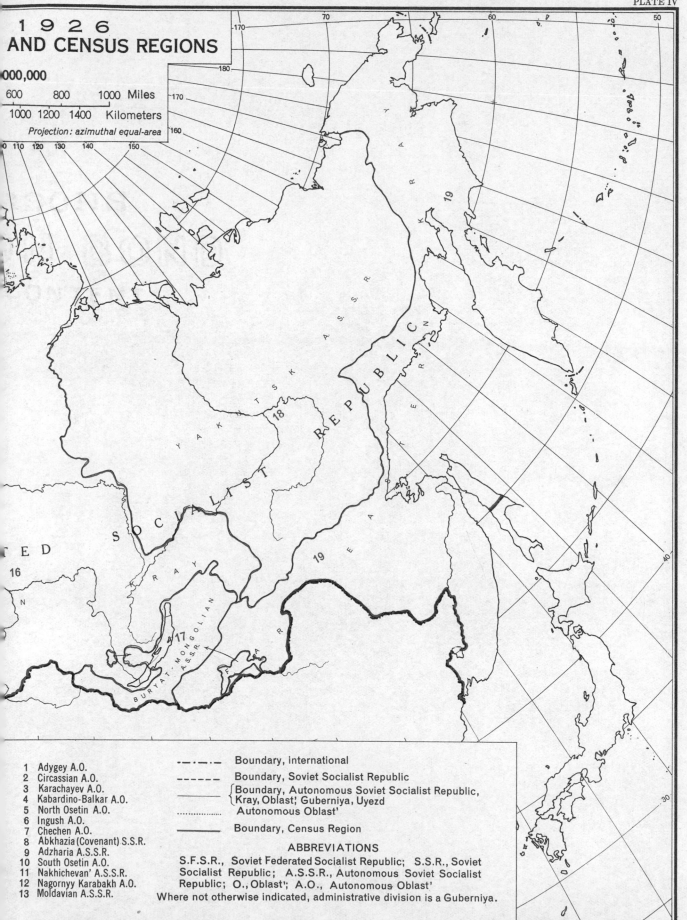

PLATE IV

1926
AND CENSUS REGIONS

000,000

| 600 | 800 | 1000 Miles |
| 1000 | 1200 | 1400 | Kilometers |

Projection: azimuthal equal-area

0 110 120 130 140 150

1 Adygey A.O.
2 Circassian A.O.
3 Karachayev A.O.
4 Kabardino-Balkar A.O.
5 North Osetin A.O.
6 Ingush A.O.
7 Chechen A.O.
8 Abkhazia (Covenant) S.S.R.
9 Adzharia A.S.S.R.
10 South Osetin A.O.
11 Nakhichevan' A.S.S.R.
12 Nagornyy Karabakh A.O.
13 Moldavian A.S.S.R.

Boundary, international
Boundary, Soviet Socialist Republic
Boundary, Autonomous Soviet Socialist Republic, Kray, Oblast', Guberniya, Uyezd
Autonomous Oblast'
Boundary, Census Region

ABBREVIATIONS

S.F.S.R., Soviet Federated Socialist Republic; S.S.R., Soviet
Socialist Republic; A.S.S.R., Autonomous Soviet Socialist
Republic; O., Oblast'; A.O., Autonomous Oblast'
Where not otherwise indicated, administrative division is a Guberniya.

Prepared by Department of State, Division
of Geography and Cartography
Drawn by American Geographical Society

tion the Transcaucasus is treated as a unit. There were four other constituent republics at this time in the U.S.S.R.: the Belorussian, Ukrainian, Uzbek (including the Tadzhik A.S.S.R.), and the Turkmen Soviet Socialist Republics (S.S.R.).[2] These give a total of 24 census regions. In the present discussion the six subregions of the Ukraine are treated as regions in the presentation of the data on migration, bringing the total to 29 units.

3. Net Redistribution among Regions

Net redistribution of living persons through previous migration among 29 regions of the Soviet Union, indicated by the 1926 census data on residence in relation to place of birth, involved 6,514,097 persons.[3] This figure is obtained by pairing each region successively with each other region, and taking the sum of the net gains. It is equal to 61 percent of the total number of native persons living outside the region of birth in 1926. This ratio of *net* to *gross* redistribution in the U.S.S.R. in 1926 may be compared with similar figures for the United States in 1930. The ratio of net to gross redistribution among the 9 geographical divisions in the United States is 50.5 percent; the comparable ratio as regards movements among the 48 states and the District of Columbia is practically identical, i.e., 50.2. Thus it appears that during the last decades of the nineteenth century and the first quarter of the twentieth century migration had been more intensively a one-way movement in Russia than within the United States. Within the United States cross movements of individuals in opposite directions made up a greater part of the whole migratory movement. The Russian population apparently had more inertia as regards change of residence, and its movements represent in greater degree the compulsive force of different pressures and opportunities in various parts of the country.

In the exchange of persons through migration among regions within the U.S.S.R. area up to 1926, 39 percent of the migrants moved in a direction opposite to the main currents of migration or participated in more or less equal exchanges between various regions. Examples of cross migration, as indicated by the data on residence in relation to place of birth, may be cited:

Against 406,000 from the Central Industrial to the Leningrad-Karelia Region—169,000 in the opposite direction

Against 47,000 from the Dnepr Prairie Right Bank to the Dnepr Prairie Left Bank—45,000 in the opposite direction

Against 104,000 from the Central Volga to the Central Industrial Region—63,000 in the opposite direction

Against 54,000 from the Central Industrial to the Lower Volga Region —36,000 in the opposite direction

Against 170,000 from the Ural to the Siberian Region—20,000 in the opposite direction

[2] The Russian names of political divisions properly include (1) the generic designation of the political unit, such as constituent republic (S.S.R.), autonomous republic (A.S.S.R.), province, district, or autonomous district, preceded by (2) the specific designation of the particular unit as an adjective, inflected to agree in gender and case with the noun that it modifies. An exact transliteration of these adjectival forms is unduly cumbersome. The arbitrary formation of an English adjectival form is also frequently awkward. Therefore, except where adjectival names are well established in English usage, e.g., Ukrainian, Belorussian, and Armenian, the nominative or root form is used here as an adjective, as Uzbek S.S.R., rather than Uzbekskaya S.S.R. or Uzbekian S.S.R. Familiar conventional forms are used for a few well-known places: Moscow rather than Moskva, Kiev rather than Kiyev, and Georgia rather than Gruzya. The endings "-iya" and "-lyand" are anglicized. On the other hand, the transliteration scheme is followed in rendering Dagestan rather than Daghestan, and Kirgiz rather than Khirgiz. The soft sign and the hard sign are generally omitted in the accompanying text. The transliteration procedure is defined at the beginning of the Bibliography.

[3] As stated, this is the sum of the net gains of each region relative to each other region or, conversely, the sum of the net losses. Column 4 of Table 21 shows the net gain or loss of each region relative to all other regions in combination.

Against 44,000 from Siberia to Kazakhstan—27,000 in the opposite
  direction

Against 53,000 from Siberia to the Far Eastern Territory—16,000
  in the opposite direction

The smaller movements were in many cases more equally balanced than the larger movements. The "cross currents" between regions do not, of course, necessarily represent movements within the same period or to and from the same localities, though such reverse movements are a general characteristic of most migration. By contrast, an extreme example of an almost purely one-way movement, except possibly as regards return migrants, is that from Belorussia to Siberia. This migration amounted to 202,000 persons, but only 3,000 persons were reported as born in Siberia and living in Belorussia.

We noted in the previous chapter that from 1897 to 1914 about 4 million more persons were added to towns and cities (1926 list) within the U.S.S.R. area than would have been expected if the growth of population in such places had merely run parallel to that of the total population. We also noted that the proportion living in urban places was apparently the same in 1926 as in 1914. Actually, the net in-migration to cities from 1897 to 1914 was probably well over 4 million, because the cities generally had lower birth rates, and during epidemic years may have had death rates that were much higher than those of rural districts.

Among the total 10,692,000 persons reported as born within the U.S.S.R. but living outside the region of birth in 1926, nearly one-half (5,074,000) were living in cities. Inter-regional migrants to cities within the European part of the U.S.S.R., excluding the Ural and Bashkir regions, accounted for 3,681,000 or 61 percent of the total 6,032,000 persons in this area living outside their native region. The relatively small movement to the Transcaucasus was also almost wholly to cities, chiefly to the petroleum center of Baku, with 190,000 out of the 214,000 native in-migrants in the Transcaucasus reported as urban residents. By contrast, the eastward expansion into the Urals, Siberia, and the Asiatic steppe region had remained largely an agrarian colonization movement, although industry, transportation, and administration in Asiatic Russia were largely in the hands of the Russian colonists. Among the 4,446,000 persons in the Asiatic part of the U.S.S.R. (exclusive of the Transcaucasus) and in the Ural and Bashkir regions who were enumerated in 1926 as living outside the region in which they were born, only 1,203,000, or 27 percent, lived in urban communities.

Migration to and from each region and the net effects of such movements, as indicated by the 1926 census data on place of residence in relation to place of birth, are shown in Plate V, with accompanying data in Table 21. It should be noted that in some cases these data may reflect in large part movements during the late nineteenth century; in other cases they may be strongly influenced by movements during the war or early postwar years.

As might be expected, the largest net gain through change of residence is found in Siberia—nearly 2,000,000 persons, representing 23 percent of the population present in that region in 1926. In addition, the net increase in the Far Eastern Territory plus that in Buryat-Mongolia amounts to slightly over 350,000. The Ural and Bashkir regions show net gains of 85,000 and 27,000, respectively. The corresponding figure for the Asiatic steppe region (Kazakh A.S.S.R.) is 617,000. The net gains for the Central Asiatic republics of Kirgizia, Uzbekistan with Tadzhikistan, and Turkmenia are small in relation to the total population in these regions but the sum of these gains, in absolute numbers, is 317,000. Summing the net gains for the Asiatic part of the Soviet Union (excluding the Transcaucasus) gives a total of 3,375,000 persons. This figure shows in a rough way the residual effect of the eastward movement of Russians

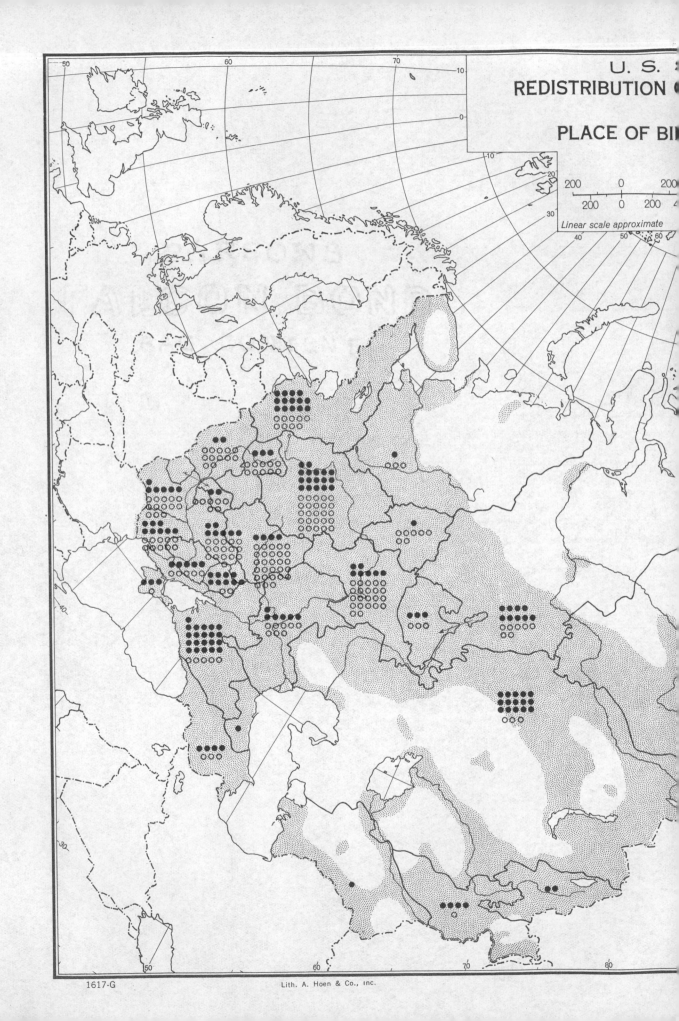

200   0   200

200   0   200

Linear scale approximate

PLATE V

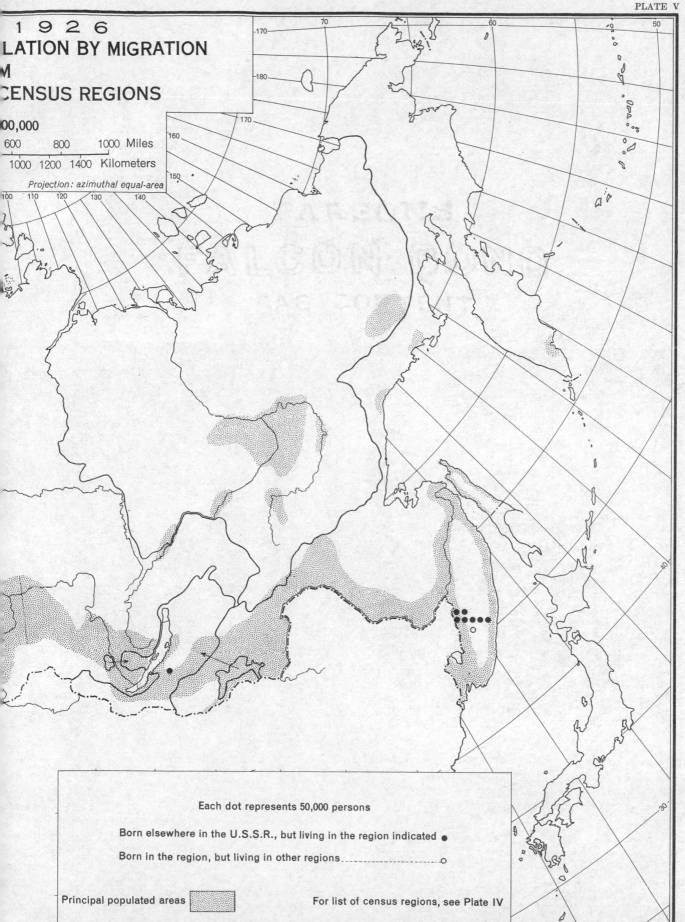

1 9 2 6
LATION BY MIGRATION
M
CENSUS REGIONS

00,000

600   800   1000 Miles

1000 1200 1400 Kilometers

Projection: azimuthal equal-area

Each dot represents 50,000 persons

Born elsewhere in the U.S.S.R., but living in the region indicated ●

Born in the region, but living in other regions ---------○

Principal populated areas

For list of census regions, see Plate IV

Prepared by Department of State, Division
of Geography and Cartography
Drawn by American Geographical Society

TABLE 21

Redistribution of Population by Migration from Place of Birth, by Census Region:
U.S.S.R., 1926

(Numbers in Thousands)

Region	Population 1926	Born Elsewhere in U.S.S.R.: Living in Specified Region	Born in Specified Region: Living in Other Regions	Net Gain or Loss (2)−(3)	Net Change as Percent of Population (4)÷(1)	Net Change as Percent of Total Exchange (4)÷(2)+(3)
	(1)	(2)	(3)	(4)	(5)	(6)
U.S.S.R.	147,028	10,692	10,692	0	—	—
Belorussian S.S.R.	4,983	132.0	602.5	−470	−9	−64
Ukrainian S.S.R. Subregions:						
Forest	2,958	100.0	349.4	−249	−8	−55
Dnepr Prairie Right Bank	8,998	303.8	653.6	−350	−4	−37
Dnepr Prairie Left Bank	7,067	351.1	811.5	−460	−7	−40
Steppe	5,568	425.2	520.6	−95	−2	−10
Dnepr Industrial	2,391	253.4	274.4	−21	−1	−4
Mining-Industrial	2,036	437.5	128.5	+309	+15	+55
Northeastern Region	2,368	62.2	142.6	−80	−3	−39
Leningrad-Karelia	6,660	728.3	439.5	+289	+4	+25
Western Region	4,299	157.5	502.1	−345	−8	−52
Central Industrial	19,314	883.4	1,298.0	−415	−2	−19
Central Black Soil	10,826	223.2	1,428.1	−1,205	−11	−73
Vyatka Region	3,463	70.8	384.6	−314	−9	−69
Ural Oblast'	6,786	444.8	360.1	+85	+1	+11
Bashkir A.S.S.R.	2,666	168.2	141.2	+27	+1	+9
Central Volga	10,268	338.3	1,127.1	−789	−8	−54
Lower Volga	5,530	321.0	433.6	−113	−2	−15
Crimean A.S.S.R.	714	149.6	61.3	+88	+12	+42
North Caucasian Kray	8,363	1,046.7	280.6	+766	+9	+58
Dagestan A.S.S.R.	788	48.1	33.6	+14	+2	+18
Siberian Kray	8,688	2,215.9	240.9	+1,975	+23	+80
Buryat-Mongolian A.S.S.R.	491	44.8	26.7	+18	+4	+25
Yakutsk A.S.S.R.	289	6.4	5.3	+1	0	+9
Far Eastern Kray	1,881	385.7	51.2	+335	+18	+76
Kazakh A.S.S.R.	6,503	780.1	162.7	+617	+9	+65
Kirgiz A.S.S.R.	993	89.2	22.8	+66	+7	+59
Uzbek S.S.R.	5,273	229.0	41.4	+188	+4	+69
Turkmen S.S.R.	1,001	82.2	19.6	+63	+6	+61
Transcaucasian S.F.S.R.	5,862	213.9	148.7	+65	+1	+18

[47]

beyond the Ural Mountains during the decades immediately preceding the First World War, plus small movements of the same sort in the early years of the Soviet regime. It can be compared with an estimated eastward migration beyond the Urals of 5,142,000 persons during the years 1894-1914, when migration to Siberia reached its largest proportions, minus an estimated return migration of 1,478,000 persons, indicating a net in-movement of 3,660,000 persons.[4] The latter figure includes migrants who died in Asiatic Russia but does not include movements before 1894 or after 1914.

Migration within European Russia had become largely a movement to cities. In 1926, the towns and cities of the Central Industrial Region held 650,000 persons born in other regions.[5] However, the migration from rural areas in the same region into these cities and to other regions, plus out-movements of city workers from this region to Leningrad, the Ukraine, or other places, more than offset this influx. Accordingly, the so-called Central Industrial Region, which includes a large rural population, shows a net loss of over 400,000 persons through exchange of migrants living and enumerated in 1926. The numbers born in other regions and living in cities of the Leningrad-Karelia Region and those of the Mining-Industrial Subregion of the Ukraine were 670,000 and 330,000, respectively. These regions, in contrast to the Central Industrial area, reveal net gains through migration—289,000 persons in the first instance and 309,000 in the second instance. The sum of the gains minus the losses in these three regions is less than 200,000 persons, although their cities, considered separately, show a net gain of nearly 2 million persons.

As a result of the mechanization of agriculture and the growth of industry elsewhere, the Black Soil Region, which was an area of opportunity in the eighteenth century, shows the heaviest net loss through migration—1,200,000 persons, equal to 11 percent of the population present in this region in 1926. The Forest Subregion of the Ukraine, the two Dnepr Prairie subregions, and even the Steppe Subregion (still referred to as "New Russia" in the late nineteenth century) also reveal net losses. In fact, the North Caucasus is the only predominantly agricultural region in European Russia that shows a significant gain through the net migration of persons living in 1926.

Plates VI and VII depict the "flow lines" of population redistribution; the 1926 census data on place of birth have been used to indicate the net transfer through migration to or from each region in relation to each other region. These lines were formed, more or less arbitrarily, by grouping those areas of origin and areas of destination, as regards net exchange of migrants, that seemed to represent similar trends. The width of the streams between different points shows the net number of persons "redistributed" in that part of its course. These streams and the volume of population redistributed through each stream, i.e., the number "picked up" through its tributaries or the equal number "deposited" through its outlets, are listed on page 49.

These streams show the tendency for migrants to move along certain well-defined channels. They also show the tendency for persons to seek locations similar to those which they have left, with interchange among industrial regions, and a tendency for migrants from the steppe regions of southern Europe to locate in the steppe regions of Asia. The sum of these nine streams accounts for 98 percent of the net exchange of population among regions, as indicated by the 1926 census data on residence and place of birth.

Migration has constantly altered the distribution of nationalities within the area now occupied by the Soviet Union. The eastward migration to Siberia, the Far East, and the northern portion of the Asiatic steppe region in the late Imperial period was predominantly a movement

---

[4] Barnes, Title 20, citing figures from Latsis and from Datsuk.
[5] Based on data from 1926 census similar to that presented here in Table 21.

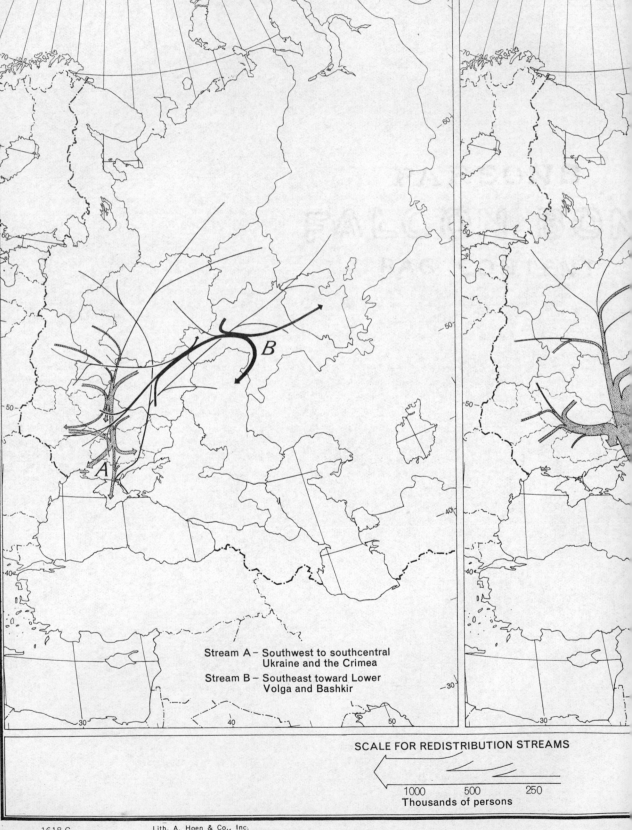

A

B

A

Stream A – Southwest to southcentral
Ukraine and the Crimea

Stream B – Southeast toward Lower
Volga and Bashkir

SCALE FOR REDISTRIBUTION STREAMS

1000   500   250
Thousands of persons

PLATE VI

1926
AMONG CENSUS REGIONS: WITHIN EUROPE AND THE TRANSCAUCASUS

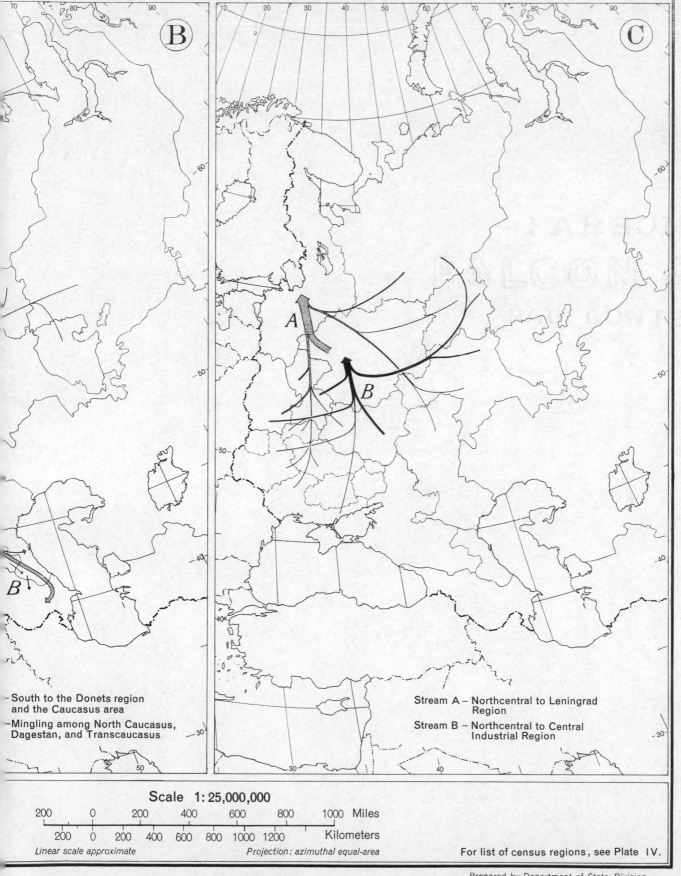

–South to the Donets region
and the Caucasus area

–Mingling among North Caucasus,
Dagestan, and Transcaucasus

Stream A – Northcentral to Leningrad
Region

Stream B – Northcentral to Central
Industrial Region

Scale 1:25,000,000

| 200 | 0 | 200 | 400 | 600 | 800 | 1000 Miles |

| 200 | 0 | 200 | 400 | 600 | 800 | 1000 | 1200 | Kilometers |

Linear scale approximate   *Projection: azimuthal equal-area*   For list of census regions, see Plate IV.

Prepared by Department of State, Division
of Geography and Cartography
Drawn by American Geographical Society

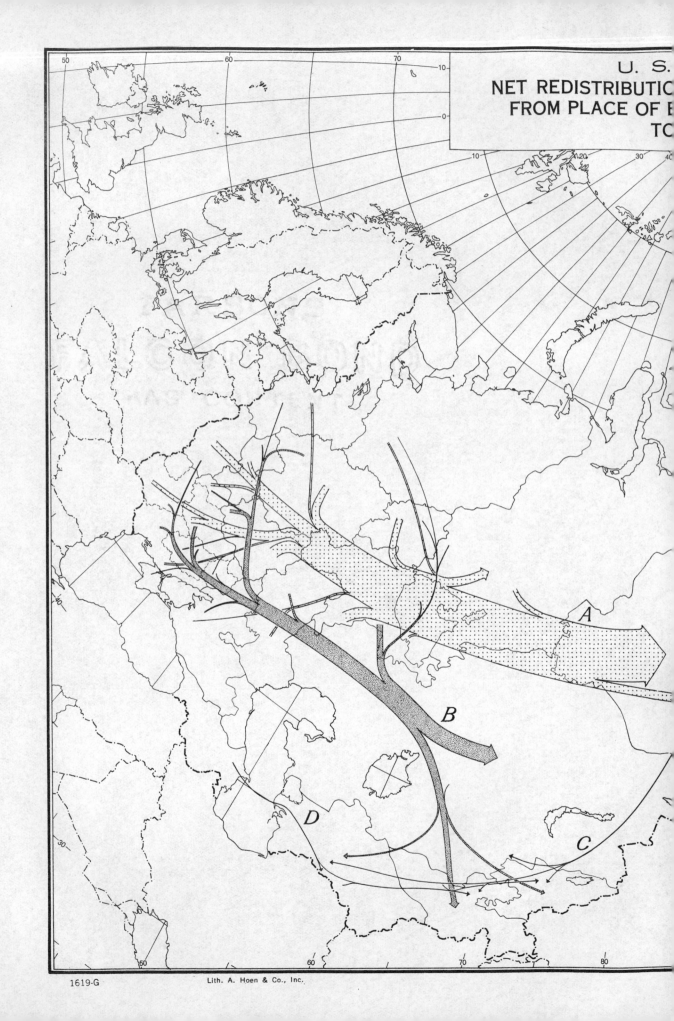

A

B

D

C

PLATE VII

D

1926
PULATION BY MIGRATION
MONG CENSUS REGIONS:
RUSSIA

Stream A – East to the Urals, Siberia, and the Soviet Far East

Stream B – Southeast to Kazakhstan and Central Asia

Stream C – South from Siberia Kray to Kazakhstan and Central Asia

Stream D – East from the Transcaucasus across Central Asia

CALE FOR REDISTRIBUTION STREAMS

2000   1000   500

Thousands of persons

Scale 1: 25,000,000

| 200 | 0 | 200 | 400 | 600 | 800 | 1000 | Miles |

| 200 | 0 | 200 | 600 | 800 | 1000 | 1200 | 1400 | Kilometers |

Linear scale approximate   *Projection: azimuthal equal-area*

For list of census regions, see Plate IV.

Prepared by Department of State, Division
of Geography and Cartography
Drawn by American Geographical Society

Streams of Population Distribution	*Volume (Net) of Migration* (Persons in Thousands)
1. Southwesterly, to the Ukraine (except the Mining-Industrial Subregion) and to the Crimea—movement declining before end of nineteenth century. Plate VI. Section A: Stream A...............	540
2. Southeasterly, to the Central and Lower Volga regions and Bashkiria—movement declining before end of nineteenth century. Plate VI. Section A: Stream B........................	268
3. Southward, to the Mining-Industrial Subregion of the Ukraine, the North Caucasus, and to Transcaucasus. Plate VI. Section B: Stream A..	1,226
4. From the Transcaucasus to the North Caucasus. Plate VI. Section B: Stream B..	50
5. Centripetal and Northern, to the Central Industrial and Leningrad-Karelia regions (including the movement from the Central Industrial to the Leningrad-Karelia Region). Plate VI. Section C: Streams A and B.............................	662
6. Eastward, to the Urals, Siberia, and the Far East. Plate VII. Section D: Stream A..	2,696
7. Eastward, to Kazakhstan and Central Asia. Plate VII. Section D: Stream B..	910
8. From Siberia, southward to Kazakhstan and Central Asia. Plate VII. Section D: Stream C...........................	24
9. From the Transcaucasus, Turkmenia, and Uzbekistan eastward within Central Asia. Plate VII. Section D: Stream D..............	27

of Russians and closely related Slavic peoples, with Ukrainians conspicuously represented in the movement across the steppe zone through the North Caucasus and south-central Volga valley to the southern Urals, Bashkiria, and Kazakhstan. As the result of the eastward movement of Russians and the slow increase or decimation of the indigenous nationalities, the whole vast area from Belorussia and the Ukraine to the Pacific Ocean came to be occupied chiefly by Russians, with interspersed islands of indigenous nationalities. In ethnic composition Kazakhstan (the Asiatic steppe region) and Kirgizia (the mountainous region to the east and south of Kazakhstan) became an intermediate zone between the predominantly Russian population of Siberia and the Turkic populations of Central Asia. The Caucasus mountain districts, the Transcaucasus, and Central Asia remained predominantly non-Slavic, with relatively few Russian inhabitants. The diversity and distribution of ethnic groups within the Soviet Union have exercised an important influence on its cultural development. This topic is given special consideration in the following chapter.

CHAPTER V

ETHNIC COMPOSITION OF THE SOVIET POPULATION, 1926

1. Groups Culturally Associated with European Russia

THE cultural diversity of the Soviet people, comprising more than 175 distinct nationalities, reflects the conflicting forces that have shaped human development in different parts of the Russian plain and adjacent regions at different times.[1] Differentiation along ethnic lines is significant for population analysis in so far as it reflects diverse historical conditions and affects present behavior. We shall, therefore, describe the ethnic groups that make up the Soviet population primarily with reference to their regional and historic associations. The treatment of linguistic or racial classifications is here subordinate to this primary purpose. The information presented in this chapter is drawn from the 1926 census, supplemented by qualitative information from other sources.[2]

The ethnic groups historically associated in the life of European Russia and taking part with Russians in the colonization of Siberia and the Asiatic steppes made up about 87 percent of the total population of the Soviet Union in 1926, amounting to 127,800,000 persons in a total population of 147,000,000 (see Table 22). Russians ("Great Russians") formed slightly more than half of the total population of the U.S.S.R. in 1926; Russians, Ukrainians, and Belorussians, together, 77 percent. These three branches of the Eastern Slavs, though exposed to different cultural influences at still earlier times, were chiefly differentiated by the long subjection of the population in the western portions of the Russian plain to Lithuanian and Polish sovereignty, a subjection that lasted from the time of the Mongol invasion in the early thirteenth century to the reign of Catherine the Great near the end of the eighteenth century. Moreover, these three nationalities have the same alphabet and speak closely related languages.

In 1926, 74 percent of the 31 million Ukrainians ("Little Russians") lived in the Ukrainian Republic; 85 percent of the 4.7 million Belorussians ("White Russians") lived in the Belorussian Republic. Each of these nationalities formed about four-fifths of the total population of the republic that bears its name. Nearly 8 million Ukrainians but only 700 thousand Belorussians were located in the U.S.S.R. outside of their respective republics. Ukrainian and Belorussian migrants tended to locate in rural areas, whereas the cities in these republics had large Jewish populations and attracted many Russians. Only 10.5 percent of the Ukrainians and 10.3 percent of the Belorussians in the U.S.S.R. lived in cities in 1926, in contrast to 21.3 percent of the Russians and 82.4 percent of the Jews. Ukrainians made up 41 percent of the total population of the North Caucasus outside the autonomous mountain republics, and an equal proportion of the population of the Kustanay section on the northern border of Kazakhstan. There were also many Ukrainians in the Black Soil and Lower Volga regions, various parts of Kazakhstan (other than Kustanay), and Siberia. In migrating eastward they tended to concentrate in southern districts where the agricultural situation resembled that of the Ukraine, but they also supplied 10 percent of the population of the Siberian Territory and 17 percent of the population of the Far Eastern Territory in 1926. Belorussians in moving eastward tended to settle in northern regions; half of all those outside the Belorussian Republic lived in Siberia.

---

[1] No exact figure on number of nationalities is possible because inexact, local designations complicate more significant distinctions. The 1926 census recognized 188 classes, plus 5 supplementary, inexact designations, but in a few cases numbers were not reported, and in a few cases only a few individuals were reported for a specified ethnic group.

[2] Mirsky, Title 203; Schultz, Title 289; Jochelson, Title 109; Hudson, Title 102; Vernadskiy, Title 343; Czaplicka, Titles 57 and 58; and others.

TABLE 22

Major Ethnic Groups: U.S.S.R., 1926[1]

Ethnic Group	Population	Percent of Total Population
Total	147,027,915	100.00
Groups Historically Associated with European Russia	127,751,265	86.89
Russian	77,791,124	52.91
Ukrainian	31,194,976	21.22
Belorussian	4,738,923	3.22
Jewish[2]	2,680,823	1.82
Finnic: Baltic Groups	588,834	0.40
European Nationalities[3]	2,870,036	1.95
Finnic: Volga Groups	2,658,700	1.81
Chuvash	1,117,419	0.76
Turkic: Volga Groups[4]	3,308,116	2.25
Bashkir and Teptyar	741,080	0.50
Gypsy	61,234	0.04
Groups Historically Associated with the Caucasus	6,975,369	4.74
Georgian	1,821,184	1.24
Armenian	1,567,568	1.07
Dagestan Mountain Groups	574,637	0.39
Other Japhetic (Caucasus Mts.)	668,596	0.45
Turkic: Caucasus Groups	1,895,900	1.29
Iranian: Caucasus Groups	447,484	0.30
Groups Historically Associated with Central Asia, Asiatic Steppes, and Siberia	11,802,382	8.03
Turkic: Central Asia and Steppes	9,747,162	6.63
Iranian: Central Asia	980,509	0.67
Mongolian	370,174	0.25
Turkic: Yakutia	241,365	0.16
Turkic: Siberian Groups	124,001	0.08
Siberian Groups (n.e.c.)[5]	129,878	0.09
Asiatic Nationalities	209,293	0.14
Other and Unknown[6]	108,514	0.07
Alien[7]	390,385	0.27

[1] For minor ethnic groups included in these major categories, see Tables 23 and 24.
[2] Including indigenous communities in Southern Russia, also Karaim.
[3] Except Baltic nationalities.
[4] Tatar, etc., except Central Asian and Siberian Tatar.
[5] N.e.c. (not elsewhere classified). Including Siberian Finnic, Samoyed, Manchu, Eskimo, and old Siberian nationalities.
[6] Census list: Nos. 46, 117, 148, 152, 184, 185, 186, 190-E (Total: 15,930), plus Miscellaneous and Unknown, Nos. 189, 190 zh.
[7] See Table 24.

Russians, Ukrainians, and Belorussians are all mainly Greek Orthodox in religious affilia-tion. Among the Belorussians, however, there is a considerable Roman Catholic minority. The adherents to the Roman Catholic religion among the Ukrainians are chiefly Uniats, who pre-serve an Eastern ritual. According to the 1897 census, there were in the Russian Empire 1,500,-

ooo Roman Catholics, including Uniats, who spoke one of the three Russian languages, giving a ratio of 5.3 per 100 *relative* to the total number of Ukrainians and Belorussians. Outside of Congress Poland, Kovno, and Vilna, which were predominantly Polish and Lithuanian districts, the largest proportions of Roman Catholics, including Uniats, in various provinces in 1897 were as follows: Grodno, 24 percent; Vitebsk, 24 percent; Kurland, 11 percent; Minsk, 10 percent; Volynia, 10 percent; Podolia, 9 percent; Kherson, Kiev, and St. Petersburg, 3 percent.

Most of the Jews in the Soviet Union have a European background, having entered Russia from Poland in the early modern period or, indirectly, from central and southern Europe. There are, however, several relatively small ancient communities near the shores of the Black Sea and in Central Asia.[3] The cultural isolation of Jews in Imperial Russia was largely due to arbitrary decrees limiting them to certain occupations and to urban residence "within the Pale," i.e., west of a prescribed line. This isolation was broken by the Revolution but the Jewish population remains predominantly urban.

The numerical dominance of Russians, Ukrainians, and Belorussians and the slow processes of cultural assimilation have lessened the significance of ethnic differences among other groups historically associated with the development of European Russia. The old Finnic, Turkic, and Chuvash peoples in the Volga-Ural region differed radically from the Russians in their cultural patterns two hundred years ago. Today these groups—Mordvian, Votyak, Mari, Komi, Tatar, Bashkir, and Chuvash, comprising about 7 million people in 1926—still form concentrated ethnic communities, but they are also represented in all parts of the Soviet Union, especially in settlements in Siberia and the Asiatic steppes. All of these people have participated in varying degrees in the agricultural, political, and cultural life of Russia, and have become gradually more assimilated to Russian patterns. Their degree of literacy was somewhat, but not greatly, below that of the Russians in 1926. The proportions of persons in the large groups described here who were able to read in any language ranged from 23 percent among the Mordvians to 38 percent among the Zyryans (a branch of the Komi), as compared with 45 percent among Russians. These groups have, however, retained distinct languages, and the Tatars and Bashkirs are predominantly Moslem rather than Greek Orthodox in religious affiliation.

The Karels, Leningrad Finns, Vepsy, Vodi, and Izhora in the northwestern part of the Soviet Union are Finnic in origin and language, but largely Russian in culture and predominantly Greek Orthodox in religion. The Finns (Suomi) and Estonians are culturally distinct. The Lapps are also Finnic-Ugrian in origin, but preserve a primitive Arctic culture. The main European nationalities in the U.S.S.R., apart from those previously included within the Russian Empire, are formed by the descendants of German, Greek, Bulgarian, and other colonists in the Black Sea, Lower Volga, and North Caucasus districts, augmented by small numbers of later immigrants.

In general, the cultural relations among Russians and other ethnic groups associated with the development of European Russia may be described at the beginning of the Soviet period as roughly analogous to those prevailing among old colonial and immigrant stocks in the United States, except that in Russia the minority groups were more definitely associated with particular regions and preserved separate languages.

2. Ethnic Diversity in the Caucasus

The Caucasus region, most of which was incorporated within the Russian Empire little more than a half century before the First World War, was characterized by far greater ethnic di-

---

[3] The Karaim, a small non-Jewish group in southern Russia, influenced by ancient Jewish culture and adhering to a distinct Hebrew sect, are arbitrarily grouped with Jews in Tables 22 and 23.

versity and conflict. The ethnic situation in this region at the time of the formation of the Soviet Union was as complicated and explosive as that in any part of southeastern Europe. Three large nationalities, Georgians, Azers (Turkic), and Armenians, meet in the Transcaucasus. These groups are similar only in size. They have been estranged by past conflicts, and by radically different historic backgrounds, language, religion, and culture. In addition to these major groups, many other groups in the Caucasus are isolated from one another, physically as in the case of nationalities occupying various parts of the Caucasus range, or by language and tradition as in the case of the thirty ethnic communities, each with its own language, in Dagestan. Moreover, even in 1926, relatively few Russians lived in or beyond the Caucasus Mountains; they formed 9.5 percent of the total population in Azerbaydzhan, 3.6 percent in Georgia, 2.2 percent in Armenia, and similar proportions in the mountain republics. Literacy was fairly high among the Georgians (39.5 percent) and Armenians (34.0 percent), but very low among the Azers (8.1 percent). In the case of the mountain nationalities, literacy was highest among the Osetins (21.2 percent), an Iranian people with a Greek Orthodox majority and a Moslem minority, and among the Cherkess or Adygey (16.9 percent), a Caucasian or Japhetic people living near the North Caucasus plain, who were chiefly Moslems. Less than 3 percent of the Chechen and only about 5 percent of the Dagestan mountaineers were able to read in any language. The nationalities historically associated with the Caucasus region made up 4.7 percent of the total population of the U.S.S.R. in 1926.

3. The Indigenous Nationalities of Asiatic Russia

The most profound cultural contrast within the U.S.S.R. is that between the groups historically identified with European Russia, who represent a primitive agricultural economy influenced by western European associations, and the indigenous nationalities of Asiatic Russia. The latter represent three main cultural types: (1) the isolated, ancient, agricultural-urban civilization of Central Asia; (2) the steppe nomads; (3) the sparse forest and tundra peoples of Siberia and the Far East. The status of the people in all these groups within the Russian Empire was essentially that of colonial subjects. Altogether they comprised 11.8 million people in 1926, or 8 percent of the total population of the U.S.S.R.

Ethnically, the Central Asian and steppe people are predominantly Turkic, with considerable Mongolian admixture—except the Iranian Tadzhiks in the southern mountain districts and adjacent plains. Turkic stocks are also represented in the Volga Tatars, the Bashkirs in the southern Urals, the Azers in the Transcaucasus, and the Yakuts in eastern Siberia. Altogether, the Turkic groups in the U.S.S.R. numbered about 16 million in 1926, or nearly 11 percent of the total Soviet population; but they include diverse nationalities with different cultural characteristics.

At the beginning of the Soviet period the position of the indigenous groups in Siberia was even less favorable than that of the North American Indians in the United States. Before the intrusion of Russians into Siberia these groups were already scattered and diverse in origin and linguistic affiliation. The two largest nationalities, the Mongolian Buryats in the vicinity of Lake Baykal and the Turkic Yakuts in the Lena Basin, represented relatively recent intrusions of steppe peoples into Siberia. The indigenous nations, especially in the case of many of the small, original Siberian tribes, were further depleted by Russian conquest and the spread of contagious diseases. The Tungusi, a Manchu people displaced and dispersed by the Yakuts, numbered only 38,000 in 1926. The only other Siberian nationalities, outside the Altay region, with 10,000 persons or more were the Finnic-Ugrian Ostyaks (22,000) in western Siberia, the Samoyeds (15,000) in western and northern Siberia, and the Chukchi or Luoravetlans (12,000) in the far northeast.

The larger Central Asian and steppe nationalities have been only slightly influenced by their contacts and conflicts with soldiers, traders, and colonists from European Russia. In 1926 the nomad cultures of the Kazakhs and Kirgiz remained intact. They were characterized by strong tribal organization, concentrated ownership of horses, cattle, sheep, and goats by hereditary family patriarchs, and the persistence of shamanistic practices in a nominally Moslem religious structure. The Turkmen around the Amu Darya delta had a slightly superior status in the Empire, as allies of the Tsar. The cultivation of cotton in Central Asia had been stimulated by trade with Moscow, and Russians and Ukrainians had established colonies in some regions; otherwise, life in Central Asia had changed little since the time of the Mohammedan conquest. Literacy was, of course, extremely low among all these groups.

4. Summary Description of Ethnic Groups in the U.S.S.R.

The composition of the Soviet population in 1926 by specific ethnic groups is shown in Table 23, which forms the basis for Table 22. In the latter, the major ethnic groups are obtained by combining particular classes, more or less arbitrarily, primarily with reference to regional association. The specific classes so combined in each major group are given in Table 23, with notes on the regions in which these classes are chiefly concentrated, their cultural affiliations, and miscellaneous information. The descriptive information is taken from various sources listed in the bibliography. Numbers of aliens, not covered by the census data on ethnic groups, are shown in Table 24.

5. Ethnic Differentiation and Political Status

The diversity in ethnic and cultural background is recognized in the political structure of the U.S.S.R. In order to secure the cooperation of ethnic minorities, obviate traditional conflicts, and contribute to the cultural advance of the population, regions containing distinct ethnic groups are organized as "autonomous" republics or districts, with special prerogatives, including representation in the All-Union Soviet of Nationalities, and special administrative responsibilities, particularly with respect to cultural affairs. Along with this constitutional recognition there has been a definite policy of encouraging or "sublimating" traditional cultural interests. Measures implementing this policy have included the use of traditional languages in schools, with Russian as a secondary language in non-Russian communities; the encouragement of traditional language publications, which in some cases has necessitated the codification of previously unwritten languages; theatrical performances, festivals, and so forth. Great effort has also been directed toward increasing economic efficiency and improving health and literacy in backward areas, and toward a closer economic and cultural integration of various regions. At the same time, the development of new industrial centers in some of the backward areas and the extensive movements of people across the Soviet Union have tended to break down the distinctive character of various regions. The policy of establishing nomadic groups in fixed residence and the revolutionary character of Soviet economy have also operated to create greater cultural uniformity. In some cases, as among the Kazakhs in the Asiatic steppes, these policies have involved sharp resistances. In general, however, the nationality policy of the Soviet Union has been acclaimed as promoting respect for cultural diversity and a high level of harmonious cooperation.

There are several types of "autonomous" areas in the U.S.S.R. with different administrative status. The "union" or "constituent" republics (Soviet Socialist Republics), located around

TABLE 23

Ethnic Groups: U.S.S.R., 1926[1]

Ethnic Group	Population	Percent			Notes on Areas of Concentration, Traditional Cultures in Pre-Soviet Period, Occupations, etc.
		Urban	Speaking Own Language	Able to Read in Any Language	
	(1)	(2)	(3)	(4)	(5)
Total	147,027,915[2]	17.9	—	39.6	
Russian	77,791,124	21.3	99.7	45.1	Predominant in European Russia, Siberia, and Soviet Far East. Greek Orthodox; Schismatic 2.5 per 100 Orthodox, 1897.
Ukrainian	31,194,976	10.5	87.1	41.3	Ukraine; Black Earth; North Caucasus; Asiatic Steppes; Siberia. Chiefly agricultural. Russian culture; some Polish influence. Greek Orthodox; Uniat (Roman Catholic, Eastern rites).
Belorussian	4,738,923	10.3	71.9	37.3	Belorussia; Siberia. Chiefly agricultural. Influenced by Polish culture. Greek Orthodox; Roman Catholic.
Jewish, etc.	2,680,823	—	—	—	
Jew	2,599,973	82.4	71.9	72.3	Ukraine, Belorussia, and all parts of U.S.S.R. Trades, handicrafts, and professions.
Crimean Jew	6,383	98.4	74.1	58.2	Ancient communities, with distinct cultural traditions.
Dagestan Jew	25,974	85.4	97.0	19.7	
Georgian Jew	21,471	72.5	99.6	32.9	
Central Asian Jew	18,698	97.9	93.8	24.2	
Karaim	8,324	94.5	36.4	84.9	An ancient Hebrew religious sect; ethnically and culturally distinct from Jews.
Finnic: Baltic Region	588,834	—	—	—	
Finn (Suomi)	19,467	37.6	85.0	76.0	Citizens of U.S.S.R. Scandinavian culture.
Leningrad Finn	115,234	6.0	97.7	70.5	Rural districts of Leningrad region. Russian culture.
Karel	248,120	2.9	95.5	41.4	Finn language; Russian culture. Agriculture, forestry, fishing. Greek Orthodox.
Estonian	154,666	23.0	88.4	72.4	Germanic culture. Protestant.
Veps	32,785	0.8	94.6	35.7	Russian culture.
Vod'	705	0.9	97.0	59.9	Russian culture.
Izhora	16,137	0.6	87.9	60.9	Russian culture.
Lapp (Lapar)	1,720	0.8	97.2	12.8	Arctic culture: Reindeer economy. Greek Orthodox.

Ethnic Groups: U.S.S.R., 1926

	(1)	(2)	(3)	(4)	(5)
European Nationalities (n.e.c.)[3]	2,870,036	—	—	—	
German	1,238,549	14.9	94.9	60.2	Settlements in southern Russia, especially in lower Volga region; dispersion throughout European and Asiatic Russia.
Pole	782,334	32.7	42.9	53.8	Belorussia and Ukraine; dispersion through European and Asiatic Russia.
Moldavian	278,905	4.9	92.3	27.6	Rumanian language. Southwest Ukraine.
Rumanian	4,651	40.4	51.9	56.4	Associated with Moldavians.
Greek	213,765	21.2	72.7	50.3	Ancient settlements in Black Sea region; concentration in southeast Ukraine.
Latvian	141,703	42.3	78.3	74.5	Own language (Slavonic-Baltic group). Protestant. Northwest Russia.
Latgal	9,707	13.1	81.4	37.0	Own language (Slavonic-Baltic group); Russian culture. Associated with Latvians.
Lithuanian	41,463	63.2	46.9	70.5	Own language (Slavonic-Baltic group). Roman Catholic. Polish culture. Northwest Russia.
Bulgarian	111,296	6.3	92.4	51.5	Balkan culture (original Bulgar communities in Volga region, circa tenth century, dispersed and absorbed).
Czech, Slovak	27,123	30.7	79.5	74.3	
Other Nationalities	20,540	—	—	—	Hungarians (5,476), Albanians, Serbs, Swedes, French, Italians, Dutch, English, and others.
Finnic: Volga-Ural Region	2,658,700	—	—	—	
Zyryan (Komi)	226,383	3.5	96.5	38.1	Northern Volga-Ural region. Russian culture on Finnic base. Hunting, fishing, agriculture, trade. Zyryans formerly active in trade and exploitation of Siberia. Greek Orthodox.
Permyak (Komi)	149,488	1.1	93.9	26.1	
Votyak (Udmurt)	504,187	1.2	98.9	25.6	Concentrations in Volga region; dispersed through other regions, especially Siberia. Agricultural and forest occupations. Russian culture, with Finnic and Bulgar survivals. Greek Orthodox.
Besermayn	10,035	0.1	99.3	16.6	
Mari (Cheremis)	428,192	0.8	99.3	26.6	
Mordvian	1,340,415	2.2	94.0	22.9	

Ethnic Groups: U.S.S.R., 1926

	(1)	(2)	(3)	(4)	(5)
Chuvash	1,117,419	1.6	98.7	32.2	Volga region. Russian culture on ancient Khazar or Bulgar base. Agriculture. Greek Orthodox.
Turkic: Volga Region	3,308,116	—	—	—	
Tatar	2,916,536	15.5	98.9	33.6	Agriculture, trade, and industry. Mohammedan culture, assimilated to Russian in varying degrees. Concentration in Volga region; widely dispersed. Moslem.
Mishar	242,640	1.5	81.2	25.6	Related to Tatar.
Kryashen	101,447	1.4	99.1	29.2	Related to Tatar ("Kryashen," local designation).
Nogay	36,274	0.4	97.2	7.1	Tatars in North Caucasus and adjacent regions. Culturally associated with Volga Tatars.
Nogaybak	11,219	0.7	95.2	42.0	
Bashkir, etc.	741,080	—	—	—	
Bashkir	713,693	2.1	53.8	24.3	A steppe people; settled in Ural region in early eighteenth century. Pastoral and agricultural. Moslem.
Teptyar	27,387	0.8	2.3	24.3	Related to Bashkir ("Teptyar," local designation).
Gypsy (Zygan)	61,234	20.9	64.2	8.3	Dispersed through U.S.S.R.
Georgian (Gruzian)	1,821,184	16.9	96.5	39.5	Agriculture, including vineyards, orchards, and livestock; handicrafts; trade. Georgian, a Japhetic language. Greek Orthodox. Minor groups vary in dialect and culture, e.g., Adzhars, in vicinity of Batum, influenced by Turkic culture. Mostly Moslem.
Including:					
Mingrel'	(242,990)	4.6	99.8	31.1	
Adzhar	(71,426)	4.1	98.7	7.8	
Svan	(13,218)	0.7	99.5	18.2	
Laz	(643)	6.8	58.3	11.8	
Armenian	1,567,568	35.4	92.4	34.0	Pastoral and agricultural; handicrafts; trade. Armenian, a Japhetic language. Religion, chiefly Armeno-Gregorian. Settlements in North Caucasus. The Transcaucasus in 1926 included 120,000 Armenians born outside present borders of U.S.S.R.
Dagestan Mountain Groups	574,637	—	—	—	
Lesgi	134,529	7.3	97.4	7.1	30 languages, mostly Japhetic. Diverse traditions. Agricultural and pastoral; handicrafts. Mostly Sunni Moslem.
Tabasaran	31,983	0.1	92.9	1.6	
Avar	158,769	1.3	99.3	6.8	
27 Other Groups	249,356	—	—	—	

TABLE 23 (*Continued*)

Ethnic Groups: U.S.S.R., 1926

	(1)	(2)	(3)	(4)	(5)
Other Japhetic or Caucasus	668,596	—	—	—	
Chechen	318,522	1.0	99.7	2.9	Mountain nationalities. Predominantly pastoral and agricultural. Chiefly Sunni Moslem.
Ingush	74,097	3.5	99.5	9.1	
Kabardian	139,925	1.3	99.3	6.8	
Beskesek-Abaza	13,825	0.6	94.4	9.6	
Cherkess (Adygey)	65,270	2.9	98.4	16.9	
Abkhazian	56,957	4.7	83.9	11.3	Northwestern Georgia (Abkhazia S.S.R.). Largely agricultural, especially tobacco. Greek Orthodox and Sunni Moslem.
Turkic: Caucasus Region	1,895,900	—	—	—	
Turk (Azer)	1,706,605	15.8	93.8	8.1	Azerbaydzhan. Persian culture. Migrated from Central Asia via Persia. Shiite Moslem. Agriculture, livestock, handicrafts, trade, industry. Also 31,795 foreign-born Azers and Turks in Azerbaydzhan.
Kumyk	94,549	7.5	99.2	11.1	North Dagestan. Sunni Moslem.
Karachay	55,123	3.2	99.5	9.2	Caucasus Mountains. Sunni Moslem.
Balkar	33,307	1.2	99.6	5.3	Caucasus Mountains near Kabardians. Sunni Moslem.
Karapapakh	6,316	—	0.1	6.2	
Iranian: Caucasus Region	447,484	—	—	—	
Osetin	272,272	7.9	97.9	21.2	Central Caucasus Mountains. Northern and southern divisions. Different dialects. Caucasian and Georgian culture. Greek Orthodox; Sunni Moslem.
Talysh	77,323	0.4	97.7	3.0	Azerbaydzhan. Agricultural or semi-nomadic. Shiite Moslem.
Tat	28,705	25.0	86.6	5.9	Near Baku; workers in petroleum industry. Shiite Moslem.
Kurd	54,661	3.4	34.4	3.7	Migrants from southern Armenia (outside U.S.S.R.). Ancient Iranian culture. Avestic.
Yezid	14,523	15.5	96.4	2.1	
Turkic: Central Asia and Steppes	9,747,162	—	—	—	
Kazakh	3,968,289	2.2	99.6	7.1	Steppe culture; nomadic. Turkic with Mongolian elements. Strong tribal traditions. Sunni Moslem with shaman survivals.

TABLE 23 (*Continued*)

Ethnic Groups: U.S.S.R., 1926

	(1)	(2)	(3)	(4)	(5)
Turkic (*Continued*)					
Uzbek	3,904,622	18.7	99.1	3.8	Sedentary. Agriculture, handi-crafts. Persian culture on steppe base. Sunni Moslem.
Kurama	50,079	0.2	16.4	2.4	Associated with Uzbeks. Mixed Turkic group, speaking a dialect of Uzbek.
Kara-Kalpak	146,317	2.9	87.5	1.3	Steppe culture, now sedentary. Amu Dar'ya oasis region.
Kirgiz	762,736	1.4	99.0	4.6	Mountain districts of eastern Central Asia. Turkic, with Mongolian elements. Pastoral, nomadic. Strong tribal traditions.
Turkmen	763,940	1.5	97.3	2.3	Steppe region, between Amu Dar'ya and Caspian. Old Turanian culture. Sunni Moslem.
Osmali Turk	8,570	30.8	86.3	19.8	
Turk of Fergana and Samarkand	537	0.6	6.5	1.1	
Kypchak	33,502	1.5	99.7	1.4	Related to Kirgiz. Now sedentary. Fergana region.
Kashgar	13,010	44.6	85.9	5.5	
Taranchi	53,010	20.2	99.5	8.5	A Turkic people, formerly living in Chinese Turkestan. Migrated to Central Asia during nineteenth century.
Uygur	42,550	6.8	52.7	4.6	A steppe people originally living in Altay Mountain region.
Iranian: Central Asia	980,509	—	—		
Tadzhik	978,680	15.2	98.3	2.2	Iranian. Valleys and mountain districts in southeast Central Asia. Persian culture. Sunni Moslem.
Yagnobts	1,829	—	99.9	—	A Galcha group in the High Pamirs. The Galchas are also Iranian, but Ismailite in religion, i.e., spiritual subjects of Aga Khan.
Mongolian	370,174	—	—		
Buryat	237,501	1.0	98.1	23.2	Buryat-Mongolia and Irkutsk region. Nomadic, passing to sedentary. Pastoral and agricultural. Lamaist Buddhist, with shaman survivals; some Greek Orthodox.
Kalmyk	129,321	1.3	99.3	10.9	Migrated to region northwest of Caspian, in early eighteenth century. Nomadic. Lamaist Buddhist.

TABLE 23 (*Continued*)

Ethnic Groups: U.S.S.R., 1926

	(1)	(2)	(3)	(4)	(5)
Mongolian (*Continued*)					
Mongolian	559	33.6	32.9	38.8	
Sart-Kalmyk	2,793	2.1	88.3	14.3	Altay region. Mohammedan Mongols.
Turkic: Yakutia	241,365	—	—	—	
Yakut	240,709	2.2	99.7	5.8	Turkic with Mongolian elements. Region formerly occupied by Tungusi. Hunting economy. Original steppe culture adapted to Arctic environment and Russian influence. Nominally Greek Orthodox.
Dolgan	656	—	99.5	1.2	
Turkic: Siberian	124,001	—	—	—	
Altay (Oyrot)	39,062	0.3	79.4	11.4	Altay Mountain region. Pastoral.
Khakas	45,608	1.1	89.9	12.9	Related to Kazakhs; formerly in Tien Shan Mountains, now in upper Yenisey or Soyan Mountain region. Pastoral. Nominally Greek Orthodox.
Buchartsi	12,012	6.2	97.9	26.1	Descendants of trading colonies from Central Asia in Siberia.
Shor	12,601	0.7	93.8	11.5	
Kurmandzh	6,335	0.1	45.7	14.3	
Telenget	3,415	—	99.5	8.8	Scattered groups of "Siberian Tatars," including some Turkicized Samoyed groups.
Karagas	2,829	—	29.1	10.5	
Teleut	1,898	0.4	57.8	19.1	
Sayonts	229	—	3.5	17.0	
Tubal Tatar	12	—	25.0	25.0	
Siberian Groups (n.e.c.)	129,878	—	—	—	
Ostyak	22,306	0.6	83.5	6.9	Western Siberia. Finnic-Ugrian. Hunting economy. Neo-Siberian culture.
Vogul	5,754	0.2	88.9	6.2	Related to Ostyak.
Samoyed	15,462	0.6	88.9	2.8	Probably related to Finnic-Ugrian groups.
Tungus	37,546	0.3	63.8	7.8	Largest indigenous Siberian nationality; related to Manchus. Scattered in northern Siberia on edges of Yakut domain.
Chukchi (Luoravetlan)	12,332	0.1	99.3	0.6	
Koryak	7,439	0.1	95.3	5.9	Various tribes in northern Siberia, Kamchatka, the Amur region, and the Pacific Coast.
Gol'd	5,309	0.7	96.7	7.2	
Kamchadal	4,217	2.8	20.4	39.6	
Gilyak	4,076	0.2	97.0	6.2	Some groups formerly in these regions are now extinct.
Eskimo	1,293	0.9	98.1	9.9	
16 Other Groups	14,144	—	—	—	

TABLE 23 (*Continued*)

Ethnic Groups: U.S.S.R., 1926

	(1)	(2)	(3)	(4)	(5)
Asiatic Nationalities (n.e.c.)[3]	209,293	—	—	—	
Korean	86,999	10.5	98.9	39.8	Soviet Far East. Chiefly agricultural.
Chinese	10,247	64.9	86.1	42.1	Soviet Far East. Chiefly commercial.
Dungan	14,600	32.2	99.2	8.6	A Turkic-Mongolian group in Kirgizia; migrated from western China in nineteenth century.
Arab	28,978	4.4	15.9	1.2	Central Asia and Caucasus.
Aysor	9,808	65.8	91.1	25.2	Indigenous group. Central Asia. Syrian language. Nestorian religion.
Persian (Iranian)	43,971	64.0	67.8	14.1	Caucasus and Central Asia. Chiefly industrial workers.
Iranian	9,188	27.2	16.3	7.9	Indigenous group. Central Asia. Shiite Moslem.
Afgan	5,348	9.7	24.0	2.1	
Hindu	61	62.3	77.0	70.5	
Japanese	93	76.3	66.7	75.3	

[1] Based on census data and notes by Mirsky, Jochelson, and Schultz's Summary of Classification by Leningrad Academy of Sciences.

[2] Including 108,514 Other and Unknown (see Table 22) and 390,385 Aliens (see Table 24).

[3] N.e.c. (not elsewhere classified). Citizens of U.S.S.R., only. See also Aliens, Table 24.

the borders of the U.S.S.R. and each having theoretically the right of secession, form the major political divisions of the Soviet Union. Between 1926 and 1939 the Transcaucasian federation was dissolved; Kazakhstan and Kirgizia, formerly part of the R.S.F.S.R., were given independent status as constituent republics; and Tadzhikistan, which had been part of the Uzbek S.S.R., was raised to the same rank. These changes brought the number of constituent republics to eleven in 1939. In the case of each constituent republic at the time of its formation, the nationality recognized in the name formed an absolute majority of its total population, but it is possible that this is no longer the case in the Kazakh S.S.R. The largest of the constituent republics is the Russian Soviet Federated Socialist Republic (R.S.F.S.R.). It stretches from the borders of the Belorussian S.S.R. and the Ukrainian S.S.R. eastward across the rest of European Russia, the North Caucasus, Siberia, and the Soviet Far East to the Pacific Ocean, and northward from the Black Sea, the Caucasus Mountains, and the Asiatic steppes to the Arctic Ocean.

Important distinct ethnic groups within the R.S.F.S.R. and in some of the other constituent republics have been recognized through the formation of subordinate "Autonomous Soviet Socialist Republics" (A.S.S.R.). In some of these subordinate republics, the ethnic group recognized by the title forms the numerically preponderant element, but in other cases Russians are more numerous than members of the titular nationality. Other areas, usually those occupied by small ethnic groups, are recognized as autonomous districts (A.O. or Autonomous Oblast')

TABLE 24

Aliens, by Country: U.S.S.R., 1926

Country	Number
Total	390,385
Europe	97,341
Greece	45,975
Poland	10,137
Germany	7,991
Austria	7,120
Czechoslovakia	3,548
Finland	4,090
Bulgaria	2,715
Rumania	2,241
Other	13,524
Turkey	25,885
Asia	266,470
Persia	92,299
Japanese Empire[1]	85,352
China	81,783
Afghanistan	6,517
Other	519
Other and Unknown[2]	689

[1] Mostly Koreans.
[2] Including United States (296).

or, in some cases, merely Autonomous Okrugs, i.e., autonomous minor civil divisions. These autonomous republics and districts have remained fixed throughout the Soviet period except for advances in rank, the formation of new autonomous areas, minor boundary revisions, and the removal of population from the Volga German A.S.S.R. for strategic reasons. Republics and autonomous districts as of 1926, with indication of major changes in status from 1926 to 1939, are shown in Table 25.

Ukrainians and Belorussians each made up four-fifths of the population in their respective republics in 1926. Russians, Jews, and Poles came next in order in the Ukraine; Jews, Russians, and Poles in Belorussia. The 172,000 Moldavians (Rumanians) in the Moldavian A.S.S.R. in the western Ukraine were only 30 percent of the population in this small autonomous republic.

Russians (Great Russians) also formed nearly four-fifths of the total population in the Russian Soviet Federated Socialist Republic, exclusive of the Kazakh and Kirgiz A.S.S.R.'s, which later became constituent republics. Russians, Ukrainians, and Belorussians were 86 percent of this total. Of the remainder, the Tatars and other minorities in the Volga-Ural region were the most numerous. Tatars, however, made up only 45 percent of the population of the Tatar A.S.S.R. On the other hand, several smaller groups such as the Chuvash, the Volga Germans, and the Mongolian Kalmyks in the Caspian steppe region were majority groups in their respective republics. In the North Caucasian Territory, exclusive of the mountain districts, 51 percent were Russians and 41 percent were Ukrainians.

[62]

TABLE 25

Political Divisions with Population and Proportion of Titular Group: U.S.S.R., 1926

Political Division, 1926[1]	Population (In thousands)	Titular Group: Percent of Total Population	Russians:[2] Percent of Total Population
1. Russian Soviet Federated Socialist Republic (R.S.F.S.R.)	100,891	73	73
R.S.F.S.R., excluding Kazakh A.S.S.R. and Kirgiz A.S.S.R., listed separately below	93,395	78	78
Including:			
Karelian A.S.S.R.	270	37	58
Komi A.O. [A.S.S.R.] (Zyryan*)	207	92*	7
Votyak A.O. [Udmurt A.S.S.R.]	756	52	43
Mari A.O. [A.S.S.R.]	482	51	44
Tatar A.S.S.R.	2,594	45	43
Chuvash A.S.S.R.	894	75	20
Bashkir A.S.S.R.	2,666	23	40
Volga German A.S.S.R.	572	66	20
Crimean A.S.S.R. (Tatar*)	714	25*	42
Kalmyk A.O. [A.S.S.R.]	142	76	11
Ingush A.O. [Checheno-Ingush A.S.S.R.]	75	93	1
Chechen A.O. [Checheno-Ingush A.S.S.R.]	310	94	3
Kabardino-Balkar A.O. [A.S.S.R.]	204	76	8
North Osetin A.O. [A.S.S.R.]	152	84	7
Adygey-Circassian A.O. (Cherkesy*)	113	45*	26
Karachayev A.O.	65	81	2
Circassian A.O. (Cherkesy*)	37	7*	4
Dagestan A.S.S.R. (31 ethnic groups*)	788	65*	12
Oyrot A.O. (Altay*)	100	36*	52
[Khakass A.O.]	89	50	47
Buryat-Mongolian A.S.S.R.	491	44	53
Yakutsk A.S.S.R.	289	82	10
2. Belorussian S.S.R.	4,983	81	8
3. Ukrainian S.S.R.	29,018	80	9
Including:			
Moldavian A.S.S.R.	572	30	9
4. Transcaucasian Soviet Federated Socialist Republics [Resolved into its constituent republics]			
Azerbaydzhan S.S.R.	2,315	62	10
Including:			
Nakhichevan' A.S.S.R. (Turk*), geographically within Armenian S.S.R.	105	84*	2
Nagornyy-Karabakh A.O. (Armenian*)	125	89*	—[3]
Armenian S.S.R.	880	84	2

TABLE 25 (*Continued*)

Political Divisions with Population and Proportion of Titular Group: U.S.S.R., 1926

Political Division, 1926[1]	Population (In thousands)	Titular Group: Percent of Total Population	Russians:[2] Percent of Total Population
Georgian (Gruzian) S.S.R.	2,666	67	4
Including:			
Abkhazia S.S.R. [A.S.S.R.]	201	28	6
Adzharia A.S.S.R.	132	54	8
South Osetin A.O.	87	69	—[3]
5. Kazakh A.S.S.R. [S.S.R.]	6,503	57	20
Including:			
Kara-Kalpak A.O. [A.S.S.R. in Uzbek S.S.R.]	305	38	2
6. Kirgiz A.S.S.R. [S.S.R.]	993	67	12
7. Uzbek S.S.R.	5,273	66	5
Uzbek S.S.R., excluding Tadzhik A.S.S.R.	4,446	74	6
Tadzhik A.S.S.R. [S.S.R.]	827	75	—[3]
8. Turkmen S.S.R.	1,001	72	8

* The figure for the titular group refers to the name in parenthesis.
[1] Political Divisions:
S.S.R.—Soviet Socialist Republic
A.S.S.R.—Autonomous Soviet Socialist Republic
A.O.—Autonomous Oblast'
[Status, 1939, in brackets]
Exact transliteration of the Russian adjectival (inflected) names is unduly cumbersome. Therefore nominative, or root, forms are used here, in text and maps—except where an adjectival form has been established in common use. The geographical boundaries of 1939 were not, in some cases, identical with those of 1926. Also, several new autonomous oblasts (districts) and autonomous okrugs (counties) were created prior to 1939, which do not correspond to political divisions of 1926. For example, a Mordva political division, which does not appear in the 1926 list, was established as an autonomous oblast in 1930 and as an autonomous republic (A.S.S.R.) in 1934.
[2] Exclusive of Ukrainians and Belorussians.
[3] Less than 1 percent.

The sparse indigenous population of Siberia is extremely heterogeneous, but except in remote regions of the Far North and Far East the demographic situation is dominated by the in-migrant Russian population. None of the indigenous Siberian people, except Mordvians from the Volga-Ural region and Tatars, was represented by so much as one percent of the total population of Siberia proper or of the Far Eastern Territory. Even in Buryat-Mongolia in 1926, Russians made up 53 percent of the total population and Buryats only 44 percent. In the more isolated Yakutia, however, the 236,000 Yakuts made up 82 percent and 13,000 Tungusi another 4.5 percent of the total population. There were only 30,000 Russians in this immense region. The Chukchi (11,000) and Koryaks (7,000) made up more than half of the scanty population of the Kamchatka section of the Far Eastern Territory. Most of the 172,000 Koreans and 92,000 Chinese in the U.S.S.R. in 1926 lived in the Far Eastern Territory. (About one-half the former and 89 percent of the latter were aliens.) These two groups made up 13 percent of the population in this territory and about one-third of that in the Vladivostok section.

[64]

Even in 1926 only 57 percent of the population in the Asiatic steppe republic, the Kazakh A.S.S.R., were Kazakhs. Russians and Ukrainians made up a third of its population, and were a majority in some districts.

The Turkic nationalities of the Central Asian republics formed the largest solid blocks of non-Slavic people in the U.S.S.R. Russians and Ukrainians had moved onto the fertile mountain soils of Kirgizia in considerable numbers and made up 18 percent of its population. But they formed less than 10 percent of the population of Uzbekistan. The mountain republic of the Iranian Tadzhiks, formerly a division of the Uzbek S.S.R., was the only republic (S.S.R. or A.S.S.R.) of the Soviet Union in 1926 in which less than one percent of the total population was Russian.

The republics of the Caucasus Mountains have distinct, and in several cases, quite homogeneous populations. Some of these nations are classified as Japhetic or Caucasian, others as Turkic, and another, the Osetin, as Iranian. On the other hand, it is almost impossible to classify the population of Dagestan along ethnic lines. In addition to the three major nationalities of the Transcaucasus—Georgians, Armenians, and Azers or Turks—several minor groups were represented in the political divisions of 1926. There were three such divisions within the Georgian Republic: the Abkhazians on the western slopes of the Caucasus, the South Osetins in the Central Caucasus, and the Adzharians in the south around Batum. There was an outlying enclave of Azers in Armenia, and one of Armenians in Azerbaydzhan, both politically subordinate to the Azerbaydzhan S.S.R. There were also fairly large scattered minorities in the Transcaucasus that had not been recognized in the formation of autonomous divisions, such as the Talysh and the Kurds. As might be expected, the population of Baku, the center of the petroleum industry, was extremely heterogeneous. There were relatively few Russians in most parts of the Transcaucasus, but they were the most numerous group in Baku, forming 35 percent of the total population.

The ethnic heterogeneity of the Soviet population and the fact that a large proportion of many minorities could neither understand any other language nor read in their own language reflect the cultural isolation of people in different parts of the former Russian Empire. These differences also tended to perpetuate their isolation. On the other hand, more remote ethnic affiliation has little social significance, except where it happens to coincide with differences in social history. For example, the Finnic stocks included some very advanced groups in the Baltic region and some very primitive groups in Siberia. Similarly, the Tatars in European Russia had a very different cultural status from that of many of the Turkic peoples in the Asiatic steppes and Central Asia. However, ethnic differences, especially when associated with different religious traditions, served to accentuate differences in levels and modes of living. They were, therefore, an underlying factor in the initial diversity of the population of various regions within the Soviet Union.

CHAPTER VI

CHARACTERISTICS OF THE SOVIET POPULATION, BY REGIONS, 1926

1. Density and Degree of Urbanization

VARIATIONS of population density within European Russia due to ancient cultural and political conditions had been largely washed out through adaptive migration before the beginning of the twentieth century. Such migration had gradually effected a distribution of population appropriate to the economic life of Russia at this time: agriculture, forestry, mining, household industries, textile and other relatively simple manufactures, and commerce. This adaptation was imperfect, as we shall see. Nevertheless, variations in population density within European Russia had become largely a function of variations in natural resources and climatic conditions. On the other hand, migration between European Russia and various parts of Asiatic Russia had been limited by formidable spatial and cultural barriers. These were only partially resolved by railway construction and slow technical advance along other lines in the late nineteenth century. Therefore, the distribution of population over this vast territory remained inefficient, even with respect to economic activities that were possible at a low technological level. Contrasts between population in different parts of the Soviet area in the early twentieth century were also profoundly influenced by variations in cultural patterns, associated with the diversity of ethnic traditions.

In a large majority of the regions treated in the presentation of 1926 census data,[1] approximately four out of every five persons at that time were living in rural communities (see Table 26 and Plate VIII). The regions with highest proportions of the total population in urban centers are listed below:

Region	Percent Urban
Crimean A.S.S.R.	46
Leningrad-Karelia Region	35
Central Industrial Region	26
Far Eastern Territory	25
Transcaucasian S.F.S.R.	24
Uzbek S.S.R. (without Tadzhik A.S.S.R.)	24
Ural District	21
North Caucasian Territory	20
Ukrainian S.S.R.	19

The proportion of population in cities was, of course, higher in particular districts: 67 percent in Leningrad Province; 42 percent in the Mining-Industrial Subregion of the Ukraine; 43 percent in Murmansk Province, which is mostly within the Arctic Circle; 40 percent in Astrakhan Province, on the Caspian Sea at the mouth of the Volga; and 38 percent in the Adzharia A.S.S.R. in southwestern Georgia, including the port of Batum. Among the three principal republics of the Transcaucasus, the percentage of population in cities was greatest in Azerbaydzhan (28 percent) because of employment in the petroleum industry around Baku.

The division between urban and rural communities is somewhat arbitrary, depending on the legal status of various communities. For example, in Uzbekistan the cities include aggregations of agricultural families, so that the total population dependent on agriculture in this republic

[1] See description of census regions in Chapter IV.

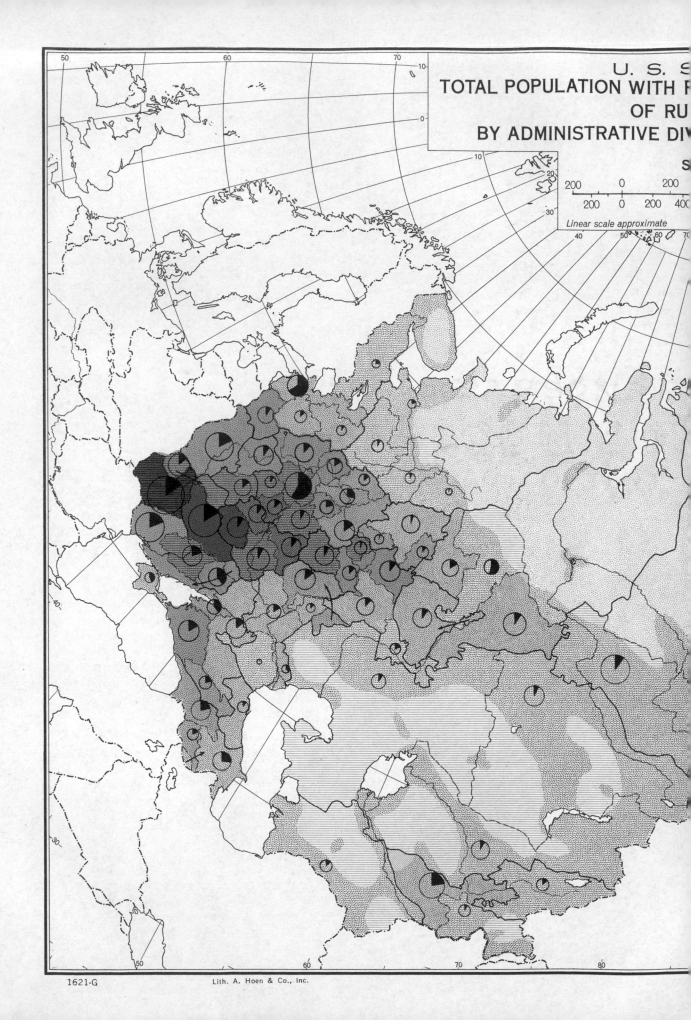

S

200   0   200
200   0   200   400
Linear scale approximate

Lith. A. Hoen & Co., Inc.

PLATE VIII

1 9 2 6

T URBAN, AND MEAN DENSITY

ULATION,

OR CENSUS SUBREGIONS

0,000

600   800   1000 Miles

1000 1200 1400 Kilometers

Projection: azimuthal equal-area

RURAL POPULATION PER SQUARE KILOMETER

| | 1 | 10 | 20 | 30 | 40 | 50 | 60 | 70 |

Areas of circles proportional to total population

The dark sectors represent the percentage of urban population.

- 10,000,000
- 5,000,000
- 1,000,000
- 0

Principal populated areas

For list of administrative divisions
and census regions, see Plate XI.

Prepared by Department of State, Division
of Geography and Cartography
Drawn by American Geographical Society

TABLE 26

Population, Density, and Percent Urban, Dependent on Agriculture, Born Outside Specified
Area, and Literate, by Administrative Divisions: U.S.S.R., 1926

| Division or Region | Population[1] | Population per Square Kilometer | | | Percent | | | | |
		Total	Rural	Urban	Urban	Dependent on Agriculture	Born Outside Specified Area	Aged 10 or Over Able to Read
U.S.S.R.	147,027,915	6.9	5.7	17.9	78.2	1.2[2]	50.2
Belorussian S.S.R.	4,983,240	39.3	32.6	17.0	81.5	6.7	53.3
Ukrainian S.S.R.	29,018,187	64.3	52.4	18.5	77.8	7.0	57.6
Forest Subregion	2,957,881	54.4	46.5	14.5	84.5	6.6	54.0
Dnepr Prairie Right Bank	8,997,757	87.6	73.4	16.1	80.9	6.6	53.2
Dnepr Prairie Left Bank	7,066,909	74.4	62.7	15.8	80.7	8.4	56.9
Steppe Subregion	5,568,233	45.9	37.1	19.1	78.5	11.7	61.4
Dnepr Industrial Subregion	2,391,155	50.9	41.0	19.4	74.7	15.3	62.9
Mining-Industrial Subregion	2,036,252	65.3	38.0	41.8	46.1	29.5	67.4
R.S.F.S.R.	100,891,244	5.1	4.2	17.3	78.3	5.8	52.8
Northeastern Region	2,368,440	2.2	1.9	9.9	86.3	5.2	59.8
Arkhangel'sk Gub.	429,184	1.0	0.7	22.5	73.1	11.7	69.9
Vologda Gub.	1,053,832	9.4	8.5	8.9	87.4	5.3	61.8
Northern Dvina Gub.	678,107	6.5	6.1	5.6	91.2	6.0	53.2
Komi Autonomous Obl.	207,302	0.5	0.5	3.3	92.3	3.6	49.7
Leningrad-Karelia Region	6,659,711	13.1	8.6	34.5	60.8	16.3	72.2
Karelian A.S.S.R.	269,734	1.9	1.4	22.6	67.6	14.7	62.2
Leningrad Gub.	2,792,129	42.2	13.9	67.2	60.5	43.9	85.2
Murmansk Gub.	23,006	0.2	0.1	42.6	46.9	58.3	75.1
Novgorod Gub.	1,050,604	20.3	17.6	13.4	77.6	9.9	66.2
Pskov Gub.	1,788,418	34.6	31.5	8.8	88.9	6.5	57.8
Cherepovets Gub.	735,818	11.7	10.9	7.3	86.7	5.7	65.7
Western Region	4,299,150	43.6	38.4	11.9	85.5	5.9	52.9
Bryansk Gub.	2,005,982	48.3	41.2	14.8	81.9	5.5	50.1
Smolensk Gub.	2,292,712	40.1	36.4	9.3	88.5	6.9	55.7

TABLE 26 (Continued)

Population, Density, and Percent Urban, Dependent on Agriculture, Born Outside Specified Area, and Literate, by Administrative Divisions: U.S.S.R., 1926

Division or Region	Population[1]	Population per Square Kilometer		Percent			
		Total	Rural	Urban	Dependent on Agriculture	Born Outside Specified Area	Aged 10 or Over Able to Read
Central Industrial Region	19,314,024	45.8	34.0	25.6	66.7	7.7	68.7
Vladimir Gub.	1,321,099	40.0	32.0	20.0	65.0	7.8	70.8
Ivanovo-Voznesensk Gub.	1,196,022	35.7	25.4	28.9	61.5	10.6	69.7
Kaluga Gub.	1,151,704	44.5	40.3	9.4	83.0	6.6	60.4
Kostroma Gub.	811,615	24.1	20.7	14.4	77.4	7.2	71.9
Moscow Gub.	4,570,877	103.0	41.9	59.2	30.9	39.9	81.6
Nizhniy Novgorod Gub.	2,743,469	33.7	28.2	16.3	77.6	6.4	56.3
Tver' Gub.	2,241,995	35.4	30.8	12.8	81.2	6.6	67.5
Yaroslavl' Gub.	1,343,159	38.6	31.0	19.7	73.4	11.5	77.7
Ryazan' Gub.	2,428,914	52.5	48.3	8.0	87.6	3.9	56.1
Tula Gub.	1,505,263	59.1	50.6	14.5	82.6	6.8	64.7
Central Black Soil Region	10,825,830	57.5	52.1	9.5	88.7	3.8	49.6
Voronezh Gub.	3,308,439	49.4	45.4	8.1	89.5	4.5	48.1
Kursk Gub.	2,906,360	66.6	60.4	9.2	88.8	4.1	51.9
Orël Gub.	1,884,533	61.3	55.1	10.0	89.4	5.2	53.7
Tambov Gub.	2,727,234	58.4	51.9	10.9	87.0	4.3	46.2
Vyatka Region	3,463,197	21.5	20.0	6.8	90.6	4.5	51.5
Votyak A.O.	756,264	24.9	22.4	10.2	87.3	8.3	42.4
Vyatka Gub.	2,224,653	20.5	19.2	6.2	91.1	4.5	55.4
Mari A.O.	482,101	21.5	20.6	4.2	93.6	6.7	47.9
Ural Oblast'	6,786,339	3.9	3.1	20.7	74.9	10.9	50.3
Cis-Ural Subregion	1,888,388	17.3	14.3	17.0	79.3	10.3[3]	51.5
Mining-Industrial Subregion	1,500,928	6.6	3.2	51.0	44.3	19.1[3]	61.5
Trans-Ural Subregion	3,205,823	12.3	11.2	9.4	85.6	13.2[3]	45.1
Tobol'sk Subregion	192,163	0.2	0.15	11.0	84.6	9.7[3]	35.2
Bashkir A.S.S.R.	2,665,836	17.6	16.0	8.8	87.7	9.5	41.4

TABLE 26 (*Continued*)

Population, Density, and Percent Urban, Dependent on Agriculture, Born Outside Specified Area, and Literate, by Administrative Divisions: U.S.S.R., 1926

Division or Region	Population[1]	Population per Square Kilometer		Percent			
		Total	Rural	Urban	Dependent on Agriculture	Born Outside Specified Area	Aged 10 or Over Able to Read
Central Volga Region	10,268,168	30.3	26.8	11.4	86.9	5.1	47.5
Orenburg Gub.	773,254	11.4	9.1	19.8	76.4	16.8	55.2
Penza Gub.	2,208,765	47.7	43.3	9.3	90.5	3.6	40.4
Samara Gub.	2,412,977	22.9	19.8	13.2	83.8	9.8	48.5
Tatar A.S.S.R.	2,594,037	38.6	34.5	10.8	87.8	4.8	48.5
Ul'yanovsk Gub.	1,384,220	40.6	35.7	12.1	85.7	5.7	50.6
Chuvash A.S.S.R.	894,478	48.9	46.4	5.1	94.5	3.6	47.3
Lower Volga Region	5,529,516	17.1	14.1	17.7	77.5	7.8	54.3
Astrakhan' Gub.	510,386	15.8	9.5	39.9	53.8	24.8	53.7
Kalmyk A.O.	141,594	1.9	1.9	—	91.1	12.6	22.3
Volga German A.S.S.R.	571,822	21.4	18.6	12.8	78.0	7.6	71.8
Saratov Gub.	2,897,363	31.8	26.9	15.2	81.9	7.2	52.0
Stalingrad Gub.	1,408,449	14.2	11.6	18.4	75.3	9.8	55.3
Crimean A.S.S.R.	713,823	27.6	14.8	46.3	52.4	27.1	72.8
North Caucasian Kray	8,363,491	28.5	22.8	19.8	74.1	16.9	55.0
Azov Subregion	1,401,076	45.4	28.0	38.4	57.3	24.9[3]	68.7
Donets-Stavropol' Subregion	2,792,953	20.2	17.4	14.0	79.9	18.0[3]	56.1
Kuban'-Black Sea Subregion	3,151,528	37.3	31.0	16.9	73.3	24.9[3]	56.1
Mountain Subregion	1,018,529	25.3	20.5	19.1	77.3	15.8[3]	27.5
Dagestan A.S.S.R.	788,098	14.5	13.0	10.8	79.6	9.1	16.7
Siberian Kray	8,687,939	2.1	1.9	13.0	81.3	29.8	41.5
Southwest Subregion	5,240,321	9.1	8.1	10.7	84.2	33.3[3]	39.7
Northeast Subregion	3,447,618	1.0	0.8	16.6	75.0	24.4[3]	44.2
Buryat-Mongolian A.S.S.R.	491,236	1.3	1.2	9.3	85.8	15.5	38.1
Yakutsk A.S.S.R.	289,085	0.07	0.07	5.3	89.9	8.6	22.2

TABLE 26 (Continued)

Population, Density, and Percent Urban, Dependent on Agriculture, Born Outside Specified Area, and Literate, by Administrative Divisions: U.S.S.R., 1926

Division or Region	Population[1]	Population per Square Kilometer		Percent			
		Total	Rural	Urban	Dependent on Agriculture	Born Outside Specified Area	Aged 10 or Over Able to Read
Far Eastern Kray	1,881,351	0.7	0.5	25.1	67.9	35.5	57.3
Transbaykal Subregion	590,101	2.2	1.8	19.3	70.7	18.4[3]	50.1
Amur Subregion	446,175	1.1	0.8	26.6	64.8	44.8[3]	62.4
Maritime Subregion	798,258	0.9	0.7	29.5	65.8	50.8[3]	60.9
Sakhalin Subregion	11,859	0.3	0.2	23.2	63.0	50.9[3]	60.1
Kamchatka Subregion	34,958	0.03	0.03	4.8	90.8	61.9[3]	25.3
Kazakh A.S.S.R.	6,503,006	2.2	2.0	8.3	89.8	16.0	22.2
Western Subregion	1,631,780	1.5	1.4	7.6	89.4	19.8[3]	24.5
Eastern Subregion	2,521,273	2.4	2.2	8.0	89.0	21.0[3]	28.5
Southern Subregion	2,349,646	2.8	2.5	9.1	89.7	11.1[3]	13.8
Kirgiz A.S.S.R.	993,004	5.1	4.5	12.2	90.0	10.7	15.3
Uzbek S.S.R. (with Tadzhik)	5,272,801	16.9	13.4	20.9	81.4	5.8	9.9
Without Tadzhik A.S.S.R.	4,445,634	28.3	21.5	23.9	79.0	5.5	11.1
Tadzhik A.S.S.R.	827,167	5.4	5.1	4.9	92.6	2.5	2.8
Turkmen S.S.R.	1,000,914	2.2	1.9	13.7	83.4	15.7	11.1
Transcaucasian S.F.S.R.	5,861,529	31.7	24.0	24.1	72.0	10.5	37.0
Azerbaydzhan S.S.R.	2,314,571	26.9	19.4	28.1	64.8	15.5	25.1
Including:							
Nagornyy-Karabakh A.O.	125,300	30.1	28.1	6.6	—	—	28.8
Nakhichevan' A.S.S.R.	104,956	19.6	16.9	14.0	—	—	11.8
Armenian S.S.R.	880,464	29.4	23.8	19.0	81.3	18.0	34.6
Georgian S.S.R.	2,666,494	38.5	29.9	22.3	75.1	8.1	47.5
Including:							
Abkhazia S.S.R.	201,016	24.8	20.8	16.1	—	—	36.5
Adzharia A.S.S.R.	131,957	51.2	31.5	38.1	—	—	39.1
South Osetin A.O.	87,375	23.6	22.0	6.6	—	—	21.7

[1] The population figures for districts other than republics or major regions are taken from the census reports for various administrative divisions. There are small discrepancies between these figures and the final figures for "population present" in the Summary Volume for the U.S.S.R.

[2] Figure for U.S.S.R. is percent of total population born outside actual borders of U.S.S.R. at time of census. Other percentages equal 100 minus "habitual" population born in same area as percent of total "present" population.

is somewhat higher than that classified as rural; this is also the case in Kirgizia. In some districts, as in the Moscow Province, Dagestan, the Transcaucasus, and some mining districts, the rural population includes a considerable proportion dependent on other occupations than agriculture, forestry, fishing, and hunting. In general, however, the rural-urban break corresponds roughly to the division between population dependent on agriculture and related occupations and that dependent on industry, mining, trade, transportation, and administration. Persons chiefly dependent on handicrafts and shop industries are divided fairly evenly between urban and rural areas.

2. Occupational Characteristics

The distribution of the populations of the various regions by occupational class in 1926 is shown in Figure 12 and, in somewhat greater detail, in Table 27. The proportion dependent on industrial occupations of all sorts (manufacturing, mining, construction, railway transportation, and other transportation) was 10 percent or over in only five cases: the Leningrad-Karelia Region (16 percent); the Central Industrial Region (15 percent); and the Ural, Crimean, and

TABLE 27

Percentage Distribution of Population of Regions by Occupational Class:
U.S.S.R., December 17, 1926[1]

Division or Region	Class I			Class II				
	Agriculture, Forestry, Fishing	Craft and Shops	Subtotal Class I	Manufacturing, Mining	Construction	Railroad Transport	Other Transport	Subtotal Class II
U.S.S.R.	78.17	3.17	81.34	4.48	.69	1.96	.80	7.93
Belorussian S.S.R.	81.46	3.70	85.16	2.08	.61	1.61	.54	4.84
Ukrainian S.S.R.	77.78	3.64	81.42	5.26	.57	1.86	.67	8.36
Northeastern Region	86.30	1.38	87.68	2.36	.31	1.33	.79	4.79
Leningrad-Karelia Region	60.80	3.02	63.82	10.58	.93	3.07	1.73	16.31
Western Region	85.46	2.03	87.49	3.48	.37	1.41	.24	5.50
Central Industrial Region	66.74	3.77	70.51	10.47	1.15	2.32	1.11	15.05
Central Black Soil Region	88.66	2.01	90.67	1.14	.33	1.85	.10	3.42
Vyatka Region	90.62	1.12	91.74	2.22	.22	.66	.18	3.28
Ural Oblast'	74.92	2.81	77.73	7.56	.69	2.60	.68	11.53
Bashkir A.S.S.R.	87.74	2.40	90.14	1.86	.40	1.05	.45	3.76
Central Volga Region	86.90	1.91	88.81	1.81	.35	1.49	.44	4.09
Lower Volga Region	77.50	4.02	81.52	3.14	.63	1.86	1.37	7.00
Crimean A.S.S.R.	52.41	7.05	59.46	4.51	1.53	1.84	3.71	11.59
North Caucasian Kray	74.08	4.14	78.22	3.55	1.06	2.58	1.05	8.24
Dagestan A.S.S.R.	79.57	5.43	85.00	1.16	.62	1.36	1.12	4.26
Siberian Kray	81.27	2.99	84.26	2.11	.88	2.22	.71	5.92
Buryat-Mongolian A.S.S.R.	85.76	1.86	87.62	.86	.45	1.35	.41	3.07
Yakutsk A.S.S.R.	89.89	2.02	91.91	.51	.27	—	.59	1.37
Far Eastern Kray	67.90	3.78	71.68	2.97	.74	6.11	2.28	12.10
Kazakh A.S.S.R.	89.77	1.47	91.24	.55	.34	.89	.31	2.09
Kirgiz A.S.S.R.	90.00	2.33	92.33	.41	.53	.21	.41	1.56
Uzbek S.S.R.[2]	81.38	5.41	86.79	.90	.65	.95	.64	3.14
Turkmen S.S.R.	83.39	1.79	85.18	.93	.46	3.58	.95	5.92
Transcaucasian S.F.S.R.	79.97	4.21	76.18	3.88	1.03	1.93	1.63	8.47

TABLE 27 (*Continued*)

Percentage Distribution of Population of Regions by Occupational Class:
U.S.S.R., December 17, 1926[1]

| Division or Region | Class III | | | | | | |
	Trade and Credit	Public Service	Miscel- laneous	No Occu- pation or Unknown	Unem- ployed	Mili- tary	Sub- total Class III
U.S.S.R.	2.18	2.89	2.18	1.82	1.14	.52	10.73
Belorussian S.S.R.	2.01	2.48	1.62	1.60	.90	1.38	9.99
Ukrainian S.S.R.	2.29	2.54	2.10	1.66	1.13	.50	10.22
Northeastern Region	1.24	2.57	1.10	1.69	.74	.20	7.54
Leningrad-Karelia Region	3.29	5.16	2.94	3.60	3.16	1.71	19.86
Western Region	1.35	2.10	.98	1.37	.62	.59	7.01
Central Industrial Region	3.06	4.29	2.23	2.58	1.82	.46	14.44
Central Black Soil Region	1.23	1.80	.94	1.18	.51	.24	5.90
Vyatka Region	.79	1.80	.79	1.24	.29	.06	4.97
Ural Oblast'	1.81	2.95	2.56	2.33	.95	.14	10.74
Bashkir A.S.S.R.	1.18	1.76	1.67	.96	.44	.08	6.09
Central Volga Region	1.47	2.21	1.14	1.33	.75	.20	7.10
Lower Volga Region	2.30	3.20	2.56	1.93	1.32	.17	11.48
Crimean A.S.S.R.	5.62	7.73	4.91	3.89	4.09	2.72	28.96
North Caucasian Kray	2.62	3.34	3.76	1.84	1.48	.50	13.54
Dagestan A.S.S.R.	2.22	2.18	2.56	2.88	.54	.36	10.74
Siberian Kray	1.69	2.61	2.68	1.61	.89	.34	9.82
Buryat-Mongolian A.S.S.R.	1.36	2.58	1.04	2.44	.65	1.25	9.32
Yakutsk A.S.S.R.	1.17	2.11	1.72	.97	.66	.09	6.72
Far Eastern Kray	2.79	4.42	3.04	2.14	1.96	1.87	16.22
Kazakh A.S.S.R.	1.29	1.54	2.58	.79	.42	.05	6.67
Kirgiz A.S.S.R.	1.61	1.39	1.87	.60	.44	.19	6.10
Uzbek S.S.R.[2]	2.73	2.20	2.75	1.15	.55	.68	10.06
Turkmen S.S.R.	2.02	2.32	.71	1.77	.49	1.58	8.89
Trancaucasian S.F.S.R.	3.47	3.92	3.50	2.41	1.12	.94	15.36

[1] Data from census, adjusted by proportional distribution of children under 10 reported as occupied but not otherwise specified. For a discussion of data available on the occupational distribution of the population, see Appendix V.

[2] Including the Tadzhik A.S.S.R.

the Soviet Far Eastern regions (each about 12 percent). The proportion dependent directly on manufacturing and mining was above 10 percent in only two cases: the Leningrad-Karelia and the Central Industrial regions; the Ural District came next with 8 percent. Manufacturing and mining supported 5 percent of the population in the Ukraine, 4.5 percent in the Crimea, 4 percent in the Transcaucasus, about 3.5 percent in the North Caucasus and in the Western Region, and about 3 percent in the Lower Volga Region and in the Far Eastern Territory. In all other major regions less than 3 percent of the population was dependent on manufacturing and mining. The proportion dependent on employment in transportation was highest in the Far Eastern Territory (8.4 percent), the Crimea (5.6 percent), and the Leningrad-Karelia Region (4.8 percent).

The occupational structure of the Crimea is most complex. This region had the lowest proportion of total population dependent on agriculture, forestry, or fishing (52 percent), although it contains some of the richest farm land in the Soviet Union. The proportion of persons *primarily* dependent on handicrafts and shop industries was unusually high in the Crimea (7 percent). Incidentally, a somewhat similar situation is indicated for several other regions with a large non-Russian population; the comparable proportion was as high as 5 percent in Uzbekistan (Central Asia) and Dagestan (a hill region northeast of the Caucasus Mountains) and 4 percent in the Transcaucasus, North Caucasus, and Lower Volga regions. The Crimea also showed higher than average proportions dependent on manufacturing and mining, construction, non-railway transportation, trade and credit, public service (influenced in this case by a greater proportion of city dwellers and many sanitoria), "miscellaneous" (independent profes-

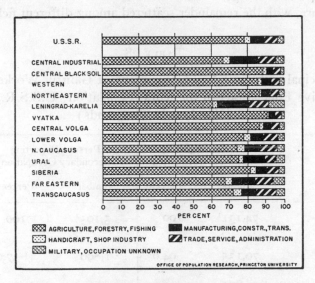

FIGURE 12. Percentage Distribution of Population of Specified Regions by Occupational Class: U.S.S.R., December 17, 1926 [Table 27]

sional, casual labor, and domestic service), no occupation or occupation unknown, unemployed, and military personnel. In the Crimea 29 percent of the total population fell in classes other than agriculture or industry: i.e., in the trade, service, miscellaneous, unemployed, and military groups. Elsewhere, the nearest approach to such complexity of the occupational pattern, as indicated by the proportion of the population not classified as immediately dependent on either agriculture or industry, is found in the Leningrad-Karelia Region (20 percent), the Far Eastern Territory (16 percent), the Transcaucasus (15 percent), and the Central Industrial and the North Caucasus regions (14 percent).

The proportions dependent on the traditional peasant or pastoral occupations (agriculture, forestry, fishing, and handicrafts and shop industry) in various parts of the Soviet Union in 1926 ran as follows:

1. Under 65 percent   Crimea, Leningrad-Karelia
2. 65-74 percent   Central Industrial, Far Eastern
3. 75-79 percent   Transcaucasus, North Caucasus, Ural
4. 80-84 percent   Ukraine, Lower Volga, Siberia
5. 85 percent or over Belorussia, Northeast, Western, Central Black Soil, Vyatka, Bashkiria, Central Volga, Dagestan, Buryat-Mongolia, Yakutia, Kazakhstan, Kirgizia, Uzbekistan, Turkmenia

It is apparent that peasant or pastoral economy dominated the life of the people in most parts of the Soviet Union at this time—with as much as one-fourth of the population dependent on other occupations only in the regions around Leningrad and Moscow and in the Crimea and the Far Eastern Territory.

Handicrafts, household industries, and part-time employment in forests, mines, or industries provided an important, though precarious, supplementary source of support for the whole rural population of the Soviet Union, especially in the forest zone and in the Crimea, the Transcaucasus, and Central Asia. Five million persons living in rural communities reported supplementary occupations in 1926 (7 percent of the rural population reporting a principal occupation). Secondary employment in agriculture or in handicraft or shop industries accounts for two-thirds of the figure, with the remainder scattered among different fields (see Table 28).

TABLE 28

Distribution by Principal and Secondary Occupations of Gainful Workers Aged 10 and Over (Active Population) in the Rural Population: U.S.S.R., 1926
(Numbers in Thousands)

Occupation	Persons Reporting Principal Occupation		Persons Reporting Secondary Occupation		Secondary per 100 Principal Occupations of Same Type
	Number	Percent	Number	Percent	
Total	74,131[1]	100	5,105[3]	100	7
Agriculture, Forestry, and Fishing	70,135	94.6	1,890	37.0	3
Handicraft and Shop Industry	870	1.2	1,754	34.4	202
Manufacturing and Mining	543	0.7	205	4.0	38
Construction	162	0.2	412	8.1	254
Railroad Transport	242	0.3	58	1.1	24
Other Transport	70	0.1	184	3.6	263
Trade and Credit	223	0.3	184	3.6	83
Public Service	508	0.7	169	3.3	33
Casual Labor, Independent Professional, Misc.	707	0.9	237	4.6	34
No Occupation or Unknown	492	0.7	12	0.2	—
Unemployed	119	0.2	—	—	—
Military	60	0.1	—	—	—
Including:					
Wage and Salary Earners ("Workers" and "Employees") All Types	(3,289)[2]	(4.4)	(1,392)[4]	(27)	42
In Agriculture, Forestry, and Fishing	(1,093)	(1.5)	(547)	(11)	50

[1] Number in total population (urban and rural): 86,220,000
[2] Number in total population (urban and rural): 9,583,000
[3] Number in total population (urban and rural): 5,425,000
[4] Number in total population (urban and rural): 1,450,000

The highest densities of rural population in 1926 are found in the Dnepr Prairie subregions of the Ukraine (Right Bank, 73 rural persons per square kilometer; Left Bank, 63), the adjacent Central Black Soil Region of the R.S.F.S.R. (52), neighboring districts in the Central Industrial Region (Tula, 51; Ryazan, 48), and in the Central Volga Region (Penza, 43; Chuvash A.S.S.R., 46). More than 80 percent of the total population in all these areas and about 95 percent of their rural population were dependent on agriculture. However, areas in which the rural population was most dense were generally areas of highly productive soil, so that this distribution does not necessarily reflect maldistribution of population within European Russia, so long as its economic life remained primarily dependent on the cultivation of the land.

3. Variations in Level of Living

Plate IX shows, according to Libkind,[2] the proportion of farms with 11 hectares (27 acres) or more of sown land in various divisions of the U.S.S.R., exclusive of the Asiatic steppe region, Central Asia, and Yakutia. Farms with less than 1 hectare (about 2.5 acres) of sown land made up 40 percent or more of all holdings in Armenia, Georgia, Dagestan, the Kalmyk District on the shores of the Caspian, the extreme northern districts of European Russia, Buryat-Mongolia, and the northern part of the Far Eastern Territory. Conversely, relatively large farms were found most frequently in the southern and eastern parts of the Ukraine, the Crimea, the North Caucasus, the Lower Volga Region, parts of the Central Volga Region, some districts in southwestern Siberia, and the Amur section of the Far Eastern Territory.

Estimates of average income per capita of rural population in various parts of European Russia, as reported by Avilov,[3] are shown in Table 29. These estimates are based on household schedules from samples of the rural population, 1926-1927, when prices were relatively free. In general, the variations shown here are fairly small. The following are indicated as the areas of lowest income (net income per capita of less than 100 rubles per year) within the European part of the U.S.S.R.:

(1) A strip along the Polish border: Belorussia, the Western Region, the Forest Subregion of the Ukraine, and the Dnepr Prairie Right Bank Subregion of the Ukraine

(2) The Central Black Soil Region and (subject to reservations about the significance of the data) the Central Volga Region

(3) Dagestan, in the hill country northeast of the Caucasus Mountains

(4) Bashkiria, in the southern Urals

The regions in the first two groups listed above were heavily dependent on crop production, and were areas of high population density. For example, in the central part of the Ukraine west of the Dnepr (Prairie Right Bank Subregion) 61 percent of the income of the rural population was derived from crop production, but only 13 percent of the farms in this area had more than 4.3 hectares (10.7 acres) of cultivated land, and less than one percent had more than 8.6 hectares. In Belorussia, the Forest Subregion of the Ukraine, and the Central Black Soil Region, the proportion of farm income from production of crops was even higher (around 70 percent), but here there were somewhat higher proportions of medium and large farms. In Dagestan, where the economy was similar to that in the Caucasus Mountains and parts of the Transcaucasus, the land was generally divided into very small plots. Bashkiria, a region of low mountains and steppes, had attracted many colonists from southern Russia. Their position was presumably improved in the new location, but the level of living of the indigenous, pastoral Bashkirs remained far below that of the Russian colonists.

[2] Libkind, Title 171. [3] Avilov, Title 6.

TABLE 29

Estimated Per Capita Income of Rural Population by Region: European U.S.S.R., 1925-1926[1]

Region	Conventional Net Income per Year Per Capita in Rubles	Percent of Rural Income from Crop Production	Percent of Farm Holdings With Over 4 Hectares of Sown Land
Belorussian S.S.R.	85	74	26
Ukrainian S.S.R.	104[2]	66[2]	—
Forest	98	71	23
Dnepr Prairie Right Bank	92	61	13
Dnepr Prairie Left Bank	111	69	37
Steppe	104	70	61
Dnepr Industrial	119	62	68
Mining-Industrial	132	71	62
Northeastern Region	106	50	7
Leningrad Region	135	50	9
Western Region	96	62	24
Central Industrial Region	140	41	15
Central Black Soil Region	84	70	36
Vyatka Region	100	53	52
Ural Oblast'	107	53	29
Bashkir A.S.S.R.	88	55	34
Central Volga Region	82[3]	58	40
Lower Volga Region	125	72	45
Crimean A.S.S.R.	143	68	52
North Caucasian Kray	135	71	54
Dagestan A.S.S.R.	88	52	3

[1] According to Avilov, Title 6.
[2] Weighted (by farm population) average of subregions.
[3] Avilov's data in detail show, in Central Volga Region, very low income in the right bank districts (Penza, Ul'yanovsk, and the Tatar and Chuvash A.S.S.R.'s) with higher, moderate income in the left bank districts (Samara and Orenburg). The whole region probably suffered at this time from incomplete recovery from famine conditions.

The North Caucasus, the Lower Volga Region, the eastern districts of the Ukraine, and the Crimea show the most favorable situation as regards agriculture—with relatively large land holdings and relatively high average income. Relatively high incomes are also indicated for the rural populations of the Central Industrial and Leningrad regions, but these were derived in large part from sources other than crop production. The rural populations in districts to the north and east (Northeastern, Vyatka, and Ural regions) were also largely dependent on sources of income other than crop production, i.e., grazing, forestry, fishing, or supplementary industrial employment; incomes in these districts were neither much above nor much below the general average.

The status of various regions on a somewhat different index of agricultural productivity is

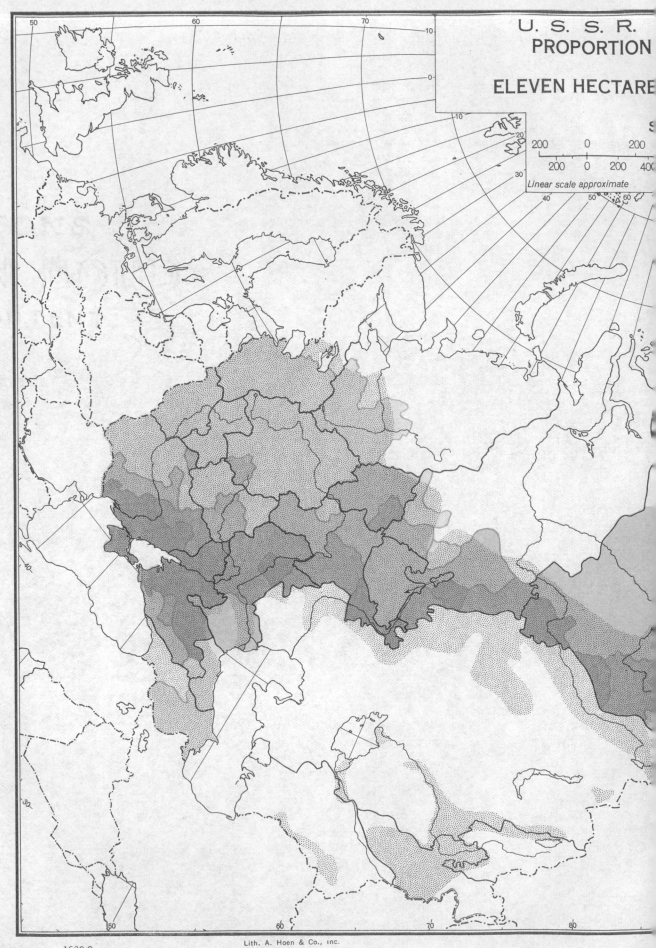

S

200   0   200

200   0   200   400

Linear scale approximate

40   50   60

Lith. A. Hoen & Co., Inc.

PLATE IX

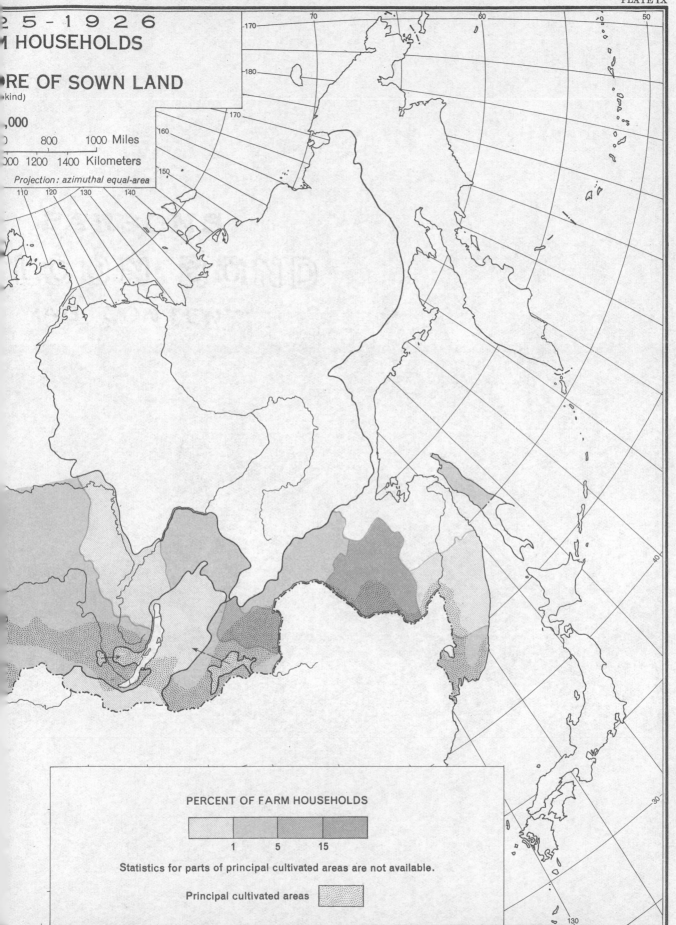

25-1926

M HOUSEHOLDS

RE OF SOWN LAND

(kind)

,000

0   800   1000 Miles

000 1200 1400 Kilometers

Projection: azimuthal equal-area

PERCENT OF FARM HOUSEHOLDS

1   5   15

Statistics for parts of principal cultivated areas are not available.

Principal cultivated areas

Prepared by Department of State, Division
of Geography and Cartography
Drawn by American Geographical Society

shown in Plate X.[4] This index is derived from official data on production for 1925-1928, the quantities of various products being weighted by average prices in the U.S.S.R. during these years. The figures represent average net values of farm production (including all major crop and livestock products, excluding fodder) in rubles per year per capita of farm population. This index differs from that presented by Avilov in that (1) it does not take account of the effect of location, transportation, or other factors on price levels in different regions; and (2) it does not take account of supplementary income from sources other than the production of crops and livestock. The relatively low status on this index of the farm population of the Central Industrial and Northeastern regions of European Russia is, therefore, not necessarily indicative of particularly low incomes. Conversely, the status of more remote districts, e.g., the Urals, Bashkiria, and Siberia, may be higher on this index than it would be on an index of average income. After these differences are taken into account, the regional variations within European Russia indicated on this index and on that prepared by Avilov appear fairly comparable. Differences in particular cases may be due to divergence of defined objectives, or to imperfections in either or both of the indices. The tier of low income regions in western Russia, indicated by Avilov, does not appear on this map. This may be due in part to the fact that the Ukraine is treated here as a unit. It also results from the surprisingly favorable status of Belorussia (generally regarded as a region of low agricultural productivity) and that of the densely populated Central Black Soil Region on this index. In these respects, the data by Avilov probably have greater significance.

The comparison between the European and the Asiatic parts of the U.S.S.R. on the index presented in Plate X is especially interesting. The productivity ratings of these two broad divisions are approximately the same: European part, 88; Asiatic part, 86. However, the European regions are characterized by relatively small variations, except the low value for Dagestan, which is economically similar to the Caucasus Mountains and parts of the Transcaucasus, and the high values shown for the Crimea and the North Caucasus. On the other hand, there is a sharp contrast in Asia between the relatively high productivity indicated for the farm population of Siberia (7 million farm persons, with an average per capita productivity valued at 117 rubles) and the low productivity shown for the farm population in the Transcaucasus (4 million persons; index 58), Uzbekistan and Turkmenia combined (5 million persons; index 69), and Kirgizia (1 million persons; index 71). The intermediate status of Kazakhstan on this index probably conceals a sharp contrast between the indigenous, nomadic population and the in-migrant Russian population.

4. Population in Relation to Resources

The evidence presented above, drawn from various sources, seems to indicate three areas of relatively high population density in relation to economic productivity in the middle 'twenties: (1) western European Russia, (2) the Transcaucasus, and (3) Central Asia. These correspond roughly to the three centers of ancient culture within the present territory of the Soviet Union; the low economic level of the population in the more isolated of these centers (the Transcaucasus and Central Asia) is most clearly indicated. The regions of relatively greatest agricultural opportunity at this time were apparently the Crimean peninsula, southern and eastern Ukraine, the North Caucasus, and Siberia. It is also apparent that the whole Soviet Union was characterized by a very low level of economic productivity.

Obviously, we have been dealing here only with the relation of population to economic op-

[4] Derived from data on agriculture in Europe and the Soviet Union presented in Wilbert E. Moore, *Economic Demography of Eastern and Southern Europe* (Geneva: League of Nations, 1945), Chapter II and Appendix I.

portunities provided by agriculture at a low technical level and by meager industrial and commercial organization. The full utilization of fuel and mineral resources in well-developed industries and a coordinated system of transportation would, of course, give a quite different pattern of economic opportunity and would demand a different population pattern.

Areas of underpopulation, in which the population was too sparse to give the basis for a balanced economy, have been a conspicuous feature of the Soviet scene. The following large administrative divisions, or subregions, had only about 1 person or less per square kilometer in 1926:

Areas	*Persons per Square Kilometer*
Northern European Areas	
Murmansk Gub.	0.2
Arkhangel'sk Gub.	1.0
Komi A.O.	0.5
Northern Asiatic Areas	
Tobol'sk Subregion (part of the Siberian plain included in the Ural Oblast' in 1926)	0.2
Siberian Territory: Eastern Subregion (including all the Arctic territory between the Ural Oblast' and Yakutia)	1.0
Buryat-Mongolian A.S.S.R.	1.3
Yakutsk A.S.S.R.	0.07
Far Eastern Territory	0.7
Including:	
Amur Subregion	1.1
Maritime Subregion	0.9
Sakhalin	0.3
Kamchatka	0.03
Asiatic Steppes	
Kazakh A.S.S.R.: Western Subregion	1.5

The population of Siberia, Buryat-Mongolia, Yakutia, and the Far Eastern Territory was, and to a somewhat lesser degree still is, largely concentrated in the narrow strip of cereal lands between the *taiga* and the *steppes*, through which the Trans-Siberian Railway passes, or along river valleys. In addition, there are concentrations in the vicinity of Vladivostok, and in isolated mining or forest communities.

Kazakhstan and Turkmenia (each with an average density in 1926 of 2 persons per square kilometer) constituted another great, sparsely populated area within the Soviet Union. The margins of this region supported agricultural settlements, but its deserts and dry grasslands maintained only a sparse nomadic population.

The economic and political integration of the Atlantic and Pacific spheres of the Soviet Union, and the integration of Central Asia with European Russia, Siberia, and the Transcaucasus necessarily awaited the mechanical development of natural resources, the utilization of improved transportation facilities, and the attraction of a larger resident population to the usable lands that form a corridor between European Russia and the Far East and between Central Siberia and Central Asia—along with the systematic exploitation of particularly promising remote regions. The construction of the Trans-Siberian Railway in the late Imperial period and the construction of the Siberian-Turkestan Railway in the early Soviet period forged important links toward such integration, which has been carried forward by complicated advances during the later Soviet regime.

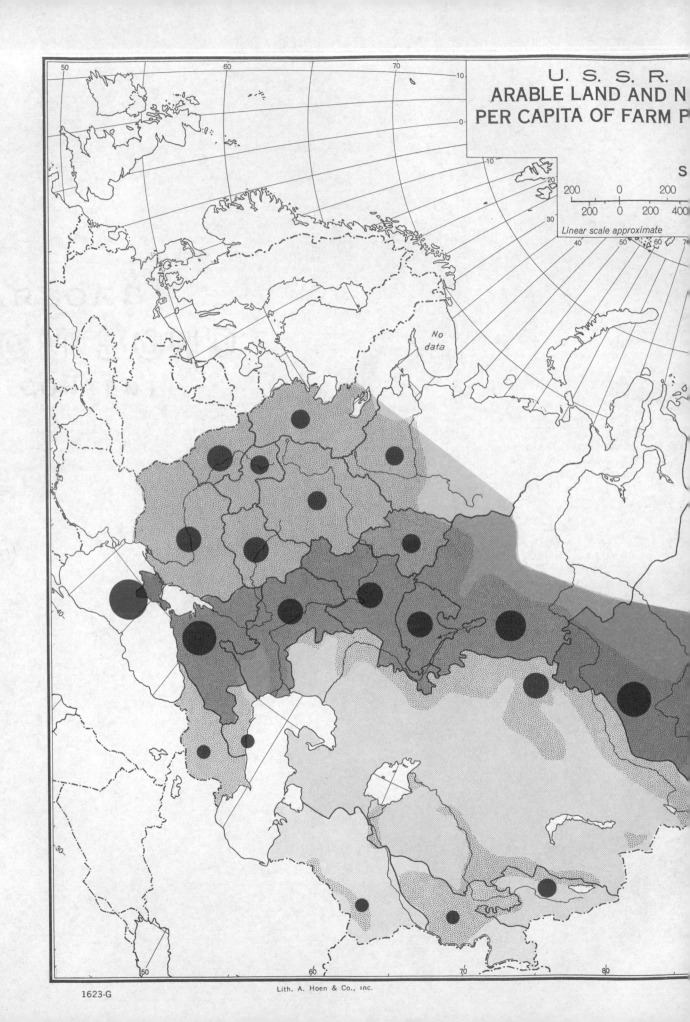

No data

S

200   0   200
200   0   200   400
Linear scale approximate
40   50   60

50   60   70   10
0
-10
20
30
40

40

30

50   60   70   80

Lith. A. Hoen & Co., Inc.

PLATE X

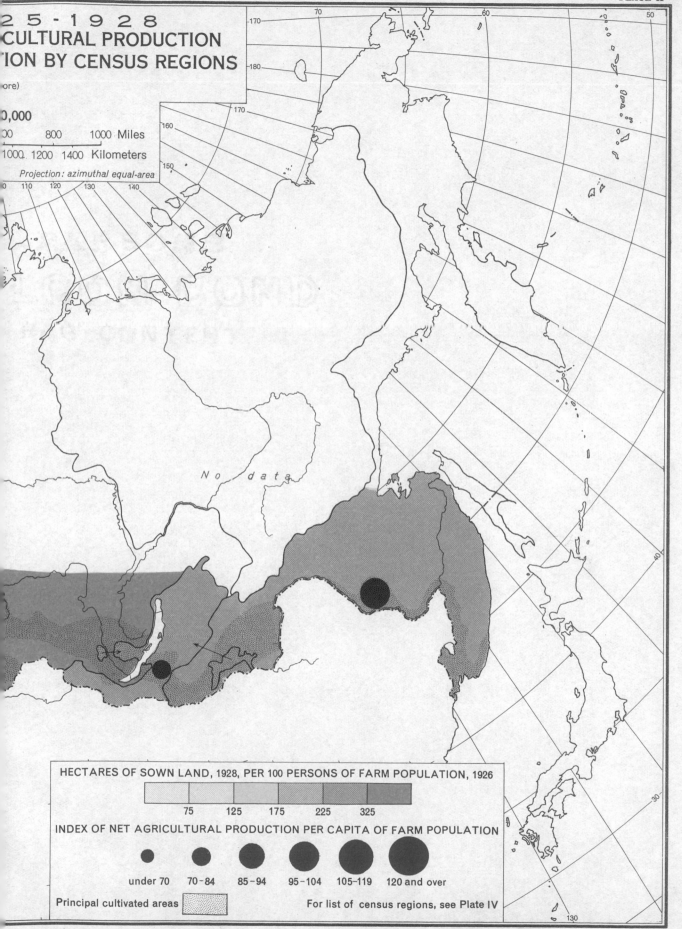

25-1928
CULTURAL PRODUCTION
TION BY CENSUS REGIONS
(ore)

0,000

00   800   1000 Miles

1000 1200 1400 Kilometers

Projection: azimuthal equal-area

No data

HECTARES OF SOWN LAND, 1928, PER 100 PERSONS OF FARM POPULATION, 1926

75   125   175   225   325

INDEX OF NET AGRICULTURAL PRODUCTION PER CAPITA OF FARM POPULATION

under 70   70-84   85-94   95-104   105-119   120 and over

Principal cultivated areas

For list of census regions, see Plate IV

Prepared by Department of State, Division
of Geography and Cartography
Drawn by American Geographical Society

5. Literacy

Literacy in European Russia was generally associated with urbanism. In 1926 slightly over two-thirds of the population aged 10 years or over in the Central Industrial Region were able to read (see Table 26, above, and Plate XI). The proportion reached 82 percent in Moscow Province, 85 percent in Leningrad Province, and 73 percent in the Crimea. About one-half of the people (excluding those under 10 years) were able to read in Belorussia, the Ukraine, and the Western, Central Black Soil, Central Volga, Lower Volga, North Caucasus, Vyatka, and Ural regions. The low literacy rates of the non-Russian nationalities, except the Volga Germans, in the Volga regions and in the North Caucasus are masked, in the figures for total population, by the large number of Russian and Ukrainian settlers. The same factor raises the figures on proportion of literate persons in Bashkiria, Buryat-Mongolia, Yakutia, and many other areas. Owing to their preponderant Russian population, Siberia (42 percent) and the Far Eastern Territory (57 percent) show proportions similar to the general average for the U.S.S.R.; but the isolation of many Siberian villages lowers the figure for this territory. The proportion of the population that was literate amounted to slightly less than one-half in Georgia, about one-third in Armenia, and about one-fourth in Azerbaydzhan.

The people of the Asiatic steppes (except where there had been a large influx of Russians and Ukrainians) and those of Central Asia were predominantly illiterate. The proportions of literate persons in these regions ran as follows:

Region	Percent Able to Read
Kazakhstan: Western Subregion	25
Eastern Subregion	29
Southern Subregion	14
Kirgizia	15
Turkmenia	11
Uzbekistan (except Tadzhik)	10
Tadzhikistan	3

Extremely low rates of literacy were also characteristic of most of the mountain republics of the Caucasus and some of the extreme northern districts of European Russia that were inhabited mainly by indigenous tribes. The cultural isolation and poverty of the people in many of the outlying regions of the U.S.S.R. were, therefore, quite as marked as their economic isolation and low plane of living.

The general level of literacy was low throughout the nation. Even in Leningrad and Moscow provinces, about 15 percent of the population aged 10 years and over were unable to read in any language in 1926. As a whole, the population of the Soviet Union at this time was only half literate. And of course it cannot be assumed that all persons reported as literate in a census are able to derive great pleasure and profit from scientific literature and *belles lettres*.

Writers have sometimes described the people of the Soviet Union as a population "sprawled across a vast territory." The description is not inappropriate to the situation in the early Soviet period. But here, as in the treatment of the economic structure of the Russian Empire, we find that many of the constructive factors that were released with great force during the Soviet period were already slowly at work before the Soviets came to power. This slow progress, however, had not advanced sufficiently to have had much effect on the economic and the cultural life of the people living in outlying regions, especially where such people were also isolated by linguistic and cultural barriers.

CHAPTER VII

REGIONAL VARIATIONS IN NATALITY, MORTALITY, AND REPRODUCTION, 1926-1927

THE analysis of the changing frequencies of births and deaths in the Soviet Union involves many interesting but difficult problems. In dealing with these it is necessary to examine vital statistics critically, and to make some corrections for apparent deficiencies. The matter of corrections will be treated in a later chapter. Here we are concerned merely with regional variations around the time of the 1926 census, the only period for which we have definite data on this subject. Information about the registration of births and deaths at this time is lacking for some regions. In the case of some other regions there is evidence that the registration data may be seriously affected by incomplete reporting. Moreover, it is desirable to use statistics that eliminate the effects of regional variations in age composition on natality and mortality. For these reasons, we shall base our treatment of natality primarily on census data. When these are combined with reasonably appropriate data on mortality, they yield approximate indices of reproduction for all parts of the U.S.S.R.

1. Variations in Mortality

The treatment of mortality in this chapter is limited to a consideration of variations among regions, with breakdown between urban and rural areas. The infant mortality rates (q_0 values) from the official Soviet life tables for 1926-1927, prepared by Novosel'skiy and Payevskiy, provide the most significant index of variations in conditions affecting health. These rates are presented graphically in Plate XII. The rates differ from the ordinary type of infant mortality rates (ratio of deaths under one year to births during the same interval) in that deaths are related to births in preceding months so as to give a more accurate index of the force of mortality. The basic data were examined before these tables were computed, and regions for which the data were most obviously defective have been omitted from this series.[1] The official crude birth, death, and infant mortality rates as reported by region for 1926 and 1927 are shown in Table 30. All of these statistics must be used with some caution; the question of possible sources of error is reserved for later consideration (see Chapter IX).

The life-table infant mortality rate for the whole European part of the U.S.S.R., 1926-1927, is 187 deaths per 1,000 births (males, 201; females, 172). With 52 additional deaths in the second year of life, only 76 percent of the children born alive are shown as living to the second anniversary of their birth (see Table 31). From Plate XII it is evident that the lowest infant mortality rate, according to life-table values, is that for Belorussia, where there were only about 100 deaths under one year of age per 1,000 live births. This region had been most subject to western European influences and it contained a large Jewish minority. The degree of its divergence from other regions is, nevertheless, rather surprising, but the contrast appears both in the urban and in the rural rates. Next to Belorussia the lowest rates are found in the Ukraine and

---

[1] The life-table infant mortality rates are shown separately for the urban and rural parts of each region, except in the case of the Crimea, where the validity of the results are somewhat questionable in any case and for which separate urban and rural tables were not computed. The original data were used without adjustments for possible errors in reporting, except in the case of the rural population of the Bashkir Republic. The rates for rural Bashkiria are a rough estimate based on an arbitrary adjustment of defective data by the author of the life tables. Apart from Bashkiria, the data most subject to question as possibly biased by incomplete registration are those for the Crimea, Siberia (based on data for one year only), and for the southeastern regions of European Russia, i.e., the Central Volga, Lower Volga, and North Caucasus.

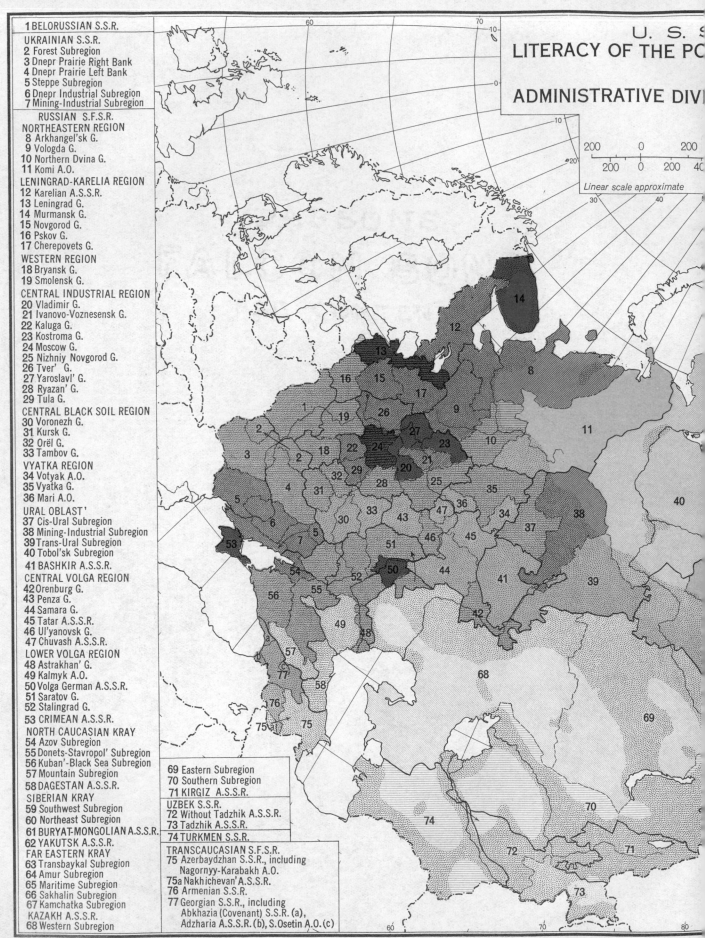

200   0   200
200   0   200   4

Linear scale approximate

1 BELORUSSIAN S.S.R.

UKRAINIAN S.S.R.
2 Forest Subregion
3 Dnepr Prairie Right Bank
4 Dnepr Prairie Left Bank
5 Steppe Subregion
6 Dnepr Industrial Subregion
7 Mining-Industrial Subregion

RUSSIAN S.F.S.R.
NORTHEASTERN REGION
8 Arkhangel'sk G.
9 Vologda G.
10 Northern Dvina G.
11 Komi A.O.
LENINGRAD-KARELIA REGION
12 Karelian A.S.S.R.
13 Leningrad G.
14 Murmansk G.
15 Novgorod G.
16 Pskov G.
17 Cherepovets G.
WESTERN REGION
18 Bryansk G.
19 Smolensk G.
CENTRAL INDUSTRIAL REGION
20 Vladimir G.
21 Ivanovo-Voznesensk G.
22 Kaluga G.
23 Kostroma G.
24 Moscow G.
25 Nizhniy Novgorod G.
26 Tver' G.
27 Yaroslavl' G.
28 Ryazan' G.
29 Tula G.
CENTRAL BLACK SOIL REGION
30 Voronezh G.
31 Kursk G.
32 Orël G.
33 Tambov G.
VYATKA REGION
34 Votyak A.O.
35 Vyatka G.
36 Mari A.O.
URAL OBLAST'
37 Cis-Ural Subregion
38 Mining-Industrial Subregion
39 Trans-Ural Subregion
40 Tobol'sk Subregion
41 BASHKIR A.S.S.R.
CENTRAL VOLGA REGION
42 Orenburg G.
43 Penza G.
44 Samara G.
45 Tatar A.S.S.R.
46 Ul'yanovsk G.
47 Chuvash A.S.S.R.
LOWER VOLGA REGION
48 Astrakhan' G.
49 Kalmyk A.O.
50 Volga German A.S.S.R.
51 Saratov G.
52 Stalingrad G.
53 CRIMEAN A.S.S.R.
NORTH CAUCASIAN KRAY
54 Azov Subregion
55 Donets-Stavropol' Subregion
56 Kuban'-Black Sea Subregion
57 Mountain Subregion
58 DAGESTAN A.S.S.R.
SIBERIAN KRAY
59 Southwest Subregion
60 Northeast Subregion
61 BURYAT-MONGOLIAN A.S.S.R.
62 YAKUTSK A.S.S.R.
FAR EASTERN KRAY
63 Transbaykal Subregion
64 Amur Subregion
65 Maritime Subregion
66 Sakhalin Subregion
67 Kamchatka Subregion
KAZAKH A.S.S.R.
68 Western Subregion

69 Eastern Subregion
70 Southern Subregion
71 KIRGIZ A.S.S.R.
UZBEK S.S.R.
72 Without Tadzhik A.S.S.R.
73 Tadzhik A.S.S.R.
74 TURKMEN S.S.R.
TRANSCAUCASIAN S.F.S.R.
75 Azerbaydzhan S.S.R., including
    Nagornyy-Karabakh A.O.
75a Nakhichevan' A.S.S.R.
76 Armenian S.S.R.
77 Georgian S.S.R., including
    Abkhazia (Covenant) S.S.R. (a),
    Adzharia A.S.S.R. (b), S.Osetin A.O.(c)

PLATE XI

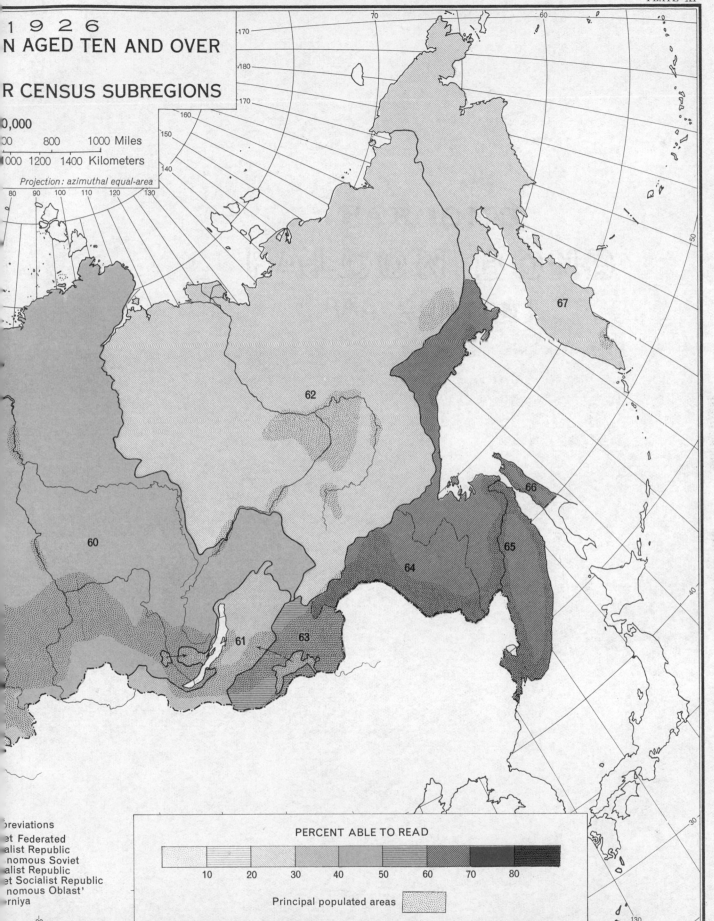

1926

N AGED TEN AND OVER

R CENSUS SUBREGIONS

0,000

| | 800 | 1000 Miles |
| 000 | 1200 | 1400 Kilometers |

Projection: azimuthal equal-area

80 90 100 110 120 130

PERCENT ABLE TO READ

10   20   30   40   50   60   70   80

Principal populated areas

breviations
et Federated
alist Republic
nomous Soviet
alist Republic
et Socialist Republic
nomous Oblast'
rniya

Prepared by Department of State, Division
of Geography and Cartography
Drawn by American Geographical Society

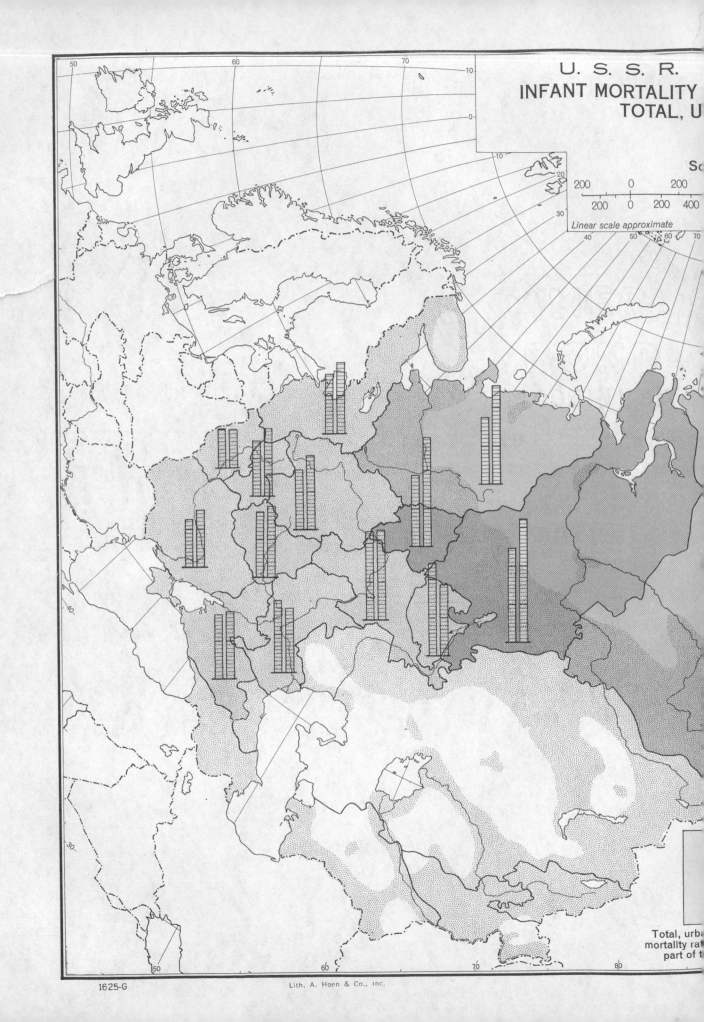

U. S. S. R.

INFANT MORTALITY

TOTAL, U

Sc

200   0   200

200   0   200   400

Linear scale approximate

Total, urb
mortality rat
part of t

PLATE XII

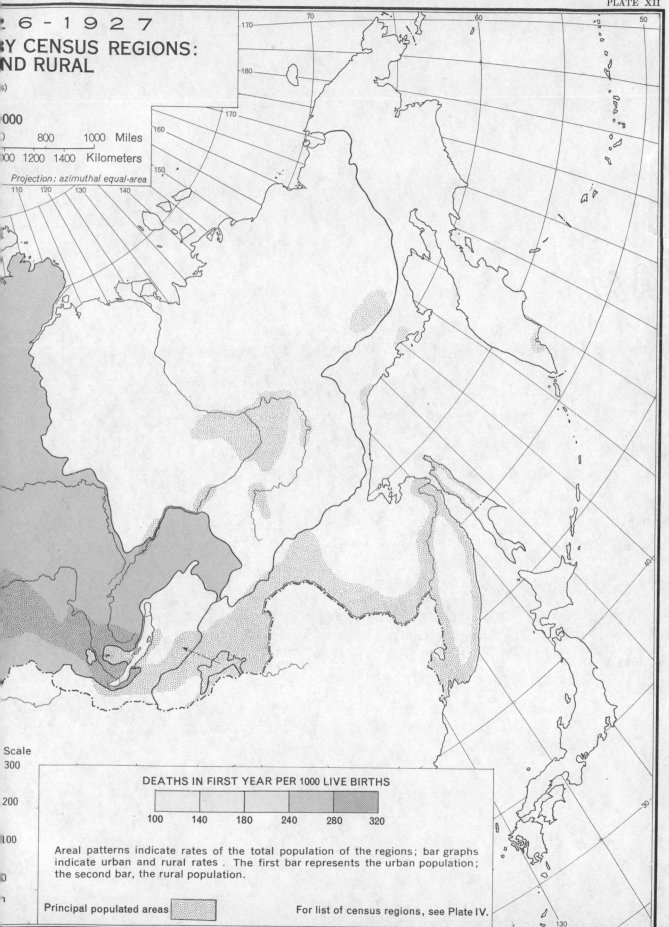

6 - 1 9 2 7

Y CENSUS REGIONS:
ND RURAL

000

800   1000 Miles

000 1200 1400 Kilometers

Projection: azimuthal equal-area

Scale

300

200

100

DEATHS IN FIRST YEAR PER 1000 LIVE BIRTHS

100   140   180   240   280   320

Areal patterns indicate rates of the total population of the regions; bar graphs
indicate urban and rural rates . The first bar represents the urban population;
the second bar, the rural population.

Principal populated areas   For list of census regions, see Plate IV.

Prepared by Department of State, Division
of Geography and Cartography
Drawn by American Geographical Society

TABLE 30

Official Vital Statistics: U.S.S.R., 1926-1927

Region	1926[1]			1927[2]		
	Live Births per 1,000 Population	Deaths per 1,000 Population	Infant Deaths per 1,000 Live Births	Live Births per 1,000 Population	Deaths per 1,000 Population	Infant Deaths per 1,000 Live Births
European Part of U.S.S.R.	43.5	19.9	172	43.0	20.8	190
Urban	33.9	16.7	159	32.1	16.8	164
Rural	45.6	20.7	174	45.5	21.7	194
Belorussian S.S.R.	40.7	14.7	102	38.6	14.1	99
Urban	31.8	13.4	109	30.4	12.1	98
Rural	42.6	15.0	101	40.3	14.5	100
Ukrainian S.S.R.	42.1	18.1	141	40.3	17.8	148
Urban	31.7	13.9	126	29.6	13.4	121
Rural	44.4	19.0	144	42.8	18.8	152
Subregions:						
Forest	41.7	19.1	141	40.8	19.1	150
Urban	31.4	14.6	116	28.6	14.2	114
Rural	43.5	19.9	144	42.9	20.0	155
Dnepr Prairie Right Bank	39.4	19.2	152	38.8	18.8	154
Urban	29.0	13.3	112	26.8	12.9	111
Rural	41.4	20.4	157	41.1	19.9	159
Dnepr Prairie Left Bank	40.7	18.4	142	38.3	17.7	147
Urban	27.7	13.2	117	25.8	12.7	108
Rural	43.1	19.3	145	40.7	18.6	151
Steppe	45.0	16.7	133	42.3	16.9	143
Urban	30.7	13.7	129	27.1	12.7	123
Rural	48.3	17.3	133	45.9	17.9	145
Dnepr Industrial	47.0	16.3	123	43.6	16.1	137
Urban	33.9	13.4	117	30.7	12.3	115
Rural	50.1	17.0	124	46.8	17.1	140
Mining-Industrial	45.8	16.4	145	44.0	16.5	147
Urban	42.7	16.1	155	41.9	16.1	147
Rural	47.8	16.6	140	45.6	16.8	147
R.S.F.S.R. Regions						
European Part:						
Northeastern	47.6	24.2	203	44.6	29.0	293
Urban	38.0	22.1	161	36.4	22.4	179
Rural	48.6	24.4	207	45.5	29.8	303
Leningrad-Karelia	37.8	18.6	165	35.4	20.2	191
Urban	29.6	15.6	144	26.6	16.9	168
Rural	41.9	20.1	172	40.1	22.0	199

TABLE 30 (*Continued*)

Official Vital Statistics: U.S.S.R., 1926-1927

Region	1926[1]			1927[2]		
	Live Births per 1,000 Population	Deaths per 1,000 Population	Infant Deaths per 1,000 Live Births	Live Births per 1,000 Population	Deaths per 1,000 Population	Infant Deaths per 1,000 Live Births
European Part: (*Continued*)						
Western	45.1	20.7	175	43.7	19.2	154
Urban	32.1	16.3	145	29.2	14.2	134
Rural	46.9	21.3	177	45.6	19.9	156
Central Industrial	41.4	19.0	175	41.0	21.1	195
Moscow	29.8	13.7	134	25.5	13.5	139
Other Urban	36.5	17.4	162	35.7	18.5	178
Rural	44.0	20.0	180	44.3	22.7	203
Central Black Soil	43.9	22.3	200	45.4	18.7	165
Urban	27.1	15.4	177	25.9	13.5	152
Rural	45.6	23.0	201	47.4	19.3	166
Vyatka	53.4	29.7	232	51.7	35.1	316
Urban	43.1	22.8	182	41.3	22.9	184
Rural	54.1	30.2	235	52.5	36.1	324
Ural Oblast'	55.6	27.3	247	53.5	33.3	346
Urban	51.4	26.6	231	48.0	27.4	248
Rural	56.7	27.5	251	55.0	34.8	369
Bashkir A.S.S.R.	44.6	16.1	140	48.5	22.0	186
Urban	43.8	20.8	195	46.2	25.4	228
Rural	44.6	15.7	135	48.8	21.6	182
Central Volga	44.0	21.8	195	47.8	25.1	212
Urban	37.0	20.8	217	36.6	21.5	207
Rural	45.0	22.0	193	49.2	25.5	212
Lower Volga	42.2	19.2	168	43.2	18.8	162
Urban	36.1	20.3	187	36.4	20.3	180
Rural	43.5	19.0	165	44.7	18.4	159
Crimean A.S.S.R.	36.6	13.2	113	36.6	15.5	124
Urban	29.6	15.7	139	28.1	16.6	143
Rural	42.2	11.2	99	43.8	14.5	114
North Caucasian Kray	42.9	17.8	155	42.7	17.1	161
Urban	32.3	15.9	157	32.9	16.6	162
Rural	45.6	18.2	155	45.1	17.2	161
Dagestan A.S.S.R.	——	——	——	——	——	——
Urban	38.1	18.8	169	——	——	——
Rural	——	——	——	——	——	——
Asiatic Part:						
Siberian Kray	51.3	25.6	235	——	——	——
Urban	39.8	24.2	234	——	——	——
Rural	52.8	25.7	235	——	——	——

TABLE 30 (*Continued*)

Official Vital Statistics: U.S.S.R., 1926-1927

Region	1926[1]			1927[2]		
	Live Births per 1,000 Population	Deaths per 1,000 Population	Infant Deaths per 1,000 Live Births	Live Births per 1,000 Population	Deaths per 1,000 Population	Infant Deaths per 1,000 Live Births
Asiatic Part: (*Continued*)						
Buryat-Mongolian A.S.S.R.	35.8	19.0	178	—	—	—
Urban	36.6	21.1	218	—	—	—
Rural	35.7	18.8	173	—	—	—
Far Eastern Kray	39.1	18.3	164	—	—	—
Urban	28.0	18.4	163	—	—	—
Rural	42.9	18.2	164	—	—	—
Transcaucasian S.F.S.R.						
Armenian S.S.R.	53.6	17.2	105	56.1	17.0	120
Urban	44.9	18.3	140	44.3	16.8	149
Rural	55.3	16.9	100	59.0	17.1	115

[1] From *Yestestvennoye Dvizheniye Naseleniya Soyuza S.S.R. v 1926 g.*, Title 419, pp. 38-48.
[2] From *Statisticheskiy Spravochnik SSSR za 1928 g.*, Title 406, pp. 76-79.

in the Crimea. The rates for the cities of Moscow (135) and Leningrad (154) are below the average for all cities but above the rates for cities in Belorussia and in the Ukraine.

Infant mortality at this time was usually higher in rural districts than in the cities. This was apparently associated with the widespread illiteracy and low economic level of the Russian peasantry. Within the European part of the U.S.S.R. the proportion of children dying within the first year of life per 1,000 births (life-table values) was 191 in the rural areas as compared with 164 in the urban areas. The worst situation, so far as our data indicate, was found in the rural districts of the Vyatka and Ural regions, with 287 and 321 infant deaths, respectively, per 1,000 live births. Only two-thirds of the children born alive in these districts survived to age 2 years. But the situation in the rural parts of the Northeastern and Central Volga regions and in Siberia was also very bad—with infant mortality rates of 255, 233, and 240 respectively.

Variations in expectation of life after passing early childhood, i.e., mean expectations of life at age 2 years, are shown in Table 31. The poorest prospect is that of males in the cities of the Northeastern Region (45 years). In general, the prospect of life at two years of age in the European part of the U.S.S.R. at this time was somewhat poorer for urban males (53.4 years) than for rural males (54.3 years), but that for urban females (60.0 years) was distinctly better than that for rural females (57.7 years). Too much reliance, however, cannot be placed on these comparisons because of possible bias due to greater incompleteness of registration in rural areas (especially in the case of females).

Owing to obvious inaccuracies in the data, examination of official information on case frequencies of specific diseases furnishes little insight into the factors responsible for regional and yearly variations in mortality around this time. For example, we can assume that an apparently steady rise in the frequency of trachoma from 4.2 per 1,000 population in 1924 to 8.5 in 1927

TABLE 31

Proportion of Infants Born Alive Who Die during First Two
Years, and Expectation of Life at Age 2: European Part of
U.S.S.R., 1896-1897, and 1926-1927 by Regions[1]

Date and Region	Proportion of Infants Dying within 2 Years Percent	Mean Expectation of Future Life at Age 2 Years Number of Years	
		Male	Female
1896-1897			
European U.S.S.R.	34.6	47.1	47.3
1926-1927			
European U.S.S.R.	23.9	54.0	58.0
Urban	21.8	53.4	60.0
Rural	24.2	54.3	57.7
Belorussian S.S.R.	14.2	57.9	60.6
Urban	13.9	58.1	62.0
Rural	14.2	57.9	60.6
Ukrainian S.S.R.	18.6	54.7	56.8
Urban	15.9	56.3	61.3
Rural	19.0	54.4	56.0
Northeastern	29.7	50.6	56.7
Urban	22.9	45.0	54.7
Rural	30.3	51.3	56.9
Leningrad-Karelia			
Leningrad City	20.4	52.0	60.0
Other Urban	21.4	49.6	57.2
Rural	22.6	53.6	59.7
Western	22.3	54.3	58.8
Urban	18.7	54.2	60.3
Rural	22.7	54.5	58.6
Central Industrial			
Moscow City	18.1	54.2	61.8
Other Urban	24.2	52.4	60.8
Rural	24.6	54.7	61.8
Ryazan'-Tula	23.6	53.3	59.0
Urban	20.1	53.1	59.8
Rural	23.9	53.5	58.9
Central Black Soil	24.3	54.9	57.2
Urban	21.4	55.9	62.0
Rural	24.4	54.8	56.7
Vyatka	35.8	49.0	52.3
Urban	25.4	47.0	55.0
Rural	36.4	49.2	52.1
Ural Oblast'	33.8	53.1	57.0
Urban	30.4	48.5	55.3
Rural	36.9	54.4	57.5

[84]

TABLE 31 (*Continued*)

Proportion of Infants Born Alive Who Die during First Two
Years, and Expectation of Life at Age 2: European Part of
U.S.S.R., 1896-1897, and 1926-1927 by Regions[1]

Date and Region	Proportion of Infants Dying within 2 Years Percent	Mean Expectation of Future Life at Age 2 Years Number of Years	
		Male	Female
Bashkir A.S.S.R.	24.8	56.0	56.8
Urban	30.6	48.4	55.0
Rural	24.0	57.0	56.9
Central Volga	29.2	51.9	55.3
Urban	29.2	50.1	57.3
Rural	29.2	52.3	55.2
Lower Volga	23.7	55.0	59.3
Urban	27.3	51.2	58.3
Rural	23.0	56.1	59.5
Crimean A.S.S.R.	16.2	55.8	60.3
North Caucasian Kray	22.8	55.1	57.2
Urban	22.9	54.0	58.4
Rural	22.8	55.7	57.0

[1] Values from life tables by Novosel'skiy and Payevskiy, Title 417.

simply represents an improvement in the registration procedures. It should, however, be reported that the morbidity statistics do not indicate any great epidemics, and they do not show sufficiently high frequencies of specific children's diseases in particular areas to contribute much to an understanding of regional variations in general or of infant mortality at this time (1926-1927).

The highest reported frequencies of tuberculosis in 1927 (i.e., over 15 reported cases per 1,000 population) are indicated for the following districts in descending order: Volga German, Kalmyk, Mari, Crimea, Astrakhan, Ural, and Yakut.[2] The data on which these ratios are based are incomplete, and in some cases the rates may be exaggerated by patients in health resorts, as in the Crimea. High frequencies of malaria (i.e., over 45 cases per 1,000 population, 1927) are given for the following districts in order: Volga German (179), Astrakhan (125), Samara (109), Orenburg, Kalmyk, Dagestan, Stalingrad, and Saratov. These data, though probably defective, clearly show the high concentration of malaria in the lower Volga valley and the adjacent steppes. Reported cases of syphilis in 1927 rise above 10 per 1,000 population in Kirgizia (30), Buryat-Mongolia (30), Kalmyk (20), Tambov, Voronezh, Dagestan, Vyatka, and Kazakhstan—i.e., among the Mongolian populations and in the Asiatic steppes, the Central Black Soil, Dagestan, and Vyatka regions. The highest reported frequencies of scurvy appear in Kazakhstan and in the Kalmyk District (5 and 4 cases, respectively, per 1,000 population, 1926), followed by Karelia and the Northern Dvina districts. The last figures can be accepted as evidence, probably very incomplete, of severe malnutrition in the steppe districts and in the

[2] People's Commissariat of Health Protection, Title 420.

Far North. The reported frequency of trachoma rises above 50 cases per 1,000 population (1927) in the Votyak District (114), Chuvash Republic (67), and the Mari District (64), i.e., three contiguous non-Slavic areas in the Vyatka and Central Volga regions.

One aspect of the bad health conditions affecting the non-Russian groups in the Volga-Ural region and in Yakutia, that is, the wide prevalence of trachoma, is also evidenced by high frequencies of blindness, according to the 1926 census data, presented in Table 32. Eight or more

TABLE 32

Proportional Frequency of Blindness by Sex, for Selected Ethnic Groups: U.S.S.R., according to the Census, 1926[1]

Ethnic Group	Persons Reported as Blind		Blind Persons per 1,000 Population	
	Male	Female	Male	Female
All Groups	101,874	132,959	1.4	1.7
Russian	51,303	60,762	1.4	1.5
Ukrainian	17,321	17,703	1.1	1.1
Belorussian	2,678	3,895	1.1	1.6
Jew	1,166	1,116	0.9	0.8
Kazakh	1,912	1,835	0.9	1.0
Armenian	1,188	1,409	1.5	1.8
Uzbek, Kurama	4,098	4,509	2.0	2.4
Karel	226	396	1.9	3.0
Mordvian	1,248	2,483	2.0	3.5
Turk (Azer)	1,808	2,910	2.0	3.6
Komi (Permyak, Zyryan)	412	727	2.3	3.6
Tatar	2,788	5,624	1.9	3.6
Mishar (Penza Gub.)	344	566	2.8	4.1
Bashkir	772	1,649	2.3	4.4
Dagestan Mountaineer	713	1,290	2.5	4.4
Kalmyk	181	328	2.7	5.2
Buryat	432	632	3.6	5.4
Turkmen	1,477	2,335	3.7	6.4
Vogul, Ostyak	91	108	6.2	8.1
Mari	1,025	2,680	5.1	11.8
Chuvash	2,251	6,967	4.2	12.0
Udmurt (Votyak)	1,067	4,315	4.5	16.1
Yakut	1,248	2,418	10.0	20.9

[1] Data from 1926 census, Title 391, Vol. 51, Table 8.

of every 1,000 women were reported as blind among the Yakuts and Vogul-Ostyaks in Siberia and among the Votyak (Udmurt), Chuvash, and Mari populations centered in the Vyatka and Central Volga regions.

On the whole, the data at our disposal indicate a general deterioration in health conditions as one moves from the west toward the east, north, or southeast, especially as one passes into areas largely occupied by non-Russian nationalities. The most striking exception appears to be the existence of very favorable health conditions in parts of the Transcaucasus, particularly in Armenia (see Table 30). Here again one is handicapped in coming to any definite conclusion because there is some evidence of incomplete registration of deaths in Armenia.[8] Data on health and mortality in Central Asia are wholly lacking or extremely fragmentary. One would expect that health conditions in the ancient cities of Central Asia during this period might be among the worst in the Soviet Union, but it is impossible either to confirm or to repudiate this supposition.

2. Variations in Fertility and Reproduction

Variations in natality in the Soviet Union at this time were apparently not closely related to the variations in mortality. The frequency of births was largely determined (in reverse) by degree of urbanization and related social-economic factors. Birth rates were much lower in cities than in the rural areas, and the decrease in natality during the early Soviet period was largely an urban phenomenon. The reported birth rates for the European part of the U.S.S.R. for the years 1926-1928 are summarized in Table 33.

TABLE 33

Births per 1,000 Population:
European Part of the U.S.S.R.,
Urban and Rural Areas, 1926-1928[1]

Area	1926	1927	1928
Total	43.6	43.2	42.0
Urban	33.9	32.1	28.3
Rural	45.7	45.8	45.0

[1] Urban rate for 1928 is derived from figures for total and rural areas. All rates are from *Sdvigi v Sel'skom Khozyaystve SSSR . . . za 1927-1930 gg.*, Title 450, p. 10. These rates for 1926 and 1927 differ slightly from those presented in Table 30, owing to later revision or to extension of area covered.

In studying regional variations in natality and in net reproduction (which takes both births and deaths into account), we shall rely primarily on census data, in combination with life-table values. The procedure is described in Appendix IV. At this point, we need merely discuss briefly its essential features and limitations. It is obvious that the relative frequency of children of any particular age in any area at any time (e.g., children two years of age in any part of the U.S.S.R., December 17, 1926) is determined by four conditions: (1) the fertility at the time when these children were born (i.e., 12/18/1923-12/17/1924) of the women who now live in this area plus that of women who died in the intervening time, (2) the reduction of the child population by death from birth to the specified age (e.g., age two years), (3) the reduction in the number of women in each age group by deaths during an equal time interval (e.g., two years), and (4) migration to or from this area of women who have borne children during this interval without their children, or of the children without their mothers. The last condition can be ignored as a factor of negligible importance. The second and third conditions can be taken into account statistically by the use of appropriate life-table values. We can thus estimate the first factor (i.e., fertility—the object of our investigation) in the case of any area for which census data and life tables are available. We can then proceed to estimate net reproduction. By applying life-table values for similar regions, we can extend the procedure to other areas for which only census data are available. Such extension involves less error than might be expected because we pick up our primary data (numbers of children aged 2 years) after the force of mortality at its highest and most variable pitch has already been expended. We begin

[8] Note the relation of rural to urban infant mortality in Armenia, and changes from 1926 to 1927.

with children who have survived infancy—working backward to estimate natality, and forward to estimate net reproduction.

It is possible to obtain indices for all parts of the Soviet Union with sufficient accuracy to show the major variations in fertility and reproduction—apart from the influence of peculiarities in the age and sex distribution of the population in different areas. The indices thus obtained are:

I. The *gross reproduction ratio* (G.R.R.), i.e., the average number of daughters borne by each woman living through the childbearing period according to the fertility (about 1924) of the women living in various areas in December, 1926.

II. The *net reproduction ratio* (N.R.R.), i.e., the ratio of female infants in two successive generations to be expected if the specific natality rates of the year 1924 and the specific death rates of the years 1926-1927 were continued indefinitely.

Several possible sources of error in the present series must be taken into account in interpreting the results:

1. If the reported number of two-year-old children in any area is smaller than the actual number, both the G.R.R. and the N.R.R. will be spuriously lowered; the converse will be true if the reported number is larger than the actual number. An examination of the child population at various ages in different areas, according to the 1926 census, shows that in some cases the numbers of children under one year and of those reported as one year of age are suspiciously low (suggesting underenumeration of infants). Also, in some cases the number aged 3 to 5 years is surprisingly low, apparently owing to disturbed conditions in some regions in 1922 and 1923. The number reported as two years of age shows a high degree of stability relative to the total number of children at other ages. We have assumed, therefore, that these figures furnish the most reliable basis for an index of natality and reproduction for various parts of the U.S.S.R. The results obtained by using these figures have been checked against available birth statistics for 1926, ignoring differences in natality between 1924 and 1926. In a few regions where birth statistics for the year 1926 gave a somewhat higher index of natality, the figures based on the birth statistics have been substituted for the values obtained by the use of census data (on the assumption that births were never over-reported in any area, although they were not reported at all in some areas and may have been under-reported in others). It is therefore assumed that, so far as this possible source of error is concerned, the results are fairly reliable.

2. The major source of error in the indices presented here arises from the dependence on life-table values. The official urban and rural life tables for each region, where available, were applied to all urban and rural areas respectively of that region, unless otherwise specified. Where no tables were available, or the available tables seemed clearly erroneous, those of some similar region were applied. The following substitutions of this sort were made:

Regions	*Life Tables Used in Deriving Gross and Net Reproduction Ratios*
Total U.S.S.R., Lower Volga Region, Crimean A.S.S.R.: urban and rural	European part of U.S.S.R.: urban and rural, respectively
Siberian Territory, Far Eastern Territory: urban and rural	Ural District: urban and rural, respectively
Transcaucasus: urban and rural	North Caucasian Territory: urban and rural, respectively
Buryat-Mongolian, Yakutsk, Kazakh, Kirgiz, Uzbek, and Dagestan republics, and Kalmyk: urban and rural	Vyatka Region: rural

Inaccuracies in the life tables or inappropriate application of substitute tables would affect the G.R.R. and the N.R.R. differently. If the life tables applied here to any region were based on death rates that were consistently too low (whether owing to incomplete registration of deaths in that region, or to the application of tables from data for a region where mortality was generally lower) the gross reproduction ratio would be spuriously *lowered* and the net reproduction ratio would be spuriously *raised*. If the tables were based on death rates that were consistently too high, the opposite effects would probably follow. Both ratios would be spuriously influenced in the same direction only if the infant mortality values were too high and the other mortality values too low, or the reverse.

The net reproduction ratios in this series are more reliable than the gross reproduction ratios. This is true because we start with the actual number of two-year-old children, and there is a much smaller margin of error in estimating the number of women at various childbearing ages to be expected from 100 two-year-old children than there is in working backward to estimate the births from which these two-year-old children were derived, because of the greater variation in infant mortality rates among different regions and the doubtful accuracy of these statistics. However, the two indices tend in a rough way to check each other. Where they deviate from their respective averages in the same direction, we can be reasonably sure of the significance of this deviation. If the indices deviate in opposite directions we must be wary of the results; but in some cases this apparent discrepancy may have a sound basis.

Both the gross and net reproduction ratios presented here for the U.S.S.R. are extremely high. (See Table 34 and Plate XIII.) The net reproduction rate of 1.72, referring to natality in 1924 in the total U.S.S.R., is similar to Kuczynski's estimate of "approximately 1.7" for the European part of the U.S.S.R., 1926-1927, based on birth-registration and life-table data.[4] Our figure for the gross reproduction ratio (2.64) is identical with his corresponding figure for the European part of the U.S.S.R. (2.6). Although these figures differ in area and in time reference, they indicate general agreement on the order of natality and reproduction characteristic of the Soviet Union at about the time of the First All-Union Census.

The gross reproduction ratio indicates an average of 2.64 daughters to each woman living through the childbearing period. Since about 106 sons were born per 100 daughters, this would give an average of 5.4 children per woman. Moreover, we used the life table for the European part of the U.S.S.R. without any adjustment in deriving this figure; but the infant mortality rate in the whole U.S.S.R. was almost certainly higher. It is, therefore, quite possible that on the average at this time about 6 children were borne by each woman living to the end of the childbearing period.

The net reproduction ratio obtained for the total U.S.S.R. is 1.72; but this is probably a little too high—if the life-table survival values are exaggerated by incomplete registration of deaths. The figure obtained here (1.72) would indicate an intrinsic natural increase (with natality of 1924 and mortality of 1926-1927) of slightly less than 2 percent a year—or a tendency toward a doubling of the population once every 36 years. It is safe to say that the intrinsic reproductivity of the Soviet population at this time was sufficient to allow an increase of well over 50 percent per generation.

From Table 34 and Plate XIII it is immediately apparent that the difference in fertility between cities and rural districts overshadows all regional variations either among urban or among rural districts considered separately. In fact the most conspicuous regional differences are largely a function of degree of urbanization. In the U.S.S.R. as a whole, the gross reproduction ratio for the rural population is 68 percent higher, and the net reproduction ratio 55

[4] Kuczynski, Title 154, p. 21.

TABLE 34

Gross and Net Reproduction Ratios, by Region: U.S.S.R., 1924, 1926-1927[1]

Region and Administrative Division	Gross Reproduction Ratio			Net Reproduction Ratio		
	Total	Urban	Rural	Total	Urban	Rural
U.S.S.R.	2.64	1.71	2.87	1.72	1.19	1.85
Belorussian S.S.R.	2.57	1.80	2.74	1.94	1.41	2.05
Ukrainian S.S.R.	2.49	1.53	2.77	1.70	1.16	1.86
Forest Subregion	2.74	1.68	2.99	1.86	1.27	2.01
Dnepr Prairie Right Bank	2.46	1.50	2.71	1.68	1.14	1.82
Dnepr Prairie Left Bank	2.48	1.43	2.76	1.69	1.08	1.85
Steppe Subregion	2.49	1.47	2.82	1.70	1.11	1.90
Dnepr Industrial Subregion	2.41	1.48	2.71	1.65	1.12	1.82
Mining-Industrial Subregion	2.29	1.75	2.68	1.61	1.33	1.80
Northeastern Region	2.95	2.03	3.07	1.76	1.31	1.82
Arkhangel'sk Gub.	2.75	2.03	3.00	1.66	1.32	1.78
Vologda Gub.	2.71	2.06	2.78	1.62	1.34	1.65
Northern Dvina Gub.	3.36	—	3.36	1.99	—	1.99
Komi Autonomous Obl.	3.35	—	3.35	1.99	—	1.99
Leningrad-Karelia Region	2.15	1.36	2.67	1.46	.92	1.82
Karelian A.S.S.R.	2.51	1.95	2.69	1.64	1.36	1.73
Leningrad Gub.	1.60	1.23	2.54	1.11	.87	1.73
Murmansk Gub.	3.05	—	3.05	1.62	—	1.62
Novgorod Gub.	2.68	1.95	2.81	1.74	1.36	1.81
Pskov Gub.	2.63	1.83	2.73	1.79	1.24	1.85
Cherepovets Gub.	2.60	1.99	2.65	1.76	1.35	1.80
Western Region	2.90	1.79	3.06	1.94	1.32	2.03
Bryansk Gub.	3.11	1.97	3.33	2.09	1.44	2.21
Smolensk Gub.	2.71	1.58	2.84	1.81	1.16	1.89
Central Industrial Region	2.53	1.63	2.91	1.72	1.12	1.97
Vladimir Gub.	2.81	2.10	3.02	1.91	1.43	2.05
Ivanovo-Voznesensk Gub.	2.43	1.68	2.81	1.66	1.15	1.91
Kaluga Gub.	2.86	1.86	2.98	1.95	1.28	2.03
Kostroma Gub.	2.44	1.76	2.57	1.66	1.21	1.75
Moscow Gub.	1.95	1.37	3.00	1.38	1.01	2.04
Nizhniy Novgorod Gub.	2.74	2.01	2.91	1.87	1.38	1.98
Tver' Gub.	2.56	1.81	2.69	1.74	1.24	1.83
Yaroslavl' Gub.	2.40	1.95	2.52	1.63	1.34	1.71
Ryazan' Gub.	3.05	1.90	3.16	2.08	1.31	2.15
Tula Gub.	2.95	1.82	3.17	2.01	1.25	2.16
Central Black Soil Region	2.86	1.78	2.99	1.83	1.26	1.90
Voronezh Gub.	2.83	1.67	2.94	1.81	1.18	1.87
Kursk Gub.	2.88	1.81	3.00	1.84	1.27	1.91
Orël Gub.	3.08	1.87	3.24	1.98	1.32	2.06
Tambov Gub.	2.73	1.81	2.85	1.75	1.28	1.82

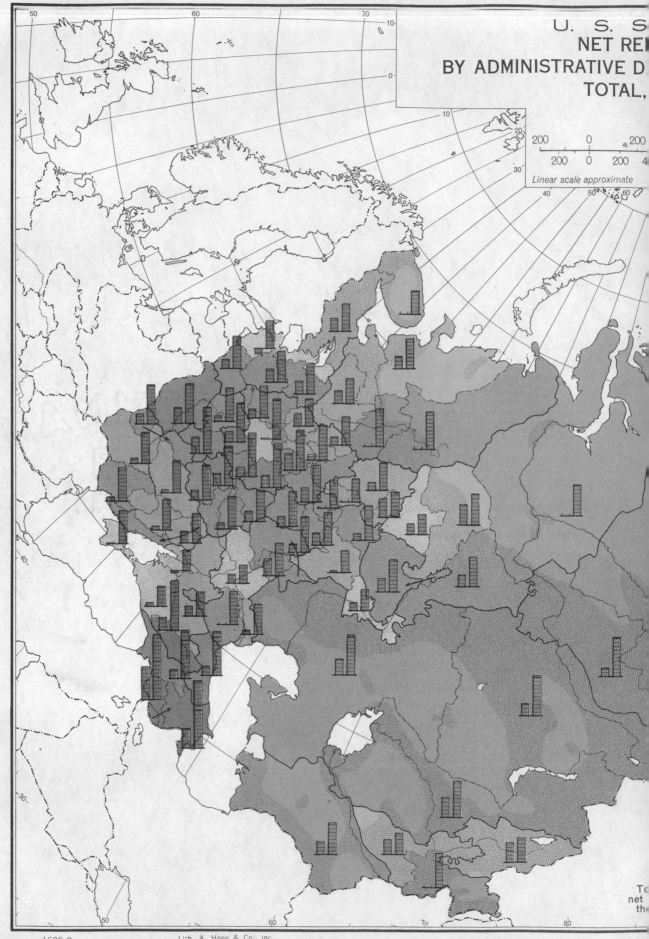

U. S. S
NET RE
BY ADMINISTRATIVE D
TOTAL,

200   0   200
200   0   200   4
Linear scale approximate

PLATE XIII

1926
ION RATIOS
OR CENSUS SUBREGIONS:
AND RURAL

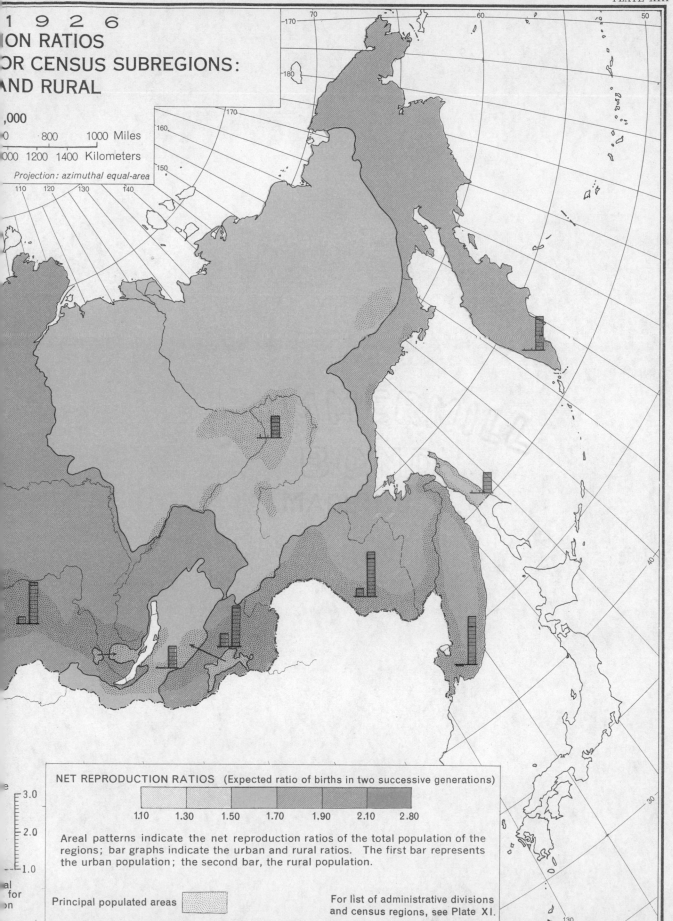

,000

| 800 | 1000 Miles |
| 000 1200 | 1400 Kilometers |

Projection: azimuthal equal-area

NET REPRODUCTION RATIOS (Expected ratio of births in two successive generations)

1.10	1.30	1.50	1.70	1.90	2.10	2.80

Areal patterns indicate the net reproduction ratios of the total population of the regions; bar graphs indicate the urban and rural ratios. The first bar represents the urban population; the second bar, the rural population.

3.0

2.0

1.0

Principal populated areas

For list of administrative divisions and census regions, see Plate XI.

Prepared by Department of State, Division
of Geography and Cartography
Drawn by American Geographical Society

TABLE 34 (*Continued*)

Gross and Net Reproduction Ratios, by Region: U.S.S.R., 1924, 1926-1927[1]

Region and Administrative Division	Gross Reproduction Ratio			Net Reproduction Ratio		
	Total	Urban	Rural	Total	Urban	Rural
Vyatka Region	3.18	2.10	3.27	1.66	1.32	1.69
Votyak A. Obl.	3.16	2.39	3.25	1.66	1.50	1.68
Vyatka Gub.	3.22	1.91	3.31	1.67	1.20	1.71
Mari A. Obl.	3.12	—	3.12	1.61	—	1.61
Ural Oblast'	3.05	2.43	3.23	1.65	1.43	1.71
Cis-Ural Subregion	2.77	2.20	2.88	1.49	1.29	1.53
Mining-Industrial Subregion	3.00	2.62	3.43	1.67	1.54	1.82
Trans-Ural Subregion	3.31	2.25	3.38	1.76	1.32	1.79
Tobol'sk Subregion	3.44	—	3.44	1.82	—	1.82
Bashkir A.S.S.R.	3.39	2.32	3.50	1.81	1.36	1.85
Central Volga Region	2.95	1.99	3.09	1.73	1.19	1.81
Orenburg Gub.	2.56	2.04	2.71	1.49	1.22	1.57
Penza Gub.	3.24	2.14	3.36	1.87	1.28	1.94
Samara Gub.	2.61	1.76	2.76	1.51	1.06	1.59
Tatar A.S.S.R.	3.17	2.00	3.34	1.84	1.19	1.93
Ul'yanovsk Gub.	3.10	2.21	3.24	1.80	1.32	1.87
Chuvash A.S.S.R.	3.00	—	3.00	1.74	—	1.74
Lower Volga Region	2.60	1.75	2.81	1.69	1.22	1.81
Astrakhan' Gub.	2.28	1.60	2.80	1.50	1.11	1.80
Kalmyk A. Obl.	3.64	—	3.64	1.88	—	1.88
Volga German A.S.S.R.	2.79	2.09	2.91	1.81	1.46	1.87
Saratov Gub.	2.79	1.75	3.01	1.81	1.22	1.94
Stalingrad Gub.	2.21	1.76	2.32	1.44	1.23	1.49
Crimean A.S.S.R.	2.19	1.46	2.94	1.45	1.02	1.89
North Caucasian Kray	2.39	1.61	2.59	1.55	1.12	1.67
Azov Subregion	1.98	1.37	2.42	1.30	.95	1.56
Donets-Stavropol' Subregion	2.46	1.85	2.56	1.60	1.29	1.64
Kuban'-Black Sea Subregion	2.23	1.58	2.37	1.37	1.10	1.52
Mountain Subregion	3.24	1.93	3.57	2.10	1.34	2.30
Dagestan A.S.S.R.	3.93	2.37	4.14	2.03	1.25	2.14
Siberian Kray	3.63	1.91	3.93	1.94	1.12	2.08
Southwest Subregion	3.67	2.08	3.83	1.95	1.22	2.03
Northeast Subregion	3.68	2.03	3.94	1.96	1.19	2.09
Buryat-Mongolian A.S.S.R.	3.06	—	3.06	1.58	—	1.58
Yakutsk A.S.S.R.	3.03	—	3.03	1.57	—	1.57
Far Eastern Kray	3.48	1.92	4.09	1.88	1.13	2.16
Transbaykal Subregion	3.55	2.29	3.90	1.91	1.34	2.06
Amur Subregion	3.50	2.08	4.11	1.89	1.22	2.17
Maritime Subregion	3.42	1.65	4.29	1.84	.97	2.27
Sakhalin Subregion	2.91	—	2.91	1.54	—	1.54
Kamchatka Subregion	3.57	—	3.57	1.89	—	1.89

TABLE 34 (*Continued*)

Gross and Net Reproduction Ratios, by Region: U.S.S.R., 1924, 1926-1927[1]

Region and Administrative Division	Gross Reproduction Ratio			Net Reproduction Ratio		
	Total	Urban	Rural	Total	Urban	Rural
Kazakh A.S.S.R.	3.79	2.68	3.90	1.98	1.41	2.04
Western Subregion	3.61	2.40	3.89	1.94	1.41	2.06
Eastern Subregion	3.91	2.28	4.01	2.03	1.31	2.07
Southern Subregion	3.74	2.66	3.81	1.94	1.53	1.97
Kirgiz A.S.S.R.	3.20	2.90	3.23	1.65	1.53	1.67
Uzbek S.S.R. (without Tadzhik)	2.98	2.66	3.06	1.54	1.40	1.58
Tadzhik A.S.S.R.	3.70	—	3.70	1.91	—	1.91
Turkmen S.S.R.	3.47	2.55	3.63	1.80	1.34	1.87
Transcaucasian S.F.S.R.						
Azerbaydzhan S.S.R.	3.62	2.19	4.31	2.36	1.52	2.77
Armenian S.S.R.	3.89	2.11	4.19	2.53	1.88	2.70
Georgian S.S.R.	3.06	1.78	3.52	1.99	1.24	2.26

[1] Fertility as of 1924; mortality as of 1926-1927.

percent higher, than the corresponding ratios for the urban population. The lowest net reproduction ratios are found in the *urban areas* of the following districts:

Leningrad Province	.87
Azov Subregion of the North Caucasus Territory, including Rostov	.95
Maritime Subregion of the Far Eastern Territory, including Vladivostok	.97
Moscow Province	1.01
Crimea	1.02
Samara Province, including Samara (Kuybyshev)	1.06
Dnepr Prairie Left Bank Subregion of the Ukraine, including Kharkov	1.08

The urban parts of the first three districts in this list are the only areas shown here in which the net reproduction ratio was below unity—indicating natality below that required for permanent population replacement with the specific mortality rates of 1926-1927—whereas a net reproduction ratio far below unity was generally characteristic of cities in Europe and the United States at this time. For the urban areas of the U.S.S.R. as a whole, the net reproduction ratio at this time was 1.19, or 19 percent above the level required for permanent population replacement. Urban net reproduction ratios in the vicinity of 1.50 or over are shown for Azerbaydzhan (1.52) and Armenia (1.88) in the Transcaucasus, Kirgizia (1.53) in Central Asia, the southern part of Kazakhstan (1.53), the Mining-Industrial Subregion of the Ural District (1.54), and the Votyak Autonomous District in the Vyatka Region (1.50).

The net reproduction ratio of the entire rural population of the Soviet Union was extremely high—1.85, indicating about 85 percent more births than would suffice for permanent population replacement. The N.R.R.'s of the rural population in western and central European Russia,

Siberia, and the Far Eastern Territory are somewhat higher: for instance, Belorussia, 2.05; Western Region, 2.03; Central Industrial Region, 1.97; Central Black Soil Region, 1.90; Siberia, 2.08; Far Eastern Territory, 2.16.

The highest N.R.R.'s are found in rural areas in the vicinity of the Caucasus Mountains: Azerbaydzhan, 2.77; Armenia, 2.70; Georgia, 2.26; the Mountain Subregion of the North Caucasus Territory, 2.30; and in the Maritime Subregion in the Far East, 2.27. The life-table values used for all these districts are the same as those for the North Caucasian Territory as a whole. We cannot be certain about the figures for net reproductive trends in the areas designated above, owing to lack of exact information on mortality, but the evidence clearly demonstrates that this is a region of extraordinary fertility.

In the case of the Dagestan, Buryat-Mongolian, Yakutsk, Kazakh, and Central Asian republics and Kalmyk we have arbitrarily used the life-table values of rural Vyatka—representing extremely high death rates. It has been pointed out that the use of high mortality rates tends to give high G.R.R.'s but low N.R.R.'s. Since the same mortality factors were used in all these districts, variations in the indices of fertility and reproduction *among* these regions are entirely a function of variations in the frequencies of two-year-old children in relation to number of women in the childbearing ages, as shown by the 1926 census.

The mountain districts with Asiatic culture (Dagestan, Tadzhikistan, and Kirgizia) and the Asiatic steppe districts (Kazakhstan and Turkmenia) generally appear as areas of high fertility. On the other hand, the N.R.R.'s for the rural districts of Uzbekistan, Buryat-Mongolia, and Yakutia are distinctly below the average obtained for the rural population of the U.S.S.R. as a whole. It is likely that unfavorable health conditions in these areas, resulting in much pregnancy wastage and extremely high infant mortality, cut down their reproductive trend sharply. However, it must be recognized that all indices for the Asiatic regions shown here are merely rough approximations of the actual situation.

The lowest *rural* net reproduction ratios are found in the following regions:

Stalingrad Province	1.49
Kuban-'Black Sea Subregion in the North Caucasian Territory	1.52
Cis-Ural Subregion in the Ural District	1.53
Sakhalin Subregion in the Far Eastern Territory	1.54
Azov Subregion in the North Caucasian Territory	1.56
Orenburg Province	1.57
Yakutia	1.57
Buryat-Mongolia	1.58
Uzbekistan (without Tadzhikistan)	1.58
Samara Province	1.59

The Stalingrad and near-by Kuban steppe regions were areas of recent settlement and larger, more commercial farms than most parts of the Soviet Union. The indices for the other areas in this list are less reliable. The relatively low net reproduction ratios in many of them were presumably due to bad health conditions, but it must be remembered that the basic data from which these rates were obtained are subject to a large margin of error.

The high frequency of early marriages in the Soviet Union, especially in rural areas and in some Asiatic districts (see Table 35), was directly associated with the high fertility. This was necessarily so, since there was little conscious control of fertility in the early Soviet period, particularly in the case of the village peasants and of the population in outlying districts.

TABLE 35

Percentage Distribution of Brides by Age: U.S.S.R., 1926[1]

Area	Years of Age						
	All Ages	19 or Less	20-24	25-34	35-44	45 and Over	Un-known
U.S.S.R., European Part	100	33.27	44.29	16.01	3.58	1.79	1.06
Cities over 50,000	100	20.26	42.68	28.06	5.95	2.48	0.59
Other Cities	100	27.36	43.71	21.21	4.64	2.28	0.80
Rural	100	35.67	44.57	13.83	3.15	1.64	1.14
Belorussia	100	28.66	46.92	18.95	3.25	1.38	0.84
Ukraine	100	35.04	43.52	15.27	3.36	1.82	0.99
R.S.F.S.R.							
European Part	100	32.74	44.50	16.18	3.70	1.80	1.08
Asiatic Part[2]	100	57.19	27.63	9.33	3.15	1.69	1.01
Armenia	100	70.09	16.15	8.98	2.48	1.14	1.16

[1] *Yestestvennoye Dvizheniye Naseleniya Soyuza S.S.R. v 1926 g.*, Title 419, p. 29.
[2] R.S.F.S.R. at this time included Kazakh A.S.S.R. and Kirgiz A.S.S.R.

3. Child-Woman Ratios by Ethnic Group

A rough index of variations in reproduction among ethnic groups in the early Soviet period can be obtained by relating the number of children to the number of women in each group, as reported in the census. Such an index automatically takes into account most of the effects of early childhood mortality in cutting down reproductivity, but does not take account of variations in the proportion of survivors from childhood to maturity. Table 36 presents child-woman ratios for various ethnic groups, showing the number of children under 5 years per 1,000 women 20-44 as given in the 1926 census. In the whole U.S.S.R. there were 844 children aged 0-4 years per 1,000 women aged 20-44 years, whereas exactly 500 children per 1,000 women at these ages would have been sufficient to maintain the population at a constant level, according to the official life tables for the European part of the U.S.S.R. The ratio of the former figure to the latter is 1.69, roughly identical with the net reproduction ratio previously obtained for the U.S.S.R. at this time. The denominator of this figure, or the "replacement quota" (i.e., the number of children 0-4 per 1,000 women aged 20-44 needed for population replacement, according to life-table values), would be different but not radically different for various ethnic groups. Its absolute lower limit is somewhat above 400; its upper range has no absolute limit, but in actual experience it never rises above 600. We can, therefore, assume that the child-woman ratio required for population replacement in any ethnic group in the U.S.S.R. in 1926 was 500±100. The observed ratios (children 0-4 years per 1,000 women aged 20-44) range from around 500 (for Jews) to around 1,200 (for several groups in the vicinity of the Caucasus). It is apparent that the Jewish population was barely replacing itself at this time, whereas some groups were tending to double their number in each successive generation.

The choice of an age class to represent the mother population is arbitrary, but ordinarily the selection of a particular broad age group (e.g., 20-44 years, 15-54 years, 15-49 years, etc.) has rather small effect on the *relative* values obtained for various groups, or on the comparison of

TABLE 36

Child-Woman Ratios by Ethnic Group: U.S.S.R., 1926

Location and Ethnic Group	Children Aged 0-4 Years per 1,000 Women Aged 20-44		
	Unadjusted Data	Data Adjusted for Variations in Number of Women Reported as 15-19 Years[1]	Average of Column 1 and Column 2
	(1)	(2)	(3)
Total: European Part, U.S.S.R.	844	844	844
Needed for Permanent Population Replacement: European Part, U.S.S.R., 1926-1927	500[2]		
Ethnic Group[3]			
1. Caucasus			
Talysh	1,219	1,376	1,298
Karachay	1,279	1,256	1,268
Ingush	1,220	1,225	1,223
Turk (Azer)	1,128	1,251	1,190
Kabardian, Balkar	1,174	1,153	1,164
Osetin	1,128	1,121	1,125
Armenian	1,091	1,127	1,109
2. Far East (Rural)			
Korean	1,051	1,063	1,057
3. Southeast Siberia			
Altay (Oyrot)	1,056	1,048	1,052
Khakas	1,058	1,043	1,051
4. Ukraine (Rural)			
Bulgarian	1,040	1,006	1,023
5. Caucasus			
Chechen	1,029	1,052	1,041
Dagestan Mountaineer	973	1,068	1,021
Kumyk	963	963	963
6. Volga-Ural			
Bashkir	1,010	980	995
Mordvian	1,006	976	991
Tatar	988	966	977
Permyak	948	951	950
Zyryan	906	907	907
7. Belorussia (Chiefly Rural)			
Belorussian	966	931	949
8. Volga-Ukraine (Chiefly Rural)			
German	933	924	929
9. Volga-Ural			
Chuvash	899	873	886
Votyak	854	848	851
Mari	839	845	842

TABLE 36 (*Continued*)

Child-Woman Ratios by Ethnic Group: U.S.S.R., 1926

Location and Ethnic Group	Children Aged 0-4 Years per 1,000 Women Aged 20-44		
	Unadjusted Data	Data Adjusted for Variations in Number of Women Reported as 15-19 Years[1]	Average of Column 1 and Column 2
	(1)	(2)	(3)
10. Ukraine (Chiefly Rural)			
Ukrainian	871	848	860
Moldavian	895	883	889
11. Caucasus			
Georgian (Gruzian)	859	875	867
Abkhazian	840	855	848
12. Asiatic and Caspian Steppes			
Kazakh	852	928	890
Turkmen	847	946	897
Kalmyk	841	869	855
Kara-Kalpak	789	914	852
13. Central Asia (Iranian)			
Tadzhik	818	915	867
14. Karelia			
Karel, Finn, Veps	861	850	856
15. Northern Siberia			
Tungus	846	858	852
16. R.S.F.S.R.			
Russian	832	827	830
17. East Siberia (Turkic)			
Yakut	788	809	799
18. Central Asia: Turkic			
Kirgiz	735	829	782
Uzbek	709	793	751
19. European			
Pole	736	732	734
Greek	738	702	720
20. East Siberia (Mongolian)			
Buryat-Mongolian	638	663	651
21. European (Urban)			
Jew	509	520	515

[1] Women reported as aged 15-44 years in total U.S.S.R. were 133.45 percent of women reported aged 20-44 years. Adjusted ratio equals ratio as in Column 1 *times* 1.3345 *times* ratio of women aged 20-44 years to women aged 15-44 years in each specified group. The adjusted ratios may, or may not, be more significant than the unadjusted ratios.

[2] From life table by Novosel'skiy and Payevskiy (Title 417), assuming 106.3 male births per 100 female births, as reported in 1926.

[3] In approximate rank with reference to last column. Nationalities grouped roughly by principal area or characteristics. Note: The data refer to the total population of each ethnic group, in all parts of the U.S.S.R.

an observed child-woman ratio and its corresponding "replacement quota." However, there were great irregularities in the number of women reported as 15-19 years old in some ethnic groups, relative to the number reported as 20-44 years old, probably owing in most cases to misinformation. We have, therefore, computed child-woman ratios, using as a base both the age classes 20-44 years and 15-44 years. However, in order to simplify the presentation we show simply (a) children 0-4 years per 1,000 women 20-44 years (Table 36, Column 1), and (b) a comparable figure *adjusted* to show the relative change from group to group indicated by ratios computed on the other basis (Table 36, Column 2). We do not know which of these figures is the more significant as an index of reproductive trend. Therefore we present the *mean* of these two figures (Table 36, Column 3), and we will cite this average value in referring to the position of various groups. The regional designations used in arranging the groups are rough characterizations of their principal location, supplied as an aid in the interpretation of the data.

It is apparent that the Caucasus Mountains and the Transcaucasus formed a general region of extraordinarily high reproductivity at this time, with the population of some ethnic groups tending to double once in every 25 or 30 years. This must be attributed to early marriage, unlimited fertility, and fairly good health conditions. The situation here is comparable to that prevailing in America in the colonial period, or that persisting to the end of the nineteenth century in the Southern Appalachian Highlands and parts of the Rocky Mountain region of the United States. Some purely rural groups in other parts of the U.S.S.R. (Koreans, Altay or Oyrots, Khakas, and Bulgarians) show a similar trend, in slightly more moderate degree, followed by the indigenous nationalities of the Volga-Ural region, and by the Belorussians, Volga Germans, Ukrainians, Moldavians, Asiatic steppe peoples, the mountain-dwelling Tadzhiks of Central Asia, and the Karelians. The child-woman ratios for all these groups are higher than those for the Russians—largely because a higher proportion of the Russians lived in urban communities.

The lowest fertility is indicated for the Jews, a predominantly urban and highly literate group. They are followed in this respect, but at some distance, by Greeks and Poles. Relatively low ratios are also shown for the Buryat-Mongolians, Uzbeks, Kirgiz, and Yakuts, but in the case of all these groups the relatively low ratios are probably less indicative of limited fertility than of the decimating effect of extremely high infant mortality. Among the Lamaist Buryats, at least, the low ratio may also be influenced by the fact that a large portion of the male population is excluded from normal family relations by religious customs. Somewhat surprisingly, the child-woman ratio of the Tungusi (the largest indigenous group of northern Siberia, excluding the Yakuts and Buryats) is slightly above that of the Russians. The three groups of Buryats, Tungusi, and Yakuts represent peoples living in Siberia before the Russian intrusion and they exist under quite primitive conditions with extremely bad health conditions.

In general, the reproductive trend of the Soviet population in the early post-revolutionary period is similar to that which the demographer usually finds in any population near the point of transition from uncontrolled to controlled fertility. It is, for example, similar to that of western Europe (except France) shortly after the middle of the nineteenth century, or that of the United States or France a few decades earlier. In the Soviet Union at this time, however, variations in health conditions still exercised great influence on reproductive trends. In the Russian Empire a few decades earlier health conditions were clearly the major factor controlling differences in natural increase, as is still the case today in eastern and southern Asia. As a sequel to the situation indicated by the data in this chapter, the demographer would ordinarily expect a gradual lowering of mortality and a rapid decrease in birth rates, characterized by widening differentials among different groups in the population. This expectation, however, is subject to the effects of changing social conditions in the U.S.S.R.—including many conditions that have no close parallel in the experience of other countries.

CHAPTER VIII

TREND OF OCCUPATIONS AND PRODUCTION IN THE SOVIET UNION,
1926-1939

THOUGH relevant to an analysis of population trends, the study of changes in the economy of the Soviet Union, including trends of national income and its distribution, level of living, and capital formation, organization and administration, involves many technical problems far beyond the scope of the present study. The treatment here is therefore limited to a brief statement about certain major features that are most directly related to population changes.[1]

In analyzing the trend of the labor force and its distribution among industrial groups and regions, we should bear in mind the three major economic problems that the Soviet regime inherited from the economic structure of the Russian Empire:

(1) The absorption of an undue proportion of the productive energies of the nation in agriculture and related activities, carried on at a low technological level.

(2) The retarded development of industry, marked by lack of capital equipment and skilled workers, in a land with great natural resources for industrial development.

(3) The inadequate economic integration of different regions, involving inefficient distribution of population, low productivity, and unnecessary transportation costs in the distribution of goods.

The development of Soviet economy can be interpreted largely as an attempt to resolve these problems, and at the same time to fulfill new social objectives, to deal with the many specific problems arising in a period of rapid transition, and to make provisions for military security.

The State Planning Board (Gosplan) was formed in 1921, soon after the period of "War Communism" had given way to the "New Economic Policy" (NEP). After preliminary experimentation during the NEP period, the First Five-Year Plan for the comprehensive control of the economic development of the Soviet Union was approved in the spring of 1929, covering the period October, 1928, to September, 1933. This was the period of rapid collectivization of agriculture. The First Five-Year Plan was, in theory, completed in 1932. The Second Five-Year Plan covers the years 1933 to 1937. The Third Five-Year Plan begins with the year 1938, although it was not finally formulated until 1939. It was interrupted by the German attack on June 22, 1941. The period covered by these Five-Year Plans is often referred to in Soviet literature as the period of "Socialist Construction." During these years a radical change was effected in the occupational structure of the Soviet population.

1. Trend of Employment and Industrial Production, 1926-1939

Data showing the trend of the employed labor force, 1926-1937, with supplementary information on planned employment, 1937-1942, are available from census materials for 1926 and employment statistics for later years. The 1926 census gives a complete description of the population by occupational class, with distinction between actively occupied persons and family dependents. The employment statistics by broad industrial divisions require some adjustment in order to make the series continuous, but these adjustments do not involve major issues affecting the interpretation of the series. The trend of planned employment from 1937 to 1942 conforms in general to the observed trend during the preceding decade. The interpolated figure for employment at the time of the 1939 census is also supported by a report on the total volume of employment in 1940.

[1] See also Appendix V for technical notes on changes in the distribution of population by occupational classes.

According to the 1926 census data, presented in Table 37, employed persons (i.e., "workers" and "employees"—the latter term referring to clerical, professional, technical, and related occupational classes) constituted only 11 percent of the potential labor force ("active popula-

TABLE 37

Number of All Occupied Persons in the U.S.S.R., 1926; Number of Employed Persons, 1926, 1930, and 1939[1]

(Numbers in Thousands)

Occupation	Total "Active Population" 12/17/1926	Employed Personnel			
		12/17/1926	1926-1927	1930	Estimated 1/17/1939
Total	86,220[2]	9,583[3]	10,944	14,531	28,539[4]
All Civilian Occupations	82,713	—	—	—	—
Agriculture and Related Occupations	71,735	1,202	2,078	2,208	3,935
Agriculture	—	—	—	1,552	2,535
Forestry	—	—	—	611	1,300
Fishing	—	—	—	45	100
Handicrafts and Shop Industry	1,866	301	423	290	400
Manufacturing, Mining, Construction, Transport, and Trade	5,606	4,734	5,338	8,482	16,955
Manufacturing and Mining	2,792	2,790	2,839	4,264	9,135
Construction	364	147	547	1,623	1,963
Railways	890	890	1,006	1,084	1,570
Other Transport	403	229	296	415	1,486
Trade and Credit	1,157	678	650	1,096	2,801
Public Administration and Social Service (including Communication)	2,030	1,893	2,400	3,152	6,932
Communication	—	—	95	153	414
Education (including Art)	—	—	715	921	2,623
Health	—	—	365	477	1,267
Municipal Service	—	—	105	131	805
Administration	—	—	1,120	1,470	1,823
Independent Professional	137	—	—	—	—
Casual Labor, Domestic Service, etc.	1,476	1,453	705	399	317
Other "Active"	3,507	—	—	—	—
Pensioners; No Occupation; Unknown	1,862	—	—	—	—
Unemployed	1,014	—	—	—	—
Military	631	—	—	—	—

[1] See Appendix V for description of sources and adjustments, and data for intervening years.
[2] All gainfully occupied persons, including peasants, members of cooperatives, etc., exclusive of children under 10 years of age, reported as gainfully occupied but not otherwise classified.
[3] Workers and employees according to census, December 17, 1926. The figures in all later columns are based on employment statistics.
[4] Figures interpolated between 1937 and 1942 estimates. The total employment figure interpolated between the 1937 and the 1940 estimates is 28,747,000.

tion"). Individual or collective enterprises in agriculture, forestry, and fishing absorbed 70,-533,000 persons (exclusive of workers and employees in these fields) or 81.8 percent of the total "active population." Individual and collective enterprises of the handicraft and work-shop type absorbed an additional 1,565,000 persons. Private enterprise in trade, construction, industrial management, professional service, and so forth provided support for approximately 1,000,000 persons. Slightly over 1,000,000 persons were reported as unemployed; 631,000 were in the armed forces; 1,862,000 persons classified as part of the "active population" were pensioners, residents in public institutions, or without known occupational status.

It should be noted that the census data on workers and employees, December 17, 1926, are based on a classification of persons by "usual occupation." In some categories, such as employment for wages in agriculture and related occupations, the average volume of employment during the year 1926-1927 was very much greater than the number of persons reporting such employment as their usual occupation at the time of the census, owing to large seasonal employment of persons usually engaged in private or collective farm enterprises or other activities. The average volume of employment during the year 1926-1927, according to current employment statistics, was 10,944,000, whereas the total number of persons reporting themselves as workers or employees by usual occupation at the time of the census was 9,583,000. This divergence must be taken into account in any comparison of census data and employment statistics.

Most persons engaged in private enterprise other than agriculture and related occupations presumably lost their previous means of support with the transition after 1928 from the period of the "New Economic Policy" to that of the "Socialist Construction," so that their absorption into the worker and employee classes represents an occupational transfer rather than an increase in the industrial, commercial, and professional force of the nation. To this extent the increase in volume of total employment from 1926-1927 to 1930, amounting to about 3.6 million, is, in part, fictitious. (The increase in trade is particularly affected by such changes.) However, since the number involved in such occupational transfers was only 1 million or less, a very real expansion of employment is indicated even during the first two years of the First Five-Year Plan. Thereafter, this expansion proceeded rapidly through 1932, with slight recession in 1933, and continued rapidly thereafter.

The trend of the employed labor force, by type of industry, over a twelve-year period (1926-1927 to January, 1939) is shown at approximately two-year intervals in Figure 13—based on data presented in Appendix Table A 10.[2] The corresponding data for 1930 and estimates for 1939, centered on the census data of January 17, are also given in Table 37. The adjustments made in the collation of these data are described in Appendix V. During a period of less than nine years, from midyear 1930 to January, 1939, the total volume of employment was practically doubled. Even more rapid expansion is recorded in many critical fields. The following ratios show level of employment in 1939 relative to that in 1930 (1930=100): manufacturing and mining, 214; non-railway transportation, 358; trade and credit, 256; communication, 271; education, 285; and health services, 266.[3] These figures undoubtedly represent the most remarkable expansion of mechanical, technical, and administrative activity ever achieved in any nation in so short a time.

The reported average number of workers in large-scale industry in 1929 was 3,365,900; the

[2] The successive years 1932 and 1933 are included to show the only slight reversal in the general trend over this period.

[3] The apparent sixfold increase in municipal services with an increase of only 24 percent in general administration may be affected by changes in classification.

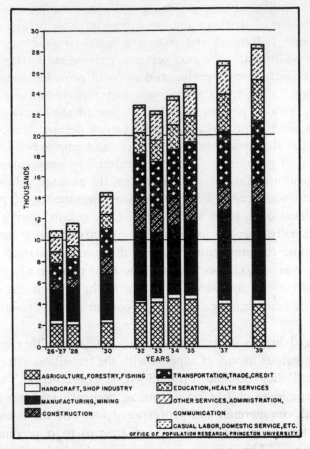

FIGURE 13. Trend of Employed Personnel: U.S.S.R., 1926-
1927 to January 1, 1939 [Table A 10]

estimated number in 1939 was 9,300,000.[4] According to these figures the index of industrial employment for 1939, relative to 1929, is 276. The corresponding index of industrial production for 1939, according to the League of Nations, is 482 (see Figure 14 and Table 38). The ratio of the production index to the corresponding employment index for 1939 is 175—indicating an increase of 75 percent in average net output per worker during the same ten-year period. The index of industrial production in the U.S.S.R. prepared by the Institut für Konjunkturforschung in Berlin (cited by the League of Nations) is 344 for 1939 relative to 1929. Even this index is well above the index for industrial employment. The gross output of industry in rubles of the 1926-1927 price level rose, according to Soviet estimates, from 18.3 billion in 1928 to 137.5 billion in 1940, a sevenfold increase in twelve years.[5] It is certain that the rapid increase in the number of industrial workers in the Soviet Union was accompanied by a marked increase in productivity per worker, though the exact degree of this increase cannot be stated categorically.

2. The Reorganization of Agriculture

It is obvious that such a rapid growth of industrial, commercial, and administrative services required the transfer from agriculture and related occupations of an appreciable proportion of

[4] Figures from sources cited in Appendix V, adjusted to dates used in industrial production series.
[5] Estimates cited by Yugoff, Title 372, p. 14.

TABLE 38

Indices of Industrial Production: U.S.S.R., 1929-1940[1]

Year	Total Industrial Production	Investment Goods	Goods Currently Consumed
1929	100	100	100
1932	168	212	136
1933	178	225	143
1935	260	356	189
1936	334	461	241
1937	372	506	272
1938	413	570	297
1939	482	676	339
1940	535	770	362

[1] According to *Statistical Year-Book of the League of Nations, 1940/41*, p. 159, on basis of official Soviet data. Industrial production covers manufacturing and mining, including production of electricity, but not construction. Pricing and weighting are as of 1926-1927.

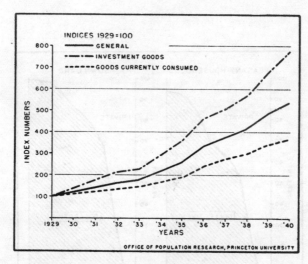

FIGURE 14. Indices of Industrial Production: U.S.S.R., 1929-1940 [Table 38]

the population previously engaged in these activities. At the same time, the expansion of industry and services required an increased volume of marketed food and other agricultural products. It was, therefore, absolutely necessary to effect a rapid increase in the per capita productivity of agricultural workers and to increase the proportion of agricultural production distributed to the families of urban workers and employees. This basic necessity, aggravated by difficulties relating to the collection of grain from the peasants and by other political considerations, led to a drastic program for the mechanization and collectivization of agriculture.

The number of tractors in use in the U.S.S.R. increased from 26,700 in 1928 to 483,500 in 1938. Changes from 1928 to 1938 in the proportions of farm families and cultivated land in the collectives are shown in Table 39 and Figure 15. In a three-year period, 1929-1931, the

TABLE 39

Percent of Peasant Households and Percent of Sown Land in
Collectives: U.S.S.R., 1928-1938[1]

Date July 1	Percent	
	Peasant Households	Sown Area
1928	1.7	2.3
1929	3.9	4.9
1930	23.6	33.6
1931	52.7	67.8
1932	61.5	77.7
1933	65.6	83.1
1934	71.4	87.4
1935	83.2	94.1
1936	90.5	98.2
1937	93.0	99.1
1938	93.5	99.3

[1] *Sotsialisticheskoye Sel'skoye Khozyaystvo SSSR*, Title 454, p. 42.

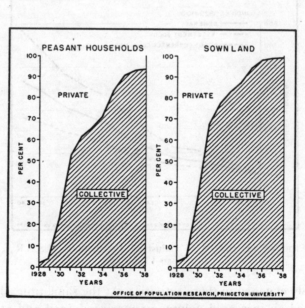

FIGURE 15. Trend of Agricultural Collectivization:
U.S.S.R., 1928-1938 [Table 39]

proportion of farm families in the collectives jumped from 3.9 to 52.7 percent; the corresponding figure for 1938 is 93.5 percent. By 1938 less than 1 percent of all sown land was cultivated by private farmers. Therefore, the few private farm families left in 1938 were largely dependent on meager subsistence agriculture or supplementary sources of income.

This revolution in Soviet agriculture and the resistance it encountered led to serious food shortages that became most acute in the spring of 1933. It also caused a serious depletion of livestock resources. An intensive campaign for the production of food crops in 1933 was rewarded with a good grain harvest, and the agricultural situation was stabilized thereafter. This crisis had far-reaching effects, including, as we shall see in a later chapter, an apparent interruption of population increase.

3. Distribution of Population by Occupational Class, 1926 and 1939

It is difficult to make an exact estimate of the change in farm population or of the number of persons in various economic classes from 1926 to 1939. According to the 1926 census, the population dependent on agriculture, forestry, and fishing was 114,056,000 persons, including 2,128,000 persons dependent on wage or salaried work in agriculture, forestry, and fishing. This was 78 percent of the total population. Two methods of estimating the farm population in 1939, similarly defined, are described in Appendix V. On one method (Assumption A), the figure obtained for January, 1939, is 97,117,000 persons, i.e., 57 percent of the total population. This may be accepted as a maximum, or very nearly a maximum, figure. An alternative method (Assumption B) gives 91,751,000 persons, i.e., 54 percent of the total population. This, in turn, may be accepted as very close to the minimum possible figure. Conversely, the population dependent on manufacturing, mining, construction, transportation, and trade rose from 14.7 million persons (10 percent of the total) to an estimated 40.9-44.9 million persons (24-26 percent of the total); persons dependent on public administration and social services rose from 4.6 million (3 percent of the total) to 16.8-18.4 million (about 10 percent of the total). There was an apparent increase in the population primarily dependent on "handicrafts and shop industries," presumably owing to the transfer of such activities from households to specialized cooperative or private enterprises. These distributions are shown in Table 40 and Figure 16.

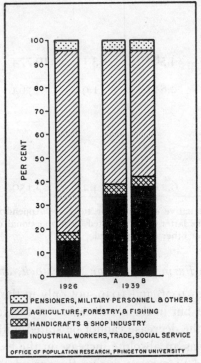

FIGURE 16. Estimated Distribution of the Soviet Population by Broad Occupational Class, 1926 and 1939 [Table 40]

TABLE 40

Estimated Distribution of the Soviet Population by Broad Occupational Class, 1926 and 1939[1]

Occupational Class	1926		1939 (Estimated)			
			Method A		Method B	
	Number (In thousands)	Percent	Number (In thousands)	Percent	Number (In thousands)	Percent
Total	147,028	100	170,467	100	170,467	100
Agriculture, Forestry, and Fishing	114,056	77.6	97,117	57.0	91,751	53.8
Collective and Private Sectors	111,928	76.1	87,634	51.4	81,332	47.7
Employed Personnel	2,128	1.5	9,483	5.6	10,419	6.1
Handicrafts and Shop Industry	4,632	3.2	7,791	4.6	7,395	4.3
Collective and Private Sectors	3,970	2.7	6,827	4.0	6,336	3.7
Employed Personnel	662	0.5	964	0.6	1,059	0.6
Industry, Trade, and Social Service	22,130	15.0	58,400	34.3	64,162	37.6
Manufacturing, Mining, Construction, Transport, and Trade	14,729	10.0	40,862	24.0	44,894	26.3
Public Administration and Social Services (plus Independent Professional, 1926, and "Nonworker," 1939)	4,588	3.1	16,774	9.9	18,429	10.8
Casual Labor, Domestic Service	2,813	1.9	764	0.4	839	0.5
Pensioners, Military Personnel, Unknown (plus Unemployed and Children Under 10 Years Reported as Gainfully Employed, 1926)	6,210	4.2	7,159	4.2	7,159	4.2

[1] For sources and discussion of alternative estimates for 1939, see Appendix V. Percentages for 1926 differ from those presented in Table 27 because the latter were adjusted by proportional distribution of children under 10 years reported as gainfully employed but not otherwise specified.

4. Changes in Farm Population, Livestock, and Sown Land

There was a decrease between 1926 and 1939, not only in the proportion of the Soviet population dependent on agriculture, but in the absolute size of the farm population. This is certain, although the exact amount of the decrease cannot be stated with any confidence. Nevertheless, during the same period there was an absolute increase in the extent of land under cultivation.[6] The acreage in grains increased 11 percent during the period 1928-1938, with most of the in-

[6] The agricultural situation did not change much between 1926 and 1928. Data for the years 1928-1938 are used for analysis of trend in sown area during the intercensus period. (See Table 41.)

crease coming in the years 1928-1932. There was also a progressive shift from rye to wheat and barley, with great expansion of the winter wheat and winter barley areas from 1928 to 1938. (See Table 41.) The acreage devoted to "technical crops" (cotton, oil plants, tobacco,

TABLE 41

Sown Area by Specified Crop: U.S.S.R., 1938;
Index of Sown Area, 1928-1938[1]

Crop	Sown Area, 1938	
	Hectares (In thousands)	As Percent of Sown Area, 1928
Total	136,943	121
Grains	102,411	111
Winter Grains	36,466	119
Winter Rye	21,181	88
Winter Wheat	14,584	236
Winter Barley	701	181
Spring Grains	65,945	107
Spring Wheat	26,928	125
Spring Barley	8,512	123
Oats	17,882	104
Buckwheat	2,085	71
Millet	3,924	69
Corn	2,609	59
Rice	164	75
Vetch	915	159
Legumes	2,519	261
Technical	10,960	127
Cotton	2,083	214
Flax for Fiber	1,882	138
Flax for Seed	352	95
Hemp (Northern)	424	46
Hemp (Southern)	231	
Sunflower	3,145	81
Soybean	194	400
Castor Bean	229	539
Mustard	344	414
Sugar Beet	1,180	153
Tobacco	95	211
Makhorka	105	289
Ether-oil and Herbs	171	—
Truck Garden and Potatoes	9,385	122
Potatoes	7,365	130
Vegetables	1,320	166
Melons	701	58
Perennial Grasses	3,395	328
Fodder Crops	14,102	364

[1] Based on data in *Posevnyye Ploshchadi SSSR*, Title 453, p. 5.

etc.) shows rapid increase to 1932, recession in 1933, and gradual increase during the following years in the case of most technical crops (but a decline in acreage used for sunflower). The area devoted to vegetables, including potatoes, expanded from 1928 to 1932 and stood at about the latter level in 1938. There was a decided rise in the production of fodder crops from 1928 to 1932, a recession in 1933, and rapid increase thereafter. There was also a constant increase in land used for perennial grasses. The land in fodder and perennial grasses was more than three times as great in 1938 as it had been ten years earlier. Since there were smaller livestock inventories in 1938 than in 1928, this increase in fodder and sown grasses represents chiefly an improvement in crop rotation and soil conservation and in feeding practices. However, because some of these crops are not sown each year, the ratio of total sown land in 1938 to that in 1928 (1.21) is several points higher than the corresponding ratio for land sown each year. The extent of land sown to grains, vegetables, and technical crops (not affected by this consideration) was 13 percent greater in 1938 than in 1928.

Apparently, there was also some increase in average yield per unit of sown land during the same period. The yields in 1928 and in 1938 were fairly representative of average conditions in the late 'twenties and late 'thirties, respectively. The reported yield per hectare for all grains in 1938 was 9.3 centners (about 14 bushels per acre) in contrast to 7.9 centners in 1928 and 8.5 centners in 1913,[7] but the 1938 figure represents "biological yield," including crops not harvested. An adjustment of 10 percent for this factor (an arbitrary figure used by some agricultural economists) would indicate quantity production per unit of land about equal to that in 1913, but higher than in 1928—with a greater proportion of wheat in the total volume of grain products. The decrease in the number of draught animals and increased use of tractors would considerably raise the *net* productivity (products available for human consumption or industry) per unit of land. The reported yields for particular grains and for most industrial crops per unit of land in 1938 were also noticeably higher than the reported yields in 1928.

Livestock inventories were seriously depleted during the collectivization drive but were built

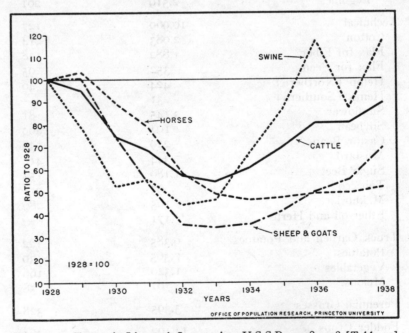

FIGURE 17. Change in Livestock Inventories: U.S.S.R., 1928-1938 [Table 42]

[7] See Yugoff, Title 372, p. 49.

up rapidly between 1934 and 1938—except in the case of horses, for which there was less need. However, even in 1938 the number of cattle and of sheep and goats had not reached the 1928 level. The movement of livestock inventories, 1928-1938, is shown in Figure 17 and the data are given in Table 42.

TABLE 42

Change in Livestock Inventories: U.S.S.R., 1928-1938

(Numbers in Millions)

Year	Cattle	Sheep and Goats	Swine	Horses
Series A[1]				
1928	70.5	146.7	26.0	33.5
1929	67.1	147.0	20.4	34.6
1930	52.5	108.8	13.6	30.2
1931	47.9	77.7	14.4	26.2
1932	40.7	52.1	11.6	19.6
1933	38.4	50.2	12.1	16.6
1934	42.4	51.9	17.5	15.7
Series B[2]				
1934	42.4	51.9	17.5[3]	15.7
1935	49.2	61.1	22.5	15.9
1936	56.7	73.7	30.5	16.6
1937	57.0	81.3	22.8	16.7
1938	63.2	102.5	30.6	17.5
Index (1928 = 100)				
1928	100	100	100	100
1929	95.1	100.2	78.4	103.3
1930	74.4	74.1	52.2	90.2
1931	67.9	53.0	55.6	78.3
1932	57.6	35.5	44.7	58.6
1933	54.4	34.2	46.4	49.4
1934	60.2	35.4	67.2	46.7
1935	69.7	41.7	86.6	47.4
1936	80.4	50.2	117.4	49.5
1937	80.8	55.4	87.7	49.8
1938	89.6	69.9	117.7	52.2

[1] Date: July 1 of each year, 1928-1934. From *Sel'skoye Khozyaystvo SSSR. Yezhegodnik 1935*, Title 451, p. 519.
[2] Date: June-July of each year, 1934-1938. From *Zhivotnovodstvo SSSR za 1916-1938 gg.*, Title 455.
[3] Given as 17.4 in original text.

Various indices of farm population density relative to extent of cultivated land near the beginning and end of the intercensus period, 1926-1939, are shown in Table 43. It is here assumed that there was no appreciable change in the size of the farm population between December 17, 1926, and the year 1928 or between the year 1938 and January 17, 1939. The simplest of these indices (rural population relative to total sown land) makes no allowance for changes in the criteria for classifying places as urban or rural, for changing proportions of rural population dependent on non-agricultural activity, or for changing proportions of sown land used for perennial crops. According to this index, during the intercensus period there was

TABLE 43

U.S.S.R.: Rural Population and Estimated Farm Population, 1926 and 1939,
Relative to Sown Land, 1928 and 1938

Population and Land Use	Period I 1926-1928	Period II 1938-1939	Period II as Percent of Period I
Rural Population, 1926 and 1939	120,713,801	114,557,278	95
Farm Population, 1926 and 1939	114,056,000	A. 97,117,000[1]	85
		B. 91,751,000[2]	80
Total Sown Land (Hectares), 1928 and 1938	112,992,400[3]	136,943,100[3]	121
Sown Land in Cereals, Vegetables, and Technical Crops (Hectares), 1928 and 1938	108,471,100[3]	122,755,900[3]	113
Indices of Density of Farm Population:			
Rural Population per 100 Hectares of Sown Land	106.83	83.65	78
Rural Population per 100 Hectares of Sown Land in Cereals, Vegetables, and Technical Crops	111.29	93.32	84
Estimated Farm Population per 100 Hectares of Sown Land	100.94	A. 70.9	70
		B. 67.0	66
Estimated Farm Population per 100 Hectares of Sown Land in Cereals, Vegetables, and Technical Crops	105.15	A. 79.1	75
		B. 74.7	71

[1] Estimate, January 17, 1939, Assumption A (see Appendix V).
[2] Estimate, January 17, 1939, Assumption B (see Appendix V).
[3] From *Posevnyye Ploshchadi SSSR*, Title 453, p. 5.

a decrease of 22 percent in the density of rural population in the Soviet Union relative to extent of sown land. Data of this type are available for different regions and will be presented in a later chapter. The most refined of these indices (farm population relative to sown land used for cereals, vegetables, and technical crops) eliminates all the sources of bias mentioned above, but depends on estimates of farm population in 1939, which unfortunately are subject to a wide margin of error. According to this index, the decrease in the density of farm population relative to sown land in the Soviet Union was between 25 percent and 29 percent, depending on the figure used for farm population. Changes in the size of the farm population and in the amount of sown land are shown graphically in Figure 18.

An exact estimate of change in net agricultural production per unit of labor would require correct estimates of changes in total agricultural production, changes in amount of agricultural production used for feed and for seed, and changes in expenditures for machinery and fertilizer, as well as changes in farm population. We have attempted to provide such an estimate.

5. Summary

It is apparent that during the period of the Five-Year Plans the Soviet Economy was transformed from extreme dependence on peasant agriculture and related occupations to an economy with a fair balance between agriculture, industry, and services. This transformation was effected at tremendous cost, but a basis was established for progressive advance in all spheres of economic activity. During the years immediately following the 1939 census, the Soviet economy

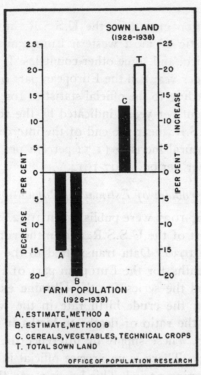

FIGURE 18. Change of Farm Population,
1926-1939, and of Sown Land, 1928-1938,
in the U.S.S.R. [Table 43]

was oriented more intensively toward preparations for the titanic struggle for survival that loomed on the horizon, until this preparatory phase was suddenly interrupted by the actual invasion which swept across White Russia, the Ukraine, and the western districts of the R.S.F.S.R. After an initial period of recovery and reconstruction, there is every reason to expect that this progress toward an efficiently balanced economy will be resumed, and that the output of Soviet industry can be directed in greater degree to raising levels of living and improving the welfare of a rapidly growing population.

CHAPTER IX

TREND OF THE SOVIET POPULATION, 1926-1939

DURING the period between the census of December 17, 1926, and that of January 17, 1939, the population of the Soviet Union increased from 147,027,915 to 170,467,186 persons. This amounted to an increase of 15.9 percent in 12 years and 1 month, or an average (geometric) increase of 1.23 percent per year.

The average rate of population growth in the U.S.S.R. in the intercensus period was far above the rate now characteristic of most western European nations, but below that of the Philippines, Puerto Rico, Mexico, and some other countries. It was below the apparent rate of natural increase (2.29 percent per year) in the European part of the U.S.S.R. at the beginning of the intercensus period, according to the official statistics for 1926-1927,[1] and below the rate of natural increase (2.05 percent per year) indicated by the reported birth rate and the ratio of births to deaths in the U.S.S.R., near the end of the intercensus period, 1938.[2] It was also below the estimated rate of natural increase (1.74 percent per year) in the European part of the U.S.S.R. area in the prewar period, 1897-1914.[3]

1. The Problem of Estimating Population Trends

The official vital statistics for 1927 were published in 1932.[4] A preliminary survey of births and deaths in the European part of the U.S.S.R. and in the rural parts of each region in 1928 had already been published in 1930.[5] Data transmitted to the Health Section of the League of Nations cover births and deaths for the European part of the R.S.F.S.R., Belorussia, and the Ukraine through 1928, and the series for the Ukraine extends through 1930. We have later official information about the crude birth rate in the whole U.S.S.R. in 1938; there is also official information on the ratio of deaths to births in 1938, and on changes in birth rates from 1935 through 1938. These supply by inference the death rate for 1938 and birth rates for 1935, 1936, and 1937. There is no precise official information on the movement of births and deaths in the intervening period. This leaves a gap that is not easily bridged.

It would appear that the Soviet statisticians who were responsible for preparing current population estimates for use in economic planning and who presumably had access to unpublished data on registered births and deaths missed the mark by a wide margin. The population estimates used in the Second Five-Year Plan, published in 1937, apparently erred (in the light of our later information) as regards the population of the Soviet Union at the beginning of this period, January 1, 1933, as well as with regard to the expected increase during these five years. The estimate was as follows:

"The planned further increase in the material security and further rise in the cultural level of the toilers find very striking expression in the tremendous growth of the population. The Second Five-Year Plan period is a quinquennium of further reduction in mortality and a rise in the birth rate as a result of which the population is increasing from 165,700,000 as of January 1, 1933, to 180,700,000 as of January 1, 1938, i.e., an increase of 15,000,000 (9.1 percent) with an average annual increase of 17.3 per thousand."[6]

---

[1] See Table 30. The birth rate minus the death rate in 1926 was .0236; in 1927, .0222. The population in the European area covered by vital statistics, 1926-1927, was equal to 78 percent of the total population of the U.S.S.R.
[2] See Table 53.
[3] See Table 15.
[4] *Statisticheskiy Spravochnik SSSR za 1928 g.*, Title 406.
[5] Gosplan, E.-S.S., Title 450.
[6] Gosplan, *The Second Five-Year Plan . . . , 1933-1937*, Title 460, p. 458.

Projecting the average rate of growth assumed in this estimate for the years 1933 through 1937 forward for 1 year and 16 days to the time of the 1939 census gives an expected population of 183,971,000 persons—13,504,000 above the number actually enumerated at that time. There is every reason to suppose that the 1939 census, which was carefully organized and supported by a great publicity campaign, was as efficient and complete as the census of 1926, so that incomplete enumeration in 1939 relative to that in 1926 can be ruled out as the explanation of this discrepancy.

A theoretical projection of the population of the U.S.S.R., prepared by the actuaries Novosel'skiy and Payevskiy, gives an expected population for January 1, 1939, which is even further from the actual population at this time than the Gosplan estimates. However, gross error in a projection of this sort, with the expected number of children under twelve years of age dependent on the extrapolation of previous birth rates, is less surprising than gross error in estimates presumably based on the reported (though unpublished) movement of births and deaths from 1926 to 1933 and their projection forward to 1939. A large part of the error in the Novosel'skiy-Payevskiy estimate arises from excessive expectation as regards natality, thus exaggerating the expected population under twelve years of age in 1939. But there was also a large error in their estimate for persons over age twelve in 1939, i.e., the survivors of persons who were living and enumerated at the time of the previous census, "aged" by applying survival ratios from the 1926-1927 life table for the European part of the U.S.S.R. (see Table 44).

TABLE 44

Population of the U.S.S.R., 1939: According to Novosel'skiy and Payevskiy, and Observed

Age	Expected Population January 1, 1939[1]			Observed Population January 17, 1939[2]			Discrepancy		
	Male	Female	Total	Male	Female	Total	Male	Female	Total
Total	93,044	98,058	191,102	81,665	88,802	170,467	11,379	9,256	20,635
Under 12	31,849	31,343	63,192	—	—	48,089	—	—	15,103
12 and Over	61,195	66,715	127,910	—	—	122,378	—	—	5,532

[1] Novosel'skiy and Payevskiy, Title 219, p. 16.
[2] Figures as reported from 1939 census, with slight adjustment by age class to give reported total population (see Table 56).

The comparison of the projection by Novosel'skiy and Payevskiy for persons over twelve years of age in 1939 with the actual number of such persons, according to the census, leads to the following conclusion: there were 5.5 million more deaths in the Soviet Union between 1926 and 1939 (apart from deaths among those born after 1926) than would have been expected if the death rates, by age and sex, of the *total* Soviet population during the whole intercensus period had been the same as the rates indicated by *recorded* deaths in the *European part* (78 percent of the total population) at the *beginning* of this period, 1926-1927. We shall consider below the critical conditions implicit in this statement (indicated by the italicized words). Our examination will lead to some revision of this conclusion; but such modification will not greatly alter its apparent significance.

2. Examination and Adjustment of Statistics on Mortality, 1926-1927

In an attempt to resolve the difficulties with which we are thus confronted, we must in the first place examine critically the data presented in the official vital statistics for the early Soviet period. Responsibility for the registration of vital statistics had been transferred at the time of the Revolution from ecclesiastical to civil authorities. This transfer encountered some resistance among conservative groups. Moreover, the organization of a new registration system within the framework of a revolutionary society, in a nation recovering from war, civil disorders, and famine and with half of the population illiterate, was a stupendous undertaking. However, great energy was devoted to this task, which was recognized as an essential requirement of the planned organization of Soviet society. The new registration system was operating over a wide area by 1923. Births and deaths were reported for that year for all the provinces and territories in the European part of the U.S.S.R. except the Ural District, part of the North Caucasus, and some small areas elsewhere; but the reported figures for several other districts were obviously defective. By 1926, the area for which vital statistics were reported had been extended to include all the European part of the U.S.S.R. (except a few outlying areas, which altogether had less than two percent of the population in the European territory),[7] Siberia, Buryat-Mongolia, part of the Far Eastern Territory, and Armenia. Meanwhile, the efficiency of registration was certainly very greatly improved in the European area. Kuczynski, after careful investigation of the data on fertility, concluded: "So far as birth statistics have been compiled, they probably are more accurate than in pre-war times."[8] He qualified this statement by the remark that "at least prior to 1926" stillborn infants may have been included in the number of births; but the official statistics for 1926 specifically define the data on births as relating to live births only. The reports of the First All-Union Census of Population also reveal a high degree of statistical efficiency, although the wide prevalence of illiteracy necessarily introduced serious irregularities in the basic data on some topics, such as distribution of population by single years of age.

The cooperation of the public in the registration of vital events was legally enforced and was stimulated by educational campaigns. Registration was also an essential feature of economic life in the U.S.S.R., specifically in relation to rationing, security benefits, and so forth. It is important to note, however, that from the standpoint of the families immediately concerned motivation for the registration of deaths may have been much less effective than that for the registration of births. One would expect any deficiencies in registration to be most serious in remote rural areas.

Novosel'skiy and Payevskiy investigated the completeness of death registration in connection with their preparation of life tables.[9] A field investigation in rural districts of Leningrad Province indicated a deficiency of 2.5 percent in the total number of registered deaths, thus indicating rather slight under-registration in this region. The highest proportions of unregistered deaths were found in the cases of infants and women. The authors suggest that deficiencies may have been more serious in some other regions; they assumed a deficiency of 12.7 percent in the number of registered deaths in the Bashkir A.S.S.R. in 1926 (but not in 1927). Except for this correction in the data for Bashkir they decided to use the registration data as reported without adjustment. With this one exception, therefore, their tables represent a statistical development of the reported vital statistics. (Adjustment of the Bashkir data for 1926 gives an increase of only 0.1 percent in the general death rate for the U.S.S.R., 1926-1927.)

The official birth rate (43.5) and death rate (19.9) reported for the European part of the

---

[7] The European areas omitted in 1926 were Dagestan A.S.S.R. (except cities), parts of Orenburg Guberniya, parts of Bashkir A.S.S.R., the Chechen and Ingush autonomous regions and two smaller districts in the North Caucasian Kray (Bataysk Rayon in the Don Okrug and Armyank Rayon in the Maykop Okrug), and "an insignificant part" of the Tatar A.S.S.R. (See Title 419, pp. 38-48.) For a complete description of the data on fertility and a partial description of the data on mortality in the U.S.S.R. through 1928, see Kuczynski, Title 154.

[8] Kuczynski, Title 154, p. 105.

[9] Novosel'skiy and Payevskiy, Title 417, pp. xi ff.

U.S.S.R. in 1926[10] may be compared with the estimated rates in approximately the same area in 1911-1913: 45.5 births and 28.6 deaths per 1,000 population, according to an official Soviet estimate, or 47.6 births and 29.6 deaths according to our previous estimate.[11] This comparison would seem to indicate a slight decrease in the crude birth rate but a large decrease in the crude death rate. The infant mortality rate in the same area apparently declined from 266 in 1909-1910 to 198 in 1925, 172 in 1926, 190 in 1927, and 155 in 1928, with the 1928 rate presumably based on preliminary data.[12] The official life-table infant mortality rates for the European part of the U.S.S.R. in 1926-1927 were: males, 201; females, 172; both sexes, 187.[13] Comparison of the last figure with that for 1909-1910 indicates a decrease of 30 percent. In spite of the disorders of the intervening years, however, such a decline in infant mortality, which is most sensitive to changing social conditions, does not seem at all impossible in view of trends in other countries. Apparent changes in infant mortality in various European countries as indicated by life-table mortality rates (q_0) for prewar and postwar periods are shown in Table 45. The territories at different periods are not always identical and the figures for some countries may be erroneous—for example, the prewar infant mortality rates for Bulgaria, India, and Japan are almost certainly too low. Nevertheless, in comparison with the changes shown in Table 45 the apparent decrease of 30 percent in infant mortality in the European area of the U.S.S.R. from 1909-1910 to 1926-1927 appears as a very moderate decline. In any case, the life-table infant mortality rate of 187 for 1926-1927 shows that, according to official statistics, the loss due to infant deaths at this time in the Soviet Union was still very great, with nearly one child among every five infants born alive dying within the first twelve months.

As one means of checking vital statistics around the time of the 1926 census, we can compare the number of children aged 2 years according to the census (the age class used in our previous analysis of natality and reproduction) with recorded births in 1924. We must limit this analysis to the area for which data on births in 1924 are available (i.e., the European part of the U.S.S.R., minus the Bashkir, Orenburg, North Caucasus, Dagestan, and Kalmyk areas). We neglect possible net migration of children under three years of age to or from this territory during the intervening period; but it is not likely that this is a source of serious error. There were 4,216,928 registered births in this "registration area" in 1924[14] and 2,977,531 children aged 2 years were enumerated in the same territory at the time of the census. This indicates the death of 29.39 percent of the infants registered at time of birth—in comparison with an expected proportion of 25.27 percent from birth to age 2 years ($1 - L_2/\text{radix}$) according to the life-table values based on registration data for 1926-1927. The former figure is 16 percent above the latter figure, but this is not a large discrepancy in view of the many complicating factors, especially the probability that infant mortality was higher in 1924 and 1925 than in 1926-1927.

There are, however, certain peculiar features about the reported mortality rates for some districts in 1926 and 1927. Although, as already noted, death rates were generally higher at this time in rural than in urban areas, the reported mortality rates for rural areas are lower than the rates for urban areas in regions where (in most cases) we would expect the poorest health conditions in rural districts and where the organization of registration procedures presumably encountered the greatest difficulties. General death rates thus *appear* to have been lower in rural than urban areas in the Bashkir A.S.S.R., Lower Volga Region, the Crimea,

---

[10] See Table 30.
[11] See Title 419, pp. 38-48, and Table 13.
[12] See Title 450, p. 20.
[13] Novosel'skiy and Payevskiy, Title 417. This infant mortality rate is 3.3 percent higher than the average of the official rates for 1926 and 1927. This may be due merely to the time adjustment of birth and death data.
[14] Kuczynski, Title 154, pp. 108 and 111.

TABLE 45

Prewar and Postwar Life-Table Infant Mortality Rates for Various Countries[1]

Area	Period I	Period II	Apparent Change as Percent of Period I
U.S.S.R., European Part	1909-1910[2]	1926-1927[2]	
Both Sexes	266	187	—30
Males	—	201	—
Females	—	172	—
Germany	1901-1910	1924-1926	
Males	202.3	115.4	—43
Females	170.5	93.9	—45
Austria	1906-1910	1930-1933	
Males	219.8	115.4	—47
Females	184.8	92.5	—50
Bulgaria	1900-1905	1925-1928	
Males	158.5	171.5	8
Females	137.8	148.8	8
Finland	1901-1910	1921-1930	
Males	134.5	99.8	—26
Females	113.1	82.8	—27
Hungary	1900-1901	1920-1921	
Males	231.2	215.3	— 7
Females	196.7	184.3	— 6
Moravia-Silesia (Czechoslovakia)	1899-1902	1929-1932	
Males	248.2	129.9	—48
Females	209.5	107.2	—49
India	1901-1910	1921-1930	
Males	290.0	248.7	—14
Females	284.6	232.3	—18
Japan	1908-1913	1921-1925	
Males	160.5	162.0	1
Females	145.0	144.0	— 1

[1] L'Institut international de statistique, Title 103, pp. 192-201, except data for U.S.S.R.

[2] Rate for 1909-1910 is not from a life-table value, but from an estimate based directly on provincial registration of births and deaths and estimated population, Title 450. The 1926-1927 values are from the official life tables, Title 417.

Buryat-Mongolia, and Armenia. There is also an apparent jump in rural death rates in several of these regions, and in some other regions, from 1926 to 1927. Infant mortality rates *apparently* increased by 35 percent or more in the rural areas of the Vyatka, Ural, and Bashkir regions, although there was no corresponding increase in the urban areas of the Vyatka or Ural regions, and the increase in the urban areas of the Bashkir Republic (where defects in the 1926 statistics have already been referred to) was only 17 percent. There were apparent increases in both rural and urban areas in the Leningrad-Karelia and Northeastern regions, but here the comparison is disturbed by boundary changes. In Armenia, the apparent increase in infant mortality rates from 1926 to 1927 was 15 percent in rural areas, but only 6 percent in urban areas. Other regions in which there were apparent increases of more than 10 percent in infant mortality in these two successive years are the rural areas of the Crimea, of the Dnepr Industrial Subregion, and of the Central Industrial Region. However, vital statistics for Siberia, Buryat-Mongolia, and the Far Eastern Territory are not included in the 1927 list, so that no such comparison is possible in these cases.

The European areas in which apparent inconsistencies in the published data give evidence of incomplete registration, especially as regards infant deaths, contain about 27 percent of the total population of the European part of the U.S.S.R.[15] An error of any given size arising from incomplete registration in this territory would, therefore, cause an error of about one-fourth that magnitude in the statistics for European Russia. If such error occurred in only one year, it would cause an error of about one-eighth that magnitude in a two-year average.

The life-table values for the European part of the U.S.S.R., 1926-1927, prepared by Novosel'skiy and Payevskiy largely on the basis of uncorrected official statistics, have a peculiar characteristic not found in tables based on well-authenticated data; namely, only a slow rise in mortality rates appears in passing from early adult to later adult years, especially in the case of females. It seems likely that this peculiarity of the Soviet tables should be attributed to incomplete registration of deaths at the later ages, particularly among women, or to gross discrepancies between ages as reported for the living population and as reported for persons at death, or to errors of both types. Adjusted tables have, therefore, been computed by accepting the life-table death rates at ages 5 to 25 years as accurate, and relating the rates for the later ages to these accepted rates as a basis, according to the general pattern of other life tables for European nations. This adjustment was carried out by Ansley J. Coale. The proportions surviving to successive years of life according to this table are shown in Table 46. Death rates according to this table are shown in comparison with those of the official table by Novosel'skiy and Payevskiy in Figure 19 (and also in Table 47). The official table gives an expectation of life at birth of 41.9 years for males, 46.8 years for females, and 44.4 for both sexes. The corresponding figures from the table by Coale are 41.0 years for males, 45.1 for females, and 43.0 for both sexes. The contrast between the adjusted table and the original table is somewhat greater, however, when measured in terms of the general death rate expected in a population having the age and sex characteristics of the U.S.S.R. in 1926. Application to this population of the specific mortality rates (m_x values) from the Novosel'skiy-Payevskiy table gives a general rate of 20.5 deaths per 1,000 population, corresponding very closely to the mean of the published rates for 1926 and 1927, as would be expected. Application of comparable rates from the Coale table gives a general rate of 21.8 deaths per 1,000 population.[16]

The expected number of deaths at ages 5 years and over obtained by applying Coale's "adjusted" table to the 1926 population is 14.6 percent above the number obtained by application of the specific rates from the Novosel'skiy-Payevskiy table. We shall assume that this represents the proportion of unregistered deaths at ages 5 years and over in the European area represented in the mortality data for 1926-1927. No assumption was made about deaths under 5 years of age in Coale's procedure. We shall, however, assume that the same proportion (14.6 percent) of deaths under 5 years was not registered. On these assumptions we have obtained

[15] Exclusive of Dagestan A.S.S.R. and Orenburg Province, which, along with some smaller areas, were not represented in the data used in calculating vital statistics for the European part of the U.S.S.R. The districts included in this figure (27 percent) are the whole Northeastern and Leningrad regions except the city of Leningrad, the whole Bashkir Republic, and the rural areas of Lower Volga, North Caucasus, Vyatka, and Ural regions, of the Crimea, and of the Dnepr Industrial Subregion.

[16] See Table 47.

TABLE 46

Adjusted Life-Table Values: European Part of the U.S.S.R., 1926-1927[1]

Numbers Surviving to Specified Age per Ten Thousand Infants Born Alive (l_x)

Age	Male	Female	Age	Male	Female
0	10000	10000	36	5835	6187
1	7990	8279	37	5786	6141
2	7457	7774	38	5735	6094
3	7211	7534	39	5682	6047
4	7074	7396	40	5627	5999
5	6971	7292			
			41	5570	5951
6	6895	7215	42	5511	5903
7	6836	7157	43	5450	5854
8	6791	7114	44	5387	5805
9	6754	7079	45	5321	5754
10	6726	7052			
			46	5252	5702
11	6704	7032	47	5181	5650
12	6686	7014	48	5108	5596
13	6670	6997	49	5032	5539
14	6652	6978	50	4952	5479
15	6633	6957			
			51	4862	5416
16	6612	6935	52	4781	5350
17	6589	6912	53	4690	5282
18	6563	6887	54	4595	5209
19	6534	6859	55	4496	5131
20	6501	6829			
			56	4393	5049
21	6466	6797	57	4286	4964
22	6429	6763	58	4174	4873
23	6391	6728	59	4058	4776
24	6352	6691	60	3936	4672
25	6312	6654			
			61	3809	4560
26	6272	6615	62	3676	4442
27	6231	6574	63	3539	4317
28	6189	6532	64	3397	4184
29	6147	6490	65	3251	4044
30	6104	6448			
			66	3100	3896
31	6061	6406	67	2944	3739
32	6018	6363	68	2784	3576
33	5974	6320	69	2622	3405
34	5929	6276	70	2458	3229
35	5883	6232			

TABLE 46 (*Continued*)

Adjusted Life-Table Values: European Part of the U.S.S.R., 1926-1927[1]

Numbers Surviving to Specified Age per Ten Thousand Infants Born Alive (l_x)

Age	Male	Female		Age	Male	Female
71	2290	3044		86	233	417
72	2117	2849		87	175	325
73	1943	2650		88	129	248
74	1771	2448		89	94	186
75	1604	2250		90	71	142
76	1440	2050		91	57	117
77	1276	1846		92	46	95
78	1116	1643		93	36	77
79	965	1448		94	28	62
80	827	1267		95	22	50
81	701	1097		96	16	39
82	585	935		97	12	30
83	480	783		98	9	23
84	386	644		99	7	17
85	303	522		100	5	13
Expectation of Life at Birth, in Years					41.0	45.1

[1] Prepared by Ansley J. Coale.

an adjusted death rate of 23.5 deaths per 1,000 population for this area. These assumptions are obviously arbitrary, but not unreasonable in the light of the evidence presented above.

The statistics for the European part of the U.S.S.R. (minus the areas for which births and deaths were not reported) represent conditions in about 78 percent of the total population of the Soviet Union. The reported death rate for Siberia in 1926 (25.6) was well above that for the European part of the U.S.S.R. (19.9); the reported rates for Buryat-Mongolia, the Far Eastern Territory, and Armenia were slightly below that for the European part,[17] but some or all of these rates may have been spuriously lowered by under-registration of deaths. We have no specific information about mortality in Central Asia, the Asiatic steppe region, or most of the Transcaucasus. It seems likely, in view of the economic and social conditions in these areas, that the average death rate of the population living outside the registration area was as high as that reported for the Vyatka and Ural regions in 1927, namely, about 35 deaths per 1,000 population, or around 50 percent above the average rate for the European part of the U.S.S.R. Combining the figures for the European and Asiatic sections of the U.S.S.R. (i.e., the populations within and outside the areas covered by the registration data for 1926 and 1927), we obtain a hypothetical death rate for the whole U.S.S.R. in 1926-1927 of 26.0 deaths per 1,000 population. This figure may be somewhat too high or somewhat too low, but it probably gives a truer representation of the actual situation as regards mortality in the Soviet Union at this time than the use, without adjustment, of the reported figure for the European part. It is probable that failure to correct for under-registration of deaths and for less favorable health conditions in areas for which vital statistics were not available led Soviet statisticians unwittingly to underestimate the force of mortality in the early Soviet period.

[17] See Table 30.

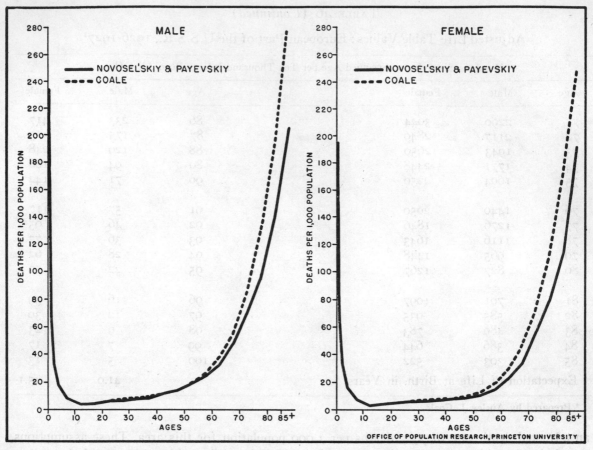

Figure 19. Age-Specific Mortality Rates: European Part of the U.S.S.R., 1926-1927 Life-Table Values (Novosel'-skiy and Payevskiy; Coale) [Table 47]

3. Conditions Affecting Mortality in the Intercensus Period

Two general conditions dominated the changing health situation in the Soviet Union between the census of 1926 and that of 1939: (1) a general improvement of health facilities, which might ordinarily have brought the average actual rate of mortality for the whole U.S.S.R. during the intercensus period to a level somewhere near that indicated by the official statistics for the European part in 1926 and 1927; (2) extraordinary changes in the economic and social organization of the U.S.S.R., which placed a particularly heavy strain on the population during these years.

Great energy was directed toward improving conditions affecting the health of the citizens of the U.S.S.R. Figures given in the previous chapter show that the total personnel employed in health work increased from 365,000 persons in 1926-1927 to 1,267,000 persons near the beginning of 1939—a more than threefold increase in about twelve years. *Socialized Medicine in the Soviet Union,* by Henry S. Sigerist, furnishes the most complete account in English of the health measures that were taken.[18] More recent information is presented in articles by the

[18] Sigerist, Title 297. It should be noted that this book contains a statement about infant mortality that might easily be misinterpreted (p. 263): "By 1936 it [the infant death rate] was further decreased to 11.8 in the U.S.S.R. and to 8.8 in the Byelorussian Republic"—with reference to Sheveler. Checking this reference, one finds that the rate ascribed to the "U.S.S.R." is that of the Ukrainian Soviet Socialist Republic, where the corresponding rate was 14.1 in 1926 and 14.8 in 1927—not that of the Soviet Union as a whole, where the rate in the European part was 17.2 in 1926 and 19.0 in 1927. The present writer cannot accept many of the theoretical positions advanced by Dr. Sigerist, but this does not affect the value of the objective material in this account.

same author, published in 1943 and 1944.[19] From 1928 to 1941, the number of general hospital beds rose from 218 thousand to 661 thousand, psychiatric hospital beds from 30 thousand to 74 thousand, and maternity beds from 27 thousand to 142 thousand. There has been an even more spectacular increase in the number of sanitaria and health resorts from some 2 thousand in 1913 to 36 thousand in 1928 and 132 thousand in 1941. The number of general medical centers has been greatly increased, and special types of medical centers that were practically non-existent in pre-revolutionary Russia have been established, such as tuberculosis stations (over 1,000), venereal disease stations (over 1,000), and women's and children's consultation centers (5,800 in 1941). Typhus, relapsing fever, typhoid, chorea, smallpox, and diphtheria have been reduced and the danger of a recurrence of great epidemics has been eliminated. According to the Commissar of Public Health of the U.S.S.R., mortality from tuberculosis has declined from 40 per 10,000 per annum in 1911-1913 to a level only 40 percent as high;[20] but an exact statistical statement of this sort is subject to variations in diagnosis and reporting. A major campaign has been directed against malaria, which was prevalent over large areas of the Russian Empire and spread to new regions during the First World War. Both the prevalence of the disease and the extensive provisions for examination are indicated by the fact that over 6 million cases were reported in 1935.[21] Provisions for examinations and medical treatment have been supplemented by control of mosquito breeding grounds, including use of airplanes in spreading oil over swamps. Special attention has also been given to the control of trachoma. The network of consultant centers for mothers and children, instruction in nutrition and child hygiene, and the care of children in nurseries has reduced infant mortality. No less important than these specific health measures have been the increase of literacy in the general population, the promotion of scientific interests, and the organization of community affairs. These have provided the basis for noticeable advances in the health of the Soviet population.

The disturbances and food shortages associated with the collectivization program, which reached the proportions of a famine in some southern European districts in the spring of 1933, reversed for a time the progress toward lower mortality and caused an undetermined excess of deaths.[22] Conditions associated with this general program and the related program for the settlement of the nomads apparently produced a crisis in the Asiatic steppe region (Kazakhstan). The population here was peculiarly dependent on livestock for its sustenance, and the depletion of livestock reached its most staggering proportions in the Kazakh Republic. The number of Kazakhs in the Soviet Union was less by one million or more than the number that would normally have been expected in 1939.[23] Finally, in the drive for rapid industrialization and the utilization of undeveloped resources, especially in remote areas such as Murmansk, Arkhangelsk, the Asiatic steppes, and northern and eastern Siberia, many new industrial workers, including dispossessed *kulaks* and political prisoners, were subjected to strains and hazards to be exceeded only by the conditions of the impending war—toward which, in large part, these stupendous efforts were directed. All of these conditions apparently reached a climax in the early 1930's.[24]

[19] Sigerist, Titles 295 and 296.

[20] Miterev, Title 204, p. 58.

[21] League of Nations, Health Section. Annual Epidemiological Report for the Year 1938.

[22] For a realistic, literary account of conditions in the Don and North Caucasus regions during the collectivization period, see *Seeds of Tomorrow* by the great Soviet novelist, Mikhail Sholokhov.

[23] See Section 9 of this chapter.

[24] The reported case frequencies of specified diseases in the *Epidemiological Reports* of the Health Section of the League of Nations show over 40 thousand cases of typhus in the European part of the R.S.F.S.R. in 1932 and in 1935 (in contrast to an average of 15 thousand reported cases, 1929-1931), and 27 thousand cases of typhus in the Asiatic part of the R.S.F.S.R. in 1932 (in contrast to an average of 2 thousand reported cases in 1929-1931). With these exceptions, these reports give no evidence of epidemics in the U.S.S.R. during this period.

4. Estimates of Mortality, 1938-1940

Official releases indicate by inference that there were 17.8 deaths per 1,000 population in the whole U.S.S.R. in 1938.[25] This is above the reported death rate in that year for any European country except Rumania, Malta, and Spain,[26] and certainly does not seem to be an unreasonably low figure. It would, however, indicate a decline of 32 percent below our hypothetical figure of 26 deaths per 1,000 population for 1926-1927. It is possible that there was still serious under-registration of deaths in the Soviet Union at this time, but this seems improbable. We shall proceed on the hypothesis that this figure correctly describes the actual situation at about the time of the 1939 census.

We have no information about specific death rates by age and sex in the U.S.S.R. in 1938, and the information about general mortality or infant mortality between 1928 and 1938 is fragmentary. We are, however, informed that in 1940-1941 (presumably referring to the twelve months before the German invasion) the infant mortality in Moscow was 101 deaths under one year per 1,000 live births.[27] In 1926-1927 the infant mortality rate (life table q_0) had been 39 percent higher in the European part of the U.S.S.R. than in Moscow—without allowance for possible differences in completeness of registration. Therefore, it is probable that around 1940 the infant mortality rate for the whole U.S.S.R. was somewhere in the vicinity of 140 or 150. According to Kazantseva mortality in the whole U.S.S.R. was generally lower in 1940-1941, especially at the early ages, "than in the year 1929." The reason for the selection of this year for comparison is not apparent, but it may have been the first year for which vital statistics were obtained for the entire U.S.S.R. (though such statistics, if collected, remain unpublished, so far as the present writer is aware). It is possible that the infant mortality rate indicated for that year represented a relatively low level which was not reached again until 1940. However, complete data on mortality are not available, so that the scientist interested in giving an objective account of population trends in the U.S.S.R. is placed in a very difficult position, and his results and interpretations generally must be treated as purely tentative.

A hypothetical series of specific death rates for the U.S.S.R. about 1940 is needed for the projection of the population to later years. We have interpolated values between two life tables representing somewhat similar mortality conditions to obtain a series of *specific* rates. When these rates are applied to the actual population at this time distributed by age and sex,[28] they give approximately the correct *general* death rate. We have obtained these values by interpolation between (1) the "adjusted" life tables for the European part of the U.S.S.R., 1926-1927, and (2) the life tables for Poland, 1931-1932. These tables were used because the general mortality corresponding to the former set (U.S.S.R., 1926-1927) was somewhat higher, while the general mortality corresponding to the latter set (Poland, 1931-1932) was somewhat lower, than that of the U.S.S.R. in 1938. Rates interpolated in fixed proportion between the two sets (closer to the latter set) give a general death rate of 17.2 deaths per 1,000 population—with the estimated age and sex distribution of the U.S.S.R. in 1938. By allowing some slight improvement from 1938 to 1940, this series is arbitrarily assumed to give an approximate description of the actual situation as regards mortality in the U.S.S.R. about 1940. Some of these specific rates are probably too high and others too low. In net effect, however, they must cor-

---

[25] See Table 53.

[26] League of Nations. *Statistical Year-Book, 1941/42*, p. 38.

[27] Kazantseva, Title 120, p. 3. The infant mortality rate reported by Kazantseva for Moscow in 1930 was 124, in contrast to 134 in 1926 and 139 in 1927 (the later figures from same sources as Table 30).

[28] The derivation of the estimated age and sex distribution of the Soviet population at the time of the 1939 census is described below in this chapter, Section 10.

respond fairly closely to actual conditions, if our information about the general death rate at this time is correct.

The specific mortality rates (m_x values) according to the various life tables described in this chapter are shown in Figure 20 and given in Table 47. The first column in Table 47 presents the death rates according to the tables by Novosel'skiy and Payevskiy for the European part of the U.S.S.R. in 1926-1927. The rates in the second column are from the same tables as "adjusted" by Coale at ages 25 years and over, and the third column gives the rates for Poland, 1931-1932. The rates in the last column are purely hypothetical, but computed so as to yield a general death rate slightly lower than that of 17.8 "observed" in 1938. One should note that the mortality rates shown here for persons under 1 year of age relate infant deaths to population under 1 year of age. Rates of this type are, by definition, higher than ordinary "infant mortality rates" since the living population under 1 year of age (the denominator of the m_0 values) is less than the corresponding number of live births. The ordinary infant mortality rates corresponding to our hypothetical series for 1938-1940 are 181 for males, 145 for females, and 158 for both sexes. These particular figures may quite possibly be too high; but we have no specific information whereby we can obtain more reliable figures. The general "life-table death rates" shown in Table 47 give the expected number of deaths per 1,000 population if any given set of specific rates prevailed in a population formed by a constant flow of births, but reduced from age to age according to the specific mortality rates of this life table. "Expected death rates" that would result from the application of any given set of specific rates to certain actual populations are also shown.

5. The Trend of Fertility in the Early Soviet Period

In considering changes in birth rates in the U.S.S.R. during the intercensus period, we assume reasonably complete registration of births in 1926 and 1927.[29] There is, in fact, no evidence of incomplete registration of births in most of the European part of the U.S.S.R. at this time, and the adjustments already made in the data on mortality were designed to bring these figures into line with comparable information on births. Data on births prior to about 1925, however, are obviously unreliable. The birth rate as reported for the European part of the U.S.S.R. *apparently* rose from 38.8 in the year 1923 to 42.9 in 1924 and 44.2 in 1925.[30] Fertility statistics for the years preceding 1923 are available only for limited areas and are probably erroneous.

We can obtain an approximate index of the trend of "effective fertility"[31] in the U.S.S.R., 1920-1926, by the use of census data on children living at each age at the time of the census (December 17, 1926), assuming constant death rates during this period according to life tables for the European part of the U.S.S.R., 1926-1927 (without adjustment since we are concerned here only with the trend from year to year). This index shows the number of births in each year that would have produced the living children enumerated by the census *if* the death rates of 1926-1927 had prevailed throughout these years. Since death rates were undoubtedly higher

[29] The situation in the Soviet Union in this respect is different from that in the United States, where motivation for the registration of births is still inadequate but where the registration of deaths is more effectively implemented.

[30] Kuczynski, Title 154, p. 110. Vital statistics for the five largest cities of the Ukraine apparently indicate a rapid upswing in 1923 from the period of relatively low fertility caused by war, civil war, and famine. The average birth rate in these cities (combined) was fairly constant during 1922: 14.8 births per 1,000 population in the first and last quarters, 12.8 in the second quarter, 16.4 in the third quarter. Then the rate apparently rose to 21.6 in the first quarter and 31.9 in the second quarter of 1923, and remained at about that level through 1924. *Ibid.*, p. 17.

[31] The term "effective fertility" has been used with different meanings in other writings, including those of the present author. In each case it has only the specific meaning defined in the context.

TABLE 47

Age-Specific Mortality Rates per 1,000 Population: European Part of the U.S.S.R., 1926-1927; the U.S.S.R., 1938-1940; Poland, 1931-1932

| Age | European Part of U.S.S.R., 1926-1927 Life-Table Mortality Rates According to | | Poland 1931-1932 | U.S.S.R. 1938-1940 |
	Novosel'skiy and Payevskiy	Adjusted by Coale	Life-Table Mortality Rates	Hypothetical Mortality Rates
Males				
Under 1	233.7	233.7	189.7	198.9
1	69.3	69.3	31.3	39.3
2	33.6	33.6	13.9	18.0
3-4	16.9	16.9	7.1	9.1
5-9	7.2	7.2	3.5	4.3
10-14	2.8	2.8	2.5	2.6
15-19	4.0	4.0	3.9	3.9
20-24	5.9	5.9	5.7	5.7
25-29	6.3	6.7	5.6	5.9
30-34	6.8	7.4	5.7	6.1
35-39	8.2	8.9	6.7	7.2
40-44	10.6	11.2	8.4	9.0
45-49	14.0	14.4	11.6	12.2
50-54	19.3	19.3	16.6	17.2
55-59	24.3	26.5	24.3	24.8
60-64	33.0	38.0	34.7	35.4
65-69	47.7	55.4	52.8	53.3
70-74	71.3	84.1	81.8	82.3
75-79	95.4	129.2	121.2	122.9
80-84	138.9	192.8	185.0	186.6
85+	205.7	277.5	302.9	302.9
Females				
Under 1	195.0	195.0	155.2	163.6
1	63.1	63.1	29.0	36.2
2	31.4	31.4	13.1	16.9
3-4	16.4	16.4	7.0	9.0
5-9	6.7	6.7	3.6	3.7
10-14	2.7	2.7	2.8	2.8
15-19	3.7	3.7	3.9	3.9
20-24	5.2	5.2	5.2	5.2
25-29	5.8	6.3	5.9	6.0
30-34	6.3	6.8	6.5	6.6
35-39	6.9	7.6	7.0	7.1
40-44	7.8	8.3	7.6	7.7
45-49	8.5	9.8	8.3	8.6
50-54	11.1	13.1	11.9	12.2
55-59	15.0	18.7	17.8	17.9
60-64	22.8	28.7	27.4	27.7
65-69	34.7	44.7	42.2	42.7
70-74	56.5	71.3	67.2	68.1
75-79	77.9	112.4	104.4	106.1
80-84	114.7	171.1	165.1	166.4
85+	192.1	248.3	277.8	277.8

TABLE 47 (*Continued*)

Age-Specific Mortality Rates per 1,000 Population: European Part of the U.S.S.R., 1926-1927; the U.S.S.R., 1938-1940; Poland, 1931-1932

| Age | European Part of U.S.S.R., 1926-1927 Life-Table Mortality Rates According to | | Poland 1931-1932 | U.S.S.R. 1938-1940 |
	Novosel'skiy and Payevskiy	Adjusted by Coale	Life-Table Mortality Rates	Hypothetical Mortality Rates
Expectation of Life at Birth in Years:				
Males	41.9	41.0	48.2	46.7
Females	46.8	45.1	51.4	50.2
Both Sexes	44.4	43.0	49.7	48.4
Life-Table Death Rates	22.6	23.3	20.1	20.7
Expected Death Rates by Application of Specified Rates:				
(a) To 1926 Population	20.5	21.8	—	—
(b) To 1938 Population	—	20.7	16.3	17.2

in the early part of this period, the actual number of children born alive in the earlier years was presumably higher than the figures shown here; but, to the extent that this was the case, these additional infants perished forthwith, owing to the troublous conditions of the years in which they were born. According to this index (see Table 48) the real peak in fertility was reached in 1923—on the rebound from the disturbed conditions of the preceding years, but before there was any widespread provision of facilities for abortion.

In the area for which the birth statistics in 1926 and 1927 were most reliable (i.e., the European part of the U.S.S.R. exclusive of the Dagestan and Bashkir republics, Orenburg Province, the Chechen and Ingush districts, and two rayons of the North Caucasian Territory) there were 4,824,942 births in 1926 and 4,846,132 births in 1927.[32] That area in 1926 contained 72.47 of all two-year-old children in the U.S.S.R. Combining these two items (and ignoring possible net migration of children under two years of age), we can estimate the total number of births in the U.S.S.R. during 1926-1927, on the assumption that the proportion of infants dying between birth and the midpoint of the third year of life in the excluded area, mostly Asiatic regions, was the same (relative to the proportion in European Russia) as in the Vyatka and Ural regions, i.e., 16.2 percent higher than in the European part of the U.S.S.R. On this basis we estimate that there were 6,716,000 births in 1926 and 6,746,000 births in 1927 in the whole Soviet Union (mean number: 6,731,000).[33] This would indicate a mean birth rate of 45.7 for the U.S.S.R. at this time. This figure is assumed to have approximate, but only approximate, validity.

[32] Same sources as Table 30. In obtaining the total for 1926, the 1927 figures for the districts of the Central Volga Region without Orenburg have been substituted for the 1926 figure for this region, which lacks breakdown by separate districts.

[33] On the assumption of a loss of 25.3 percent of the infants born in 72.47 percent of the U.S.S.R. and of 29.4 percent of the infants born in the remaining 27.53 percent of the territory (outside the registration area), making the ratio of births in the U.S.S.R. to births in the registration area: 1.392.

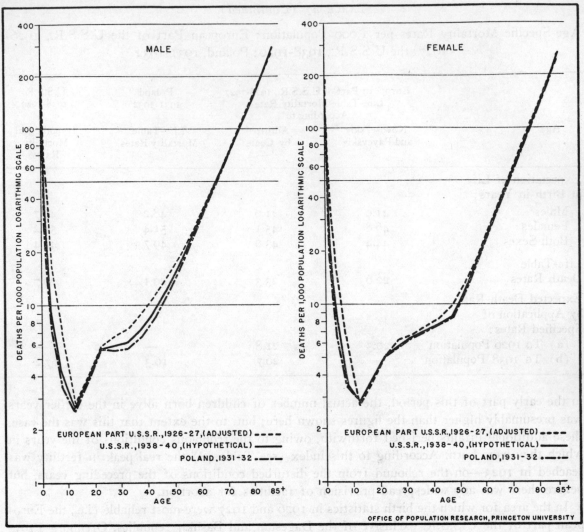

Figure 20. Age-Specific Mortality Rates: European Part of the U.S.S.R., 1926-1927 (Coale); U.S.S.R., 1938-1940; Poland, 1931-1932 [Table 47]

6. Conditions Affecting Fertility, and Estimated Trend, 1927-1938

There is evidence of wide fluctuation in the birth rates between 1928 and 1938. The Soviet code had legalized abortion shortly after the formation of the Union of Soviet Socialist Republics, and had made provision for abortion under medical auspices in public clinics. Resort to contraception as the preferable means of controlling family size was stressed in educational campaigns, but the abortion clinics were provided as an alternative for persons unable to practice contraception immediately and effectively. The response to these provisions was at first only moderate but by the middle 'thirties the number of births in the Soviet Union was sharply reduced from over six and one-half million births in 1926 and in 1927 to less than five million births in 1935.[34] The reduction in fertility was also associated with an increase in the frequency of divorce. Although these trends were by no means purely an urban phenomenon, they were most extreme in the large cities. The situation in Moscow, with regard to births and abortions, is shown in Table 49. The ratio of abortions per 100 births in Moscow rose from

[34] See Table 53.

TABLE 48

Index of Variations in "Effective Fertility": U.S.S.R., 1920-1926

Year	Hypothetical Births[1] (In thousands)	Hypothetical Births Adjusted for Estimated Errors in Census Data[2] (In thousands)	Hypothetical Rate (Adjusted) per 1,000 Population[3]	Reported Birth Rate, European U.S.S.R., per 1,000 Population[4]
1926	5,950	6,200	42.6	43.6
1925	5,774	6,248	43.9	44.7
1924	5,907	5,907	42.5	43.1
1923	6,230	6,230	45.5	38.8
1922	5,093	5,185	38.0	33.4[5]
1921	4,999	4,816	35.2	32.6[5]
1920	4,322	4,447	32.2	30.9[5]

[1] Number of children reported in each age class divided by the corresponding survival ratio from life tables for European part of U.S.S.R., 1926-1927. For example, the population aged 6 years, on December 17, 1926, divided by (L_6/radix) gives hypothetical births for 1920. The hypothetical numbers and rates shown here are generally lower than actual births and birth rates.

[2] Assuming 4.2 percent of children under 1 year and 8.2 percent of children aged 1 year not enumerated, and children aged 4, 5, and 6 years adjusted to give straight-line trend at these ages. These adjustments, though derived from the Soviet data, are in line with adjustments commonly required in the census data of other countries.

[3] Adjusted figures related to population as estimated by Volkov, and adjusted to include Khiva and Bukhara. (See Table 12.)

[4] Rates for 1924-1926 from the official vital statistics for 1926, Title 419, p. 8. The summary figure for 1926 is slightly different from that cited in Table 30, from the same source, pp. 38-48. Rates for 1920-1923 from Kuczynski, Title 154, p. 109.

[5] Twenty provinces only, *Ibid.*, p. 104.

TABLE 49

Reported Births and Abortions in Moscow: 1914, 1921-1926, and 1934-1935

Year	Reported Births per 1,000 Population[1]	Reported Abortions per 1,000 Population[1]	Abortions per 100 Births
1914	31.0	3.2	10
1921	30.6	5.7	19
1922	25.6	5.5	21
1923	30.1	5.5	18
1924	29.3	5.7	19
1925	31.0	9.7	31
1926	28.9	15.8	55
	Absolute Number[2]	Absolute Number[2]	
1934	57,000	154,584	271
1935	70,000	155,000	221

[1] Gens, Title 80.
[2] *Izvestiya*, July 12, 1936.

about 20 percent in 1924 to about 30 percent in 1925, and swung rapidly upward thereafter to the ratio of 270 abortions per 100 live births in 1934. In 1924-1925, statistics for twenty provinces in the European part of the U.S.S.R. showed an average ratio of 13 abortions per 100 live births. By 1934, the number of abortions was as large as the number of births in many areas. Resort to abortion clinics was extensive in the cities of Central Asia as well as in the Russian Federation (R.S.F.S.R.) and the Ukraine.[35]

By 1934, educational and social measures were advanced to counteract the trend toward abortion and reduced natality. Measures for the protection of mothers and children were strengthened. Regulations issued in 1935 forbade abortions in the case of first pregnancies and prescribed only curettage without anesthetic, within three months after pregnancy, with a minimum of at least six months between operations. Much attention was given in Soviet medical literature to the technique of "painless birth." That these measures were not without some effect is indicated by the increased number of births in Moscow from 1934 to 1935 (see Table 49). Moreover, increases in number of births at this time were reported from many districts.[36]

Far more drastic action was taken in 1936. The Central Executive Committee and the Council of People's Commissars of the U.S.S.R. on June 27, 1936, issued a comprehensive decree on matters relating to natality and family relations.[37] The main provisions of this code were as follows:

1. Abortion was prohibited, except operations performed in hospitals or maternity homes on specific medical or eugenic grounds. These grounds were defined by the Commissariat of Public Health, as follows:[38]

(1) Serious chronic diseases of the heart and blood vessels (described in detail)

(2) Chronic inflammatory and sclerotic processes of the kidneys

(3) Nephrolithiasis on both sides (based on X-ray evidence)

(4) Pulmonary tuberculosis (specific conditions)

(5) Tuberculosis of the urinary tract, etc.

(6) Chronic diseases of the liver with manifest functional disturbances

(7) Graves' disease, with certain complicating symptoms

(8) Pernicious anemia

(9) Leukemias

(10) Malignant tumors

(11) Epilepsy, diagnosed in a medical institution

(12) Retinitis or neuritis of the optic nerve caused by pregnancy or by disease of the peripheral vascular system

(13) Serious diseases of the cornea as a result of physical exhaustion (and specified related conditions)

(14) Pelvic conditions making natural birth impossible

(15) Presence in the prospective mother, father, or one of their children of one of the following hereditary diseases: haemophilia, idiocy, genuine epilepsy, severe schizophrenia or manic-depressive psychosis (with hospital history), hereditary eye disease causing blindness, hereditary deaf-mutism, hereditary progressive diseases of the nervous system (progressive muscular atrophy, hereditary ataxia)

A doctor performing an illegal abortion was liable to imprisonment of one to two years, with longer sentence for a medically unqualified practitioner. A pregnant woman undergoing an

[35] Gens, Title 80. [36] Akusherstvo i Ginekologiya, Title 485, 1936, pp. 120 ff.
[37] Moscow Daily News, June 28, 1936. Quoted by Sigerist, Title 297, pp. 344-353.
[38] This statement is summarized from Sigerist, Title 297, pp. 353-354.

illegal abortion was liable to social reprimand, and subject to fine up to 300 rubles in case of repeated offense.

2. The social insurance allocation to employed mothers for equipment for infants was increased from 32 to 45 rubles. The monthly allowance to nursing mothers was raised from 5 to 10 rubles per month, and provisions were made for extending this allowance to women in cooperative enterprises not previously included.

3. Maternity leave was extended to women in clerical occupations, comparable to that previously provided for women workers (56 days before and 56 days after confinement), with provisions for the protection of pregnant women as regards employment.

4. Annual allowances for five years were provided for mothers of large families, payable as follows: 2,000 rubles each year for the sixth and each subsequent child through the tenth; an initial payment of 5,000 rubles at the birth of an eleventh and each subsequent child, with 3,000 rubles payable on each birthday for four years. The allowances thus provided were made applicable to families already qualified to receive these benefits at the time of the publication of the law.

5. Plans were announced to extend greatly the network of maternity homes—through the provision of 11,000 new maternity beds before 1939 in cities and in industrial and district centers, in addition to the 4,200 beds provided in the previous plan of the same year, and the provision of 32,000 maternity beds in rural localities. Half of the latter were to be established in village hospitals, half in collective-farm maternity homes. Provision was also made for the opening of 14,400 new obstetrical stations with trained personnel to attend women for whom maternity hospital service was not available.

6. Provisions were made for doubling, within the next two and one-half years, the number of nursery beds in both urban and rural places, through the addition of 400,000 new beds in urban nurseries and 4,000,000 new beds in collective-farm nurseries. It was provided that the nursery homes in industrial communities (using two shifts of attendants) should be open sixteen hours each day, including rest days. Plans were also announced for opening 800 new dairy kitchens in cities, equipped to feed one and one-half million children under three years of age.

7. It was also proposed to triple the permanent kindergarten facilities in cities, and similarly to increase the number of permanent kindergartens and seasonal playgrounds attached to the collective farms, including provisions for training 50,000 kindergarten teachers.

8. In the related administrative and financial provisions, the allocations from state and local budgets and social insurance funds for child welfare and maternal services were increased from 875 million rubles in the 1935 budget to 2,174 million rubles in the 1936 budget. An additional 70 million rubles were assigned to allowances to mothers, exclusive of allowances to large families.

9. Finally, the laws relating to marriage and the family were revised by way of "combating light-minded attitudes toward family and family obligations." The personal attendance of both parties was made mandatory in divorce proceedings, and the fact of the divorce was henceforth entered on the passports of the divorcees. The registration fee was raised to 50 rubles for the first divorce, 150 rubles for the second, and 300 rubles for the third and subsequent divorces. The alimony payable by the father of one child was fixed at one-fourth of his wages; by the father of two children, at one-third; by the father of three or more children, at one-half. Strict provisions were made to insure the payment of alimony.

The effect of these provisions in reducing the frequency of abortion, increasing natality, and discouraging the dissolution of families was dramatic. In Moscow, 30,877 abortions were performed in the third quarter of 1935, but only 2,306 in the third quarter of 1936.[39] The birth rate in Moscow, which had risen gradually from 1934 to 1936, suddenly reached a peak in 1937. The estimated birth rates in Moscow are as follows:[40]

Year	Births per 1,000 Population
1934	14.7
1935	17.3
1936	19.9
1937	35.4
1938	28.5

In the whole U.S.S.R., the number of abortions performed on medical certification decreased by 97 percent from the first half of 1936 to the second half of 1937, and the number of uncertified abortions (outside of hospitals) was also reduced. The decrease in abortion was said to have been most spectacular in Central Asia, and somewhat less so in the Ukraine and Georgia.[41] Conversely, the average number of patients per year per hospital maternity bed in the U.S.S.R. rose from 24.1 in 1935 to 30.8 in 1937, although the number of attended deliveries at home also rose—from 469,000 in 1935 to 544,000 in 1937. However, hospital deliveries and professionally attended deliveries at home apparently accounted for less than half of all births in the U.S.S.R. in 1937·(16.8 such deliveries per 1,000 total population[42] as compared with 39.6 births per 1,000 total population[43]).

There has been little discussion of contraception in Soviet medical literature since 1936. So far as the writer can learn, there has been no public effort in recent years to extend the use of contraception, but contraceptive facilities are generally available, at least in cities, and there is certainly no legal obstacle to their dissemination. Levi, writing in a Soviet medical journal in 1937, described a tendency in some medical circles, following the 1936 anti-abortion decree, to combat contraception, but he asserted that such conduct was due to a misunderstanding of the official position on this subject and should be corrected.[44] As an official of the Commissariat of Health, he directed that in the case of women in poor health positive encouragement and help should be extended in the use of contraceptives.

Reports concerning the change in natality between successive years and the birth rate reported for 1938 make it possible to reconstruct the series from 1935 to 1938, as follows (see Table 53 presented in a later section of this chapter):

Year	Births per 1,000 Population
1938	38.3
1937	39.6
1936	33.6
1935	30.1

If we assume that the birth rate in 1934 for the U.S.S.R. was about the same as in 1935, and that the decline in the birth rate from 1928 to 1934 proceeded in equal steps each year, we obtain the hypothetical series shown in Figure 21.

7. Estimates of Natural Increase and Net Reproduction, 1926 and 1938

Combining our hypothetical birth and death rates for the U.S.S.R. in 1926-1927 (birth rate,

---

[39] *Akusherstvo i Ginekologiya*, Title 485, 1939, pp. 126-127.

[40] Prokopovich, Title 261, p. 118. Data from *Pravda*; February 20, 1936; January 6, 1938; June 28, 1938; June 2, 1939.

[41] *Akusherstvo i Ginekologiya*, Title 485, 1936, pp. 120 ff.

[42] *Ibid.*   [43] Table 53.   [44] Levi, Title 170.

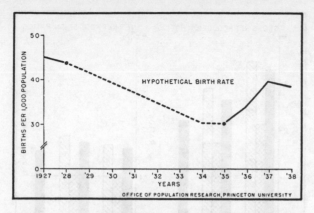

Figure 21. Hypothetical Birth Rates: U.S.S.R., 1927-1938
[Table 53]

45.7; death rate, about 26.0) gives an estimated rate of natural increase at this time of about 20 per thousand per year—somewhat less than that indicated by the official statistics for the European part of the U.S.S.R. (23 per thousand per year). The official information for the year 1938, which we assume to be substantially correct (birth rate, 38.3; death rate, 17.8), indicates approximately the same rate of natural increase at that time (20.5 per thousand per year).

Estimated gross and net ratios around the time of the 1897, 1926, and 1939 censuses are shown in Table 50 and Figure 22. The ratios are by no means exact, but they give a rough

TABLE 50

Estimated Gross and Net Reproduction Ratios: European Part
of the U.S.S.R., 1897; U.S.S.R., 1926 and 1938[1]

Date	Total		Urban		Rural	
	G.R.R.	N.R.R.	G.R.R.	N.R.R.	G.R.R.	N.R.R.
1897[2]	3.29	1.60	2.13	1.05	3.46	1.68
1926[3]	2.64	1.72	1.71	1.19	2.87	1.85
1938	2.19	1.54	—	—	—	—

[1] For description of procedures, see Appendix VI. Dates refer to census.
[2] Fertility: European part of U.S.S.R., about 1894.
  Mortality: European part of U.S.S.R., 1896-1897.
[3] Fertility: U.S.S.R., about 1924.
  Mortality: European part of U.S.S.R., 1926-1927.

indication of the situation at these dates with some important reservations. The apparent decrease in gross fertility from 1897 to 1926 may be in part fictitious, in so far as the official mortality rates (used here without adjustment) for the European part of the U.S.S.R., 1926-1927, inadequately represent the force of mortality at that time in the total U.S.S.R., and in view of the possibility that infant deaths may have been less completely reported in the early Soviet period than in the late Imperial period. Similarly, the apparent increase in the net reproduction ratio from 1.60 (European area of the later U.S.S.R., about 1897) to 1.72 (total U.S.S.R., about 1926) may also be, in part, fictitious and the apparent decrease to 1.54 in 1938 may be exaggerated.

[131]

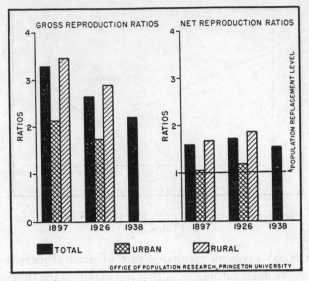

Figure 22. Estimated Gross and Net Reproduction Ratios:
European Part of the U.S.S.R., 1897; U.S.S.R., 1926 and
1938 [Table 50]

In obtaining the gross reproduction ratios for 1938, we used separate maternal frequencies for urban and rural areas. The corresponding maternity schedule for the total population is shown in Table 51. These specific fertility rates have only approximate accuracy. Some may be

TABLE 51

Hypothetical Specific Fertility Rates: U.S.S.R., 1938[1]

Age of Mother	Births per 1,000 Women
15-19	33.4
20-24	225.3
25-29	231.8
30-34	186.3
35-39	140.0
40-44	67.5
45-49	18.6

[1] The procedure used here is analogous to that used in getting estimated mortality rates by age and sex at about this time. We have assumed that the *proportional* distribution of births by age of mother in the urban and rural parts of the U.S.S.R., considered separately, was the same as that observed in the urban and rural parts of the Ukraine, respectively, in 1926 (for which figures were available). We then weighted these proportional distributions by urban and rural populations of the U.S.S.R. in 1939, and adjusted the schedule thus obtained by equal proportions to give the required total number of births, when applied to the estimated distribution of the population by age and sex in 1938, assuming 38.3 births per 1,000 population in 1938.

too high and others may be too low, but in net effect they account for the reported crude birth rate in 1938.

Additional information is available on the *relative* frequencies of births in hospitals by age of mother in urban and rural areas in 1928 and in 1934. It is, however, impossible to derive maternal frequencies directly from these data because they relate only to hospital deliveries and because we lack information both about the age distribution of the populations concerned and about the absolute level of natality in any of these populations (see Table 52).

TABLE 52

Relative Frequency of Deliveries in Maternity Hospitals, by Age of Mother: R.S.F.S.R., Ukrainian S.S.R., and Belorussian S.S.R., 1928 and 1934[1]

| | 1928 | | 1934 | |
Age of Mother	Urban	Rural	Urban	Rural
Total	1,000	1,000	1,000	1,000
Under 20	69	48	48	38
20-24	352	298	404	305
25-29	301	279	306	288
30-34	155	174	152	188
35-39	89	130	68	120
40-44	29	57	18	46
45 and Over	5	14	4	15

[1] From Kraval', Editor, Title 476. The data given above were copied from the First Edition.

8. Analysis of Population Change, 1926-1939

In order to analyze the trend of the Soviet population from 1926 to 1939, we shall, in the first experiment, ignore possible fluctuations in mortality during the intercensus period, assuming a straight-line relation between the (estimated) general death rate for the U.S.S.R. in 1926-1927 and that in 1938. However, we shall take account of apparent fluctuations in natality, assuming a steady decline to 1934, and a constant rate in 1934-1935 at the 1935 level. On this basis we obtain the hypothetical series shown in Table 53 and Figure 23. The rates of natural increase for successive years, obtained in this way, are used to carry forward the population from 1926 to January 1, 1934, and to carry backward the population from 1939 to the same date. If there had been no great fluctuations in death rates during the interval and if our adjustments for under-registration of deaths and so forth are correct, the forward and the backward projections to January 1, 1934, should meet at the same point.

Actually, there is a discrepancy of about 5.5 million.[45] One possible interpretation of this discrepancy is that it represents the magnitude of "excess mortality" beyond that normally expected during the period of the collectivization of agriculture, the settlement of the nomads, and the initial phases of the drive for the use of undeveloped resources and for rapid industrialization. The only alternative interpretations are: (1) that mortality in the Soviet Union was higher than our estimate for 1926-1927 (which in turn is higher than that indicated by the official statistics), or higher than our figure for 1938 (derived directly from official information), or both; or (2) that the decrease in births during the late 'twenties and early 'thirties was even more spectacular than the available information indicates. The last of these alternatives would seem to be the least likely (see Figure 23).

In view of our ignorance of the exact nature of the discrepancy (5,522,000 persons) between the increase indicated by the hypothetical series of births and deaths shown in Table 53

[45] It will be noted that the estimated deficit for the total population indicated by these projections happens to be almost identical with the estimated deficit in the population *over 12 years of age* indicated by comparison of the projection by Novosel'skiy and Payevskiy with the observed population in 1939 (see Table 44).

TABLE 53

Hypothetical Trend of the Soviet Population and Vital Statistics, 1927-1934 and 1934-1939[1]

Year	Population January 1 (In thousands)	Births per 1,000 Population	Deaths per 1,000 Population	Births (In thousands)	Deaths (In thousands)
1927	147,135[2]	45.0[3]	26.0[3]	[6,731]	[3,862]
1928	[150,004]	43.7[4]	24.2[5]	[6,620]	[3,666]
1929	[152,958]	(41.4)	25.1[5]	[6,384]	[3,871]
1930	[155,471]	(39.2)	(24.3)	[6,140]	[3,806]
1931	[157,805]	(36.9)	(23.5)	[5,862]	[3,733]
1932	[159,934]	(34.6)	(22.7)	[5,567]	[3,652]
1933	[161,849]	(32.4)	(21.8)	[5,272]	[3,547]
1934	[163,574]				
Discrepancy	—5,522				
1934	[158,052]	[30.1]	(21.0)	[4,779]	[3,334]
1935	[159,497]	[30.1]	(20.2)	4,829[6]	[3,238]
1936	[161,088]	[33.6]	(19.4)	5,447[7]	[3,147]
1937	[163,388]	[39.6]	(18.6)	6,542[8]	[3,071]
1938	[166,859]	38.3[9]	17.8[10]	[6,457]	[3,001]
1939	170,315[2]				

1927-1939

Actual Increase	23,180
Expected Births	70,630
Expected Deaths	41,928
Births — Deaths	28,702
Discrepancy	—5,522

[1] Population figures obtained by working forward from 1927 to 1934, and by working backward from 1938 to 1934. Interpolated figures in parentheses. Figures in brackets are derived from other figures in this table. There are minor discrepancies in this table that do not affect the essentials of the argument. For example, the number of births for 1927 is compatible with a birth rate of 45.3 instead of the assumed rate of 45.0.

[2] Population, January 1, 1927, from census of December 17, 1926, plus estimated increase (15 days). Population, January 1, 1939, from census of January 17, 1939, minus estimated increase (16 days).

[3] Estimated rates for total U.S.S.R.

[4] Applying relative change in birth rates 1928/1927 in European U.S.S.R., except Dagestan (see Kuczynski, Title 154, p. 112), to previous estimated rate for U.S.S.R.

[5] Applying relative change in death rates 1928/1927 and 1929/1928 in Ukraine (Kuczynski, Title 154, p. 18) to previous estimated rate for U.S.S.R. Note: Partial data indicate improvement in mortality in other parts of European U.S.S.R., 1927-1928.

[6] Natality 1938/1935: 1.337. *Izvestiya*, June 27, 1939. Birth rate 1934 assumed to be same as in 1935.

[7] Natality 1936/1935: 1.128. Sautin, *Pravda*, June 27, 1939.

[8] Natality 1937/1936: 1.197. Sautin, *Ibid.* Corresponding ratios for 1937/1936, cited in *Pravda*, March 2, 1938, are: births 1.18, deaths .974.

[9] Sautin, *Ibid.*

[10] Ratio births/deaths in 1938: 2.157. Buzin and Dubrovitskiy, Title 43, p. 14.

and the actual increase observed in the census, it is impossible to make a reliable estimate of the movement of population in the U.S.S.R., 1927-1939. If we assume that the discrepancy represents "excess deaths" associated with the tempo of industrial expansion, the collectivization of agriculture, and the settlement of nomads, and if we arbitrarily assign one-third of this excess to the critical year 1932 with the remainder distributed over the adjacent years in either

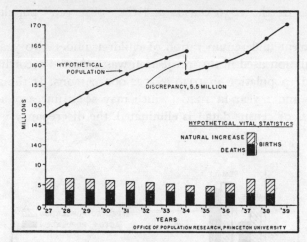

Figure 23. Hypothetical Trend of the Soviet Population
and Vital Statistics, 1927-1934 and 1934-1939 [Table 53]

direction in a straight-line relation, assuming no excess deaths in 1927 and 1937, the series shown in Table 54 results. This is a highly arbitrary series, but it may represent as close an approximation to the actual change as can be obtained in the absence of more explicit information.

A somewhat similar result is obtained by "aging" the population as reported in the 1926 census to give the "expected" population aged 12 or over in 1939—similar to the procedure followed by Novosel'skiy and Payevskiy, but using the life tables as adjusted by Coale. These tables relate to the European part of the U.S.S.R. in 1926-1927. If there had been a gradual decline in mortality between 1926 and 1939, they should be fairly appropriate to the whole U.S.S.R. during the intercensus period. The results are shown graphically in Figure 24, based on data in Table A 19, Appendix VI. The discrepancy between the "expected" population aged

TABLE 54

Hypothetical Population: U.S.S.R., January 1 of
Each Year, 1927-1934

Year	Population (In thousands)
1927	147,135
1928	150,004
1929	152,774
1930	154,919
1931	156,701
1932	158,094
1933	158,168
1934	159,156
1935	160,049
1936	161,272
1937	163,388
1938	166,859
1939	170,315

12 or over at the time of the 1939 census and the "observed" population at these ages is 4,844,000 persons.[46]

In view of the apparent underenumeration of children under two years of age in the 1926 census, the initial population used in this projection was adjusted accordingly. This adjustment increases the "expected" population in 1939 by 522,000 persons. If the adjustment for under-enumeration at ages 0 and 1 year in 1926 (which may seem unreasonable to persons not familiar with the vagaries of census data) is eliminated, the discrepancy is reduced to 4,322,000

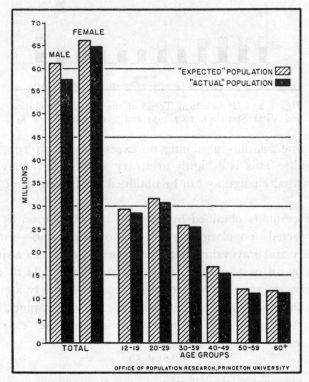

Figure 24. Population of the U.S.S.R. Aged 12 Years and Over, 1939: (A) "Expected"; (B) "Actual" [Table A 19]

persons. Since we must suppose that if there was excess mortality during the intercensus period in the population already living in 1926, there was also some excess mortality among infants born during these years, either of these figures (4.8 million or 4.3 million) might be supposed to fit reasonably well with the discrepancy (5.5 million) indicated by the interpolation of birth and death rates.

All of these procedures are subject to error, and the discrepancy here indicated therefore has a large margin of error. Our information does, however, indicate the loss of some 5 million lives during the intercensus period above the number of deaths that would normally have been expected. On the basis of the interpolated death rates, the "expected" number of deaths from December 17, 1926, to January 17, 1939, was about 42 million (see Table 53). The actual number of deaths, therefore, appears to have been about 12 percent above the number expected. The relative variance is greater if we compare the apparent discrepancy between "expected" and "observed" populations aged 12 and over in 1939. In this case the expected number of deaths (20.4 million) during the interval to persons living in 1926 would have to be increased

[46] For description of procedure, see Section 10 of this chapter, and Appendix VI.

by 23.7 percent to bring the "expected" population down to the "observed" number of persons aged 12 and over in 1939.[47] Nevertheless, it is possible that the apparent "excess" in deaths during the interval should be explained as due in part, if not wholly, to higher "normal" death rates at the beginning or end of the period, or both, than we have assumed. In the end we are faced with the conclusion that mortality in the Soviet Union has generally been much higher than the available data seem to indicate, or that there was some depletion of the population during the intercensus period owing to special conditions at that time.

9. Changes in Ethnic Affiliation

Evidence about the relative increase of different ethnic groups between 1926 and 1939 is ambiguous. A preliminary report on population by "nationality," according to the 1939 census, has been published, but since it is based on incomplete returns, no data are presented for Buryats, Yakuts, and other ethnic groups located principally in northern Asiatic regions. Otherwise, figures are apparently given for each nationality with 20,000 persons or more. However, the definition of "nationality" (*natsionalnost*) in the 1939 census differs radically from the earlier classification by "nationality" (*narodnost*—officially translated as "group ethnique") in the 1926 census reports. The question of "nationality" in 1939 was given a purely psychological-cultural definition, indicating the group with which each individual or parent felt that he and his children were most closely identified.[48] Furthermore, since the data are incomplete and no distribution by administrative divisions or by language is yet available, the classes reported for 1939 (which are obviously in many cases less precise and more inclusive than the ethnic groups described in the 1926 census) cannot always be related exactly to corresponding classes as reported in 1926. An attempted comparison on the basis of the available data supplies some interesting information, but the comparison undoubtedly contains some inaccuracies and must be used with caution.

From Table 55 it is apparent that there has been a cultural-psychological trend toward the association of individuals in larger ethnic groups, and toward the substitution of identification with political units in place of identification with traditional ethnic groups. The number reported as Jews increased, but the proportional increase of this group is slightly below that of the general population, presumably because of the lower rate of natural increase characteristic of Jews.[49] There were also small increases, at less than average rates, in the numbers reported as Greek and as Finn. There was little apparent change in the number of Koreans in the U.S.S.R. between 1926 and 1939, if the number of aliens is added to the 1926 base, possibly owing to some net emigration of Koreans during this period. All other groups *not identified with an autonomous republic or district* in the U.S.S.R. (i.e., Pole, Estonian, Latvian and Latgal, Bulgarian, Kurd, Iranian, Lithuanian, Chinese—if non-citizens are included in the 1926 base, Czecho-Slovak, and Arab) show absolute decreases in number between 1926 and 1939. In some cases such decreases may be associated with net emigration; in most cases, however, the decline is probably not demographic at all, but simply indicates the cultural identification of such persons with one of the major Soviet nationalities.

The number of persons reporting themselves as Russians in 1939 was 27 percent higher than the number classified as "Russians" in 1926, in contrast to an increase of slightly less than 16 percent for the total population. Higher than average increase is also indicated for Tatars— even using as the 1926 base the sum of various ethnic groups which are commonly referred to as "Tatars" and which do not appear elsewhere in the 1939 list. In both cases these relative

---

[47] See Appendix VI, Table A 18 and Table A 19. [48] Somerville, Title 304.
[49] See Chapter VII.

TABLE 55

U.S.S.R.: Population by Nationality, 1939, Compared with Population by Ethnic Group, 1926

Designation in 1939	Number, 1926, in Possible Corresponding Group	Number 1939	Ratio of 1939 to 1926 (B)÷(A)	Notes on Composition of Possible Corresponding Group in 1926
	(A)	(B)	(C)	(D)
Total	147,027,915	170,467,186	1.159	
Total, Tabulated	147,027,915	169,519,127	1.153	
Citizens, U.S.S.R.	146,637,530	——	——	
Russian	77,791,124	99,019,929	1.273	
Ukrainian	31,194,976	28,070,404	0.900	
Belorussian	4,738,923	5,267,431	1.112	
Uzbek	3,954,701	4,844,021	1.225	Including 50,079 Kurama
Tatar	3,477,507	4,300,336	1.237	Tatar, 2,916,536; Mishar, 242,640; Kryashen, 101,447; Nogay, 36,274; Nogaybak, 11,219; Siberian Tatar: Shor, Kurmandzh, etc., 27,319; Central Asia: Kypchak, 33,502; Kashgar, 13,010; Taranchi, 53,010; Uygur, 42,550
Kazakh	3,968,289	3,098,764	0.781	
Jew	2,672,499	3,020,141	1.130	Including ancient Jewish settlements but not Karaim
Azer	1,706,605	2,274,805	1.333	
Georgian	1,821,184	2,248,566	1.235	
Armenian	1,567,568	2,151,884	1.373	
Mordvian	1,340,415	1,451,429	1.083	
German	1,246,540	1,423,534	1.142	Including 7,991 aliens
Chuvash	1,117,419	1,367,930	1.224	
Tadzhik	980,509	1,228,964	1.253	Including 1,829 Yagnobts
Kirgiz	762,736	884,306	1.159	
Peoples of Dagestan	669,186	857,371	1.281	Dagestan Mountain groups, except Jews (census lists: 119-146, 151, 190a), plus Kumyk (94,549)
Bashkir	741,080	842,925	1.137	Including 27,387 Teptyar
Turkmen	763,940	811,769	1.063	
Pole	792,471	626,905	0.791	Including 10,137 aliens
Udmurt	504,187	605,673	1.201	Votyak
Mari	428,192	481,262	1.124	
Komi	375,871	408,724	1.087	Zyryan, Permyak
Chechen	318,522	407,690	1.280	
Osetin	272,272	354,547	1.302	
Greek	259,740	285,896	1.101	Including 45,975 aliens
Moldavian	278,905	260,023	0.932	Not including 4,651 Rumanians and 2,241 aliens from Rumania

TABLE 55 (*Continued*)

U.S.S.R.: Population by Nationality, 1939, Compared with Population by Ethnic Group, 1926

Designation in 1939	Number, 1926, in Possible Corresponding Group	Number 1939	Ratio of 1939 to 1926 (B)÷(A)	Notes on Composition of Possible Corresponding Group in 1926
	(A)	(B)	(C)	(D)
Karel	248,120	252,559	1.018	
Kara-Kalpak	146,317	185,775	1.270	
Korean	172,000	180,412	1.049	Including 85,000 subjects of Japanese Empire
Kabardian	139,925	164,106	1.173	
Finn	138,791	143,074	1.031	Finn (Suomi), Leningrad Finns, including 4,090 aliens
Estonian	155,963	142,465	0.913	Including 1,297 aliens
Kalmyk	129,321	134,327	1.039	
Latvian and Latgal	154,239	126,900	0.823	Including 2,829 aliens
Bulgarian	114,011	113,479	0.995	Including 2,715 aliens
Ingush	74,097	92,074	1.243	
Adygey	65,270	87,973	1.348	Cherkess
Karachay	55,123	75,737	1.374	
Abkhazian	56,957	58,969	1.035	
Khakas	45,608	52,602	1.153	
Oyrot	39,062	47,717	1.222	Altay
Kurd	54,661	45,866	0.839	
Balkar	33,307	42,666	1.281	
Iranian	43,971	39,037	0.888	"Persians," but *not* including 92,299 aliens, subjects of "Persia," or 9,188 "Irani"
Lithuanian	42,709	32,342	0.757	Including 1,246 aliens
Chinese	92,030	29,620	0.322	Including 10,247 citizens; 81,783 aliens
Czech, Slovak	30,671	26,919	0.878	Including 3,548 aliens
Arab	28,978	21,793	0.752	
All Other	1,221,423	1,775,545		
Including:				
Other Nationalities		827,486[1]		
Late Returns, Not Tabulated		948,059[2]		

[1] Including 20,207 Assyrians. All others reported as specific groups in the 1939 preliminary figures are shown separately in this table.

[2] Total tabulated returns amount to 99.44 percent of total population.

increases probably point to the cultural assimilation of kindred ethnic groups. Conversely, the decrease in the number of persons reported as Ukrainian was probably due, in the main, to increasing identification with the Russians, especially in the case of Ukrainians living in the R.S.F.S.R. In like manner, some persons formerly reported as Karelians may have described themselves in 1939 as Russians or as Finns.

On the other hand, the relatively rapid growth of distinctive ethnic groups characterized by high child-woman ratios in 1926 undoubtedly reflects rapid natural increase. This is the case with respect to most groups in the vicinity of the Caucasus Mountains, namely, the Armenian, Azer, Georgian, Osetin, Chechen, Ingush, Adygey, Karachay, Balkarian, Kabardian, and peoples of Dagestan. The same may be said of the Oyrots of southeast Siberia and some groups in the Volga region (Chuvash and Udmurt, as well as Tatar). The increase of several Central Asiatic nationalities (Uzbek, Tadzhik, Kara-Kalpak, and Kirgiz) may also be attributed, in large part at least, to high natural increase.

One of the most striking declines is that of the Kazakhs of the Asiatic steppe region. This is an ethnically distinct group, associated with a constituent republic and not easily assimilated by other nationalities, though a few Kazakhs may have reported themselves in 1939 as Tatars, Uzbeks, Kirgiz, Turkmen, or Russians. There was an absolute decrease of about 869,000 persons in the number reported as Kazakhs between 1926 and 1939, whereas at the average rate of increase of the whole Soviet population (15.9 percent) we would have expected an absolute increase of 631,000 persons. The sum of these figures gives a deficit of exactly 1.5 million below the expected number in 1939. We must also take into account the fact that there was a terrific depletion of livestock in this region, more serious than in any other part of the Soviet Union, between 1928 and 1934, with a loss of 73 percent of the cattle, 87 percent of the sheep and goats, and 88 percent of the horses.[50] This occurred during the period of collectivization and the settlement of nomads, which were vigorously opposed by tribal chiefs and many of their followers. It is impossible to escape the conclusion that there must have been heavy losses in this region due to excess deaths. There may have been a considerable exodus of Kazakhs into other parts of the Soviet Union, especially into Central Asia, and small movements across the closed borders of the U.S.S.R. into Sinkiang or Iran.[51] It is also possible that the apparently stationary status of the Kalmyk reflects difficulties associated with the policy of converting nomad bands into collective farmers.

In some cases, as noted, a difference in the relative numbers of persons reported in ethnic groups in 1926 and in 1939 presumably indicates actual population change. In most cases, however, the data should be interpreted in cultural terms. They point to the increasing importance of the major nationality, the Russian. They also indicate, in more general terms, a trend toward the cultural amalgamation of diverse groups into the major nationalities associated with the recognized political divisions of the U.S.S.R.

10. Changes in the Age and Sex Composition of the Population

To date, the published information from the 1939 census gives a distribution of the population by sex *without age*, and by broad age classes *without sex*. These distributions are shown in Table 56, Column 1.

By the simple procedure of assuming that the proportion of each sex in the population under

[50] *Sel'skoye Khozyaystvo SSSR. Yezhegodnik 1935*, Title 451, pp. 514-519.

[51] Movement of Kazakhs into Iran was presumably negligible, but migration across the mountains into Sinkiang may have been fairly large. In earlier times there were frequent movements back and forth between "Russian Turkestan" and "Chinese Turkestan." Eleanor Lattimore gives the total number of Kazakhs in Sinkiang, about 1940, as 247,000—including original inhabitants, those who fled to escape conscription in 1916, and those who fled to escape collectivization during the Soviet regime. (See E. Lattimore, "Behind the Sinkiang Incident," *Far Eastern Survey*, Vol. 13, No. 9, pp. 78-81, May 3, 1944.) It has been stated that "many ten-thousands" moved from the Soviet Union into Sinkiang each year over several successive years. (See Hans Übersberger, Editor, *Kazak, Fuad. Ostturkistan zwischen den Grossmächten. Ein Beitrag zur Wirtschafts-Kunde Ostturkistans*. Osteuropäische Forschungen. New Series, Vol. 23. 160 pp.) This writer states that Chinese settlers in Sinkiang were unwelcome, but that settlers from Soviet territory were welcomed, particularly those who came with their herds. (*Ibid.*, p. 10.) A few of the Kazakhs who passed the Soviet borders apparently trekked still farther and settled in India. Part of the depletion both of population and of livestock in Kazakhstan may therefore have been due to such movements.

15 years of age in 1939 was approximately the same as in 1926, we can obtain comparable distributions under and over 15 years by sex for 1926 and 1939. The distribution for 1939 shown in Table 57 is based on the fact that according to the 1926 census males formed 50.35 percent

TABLE 56

Distribution of Population by Broad Age Class and by Sex: U.S.S.R., January 17, 1939

Age Class	Distribution as Reported[1]	Adjusted to Equal Total Population	Age Unknown Distributed in Proportion to Total Population Aged 15 and Over	Adjusted Distribution (2)+(3)
	(1)	(2)	(3)	(4)
Total	169,519,127	170,467,186		170,467,186
0-7	31,412,232	31,587,909		31,587,909
8-11	16,409,098	16,500,868		16,500,868
12-14	13,336,151	13,410,736		13,410,736
15-19	15,124,176	15,208,760	4,615	15,213,375
20-29	30,639,041	30,810,394	9,349	30,819,743
30-39	25,332,993	25,474,671	7,731	25,482,402
40-49	15,235,864	15,321,073	4,649	15,325,722
50-59	10,867,408	10,928,186	3,316	10,931,502
60 and Over	11,129,290	11,191,532	3,397	11,194,929
Age Unknown	32,874	33,057		
Total	170,467,186			
Males	81,664,981			81,664,981
Females	88,802,205			88,802,205

[1] Based on tabulation of age distribution of persons covered by reports on 99.44 percent of complete population. The population not covered (0.56 percent) is here distributed in proportion to the distribution of the covered population. This may involve an error (see Appendix VI) but information on which to base any other adjustment is lacking.

of the actual population under 15 years of age.[52] The proportion of the total population in the juvenile group under 15 years of age was somewhat smaller in 1939 than in 1926. This is not surprising. But it is surprising to find that the percentage of men in the population aged 15 years and over was apparently *lower* in 1939 than in 1926. One would have expected that the maturing of boys and girls, in about equal numbers, during the years 1926-1939 would have tended to make the numbers of men and women more nearly equal in 1939. This comparison suggests, therefore, that during the difficult years of forced collectivization in agriculture and forced industrial expansion the male population was subject to special hazards and suffered particularly heavy losses.

Using more refined procedures, we can distribute the population aged 0-7 and 8-11 years, as reported in the 1939 census, into more detailed age and sex groups on the basis of our hypothetical data on births and life-table values. We can then use the projected population of the U.S.S.R., obtained by "aging" the population as reported in the 1926 census, to distribute the

[52] The proportion of males in the life-table population under 15 years (European part of U.S.S.R., 1926-1927), with male and female life-table populations weighted by sex ratio at birth according to the vital statistics for 1926 (1.063 males per 1 female), is similar, namely, 50.43 percent. Likewise, the proportion of males in the expected population under 12 years of age, 1939, according to Novosel'skiy and Payevskiy is 50.40 percent (see Table 44).

TABLE 57

Distribution of Population Under and Over 15 Years of Age, by Sex:
U.S.S.R., 1926 and 1939 (Estimated)

Sex	Age					
	1926			1939		
	Under 15 Years	Over 15 Years	Percent Under 15 Years	Under 15 Years	Over 15 Years	Percent Under 15 Years
Total	54,682,717	92,345,198	37.2	61,499,513	108,967,673	36.1
Males	27,530,718	43,512,634[1]	38.8	30,962,729[2]	50,702,252[1]	37.9
Females	27,151,999	48,832,564[1]	35.7	30,536,784[2]	58,265,421[1]	34.4
Percent Males in Total Population	50.3463	47.12	—	50.3463[2]	46.53	—

[1] Persons of unknown age included in populations aged 15 years and over.
[2] Population under 15 years of age distributed by sex according to proportions in 1926. A slightly different estimated distribution by age and sex, 1939, is obtained in Table 58 by more refined procedures described in Appendix VI.

total number in each broad age class into smaller groups by five-year age classes and by sex. The hypothetical values and the projected population are used only to distribute the population by age and sex *within* broad age classes, as reported by the census (with the minor adjustments shown in Table 56). The only exception is made in the case of the age classes 12-14 and 15-19 years. The total of these two classes is kept as reported, but the distribution within this total is adjusted. The procedure is described in detail in Appendix VI. In the absence of complete census data, the results thus obtained are presumed to give a reasonably satisfactory, though merely approximate, distribution of the population of the U.S.S.R., 1939, by five-year age classes and by sex. (See Table 58.)

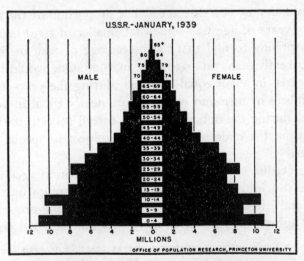

Figure 25. Estimated Distribution of Population, by Age
and Sex: U.S.S.R., January 17, 1939 [Table 58]

The estimated distribution of the Soviet population, shown in Figure 25, has certain peculiarities that reflect the disturbed conditions of the preceding decades. The deficiency of men, relative to women, caused by World War I and conditions during the revolutionary period, was apparently aggravated during the interwar period. The Soviet population, therefore, entered World War II with an adult male population, which, though very large, had been appreciably depleted by previous calamities, hardships, and hazards. During World War II this situation placed on the women of the Soviet Union a special strain and responsibility which they have met in heroic fashion.

TABLE 58

Estimated Distribution of Population, by Age and Sex:
U.S.S.R., January 17, 1939[1]

Age	Male	Female	Total
Total	81,664,981	88,802,205	170,467,186
Under 1	2,693,498	2,605,311	5,298,809
1	2,553,215	2,492,989	5,046,204
2	2,210,019	2,165,876	4,375,895
3	1,931,436	1,894,051	3,825,487
4	1,639,318	1,621,060	3,260,378
0-4	11,027,486	10,779,287	21,806,773
5-9	8,737,364	8,763,726	17,501,090
10-14	10,454,656	10,521,232	20,975,888
15-19	8,109,611	8,319,526	16,429,137
20-24	7,163,791	7,207,163	14,370,954
25-29	7,936,949	8,511,840	16,448,789
30-34	6,540,583	7,193,950	13,734,533
35-39	5,329,803	6,418,066	11,747,869
40-44	3,747,754	4,771,555	8,519,309
45-49	2,985,545	3,820,868	6,806,413
50-54	2,690,476	3,286,951	5,977,427
55-59	2,234,508	2,719,567	4,954,075
60-64	1,764,812	2,276,368	4,041,180
65-69	1,320,739	1,776,982	3,097,721
70-74	865,489	1,236,148	2,101,637
75-79	506,914	775,279	1,282,193
80-84	192,276	305,329	497,605
85+	56,225	118,368	174,593

[1] The population under 2 years (otherwise obtained) has been adjusted, on the basis of estimated underenumeration of such children in 1926, to give expected census figures by deduction of 678,400 (6 percent), arbitrarily distributed among the four age-sex classes concerned. If this adjustment had not been made, the difference between the number under 5 years and the number aged 5-9 would have been greater than the figures shown here. The population over 60 years of age is distributed in proportion to 1926 population in same cohorts, "aged" by life-table ratios. Complete census data would probably show a higher proportion in the class reported as 85 years and over; but part of this apparent difference would be fictitious.

Numbers of children aged 3, 4, and 5-9 years in January, 1939, born during 1929-1935, appear relatively small—reduced by the widespread resort to the abortion clinics during that period and by the difficult conditions that prevailed at the time of their birth. On the other hand, the cohort aged 10-14 years in January, 1939, is exceptionally large. We may assume that the same is true as regards those aged 15-16 at the time of the census (born 1923-1924), who reached their eighteenth birthdays in 1941 and in 1942, respectively. The Soviet Union has been strengthened during the present war by the large company of youths who have reached military age during recent years. The child population has apparently again been augmented by a bumper crop of babies born during the years immediately preceding World War II. In the postwar period this will in some measure offset the inevitable drop in births during wartime.

The Soviet population is, and for some decades will continue to be, an extremely young population—in the sense of having a large proportion of children and young adults and a small proportion of older adults. This situation will presumably change consistently and fairly rapidly during the coming decades. A gradual maturing of the population, with an increasing proportion of older persons, may be expected in the Soviet Union as in most other countries.

CHAPTER X

POPULATION REDISTRIBUTION WITHIN THE SOVIET UNION, 1926-1939

1. The Changing Population Pattern

ON the eve of the Second World War the spatial pattern of the population of the Union of Soviet Socialist Republics reveals the persistent force of geographic conditions—temperature, rainfall, soils, topography, and distance. (See Plate XIV, considered in relation to Plates I and II in Chapter I.) Large areas remain uninhabited or very sparsely settled. But important industrial cities also appear in regions remote from the population center. A series of population maps for successive years would demonstrate the force of new dynamic factors: (1) the progressive penetration of population into remote regions, (2) the increasing density of population along communication lines, and (3) the rapid increase of population in many established centers of commerce and industry, along with the formation of new industrial or commercial centers in previously uninhabited or sparsely settled areas.

These dynamic aspects of population distribution in the U.S.S.R. represent the advance of technology, changing the relations between man and environment. The primary relation of geography to the production of foodstuffs, which formerly dominated the distribution of population, is modified by new agricultural techniques. Furthermore, this relation, even as so modified, has ceased to be all important because of the emergence of new industrial techniques. A unit of land can no longer be appraised merely in terms of soil, slope, sunshine, and rainfall. In fact, such conditions may now be relatively unimportant where the underlying formation holds rich mineral or fuel deposits, or where a locality is situated beside a river with high potentiality for the production of electric power, or where it has become a cultural, administrative, and commercial center. Similarly, the sheer factor of distance between central and outlying regions diminishes rapidly with the growth of transportation and communication.

Nevertheless, the Russian landscape remains powerful in its influence on the lives of its occupants. Its deep forests, its arctic and desert regions, the great mountains along its southern borders, and the ranges of east Siberia still obstruct human endeavors and present a challenge to physical and intellectual courage. As the people of the Soviet Union are released from the confines of villages, many are drawn into new types of pioneer experience. Many others are stimulated by travel and by contact with diverse scenes and a variety of ancient cultures, as well as by the motifs of a new social order.

The impact of technology on the Russian landscape did not begin with the Soviet regime. In fact, the greatest single advance was undoubtedly the construction of the Trans-Siberian Railway in the late Tsarist period. But technological progress has received a tremendous impetus in the era of "Socialist Construction," and has been given new directives and meanings.

2. The Growth of Cities

The rapid growth of cities in all parts of the U.S.S.R. has been the outstanding and controlling factor in the redistribution of population under the Soviets. This is, of course, an expression of the rapid expansion of industry, commerce, and services. Plate XV shows the distribution of all cities of 50,000 inhabitants or over in 1939. The census figures for these cities are given in Appendix VII, Table A 24. On Plate XV the area of the symbol for each city is proportional to the number of inhabitants in 1939. The shading shows the rapidity of population increase, 1926-1939. The legend "Percentage Growth" must be interpreted as meaning "population in 1939 as percent of population in 1926." The lowest class (cities with growth ratios up to 250 percent) includes the cities that doubled in population during the inter-census period. There was no city in this class that did not have a larger population in 1939 than in 1926. It will be noted that cities characterized by extremely rapid growth are found both in the older European centers, especially around Moscow and in the Ukraine, and in new, previously undeveloped regions.

Most of the large cities, as well as most of the smaller urban communities, grew rapidly between 1926 and 1939. There were 12 cities with more than 200,000 inhabitants in 1926, including Leningrad with 1,690,000 and Moscow with 2,029,000 inhabitants. In 1939, there were 39 cities over the 200,000 mark, including Leningrad with 3,191,000 and Moscow with 4,137,000 inhabitants. The 12 cities which had more than 200,000 inhabitants in 1926 are (in order of population, 1939): Moscow, Leningrad, Kiev, Kharkov, Baku, Gorkiy, Odessa, Tash-kent, Tbilisi, Rostov, Dnepropetrovsk, and Saratov. These cities had a combined population of 13,557,000 persons in 1939, a figure 90 percent above their combined population in 1926. Among them, the highest percentage increases were in Gorkiy (190 percent), Dnepropetrovsk (112 percent), and Moscow (104 percent). Gorkiy, northeast of Moscow and in the Old In-dustrial Region, has a variety of metallurgical, chemical, and woodworking industries, includ-ing the great Gorkiy Motor Works. Dnepropetrovsk, supplied with new electric power, is situated on the route between the iron ore of Krivoy Rog and the coal deposits of the Donbas Basin. It is the center of the rapidly expanding Dnepr Industrial Combine, a complex of varied metallurgical and chemical industries.

The general expansion of administrative centers in the Soviet Union is indicated by the rapid growth of Moscow, the capital of the U.S.S.R., and that of the four other capital cities mentioned in the previous paragraph—Kiev, capital of the Ukrainian S.S.R., 65 percent in-crease; Baku, capital of the Azerbaydzhan S.S.R., 79 percent increase; Tbilisi, capital of the Georgian S.S.R., 77 percent increase; Tashkent, capital of the Uzbek S.S.R., 81 percent in-crease. Such cities are centers for a variety of industrial, commercial, and cultural activities. Some of the smaller capital cities show even more conspicuous increases. Erivan, capital of the Armenian S.S.R., grew from 65,000 in 1926 to over 200,000 in 1939. Alma Ata, capital of the Kazakh S.S.R., grew from 45,000 in 1926 to 231,000 in 1939. Stalinabad (formerly Diushambe), the capital of the Tadzhik S.S.R., rose from an isolated town of 5,607 inhabi-tants in 1926 to a city, connected by railroad with the rest of the Soviet Union, with 82,540 persons in 1939.

Along with the rapid growth of Moscow, there was a movement of population into its periphery. Several of the suburbs around Moscow increased threefold and more during the intercensus period. For example, Lyublino and Kuntsevo grew from places with less than 10,000 persons in 1926 to cities of over 60,000 in 1939. In fact, the population of all places outside the city of Moscow but within the Moscow District that were classed as urban in 1939 was over three times as large as the population of such places in 1926.[1] The same centrifugal movement into the environs influenced the rural population of the Moscow District, which in-creased 29 percent, in contrast to the absolute decrease of rural population characteristic of most parts of European Russia.

The port of Odessa, with an increase of 44 percent, had the slowest growth of any of the twelve major cities of 1926. It had achieved its importance as the center of the grain export trade. However, smaller ports serving different interests increased rapidly. Mariupol, terminal of a railway through the Donbas Basin to the Azov Sea, increased three and a half times to become a city of 222,000 inhabitants in 1939. The principal Arctic ports in the European part

[1] Konstantinov, Title 512.

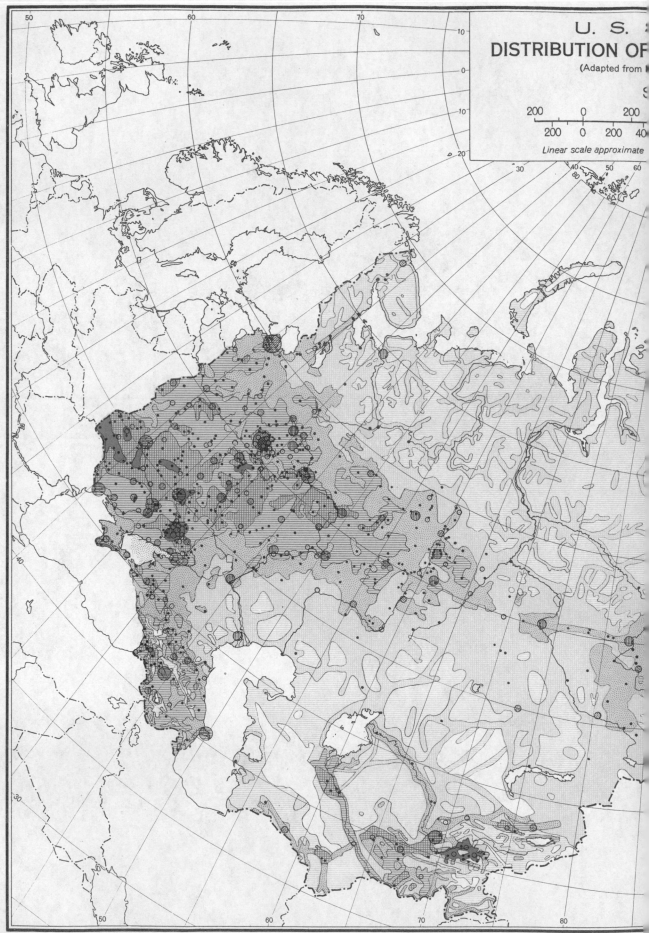

U. S.

DISTRIBUTION OF

(Adapted from

S

200   0   200

200   0   200   40

Linear scale approximate

50   60   70   10

0

10

20

30   40   50   60

40

50

60

70

80

PLATE XIV

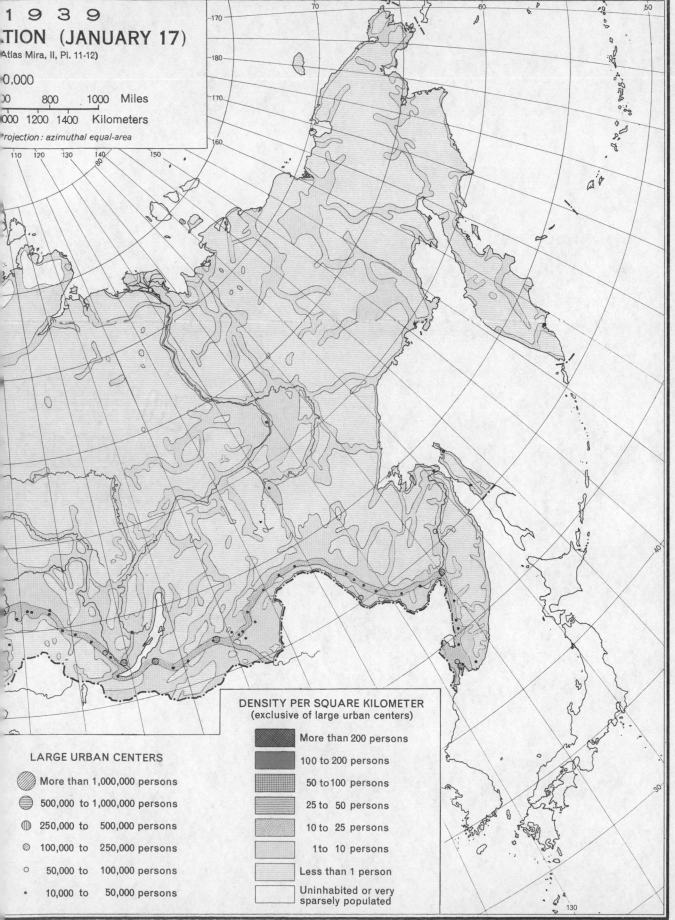

1939
TION (JANUARY 17)
(Atlas Mira, II, Pl. 11-12)

0,000

| 00 | 800 | 1000 Miles |

| 000 | 1200 | 1400 | Kilometers |

Projection: azimuthal equal-area

LARGE URBAN CENTERS

More than 1,000,000 persons

500,000 to 1,000,000 persons

250,000 to 500,000 persons

100,000 to 250,000 persons

50,000 to 100,000 persons

10,000 to 50,000 persons

DENSITY PER SQUARE KILOMETER
(exclusive of large urban centers)

More than 200 persons

100 to 200 persons

50 to 100 persons

25 to 50 persons

10 to 25 persons

1 to 10 persons

Less than 1 person

Uninhabited or very
sparsely populated

Prepared by Department of State, Division
of Geography and Cartography
Drawn by American Geographical Society

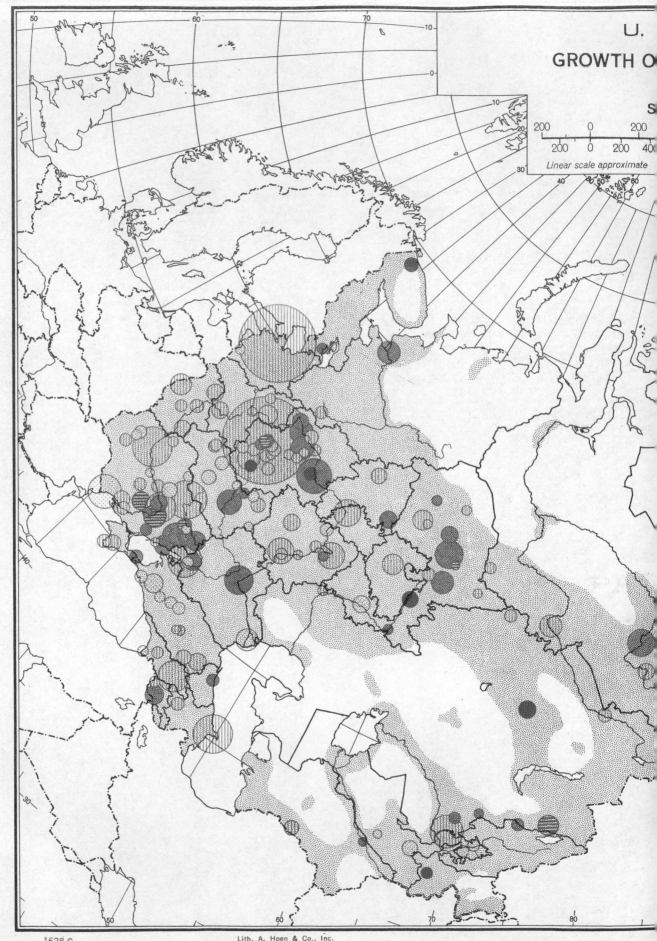

S

200	0	200	
200	0	200	400

Linear scale approximate

PLATE XV

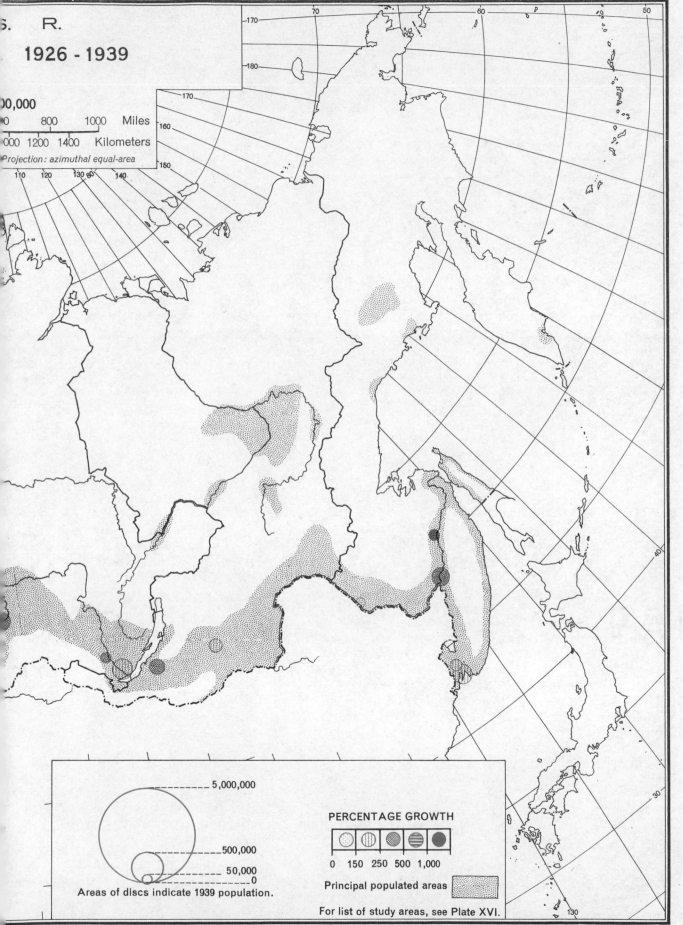

5.   R.

1926 - 1939

00,000

0	800	1000 Miles
000	1200 1400	Kilometers

Projection: azimuthal equal-area

Areas of discs indicate 1939 population.

5,000,000

500,000

50,000

0

PERCENTAGE GROWTH

0   150   250   500   1,000

Principal populated areas

For list of study areas, see Plate XVI.

Prepared by Department of State, Division
of Geography and Cartography
Drawn by American Geographical Society

of the Soviet Union grew at a phenomenal pace—Murmansk rose from 9,000 to 117,000 persons and Arkhangelsk from 77,000 to 281,000 persons. The principal Pacific port, Vladivostok, increased from 108,000 persons in 1926 to 206,000 persons in 1939.

As might be expected, extremely rapid growth is registered for cities and clusters of cities in various mining and industrial regions. The largest new city in the U.S.S.R. is Karaganda, with a population in 1939 of 165,937. This is the center of new coal mining operations in the north-central part of the Asiatic steppes. The second largest new city is Magnitogorsk (1939 population, 145,870) at the site of the "Magnetic Mountain"—a new metallurgical center in the southern Urals. Komsomolsk (1939 population, 70,746) is one of the most remarkable towns in the whole Soviet Union. It was founded in 1932 on the banks of the lower Amur River in a remote wilderness by 4,000 members of the Communist Youth Organization (whence its name). By 1939, it was equipped to launch steel vessels for duty in the Pacific Ocean. A fourfold increase in its population was projected in plans for the next four years. This city is served by a new railway running north along the Amur from Khabarovsk on the Trans-Siberian. It is also on the line of the partially completed railway across eastern Siberia north of Lake Baykal, through Yakutia and the Far East.[2] These lines are projected to reach the Pacific at Nikolayevsk at the mouth of the Amur and at Sovyetskaya Gavan on the Sea of Japan.

There are 49 "boom cities" in the Soviet Union—defined (1) as having increased threefold or more during the twelve-year intercensus period, and (2) as having 50,000 or more inhabitants in January, 1939. These cities are listed in Table 59. They may be grouped as follows: (1) 15 cities in the Dnepr-Donets-Don industrial belt across the southern and eastern part of the Ukraine (from the iron mines at Krivoy Rog, around the electric power stations of the lower Dnepr, through the Donbas Coal Basin, and beyond the Ukraine into the Rostov District); (2) 6 cities in the environs of Moscow; (3) 13 cities in the Urals-Kuznets-Karaganda triangle (including Ural mining-industrial towns, the Kuzbas Coal Basin and associated industries in Novosibirsk District, and the Karaganda Coal Basin in north-central Kazakhstan); (4) 4 cities in the eastern R.S.F.S.R. (from the Cheremkhovo coal fields in the Irkutsk District, west of Lake Baykal, eastward along the Mongolian and Manchurian borders, to the Amur and Ussuri rivers in the Far East); (5) 4 cities in southeastern Kazakhstan and Central Asia; (6) 2 cities in the European Arctic region; and (7) 5 cities (including one new city, Stalinogorsk, southeast of Tula) in other parts of the U.S.S.R.

The number of people living in places classified as "urban" rose from 26.3 million in 1926 to 55.9 million in 1939, an increase of 112 percent in 12 years and 1 month. The proportion of the whole Soviet population living in such places in 1926 was only 17.9 percent—less than the proportion living in incorporated places of 2,500 population or more in the United States in 1860. The proportion of the Soviet population reported as living in urban communities in 1939 was 32.8 percent—less than the corresponding figure for the United States in 1890. In the U.S.S.R. the designation of a community as "urban" is a matter of legal definition (actually determined by its economic functions) and does not strictly imply any specific size or density. Changes in the number of urban places or in population living in such places are, therefore, subject to variations in legal codes. However, it does not appear that the growth indicated by the figures cited here is appreciably affected by this consideration. The total population in places which had 50,000 inhabitants or more in 1939 (subject to administrative changes only as regards their city limits) grew from 16,163,000 in 1926 to 34,137,000 in 1939—an increase of 111 percent.[3]

---

[2] This line may also have been completed before the publication of this text.

[3] The figures cited here, unless otherwise specified, are derived directly from official census data.

TABLE 59

Cities with 50,000 or More Inhabitants, 1939, and with Threefold or Greater Increase, 1926-1939[1]

City in Order of Increase	Administrative Division	Population 1926	Population 1939	Ratio 1939/ 1926
Karaganda	Kazakh S.S.R.	—	165,937	—
Magnitogorsk	Chelyabinsk Obl.	—	145,870	—
Stalinogorsk	Tula Obl.	—	76,207	—
Komsomol'sk	Khabarovsk Kray	—	70,746	—
Stalinsk	Novosibirsk Obl.	3,894	169,538	43.5
Stalinabad	Tadzhik S.S.R.	5,607	82,540	14.7
Murmansk	Murmansk Obl.	8,777	117,054	13.3
Dzerzhinsk	Gor'kiy Obl.	8,910	103,415	11.6
Prokop'evsk	Novosibirsk Obl.	10,717	107,227	10.0
Kamensk Ural'skiy	Chelyabinsk Obl.	5,367	50,897	9.5
Lyublino	Moscow Obl.	8,391	64,332	7.7
Kramatorskaya	Ukr. S.S.R.: Stalino Obl.	12,348	93,350	7.6
Kemerovo	Novosibirsk Obl.	21,726	132,978	6.1
Kuntsevo	Moscow Obl.	9,978	60,963	6.1
Zaporozh'ye	Ukr. S.S.R.: Zaporozh'ye Obl.	55,744	289,188	5.2
Krivoy Rog	Ukr. S.S.R.: Dnepropetrovsk Obl.	38,228	197,621	5.2
Alma Ata	Kazakh S.S.R.	45,395	230,528	5.1
Orsk	Chkalov Obl.	13,581	65,799	4.8
Gorlovka	Ukr. S.S.R.: Stalino Obl.	23,125	108,693	4.7
Chelyabinsk	Chelyabinsk Obl.	59,307	273,127	4.6
Cheremkhovo	Irkutsk Obl.	14,485	65,907	4.6
Ulan-Ude	Buryat-Mongolian A.S.S.R.	28,918	129,417	4.5
Losinoostrovsk	Moscow Obl.	15,624	70,480	4.5
Dneprodzerzhinsk	Ukr. S.S.R.: Dnepropetrovsk Obl.	34,150	147,829	4.3
Chapayevsk	Kuybyshev Obl.	13,529	57,995	4.3
Leninsk-Kuznetskiy	Novosibirsk Obl.	19,645	81,980	4.2
Nikopol'	Ukr. S.S.R.: Dnepropetrovsk Obl.	14,214	57,841	4.1
Krasnyy Luch	Ukr. S.S.R.: Voroshilovgrad Obl.	12,425	50,829	4.1
Nizhniy Tagil	Sverdlovsk Obl.	38,820	159,864	4.1
Sergo	Ukr. S.S.R.: Voroshilovgrad Obl.	17,224	68,360	4.0
Berezniki	Perm' Obl.	16,138	63,575	3.9
Chardzhou	Turkmen S.S.R.	13,950	54,739	3.9
Khabarovsk	Khabarovsk Kray	52,045	199,364	3.8
Shakhty	Rostov Obl.	41,043	155,081	3.8
Konstantinovka	Ukr. S.S.R.: Stalino Obl.	25,303	95,087	3.8
Arkhangel'sk	Arkhangel'sk Obl.	76,774	281,091	3.7
Podol'sk	Moscow Obl.	19,793	72,422	3.7
Ordzhonikidze	Ukr. S.S.R.: Stalino Obl.	24,329	88,246	3.6
Mytishchi	Moscow Obl.	17,054	60,111	3.5
Chimkent	Kazakh S.S.R.	21,018	74,185	3.5
Mariupol'	Ukr. S.S.R.: Stalino Obl.	63,920	222,427	3.5
Voroshilovsk	Ukr. S.S.R.: Voroshilovgrad Obl.	16,040	54,794	3.4
Novosibirsk	Novosibirsk Obl.	120,128	405,589	3.4
Perovo	Moscow Obl.	23,711	77,727	3.3
Lipetsk	Voronezh Obl.	21,439	66,625	3.1
Erivan	Armenian S.S.R.	64,613	200,031	3.1
Makeyevka	Ukr. S.S.R.: Stalino Obl.	79,421	240,145	3.0
Sverdlovsk	Sverdlovsk Obl.	140,300	425,544	3.0
Melitopol'	Ukr. S.S.R.: Zaporozh'ye Obl.	25,289	75,735	3.0

[1] For the complete list of cities with over 50,000 inhabitants in 1939, see Appendix VII, Table A 24.

Migration was clearly the main factor in the growth of cities. In analyzing the increase of the urban population we must take account of the changed legal status of communities classified as "rural" in 1926 and as "urban" in 1939. The estimated number of persons living in such communities in 1939 was 5.8 million.[4] However, since many of these places were rapidly growing communities, like Karaganda, Magnitogorsk, and Stalinogorsk, in-migrants presumably made up a large proportion of their population at this time. We can, therefore, assume that about 28 million people were living in 1926 in places that were classified as urban in 1939 (i.e., about 1.7 million more than the number reported as living in cities in 1926). This figure is presumably subject to an error of less than one million, in either direction.

A population of 28 million persons, growing at the average rate of increase indicated for the whole Soviet population, would have become a population of 32.45 million persons in 1939, or 23.5 million less than the number reported as living in cities in 1939. Unless the natural increase of the urban population was *higher* than that of the rural population, migration from rural communities to cities must have involved the net transfer of at least 23 million people (minus births, plus deaths in the population so transferred).

According to the official statistics for the European part of the U.S.S.R. for 1926, the crude rate of natural increase of the urban population was 17.2 per thousand, whereas that of the rural population was 24.9 per thousand.[5] According to these statistics, natural increase was about 50 percent higher in rural than in urban communities in the European part of the U.S.S.R. at the beginning of the intercensus period. The rate of natural increase may, however, have been lower in rural districts not covered by registration data. On the other hand, the sharp drop in natality between 1926 and 1934 was certainly more pronounced in cities than in rural communities, but we have no exact information on this subject, and the heavy weighting of the city population with young adults in the reproductive years would tend to dampen the differential. Again, if there was heavy excess mortality in some districts in the early 'thirties, as the data seem to show, this loss may have occurred chiefly in rural districts. It is impossible to estimate with any accuracy the natural growth of the urban and rural segments of the Soviet population during the intercensus period. But the "expected" natural increase of the initial urban population at the average rate for the whole U.S.S.R. is only 4.5 million persons, so that an appreciable difference in rates of natural increase would not greatly alter the figure for net migration (about 23 million persons) suggested in the previous paragraph.

Sul'kevich reports the net rural-urban migration during the intercensus period as 18.5 million, apart from migration into places classified as rural in 1926.[6] If we assume that these new cities received a net in-migration of about 4.5 million persons, we again bring the total estimated net rural-urban migration to about 23 million. Estimates of net rural-urban migration are available for the years 1928-1935.[7] In order to reconcile these figures with that just given for the total intercensus period, we must assume that the net movement to cities in 1936, 1937, and 1938 was only about 1.5 million each year, rather than about 2.5 million as reported for 1934 and for 1935, assuming 0.8 million as a net figure for 1927. This assumption as regards the years 1936-1938 seems unlikely; it is probable that the earlier figures were somewhat exag-

---

[4] Sul'kevich, Title 323, p. 30.

[5] See Table 30. According to the registration data, there was practically no change in the death rate but a marked decline in the birth rate for cities in the following year, bringing the rate of natural increase to 15.3 per thousand in 1927. On the other hand, the birth rate of the rural population changed very slightly, whereas there was an apparent increase in the death rate, making the rate of natural increase of the rural population 23.8 per thousand in 1927. In the light of our previous discussion it appears probable that the decline in natality in cities from 1926 to 1927 was real, but that the apparent increase in mortality in rural communities was largely spurious, owing to improvement in registration.

[6] Sul'kevich, Title 323, p. 30.

[7] *Sotsialisticheskoye Stroitel'stvo, 1936*, Title 409, p. 545.

gerated by double-counting of migrants in the community registers. However, accepting all the information at face value and arbitrarily filling in the missing figures, the hypothetical series runs as follows:

Net Migration to Towns and Cities
(In Thousands)

1927	[800]
1928	1,062
1929	1,392
1930	2,633
1931	4,100
1932	2,719
1933	772
1934	2,452
1935	2,527
1936	[1,514]
1937	[1,514]
1938	[1,515]
1927-1938	23,000

The information on rural-urban migration in the U.S.S.R. during the intercensus period lacks precision, but its broad import is clear enough. People who had come from rural communities within the preceding twelve years made up at least two-fifths of the population of Soviet cities in 1939. These recent in-migrants from the countryside to the cities represented an eighth or more of the total Soviet population. There is always a large movement back and forth wherever there is a large net migration, so these statements are conservative. Meanwhile, the organization and mechanization of agriculture and the development of rural industries were beginning to break down the traditional contrasts between peasants and proletariat in the activities and culture of the whole population.

3. *Method of Analyzing Population Redistribution, 1926-1939*

Analysis of population changes by regions within the U.S.S.R. between 1926 and 1939 involves serious difficulties. The administrative divisions of the U.S.S.R. were reshuffled and their boundaries changed at various times during the intercensus period. The preliminary 1939 census reports give official information on changes from 1926 to 1939 only with respect to the eleven constituent republics, as units, and individual cities.[8] In order to present a consistent account of population change in different parts of the vast R.S.F.S.R., reaching from Belorussia and the Ukraine to the Pacific, it is necessary to piece together previous census data for minor divisions or fractions thereof.[9] This involves considerable labor and risk of error. In order to reduce labor and errors, we have carried through this operation only for large areas (representing in each case a group of oblasts or comparable units, as constituted in 1939). These are referred to here as "Study Areas." They are arbitrary divisions of the Soviet territory, but they correspond roughly in most cases to natural or administrative regions. It should be emphasized that these Study Areas are *not identical* with similar regions as defined in the

[8] The number of constituent republics was raised to sixteen in 1940 through annexations and related changes in the Soviet constitution.
[9] Such a reconstruction of data on sown land by oblasts (as of 1938), 1928-1938, has been reported and is cited below in connection with the data on rural population.

1926 census, on the basis of the administrative divisions in use at that time. In some cases the divisions are frankly arbitrary and must be so recognized.[10] The Study Areas, with the political divisions as of 1939 included within each area, are shown in Plate XVI.

After this study had been completed, we received a report of a comparable investigation by a Soviet geographer, Konstantinov. In view of the superior resources at his disposal, we assume that his results are more accurate than those obtained by our investigation. An exact comparison of the two series at all points is not possible, because the "Regions" used by Konstantinov differ from our "Study Areas," but in most cases the areas can be adjusted so as to permit comparison (see Table 60). Such a comparison indicates that the estimates of population change by Study Areas, as shown here, contain fairly large inaccuracies. Thus, to cite the largest discrepancy in cases where a direct comparison is possible, our series shows an increase of 88 percent for the urban part of the Western Study Area, which includes only Smolensk and Kalinin districts as of 1939, whereas the increases of urban population in these districts as reported by Konstantinov give a weighted average increase of only 77 percent. The direction and magnitude of changes are, however, roughly similar in the two series. Konstantinov and other Soviet writers have also reported intercensus changes for selected administrative divisions within these regions. We shall make use of such information in the interpretation of our findings.

We shall postpone the consideration of migration and natural increase as distinct factors in population change, until we have examined (1) changes in urban population, and (2) changes in rural population, in various parts of the U.S.S.R. from 1926 to 1939. In taking account of the absolute increase or decrease in each area, we can compare the apparent change with the increase that would have been expected if the population of each community had increased at the same rate as the entire Soviet population (15.9 percent). We shall refer to the difference between these figures (*"actual" change minus "expected" increase*) as a *redistribution increment*.[11] It represents the number of people added to the urban or rural population of any area *above* the number needed to maintain its share of the total Soviet population—or the loss below that number, in the case of a negative increment or "decrement." For the present, we make no assumption as to whether this "redistribution" was caused by migration or by different rates of natural increase or by both.

4. Changes in Urban Population by Study Areas

There were 29,596,000 more people living in urban places in the U.S.S.R. in 1939 than there were in 1926. Of this number, nearly 19.6 million were added to cities in the European part, exclusive of the Urals, Bashkiria, and Dagestan; 6.5 million were added to cities in the eastern part of the R.S.F.S.R.; and about 1 million each to the cities of (1) the Transcaucasus and Dagestan, (2) Kazakhstan, and (3) the Central Asia republics. In terms of percentage increase, the growth of cities in the European part of the U.S.S.R. was more rapid than in the Transcaucasus or Central Asia, but not so rapid as in the eastern part of the R.S.F.S.R. or in Kazakhstan. The Urals, Bashkiria, Siberia, the Far East, and Kazakhstan had only 15 percent of the total urban population in 1926 but over 20 percent in 1939. These findings in regard to the growth of urban population in the major divisions of the U.S.S.R. are summarized in Table 61.

[10] These areas were drawn in such a way as to make comparison between 1939 and 1926 data, or between 1926 and 1897 data, as simple as possible. Even so, the estimates of population within specified areas at previous census dates frequently involved difficulties and are subject to an unknown margin of error. For statement of procedure and description of areas, see Appendix VII.

[11] We are forced to ignore changes in the legal status of communities in these calculations, because we lack the information needed to take such changes into account.

TABLE 60

Estimate of Changes in Population Study Areas of the R.S.F.S.R., 1926-1939, Compared with Changes by Region as Reported by Konstantinov[1]

As Reported by, or Derived from Figures Reported by, Konstantinov				As Estimated in This Study			
Region	1939 Population as Per- cent of 1926 Population			Study Area	1939 Population as Per- cent of 1926 Population		
	Urban	Rural	Total		Urban	Rural	Total
Central Industrial	229	100	141	Old Industrial Center	224	96	132
				Except Ryazan[2]	229	99	140
Central Black Soil	142	89	94				
Orel, Kursk, Voronezh, Tambov[3]	147			Central Black Soil	144	90	96
Western R.S.F.S.R.	193	86	112				
Except Leningrad Obl.[4]	177	81	91	Western	188	84	94
Leningrad Obl.[5]	198	97	144	Leningrad	196	94	141
				Northeast	276	92	110
				Karelia-Murmansk	558	164	259
European North	324	96	121	N.E. and K-M.	335	98	123
Volga Area	197	90	105				
				Vyatka	258	100	112
				Tatar	221	99	113
				Central Volga	165	83	94
				Lower Volga and Don	188	80	104
Southern R.S.F.S.R.	176	100	116				
(Including part of Lower Volga and Don Study Area)				Crimea	178	141	158
				North Caucasus	163	105	115
				Dagestan	258	120	135
				Ural	274	94	131
				Bashkir	228	112	123
				Ural, and Bashkir and			
Ural Area	258	96	121	Udmurt A.S.S.R.'s	264[6]	99	127[6]
Western Siberia	291	97	120	West Siberia	287	95	117
				Central Siberia	312	107	138
				East Siberia	384	120	159
Central Siberia and Soviet				Soviet Far East	329	136	188
Far East	334	118	157	C.S., E.S., and S.F.E.	334	117	156

[1] Konstantinov, Title 512. In some cases comparable figures have been obtained only by arbitrary adjustments; in other cases it is impossible to obtain comparable figures. The figures in both series for constituent republics, not shown here, are given in official reports. Figures for identical areas in the two series are given in each case on the same line.

[2] Subtracting figures for Ryazan Oblast', assuming urban change as reported by Konstantinov (11.4 percent increase), and same rural change as reported for Tula Oblast' (15.5 percent decrease).

[3] Weighted average of ratios reported by Konstantinov for urban parts of four districts.

[4] Weighted average of ratios for Kalinin and Smolensk districts.

[5] Urban: weighted average of components.

[6] Urban figure for Udmurt area in 1926 obtained on arbitrary assumption of increase proportional to that in Bashkir area.

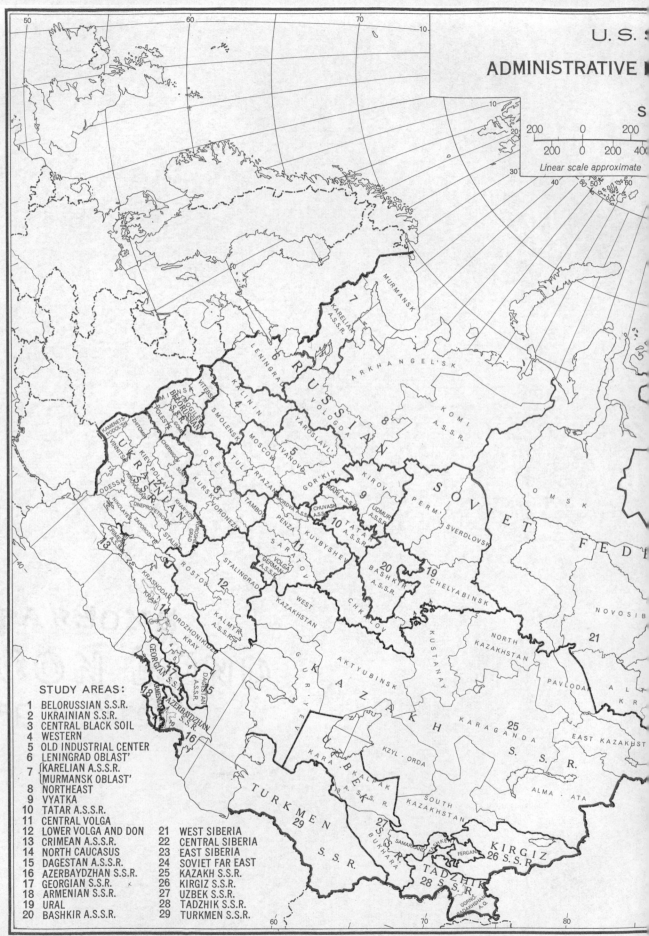

U.S.

ADMINISTRATIVE

STUDY AREAS:

1 BELORUSSIAN S.S.R.
2 UKRAINIAN S.S.R.
3 CENTRAL BLACK SOIL
4 WESTERN
5 OLD INDUSTRIAL CENTER
6 LENINGRAD OBLAST'
7 KARELIAN A.S.S.R.
  MURMANSK OBLAST'
8 NORTHEAST
9 VYATKA
10 TATAR A.S.S.R.
11 CENTRAL VOLGA
12 LOWER VOLGA AND DON
13 CRIMEAN A.S.S.R.
14 NORTH CAUCASUS
15 DAGESTAN A.S.S.R.
16 AZERBAYDZHAN S.S.R.
17 GEORGIAN S.S.R.
18 ARMENIAN S.S.R.
19 URAL
20 BASHKIR A.S.S.R.

21 WEST SIBERIA
22 CENTRAL SIBERIA
23 EAST SIBERIA
24 SOVIET FAR EAST
25 KAZAKH S.S.R.
26 KIRGIZ S.S.R.
27 UZBEK S.S.R.
28 TADZHIK S.S.R.
29 TURKMEN S.S.R.

PLATE XVI

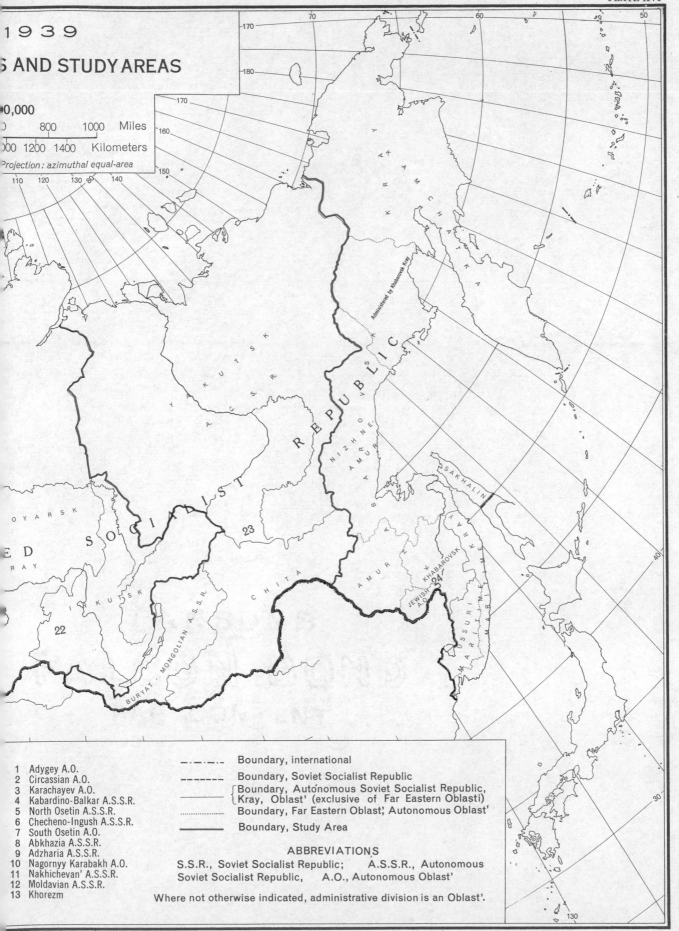

1939

S AND STUDY AREAS

0,000

0	800	1000 Miles
000	1200 1400	Kilometers

Projection: azimuthal equal-area

1 Adygey A.O.
2 Circassian A.O.
3 Karachayev A.O.
4 Kabardino-Balkar A.S.S.R.
5 North Osetin A.S.S.R.
6 Checheno-Ingush A.S.S.R.
7 South Osetin A.O.
8 Abkhazia A.S.S.R.
9 Adzharia A.S.S.R.
10 Nagornyy Karabakh A.O.
11 Nakhichevan' A.S.S.R.
12 Moldavian A.S.S.R.
13 Khorezm

_._._._ Boundary, international
- - - - - Boundary, Soviet Socialist Republic
{ Boundary, Autonomous Soviet Socialist Republic,
{ Kray, Oblast' (exclusive of Far Eastern Oblasti)
.... Boundary, Far Eastern Oblast', Autonomous Oblast'
━━━━━ Boundary, Study Area

ABBREVIATIONS
S.S.R., Soviet Socialist Republic;   A.S.S.R., Autonomous
Soviet Socialist Republic,   A.O., Autonomous Oblast'

Where not otherwise indicated, administrative division is an Oblast'.

Prepared by Department of State, Division
of Geography and Cartography
Drawn by American Geographical Society

TABLE 61

Increase of Population in Places Classified as Urban: U.S.S.R. and Principal Divisions,
1926-1939[1]

(Numbers in Thousands)

Division	Population		Increase 1926-1939		Expected Increase[2]	Redistribution Increase[3]
	1926	1939	Absolute	Percent		
U.S.S.R.	26,314	55,910	29,596	112	4,195	25,401
European Part, except Ural, Bashkir, and Dagestan	19,495	39,073	19,578	100	3,108	16,470
Transcaucasus with Dagestan	1,486	2,790	1,304	88	237	1,067
Ural, Bashkir, and Asiatic R.S.F.S.R.	3,436	9,957	6,521	190	548	5,973
Kazakhstan	519	1,706	1,187	229	83	1,104
Central Asia	1,378	2,384	1,006	73	220	786

[1] Based on Table 62.   [2] 1926 population multiplied by .15942.
[3] Actual change minus expected increase—ignoring changes in legal status of communities.

In every Study Area there was an appreciable increase of urban population between 1926 and 1939, as is shown in Table 62 and Plate XVII. Even the units with the slowest urban growth show an increase of over 40 percent in the number of persons living in cities. The two Study Areas with the lowest rate of urban increase, the Central Black Soil area and Uzbekistan, are predominantly agricultural, and the urban workers in these areas during this period were largely engaged in textile or food-processing industries. In general, cities chiefly dependent on the production of consumer goods show less rapid growth than the centers of metallurgical, chemical, and machine industries—except in the case of important administrative centers, which are generally characterized by rapid population increase.

The total urban population of the Ukraine increased from 5.4 million in 1926 to 11.2 million in 1939. The total (urban and rural) population of the Stalino District, in the heart of the Donets mining-industrial region, increased by 91 percent.[12] This district includes some of the most rapidly growing cities in the U.S.S.R., such as Kramatorskaya, Gorlovka, Konstantinovka, Ordzhonikidze, Mariupol, and Makeyevka, in each of which the 1939 population was at least three times as large as that of 1926. (See Table 59.) Aside from Kiev, the large industrial cities in the Ukraine—Karkov, Dnepropetrovsk, and Stalino—almost doubled or more than doubled their population during the intercensus interval. A tabulation of the change in all Ukrainian cities with 50,000 inhabitants or more in 1939 shows a striking difference between the trends in the mining and industrial districts and in other parts of the Ukraine.[13]

Area Distribution of Cities With 50,000 Population in 1939	Percent Increase 1926-1939
Don Basin	212
Dnepr Subregion	215
Dnepr Prairie Left Bank Subregion	86
Dnepr Prairie Right Bank Subregion	55
Steppe Subregion	57

[12] *Ekonomicheskaya Geografiya SSSR*, Title 464, p. 152.   [13] Konstantinov, Title 512.

TABLE 62

Urban Population Change by Study Area: U.S.S.R., 1926-1939
(Numbers in Thousands)

Population Study Area	Population		Increase, 1926-1939	
	1926	1939	Absolute	Percent
U.S.S.R.	26,314	55,910	29,596	112
European Part, except Ural, Bashkir, and Dagestan	19,495	39,073	19,578	100
Belorussia	848	1,373	525	62
Ukraine	5,374	11,196	5,822	108
Central Black Soil	1,335	1,918	583	44
Western	612	1,151	539	88
Old Industrial Center	4,626	10,382	5,756	124
Leningrad	2,098	4,119	2,021	96
Karelia-Murmansk	71	396	325	458
Northeast	271	749	478	176
Vyatka	332	858	526	158
Tatar	281	622	341	121
Central Volga	1,171	1,936	765	65
Lower Volga and Don	1,164	2,191	1,027	88
Crimea	330	586	256	78
North Caucasus	982	1,597	615	63
Transcaucasus with Dagestan	1,486	2,790	1,304	88
Azerbaydzhan	650	1,161	511	79
Georgia	594	1,067	473	80
Armenia	167	366	199	119
Dagestan	76	196	120	158
Ural, Bashkir, and Asiatic R.S.F.S.R.	3,436	9,957	6,521	190
Ural	1,421	3,893	2,472	174
Bashkir	233	531	298	128
West Siberia	891	2,555	1,664	187
Central Siberia	357	1,113	756	212
East Siberia	196	753	557	284
Soviet Far East	338	1,112	774	229
Kazakhstan	519	1,706	1,187	229
Central Asia	1,378	2,384	1,006	73
Kirgiz	122	271	149	122
Uzbek	1,012	1,445	433	43
Tadzhik	106	252	146	138
Turkmen	137	416	279	204

As already noted, Moscow City and the cities and towns in the surrounding district grew rapidly between 1926 and 1939; the urban population of the Moscow District as a whole increased by 130 percent during this period. The increase of urban population in the Gorkiy District was even greater (157 percent),[14] and this included a new industrial city, Dzerzhinsk. According to Konstantinov, the urban population of the Ryazan District increased by only 11.4

[14] *Ibid.*

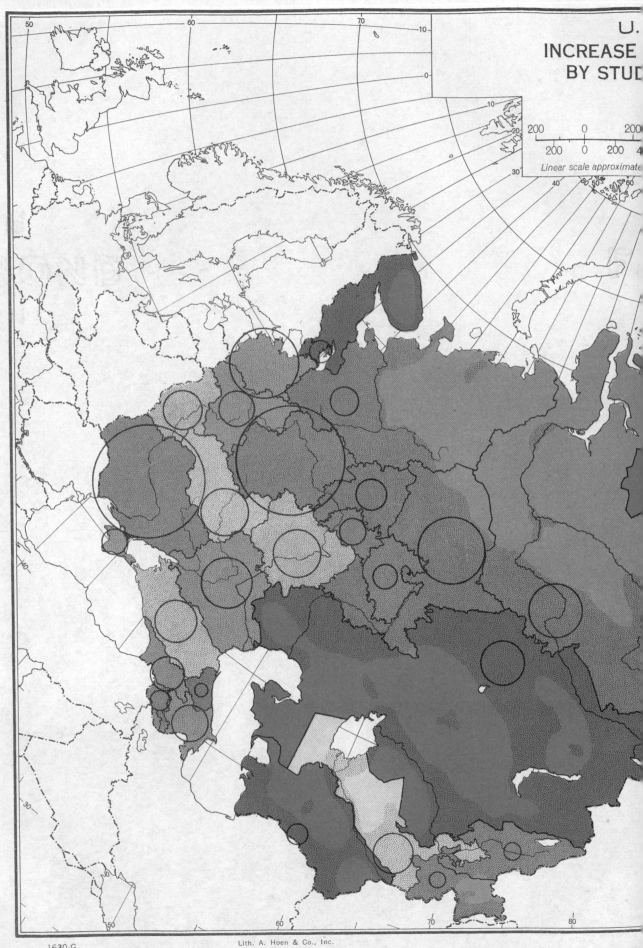

U.
INCREASE
BY STUD

200   0   200

200   0   200   4

Linear scale approximate

Lith. A. Hoen & Co., Inc.

PLATE XVII

S. R.
N POPULATION
5, 1926-1939

000,000

600   800   1000   Miles
1000 1200 1400   Kilometers
Projection: azimuthal equal-area

10,000,000

5,000,000

1,000,000
500,000

0

Areas of circles proportional
to urban population, 1939

PERCENTAGE INCREASE

25   50   75   100   150   200

Principal populated areas

For list of study areas, see Plate XVI.

Prepared by Department of State, Division
of Geography and Cartography
Drawn by American Geographical Society

percent; there must therefore have been an absolute decrease of population in the cities and towns of this district other than Ryazan City.[15] These communities were largely engaged in service to the surrounding farm villages and in food-processing industries partly dependent on seasonal labor. This district is here included in the "Old Industrial" area, in conformity with the grouping followed in the 1926 census. Even so, the urban population of this whole Study Area increased by 124 percent from 1926 to 1939. Excluding Ryazan District, the number of persons in cities in the Central Industrial Region (as defined by Konstantinov) increased 129 percent.

The urban population of the Leningrad District nearly doubled between 1926 and 1939. The towns and cities in the environs of Leningrad grew more rapidly than the metropolis itself, as in the case of Moscow. Only moderate increases of urban population occurred in the Kalinin District (86 percent) and in the Smolensk District (66 percent); both of these are in the Western Area of the R.S.F.S.R. The growth of urban population was even less rapid in Belorussia (62 percent), as in the western part of the Ukraine.[16]

The growth of urban population in the far northern part of European Russia was most spectacular. In 1926 there were only 342,000 persons in urban places in all districts of the Karelia-Murmansk and Northeastern areas but 1,145,000 persons were living in cities in these areas in 1939. Moreover, this increase was concentrated in the extreme northern districts. The total (urban and rural) population of the Murmansk District grew ninefold.[17] The population growth of the Northeast Region was due to increase in the Arkhangelsk District, and in the Komi A.S.S.R., whereas the Vologda District was regarded as a labor supply region.[18] There was an absolute decrease of total population in the Vologda District.[19] The Murmansk District, extending across the Kola Peninsula between the White Sea and the Arctic Ocean, has important mineral and forest resources. It has the largest apatite mines in the world, with which is associated a plant for production of fertilizer. It also has a wide variety of valuable metals. Its strategic importance is obvious, since it has the only year-round Soviet port on the Arctic Ocean. The electrification of the railway to Murmansk above the Arctic Circle, with an underground power station, was one of the important achievements in the economic and military development of the U.S.S.R.

There was a rapid growth of urban population, from a small initial base, in most of the autonomous republics of the Volga region, with a twofold increase or better in the Tatar A.S.S.R., the Chuvash A.S.S.R., and the Mari A.S.S.R.—and also in some of the autonomous republics of the North Caucasus area.[20] Elsewhere, the growth of cities and towns in the Volga and North Caucasus areas was generally moderate—with the notable exception of Stalingrad, where the number of inhabitants increased from 151,000 in 1926 to 445,000 in 1939. The moderate increase of Groznyy (78 percent), like that of Baku in the Transcaucasus, was less than might have been expected in view of the rapid expansion of the petroleum industry in these centers. This is attributed to technological advances that brought about great increase in productivity per worker, with consequent reduction in the demand for labor.[21]

The great industrial development of the Urals was effected by linking its rich mineral resources with the coal reserves of the Kuznets region across the broad level plain of western Siberia, and later by tapping the excellent, but previously undeveloped, coal reserves of the Karaganda Basin in northern Kazakhstan, which is nearer the Ural region than the Kuzbas Basin (Kuznets). The varied industries of the Urals are served now by a single electric power

---

[15] Ryazan City, population, 1926: 50,919; 1939: 95,358. Total urban population of Ryazan District, 1939: 218,797.
[16] Konstantinov, Title 512.
[17] *Ekonomicheskaya Geografiya SSSR*, Title 464, p. 152.
[18] Sonin, Title 308, p. 82.
[19] Konstantinov, Title 512.
[20] *Ibid.*
[21] *Ibid.*

system—from Berezniki in the north to Magnitogorsk in the south (435 miles). Some two hundred important new enterprises were established here during the first two Five-Year Plans.[22] The region has many chemical as well as metal industries, and some local coal resources. It receives petroleum from the Emba region in western Kazakhstan, and efforts have been directed toward developing new petroleum districts in the Urals. The urban population of the area increased from 1,421,000 persons in 1926 to 3,893,000 in 1939, an increase of 174 percent. The small urban population of the adjacent Bashkir A.S.S.R. also more than doubled, amounting to 531,000 persons in 1939. Siberia's city population rose rapidly—somewhat more rapidly than that of the Urals. This was most marked in the Kuznets region, where important industries as well as coal mining have been developed.

There was a phenomenal growth of cities in Kazakhstan. Their population increased more than threefold during the intercensus period. In addition to the rise of Karaganda, several cities in the southeastern part of the Kazakh Republic grew rapidly.

The territory beyond West Siberia includes the valley of the Yenisey River, mountainous plateaus and valleys to the east, and the Pacific coast region. This whole terrain is sometimes referred to as Eastern Siberia or as the Far East.[23] Here it is divided into three areas: (1) Central Siberia, including Krasnoyarsk Territory, which reaches north through the Yenisey valley to the Arctic Ocean, and the Irkutsk District, west of Lake Baykal; (2) East Siberia, including the Buryat-Mongolian A.S.S.R., east of Lake Baykal, the Yakutsk A.S.S.R. in the northern interior, and the Chita District along the Mongolian and Manchurian borders; and (3) the Soviet Far East. This last area includes two political divisions: Khabarovsk Territory (most of the upper as well as lower Amur regions, the northern coastal areas, the Kamchatka Peninsula, and the Soviet part of Sakhalin Island), and the Maritime Territory (Vladivostok, the Lake Khanka and Ussuri River regions, and a coastal strip between high mountains and the Japan Sea). Most of this vast territory, except in the Maritime Territory, has an extremely severe climate but it contains great known and perhaps still greater unknown resources.

These areas beyond West Siberia are closely linked in economic and strategic importance. Their towns and cities held only 891,000 persons in 1926, but these cities and the new ones founded during the next twelve years received over 2 million additional persons in the intercensus period, giving a total urban population of 2,978,000 persons in 1939. These urban pioneers of the eastern R.S.F.S.R. can undoubtedly be regarded as the forerunners of a much greater movement in the future. The population here is still highly concentrated along the Trans-Siberian line, but with a new railway under construction (or already completed) north of Lake Baykal, new motor highways, airways, and the development of Arctic shipping, the isolation of many parts of this territory is gradually yielding to human advance. For example, a long motor highway now reaches from Magadan on the Okhotsk Sea across the mountains into the Kolyma River gold region, which lies within the Arctic Basin. At the time of the 1939 census the Yakutsk A.S.S.R. had no city of 50,000 population or over, but its capital, Yakutsk, in the Lena valley half way between the Trans-Siberian Railway and the Arctic Ocean, is reported to have passed this point shortly thereafter. The new gold-mining towns in the Aldan River region, southeast of Yakutsk, are also reported to have, altogether, some 50,000 inhabitants.[24] The rise of Komsomolsk has already been mentioned. The city of Khabarovsk, itself, increased nearly fourfold, to a population of practically 200,000 persons in 1939. Cheremkhovo, center of a new coal-mining development in Irkutsk, increased four and a half times, reaching 66,000 population. Ulan-Ude, capital of the Buryat-Mongolian A.S.S.R. and site of a large

---

[22] Mikhailov, Title 194, p. 153.
[23] The Soviet Far East is defined by some writers as including Chita Oblast and Buryat-Mongolia.
[24] Davies and Steiger, Title 59, p. 10.

locomotive and railway carriage works, grew at a similar pace to 129,000 population in 1939.

The construction of the Turkestan-Siberia Railway, linking Central Asia with West Siberia, stimulated the development of both regions. The population of Tashkent, the largest city in Central Asia, increased from 324,000 to 585,000 persons during the intercensus period. There are other rapidly growing industrial and commercial centers in the Central Asian republics, but since they lack great mineral or fuel resources their economy has been focused chiefly on agriculture and the development of consumer industries—though some industrial plants have been moved there during the war. Accordingly, the growth of cities was less marked in the Central Asian republics prior to 1939 than in the R.S.F.S.R., the Ukraine, or Kazakhstan. There was also, in general, only a moderate increase of urban population in the Transcaucasian republics.

5. Changes in Rural Population by Study Areas

The changes in the rural population of different parts of the U.S.S.R. present a very different picture. This is evident from a comparison of Table 63 and Plate XVIII with Table 62 and Plate XVII. The Transcaucasus (plus Dagestan) and Central Asia stand out as regions of rapid rural increase. All of the eight republics in these regions, with the exception of Turkmenia, show rural increases of 19 to 36 percent, in contrast to an absolute *decrease* of 5 percent in the rural population of the whole U.S.S.R. The number of persons outside of cities remained stationary in the eastern part of the R.S.F.S.R., treating the Urals, Bashkiria, Siberia, and the Far East as a unit. The rural population in the European part of the U.S.S.R. decreased by 10 percent, with decreases by this percent or more in the Lower Volga and Don, Central Volga, Ukraine, Western, and Central Black Soil areas. The only European areas showing rapid increases in rural population were Karelia-Murmansk (64 percent) and the Crimea (41 percent). There was a small increase in the North Caucasus area (5 percent), probably owing to increases in the mountain districts. The rural population of Kazakhstan decreased by 20 percent during the intercensus period.

The absolute decrease of rural population, as well as the still greater absolute decrease of population dependent on agriculture, forestry, and fishing, in the U.S.S.R. as a whole was associated with an absolute increase of cultivated land. The ratio of rural population to sown land, therefore, declined by about 22 percent during the intercensus period, as indicated in Table 43. In other words, there was about 22 percent more sown land per person in the rural population of the Soviet Union at the end than there had been at the beginning of this interval. Ratios of sown land to rural population have also been computed for 1926-1928 and 1938-1939 for the various Study Areas; these are presented in Plate XIX and Table 64. Subject to certain reservations, the changes in these ratios afford a significant index of change in the potential productivity of the rural population in each region. The change during the intercensus interval is, in general, more significant than the absolute height of the ratio in any Study Area at the beginning or at the end of the interval, because the extent to which the rural population is dependent on the production of crops varies widely in different parts of the U.S.S.R. During the intercensus years, the rural population of some areas probably became more dependent on crop production, through a shift from grazing to agriculture, as in Kazakhstan. Conversely, the rural population of other regions undoubtedly became less dependent on crop production, through a shift to industrial and service occupations, for example, in the Soviet Far East, Karelia-Murmansk, the Old Industrial Center, the Crimea, and parts of the Ukraine. However, regional variations in the trend of these relations during the intercensus period were probably

TABLE 63

Rural Population Change by Study Area: U.S.S.R., 1926-1939
(Numbers in Thousands)

Population Study Area	Population		Change, 1926-1939	
	1926	1939	Absolute	Percent
U.S.S.R.	120,714	114,557	—6,157	— 5
European Part, except Ural,				
Bashkir, and Dagestan	85,275	77,009	—8,266	—10
Belorussia	4,135	4,195	60	1
Ukraine	23,669	19,765	—3,904	—16
Central Black Soil	11,332	10,194	—1,138	—10
Western	5,662	4,752	— 910	—16
Old Industrial Center	12,078	11,650	— 428	— 4
Leningrad	2,462	2,316	— 146	— 6
Karelia-Murmansk	222	365	143	64
Northeast	2,630	2,431	— 199	— 8
Vyatka	4,235	4,246	11	0
Tatar	2,313	2,298	— 15	— 1
Central Volga	7,429	6,133	—1,296	—17
Lower Volga and Don	4,039	3,213	— 826	—20
Crimea	384	541	157	41
North Caucasus	4,683	4,910	227	5
Transcaucasus with Dagestan	5,074	6,174	1,100	22
Azerbaydzhan	1,664	2,049	385	23
Georgia	2,083	2,476	393	19
Armenia	714	915	201	28
Dagestan	613	734	121	20
Ural, Bashkir, and Asiatic R.S.F.S.R.	18,590	18,838	248	1
Ural	5,522	5,182	— 340	— 6
Bashkir	2,332	2,614	282	12
West Siberia	6,721	6,354	— 367	— 5
Central Siberia	1,983	2,114	131	7
East Siberia	1,129	1,349	220	20
Soviet Far East	903	1,226	323	36
Kazakhstan	5,555	4,440	—1,115	—20
Central Asia	6,220	8,097	1,877	30
Kirgiz	879	1,189	310	35
Uzbek	3,553	4,837	1,284	36
Tadzhik	926	1,233	307	33
Turkmen	861	837	24	3

less extreme than the regional variations in degree of dependence on crops at either the beginning or the end of the period in question.

There was an absolute increase of sown land in every Study Area with two exceptions. There was a slight decrease in Belorussia, although large tracts of marshland had been drained and opened to settlement, but this region is on the whole a relatively poor area for crop production. It is more surprising to find that there was a marked decrease of sown land in the Soviet Far

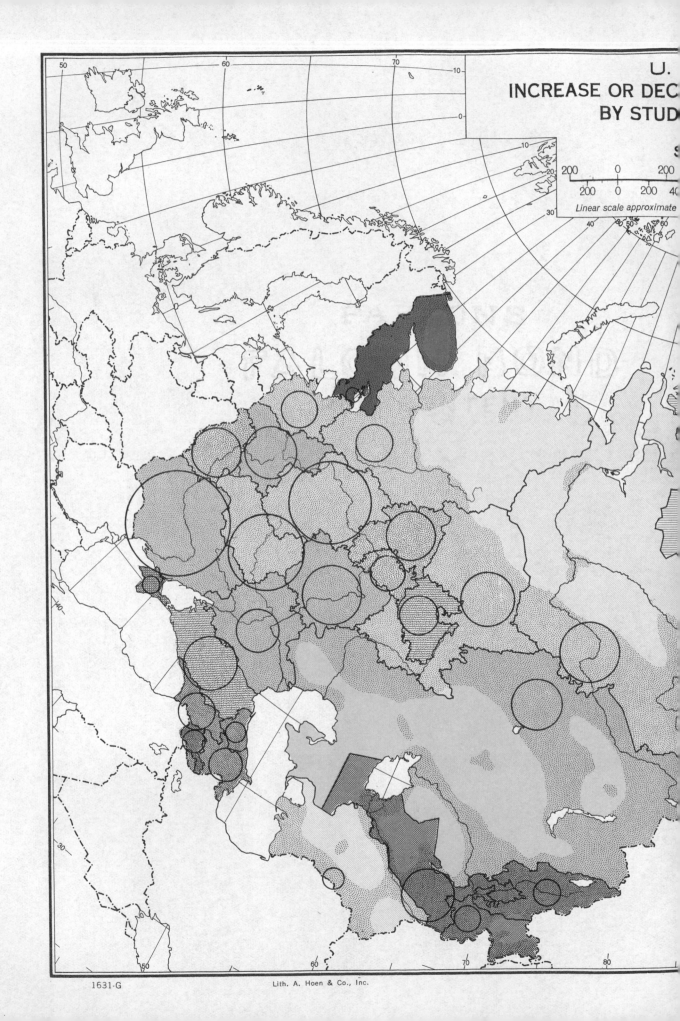

PLATE XVIII

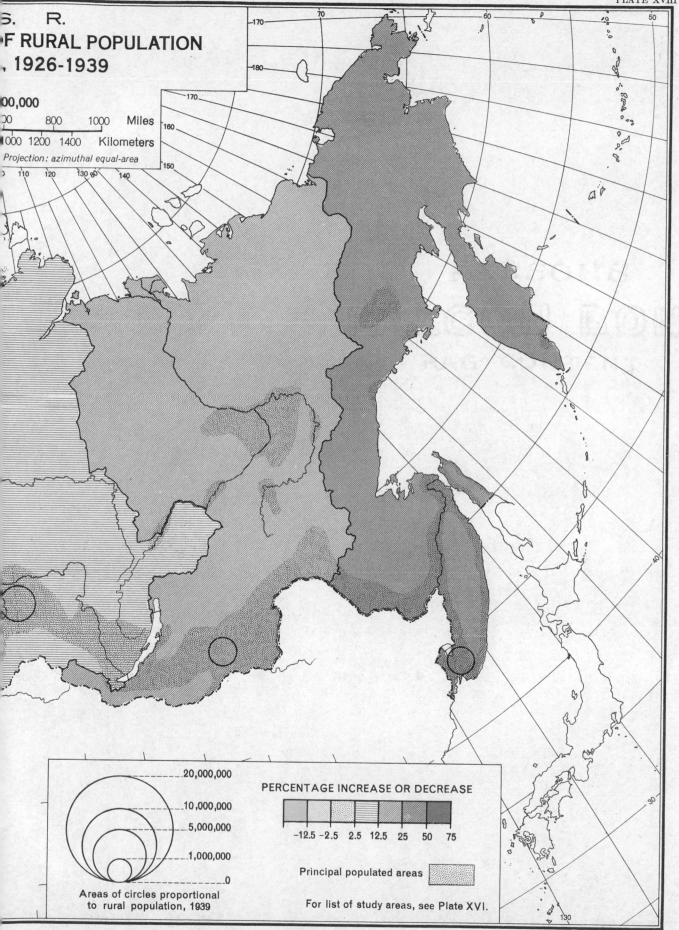

S.   R.

F RURAL POPULATION

, 1926-1939

00,000

0   800   1000   Miles

000 1200 1400   Kilometers

Projection: azimuthal equal-area

20,000,000

10,000,000

5,000,000

1,000,000

0

Areas of circles proportional
to rural population, 1939

PERCENTAGE INCREASE OR DECREASE

-12.5 -2.5   2.5   12.5   25   50   75

Principal populated areas

For list of study areas, see Plate XVI.

Prepared by Department of State, Division
of Geography and Cartography
Drawn by American Geographical Society

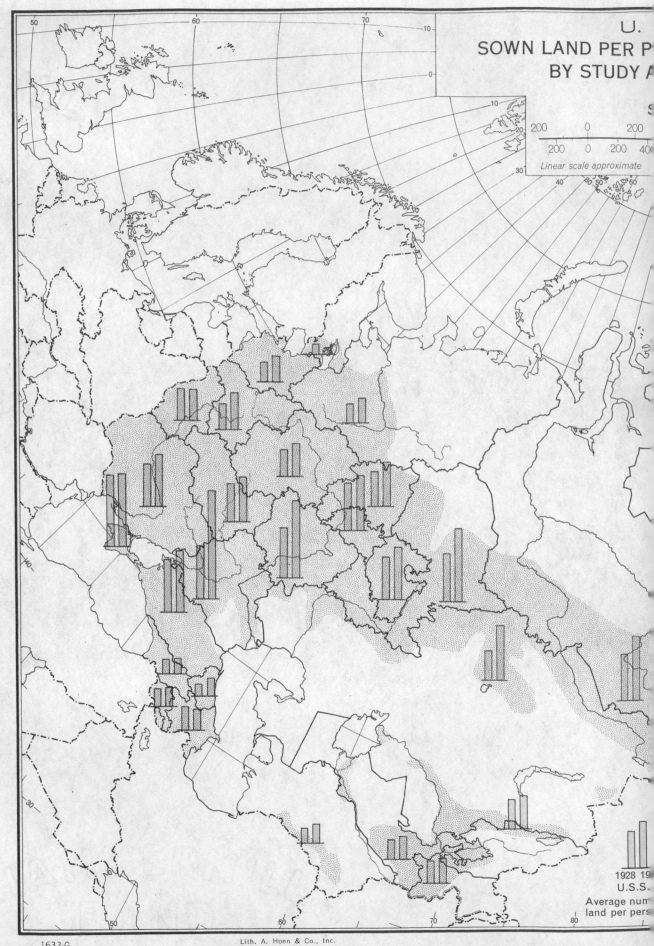

U.
SOWN LAND PER P
BY STUDY A

200   0   200
200   0   200   40
Linear scale approximate

1928 19
U.S.S.
Average num
land per pers

PLATE XIX

S.   R.

N RURAL POPULATION

28 AND 1938

0,000

800   1,000   Miles

000 1200 1400   Kilometers

Projection: azimuthal equal-area

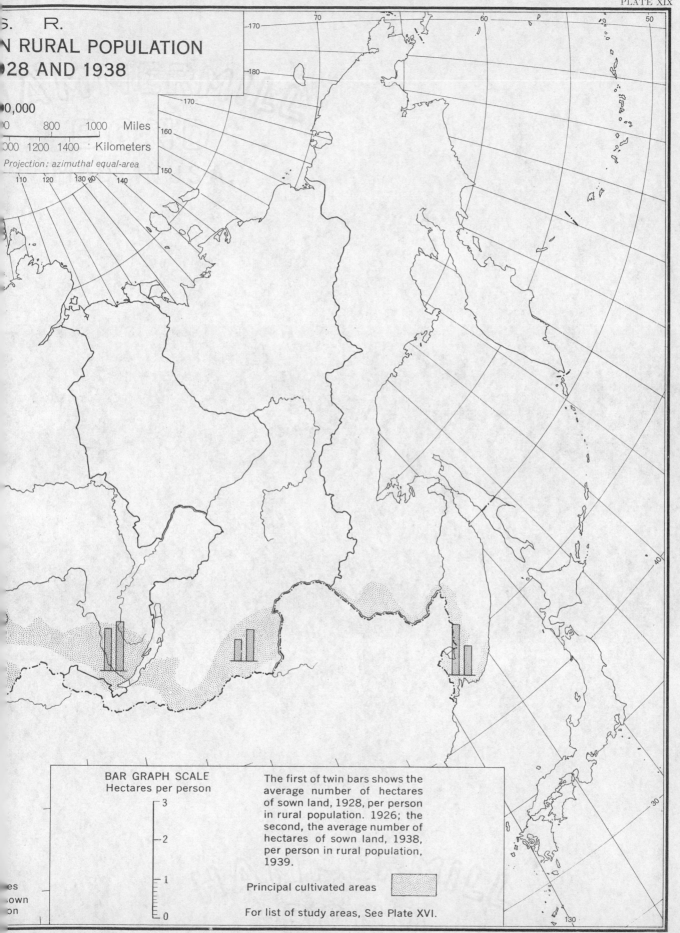

BAR GRAPH SCALE
Hectares per person

— 3

— 2

— 1

— 0

The first of twin bars shows the average number of hectares of sown land, 1928, per person in rural population. 1926; the second, the average number of hectares of sown land, 1938, per person in rural population, 1939.

Principal cultivated areas

For list of study areas, See Plate XVI.

Prepared by Department of State, Division of Geography and Cartography
Drawn by American Geographical Society

TABLE 64

Change in Sown Land Per Capita of Rural Population, 1928-1938

Population Study Area	Sown Land, 1938, as Percent of Sown Land, 1928	Hectares, 1928, Per Capita of Rural Population, 1926	Hectares, 1938, Per Capita of Rural Population, 1939	Ratio of Hectares Per Capita 1938/1928 (Percent)
	(1)	(2)	(3)	(4)
U.S.S.R.	121	.936	1.195	128
European Part, except Ural, Bashkir, and Dagestan	116	.965	1.234	128
Belorussia	98	.822	.795	97
Ukraine	103	1.053	1.295	123
Central Black Soil	106	.951	1.121	118
Western	118	.663	.934	141
Old Industrial Center	116	.694	.836	120
Leningrad	123	.501	.657	131
Karelia-Murmansk	117	.243	.173	71
Northeast	118	.505	.647	128
Vyatka	126	.892	1.122	126
Tatar	119	1.175	1.403	119
Central Volga	126	1.262	1.926	153
Lower Volga and Don	160	1.364	2.751	202
Crimea	142	1.833	1.843	101
North Caucasus	121	1.359	1.573	116
Transcaucasus with Dagestan	123	.458	.463	101
Azerbaydzhan	107	.614	.533	87
Georgia	126	.377	.398	106
Armenia	132	.465	.478	103
Dagestan	187	.302	.470	156
Ural, Bashkir, and Asiatic R.S.F.S.R.	134	1.133	1.496	132
Ural	143	1.201	1.835	153
Bashkir	141	1.059	1.328	125
West Siberia	133	1.155	1.622	140
Central Siberia	126	1.046	1.235	118
East Siberia[1]	160	.714	.953	133
Soviet Far East	78	1.277	.733	57
Kazakhstan	144	.764	1.375	180
Central Asia	149	.548	.625	114
Kirgiz	152	.767	.860	112
Uzbek	153	.522	.585	112
Tadzhik	147	.589	.649	110
Turkmen	123	.386	.490	127

[1] Omitting Yakutsk A.S.S.R., for which 1928 figures on sown land are lacking; 100,000 hectares (.3 hectares per capita of rural population) were sown here in 1938. The corresponding figures for 1928 would have been much lower.

East (see Table 64, Column 1). The Far East suffered at this time from the rapid population turnover characteristic of a pioneer region, accentuated by much political turmoil. It is possible that partial relocation of the large Korean farming population affected the situation. However, the principal factor was undoubtedly the acute industrial labor shortage in the Far East, and the attraction of rapidly expanding industrial opportunity for persons engaged in farming under difficult conditions.[25] In the Karelia-Murmansk area there was an expansion of sown acreage, but the increase of rural population outstripped the increase of sown land (necessarily limited by climatic conditions).

Apart from Belorussia, Karelia-Murmansk, and the Soviet Far East, the only areas which do not show a marked advance during the intercensus period in the ratio of sown land to rural population are the Crimea, the Transcaucasus, and Central Asia. The Crimea received the highest ratings of any part of the U.S.S.R. on the indices of agricultural productivity and average real income of rural population in 1926; it was also the area of most diverse occupational structure. There was a great development of health resorts and recreational facilities in the Crimea under Soviet rule. In view of these factors, it is not surprising that there was a rapid increase of rural population and also a rapid increase of sown land in this area—and that these two developments were roughly parallel—so that there was little change here in the index for sown land relative to rural population. The low ratio of sown land to rural population in Dagestan also rose rapidly (56 percent), owing to a rapid expansion of sown area that more than offset the absolute increase of the rural population. There was a similar, but less marked advance, in this respect in Turkmenia.

The Transcaucasus, as a whole, shows little change in economic status on this index. The change in Central Asia, in spite of a very considerable increase in extent of sown land, is only half as great as the average for the U.S.S.R. These lags were associated with rapid growth of the rural population in both of these regions. The Transcaucasus and Central Asia showed low productivity per capita of farm population on all indices for the early Soviet period. However, strenuous efforts were directed during the Five-Year Plans toward forcing the expansion of semitropical agriculture, including cotton, citrus fruits, essences, tobacco and kok-sagyz (a substitute for rubber), so as to make the U.S.S.R. largely independent of foreign imports. The expansion of the sown land area in southern Kazakhstan and Central Asia was made possible by a great extension of irrigation, and new irrigation projects were introduced in parts of the Transcaucasus. There was clearly an important advance in the economic productivity of the southern regions of the U.S.S.R. during these years, but the relation of people to economic opportunity was strongly affected by demographic factors, which we shall consider below in discussing total population changes.

Some of the districts showing a drop in rural population have rather unfavorable soil conditions, notably the Smolensk and Kalinin districts of the Western area, where there was an absolute decrease of 16 percent in the rural population between 1926 and 1939. The rural populations of the Leningrad and Old Industrial Center regions also decreased somewhat, but not greatly. On the other hand, the rural population of Belorussia and the Vyatka area (be-

[25] The sown area in Khabarovsk Territory dropped sharply from 740 thousand hectares in 1928 to 474 thousand hectares in 1932 (during a period when difficult conditions led to the return of many migrants), but rose irregularly to 581 thousand hectares in 1938 (stimulated, in part, by new settlements in the Jewish Autonomous Region). In the Maritime Territory, after a rise from 413 thousand hectares in 1928 to 462 thousand in 1932, there was a gradual decline to 318 thousand in 1938. In view of this situation great emphasis, near the end of the intercensus period, was laid on the expansion of agriculture in this region in order to establish an efficient local balance between industry and agriculture (see Sonin, Title 308). The Third Five-Year Plan carried provisions for a great increase in sown area in the Far East.

tween the upper Volga and the Urals) remained constant, whereas that of Dagestan (as already noted) and presumably that of the Caucasus Mountain districts increased rapidly.

The most striking decreases of rural population, however, did not occur in areas of low agricultural productivity, but in the fertile steppe zone across southern Russia, western Siberia, and Kazakhstan, i.e., in the regions most adapted to mechanized, large-scale farming. The apparent percent declines in rural population in this zone were as follows: Ukraine, 16 percent; Central Black Soil, 10; Central Volga, 17; Lower Volga and Don, 20; Ural, 6; West Siberia, 5; and Kazakhstan, 20. The *redistribution decrements* (i.e., the loss below "expected" increase at the average rate of the whole U.S.S.R.) of the rural population in these seven areas represent a combined total of 19,236,000 persons.[26] These areas held large rural populations in 1926, having altogether 53 percent of the entire rural population of the Soviet Union. They supplied 76 percent of the total rural redistribution decrement (25.4 million persons).

The principal reason for this trend is simple. These are the areas where the reorganization and mechanization of agriculture could release the largest number of potential industrial workers, simultaneously with an extension of sown area and an increase in agricultural production. This situation is well illustrated in the case of the Rostov and Stalingrad districts, grouped here with the Kalmyk A.S.S.R. as the Lower Volga and Don area.[27] With the exception of the Crimea, this area had the highest ratio of sown land, 1928, to rural population, 1926. With the exception of Dagestan and East Siberia, it had the highest absolute increase of sown land, 1928-1938. Finally, with the exception of Kazakhstan, it sustained the heaviest proportional loss in rural population. Accordingly, in this area the average amount of sown land per capita of rural population increased 100 percent during the intercensus period, and reached 2.75 hectares per person, which was the highest level in the U.S.S.R.

This economic advance, however, was not accomplished without tragic losses. The depletion of livestock during the collectivization drive was generally heaviest across this fertile steppe zone. Nowhere else, however, did this loss reach such proportions as in Kazakhstan, where the nomad population was almost wholly dependent on livestock for its sustenance. Commercial farming, prior to 1928, had become most firmly established in the steppe zone. And in Kazakhstan tribal structure and traditional property relations constituted a formidable obstacle to the collectivization program, although this was apparently not the case, at least to the same degree, among other nomad groups.

There were large movements of peasants from many relatively overpopulated rural districts in European Russia to the near-by expanding industrial centers. According to Sonin, 5.5 million persons migrated to Moscow, Leningrad, Gorkiy, and five smaller cities from the districts of Vologda in the Northeast Study Area; Kalinin and Smolensk, comprising the Western Area; Yaroslavl and Ryazan in the Old Industrial Center; Orël, Kursk, Voronezh, and Tambov, which constitute the Central Black Soil Area; and Penza, Kuybyshev, and the Mordva A.S.S.R., in the Central Volga.[28] There was undoubtedly heavy movement from rural communities to cities within the Ukraine. Moreover, the rural population of West Siberia apparently supplied enough surplus personnel to offset, in net effect, the labor demands of industrial communities in this general region, leaving the proportion of the total Soviet population in this area constant from 1926 to 1939. On the other hand, rural as well as urban communi-

[26] See Table 66.

[27] Rapid increases in the ratio of sown land to rural population took place in each of these three component areas, although the absolute amount of sown land in the arid Kalmyk steppes was still small in 1938.

[28] Sonin, Title 308, p. 80. This information may have been drawn from registration data, or from a preliminary tabulation of 1939 census returns.

ties in the areas farther to the east increased more rapidly than the Soviet population as a whole, resulting in large redistribution increments in these areas.

6. Population Redistribution: Migration and Differential Natural Increase

The net population change of the various Study Areas from 1926 to 1939 is shown in Plate XX and the redistribution increments in Plate XXI. The estimates on which these maps are based are given in Tables 65 and 66. It is possible in a few cases to supplement these findings with information on particular districts.

TABLE 65

Total Population Change by Study Area: U.S.S.R., 1926-1939

(Numbers in Thousands)

Population Study Area	Population		Change, 1926-1939	
	1926	1939	Absolute	Percent
U.S.S.R.	147,028	170,467	23,439	15.9
European Part, except Ural,				
Bashkir, and Dagestan	104,770	116,081	11,310	11
Belorussia	4,983	5,568	585	12
Ukraine	29,043	30,960	1,917	7
Central Black Soil	12,667	12,112	—555	—4
Western	6,275	5,902	—373	—6
Old Industrial Center	16,704	22,032	5,328	32
Leningrad	4,560	6,435	1,875	41
Karelia-Murmansk	293	760	467	159
Northeast	2,901	3,180	279	10
Vyatka	4,567	5,103	536	12
Tatar	2,594	2,919	325	13
Central Volga	8,600	8,069	—531	—6
Lower Volga and Don	5,203	5,404	201	4
Crimea	714	1,127	413	58
North Caucasus	5,665	6,508	843	15
Transcaucasus with Dagestan	6,561	8,964	2,403	37
Azerbaydzhan	2,314	3,210	896	39
Georgia	2,677	3,542	865	32
Armenia	881	1,282	401	46
Dagestan	689	931	242	35
Ural, Bashkir, and Asiatic R.S.F.S.R.	22,026	28,795	6,769	31
Ural	6,943	9,074	2,131	31
Bashkir	2,565	3,145	580	23
West Siberia	7,612	8,909	1,297	17
Central Siberia	2,340	3,227	887	38
East Siberia	1,325	2,102	777	59
Soviet Far East	1,241	2,338	1,097	88
Kazakhstan	6,074	6,146	72	1
Central Asia	7,597	10,480	2,883	38
Kirgiz	1,002	1,459	457	46
Uzbek	4,565	6,282	1,717	38
Tadzhik	1,032	1,485	453	44
Turkmen	998	1,254	256	26

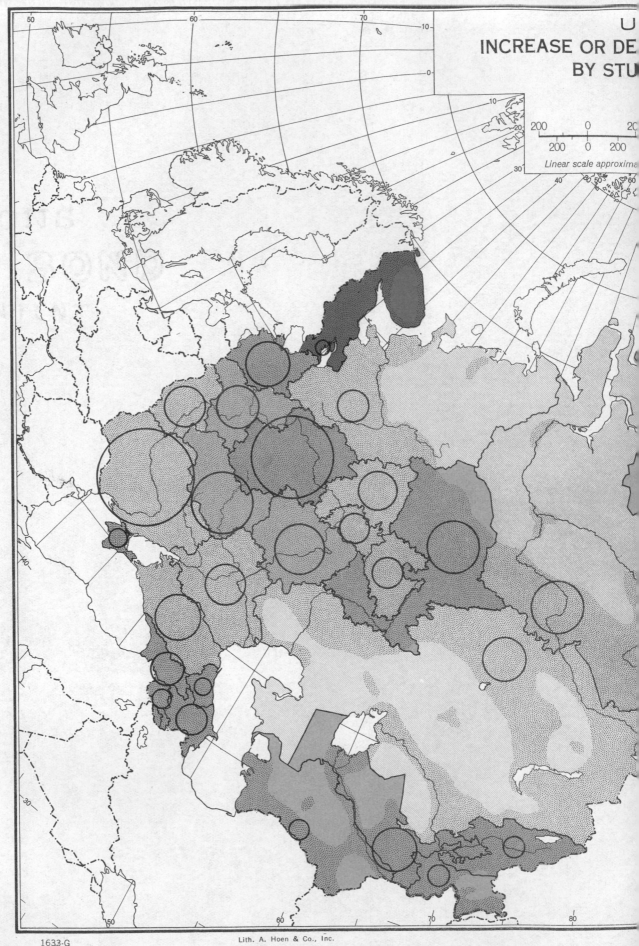

200   0   20
200   0   200
Linear scale approxima

Lith. A. Hoen & Co., Inc.

PLATE XX

S. R.
OF TOTAL POPULATION
S, 1926-1939

,000,000

| 600 | 800 | 1000 Miles |
| 1000 | 1200 1400 | Kilometers |

Projection: azimuthal equal-area

PERCENTAGE INCREASE OR DECREASE

-12.5 -2.5   2.5 12.5   25   50   75   100   150   200

30,000,000

10,000,000
5,000,000

1,000,000

0

Areas of circles proportional
to total population, 1939

Principal populated areas

For list of study areas, see Plate XVI.

Prepared by Department of State, Division
of Geography and Cartography
Drawn by American Geographical Society

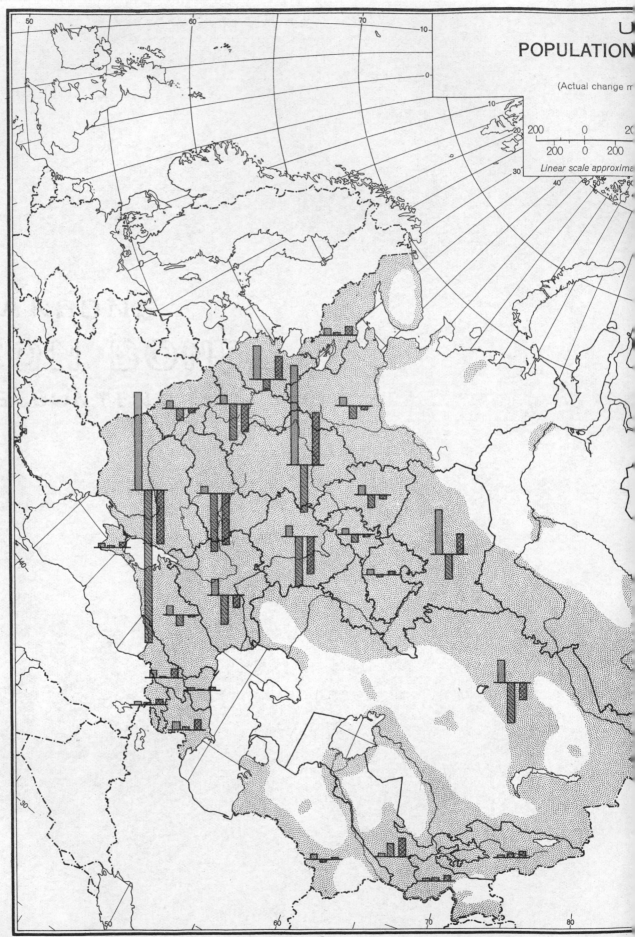

PLATE XXI

S. R.
BY STUDY AREAS
939

rease": urban, rural, and total)

,000,000

| 600 | 800 | 1000 | Miles |

| 1000 | 1200 | 1400 | Kilometers |

Projection: azimuthal equal-area

100 110 120 130 60 140

PH SCALE
of persons

- 5.000
- 4.000
- 3.000
- 2.000
- 1,000
- 0

Bar above the line indicates an increase above that expected on basis of total population growth of U.S.S.R.; bar below, a relative decrease. The first bar of each group represents the urban population; the second bar, the rural population; and the third bar, the total population (the net of the first two).

Principal populated areas

For list of study areas, see Plate XVI.

Prepared by Department of State, Division of Geography and Cartography
Drawn by American Geographical Society

TABLE 66

Difference between Actual and Expected Population Change by Study Area: U.S.S.R., 1926-1939

Population Study Area	Expected Increase[1]		Redistribution Increment (+) or Decrement (—)[2]		
	Urban	Rural	Urban[3]	Rural[3]	Total[3]
U.S.S.R.	4,195	19,244	25,401	—25,401	0
European Part, except Ural, Bashkir, and Dagestan	3,108	13,595	16,471	—21,860	—5,389
Belorussia	135	659	390	—599	—209
Ukraine	856	3,773	4,966	—7,678	—2,712
Central Black Soil	213	1,807	370	—2,946	—2,576
Western	98	903	441	—1,813	—1,372
Old Industrial Center	737	1,925	5,019	—2,353	+2,666
Leningrad	334	392	1,687	—538	+1,149
Karelia-Murmansk	11	35	314	+108	+422
Northeast	43	419	435	—618	—183
Vyatka	53	675	473	—664	—191
Tatar	45	369	296	—384	—88
Central Volga	187	1,184	578	—2,481	—1,903
Lower Volga and Don	186	644	841	—1,470	—629
Crimea	53	61	203	+96	+299
North Caucasus	157	747	458	—520	—62
Transcaucasus with Dagestan	237	809	1,067	+291	+1,358
Azerbaydzhan	104	265	408	+120	+528
Georgia	95	332	379	+61	+440
Armenia	27	114	172	+87	+259
Dagestan	12	98	108	+23	+131
Ural, Bashkir, and Asiatic R.S.F.S.R.	548	2,964	5,973	—2,716	+3,257
Ural	227	880	2,244	—1,221	+1,023
Bashkir	37	372	261	—90	+171
West Siberia	142	1,071	1,522	—1,439	+83
Central Siberia	57	316	699	—185	+514
East Siberia	31	180	527	+40	+567
Soviet Far East	54	144	720	+179	+899
Kazakhstan	83	886	1,104	—2,001	—897
Central Asia	220	992	786	+885	+1,671
Kirgiz	19	140	130	+170	+300
Uzbek	161	566	271	+717	+988
Tadzhik	17	148	129	+159	+288
Turkmen	22	137	256	—161	+95

[1] At average rate of entire Soviet population. 1926 population multiplied by .15942.

[2] Absolute change (from Tables 62 and 63) minus expected increase.

[3] Last digits of largest figures are raised or lowered one point where necessary to give correct totals for urban and rural, separately; total decrement of each area is taken as algebraic sum of urban and rural figures.

Unfortunately, we have not succeeded in locating 1939 population data for the Ukraine by minor political divisions. We know that there was an absolute increase of 108 percent in urban population and an absolute decrease of 16 percent in the rural population of this republic (see Tables 62 and 63). We can assume that the districts in the southern and eastern Ukraine, where there were many rapidly growing towns, increased rapidly. It is not surprising, therefore, to learn that the population of the Stalino District increased 91 percent and that of the Voroshilovgrad District increased 37 percent, 1926-1939.[29] Most of the predominantly rural oblasts presumably lost population, but we are unable to describe the regional incidence of such changes within the whole republic.

Within the Old Industrial Center, where our data indicate a total population increase of 32 percent, there was a reported increase of 74 percent in the Moscow District and of 28 percent in the Gorkiy District.[30] This would indicate a slow average increase of about 8 percent between 1926 and 1939 for the population in the remaining districts: Ivanovo, Ryazan, Tula, and Yaroslavl.

The extremely rapid growth of the Karelia-Murmansk population, which, according to our data, grew to more than two and a half times its number in 1926, was due chiefly to a ninefold increase in the Murmansk District.[31] But since the initial population here was small, there was also apparently a very considerable growth in the Karelian A.S.S.R.

Our data indicate an absolute increase of 6.8 million persons in the eastern part of the R.S.F.S.R. (Urals, Bashkiria, Siberia, and the Far East)—or 6.2 million, excluding Bashkiria. This is above the figure cited by Sonin and others for the Urals, Siberia, and the Far East, i.e., an absolute increase of 5.9 million between 1926 and 1939,[32] and is apparently somewhat too high.

The redistribution increment for the entire eastern R.S.F.S.R., 1926-1939, is 3,257,000, or 3,086,000 excluding Bashkiria. If we assume, as seems probable, that this change should be credited to net in-migration, our estimate is in agreement with the statement that "more than three million people (exclusive of returned migrants) moved to the Urals, Siberia, and the Far East" during the interval between 1926 and 1939.[33] On the assumption that in these areas the redistribution increments represent the approximate amount of net migration, this total is distributed as follows:

Area	Approximate Net Number of In-migrants, 1926-1939
Ural	1,023,000
Bashkir	171,000
West Siberia	83,000
Central Siberia	514,000
East Siberia	567,000
Soviet Far East	899,000

[29] *Ekonomicheskaya Geografiya SSSR*, Title 464, p. 152.

[30] *Ibid*. Inferential increases for other districts obtained by use of 1939 data by oblasts given in Appendix VII, Table A 22.

[31] *Ibid*.

[32] Sonin, Title 308, p. 79.

[33] Sonin, Title 308. This interval is referred to in the text as a fourteen-year period, but the same figure also appears in the Academy publication, where the reference is clearly to the intercensus period of twelve years and one month.

Percentage increases for selected districts in these areas are reported in a Soviet source as follows:[34]

Study Area and Political Division	Percent Increase, 1926-1939
Ural	
Sverdlovsk Oblast	53
West Siberia	
Novosibirsk Oblast	53
Central Siberia	
Irkutsk Oblast	49
East Siberia	
Chita Oblast	73
Buryat-Mongolian A.S.S.R.	39
Soviet Far East	
Khabarovsk Kray	136
Maritime Kray	42

The reported information for the two divisions of the Soviet Far East agrees approximately with our figures for the Study Area. The reported increases for Buryat-Mongolia and the Chita District, in combination with our estimate for East Siberia, would allow an increase of about 50 percent in the Yakutsk A.S.S.R., which would seem to be surprisingly high for that region. There is probably an error in our estimates. The information on the Irkutsk District and our estimate for Central Siberia give an increase of 32 percent for Krasnoyarsk Territory. Our estimate for West Siberia and the reported data on the Novosibirsk District indicate practically no net intercensus change for the combined population of Omsk and the Altay Territory. An increase of about 23 percent is indicated for the Ural area, exclusive of the Sverdlovsk District.

In discussions of migration within the U.S.S.R. there has been much emphasis on the difficulty of securing permanent migrants for the eastern regions and on heavy return movements —a phenomenon almost universally characteristic of pioneer communities. Nevertheless, the observed redistribution increments for the twelve-year period, 1926-1939, in the case of the Urals, Siberia, and the Soviet Far East are reasonably close to early expectations of migration to these areas for a somewhat shorter interval, 1926-1936. Plans for migration during this period (1926-1936) prepared by the Commissariat of Agriculture, and cited by Babynin in the *Bulletin* of the R.S.F.S.R. Planning Commission in 1927, included 500,000 migrants to the Urals, 1,812,000 to Siberia, and 1,145,000 to the Far East, or a total of 3,457,000 persons.[35] The redistribution increments for the corresponding Study Areas (with Siberia having a more inclusive and the other areas a more restricted reference) are: Ural Area, 1,023,000; Bashkiria, 171,000; Siberia (West, Central, and East), 1,164,000; Soviet Far East, 899,000; total, 3,257,000 persons. However, this rough agreement may be purely accidental. The eastward migration up to 1939 did not include a large number of agricultural settlers, as was originally intended, but was predominantly a movement of potential industrial workers and their families.

The distribution of population in various parts of the Khabarovsk Territory in 1939 is indirectly suggested on the basis of a list of electoral precincts set up according to regulations formulated in July, 1939, so as to include about 15,000 persons in each district.[36] There were altogether 108 such precincts. This figure multiplied by 15,000 gives a hypothetical population

[34] *Ekonomicheskaya Geografiya SSSR*, Title 464, p. 157.
[35] Babynin, Title 10, pp. 46-58.
[36] *Tikhookeanskaya Zvezda* (Khabarovsk), October 26, 1939.

of 1,620,000 persons, as compared with 1,430,875 persons according to the census taken on January 17 of the same year. The difference between these figures may represent actual increase, or it may be due simply to the effect of rounding numbers in the composition of districts; it is probably influenced by both of these factors. Treated literally, this difference would indicate an increase of 13 percent in six months, which is hardly probable but not absolutely impossible. On the same basis, the estimate for the city of Khabarovsk is 225,000 persons, or 13 percent above the census figure; that for Komsomolsk is 105,000, or 48 percent above the census figure. Similarly, the population indicated for the Jewish Autonomous District is 135,000, which is 24.5 percent greater than the census figure. These were probably among the areas with most rapid increase. The hypothetical population in all other areas is 1,155,000 persons, which is 9.7 percent above the corresponding census figure. This remainder is distributed as follows:

Area	*Hypothetical Population, July, 1939*
Amur District: the region west of the Amur River along the Trans-Siberian Railway, extending north across the mountains to include a section (Yakutia to Komsomolsk) of the new, partially completed northern line	570,000
Areas subordinate to the Khabarovsk Organization, including two non-contiguous regions: (1) the region in the vicinity of the city of Khabarovsk; (2) a special area in the north that includes the Kolyma River region and Magadan, with one precinct allotted to this city	240,000
Lower Amur District, including the city of Nikolayevsk and a part of the Okhotsk coast	105,000
Sakhalin District: the Soviet portion of Sakhalin Island	120,000
Kamchatka District: the far northeastern region between the Okhotsk Sea and the Arctic Ocean and the Kamchatka Peninsula	120,000

The Jewish Autonomous District (formerly, Biro-Bidzhan District), mostly south of the Trans-Siberian Railway, lies in a bend of the Amur River near its junction with the Sungari River from Manchuria. The progress of this district, located in a strategically vital and precarious situation and handicapped by swampy soil, has been the subject of much controversy. It had a population of about 34,000 persons (78 percent Russian, 12 percent Korean and Chinese, and 10 percent indigenous) when it was set apart in 1928 as a national district for Jewish settlement. It received its present political status on May 7, 1934. The district has been characterized by a large flow of in-migrants, but also by large return movements.[37] In January, 1939, its total population was 108,419 persons, of whom about one-fourth or perhaps somewhat more were Jews.[38] Some of the Jewish refugees from German-occupied Poland were later settled in this region.

The population of the Soviet portion of Sakhalin Island was only 12,000 persons in December, 1926, but even this number apparently represents a gain of about 20 percent above the population in 1925, when the Soviets acquired title. This area is reported to have had a ten-

[37] Yarmolinsky, Title 369.
[38] The proportion of Jews was reported as 23.8 percent in *Emes* (periodical published in Moscow), June 3, 1937.

fold increase in population from 1925 to 1936.[39] The hypothetical figure for 1939, as noted above, is 120,000 persons.

In addition to its strategic and commercial importance, the Soviet Far East is reputed to be rich in mineral resources, forests, and vegetation including many varieties not found elsewhere in the Soviet Union. It has some excellent farm lands, and will undoubtedly support a rapid population increase during the next few decades. The region provides a fourth of the fish supply of the whole U.S.S.R. Many of the indigenous nationalities of the Far Eastern districts gain their livelihood from this activity. As they become members of cooperative artels, their traditional skills in hunting, fishing, and other forest occupations become integrated and modified in the organized enterprises of a modern economy.

Soviet policy during the Third Five-Year Plan (1938-1942) was directed toward making the Far East "an economically balanced, first-rate industrial region, strengthening the economic and military power of the USSR in the East."[40] Ten percent of the total budget in the Third Five-Year Plan was devoted to the development of this area and adjacent regions in eastern Siberia. Much energy, therefore, has been spent on the promotion of complementary industries, such as cement and lumber for industrial and residential construction, fuel for regional industries (including petroleum, as well as coal from the older fields near Vladivostok and from new mines on the Bureya River and elsewhere), and the development of an adequate transportation system. Plans for the region include a proposed increase in livestock to a level per capita above the average for the U.S.S.R. and a projected increase in sown land.

The Arctic region has captured the attention of scientists, economists, writers, and the Soviet public. Some developments in the European Arctic and the Far East have already been mentioned. There are also important new settlements along the Yenisey River in Krasnoyarsk Territory. Igarka, far to the north in Central Siberia, has about 20,000 inhabitants.[41] It now has a permanent quay for Trans-Arctic transportation. This was built into frozen banks and through thick ice during two winters, when the water level was low, to provide a structure that could resist the terrific spring floods. Below Igarka, the port of Dudinka is connected by a ninety-mile railway across the tundra with Norilsk, a town of 30,000 inhabitants, center of the Northern Polymetallic Combine which augments the Soviet output of molybdenum, mercury, zinc, copper, and nickel.[42] Even Verkhoyansk in Yakutia, described as the cold pole of the world with a temperature sometimes reaching —94° Fahrenheit, is the scene of tin mining operations. Agriculture has been developed in far northern districts, with special preparation of seeds and other experimental techniques, including hothouse cultivation in remote Arctic stations. The Lena valley, winding through Yakutia halfway between the Trans-Siberian Railway and the Arctic Ocean, has long been used for farming, but its sown area was greatly increased in the late 'thirties. In 1938 there were 100,000 hectares of sown land (chiefly in spring rye, spring wheat, and spring barley) above permanently frozen subsoil in the Yakutsk Republic, where only 42,000 hectares were sown in 1930.[43] In planning the development of the Far North emphasis has been laid on the provision of health, educational, and cultural facilities both for new communities and for the indigenous people scattered through the northern taiga and tundra, and along the shores of the Arctic and northern Pacific.

The extension of agriculture northward, involving great expansion of wheat areas in central Russia and the development of gardening in the Arctic, has its counterpart in the construction of large irrigation projects and the introduction of new methods of farming in the arid steppe zone. New techniques here include the preparation of seeds to resist drought, the cultivation of

[39] Mikhailov, Title 194, p. 204.
[41] Davies and Steiger, Title 59, p. 190.
[43] *Posevnyye Ploshchadi SSSR*, Title 453.
[40] Sonin, Title 308, p. 77.
[42] *Ibid.*, p. 82.

crops in deep trenches in desert areas, and similar measures. Likewise, mining operations have been initiated in regions where the temperature may rise to $+160°$ Fahrenheit, such as the sodium sulphate industry at Kara-Bogaz-Gol on the Aral Sea and a sulphur plant in the Kara-Kum Desert, which is linked with Ashkabad by an auto speedway.[44]

We have attributed to net in-migration almost the entire growth increment of cities in general, and the increments of total population both in the remote districts of the Far North and, more particularly, in the Urals, East Siberia, and the Soviet Far East. The population increase of the Transcaucasus republics presents a striking contrast in this respect. Here the redistribution increments seem to have been due mainly to rapid natural increase and the relative *immobility* of the population.

During the intercensus period there was an increase of 46 percent in the population of Armenia, 39 percent in Azerbaydzhan, and 32 percent in Georgia. There was also an increase of 35 percent in the population of the Dagestan A.S.S.R., across the eastern portion of the Caucasus range. Population growth probably proceeded at about the same rate in the Caucasus Mountain districts. These increases may be compared with the average of 15.9 percent for the whole U.S.S.R. during the same period.

The net exchange between the Transcaucasus and the rest of the U.S.S.R., as indicated by data on birth and place of residence in 1926, was only 65,000 persons (213,900 in-migrants minus 148,700 out-migrants), or 1 percent of the total population of the region at that time (5,862,000 persons).[45] Thus, in the early Soviet period the Transcaucasus appeared as an area of relatively low mobility, and there is no evidence of large movements to or from the republics of this region during more recent years. On the other hand, there is evidence that this is an area of unusually high natural increase. This is shown by the vital statistics of the early Soviet period (available only for Armenia), and by the net reproduction ratios based on age-distribution data.[46] Similar evidence is contained in later occasional reports on ratios of births to deaths.[47] It is, in general, a region of early marriages, high fertility, and good health conditions. Furthermore, economic changes here have been progressive but less drastic than in many other parts of the Soviet Union.

Changes in numbers of persons classified by "ethnic group" in 1926 and by "nationality" in 1939 can be used to obtain indices of natural increase during the intercensus period, subject to the important limitations described in Chapter IX.[48] These limitations are important in the case of Russians, Ukrainians, Belorussians, Tatars, and other nationalities where the data are strongly influenced by trend toward cultural assimilation, uncertainty as to minor groups included in the broad 1939 definition, or the possible influence of political status in the case of titular groups recognized in the formation of autonomous republics. These factors may affect some nationalities of the Caucasus region or Central Asia with respect to one another. For example, the apparent decrease in the number of Kurds probably has no relation to the demographic changes. However, these limitations presumably do not seriously affect the data for the main nationalities of the Caucasus region or Central Asia, when the data for various groups in the same region are treated in combination.

All the nationalities of the Transcaucasus and Caucasus Mountain districts listed in Table 55 show increases *above* the average increase of the entire population of the U.S.S.R., 1926-1939, with the exception of two small groups, Kurds and Abkhazians. If we apply the percentage increases shown in Table 55 for each group listed there (except Russians and Ukrain-

[44] *Ibid.*, p. 153.   [45] See Chapter IV, Table 21.   [46] See Chapter VII.

[47] Such ratios for 1938 were reported as 3.35 for Armenia, 3.34 for Georgia, and 2.32 for Azerbaydzhan, in contrast to 2.157 for the whole U.S.S.R. See Buzin and Dubrovitskiy, Title 43, p. 24.

[48] See Section 9 of Chapter IX.

ians) to the number of such persons listed in the Transcaucasus republics in 1926 and assume that the rest of their populations increased at the average rate of the whole Soviet population, we obtain the following estimated percentages of natural increase, 1926-1939: Azerbaydzhan, 28.7 percent; Georgia, 24.6 percent; Armenia, 35.5 percent. These "natural increases" account for 76 percent of the total population growth of the Transcaucasian republics. If the remainder is attributed to migration, there was an estimated net migration during these years of 232 thousand persons to Azerbaydzhan, 206 thousand persons to Georgia, and 80 thousand persons to Armenia. It is probable that many of the in-migrants settled in cities, and that the growth of rural population in the Transcaucasus and Caucasus Mountain districts was due to rapid natural increase and relatively low mobility. As already noted, rural population increase was a major factor in the total population change of all these areas; and the increase of rural population outstripped the increase of sown land in the Transcaucasus republics.

A somewhat similar but more complicated situation is indicated with regard to Central Asia. All of the Central Asian republics show "redistribution increments" for the period 1926-1939 (see Table 66). This is true of the rural as well as the urban areas, considered separately, except in Turkmenia, where the rural population decreased slightly. Using the procedure described in the previous paragraph, we obtain the following estimates of proportional increases through excess of births over deaths, 1926-1939: Uzbekistan, 20.4 percent; Tadzhikistan, 24.3 percent; Turkmenia, 10.0 percent; Kirgizia, 16.7 percent. Incidentally, on the basis of the nationality data, the Turkmen show an increase below that of other groups in this region, standing somewhat intermediate in this respect between the other Central Asian nationalities and the Kazakhs. With the same procedure, the estimated net in-migration to these republics was: Uzbekistan, 786 thousand persons; Kirgizia, 290 thousand; Tadzhikistan, 202 thousand; and Turkmenia, 156 thousand—giving an estimated total of 1,434,000 persons. This is below the figure of 1.7 million reported in the Soviet text on *Economic Geography*, as the number of persons who moved from other sections of the U.S.S.R. to these republics during the intercensus period.[49] Kazakhs, migrating from the arid steppe region, probably formed an important element in this movement, especially during the collectivization period.

Apparently, differential natural increase was a major factor in causing positive redistribution increments in the Uzbek and Tadzhik republics in Central Asia, and in the Transcaucasus (probably also in the adjacent mountain districts of the North Caucasus Area). The same may have been true of some minor districts of the R.S.F.S.R., concerning which we have no definite information. Elsewhere, the positive redistribution increments can be attributed, at least for the most part, to net in-migration. As regards areas of relative population loss (redistribution decrements), the evidence is more ambiguous. In most cases, except Kazakhstan and possibly some predominantly rural districts in the European steppe region, such redistribution decrements should probably be attributed directly to net out-migration. Inter-regional migration was thus the major factor determining changes in the distribution of the Soviet population during the intercensus period.

7. Comparison of Changes in Two Intercensus Periods

A brief comparison of regional population trends for the periods 1897-1926 and 1926-1939 brings out some interesting similarities and contrasts. The earlier intercensus period (1897-1926) extended over nearly thirty years. It included seventeen years of normal increase in the prewar period at an estimated average rate of 1.7 percent per year (38 percent higher than the average rate of natural increase during the Soviet intercensus period, which was 1.23 percent).

---

[49] *Ekonomicheskaya Geografiya SSSR*, Title 464, p. 152.

There was no net increase during the years from 1914 to 1923, but after this there was a spurt of very rapid natural increase before the time of the First All-Union Soviet Census. The total increase of population within the U.S.S.R. during the thirty years from 1897 to 1926 was 38.6 percent, in contrast to an increase of 15.9 percent in the later twelve-year period, 1926-1939. This difference in the rate of total population increase in the two periods is eliminated in comparing the respective "redistribution increments." However, a redistribution increment in the later period represents the effects of migration or differential natural increase during a twelve-year interval, whereas an increment of the same size during the earlier period would indicate that the forces making for redistribution of population worked at a slower tempo or were checked by conflicting trends. Nevertheless, the gross transfer of population among the Study Areas used in this comparison, as indicated by the sum of all redistribution increments with the same sign (plus or minus), was much greater in the later twelve-year period (10,577-000 persons) than in the earlier thirty-year period (5,154,000 persons). (See Table 67.)

TABLE 67

Total Population Change by Study Area: U.S.S.R., 1897-1926 and 1926-1939
(Numbers in Thousands)

Population Study Area	Population		Percent Increase	Redistribution Increment (+) or Decrement (−)	
	1897[1]	1926		1897-1926	1926-1939
U.S.S.R.	106,070	147,028	38.6	0	0
European Part, except Ural and Bashkir, but including Dagestan	78,739	105,459	34	−3,684	−5,258
Belorussia	3,722	4,983	34	−176	−209
Ukraine	21,246	29,043	37	−407	−2,712
Central Black Soil	9,328	12,667	36	−263	−2,576
Western	4,801	6,275	31	−380	−1,372
Old Industrial Center	12,201	16,704	37	−208	+2,666
Northern (Leningrad, Karelia-Murmansk, Northeast)	5,985	7,754	30	−542	+1,388
Vyatka and Tatar	6,222	7,161	15	−1,462	−279
Central Volga	6,666	8,600	29	−639	−1,903
Lower Volga and Don	3,689	5,203	41	+89	−629
Crimea	524	714	36	−12	+299
North Caucasus and Dagestan	4,355	6,354	46	+316	+69
Transcaucasus	4,493	5,872	31	−356	+1,227
Ural, Bashkir, and Asiatic R.S.F.S.R.	12,702	22,026	73	+4,419	+3,257
Ural and Bashkir	6,951	9,508	37	−127	+1,194
West Siberia	3,361	7,612	126	+2,953	+83
Central Siberia	1,073	2,340	118	+853	+514
East Siberia	968	1,325	37	−17	+567
Soviet Far East	349	1,241	256	+757	+899
Kazakhstan	4,248	6,074	43	+186	−897
Central Asia	5,888	7,597	29	−565	+1,671

[1] Compare Chapter III, Footnote 3.

In the following comparison of particular areas, it must be emphasized that the figures shown here for 1897 are even more subject to error than the estimates for various areas in 1926. In the case of Central Asia, the 1897 estimate is based on the arbitrary assumption that the population changes in the territory of the former Khanates of Khiva and Bukhara from 1897 to 1926 were proportional to changes in the rest of Central Asia. In other cases errors in these figures may arise from incorrect allocation of minor political divisions. In order to reduce errors of this sort and also to reduce the labor involved, some of the Study Areas used for the later period have been combined into larger units.

Most of the European areas showing redistribution decrements during the earlier period, i.e., Belorussia, Ukraine, the Central Black Soil, Western, Vyatka and Tatar, and Central Volga areas, also appear as areas with relative population loss in the later period. The notable exceptions are the Old Industrial Center, the northern part of European Russia (Leningrad, Karelia-Murmansk, and the Northeast areas combined), and the Crimea. These areas had redistribution decrements from 1897 to 1926, but positive increments during the Soviet period, 1926-1939.

A similar contrast appears in the case of both the Transcaucasus and Central Asia, each considered as a unit. These regions failed to hold their share of the total growth during the earlier period, but were areas of rapid increase from 1926 to 1939. Apparently, population growth in these regions had been previously checked by high mortality, especially in Central Asia, and by violent disturbances during the era of war and revolution. High mortality among the Yakuts and Buryats probably also accounts for the lag in population growth indicated for East Siberia between 1897 and 1926. There were also movements across the border into Sinkiang and Mongolia from Kirgizia and from Buryat-Mongolia during World War I and the early revolutionary period. High mortality among the Finnic and Turkic nationalities in the region between the Volga and the Urals and the effects of the famine in the Volga region in 1921-1922, combined with migration across the Urals, presumably account for the large decrement in the combined Vyatka-Tatar Area and in the Central Volga Area, 1897-1926. High mortality, as well as eastward migration, may also account for the apparent failure of the Ural and Bashkir region to increase more rapidly than the entire population within the U.S.S.R. from 1897 to 1926. In general, it appears that most of the areas largely occupied by non-Slavic elements increased less rapidly than the Slavic population prior to the Soviet regime. This relation was generally reversed, with the conspicuous exception of Kazakhstan, during the Soviet period, 1926-1939.

The redistribution increment of Siberia, plus the Ural and Bashkir areas and the Soviet Far East (i.e., the eastern part of the R.S.F.S.R.), was larger during the earlier period, 1897-1926, than during the Soviet period; the increment of the former was 4,400,000 persons, in contrast to 3,300,000 persons during the latter. The earlier figure is roughly 25 percent above the estimated net in-migration to this area during the years 1897 to 1914; and there was little net migration to Siberia between 1914 and 1926. One must bear in mind that the migrants to Siberia before 1914 who remained in this area contributed their natural increase over two decades to the growth of the Siberian population. Furthermore, Siberia as a whole suffered much less devastation than European Russia during the period of war and revolution. On the other hand, the redistribution increment of the eastern part of the R.S.F.S.R., 1926-1939, can be attributed almost wholly to the immediate effect of migration.

The urban population in the Asiatic part of the U.S.S.R., excluding the Transcaucasus but including the Ural and Bashkir regions, showed a considerable upward trend from 1897 to 1926, following the construction of the Trans-Siberian and Tashkent railroads. It apparently rose from about 2 million in 1897 to 5.3 million persons in 1926—an absolute increase of 3.3 million in about thirty years. (However, part of this apparent increase may have been spurious because of the rapid extension of the list of urban places in the early Soviet period.) During the second intercensus period the urban population of the same area rose much more rapidly from 5.3 million to 14 million persons, or an absolute increase of 8.7 million in twelve years. On the other hand, the rural population of this territory, which had increased from 20.8 million in 1897 to 30.4 million in 1926, had only a slight additional increase to 31.4 million persons in 1939. The eastward movement of population, which had been chiefly agricultural in the preceding period, became predominantly industrial during the Soviet regime.[50]

8. Migration Policies

Migration within the Soviet Union has been determined, in the main, by the free adjustment of individuals to variations in economic opportunity, as in other countries; but variations in economic opportunity here have been determined, especially since the inauguration of the successive Five-Year Plans, by the central instruments of national planning and administration. Modifications and exceptions to this general statement are described below. The theoretical underlying principles in the redistribution of population within the U.S.S.R. are described by Voshchinin, writing in 1934, as follows: "The principle of freedom and voluntary decision remains valid as before for every citizen of the U.S.S.R., but the principle that government help is given only to the type of migration that corresponds to the general policy and real potentialities of the state is being put into operation now more than ever before."[51]

During the Imperial regime there had been a long period of relative indifference to the colonization of Asiatic Russia, usually attributed to the opposition of the dominant landholding aristocracy to any diminution of the labor supply in European Russia. However, in the last two decades before the First World War the Imperial administration took an active interest in promoting migration to Siberia and appropriated funds to aid in the establishment of new settlements. Subsidization and systematic direction of migration beyond the Urals began after the Revolution with the establishment of the All-Union Migration Committee in 1925, but the funds allotted for this purpose did not reach the level of expenditures of the late Imperial regime until 1928.[52] It is interesting to note, however, that as late as 1928 Kazakhstan and the Buryat-Mongolian and Bashkir republics were still closed to in-migration from European Russia. Responsibility for promoting migration and settlement was transferred to the Commissariats of Labor and Agriculture in 1930. Subsidized agricultural settlement declined, except in combined industrial-agricultural colonization projects and except for special provisions for the development of Biro-Bidzhan, reorganized in 1934 as the Jewish Autonomous District. "The second Five-Year Plan [1933-1937] contained no unified schedule of migration."[53] At this time migration was determined by the response of workers to new opportunities, the initiative of industrial administrations in recruiting workers for new enterprises, including subsidized transportation and preferential wage rates, and the spontaneous or induced interest of collective farm organizations in releasing surplus workers. However, in 1936 responsibility for the promotion of colonization programs was assigned to the People's Commissariat for Internal Affairs.

The industrial labor force, especially in such fields as lumbering, mining, industrial construction, and railway, canal, and road building was augmented by the assignment of prisoners,

---

[50] The data for rural and urban areas were compiled separately for 1897, as well as for 1926 and 1939. These data are not presented separately, chiefly because of the lack of comparability, resulting from radical changes in the legal status of communities with similar characteristics between 1897 and 1926.

[51] Voshchinin, Title 353, p. 269.   [52] Barnes, Title 20.   [53] Sonin, Title 308, p. 80.

deported kulaks, and those condemned for political deviations to various undertakings, especially in remote and relatively undeveloped areas. There is no reliable estimate of the number of persons in the "controlled" labor force, but the assignment of such persons to labor in some of the far northern and eastern regions was undoubtedly an important factor in some of the population changes described above.

"Planless" movements involved much seasonal and cross migration, and were associated with the heavy turnover characteristic of Soviet industries. Moreover, under these conditions, the state farms and collectives in relatively undeveloped areas were unable to recruit workers or members in sufficient force to meet food-consumption needs and to promote a sound and balanced regional economy around rapidly expanding industries in such regions as the Soviet Far East. The Program and Rules of the Communist Party in 1938 included the following provision: "It is imperative for the planned development of our national economy that there be maximum utilization of the labor force and that it be so distributed, both territorially and throughout the various branches of economy, as to result in its most efficient use. The Soviet Government must immediately address itself to this problem."[54] Thereafter, earlier measures for the planning and indirect control of migration were intensified, and new measures of more direct control were inaugurated.

These new measures did not affect the movements treated in this chapter, but the most important features of the new program can be most conveniently mentioned at this point. Its main principles, including measures previously in force, may be listed as follows:[55]

(1) Allocation of areas for industrial recruiting by officials responsible for labor recruitment; for example, in 1940 industrial workers for the Far East could be recruited only from the Tatar, Bashkir, Chuvash, and Mordva A.S.S.R.'s and the Vyatka, Kuybyshev, Tambov, and Kursk districts. The fishing industry of the Far East was limited in drawing new personnel to Krasnodar Territory in the North Caucasus, and the adjacent Stalingrad and Saratov districts. Other limited zones were fixed for the recruitment of collective farm members for labor in Moscow, Leningrad, Arkhangelsk, and other cities with a large demand for workers.

(2) Preferential wages in districts with acute need of new workers, or where conditions of labor are unusually severe, as in the Far North.

(3) Free transportation of persons and their effects and equipment to designated areas, or reduced transportation costs. Provisions for medical care en route.

(4) Special provisions in new communities for cultural institutions and social services, such as schools, libraries, theaters, social centers, hospitals and medical services, and nurseries.

(5) Planning and preparation of sites for new agricultural settlements before the families of the workers are moved to these new locations, including forest-clearing, drainage, irrigation, road construction, and erection of buildings. While engaged in the preparatory work the family heads of new collective farms receive credits in the new enterprise, and their families prior to migration are cared for by the collective farms which they are leaving.

(6) Credit for personally owned provisions, equipment, and livestock, and the supply and the provision of comparable goods at the new site.

(7) Cancellation of tax debts, and tax exemptions for five to ten years in the new situation.

(8) Long-term credits for construction and repair and, where possible, public provision of houses and barns.

(9) Selection, in so far as possible, of groups of families with previous experience in working together.

[54] *Ibid.*, p. 74.   [55] Based chiefly on article by Sonin, Title 308.

Several important measures, introduced after the outbreak of war in Europe, provided new types of public control over individual movements:

(1) In June, 1940, the right of workers voluntarily to quit employment in any state, co-operative, or social enterprise or institution was abrogated, and individuals were obliged to secure the permission of the head of the enterprise in order to terminate a work agreement. The granting of such permission was obligatory only under specified conditions, such as illness, entrance to a middle or higher technical school, old age, etc.[56]

(2) In October, 1940, certain specified categories of technical workers were made subject to official assignment as regards industry and location.[57]

(3) The new educational program, also established in 1940, provided that pupils in special vocational schools (which now became the only free schools above the primary level) should be required to accept assigned work anywhere in any industry during a four-year period after the completion of courses.[56]

Some of these measures will undoubtedly be modified in the postwar period, but the principle of planned migration, as well as measures for raising technical levels of performance and maintaining standards of industrial discipline, is likely to be carried forward, at least during the period of initial reconstruction.

Inter-regional population movements within the Soviet Union during the three successive Five-Year Plans conformed in part to official plans, but they were also influenced by individual responses to economic forces and by differential natural increase. In general, these movements have tended to bring about a far more efficient balance between persons, resources, and economic operations. They have also contributed to the diffusion of common cultural patterns and the emergence of national consciousness. Obviously, the pattern of population distribution recorded in 1939 is not final but transitional. Rural-urban and inter-regional population exchanges were progressing rapidly when the war interrupted them. The war has created profound dislocations and new adjustments. Apart from this, the population movements between 1926 and 1939 should be considered as the initial phases of dynamic trends that are likely to be projected, with various modifications, far into the future.

[56] *The American Review on the Soviet Union*, Vol. 4, No. 2, pp. 11-32, June, 1941.
[57] *International Labour Review*, Vol. 43, No. 2, p. 207, February, 1942.

CHAPTER XI

WAR CHANGES AND POPULATION PROSPECTS

1. Population Projections: Assumptions and Procedure

BIRTHS and deaths in the U.S.S.R. during the years immediately preceding the Second World War might have been predicted with approximate accuracy from trends in the years prior to World War I, considered in relation to the experience of other countries; but the fluctuations in natality and mortality during the 'twenties and early 'thirties could not have been thus predicted. Similarly, trends in the redistribution of population in the Soviet Union have in large part followed the lines of migration within the Russian Empire. On the other hand, the rapid acceleration in the growth of cities reflects the new tempo of changes in economic organization and technology that have taken place under the Soviets. Such observations suggest both the value and the limitations of estimates of future population changes. Any projection of trends into the future must rest on the major assumption that the underlying conditions controlling the events in question will continue to operate in a fairly orderly way. In so far as this is not the case, future events may follow a course quite different from any that can be charted in advance. Therefore, in considering population projections, it is essential to examine carefully the specific assumptions on which they rest and to recognize clearly their limitations. Subject to these limitations, such projections have predictive value.

Projections of population growth in the U.S.S.R. are presented here, first, without adjustment for war losses, and then with adjustment for war losses on the basis of certain hypotheses. The projections will concern the population of the Soviet Union within the area covered by the 1939 census, with a later discussion of the demographic significance of possible changes of international boundaries. We shall not attempt to give quantitative expression to trends in the redistribution of population, because the complexity of such movements makes their mathematical projection difficult and of little use; but the analysis of previous rural-urban and inter-regional movements gives a rough indication of the probable future course of migration. Population changes during the war present a special problem, and we shall deal with them only in a tentative way.

The basic projection of the population of the U.S.S.R. from 1940 to 1970 was developed by the authors of *The Future Population of Europe and the Soviet Union.*[1] They accepted, as initial data, the account of population trends in the U.S.S.R. reported in the chapters above, with an estimated distribution of population by age and sex, January 1, 1940, adapted from that given here for January 17, 1939. They developed these data on the hypotheses and with the methods used in obtaining population projections for various European countries.

These basic hypotheses are not static; they assume a dynamic but orderly development of natality and mortality rates. The framework of the procedure is, nevertheless, identical for all European countries and for the Soviet Union. In this case, the procedure involves the assumption that the future development of population trends in the Soviet Union will conform to previous European experience. We shall presently consider the validity of this assumption in regard to both mortality and fertility with reference to specific conditions in the Soviet Union, but one advantage of it is immediately apparent. Divergence in the trend of the population projections for the Soviet Union from those of other European countries is solely a function of deviations in the initial observations, or estimates of actual events. The necessity of setting

---

[1] The reader is referred to this monograph by Notestein and others, Title 213, for a complete statement of the general hypotheses and methods by which the population projections are derived.

up arbitrary hypotheses about expected future changes in each country is obviated. Therefore, the projections for various countries are strictly comparable. Since the exact procedure is fully described in the monograph mentioned above, the statement here can be brief, designed simply to equip the reader for appraising the nature, value, and limitations of the results that are presented below.

In principle, the process of projecting a population is a simple one. An initial population distributed by sex and by five-year age groups is carried forward over a five-year interval by subtracting the expected number of deaths (as each group becomes five years older), adding the estimated births during the interval, and subtracting the estimated number of deaths from the cohorts of the new-born. The population obtained in this way serves as the starting point for a repetition of the operation. Given initial schedules of mortality by sex and by age, and the fertility of women at different ages, the procedure depends entirely on the modification of these schedules as they are projected into the future. The methodological problem was to find ways of projecting these vital rates that would be at once systematic and sufficiently flexible to be appropriate to widely varying conditions in Europe and the U.S.S.R. The procedures finally selected for treating mortality and fertility are similar in effect but based on different specific assumptions.

A careful study was made of all available death rates at particular ages for European countries at different times, using life-table probabilities of survival from given ages through a specific number of years. It was found that particular rates (i.e., rates of a given height) had rather characteristic declines, regardless of the time when these particular rates were observed in different countries. The declines had been rapid where rates were high, and slow where rates were already low. Height-slope relations (i.e., relations between the level of the death rate and the rate of decline) that had remained intact so long were deemed pertinent to the projection of mortality rates into the future. Following this cue, for each age-sex group the past experience of European countries was combined to give a single "average" curve that represents the course through which peacetime death rates for that group have moved from high to low in European experience (see Figure 26). The expected future death rates for each age-sex group in any country are then read off by locating the initial rate on the curve for that group and moving forward at five-year intervals. This process yields death rates ($_nq_x$) for each age-sex group at the required intervals from 1940 to 1970. Complete life tables for each country at successive intervals are then derived from these rates; these in turn give the survival ratios used to move the population forward five years in age and time.

Applied to the Soviet Union the method carries the assumption that Russian death rates will move from their observed positions in the life table for the U.S.S.R., 1938-1940, in the same way that death rates of European countries have moved from identical positions in the past.[2] On this basis, the expectation of life at birth for males progresses from 46.7 years in 1940 to 52.7 in 1955 and to 58.2 in 1970; that for females changes from 50.2 years in 1940 to 56.2 in 1955 and to 61.5 in 1970. The expected decline of mortality in the future, indicated by this method for the Soviet Union, is more rapid than that for most European countries; but this faster decline is simply a function of the higher initial mortality of the Soviet population.

Actually, three factors are likely to make for even more rapid improvement of health conditions and more rapid decline of mortality in the U.S.S.R. In the first place, any country with moderately high mortality rates today has at its disposal scientific techniques in sanitation and medicine that were not available to western European countries at the time when their mor-

[2] The assumptions implicit in the construction of this hypothetical life table are described in Chapter IX, Section 4.

tality rates were at the same level. Secondly, in view of the natural resources of the Soviet population and the strides made during the last fifteen years in the development of basic industries, there is reason to expect extraordinary progress in economic productivity after recovery from the devastation of war. This would bring a rise in level of living and provide the economic basis for improvement in health. The rapid rise in literacy will have a similar influence. Finally, measures already inaugurated in the organization of health services in the U.S.S.R. may be expected to have far-reaching effects as these measures pass into the hands of technically trained administrators, doctors, and nurses, whose number is being steadily increased. The effect of these conditions cannot be measured on the basis of past European experience because they have not previously existed in the same combination to the same degree. In so far as these considerations are valid, we may anticipate a faster advance in expectation of life than

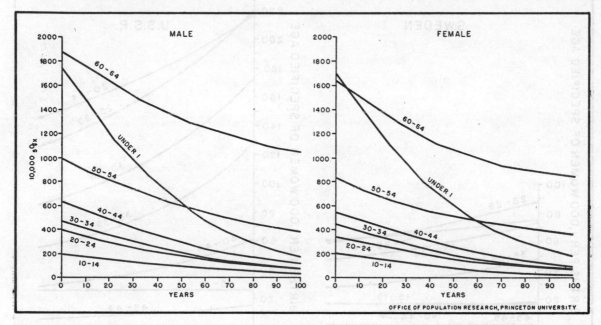

Figure 26. Basic Curves for the Projection of Mortality for Selected Age Groups, by Sex [Based on data from Notestein and others, Title 213]

that indicated by the procedures used in this projection—which would tend to cause more rapid population growth than that indicated here.

The fertility rate for each five-year age group of potential mothers was projected on a rectangular hyperbola, having the height "observed"[3] for the base period and the initial downward slope found to be consonant with this height in the recent experience of European countries.[4] Under this procedure, countries having identical rates in the same base period would have identical projected rates, as in the case of mortality. This procedure is based on the observation that in the interwar period the height and downward slope of fertility were rather highly correlated. Fertility fell rapidly where it was highest and slowly where it was lowest. Unlike the case of mortality, however, this height-slope relation was not independent of time.

[3] The "observations" in this case, as in the case of death rates for the Soviet population, are estimated values (see Chapter IX).

[4] Rates for women aged 15-19 were held constant at the value for 1940. The experience of Australia and of New Zealand was included with that of the available European countries. The procedure was centered on 1930 as the starting point; but the basic fertility schedule used in the projection of the population of the U.S.S.R. is that corresponding to the reported birth rate in 1938. See Chapter IX for description of this schedule, and see Notestein and others, Title 213, for a discussion of the general procedure followed in projecting fertility rates.

European rates of given levels have tended to drop with increasing rapidity in recent decades. The "observed" rates in the base period and the height-slope relations derived from recent European experience determine the course of the hyperbolas. It may be noted that such hyperbolas cannot assume negative values, and that the declines become progressively slower as time goes on.

The method yields very rapid declines in natality for the Soviet Union during the period under consideration, in agreement with the observed fact that in general European experience high rates have dropped most rapidly. The declines in fertility projected for the Soviet Union are contrasted with those for Sweden in Figure 27. In 1940 the gross reproduction ratio is

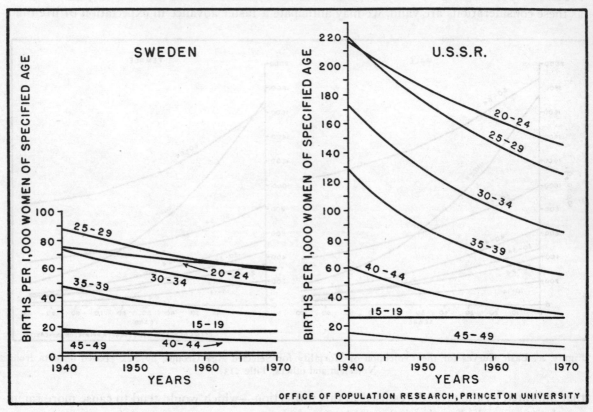

Figure 27. Fertility Rates Projected for Sweden and the U.S.S.R., 1940-1970 [From Notestein and others, Title 213, p. 33]

2.06 for the U.S.S.R. and 0.79 for Sweden. The projected gross reproduction ratio for the U.S.S.R. drops by 1970 to 1.16 (somewhat above that of the United States in 1935-1940), whereas that for Sweden tends to level off and is 0.54 in 1970. The projected decline in the interval is about 44 percent in the case of the U.S.S.R., but only about 32 percent in Sweden.

As in the case of the assumptions relating to mortality, the question arises whether this underlying hypothesis in regard to fertility is appropriate to the specific conditions of the Soviet Union. The evidence reviewed in Chapter IX indicates a rapid drop in natality in the U.S.S.R. between 1926 and 1934, during a period when economic conditions were difficult and when facilities for abortion were freely provided in public clinics. Given a repetition of both these conditions, a similar drop, below the trend indicated here, might be expected; but such repetition is quite unlikely. However, even on the reasonable assumptions that there is orderly economic progress, that contraception continues to be officially sanctioned, and that contraceptive means become more generally available, the trend of natality in the U.S.S.R. in the future may be quite different from that in European countries during the interwar period. The fact that the economic cost to parents of bearing and rearing children in the Soviet Union is less than it has been in European countries, because of greater public provisions for maternal and child care, may have a powerful effect in retarding the decline of fertility. Subtle ideological and attitudinal factors may reinforce this deviation. In the judgment of the present writer, such considerations would make a projection of natality rates for the Soviet population very far into the future extremely dubious. On the other hand, the trend toward urbanization and industrialization and the breakdown of traditional peasant attitudes may be expected to bring natality during the next few decades well below its prewar level in the Soviet Union.

In these projections no account is taken of the possible effect on fertility of state policies specifically designed to influence parenthood and population trends. There is, in fact, at the present time no proper basis for estimating the probable effects of particular kinds of population policy; but it is now apparent, both on theoretical grounds and from the observation of recent experience in various countries, that measures taken to implement population policies may have considerable influence on actual population trends. Measures adopted in the Soviet Union during 1934, 1935, and 1936 forecast the emergence of a positive population policy in that country.[5] This trend was given more advanced expression in an Edict of the Supreme Soviet of the U.S.S.R. on the increase of state aid for mothers and children, July 8, 1944.[6] Although these measures have not been so freely proclaimed as means for the promotion of more rapid population increase as have comparable measures in other countries, they constitute in effect one of the most decisive pro-natalist programs ever inaugurated in any country.

The allowances and awards to mothers of large families provided in the Edict of July 8, 1944, are shown below in schematic form. In appraising the value of the allowances the reader can bear in mind the figure 4,020 rubles, representing Yugoff's estimate of the average annual wage of workers in the U.S.S.R. in 1940.[7]

The current allowances are computed and paid in monthly installments. The discontinuance of payments when the child reaches the fifth year has no clear relation to any change in the economic needs of the family, except on the assumption that before the expiration of this period the mother will be entitled to a still larger allowance on behalf of a subsequent child. In the case of unmarried mothers, payments are continued until children reach the twelfth year in the following amounts per year: one child, 1,200 rubles; two children, 1,800 rubles; three or more children, 2,400 rubles. Unmarried mothers with three or more children are also entitled to common allowances for mothers of large families. The special grant to unmarried mothers is retained in case of later marriage, presumably in order to avoid creating any economic incentive against marriage. The unmarried mother, if she so desires, may entrust her child to the permanent nurture of a state institution, but in this case, of course, she does not continue to receive a grant on behalf of the child. Widows with children receive allowances equal to, but no larger than, those paid to mothers with living husbands.

Conversely, special taxes are levied on men aged 20 to 50 years and on women aged 20 to 45 years who have less than three children. For those paying income taxes (with different but comparable provisions for collective farm members and other classes not paying income taxes) such taxes amount to 6 percent of the income of persons with no children, 1 percent of the income of persons with only one child, and one-half of one percent of the income of persons

---

[5] See above, Chapter IX.

[6] For an authoritative English translation of the text of this Edict, see Embassy of the Union of Soviet Socialist Republics, *Information Bulletin*, Washington, D.C., July 25, 1944.

[7] See Yugoff, Title 372, p. 165.

Allowances and Awards to Mothers of Large Families

On Behalf of Child of Specified Order, Relative to Previous Children Living, or Killed or Missing in War	Allowance Paid at Birth (Rubles)	Current Allowance from Beginning of Second to Beginning of Fifth Year of the Child's Life, or Until Payments on Behalf of a Child of Higher Order Come Into Effect. Value per Year (Rubles)	Honors When Specified Child Reaches the Age of One Year
Third	400	—	—
Fourth	1,300	960	—
Fifth	1,700	1,440	Motherhood Medal, Second Class
Sixth	2,000	1,680	Motherhood Medal, First Class
Seventh	2,500	2,400	Order of Glory of Motherhood, Third Class
Eighth	2,500	2,400	Order of Glory of Motherhood, Second Class
Ninth	3,500	3,000	Order of Glory of Motherhood, First Class
Tenth	3,500	3,000	Order of Mother Heroine (Gold Star), with Scroll from the Presidium of the Supreme Soviet of the U.S.S.R.
Eleventh and Each Subsequent Child	5,000	3,600	

with only two children—with certain exceptions, such as wives of soldiers and sailors, invalids, and students up to 25 years of age.

The Edict also enlarges public provisions for the welfare of mothers and children, covering such matters as increase in supplementary rations for expectant and nursing mothers, extension of the prescribed period of maternity leave with pay, et cetera. Over 100 million rubles were allocated in the wartime budget of 1944 for the construction of new nursery schools, and it was estimated that Soviet nursery schools in that year would care for 1,837,840 children.[8] The Edict of July 8, 1944, also includes legal measures designed to strengthen the family—specifically, regulations with respect to divorce even more stringent than those previously in force.

Some of the features of the legislation described above may represent a temporary accommodation to conditions created by the war. The special provisions for unmarried mothers would seem to be especially designed to meet these situations. In any case, the whole program will be subject to modification in the light of future experience and the emergence of new conditions. It is possible that Soviet provisions relating to families and children may be revised in the future, with less emphasis on the stimulation of births, in order to meet more exactly the varying economic needs of families of different types. Although it is impossible to make any exact estimate of the probable effect of measures now in force on the frequency of births

[8] Embassy of the Union of Soviet Socialist Republics. *Information Bulletin*, Washington, D.C., Sept. 22, 1944.

in the Soviet Union, it is only reasonable to suppose that they will very appreciably retard the trend toward smaller families that might otherwise be expected.

Examination of specific conditions in the U.S.S.R., as they affect expected trends both in mortality and in fertility, suggests that the growth of Soviet population is likely to be considerably more rapid in the near future than that indicated in the projections presented below—in spite of the fact that, in comparison with most European countries, the growth as thus projected appears to be extraordinarily high. A consideration of the history of various Soviet measures affecting fertility also suggests that population change in a nation having the social structure of the Soviet Union may be in considerable degree influenced from time to time by changes in public policy.

2. Hypothetical Adjustment for War Losses

It is, of course, impossible to estimate the effect of World War II on the future population of the Soviet Union. However, some idea of its possible effect, apart from boundary changes and migrations across the January-1939 borders, can be obtained by setting up a series of purely arbitrary hypotheses.

Let us assume, as an experiment, that the population as projected to 1945 is reduced through the effects of war by 20 million persons. We include in this hypothesis war losses occurring after as well as before January 1, 1945, but ignore the effect of the war in reducing births after this date except the reduction due to loss of potential parents. In applying this hypothesis we shall assume that the loss is distributed as follows:

(1) A loss of male military personnel amounting to 5,000,000 persons, with relative losses by five-year classes in 1945 in proportion to the relative losses by corresponding age classes in the German population in 1920. (This hypothesis can be compared with the announcement by Stalin in *Pravda* on June 22, 1943, that the Soviet army had lost 4,200,000 dead and missing persons during the first two years of the war. This figure includes missing persons who will survive, but it does not include deaths after this date from earlier wounds or sickness, or from later military action. The number of killed, missing, or captured persons in the Soviet forces to June 22, 1944, was officially estimated as 5,300,000 persons.[9] It should be noted that this estimate, in contrast to that of the previous year, apparently includes Soviet military personnel captured by German forces.)

(2) A reduction of about 25 percent in the number of children under five years of age otherwise expected in 1945, i.e., a loss of about 6,000,000 children due to a deficit in births and to excess infant mortality caused by the war. (In the light of European experience during the First World War this assumption may be considered rather conservative.)

(3) A reduction of 9,000,000 persons in other age and sex classes due to excess civilian deaths among persons living on January 1, 1940, or born during the next five years. (We distribute this loss by age and sex in proportion to the initial population in each cohort at the beginning of the preceding five-year period, except that two-fifths of the males aged 15-39 years in 1940 are withdrawn—as not subject to excess risk of death as civilians—before the proportional distribution of excess civilian deaths is carried out.)

It must be emphasized that this statement of possible war losses is an *hypothesis*, and not an *estimate*. Errors in the distribution of the hypothetical total war loss might have small effect on resultant total populations but larger effects on expected distributions by age and sex classes. For example, if the figure for military losses were too low and the figure for civilian losses were too high, our adjustments for war losses would not fully reflect the depletion in the

---

[9] Associated Press, London, June 22, 1944.

number of adult males caused by the war. These hypothetical adjustments for war losses in the population projected to 1945 are shown in Table 68.

TABLE 68

Hypothetical War Losses to the Population of the U.S.S.R., as of 1945: By Age and Sex
(Numbers in Thousands)

Age in 1945	Losses Due to Deficit in Births and Excess Civilian Deaths[1]		Losses Due to Male Military Deaths[3]	All Losses of Males
	Male	Female		
Total Losses	6,917.6	8,082.8	5,000.0	11,917.6
0-4	3,019.7[2]	2,980.3[2]	—	3,019.7
Total Losses Over Age 5	3,897.883	5,102.456	5,000.0	8,897.883
5-9	672.9	657.1	—	672.9
10-14	497.8	499.3	—	497.8
15-19	595.6	599.6	266.7	862.3
20-24	277.2	474.0	1,114.4	1,391.6
25-29	244.9	410.6	1,471.3	1,716.2
30-34	271.3	484.9	1,100.8	1,372.1
35-39	223.6	409.8	677.8	901.4
40-44	182.2	365.7	254.4	436.6
45-49	213.5	271.9	114.6	328.1
50-54	170.1	217.7	—	170.1
55-59	153.3	187.3	—	153.3
60-64	127.3	154.9	—	127.3
65-69	100.6	129.7	—	100.6
70-74	75.24	101.2	—	75.24
75-79	49.31	70.45	—	49.31
80-84	28.88	44.17	—	28.88
85-89	10.95	17.39	—	10.95
90+	3.203	6.746	—	3.203

[1] Hypothetical 9,000,000 excess deaths (exclusive of excess infant deaths) are distributed in proportion to population of each cohort in 1940, minus 40 percent of males in cohorts aged 15-39 years in 1940 (as not exposed to risk of excess civilian death). Military deaths to women in armed forces and to males outside the military group are included in civilian deaths. (All computations in this table were based on figures before rounding.)

[2] Hypothetical 6,000,000 loss due to deficit in births and excess infant mortality is distributed in proportion to males and females in projected population under 5 years in 1945.

[3] Hypothetical 5,000,000 loss due to military deaths is distributed by age in proportion to age-distribution of German military deaths in First World War. Estimates of excess mortality, 1910-1925, in Germany above that expected at the mean death rates for 1910 and 1925 were supplied by Dudley Kirk. The proportional losses in cohorts of males for the classes 15-19 years through 45-49 years were as follows: 2.81 percent, 15.25 percent, 22.90 percent, 15.48 percent, 11.60 percent, 5.38 percent, and 3.49 percent. These proportions multiplied by .9129919, applied to the previously projected male population of the U.S.S.R. in the same age classes in 1945, give the hypothetical total of 5,000,000.

We assume that mortality and fertility after January 1, 1945, develop as previously expected, except that a further adjustment is made to take account of the possible effect of the depletion of the male population on the number of births in each succeeding five-year period to 1970. The factors used for this adjustment are shown in Appendix VIII, Table A 27. These factors were worked out prior to the announcement of the Edict of July 8, 1944, described above. It may be that the provisions of this Edict, especially those relating to unmarried mothers, will obviate part of the loss of births attributed to depletion of the male population. This is not, however, a major factor in the total effect of the war on the future population of the U.S.S.R., indicated by our procedure.

The actual war losses of the Soviet population may not be so great as those represented by these hypothetical figures—or, conceivably, they may be even greater. The adjusted estimates simply show the expected development to 1970 of the population resident within the U.S.S.R. at the time of the last census on the basis of the specified *hypotheses*, with expected distribution by age and sex at successive dates. The reader can obtain an adjustment between, or outside, the values shown here to fit any alternative assumption regarding the magnitude of the population loss resulting from the war, if the relative distribution of this loss among various sex and age classes as presented here is accepted as approximately accurate. For example, with a total war loss of 12 million persons (as of 1945) but with other factors constant, the expected number in any sex and age class at any time would be equal to the number obtained on the basic projection *minus* .6 times the difference between this figure and that obtained on the projection adjusted for a hypothetical loss of 20 million persons.[10]

3. Population Projections, U.S.S.R. (January-1939 Area), 1940-1970

The total population of the U.S.S.R., projected with and without this adjustment for hypothetical war losses, is presented in Table 69 by five-year intervals from 1940 to 1970.

TABLE 69

Total Population of the U.S.S.R. (January-1939 Area) Projected by Five-Year Intervals with and without Hypothetical War Losses, 1940-1970

Year	Without Adjustment for War Losses (In millions)	Adjusted for Hypothetical War Losses (In millions)
1940	173.8	173.8
1945	189	169
1950	203	181
1955	216	192
1960	228	203
1965	240	213
1970	251	222

Apart from the effects of war, the first series gives an expected increase of 77 million persons in a thirty-year period. The indicated increase for the first decade, 1940-1950, is 16.9 percent; that for the second decade is 12.5; for the third decade it is 10.0; and over the entire thirty years the expected increase is 44.6 percent. The first of these percentages is intermediate between the estimated natural increase of the white population of the United States, 1880-1890, and the corresponding figure for the previous intercensus period.[11] The 10 percent in-

[10] In applying the hypotheses described above, the projection with adjustment for war losses was actually reduced by 20,156,990 persons in 1945, because of chance effects of the procedure followed in rounding decimals. The figure .59533 should, therefore, be substituted for .6 in this statement.

[11] Warren S. Thompson and P. K. Whelpton, *Population Trends in the United States* (New York: McGraw-Hill, 1933), combining information on pp. 8 and 303. These statements would remain valid for exact ten-year intervals.

crease indicated for the third decade is intermediate between the estimated natural increase of the white population of the United States in 1930-1940 and the corresponding figure for 1920-1930. The increase anticipated in the Soviet population is therefore quite conservative. The hypothetical war loss is cumulative in its effect, involving an estimated loss of 29 million persons by 1970. As a proportion of the total population otherwise expected, the loss also rises from 10.66 percent in 1945 to 11.56 percent in 1970, owing to the effect on births of changes in the population in the childbearing ages; but this proportion would remain fairly constant thereafter. Nevertheless, the series with adjustment for war losses indicates an expected population in 1950 somewhat above that living in 1940, with rapid increase thereafter in each successive five-year period. This series gives a net increase of 48 million persons between 1940 and 1970, equal to nearly 28 percent of the initial population.

Figure 28 presents the contrast between the projected growth of the population of the U.S.S.R. and that of various divisions of Europe, each defined with reference to its 1937 boundaries and projected without adjustment for war losses. It will be noted on this chart that shortly after 1960 the Soviet projection rises above that for Northwestern and Central Europe (i.e., the United Kingdom, Ireland, Denmark, Norway, Sweden, Finland, Estonia, Latvia, Germany, the Netherlands, Belgium, France, Switzerland, Czechoslovakia, Austria, and Hungary combined). Moreover, a continued increase is indicated for the U.S.S.R. population at the end of this period, whereas the projection of the population of Northwestern and Central Europe turns downward after 1955.

4. Possible Effect of Boundary Changes

The question arises as to the possible effect of boundary changes on the future population of the U.S.S.R. The legal boundaries of the Soviet Union and, consequently, the composition of its population are at present indeterminate.[12] We must, therefore, proceed on the basis of hypotheses that carry no explicit or implicit assumptions as to the probable limits of the Soviet Union. In describing changes during the war, we shall, as a matter of convenience, use the terminology of the context from which the material is drawn, without any elaborate attempt to make the terms conform to any particular political theory, referring indifferently, for example, to the same areas as "eastern Poland" or "western Belorussia and western Ukraine." In projecting demographic trends into the future, the populations of all countries were necessarily defined in terms of their prewar boundaries, for which vital statistics are available or can be estimated. The projection to 1970 of the population of the U.S.S.R. as defined in the 1939 census carries no implication that the future population of the Soviet Union will, or will not, correspond to these limits. Projections were also prepared in the same series for the various countries of Europe, including national areas which, according to the Soviet constitution, are now in whole or in part included within the U.S.S.R. A summary of certain relevant findings are presented below. The reader can adjust the materials so presented to obtain a rough approximation to conform to the course of future events.

The German occupation of western and central Poland, beginning September 1, 1939, was followed immediately by the Russian occupation of eastern and southeastern Poland, Bessarabia, and northern Bukovina. Soviet military bases were established by treaty agreements in

[12] The text of this chapter was written prior to the conference at Yalta in the Crimea between the heads of government of the Union of Soviet Socialist Republics, the United Kingdom, and the United States of America. The agreement announced at this conference gives recognition to the inclusion within the U.S.S.R. of areas that are substantially identical with those referred to here as claimed by the U.S.S.R. Some of the phraseology used here, in an attempt to preserve strict objectivity with reference to pending political issues, would seem to be obsolete or gratuitous in the light of this Yalta agreement. However, since this text was designed to be appropriate to any later political decisions, it has been left without revision.

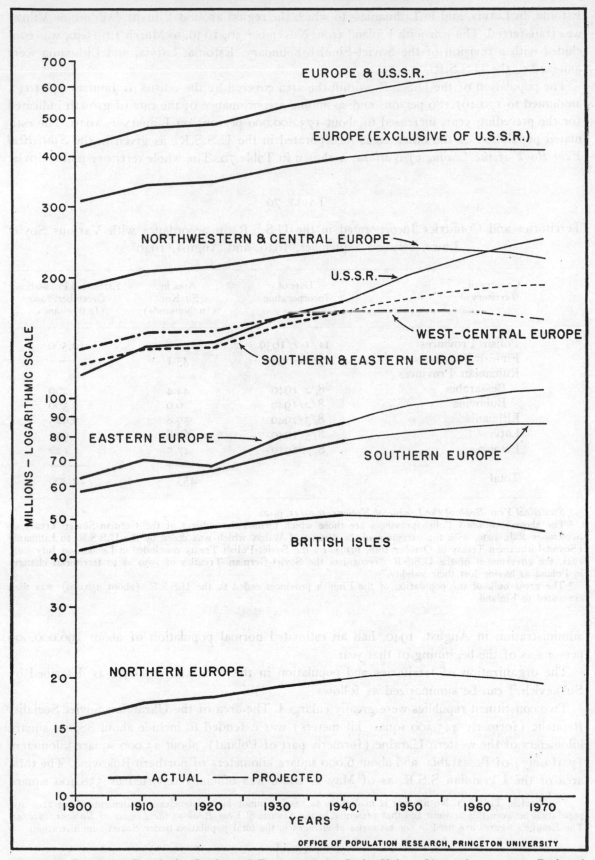

Figure 28. Population Trends for Regions of Europe and the Soviet Union: Observed, 1900-1940; Projected, 1940-1970 [From Notestein and others, Title 213, p. 58]

Estonia, in Latvia, and in Lithuania—to which the region around Vilnyns (Wilno, or Vilna) was transferred. The war with Finland from November 30, 1939, to March 12, 1940, was concluded with a revision of the Soviet-Finnish boundary. Estonia, Latvia, and Lithuania were annexed to the U.S.S.R.

The population of the U.S.S.R. within the area covered by the census of January 17, 1939, amounted to 170,467,186 persons and, assuming a continuance of the rate of growth indicated for the preceding year, increased to about 173,800,000 persons on January 1, 1940. The estimated population of the other areas incorporated in the U.S.S.R., as given in the *Statistical Year-Book of the League of Nations*, is shown in Table 70. The whole territory under Soviet

TABLE 70

Territories and Countries Incorporated in the U.S.S.R. in accordance with Various Soviet Laws, between September, 1939, and August, 1940[1]

Country or Territory	Date of Incorporation	Area in Sq. Km. (In thousands)	Estimated Population December, 1939 (In thousands)
Polish Provinces[2]	11/1-2/1939	194.8	12,500
Finnish Provinces	3/12/1940	35.1	——[3]
Rumanian Provinces			
Bessarabia	8/2/1940	44.4	3,200
Bukovina	8/2/1940	6.0	500
Lithuania	8/3/1940	59.8	2,925
Latvia	8/5/1940	65.8	1,951
Estonia	8/7/1940	47.5	1,122
Total		453	22,200

[1] *Statistical Year-Book of the League of Nations, 1940/41*, p. 20.

[2] The above-mentioned Polish provinces are those which formed the subject of the German-Soviet Treaty of September 28th, 1939, with the exception of the district of Wilno, which was ceded by the U.S.S.R. to Lithuania (Soviet-Lithuanian Treaty of October 10th, 1939). By the Soviet-Polish Treaty concluded in London on July 30th, 1941, the government of the U.S.S.R. "recognises the Soviet-German Treaties of 1939 as to territorial changes in Poland as having lost their validity."

[3] The great bulk of the population of the Finnish provinces ceded to the U.S.S.R. (about 450,000) was then evacuated to Finland.

administration in August, 1940, had an estimated normal population of about 196,000,000 persons as of the beginning of that year.

The organization of territories and population in the U.S.S.R. in 1940, as described by Sul'kevich,[13] can be summarized as follows:

Two constituent republics were greatly enlarged. The area of the Ukrainian Soviet Socialist Republic (formerly 445,300 square kilometers) was extended to include about 88,000 square kilometers of the western Ukraine (formerly part of Poland), about 15,000 square kilometers (part only) of Bessarabia, and about 6,000 square kilometers of northern Bukovina. The total area of the Ukrainian S.S.R. as of May 1, 1940, was officially reported as 558,400 square

[13] Sul'kevich, Title 323. No attempt is made here to resolve minor inconsistencies in statements about area and population between this account and that presented in the *Statistical Year-Book of the League of Nations, 1940/41*. The League's figures are used in our estimates of changes in the total population under Soviet administration.

kilometers.[14] As the density of population in the areas added to the Ukrainian Republic, though they were predominantly rural, was higher than that of the former Ukrainian S.S.R., there was an even greater proportional increase of population—with the addition of 8 million persons from the western Ukraine, 1.05 million from Bessarabia, and 0.5 million from Bukovina. Part of the Moldavian A.S.S.R., formerly a part of the Ukrainian S.S.R., was assigned to the newly formed Moldavian Soviet Socialist Republic, involving the political transfer of 310 thousand persons. The net increase imputed to the Ukrainian S.S.R., therefore, was 9,240,000 persons; this republic had a total population of over 30,960,000 persons at the time of the 1939 census.

The newly established boundaries of the Belorussian S.S.R. covered 228,300 square kilometers and included an estimated 10,400,000 persons. The original area had 126,800 square kilometers, with a population of 5,567,976 persons. The added territory was around 108,000 square kilometers with about 5 million persons, but this total was reduced somewhat by the transfer to Lithuania of certain areas inhabited chiefly by persons of Lithuanian ancestry.

Two new Soviet Socialist Republics were established, embracing parts of former divisions of the U.S.S.R. with lower political rank. The Moldavian S.S.R. was formed by the major portion of Bessarabia (28,800 square kilometers with an estimated 2,100,000 persons) and part of the former Moldavian A.S.S.R. (3,900 square kilometers with 310,000 persons). The remainder of the latter area, with a large Ukrainian population, remained within the Ukrainian S.S.R. and was transferred to the Odessa District.

The Karelo-Finnish Soviet Socialist Republic included the former Karelian A.S.S.R., which had 136,400 square kilometers and 469,145 persons in January, 1939. At that time this was part of the Russian Republic (R.S.F.S.R.) but organized as a subordinate Autonomous Soviet Socialist Republic. The Karelians are cognate in origin and language to the Finns. The newly constituted republic, with areas annexed from Finland, covered 196,000 square kilometers. The number of Finns remaining in the annexed areas was negligible.

Three other newly constituted constituent republics were formed: (1) the Estonian S.S.R. (area, 47,500 square kilometers; population, 1,120,000 persons); (2) the Latvian S.S.R. (area, 65,800 square kilometers; population, 1,950,000 persons); and (3) the Lithuanian S.S.R. (area, 59,700 square kilometers; population, 2,880,000—exclusive of area and population transferred from Belorussia, but after incorporation of former Polish territory).

The Soviet government has announced that its future boundaries with Poland are subject to negotiation, and has proposed that the "Curzon Line" be recognized as a basis for such negotiations. The implications of this proposal as regards "the Soviet population" in terms of territorial boundaries can be explored, and we can obtain a rough idea of how this population might be projected to 1970—apart from the effect of war losses. This calculation, as in the case of the population defined by the 1939 census, carries no implication that the future population of the U.S.S.R. will, or will not, correspond to these limits.

The population in Poland east of the Curzon Line, as shown in *Philips International Atlas*, can be estimated on the basis of Polish census data as about 10,208,000 persons in 1931. This figure is equal to 89.16 percent of the estimated 1931 population in the part of Poland brought under Soviet or Lithuanian control in 1939. The estimated population of the latter area on December 31, 1939, according to the *Statistical Year-Book of the League of Nations, 1940/41*, was 12,983,000 persons (including 483,000 persons in the district around Vilna, annexed by

[14] *SSSR Administrativno-Territorial'noye Deleniye Soyuznykh Respublik*, Title 481. It will be noted that this figure is somewhat higher than that indicated by reference to the component parts. Moreover, about 4,000 square kilometers were transferred from the Ukrainian S.S.R. when the new Moldavian S.S.R. was established.

Lithuania). We assume, therefore, that on January 1, 1940, there were about 11,576,000 persons east of the Curzon Line within the prewar boundaries of Poland, ignoring military and civilian movements during the previous months.

The normal 1940 population of areas west of the January-1939 Soviet borders now considered by the Soviet government to be a permanent part of the U.S.S.R., distributed by 1938 political divisions was, therefore, as follows:

Estonia	1,122,000	(From Table 70)
Latvia	1,951,000	(From Table 70)
Lithuania	2,442,000	(Excluding Vilna area)
Poland (Part)	11,576,000	(See preceding paragraph)
Rumania (Part)	3,200,000	(Bessarabia, from Table 70)
Total	20,291,000	(Ignoring small numbers of persons in parts of Finland annexed by the U.S.S.R., 1940)

This figure is equal to 22.34 percent of the estimated 1940 population of Eastern Europe (Poland, Lithuania, Rumania, Bulgaria, Greece, Yugoslavia, and Albania, plus Estonia and Latvia).[15] The expected future growth of the area in question would probably not be very different from that of this larger region as a whole. On this assumption, we can divide the population as projected for this region, without adjustment for war losses, to obtain the figures given in Table 71, Columns 2 and 3.

TABLE 71

Hypothetical Population in Specified Parts of Europe and the U.S.S.R., 1940-1970, without Adjustment for War Losses and Migration[1]
(Numbers in Millions)

Year	U.S.S.R. January-1939 Area[2]	Other Areas Claimed by U.S.S.R.[3]	Other Parts of Eastern Europe[3]	Northwestern and Central Europe (except Estonia and Latvia)[4]	Southern Europe[5]
	(1)	(2)	(3)	(4)	(5)
1940	173.8	20.3	70.5	230	77
1945	189.0	21.2	73.5	233	80
1950	203.1	22.0	76.3	234	82
1960	228.5	23.4	81.1	231	85
1970	251.3	24.1	84.0	222	86

[1] Based on figures in *The Future Population of Europe and the Soviet Union*, Title 213.
[2] Exclusive of Bessarabia, not legally ceded to Rumania, but under Rumanian administration, January 17, 1939.
[3] See text. "Eastern Europe," as defined in the text of Title 213, includes Lithuania but not Latvia and Estonia.
[4] European countries not included in other specified areas.
[5] Italy, Spain, and Portugal.

If the population of the western areas now claimed by the U.S.S.R. has suffered war losses merely proportional to hypothetical losses of the population within the January-1939 borders of the U.S.S.R. (10.66 percent in 1945, rising to 11.56 percent in 1970), this would cause a

[15] Estonia and Latvia are included in Northwestern and Central Europe in the population projections presented in Title 213.

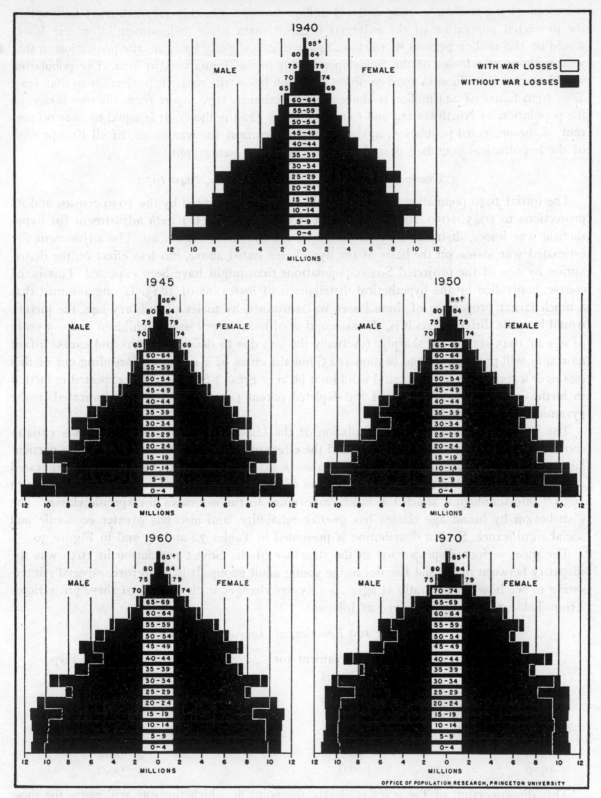

Figure 29. Population of the U.S.S.R., 1940, and Projected Populations, 1945, 1950, 1960, and 1970: (I) Without Adjustment for War Losses; (II) Adjusted for Hypothetical War Losses [Appendix VIII]

[189]

reduction of 2.2 million in 1945 and 2.8 million in 1970. On this very arbitrary assumption the projected population of the enlarged U.S.S.R. area after "adjustment" for war losses would be 188 million persons in 1945—a figure that is slightly less than the projection to that year without war losses of the Soviet population in the January-1939 area. The population would reach 244 million in 1970 or about 8 million below the original projection to that year. This 1970 figure of 244 million is above the projection to 1970, *apart from the war losses*, of the population of Northwestern and Central Europe (222 million). It is equal to over 60 percent of the projected population, again without adjustment for war losses, of all Europe west of the hypothetical boundary described in the preceding paragraphs.

5. *Changes in Age and Sex Composition, 1940-1970*

The initial 1940 population of the U.S.S.R. in the area covered by the 1939 census, and its projections to 1945, 1950, 1960, and 1970 (I) *without*, and (II) *with* adjustment for hypothetical war losses, distributed by sex and age, are shown in Figure 29. The adjustment for estimated war losses, on the basis of the hypotheses stated above, has less effect on the distribution by age of the projected Soviet populations than might have been expected. This is, of course, controlled by the hypothetical distribution of losses, as of 1945. If one assumed that a much larger proportion of these losses was sustained by males of military age, the picture would be quite different. As it is, the assumption of heavy war losses in children under 5 years of age in 1945 stands out sharply. (Actually the loss due to deficit in births and excess infant mortality will probably extend beyond 1945, but the effect of a moderate spreading out of this loss over a somewhat longer period would not be very great.) Similarly, the expected reduction in births in later years because of the depleted parent population is clearly indicated in the pyramids for 1960 and 1970.

The initial distribution of the population of the U.S.S.R. by five-year age classes (1940) shows some pronounced irregularities, and the effect of the hypothetical war losses on particular classes at later dates is fairly striking in some cases. However, in view of the complicated adjustments underlying the initial distribution of the Soviet population by five-year classes in 1939,[16] one should not attach too much importance to the estimates for specific classes. The distribution by broad age classes has greater reliability, and also has greater economic and social significance. Such a distribution is presented in Tables 72 and 73 and in Figure 30.

The most serious disproportion in the structure of the Soviet population in 1940 was the disparity between males and females in the young adult group. It is, therefore, especially interesting to see how the sex ratio at ages 20-44 years changes in the course of these projections. From Table 72 it may be derived as follows:

Males per 100 Females, at Ages 20-44 Years

Year	I. Without Adjustment for War Losses	II. Adjusted for Hypothetical War Losses
1940	90.1	—
1945	93.2	82.2
1950	96.2	86.1
1960	99.7	93.8
1970	100.6	99.9

This disproportion of the sexes is clearly the point at which the war will cause the most serious dislocation in the structure of the Soviet population, although the degree of this effect

[16] See Section 10 of Chapter IX.

TABLE 72

Distribution by Age and Sex of Projected Population in Specified Parts of Europe and the U.S.S.R., 1940-1970

Area and Date	Total	Both Sexes Under 20 Years	Males 20-44 Years	Males 45-64 Years	Females 20-44 Years	Females 45-64 Years	Both Sexes 65 Years and Over
U.S.S.R. (January-1939 Area) Unadjusted							
1940	173,788	79,070	31,040	9,780	34,450	12,230	7,218
1945	189,033	85,100	34,410	10,820	36,940	13,850	7,913
1950	203,080	86,050	38,600	12,990	40,120	16,650	8,670
1960	228,457	89,600	42,670	19,570	42,810	23,070	10,737
1970	251,310	87,500	49,610	23,600	49,320	25,640	15,640
U.S.S.R. (January-1939 Area) Adjusted for Hypothetical War Losses							
1940	173,788	79,070	31,040	9,780	34,450	12,230	7,218
1945	168,876	75,150	28,590	10,040	34,800	13,020	7,276
1950	181,053	75,080	32,510	11,990	37,740	15,670	8,063
1960	203,186	76,320	37,820	16,940	40,330	21,720	10,056
1970	222,262	77,100	43,580	19,220	43,640	24,160	14,562
Eastern and Baltic Europe							
1940	90,812	38,862	16,677	6,261	17,140	7,333	4,539
1945	94,735	38,643	18,130	6,921	18,156	8,094	4,792
1950	98,285	37,158	19,524	8,010	19,219	9,118	5,254
1960	104,531	34,503	21,176	10,695	20,383	11,393	6,381
1970	108,053	32,185	21,914	12,043	21,044	12,244	8,624
Northwestern and Central Europe, except Estonia and Latvia							
1940	230,425	72,630	43,995	22,676	44,905	26,533	19,687
1945	233,280	69,053	45,223	23,961	45,034	28,209	21,800
1950	234,248	64,942	44,889	26,418	44,328	30,130	23,543
1960	231,391	56,074	42,622	31,217	41,673	33,022	26,784
1970	222,296	47,043	40,487	31,233	39,472	31,735	32,327
Southern Europe							
1940	77,464	29,750	14,087	6,289	14,538	7,339	5,461
1945	80,065	29,145	15,170	6,715	15,225	7,933	5,877
1950	82,295	27,739	16,227	7,393	15,961	8,637	6,338
1960	85,492	24,743	17,093	9,452	16,532	10,233	7,439
1970	86,452	22,120	17,004	10,807	16,407	11,021	9,093

is uncertain. Moreover, this effect will persist as a serious drag, but with diminishing force, through the next quarter century.

Young adults 20-44 years form a surprisingly constant proportion of the total population in all these projections. However, with the hypothetical war losses, the number of males in this age group in the U.S.S.R. drops in 1945, constituting only 16.9 percent of the total rather

TABLE 73

Percent Distribution by Age and Sex of Projected Population in Specified Parts of Europe and the U.S.S.R., 1940-1970

Area and Date	Total	Both Sexes Under 20 Years	Males		Females		Both Sexes 65 Years and Over
			20-44 Years	45-64 Years	20-44 Years	45-64 Years	
U.S.S.R. (January-1939 Area) Unadjusted							
1940	100	45	18	6	20	7	4
1945	100	45	18	6	20	7	4
1950	100	42	19	6	20	8	4
1960	100	39	19	9	19	10	5
1970	100	35	20	9	20	10	6
U.S.S.R. (January-1939 Area) Adjusted for Hypothetical War Losses							
1940	100	45	18	6	20	7	4
1945	100	45	17	6	21	8	4
1950	100	41	18	7	21	9	4
1960	100	38	19	8	20	11	5
1970	100	35	20	9	20	11	7
Eastern and Baltic Europe							
1940	100	43	18	7	19	8	5
1945	100	41	19	7	19	9	5
1950	100	38	20	8	20	9	5
1960	100	33	20	10	19	11	6
1970	100	30	20	11	19	11	8
Northwestern and Central Europe, except Estonia and Latvia							
1940	100	32	19	10	19	12	9
1945	100	30	19	10	19	12	9
1950	100	28	19	11	19	13	10
1960	100	24	18	13	18	14	12
1970	100	21	18	14	18	14	15
Southern Europe							
1940	100	38	18	8	19	9	7
1945	100	36	19	8	19	10	7
1950	100	34	20	9	19	10	8
1960	100	29	20	11	19	12	9
1970	100	26	20	13	19	13	11

than 18.2 percent as would otherwise be expected. After 1945, the expected proportion of young adult males rises in all the populations considered here—except in the case of Northwestern and Central Europe, where the moderate decline here indicated will actually be accentuated by war losses. Women in the same age group form a fairly constant proportion of the expected total for each population at each date. Again, however, Northwestern and Central Europe shows a slight relative decline, which is intensified by an expected shift from the younger to the older ages within this group (not shown here).

There are striking changes in the expected proportions of those under 20 years. In both series for the U.S.S.R., the proportions in the juvenile group decline from 45 percent in 1940 to 35 percent in 1970; but even with this drop, the expected proportion for the U.S.S.R. in

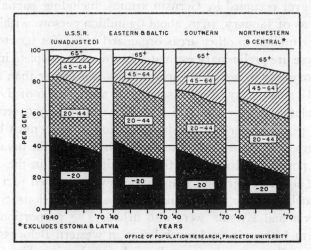

Figure 30. Distribution of Population by Broad Age Classes as Projected for Specified Parts of Europe and the U.S.S.R., 1940-1970 [Table 73]

1970 remains above the proportion of children and youth observed in 1940 in Northwestern and Central Europe (32 percent) and far above the 21 percent expected in 1970. Conversely, the expected proportion of persons aged 65 years and over rises in the U.S.S.R. from 4 percent in 1940 to 6 percent in 1970, or to 7 percent in the "adjusted" series. Even so, it does not reach the proportion of such older persons already present in Northwestern and Central Europe (9 percent in 1940), and is less than half the expected proportion in this area in 1970 (15 percent).

If our hypotheses have any relation to reality, the population of the Soviet Union will continue to grow rapidly through the next quarter century. It will also continue to be a relatively young population, as regards its age composition. It will almost inevitably begin to approach the more "mature" structure of western European nations, because of improved health conditions with consequent decline in the death rate and because of retardation of natural increase. But, in spite of such trends, the differential between the Soviet and the European age structures is likely to persist in marked degree for a long time.[17]

6. Population Displacement during the Second World War

According to the estimates discussed in Section 4 above, the area under Soviet administration in January, 1940, had a population of about 196 million persons at that time. There must

[17] The complete projections for the population of the U.S.S.R. (with and without adjustment for war losses) are given in Appendix VIII. See also the more extended treatment (without adjustment for war losses) in Notestein and others, Title 213.

have been about 200 million persons under Soviet administration when the German armies crossed the new Soviet frontier on June 22, 1941. The persons in areas incorporated in the U.S.S.R. during the previous two years, except those moved eastward beyond the path of the invasion, immediately fell under German control. The estimated population in these areas, as of December 31, 1939, was over 22 million persons. In addition, the German armies during the next five months moved across territory normally containing over one-third of the total population within the January-1939 borders of the U.S.S.R. The Soviet resistance before Moscow and the subsequent winter campaign recovered populous areas in central Russia which remained free thereafter. The German campaign in the summer of 1942 ended at Stalingrad and in the North Caucasus mountains.

All Soviet territory ever occupied by German armies, including partially occupied cities, is estimated to have held, as of January, 1939, about 63 million persons within the prewar borders of the U.S.S.R. and 22 million in other areas organized as Soviet territory, giving a total of 85 million persons. These are preliminary estimates based on incomplete information. It should be noted that the territory *ever occupied* at various times was larger than the greatest area held at any one time by the German army. Even assuming an acceleration of the eastward movement of industries and population within the U.S.S.R. between the 1939 census and June, 1941, about 43 percent of all people under Soviet administration in 1940 must have had their homes in communities that were overrun at some time during the war by the invading German armies. The proportion of the population living in cities was slightly less in the ever-occupied part of the original U.S.S.R. (about 31 percent) than in the never-occupied part (about 34 percent); but the rural-urban distribution was very similar in these two divisions. Similar proportions of the population of Latvia and Estonia were also urban. The proportion of inhabitants who were urban was lower in Lithuania, and much lower in western Belorussia, western Ukraine, and Moldavia, which are all areas of high rural population density. The division of Soviet territory between ever-occupied and never-occupied areas is shown in Plate XXII.

In analyzing migratory movements during the war several distinct currents must be differentiated. Before the U.S.S.R. was involved in the war, treaty arrangements had provided for the transfer of persons between Soviet and German territories—with reference to ethnic or legal status, or on the basis of individual options under specific conditions. Prior to Soviet annexation, 63,800 persons were transferred from Lithuania, Latvia, and Estonia to the Reich. After Soviet annexation, 66,700 persons were transferred in the same direction, but 21,000 Lithuanians and Russians were transferred from German-held territory to Lithuania. Similarly, about 30,000 or 40,000 Belorussians and Ukrainians were transferred to Russian territory in exchange for about 130,000 Germans and some Poles (perhaps 14,000 or even more) who elected transfer to the Reich. The effect of these transfers was a net loss of some 200,000 persons from the extended territory of the U.S.S.R.[18]

The net movement of refugees, however, was in the opposite direction and brought a larger number of persons into Soviet territory. According to Lithuanian sources there was an influx to that country of 14,000 soldiers and 75,000 to 80,000 civilians from Poland (all but 10,000 of the civilians being Jews). According to other, more conservative estimates, the number of such civilian refugees was about 30,000. A few thousand also entered Latvia. An estimated 100,000 to 130,000 Jews crossed into Soviet territory from Rumania, fleeing German occupation, but 35,000 to 40,000 Rumanians (as distinct from the Moldavian population of that area) moved from Bessarabia and northern Bukovina to escape Russian occupation. Many Polish citizens, Jews and others, fled from the German to the Soviet zone in Poland, prior to

---

[18] Figures in this and the paragraphs immediately following are from Kulischer, Title 157.

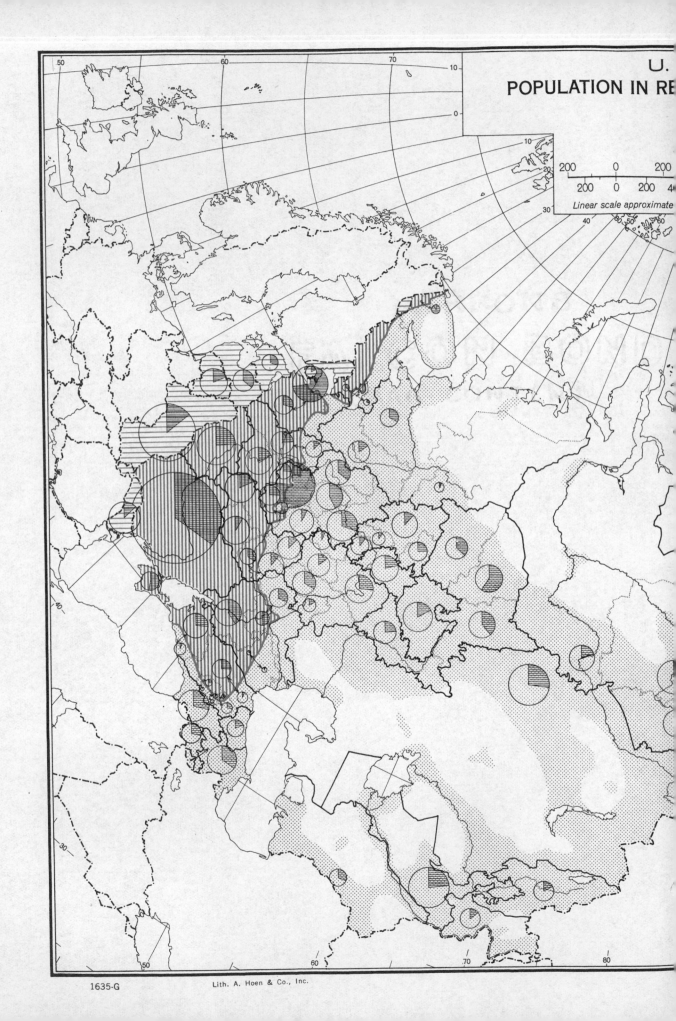

U.
POPULATION IN R...

PLATE XXII

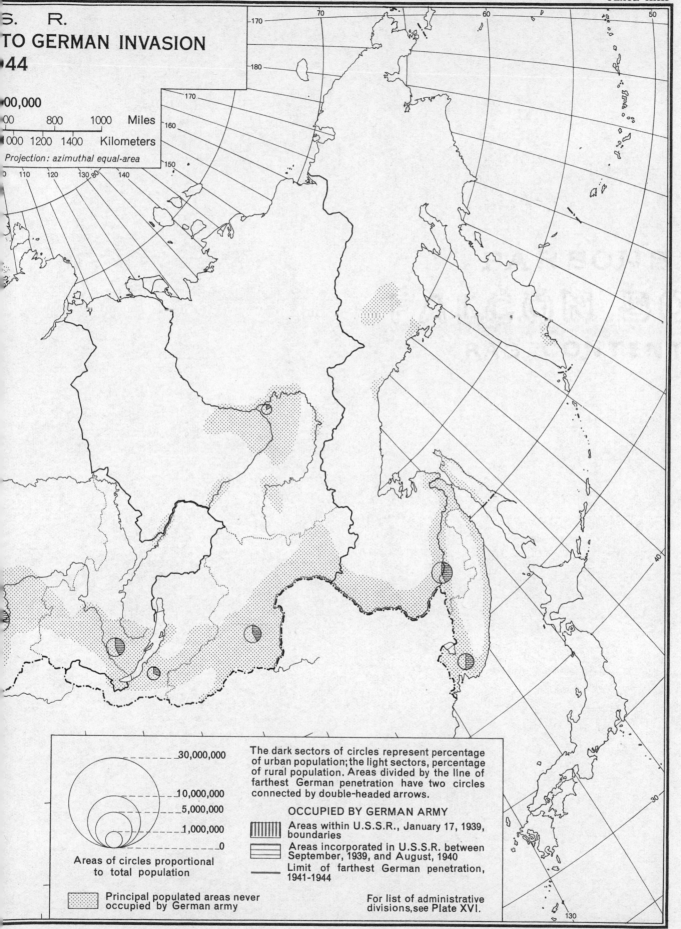

S. R.

TO GERMAN INVASION

44

00,000

| 00 | 800 | 1000 | Miles |

| 000 | 1200 | 1400 | Kilometers |

Projection: azimuthal equal-area

The dark sectors of circles represent percentage
of urban population; the light sectors, percentage
of rural population. Areas divided by the line of
farthest German penetration have two circles
connected by double-headed arrows.

OCCUPIED BY GERMAN ARMY

Areas within U.S.S.R., January 17, 1939,
boundaries

Areas incorporated in U.S.S.R. between
September, 1939, and August, 1940

Limit of farthest German penetration,
1941-1944

30,000,000

10,000,000

5,000,000

1,000,000

0

Areas of circles proportional
to total population

Principal populated areas never
occupied by German army

For list of administrative
divisions, see Plate XVI.

Prepared by Department of State, Division
of Geography and Cartography
Drawn by American Geographical Society

the transfer already noted of Ukrainians and Belorussians in exchange for Germans. The total number of Jewish refugees who crossed the Soviet line in Poland has been estimated by the Institute of Jewish Affairs at 200,000. The number of non-Jewish refugees was apparently smaller.

There was apparently a net in-movement of refugees and transferred persons, combined, to the Soviet territory, but the number so added was relatively small. This movement, however, takes on added significance in view of the fact that several hundred thousand persons thus added to the Soviet population were settled in Central Asia, Kazakhstan, and the northern and eastern districts of the R.S.F.S.R. a year or more before the German army launched its attack on the Soviet Union. These persons are not covered in the estimates given below for the population evacuated from the occupied parts of the U.S.S.R.

Another wartime movement, begun on a relatively small scale at an early stage and augmented just before and after the German attack, was the selective evacuation of such persons as former army officers, government officials and executives, and, later, workers of various kinds from areas annexed by the U.S.S.R. to the interior of the Soviet Union. The earlier movements involved arrest in most cases; the later were predominantly voluntary. Kulischer estimates the total number of civilians evacuated from the annexed areas at 1,500,000 to 2,000,-000 persons. There was also the transfer of the Volga German population and persons of German extraction in other exposed areas.[19] The total number reported as "German" in the U.S.S.R. in 1939 was 1.4 million. It is impossible to say exactly how many of this number were relocated as a military measure. Most of the Volga Germans were transferred to the Altay region, a relatively undeveloped but fertile agricultural area in the southeastern corner of western Siberia. A similar, but apparently more limited and selective, relocation of persons of Oriental nationalities in the Soviet Far East had been previously carried out.

The free movement of refugees within the Soviet Union beyond the reach of the German army as it rolled eastward in the initial stages of the invasion is generally regarded as relatively negligible. Such escape was, for the most part, impossible, and it was essential to keep the highways open for military use. However, as the initial invasion reached its limits in the winter of 1941-1942, and during the later stages of the war, there may have been larger movements over relatively short stages. The exodus from Leningrad, which was cut off but never occupied, represents a movement of somewhat similar character. It has been unofficially reported that the population of Leningrad was reduced from 3 million persons in 1939 to 1 million in 1943; but it is impossible to know how much of this depletion, if correctly reported, was due to starvation, exposure, disease, and bombardment and how much represents evacuation or escape to other districts.

Finally, we come to the most important population movement in the U.S.S.R. during the war—apart from the mobilization of military personnel, which we shall not attempt to estimate—namely, the planned, selective evacuation of persons from the path of the invader. When the Germans crossed the frontiers, plans were immediately put into effect for the rapid removal of people and equipment. In fact, large-scale evacuation of persons from the annexed areas bordering on the German zone seems to have been initiated at least several days before June 22, 1941. Most of this evacuation was by railway. Whole factories were dismantled and set up in the interior; a large part of the farm machinery and much of the livestock were removed. There is no precise official information about the number of persons evacuated, and widely divergent estimates have been made by competent authorities.

[19] About 66 percent of the population of the Volga German A.S.S.R. in 1926 was classified by ethnic affiliation as German; the total population of this division was 606,000 in 1939. There were also many Germans in the Ukraine, Moscow, and other districts.

These estimates are reviewed by Kulischer, and two lines of evidence are followed in the attempt to obtain a reliable result. Information is available from German sources about the population of various cities in the Ukraine. Figures cited by Kulischer from *Novoye Slovo* (Berlin), January 7, 1942, and July 22, 1942, are supplemented in Table 74 by figures from the

TABLE 74

Population of Ukrainian Cities, 1939 and 1942-1943
(Numbers in Thousands)

City	Population January 17, 1939	Population[1] 1942-1943
Kiev	846	330[2]
		305
Odessa	604	300[3]
Dnepropetrovsk	501	152[4]
		280
Zaporozh'ye	289	120
Mariupol'	222	178[4]
Krivoy Rog	198	125
Nikolayev	167	84
Dneprodzerzhinsk	148	75
Poltava	130	75
Kirovograd	100	63
Kherson	97	59
Zhitomir	95	42
Vinnitsa	93	42
Melitopol'	76	65
Total	2,740[5]	1,335[5]

[1] Figures, unless otherwise specified, are from *Deutsche Ukraine Zeitung*, February 2, 1943. Data refer to January 1, 1943.
[2] *Izvestiya*, October, 1942. (Cited by Kulischer, p. 90.)
[3] *Novoye Slovo*, July 22, 1942. (Cited by Kulischer, p. 90.)
[4] *Ibid.*, January 7, 1942. (Cited by Kulischer, p. 90.)
[5] Totals include only those cities for which 1942-1943 figures were obtained from *Deutsche Ukraine Zeitung*.

Deutsche Ukraine Zeitung, February 2, 1943. It is interesting to note that the earlier figure for Dnepropetrovsk cited here (published, January 7, 1942) is much smaller than the later figure, referring to January 1, 1943. If the two estimates are equally accurate, this may indicate that movement of persons from other parts of the occupied zone to this industrial city had partially restored the population as initially depleted by evacuation. In general, the population of Ukrainian cities in 1942 seems to have been half as large or less than it was in 1939. The reference cited for Mariupol gives the number of males as 76,730 and that of females as 101,628.[20] The depletion of urban population by evacuation may have been less marked in the most western districts of the annexed area than in the Ukraine as a whole, but scattered Soviet references indicate far greater depletion of population in some other cities, such as Smolensk and Kalinin. German discussions of agricultural problems in the occupied area give added evidence of the large-scale removal or destruction of farm equipment, but indicate that shortage

[20] Kulischer, Title 157, p. 90.

of agricultural labor was not serious except in certain districts. (The fact that many of the Ukrainian cities had been largely stripped of their population before the re-entry of Soviet forces in 1943 and 1944 does not, of course, bear directly on the problem now under discussion.) This evidence furnishes some reason for believing the thesis of the Chief of the War Economy Department in the German Economic Administration in the East that the evacuation from the area occupied in 1941 was equal to about half of its urban population, with refugee movements to rural districts about offsetting the evacuation of rural population. This German authority estimated on this basis that the number evacuated from occupied to free Soviet territory in 1941 was about 12.5 million persons.[21]

Two estimates by independent authorities, based on an analysis of the railway carrying capacity, result in divergent figures for evacuation from areas occupied prior to 1942. Habicht estimates 15 million as a maximum, and Vassiliev places the total number of evacuees as from 7.5 to 10 million.[22]

Estimates based on population changes in the occupied area would necessarily include military personnel mobilized from its civilian population. Figures based on transportation possibilities would also include military personnel recruited from areas threatened by imminent invasion, to the extent that the newly mobilized individuals were not immediately used in the same area. The evidence presented above suggests a possible evacuation of about 10 million persons from areas occupied by the German army during 1941, *including* military personnel moved eastward, but *excluding* refugee movements near the line of farthest advance. However, it is not clear that these lines of evidence can be applied to the areas occupied in the 1942 campaign (the procedure followed by Kulischer); the proportion of the population evacuated from these areas may have been much larger. Kulischer estimates the grand total of evacuees from both the annexed and original Soviet territories at 12 million persons, excluding only military personnel mobilized before the German invasion.[23] This is a very possible figure, but the margin of error in either direction would seem to be well over the 15 percent that Kulischer suggests as a probable maximum.

Scattered evidence as to the location of refugees and evacuees within the U.S.S.R. during the war can be briefly summarized as regards their general import. In general, these displaced people were located in the areas east of the Central Industrial Region which had been marked by most rapid expansion during the preceding decade, except that they were apparently not settled to any great extent in the Far East. It would appear that large numbers were located in regions near the Turkestan-Siberian Railway, and that Tashkent was an important distributing point for refugees and evacuees. A great many were assigned to various established and relocated industries in the Central Volga Region, the Urals, western and central Siberia, Kazakhstan, Central Asia, and the Far North. The industrial output of the Ural region is reported to have increased threefold during the war.[24]

Millions of persons, other than refugees and evacuees, moved to new locations in response to the labor demands of war industries. Many others, especially women and children, were also drawn into new occupations without change of residence.

7. Relation of War Movements to Long-Range Perspectives

Migration in the Soviet Union, as in China, has brought new population to, and stimulated the development of, areas potentially important for the future economy of these great nations.

[21] Kulischer, Title 157, p. 91. Reference to article by Rachner, *Reichsarbeitsblatt*, March 5, 1942. Kulischer indicates that this may involve an overestimate of urban population.
[22] *Ibid.*, pp. 91-92.   [23] *Ibid.*, p. 93.
[24] *New York Times*, January 2, 1943, referring to an article by Yaroslavsky.

The eastward movement of the Soviet population and the westward movement of Chinese have focused attention on the sparsely populated interior of the Eurasian land mass. The major difference between these cases is that in the U.S.S.R. the migration of the preceding years had provided a broad foundation for this war movement. Along with the acceleration of industrial production, during the war there was a great expansion of sown area in Siberia, Kazakhstan, and Central Asia. This was necessary in order to compensate so far as possible for temporary loss of great fertile areas in the western part of the U.S.S.R., especially in the Ukraine, the Crimea, and the North Caucasus. Though much of this expansion of agriculture in the geographical center of the Union must have been effected at a relatively low technological level, this enforced trend will have a positive influence on the future development of areas far removed from the old center of population.

In February, 1942, the Council of People's Commissars issued an order requiring local authorities in the eastern regions to make arrangements for the permanent absorption of workers and employees transferred there with their factories and equipment. Yaroslavsky, writing in *Pravda* at the beginning of 1943, called attention to the fact that the wartime movement to the Urals had brought many technicians and highly skilled workers into that region. He mentioned the evacuation of the Soviet Academy of Science from Moscow to Sverdlovsk, where many of its experts were engaged in research relating to industrial resources, and the location of the Ukrainian National Theater in a Ural city. He urged large appropriations in order to bring the cultural and health facilities of such cities up to the standards set for Russia's older western cities. The reconstruction of devastated areas will draw many workers and their families back into the western districts. But the acceleration of industrial and agricultural expansion in the central and eastern part of the U.S.S.R. will undoubtedly have a permanent effect on the whole future economy of the Union. However, one cannot for a moment presume that these constructive aspects of wartime population displacement in the Soviet Union can be measured against the dislocations, the destruction of capital equipment, the loss of life, and the crippling and exhaustion of survivors wrought by the war.

8. Cultural Trends

Migration during the interwar period and the great movements during the war have tended to break down the isolation of communities and regions and ethnic groups within the Soviet Union. Similarly, the rapid advance of technology, education, and literacy is bringing the whole population to a higher level of communication, productivity, and capacity for participation in public affairs. Many of the most important phases of such qualitative changes in the Soviet population cannot be easily defined in statistical terms. Figures on education and literacy do, however, supply suggestive evidence on one aspect of this subject.

Data on literacy from the censuses of 1897, 1926, and 1939 were summarized in the second release on the 1939 census (with the data for 1897 adjusted to cover the territory embraced within the January-1939 boundaries of the U.S.S.R., and similar adjustment by republics for 1926). According to this release, the proportion of "literacy" among all persons aged 9 years or over in the U.S.S.R. area rose from 24.0 percent in 1897 to 51.1 percent in 1926 and 81.2 percent in 1939. The comparable series for persons aged 9-49 years of age rose from 26.3 percent in 1897 to 56.6 in 1926 and to 89.1 in 1939.

The figures on literacy by republics are even more striking, as indicative of the rapid leveling of cultural opportunity among various segments of the Soviet population (see Table 75). Thus, to cite the most extreme case, less than 1 percent of all women in Tadzhikistan were reported as "able to read" in 1926 but 65 percent were reported as "able to read or write" in

TABLE 75

Literacy of the Population of the U.S.S.R.: By Republics and by Sex, 1926 and 1939[1]

| Republic | Percent of Population Aged 9 Years or Over Able to Read or Write | | | | | |
| | 1926[2] | | | 1939[3] | | |
	Male	Female	Total	Male	Female	Total
U.S.S.R.[4]	66.5	37.1	51.1	90.8	72.6	81.2
R.S.F.S.R.	72.0	40.2	55.0	92.3	73.0	81.9
Ukrainian S.S.R.	75.5	40.9	57.5	94.8	76.8	85.3
Belorussian S.S.R.	71.5	35.8	53.1	90.7	68.1	78.9
Azerbaydzhan S.S.R.	33.2	16.4	25.2	81.5	64.5	73.3
Georgian S.S.R.	55.5	39.4	47.5	66.1	74.6	80.3
Armenian S.S.R.	49.5	19.2	34.5	85.0	62.4	73.8
Turkmen S.S.R.	16.5	7.7	12.5	73.3	60.6	67.2
Uzbek S.S.R.	14.2	6.5	10.6	73.6	61.6	67.8
Tadzhik S.S.R.	6.2	0.8	3.7	77.7	65.2	71.7
Kazakh S.S.R.	32.6	12.5	22.8	85.2	66.3	76.3
Kirgiz S.S.R.	22.1	7.4	15.1	76.7	63.0	70.0

[1] According to second release on the 1939 census.
[2] "Able to read," according to 1926 census definition.
[3] "Able to read or write," according to 1939 census definition.
[4] Excluding Western Ukraine and Western Belorussia.

1939. The change in definition would appear to indicate a relaxation of standards in census procedure, but it would be gratuitous to attribute the phenomenal change mainly to this factor. The apparent trend is supported by an abundance of circumstantial evidence.

The statistics on elementary and secondary school enrollment give supplementary evidence of the rise and equalization of cultural opportunity in all parts of the U.S.S.R. For this purpose, the administrative statistics on school enrollment have been used, and the number of pupils in 1938 and 1939 has been related to total population on January 17, 1939. Such ratios are shown for the urban and rural parts of each republic in Table 76. (For proportions in 1939, see also Figure 31.)

In both urban and rural areas a decrease in the number of pupils in lowest grades is shown for the whole U.S.S.R. from 1938 to 1939 (numbers of pupils in both years being related here to the same base population). The trend is indicative of the decrease in births in the U.S.S.R. in the early 1930's, which has been previously noted. The higher ratios for elementary schools in rural as compared with urban areas can also be interpreted in purely demographic terms, as suggestive of the greater proportion of children in the rural population. It is apparent from these statistics that elementary school attendance has become universal in all parts of the U.S.S.R., and the variations in pupil-population ratios at the elementary school level conform closely to probable variations in ratios of children of school age to total population. This is supported by the data for administrative districts (not presented here in detail). On the other hand, it is clear that attendance at educational levels higher than the first four grades drops off fairly sharply, and that, in this respect, the rural communities in some republics lag far behind the more industrial areas. This is conspicuously the case in Tadzhikistan, but it is scarcely surprising in a region where 99 percent of the women were reported as illiterate in 1926. A rapid increase in proportions attending higher grades is evident, especially in the regions previously characterized by general illiteracy.

TABLE 76

Pupils in Specified Grades, 1938 and 1939, per 100 Persons in Total Population,
January 17, 1939: Urban and Rural Areas, by Republics of the U.S.S.R.[1]

| Republic | Grades 1-4 | | | | Grades 5-7 | | | | Grades 8-10 | | | |
| | Urban | | Rural | | Urban | | Rural | | Urban | | Rural | |
	1938	1939	1938	1939	1938	1939	1938	1939	1938	1939	1938	1939
U.S.S.R.	9.4	9.2	13.9	13.4	5.7	6.4	4.9	5.4	1.5	2.0	0.5	0.7
R.S.F.S.R.	9.5	9.4	14.2	13.6	5.9	6.6	4.9	5.3	1.5	1.9	0.4	0.6
Ukraine	8.5	8.1	12.1	11.2	5.6	6.0	5.7	6.0	1.6	2.1	0.8	1.0
Belorussia	9.1	9.2	14.0	13.9	5.9	6.5	5.2	5.7	2.4	3.1	0.5	0.8
Azerbaydzhan	10.7	10.4	15.0	14.9	5.0	5.6	5.2	5.7	1.3	1.7	0.6	1.1
Georgia	8.5	8.6	14.2	14.0	5.4	6.0	5.5	6.0	2.4	2.9	1.1	1.4
Armenia	12.8	12.7	17.1	17.4	6.4	6.8	6.2	6.9	2.1	2.6	1.3	1.8
Turkmen	10.0	9.8	14.4	14.8	3.9	4.9	2.4	4.0	0.5	0.8	0.03	0.06
Uzbek	10.7	11.1	15.2	15.5	4.4	5.5	2.6	3.7	0.8	1.3	0.09	0.21
Tadzhik	9.4	10.5	17.1	18.2	3.0	4.0	0.6	1.3	0.5	0.7	0.02	0.04
Kazakh	10.8	10.4	13.7	12.5	5.5	6.8	4.0	5.2	1.0	1.5	0.3	0.5
Kirgiz	12.2	11.6	16.8	16.9	5.4	6.6	3.3	4.7	1.3	1.7	0.3	0.4

[1] Data on pupils from *Kul'turnoye Stroitel'stvo SSSR, 1940*, Title 475.

9. Summary and Prospect

The evidence reviewed above leads naturally to certain major conclusions that can be stated in summary fashion.

The dynamics of the Soviet population will bring continued population increase in the post-war period, with a large though gradually decreasing proportion of children, youth, and young adults. There is also the prospect of an increasingly efficient distribution of population in relation to economic resources and production. Finally, rapid advances in health, skills, cultural resources, and equipment will enhance the postwar prospects of the Soviet population.

It is necessary to raise seriously the question as to whether or not the population of the Soviet Union is beginning to reach a magnitude beyond which a continued rapid increase in numbers would jeopardize the level of living that might otherwise be attained among its citizens. It is clear that the efficient development of its varied resources in a vast territory requires a large population. On the other hand, it is clear that its resources, especially with respect to agriculture, are limited by severe climatic conditions. No dogmatic answer can be given to this question at the present time, especially in view of the rapidity of technological changes in the modern world and their implications for the relation of population to resources. The question is raised here merely to indicate a problem that will merit careful examination in the future.

In August, 1914, the people of the Russian Empire were brought into the First World War. They were numerous but unhealthy, illiterate, and bound by an economy that utilized a relatively small part of their resources at a low technological level. The next thirty years brought inconceivable hardships and tremendous losses. The loss of human lives during these past thirty years, counting both excess deaths and deficits of births under abnormal conditions, approaches and may pass fifty million persons. The Russian population entered this period of trial with one great physical asset: a low density of persons to resources, which gave it the highest potentiality for rapid industrial progress of any nation in the world. The will of the people and the quality of their leadership, by taking advantage of this basic physical asset, created at terrific cost a nation that has proved itself capable of withstanding the most powerful military aggression in human history. Having achieved the foundations of new economic and social progress and having survived this ordeal, the people of the Union of Soviet Socialist Republics today face prospects far different from those of the previous generation.

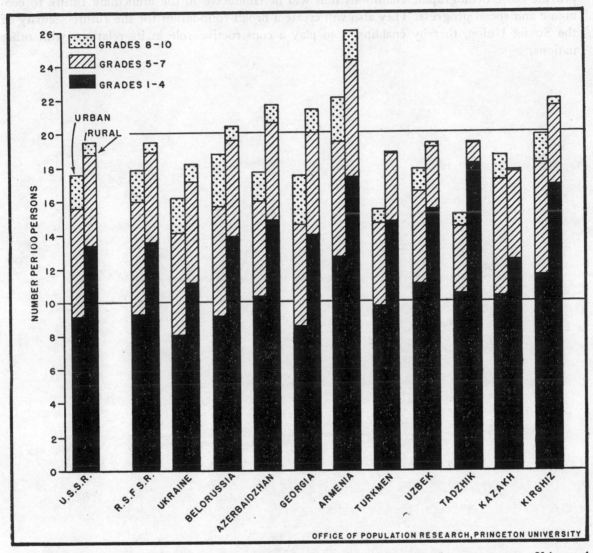

Figure 31. Pupils in Specified Grades, 1939, per 100 Persons in Total Population, January 17, 1939: Urban and Rural Areas, by Republics of the U.S.S.R. [Table 76]

During these last thirty years there have been great fluctuations of births and deaths; the present composition of the Soviet population shows the effects of these fluctuations. There have also been violent displacements of population and flights, as well as orderly migration in response to new opportunities. These more erratic movements will give way, if the war is followed by a long peace, to more orderly patterns of population change. There is little likelihood of a repetition of the pattern of uncontrolled fertility with great wastage in death, which was characteristic of the old Russian Empire and of mediaeval Europe and which still persists in most Asiatic countries. On the other hand, the Soviet population may not pass through the trend toward population decrease that is now characteristic of most western European nations.

We have attempted to project over a few decades the probable course of population in the Soviet Union, assuming the continuance and gradual modification of prewar trends. But population movements within the U.S.S.R., as well as its economy and culture, are still fluid and unpredictable. It is clear, however, that the forces now implicit in Soviet population trends provide basic demographic conditions that will be conducive in the immediate future to economic and social progress. They also will create a broad foundation for the future security of the Soviet Union, thereby enabling it to play a constructive role in its relations with other nations.

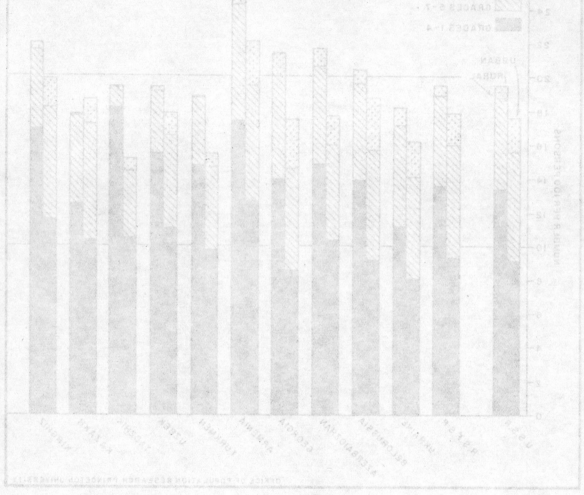

APPENDIX I

NOTES ON ESTIMATION OF THE GROWTH AND DISTRIBUTION OF RUSSIAN POPULATION, 1724-1897

1. Estimates prior to 1897 are based on enumerations of males for purposes of taxation. Each enumeration extended over a period of several years, and reference to any exact date has only approximate value. Males of all ages from birth to death in taxable classes were subject to enumeration, but males in classes not conveniently taxable were exempt, such as members of the nobility, clergy, court, and militia. The enumerations are referred to in Russian literature as "revisions." The "first revision" was made as of 1724 (or 1723), near the end of the reign of Peter the Great— leaving out of account an earlier revision (about 1710), which was repudiated by Peter as defective and unsatisfactory.

2. The "first revision" relates to an area referred to here as "Peter's realm," covering central and northern Russia with certain exceptions. It does not include two European regions also subject to Peter at this time: (1) the recently conquered Baltic provinces and (2) Little Russia on the south-western frontier. The former region, including the Kurland, Estland, and Lifland gubernii, is omitted in our treatment. The latter region corresponds to the later Poltava and Chernigov gubernii, plus the city of Kiev, and is combined with the border region (*ukrain*) outside Peter's jurisdiction (i.e., the remainder of Kiev Guberniya, plus Podolia and Volynia gubernii). This combined region is here referred to as the Ukrainian region. It does not include the Black Sea districts that form part of the present Ukrainian S.S.R.

Peter's realm did not include the territory to the west inhabited chiefly by Belorussians and Lithu-anians (Grodno, Kovno, Minsk, Mogilëv, Vil'na and Vitebsk gubernii, as of 1897). This is here referred to as the Lithuanian-Belorussian region.

Moreover, Peter's realm did not include the regions of southern Russia not yet effectively occupied by Russians. These regions are divided in our treatment as follows:

Designation	Gubernii as of 1897
Black Sea Districts	Kherson, Tavrida (including the Crimea), and Yekaterinoslav (Bessarabia is omitted in our treatment)
Don Region	Voyska Donskogo Oblast'
North Caucasus	Dagestan, Black Sea (Chernomore), Stavropol', and Terek
Southeast (New)	Astrakhan', Orenburg (including Asiatic part), and Samara

Peter's authority extended into Siberia, but the estimated population living beyond the Urals at this time (including the Trans-Ural part of Perm' Guberniya) is subtracted and given separate treatment. The 1897 political divisions that comprised Peter's realm, i.e., the area of the "first revision," as described by Milyukov,[1] are shown in Table A 1. This table also gives the number of enumerated males, in 1724, and Milyukov's estimates of persons per square verst at that time.

3. Our estimate of the population of Peter's realm in 1724 is based on the following items: (1) the number of enumerated males is taken as 5,794,928, using a revised figure from Schnitzler,[2] which is slightly higher than the sum of figures in Table A 1; (2) the ratio of non-taxable to tax-able classes is assumed to be 1.06955, as in 1835;[3] and (3) the ratio of total population to total number of males is assumed to be 2.06, as in 1926 (a postwar year, comparable in this respect to 1724). These factors give an estimated population of 12,774,000. The final estimate is rounded to 13,000,000, which is also Milyukov's estimate of total population in Peter's realm at this time.

This estimate is subject to serious error in so far as the enumeration data were grossly defective or inaccurate, e.g., if a considerable proportion of taxable males escaped enumeration by the Tsar's agents. Such error may amount to 5 or perhaps 10 percent.

4. Milyukov gives estimated densities by regions within Peter's realm, but these estimates appear to demand revision. Unfortunately he does not give his absolute estimates of area or population.

[1] Milyukov, Title 199. [2] Schnitzler, Title 288, p. 107. [3] *Ibid.*, p. 86.

TABLE A 1

Divisions of the Russian Empire, 1897, within Specified Divisions of the Realm of Peter the
Great, with Number of Enumerated Males, 1724, and Estimated Density
according to Milyukov[1]

Division	Enumerated Males	Persons per Square Verst
I. Center (old Moscow Guberniya)	1,622,033	29.4
Moscow Gub.		
Vladimir Gub., except part in VI		
Kaluga Gub., except part in III		
Ryazan' Gub., except parts in V and VI		
Tula Gub., except parts in III, IV, and V		
Kostroma Gub.: 3 western uyezds (Buysk, Nerekhot, Kostroma)		
Yaroslavl' Gub.: Rostov uyezd		
II. Northwest (old St. Petersburg Guberniya)	923,211	5.2
St. Petersburg Gub.		
Novgorod Gub.		
Pskov Gub.		
Tver' Gub., except part in III		
Yaroslavl' Gub., except part in I		
Olonets Gub., except part in VII		
III. West (old Smolensk Guberniya)	271,879	7.6
Smolensk Gub.		
Kaluga Gub. (major part); 6 western uyezds (Zhizdra, Kozel'sk, Likhvin, Meshchovsk, Mosal'sk, Peremyshl'sk)		
Tver' Gub.: Zubtsov uyezd		
Tula Gub.: Odoyes uyezd		
IV. Old Southwest (old Kiev Guberniya)	532,656	11.2
Kursk Gub., except part in V		
Orël Gub., except part in V		
Khar'kov Gub., except part in V		
Tula Gub.: Novosel'sk and Byelyev uyezds		
V. Old South (old Azov Guberniya)	434,536	3.9
Voronezh Gub.		
Penza Gub., except part in VI		
Ryazan' Gub. (major part): 5 southern uyezds (Rankov, Ryazhsk, Ranenburg, Skopin, Sapozhkov, Pronsk)		
Tambov Gub., except part in VI		
Tula Gub.: Efremov and Chern uyezds		
Saratov Gub.: 4 western uyezds (Atkarsk, Balashov, Petrovsk, Serdobsk)		
Khar'kov Gub.: 5 eastern uyezds (Izyum, Kupyansk, Zmiyev, Starobel'sk, Volchansk)		
Kursk Gub.: Novo-Oskol'sk uyezd		
Orël Gub.: Yeletsk uyezds		

TABLE A 1 (*Continued*)

Divisions of the Russian Empire, 1897, within Specified Divisions of the Realm of Peter the
Great, with Number of Enumerated Males, 1724, and Estimated Density
according to Milyukov[1]

Division	Enumerated Males	Persons per Square Verst
VI. Old Southeast (old Kazan' and Astrakhan' gubernii)	591,925	2.6
Kazan' Gub.		
Nizhniy Novgorod Gub.*		
Simbirsk Gub.		
Ufa Gub.		
Saratov, except part in V		
Ryazan' Gub.: Kasimov and Spassk uyezds		
Tambov Gub.: Elatomsk and Temnikov uyezds		
Penza Gub.: 3 southeast uyezds (Penza, Morshansk, Gorodishche)		
Vladimir Gub.: 4 eastern uyezds (Vyaznikov, Gorokhov, Melenki, Murom)		
Kostroma Gub.: 2 southeast uyezds (Vetluga and Varnavinsk)		
Vyatka Gub.: 6 southern uyezds (Yelabuga, Malmyk, Nolinsk, Sarapul, Uyzhum, Yaransk)		
Perm' Gub.: 2 southern (European) uyezds (Krasnoufinsk, Osa)		

   *Note: Enumerated males in "Nizhegorodskaya
Guberniya" formed during Peter's reign prior to
the "first revision" (assumed as properly added
to the number given above in calculating total
population of this region, but apparently neglected by Milyukov in his estimate of density):
473,657

Division	Enumerated Males	Persons per Square Verst
VII. North (old Arkhangel'sk Guberniya)	315,975	0.7
Arkhangel'sk Gub.		
Vologda Gub. (Note: Two eastern uyezds here, Ust'sysol'sk and Yarensk, were not used by Milyukov in computing density)		
Kostroma Gub., except parts in I and VI (Note: Vetluzhsk uyezd, included here, was not used by Milyukov in computing density)		
Olonets Gub.: northern part (Kargopol'sk uyezd)		

   Area used by Milyukov: 418,700 square miles
   Total area: 512,200 square miles

Division	Enumerated Males	Persons per Square Verst
VIII. East (old Siberian Guberniya: European part)	404,626	1.9
Vyatka Gub., except part in VI		
Perm' Gub.: Cis-Ural uyezds, except part in VI (Kungur, Okha, Perm', Solikamsk, and Cherdyn uyezds)		

   Note: Enumerated males = European part plus Asiatic
      part
      Density = European part

[1] List (adapted) and figures from Milyukov, Title 199, pp. 21-37.

For the present study the land area of each region was first estimated from the 1897 census report, by summing the areas for 1897 gubernii or uyezds within each of the old gubernii as described by Milyukov. The density figures (persons per unit of land, as computed by Milyukov) were then applied to each area and a tentative series of population estimates obtained. These were compared with the reported number of males enumerated in each region; the proportion was constant in most cases but there were certain exceptions.

It may be noted here that Milyukov was a scholarly historian, concerned with the history of Russian colonization, economy, and culture. He was not interested in the absolute but merely in the relative values of his data.[4] He knew the history of the regions, but he did not report his exact procedures or the complete basic data.

Milyukov, in dealing with the eastern region, apparently assumed that about one-half the population of the old "Siberian Guberniya" (which includes European parts of Perm' and most of Vyatka, also in Europe) lived east of the Urals. His density ratio for this region applies, therefore, only to its European part (in Perm' and Vyatka). We have followed him in this assumption. Milyukov's density figure for the southeastern portion of Peter's realm, referred to in his text as "the Kazan' and Astrakhan' gubernii" of that time, appears to be erroneous. It corresponds to the enumerated number of males in these two old gubernii, but the Nizhegorod Guberniya had been formed from parts of these gubernii during Peter's reign and its area is definitely included in this region by Milyukov. We have, therefore, adjusted the population of this region to correspond to the adjusted sum of the enumerated males in old Kazan', Astrakhan', and Nizhegorod gubernii (as of 1724).

Finally, the sum of the population figures indicated by his density values applied to the respective areas gives a total that is much too low (about 10 million instead of 13 million). Apparently, Milyukov, in computing area densities, assumed about equal numbers of males and females; but, in estimating the *total* population of Peter's realm, he followed other students who introduced corrections to give a much higher total (as indicated above). We have, therefore, adjusted the regional population figures proportionately to give the estimated total.

5. The estimates for regions outside Peter's realm are even more dubious. It is assumed that the density of population at this time in the region referred to here as Lithuania-Belorussia was equal to the average density of the three central districts of Peter's realm (Northwest, West, and Central), i.e., higher than in the western region (Smolensk) but much lower than in the central region (Moscow). It is also assumed that the density in the area defined above in Section 2 as the Ukrainian region ("Little Russia" plus the *ukrain* of Peter's time) is equal to that of the three southern regions within Peter's realm combined—taking into account the higher density in the vicinity of Kiev in the twelfth century, but also the terrific devastation of this region during the Mongol invasion and subsequent campaigns between Poland and Moscow. These estimates have been discussed with several Russian scholars, and checked, as regards indicated growth, against the data from later "revisions." The figures probably indicate the order of magnitude with reasonable accuracy, but are obviously mere guesses and subject to a large margin of error.

The same must be said of the figure for the Russian population in 1724 in the territory of the semi-independent Don Cossacks and in the districts dominated by Tatar nomads in southern Russia. The estimated Cossack population in the Don region in 1838 was only 215,000, after transfers from the Dnepr region to the Don, under Catherine II, according to Koeppen.[5] Veynberg estimates the total population of the Don region within the Russian Empire in 1724 as 50,000, assuming a change proportional to the estimated increase in Orenburg and Astrakhan' gubernii (1897 limits).[6] Milyukov estimates that there were "less than 50,000 Russians" in southern Russia (Black Sea districts, as defined above) about the middle of the eighteenth century. We have arbitrarily used the figures: 100,000 Russians in the Don region; 50,000 Russians in Black Sea districts; 50,000 Russians in the Volga steppe region; none in the North Caucasus. Relatively large errors in these figures, in view of their small absolute value, would not have a great effect on the estimate of the total Russian population at this time or on the estimates of increase of population in different parts of Russia during the next two centuries.

6. The figures for January 1, 1859, are based on the data of the "tenth revision." In this case we have official estimates of total population by gubernii, which remained fixed until 1914 in regard to

[4] Conversation with Milyukov as reported by Dr. Eugene Kulischer to writer.
[5] Schnitzler, Title 288, p. 90.   [6] Veynberg, Title 344, Table 1, Note 14.

the territory treated here, except for changes in the North Caucasus Kray and the Don Oblast', and in the Ufa Guberniya (formed after 1859 from parts of other gubernii in our "New Southeast"). We therefore used the figures supplied by A. A. Troynitskiy.[7] These "official estimates" are, of course, not necessarily superior to our unofficial guesses, except that they are based on more intimate knowledge of conditions; the values for this period must, consequently, also be accepted with reservations. The estimate of Russian and non-Russian population is discussed below.

7. The figures for 1897 are taken from the census.[8] "Peter's realm" as defined in Table A 1, plus the Lithuanian-Belorussian and the Ukrainian regions, is assumed to represent the *original land base* of the Russian population in 1724. The *total* population within this area *plus* Russians, Ukrainians, and Belorussians, classified on the basis of mother tongue, in districts to the south and east is assumed to represent the total "Russian population" in 1897. (The number of persons reported as having one of the three Russian languages as a mother tongue is usually somewhat larger than the sum of Orthodox, "Schismatic," and several minor Christian sects, classified on the basis of religion.) This total Russian population is assumed to represent roughly the number of the descendants in this region of the parent "Russian population" of 1724, although it was affected by absorption of some old Slavic colonists from the Danubian region, Armenian colonists, and others through acculturation and intermarriage. Jews, Germans, Poles, and other non-Russian ethnic groups in these districts are not included, although in some cases they were drawn from the parent population of 1724. This procedure is based on the assumption that if non-Russian elements are deducted from the population in the regions of rapid colonization and development, the *net* migration across the western boundary to and from European Russia (excluding Bessarabia, Poland, Finland, and the three Baltic provinces) can be regarded as relatively negligible.

8. A more complicated procedure is required in order to estimate Russian and non-Russian population in southern Russia in 1724 and in 1859. We first estimate the indigenous population (as contrasted with both Russian and other non-Russian in-migrant groups), which is assumed to have been fairly constant from 1724 to 1859, and to have increased about one-half as rapidly as the total population of European Russia from 1859 to 1897. The indigenous population of various districts as of 1897, according to a classification by religion, is taken as the sum of Mohammedans, Buddhists, Jews (Taurida and North Caucasus only), Karaims, "other non-Christians," and Armenians (North Caucasus only). The following figures are obtained in this way: Black Sea region, 263,000; Don region, 36,000; North Caucasus, 1,254,000; and New Southeast, 1,104,000; with a total of 2,657,000. The corresponding total in 1859 is assumed to have been about 2,000,000 persons, distributed among districts in the same proportions. The indigenous population of the Black Sea and Don regions was apparently included in the official estimates of total population in 1859. But the mountain people of Dagestan and the North Caucasus and the nomads in the eastern steppe regions were not so included. The estimates of non-indigenous population in 1859 run as follows: Black Sea region (official figure minus estimated indigenous), 2,527,000; Don region (same procedure), 867,000; North Caucasus (official figure), 843,000; New Southeast (official figure), 2,822,000.[9]

It is then assumed that the Russian population constituted the same proportion of the total non-indigenous population in 1859 as in 1897: namely, Black Sea region, 81.6 percent; Don region, 96.6 percent; North Caucasus, 93.7 percent; and New Southeast, 84.9 percent. These percentages, applied to the adjusted non-indigenous totals, give estimates of Russian population in 1859. The estimated indigenous population in the North Caucasus and New Southeast is added to the official figures to give estimated total population in these regions in 1859. The estimate of non-Russian population in southern Russia in 1724 (taken as equal to indigenous population in 1859) probably gives a maximum value.

No attempt is made to estimate the non-Russian population in Asiatic Russia prior to 1897.

9. The 274,000 given as the estimated Russian population of Siberia in 1724 is an interpolation between the estimates of Slovtsol for 1709 (220,227) and for 1737 (297,810).[10] The population of Perm' Guberniya in 1724, as estimated on the basis of the "first revision" data, was 252,000 persons, divided equally between European and Asiatic parts (see Section 4, above), giving 126,000 in the

---

[7] Troynitskiy, Title 331.   [8] Census of 1897, Title 381.
[9] Official figures from Troynitskiy, Title 331; estimates of indigenous population are described above.
[10] Cited in *Aziatskaya Rossiya*, Title 415, Vol. I, p. 81.

Asiatic part. Summing these figures gives 400,000 as the estimated number of Russians beyond the Urals at this time.

It is assumed that there was no Russian population in the Asiatic steppes, Turkestan, or the Transcaucasus in 1724. The Russian population of the Transcaucasus and Turkestan in 1859 is also ignored as negligible. The official estimates for Asiatic regions in 1859, aside from estimates of nomads, are assumed to refer only to Russian population as here defined.

10. Distribution of population within "Peter's realm" in 1859 by three major divisions was ob-

TABLE A 2

Estimated Growth and Distribution of the Russian Population, 1724-1897
(Numbers in Thousands)

Area	Land Area Sq. Km.	1724		1859		1897	
		All Classes	"Russian Population"	All Classes	"Russian Population"	All Classes	"Russian Population"
Total[1]	21,197	—	17,900		58,629	111,916	94,331
Total European Part	4,800	19,500	17,500	58,024	55,205	92,075	87,384
Peter's Realm (European Part)	3,051	12,600	12,600	35,275	35,275	48,800	48,800
Central Russia	617	6,690	6,690	11,542	11,542	15,741	15,741
Center	127	3,850	3,850			5,788	5,788
Northwest	408	2,200	2,200			7,472	7,472
West	82	640	640			2,481	2,481
Old South	869	4,640	4,640	20,233	20,233	28,173	28,173
Old Southwest	108	1,240	1,240			5,408	5,408
Old South	257	1,000	1,000			9,846	9,846
Old Southeast	504	2,400	2,400			12,919	12,919
North and East	1,565	1,270	1,270	3,500	3,500	4,886	4,886
North	1,327	770	770			2,609	2,609
European East	238	500	500			2,277	2,277
Lithuania-Belorussia	303	3,300	3,300	5,399	5,399	10,063	10,063
New South	1,446	3,600	1,600	17,350	14,531	33,212	28,521
Ukraine Region	267	1,400	1,400	8,441	8,441	14,643	14,643
Black Sea Region	195	250	50	2,527	2,060	6,295	4,921
Don Region	164	130	100	897	840	2,564	2,442
North Caucasus	259	940	—	1,783	790	4,355	2,906
Volga Steppe	561	880	50	3,702	2,400	5,355	3,609
Total Asiatic Part[1]	16,397	—	400	—	3,424	19,841	6,947
Trans-Ural Perm'	133	—	126	—	917	1,401	1,342
Siberia	12,479	—	274	—	2,288	5,758	4,659
Steppe Region	1,853	—	—	—	219	2,466	493
Turkestan[1]	1,722	—	—	—	—	5,281	204
Transcaucasus	210	—	—	—	—	4,935	249

[1] Not including Khiva and Bukhara.

tained as follows. Ratios of population change from 1859 to 1897 were computed for groups of gubernii, without adjustment for parts of gubernii falling in different divisions. These ratios were then applied to the 1897 population figures for the exact areas to give estimated distribution in 1859.

11. The development of these estimates has involved many trivial and dubious adjustments. All of the figures, except perhaps those drawn directly from the 1897 census, are subject to question and many undoubtedly involve serious errors. No claim is made with regard to the reliability of the results *except* for the broad features of the growth and distribution of the Russian population, thus indicated, as set forth in the text and subject to the reservations there stated.

TABLE A 3

Parts of the Russian Empire Outside the U.S.S.R., 1923

Division of the Russian Empire	Land Area Outside U.S.S.R. Sq. Km. (In thousands)	Population as of 1897 in Area Outside U.S.S.R. (In thousands)	Percent of Land Area Outside U.S.S.R.	Percent of Population as of 1897 in Area Outside U.S.S.R.
Total	847.5	24,134.1	—	—
Vistula Gubernii ("Congress Poland")	126.9[1]	9,402.3[1]	100	100
Duchy of Finland	325.5[2]	2,400.0[3]	100	100
European Russia	354.4[4]	11,882.0[5]	—	—
Estland	20.2[6]	412.7[6]	100[6]	100[6]
Lifland	47.0	1,299.4	100	100
Kurland	27.0	674.0	100	100
Kovno	40.2	1,544.6	100	100
Grodno	38.6	1,603.4	100	100
Bessarabia	45.6	1,935.4	100	100
Vil'na	41.5	1,574.6	99.0	99.0
Volynia	40.2	1,510.4	56.0	50.6
Vitebsk	14.1	510.0	32.0	34.2
Minsk	27.3	706.8	30.0	32.4
Pskov	3.5	80.8	8.0	7.2
St. Petersburg	0.9	28.9	2.0	1.4
Arkhangel'sk	8.4	1.0	1.0	0.3
Transcaucasus	26.8	441.2	—	—
Kutais	4.8	70.4	13.2	6.7
Kars	18.3	281.7	96.6	96.6
Erivan	3.7	89.1	14.0	10.7
Sakhalin	13.9	8.6[7]	18.3	30.4

[1] Census of 1897, Title 381.

[2] Saucerman, Title 338, p. 100. See this source for distribution of territory received by other nations.

[3] Figure for legal population, December 31, 1896, 2,555.5 from *Statistical Year-Book of Finland, 1939*, adjusted to give approximate actual population.

[4] Saucerman, Title 338, has an alternative estimate of 354.2.

[5] An independent estimate by Volkov, Title 352, is 11,855.8.

[6] Volkov, Title 352, pp. 16-19. Area figures obtained by applying percentage of territory lost according to Central Statistical Committee (as cited by Volkov) to areas of total gubernii as given in the census of 1897.

[7] Area ceded to Japan at end of Russo-Japanese War. Estimated fraction of total area and population.

TABLE A 4

Estimate of Land Areas of the Russian Empire and of the U.S.S.R.
(In Thousand Square Kilometers)

Area	Total	Europe	Asia
I. U.S.S.R., 1926	21,176[1]	5,999[2]	15,177[2]
Adjustments to give area of Russian Empire without Finland, Khiva, and Bukhara:			
Khiva	—	—	—62[3]
Bukhara	—	—	—207[4]
Poland	—	+127[5]	—
Parts of 50 gubernii of European Russia	—	+354[5]	—
Parts of Transcaucasus	—	—	+27[5]
Parts of Sakhalin (ceded to Japan)	—	—	+14[5]
Total	21,429	6,480	14,949
II. Russian Empire, 1897, according to Census	21,464	5,200[6]	16,264[6]
Adjustments to give area used in study of growth and distribution of Russian population:			
Poland	—	—127	
Bessarabia, Kurland, Lifland, and Estland	—	—140	
Trans-Ural Perm'	—	—133	+133
Total	21,197	4,800	16,397

[1] Census of 1926, Title 391.

[2] Division between Europe and Asia from *Statistical Year-Book of the League of Nations, 1934/35*, p. 22. The division between "Europe" and "Asia" is arbitrary. The large discrepancy between the figures in these columns is, therefore, not surprising. The smaller discrepancies for the total area of the Russian Empire are due to differences in estimates of land area.

[3] *Bol'shaya Sovetskaya Entsiklopediya*, Title 471, Vol. 59.

[4] Heilperin, *Gazetteer* (Lippincott). Somewhat different estimates are cited in Ritter and in Bausense.

[5] See Appendix, Table A 3.

[6] Arbitrary division between Europe and Asia (unofficial). "Europe" includes only Cis-Ural part of Perm' Guberniya, but all of Orenburg and Ufa gubernii, the North Caucasus districts, and Dagestan.

APPENDIX II

DATA USED IN ESTIMATING THE TREND OF AGRICULTURAL PRODUCTION, 1883-1914

1. The division of provinces between black soil (including steppe) and other zones, according to Obukhov, is as follows:

Black Soil Provinces	Non-Black Soil Provinces
Kursk	Arkhangel'sk
Orël	Olonets
Tula	Vologda
Ryazan'	Novgorod
Tambov	St. Petersburg
Voronezh	Pskov
Simbirsk	Estland
Penza	Lifland
Kazan'	Kurland
Saratov	Kovno
Samara	Vil'na
Orenburg	Grodno
Astrakhan'	Vitebsk
Don	Minsk
Khar'kov	Mogilëv
Poltava	Smolensk
Chernigov	Kaluga
Volynia	Tver'
Kiev	Moscow
Podol'sk	Vladimir
Kherson	Yaroslavl'
Bessarabia	Kostroma
Tavrida	Nizhniy Novgorod
Yekaterinoslav	Vyatka
Ufa	Perm'

2. The absolute figures (sums of figures for specified years) used for the ratios shown in the text are as follows:

Period	Sown Area in Thousand Desyatin[1]		"Bread Grains" in Thousand Puds[1]	
	Black Soil	Non-Black Soil	Black Soil	Non-Black Soil
1883-1887	207,995	90,492	7,597,345	3,422,428
1888-1893	260,246	107,689	9,135,702	4,218,080
1894-1898	216,614	91,274	9,197,272	4,064,859
1899-1903	240,813	93,148	11,048,568	4,137,913
1904-1909	310,126	110,917	14,034,474	5,087,031
1910-1914	269,999	93,316	13,435,917	4,527,155

[1] Sums of figures for specified years, as given by Obukhov, Title 223, pp. 56-58.

[211]

APPENDIX III

NOTES ON ESTIMATES OF THE DEFICIT IN GROWTH OF THE POPULATION IN THE U.S.S.R., 1897-1926

1. Estimates of net emigration, 1897-1913, are based on data presented by Ferenczi[1] and by Obolensky-Ossinsky.[2] Estimates were first made of the number of emigrants by linguistic groups, from the whole Russian Empire to the United States and Canada during these years (from Ferenczi, pp. 464, 466, 468, and Obolensky-Ossinsky, p. 530). Omissions for the years 1897 and 1898 were filled by assuming the same number in each of these years as in 1899. Data for Poles and Finns were omitted on the assumption that emigration of these classes from European Russia was equaled or exceeded during this period by migration from Congress Poland and the Duchy of Finland to European Russia. The following totals were obtained:

Hebrews	1,072,000
Russians, Belorussians, Ukrainians	260,000
Lithuanians, Letts	237,000
Germans	149,000
Others (except Poles and Finns)	22,000

These totals were adjusted to give estimated *net* migration to United States and Canada by applying the following ratios of net to gross emigration, based on data for the years 1908-1913 (Obolensky-Ossinsky, p. 530): Hebrews, .932; Russians and related groups, .588; Lithuanians and Letts, .765; Germans, .967; Others, assumed to be .8. The adjusted total for each ethnic group was then distributed among specified divisions of the Russian Empire in proportion to the distribution of corresponding groups as shown by the 1897 census. The resultant figures in thousands run as follows:

	Russian Empire	All European Russia (50 Provinces and North Caucasus)[3]	European Part of U.S.S.R.[4]
Hebrews	999	735	478
Russians, Belorussians, Ukrainians	153	153	135
Lithuanians, Letts	181	134	—
Germans	144	107	119
Others (except Poles and Finns)	18	14	15
Total		1,143	747

It was then assumed, after consideration of the evidence, that net emigration from the Russian Empire to all countries was between 1.1 and 1.2 times the net emigration to the United States and Canada.[5] The final estimates of net emigration, 1897-1913, were: All European Russia (50 provinces and North Caucasus): 1,345,000 persons; European part of the U.S.S.R.: 875,000 persons. These figures are used in the estimates discussed in Chapter III.

2. Table A 5 presents the survival ratios used in "aging" the 1897 population in the U.S.S.R. area to 1926. The expected number of children under 5 years of age at successive five-year intervals, and the survival ratios used in "aging" these cohorts to 1926, are shown in Table A 6.

[1] In Willcox, Title 358.
[2] Obolensky-Ossinsky, Title 221.
[3] Excluding Poland and Finland.
[4] This calculation was carried out for the total U.S.S.R. area (including Asiatic parts) but was applied without adjustment to the European part of the U.S.S.R. area.
[5] The final estimates were taken as net emigration to the United States and Canada from all European Russia (1,143,000) times 1.177, and that from the European part of the U.S.S.R. (747,000) times 1.172. These adjustment factors, though carried out in detail, are merely rough approximations. The whole procedure and the resultant estimates are subject to a wide margin of error.

TABLE A 5

Thirty-Year Survival Ratios Used in Projecting the Population in the U.S.S.R. Area, 1897-1927[1]

| Age | | Survival Ratios | |
February 9, 1897	February 9, 1927	Male	Female
0-4	30-34	.697	.697
5-9	35-39	.798	.790
10-14	40-44	.787	.778
15-19	45-49	.751	.749
20-24	50-54	.707	.715
25-29	55-59	.649	.663
30-34	60-64	.575	.591
35-39	65-69	.474	.486
40-44	70-74	.355	.363
45-49	75-79	.239	.243
50-54	80-84	.148	.151
55-59	85-89	.085	.091
60-64	90-94	.048	.051
65-69	95-99	.028	.033

[1] Derived from Novosel'skiy and Payevskiy, Title 417, Table 55.

TABLE A 6

Values Used in Estimating Expected Population Under 30 Years of Age in 1926

| | Extrapolated Population | | Survival Values to December 17, 1926 | | | |
Date Dec. 17	Total (In thousands)	Ages 0-4 (In thousands)[1]	Using 1896-97 Life Table[2]	Using 1926-27 Life Table[3]	Weight of Values in Col. A	Weighted Mean
			(A)	(B)	(W)	(W)(A)+[1-(W)](B)
1901	115,072	17,537	.7272	.8291	.3134	.7852
1906	124,993	19,049	.7558	.8538	.2606	.8200
1911	135,875	20,707	.7815	.8744	.2021	.8504
1916	147,471	22,475	.8025	.8881	.1384	.8734
1921	160,186	24,412	.8363	.9067	.0721	.9007
1926	173,996	26,517	—	—	—	

[1] Figures in previous column multiplied by .1524, which was the proportion of children under 5 in the total population in the area of the R.S.F.S.R., Ukraine, Belorussia, and Transcaucasus in 1897, according to the All-Union Census of the U.S.S.R., 1926, Vol. 17.

[2] Novosel'skiy and Payevskiy, Title 417, Table 55.

[3] Novosel'skiy and Payevskiy, Title 417, Table 1.

[213]

APPENDIX IV

THE DERIVATION OF GROSS AND NET REPRODUCTION RATIOS, U.S.S.R. AREAS, 1924-1926

Data from the First All-Union Census, December 17, 1926, are used in combination with life-table values to give gross and net reproduction ratios for the urban and rural population of administrative divisions. The "net reproduction ratio" shows the expected ratio of births in two successive generations, i.e., the ratio of births in the second generation to births in the first generation. It takes account of the frequency of births to women at different ages and the survival of daughters from birth to the same ages during the childbearing years, so as to show the net effect of natality and mortality on the succession of generations—apart from the temporary effects of the age distribution of the population at any particular time. A net reproduction ratio of 1.00 indicates that women as they pass through the childbearing period have just enough daughters to supply an equal number of potential mothers in the next generation, after the ranks of the daughters have been decimated by death—if the birth and death rates prevailing at the time of the study remain constant. The corresponding "gross reproduction ratio" shows the average number of potential mothers (i.e., daughters) borne by each woman who lives through the childbearing period—leaving the effects of mortality out of account. The average number of children borne by each woman living to the end of the childbearing period is usually a little more than twice this figure, because somewhat more than half the babies born are usually boys.

Ordinarily the natality values used in these ratios are derived from birth registration data. However, birth registration data are not available for all parts of the Soviet Union at any one time. This difficulty can be overcome, without any sacrifice in theoretical accuracy, by the use of age distribution data, following a technique developed by Wilson H. Grabill and described in his monograph, *A Method for Calculating Gross and Net Reproduction Rates from Census Data*.[1] Practically, the relative accuracy of the Grabill method, as compared with the usual procedure (developed independently by Alfred J. Lotka and by R. R. Kuczynski), depends on the accuracy of census data for children in the selected age class as compared with registration data on births—with the added consideration that as regards the *net* reproduction ratio the Grabill method can be so applied as to escape any dependence on data concerning infant mortality (which is often subject to serious error), although the *gross* reproduction ratio does then become dependent on such data.

We have selected the single-year age class at 2 years as providing the most reliable ratios on the basis of the Soviet census data at this time. This refers the indices of natality to the year 1924, i.e., the year of birth of most children aged 2 years on December 17, 1926. The mortality data are taken from life tables, representing death rates in 1926-1927. However, birth rates and death rates for all regions for which data are available were fairly constant during the period covered by these statistics. We have also compared the ratios thus obtained, wherever possible, with reproduction ratios based on birth registration data for the year 1926. The census data on children were narrowed to a single year, age 2, because the number of children over 2 years was disturbed in some regions by abnormal conditions of counter-revolution and the aftermath of famine, whereas the data for children under 2 years seemed to be seriously deficient in some other areas, presumably because of underenumeration. However, our procedure puts a heavy statistical responsibility on the shoulders of the Russian two-year-olds, and any deficit or surplus in the enumeration of this class would bias the results. For this reason we have adjusted the ratios to those based on 1926 birth registration data (where available) wherever the values obtained by the latter procedure were *higher* than those based on data on two-year-old children (on the assumption that, although births might be under-reported, they were presumably never over-reported). These adjustments were small except in the case of the Ukraine, where the ratios were raised by 8.7 percent.[2] It is, of course, possible that undiscovered bias of equal or greater magnitude may influence the ratios of other areas, but evidence to this effect has not been found.

[1] Master's Thesis, The American University, Washington, D.C. [Abstract to be published].
[2] This rather surprising result is in line with the results of an investigation by Ptoukha, who also found evidence of serious underenumeration in the 1926 census of children aged 2 years in the Ukraine. See Title 268.

Except where specific data on children by age of mother are available, the use of census data in computing gross and net reproduction ratios requires indirect standardization, which is also necessary in obtaining such ratios from registration data if births are not distributed by age of mother. Hypothetical age-specific ratios of children to women in each age class are used to apportion the number of children reported born to women in different age classes as actually reported in the census. The *hypothetical* age-specific ratios applied to each area are derived from a "standard" schedule of fertility and the life-table values used in that particular area.[3] These hypothetical ratios are then corrected so as to give the observed number of children. This correction applied to the gross reproduction ratio of the standard population (i.e., the sum of the age-specific maternal frequencies, daughters only) gives the estimated gross reproduction ratio of the observed population. The *estimated* age-specific ratios of children to women (i.e., the corrected hypothetical ratios) are then combined with life-table survival values to give the estimated net reproduction ratio for the observed population.

The *level* of fertility represented by the "standard" schedule does not affect the ratio finally obtained (which is corrected by relating the observed number of children, or births, in the population studied to the number "expected" by application of the standard schedule). However, the accuracy of the results is impaired by any wide divergence between *relative* frequencies of births to women at different ages in the standard as compared with any observed population. For this reason, throughout the series we have used different standards for the rural and for the urban parts of each administrative area, on the hypothesis that differences in the relative distribution of births by age of mother in the U.S.S.R. at this time were most profoundly affected by urbanization. The "standard" schedules actually used in this way are those for the urban and rural parts of the Ukraine, 1926-1927, as reported by Kuczynski.[4] The gross reproduction ratio of any administrative area is then obtained by averaging (using population as weights) the gross reproduction ratios of its urban and rural populations. The net reproduction ratio of any area is obtained in the same way from the net reproduction ratios of its urban and rural populations.

In the Grabill procedure one begins by picking up data for children in some specific age class (here, children aged 2 years) and working backward with life-table values to obtain gross reproduction ratios, and then forward with life-table values to obtain net reproduction ratios. Therefore, high death rates tend to *raise* the G.R.R.'s and to *lower* the N.R.R.'s. The use of a life table which has *consistently* higher or lower values than those actually prevailing in any area would, therefore, tend to bias the two sets of rates in opposite directions.

The life-table values for the urban and rural parts of various regions were taken from the Novosel'skiy-Payevskiy series, wherever apparently reliable life tables were available. These values were applied to the data for the urban and rural parts of each administrative division in that region. Where such regional tables were not available, the table judged to represent a most nearly comparable condition was arbitrarily selected for application. As already noted, the selection of an inappropriate table would in general tend to bias the gross reproduction ratio in one direction (up or down) and the net reproduction ratio for that area in the opposite direction. The selected life tables applied to various regions are reported in Chapter VII.

The standard fertility schedules used here, and an example of the derived life-table values (i.e., values from the tables for the European part of the U.S.S.R., 1926-1927) used in this procedure are shown in Tables A 7, A 8, and A 9.

[3] The "standard" fertility schedules by the age classes, 15-19 . . . 45-49 were first translated by interpolation into fertility schedules by the age classes, 12.5-17.49 . . . 42.5-47.49. These fertility schedules were then used, by application of life-table values for survival of children from birth to midyear of age two and for survival of women from various ages to ages 2.5 years higher, to obtain the hypothetical age-specific child-woman ratios.

[4] Kuczynski, Title 154, p. 155. The specific fertility rates for Moscow were used for the cities of Moscow and Leningrad.

TABLE A 7

Standard Age-Specific Fertility Schedules

Age of Women	Births per Year per 1,000 Women in Specified Age Class		
	Ukraine, Rural	Ukraine, Urban	Moscow
I. Observed[1]			
15-19	37.3	33.7	26.4
20-24	273.6	182.6	146.1
25-29	291.6	167.5	133.5
30-34	240.8	121.4	92.4
35-39	184.3	84.4	54.1
40-44	92.1	34.3	21.4
45-49	25.9	8.3	3.7
Total Fertility[2]	5,728.4	3,160.6	2,388.3
Gross Reproduction Ratio[3]	2.773	1.530	1.167
II. Interpolated Values			
12.5-17.4	9.3	8.4	6.6
17.5-22.4	156.5	111.8	89.1
22.5-27.4	306.2	191.0	152.9
27.5-32.4	268.8	144.0	113.4
32.5-37.4	215.1	103.1	72.5
37.5-42.4	139.3	58.8	36.4
42.5-47.4	54.0	18.1	10.5

[1] Kuczynski, Title 154, p. 155.
[2] Sum of age-specific rates multiplied by 5.
[3] Total fertility x (female births/total births) x 1/1,000.

TABLE A 8

Hypothetical Age-Specific Child-Woman Ratios (Children Aged 2 Years); Example of Life-Table Values for the European Part of the U.S.S.R., 1926-1927

Area Type and Age of Women at Time of Census ($= x$)	Life-Table Adjustment Factors				Hypothetical Child-Woman Ratios[1]
	L_2	$_5L_x$	$_5L_{x-2.5}$	$L_2(_5L_{x-2.5}/_5L_x)$	
	(1)	(2)	(3)	(4)	(5)
Rural					
15-19	.74351	3.41894	3.44778	.750	.0070
20-24	"	3.34082	3.38195	.752	.1177
25-29	"	3.24635	3.29266	.754	.2309
30-34	"	3.14791	3.19593	.755	.2029
35-39	"	3.04365	3.09425	.756	.1626
40-44	"	2.93459	2.98817	.757	.1055
45-49	"	2.81724	2.87411	.758	.0409
Urban					
15-19	.77067	3.63094	3.65689	.776	.0065
20-24	"	3.54969	3.59721	.781	.0873
25-29	"	3.47138	3.51518	.781	.1492
30-34	"	3.37629	3.42292	.781	.1125
35-39	"	3.27297	3.32381	.783	.0807
40-44	"	3.15861	3.21561	.785	.0462
45-49	"	3.02891	3.09295	.787	.0142

[1] Final life-table adjustment factor (Column 4) multiplied by the interpolated age-specific fertility ratio at age x-2.5 (as given for each area-type in Table A 7) divided by 1,000.

TABLE A 9

Net Reproduction Factors; Example of Life-Table Values for the European Part of the U.S.S.R., 1926-1927[1]

Age of Women	Rural	Urban
15-19	2.239	2.305
20-24	2.187	2.227
25-29	2.125	2.203
30-34	2.061	2.142
35-39	1.992	2.077
40-44	1.922	2.005
45-49	1.844	1.922

[1] The estimated (corrected hypothetical) specific child-woman ratios in each area are multiplied by these factors, and summed to give the net reproduction ratio for that area. The N.R.R. factors for each five-year age class were obtained as follows:
For ages 15-19: (L_{17}/L_2) x 5 [years in interval] x .4978 [female births/total births].
For ages 20-24: (L_{22}/L_2) x 5 x .4978.
Similar procedures were used to obtain the N.R.R. factors for the other five-year age classes.

APPENDIX V

NOTES ON THE EMPLOYED LABOR FORCE AND ECONOMIC CLASSES
IN THE SOVIET UNION, 1926-1939

Data are available on the distribution of the population by occupation and family status at the time of the census, December 17, 1926. There are also current statistics on employment for the period 1926-1937, an estimate of total employment in 1940, a forecast of planned development for 1937-1942, and certain "social classifications" of the population of the Soviet Union for 1937 and 1939.

The 1926 census data are based on a classification of all persons according to "usual occupation" or family status in relation to gainfully occupied persons. Employed personnel in the Soviet Union refers to two classes: "workers" and "employees." The latter term includes clerical and professional employees and some types of technical and service workers. All others are classified as "workers." The category here referred to as "handicrafts and shop industry" is designated "small household and handicraft industry" in the census (melkaya i kustarno-remeslennaya promyshlennost). It includes weaving, spinning, and sewing; garment, boot, and harness shops; builders, blacksmiths, tinsmiths, jewelers, bakers, barbers, et cetera. The category "agriculture, forestry, and fishing" also apparently includes some handicraft workers, as is shown by the detailed classification of workers and employees in this group. The classification scheme obviously reflects the primitive, unspecialized character of much of the economic activity of the Soviet population at this time.

Various sources follow somewhat different schemes in the classification of workers by industry, so that some adjustment is necessary to give comparable results. The division between "large-scale industry" (roughly comparable to manufactures and mining in the 1926 census classification) and "small industry" (roughly comparable to handicrafts and shop industries in the 1926 census) is dropped for 1937 and later years; the single figure for "industry" thereafter also includes part of the labor force previously classed under forestry, construction, and transportation, although these categories are retained with restricted application.[1] Therefore some adjustment is necessary in order to give comparable figures on the employed labor force by major industrial groups for the whole intercensus period, 1926-1939. These adjustments do not affect the figures on total employment. They are made only to give some indication of trend by major groups. The results are presented in Table A 10.

The sources and adjustments are as follows:

Data for December 17, 1926, are from the census, Volume 34, giving classification by "principal occupation."

Data for 1926-1927 through 1935 are from *Trud v SSSR, 1935*, Title 448, pp. 10-11. (Compare *Sotsialisticheskoye Stroitel'stvo, 1935*, Title 409, pp. 308-309, and *1936*, pp. 508-509.) These data refer to average annual volume of labor, as reported by industries. "Large industry" in these tables is assumed to be equivalent to manufacturing and mining in the census classification. "Small industry" is assumed to be equivalent to handicrafts and shop industry in the census classification. Communication is transferred to public service ("institutions") to conform to the census classification.

Data for 1937 and planned figures for 1942 are from *Tretiy Pyatiletniy Plan*, Title 461, pp. 228-229. The new classification scheme used in this source differs from that used in 1926-1927 through 1935. The new classification is also used in *Sotsialisticheskoye Stroitel'stvo, 1933-1938*, Title 410, p. 138, which gives data for 1932, making possible a comparison and partial adjustment of the two schemes. The figures in our table conform to the earlier scheme, so far as possible. Figures for forestry, fishing, and small industry are carried forward from 1935. In the later sources giving data for 1932, 1937, and 1942 the figure for "industry" includes workers in forestry, fishing, and handicrafts and shop industries, except for a specific part of the forestry group which is separately reported (196,000 in 1932; 248,000 in 1937; 325,000 in 1942). "Manufacturing and mining," therefore, is here estimated as "industry" *plus* "forestry" (specific part) *minus* the estimated total number in

---

[1] Compare treatment of 1932 data in *Sotsialisticheskoye Stroitel'stvo, 1935*, Title 409, and *Ibid., 1933-1938*, Title 410. The change is large in the case of forestry, but less important as regards construction and transportation.

TABLE A 10

Trend of the Employed Labor Force: U.S.S.R., 1926-1939
(Numbers in Thousands)

Occupation	Total "Active" Population 12/17/1926	Employed Personnel (Workers and Employees)		
		12/17/1926	1926-1927	1928
Total	86,220[1]	9,583[2]	10,944	11,599
All Civilian Occupations	82,713	—	—	—
Agriculture and Related Occupations	71,735	1,202	2,078	2,037
Agriculture	—	—	—	1,676
Forestry	—	—	—	331
Fishing	—	—	—	30
Handicrafts and Shop Industry	1,866	301	423	408
Manufacturing, Mining, Construction, Transport, and Trade	5,606	4,734	5,338	5,771
Manufacturing and Mining	2,792	2,790	2,839	3,096
Construction	364	147	547	723
Railways	890	890	1,006	971
Other Transport	403	229	296	299
Trade and Credit	1,157	678	650	682
Public Administration and Social Service (including Communication)	2,030	1,893	2,400	2,574
Communication	—	—	95	95
Education (including Art)	—	—	715	789
Health	—	—	365	399
Municipal Service	—	—	105	117
Administration	—	—	1,120	1,174
Independent Professional	137	—		
Casual Labor, Domestic Service, etc.	1,476	1,453	705	809
Other "Active"	3,507	—	—	—
Pensioners; No Occupation; Unknown	1,862	—		
Unemployed	1,014	—		
Military	631	—		

forestry, fishing, and handicrafts and shop industry (i.e., reported figures for 1935). Minor differences in classification of construction and transportation are ignored and the reported figures are used without adjustment.

The figures for January 17, 1939, are interpolated between the figures for 1937 and 1942 (1937 *plus* .3092 x difference) with an alternative interpolation for the total number, using the 1940 estimate (see notes 3 and 4 of Table A 10).

According to the employment statistics the average number of workers and employees during 1926-1927 was 10,944,000. This figure is 14.2 percent above the corresponding census figure of 9,583,000 for December 17, 1926. The figures have a somewhat different time reference, but this is probably a minor source of difference. As might be expected, the greatest discrepancies appear in construction, agriculture and related occupations (employed personnel), and handicrafts. The employment figure for agriculture and related activities is 73 percent above the corresponding census figure (a difference of 876,000 persons) and that for handicraft and shop industries is 41 percent

TABLE A 10 (*Continued*)

Trend of the Employed Labor Force: U.S.S.R., 1926-1939
(Numbers in Thousands)

Occupation	Employed Personnel (Workers and Employees)				
	1930	1932	1933	1934	1935
Total	14,531	22,943	22,325	23,681	24,770
All Civilian Occupations	—	—	—	—	—
Agriculture and Related Occupations	2,208	4,097	4,123	4,414	4,374
Agriculture	1,552	2,858	2,819	3,094	2,974
Forestry	611	1,140	1,193	1,209	1,300
Fishing	45	99	111	111	100
Handicrafts and Shop Industry	290	248	327	348	401
Manufacturing, Mining, Construction, Transport, and Trade	8,482	13,884	12,933	13,849	14,479
Manufacturing and Mining	4,264	6,481	6,229	6,531	7,066
Construction	1,623	3,126	2,361	2,618	2,204
Railways	1,084	1,527	1,474	1,603	1,789
Other Transport	415	696	831	952	1,133
Trade and Credit	1,096	2,054	2,038	2,145	2,287
Public Administration and Social Service (including Communication)	3,152	4,373	4,526	4,660	5,122
Communication	153	224	257	295	334
Education (including Art)	921	1,347	1,463	1,568	1,725
Health	477	647	681	739	809
Municipal Service	131	237	373	378	509
Administration	1,470	1,918	1,752	1,680	1,745
Independent Professional	—	—	—	—	—
Casual Labor, Domestic Service, etc.	399	341	416	410	394
Other "Active"	—	—	—	—	—
Pensioners; No Occupation; Unknown	—	—	—	—	—
Unemployed	—	—	—	—	—
Military	—	—	—	—	—

above the census figure (a difference of 122,000 persons). These differences are consistent with the large amount of seasonal employment characteristic of Russian economy, especially in rural industries. According to the 1926 census, 5,425,000 persons, chiefly resident in rural areas, reported secondary occupations, of whom 2,047,000 gave agriculture or related activities and 1,804,000 listed handicrafts and shop industry as the chief source of supplementary income. The industrial employment figure for manufacturing and mining is only 2 percent above the corresponding census figure.

The handicraft and shop industry class represents a heterogeneous group including traditional handicrafts, small weaving establishments, et cetera. (Forestry and fishing cooperatives are apparently included in this category in the later "social classifications" of 1937 and 1939.) The trend of this group is difficult to interpret. Apparently it reflects two tendencies, which are phases of the same general development but which have opposite effects on the classification of persons in this category: (1) the transfer of economic activities from the traditional handicraft field to manufacturing and mechanical industries, and (2) the transfer of supplementary lines of peasant activity into more highly organized cooperative enterprises, owing to greater specialization in agriculture.

TABLE A 10 (*Continued*)

Trend of the Employed Labor Force: U.S.S.R., 1926-1939
(Numbers in Thousands)

Occupation	1937	1940	Employed Personnel (Workers and Employees) Planned 1942	Estimated 1/17/1939
Total	26,989	30,400[3]	32,000	28,539[4]
All Civilian Occupations	—	—	—	—
Agriculture and Related Occupations	3,883	—	4,050	3,935
Agriculture	2,483	—	2,650	2,535
Forestry	1,300	—	1,300	1,300
Fishing	100	—	100	100
Handicrafts and Shop Industry	400	—	400	400
Manufacturing, Mining, Construction, Transport, and Trade	15,950	—	19,200	16,955
Manufacturing and Mining	8,561	—	10,416	9,135
Construction	2,023	—	1,829	1,963
Railways	1,512	—	1,700	1,570
Other Transport	1,272	—	1,965	1,486
Trade and Credit	2,582	—	3,290	2,801
Public Administration and Social Service (including Communication)	6,415	—	8,085	6,932
Communication	375	—	500	414
Education (including Art)	2,425	—	3,065	2,623
Health	1,118	—	1,600	1,267
Municipal Service	754	—	920	805
Administration	1,743	—	2,000	1,823
Independent Professional	—	—	—	—
Casual Labor, Domestic Service, etc.	341	—	265	317
Other "Active"	—	—	—	—
Pensioners; No Occupation; Unknown	—	—	—	—
Unemployed	—	—	—	—
Military	—	—	—	—

[1] All gainfully occupied persons, including peasants, members of cooperatives, etc. The census data on gainful workers (first two columns) are exclusive of 1,134,000 children, under 10 years of age, reported as gainfully occupied but not otherwise classified.

[2] Workers and employees according to the census, December 17, 1926. The figures in all later columns are based on employment statistics (see text for sources).

[3] Voznesenskiy, *Pravda*, February 19, 1941.

[4] Figures interpolated between 1937 and 1942 estimates. The total employment figure interpolated between the 1937 and the 1940 estimates is 28,747,000.

The most significant division within Soviet economy is that between (I) agriculture, forestry, fishing, and handicrafts and shop industry, and (II) manufacturing, mining, construction, transportation, trade, and public service. The trend of personnel in the latter division (Group II) is shown with approximate accuracy by the employment statistics from 1928 through 1939. Other data must be used to study the trend in the first of these broad divisions (Group I). The use of employment data alone (in contrast to census data) gives a slightly exaggerated picture of the expansion in economic opportunity in the Soviet Union from 1926 to 1930, because persons privately engaged in certain types of economic activity, e.g., trade in 1926 (during the NEP period), became workers and employees after 1928; but this has little effect on the figures for industrial employment. However, comparison of census data and employment statistics is complicated by factors already mentioned.

The problem of the changing size of the farm population, exclusive of employed personnel on state farms, machine tractor stations, and in similar situations, is bound up with the classification of the whole Soviet population by major occupational groups. This involves great difficulties. We have no data on number of persons actively engaged in agriculture at any time since 1926. There are data relating to "social classes" in 1939, but their interpretation is ambiguous. The census schedule used in 1939 contained two distinct questions relating to economic status: Question 14, "Occupation," and Question 16, "Social Class." The census procedures are officially interpreted in a treatise by Voblyy and Pustokhod.[2] It is explicitly stated that the answer to Question 14 does not necessarily determine the answer to Question 16.

"Social classifications" of the population of the Soviet Union have been reported for the years 1937 and 1939. The latter was based on the 1939 census. The source of the former was not specified; it may possibly have been based on unpublished results of the 1937 census.[3] The contrast between these two classifications is shown in Table A 11.

We will first take account of a relatively minor discrepancy. In 1937 persons dependent on public support, including pensioners, subsidized students, invalids in hospitals, prisoners, and so on, plus military personnel, plus persons of undesignated social status, were assigned to a miscellaneous group that included 4.2 percent of the population. In 1939 this miscellaneous group apparently included only "non-workers" ("employees of cults," et cetera)[4] and persons of "undesignated social class," together comprising 0.77 percent of the population. The difference (3.43 percent) represents about 5,850,000 persons in 1939. The description of the 1939 census procedures shows that pensioners were classified according to last occupation or the social status of their families; but it is *possible* that some elements (such as military personnel) included in the miscellaneous group in 1937 were assigned *in toto* in 1939 to one of the specified social classes, for example, workers or employees.

The really serious discrepancy between these two classifications, as regards an understanding of the development of Soviet economy between 1926 and 1939, is the divergent distribution of population between major occupational divisions. The worker-employee group (including employed personnel in agriculture and handicrafts) in 1937 was reported as 34.7 percent of the total population. This proportion applied to the 1939 population would represent a total of 59,152,000, which is more than 25 million below the corresponding figure indicated by the 1939 classification. In 1937, the cooperative and private enterprise group in agriculture and handicrafts was reported as including 61.1 percent of the total population. This proportion applied to the 1939 population would represent 104,155,000 persons, which is nearly 20 million above the number assigned to this group in 1939. The employed labor force was increasing more rapidly than the total population during this period. This trend could account for a small increase during a period of less than three years in the percentage of the population in the worker-employee sector, but not for an increase of the order indicated by these figures. Also, the discrepancy is too great to be due to ordinary errors in census data. There are two possible interpretations: (1) If the 1937 social classification was based, not on unpublished census data, but on some estimate of worker-employee population with the residual (de-

[2] Voblyy and Pustokhod, Title 346. See also Pisarev, Titles 246 and 247. A partial description of the procedures (based on these sources) is given by Somerville, Title 304.

[3] According to Soviet authorities, the 1937 census was suppressed because of (1) inaccuracy, and (2) ideological errors in the formulation of questions and development of data. Current estimates of the Soviet population at this time were greatly in error. The expected population in 1937 (see Preface, prepared in 1936, to *Second Five-Year Plan*, Title 460) was 180,700,000 in contrast to an observed population of only 170,467,000 almost two years later. Great efforts were directed toward insuring completeness in the 1939 census returns, including an extensive publicity campaign prior to the census. It is possible that the suspicion of gross inaccuracy in the 1937 data was not confirmed by comparison with the 1939 returns, but the population indicated by the 1937 data may have seemed impossibly low at the time. In the judgment of the present writer, the 1939 data are presumably more accurate as regards all purely objective inquiries; but, quite apart from the merits of the ideological issues involved, the 1937 procedures were presumably designed to give results that would have been more comparable with the 1926 data than are the 1939 results.

[4] This small group (0.04 percent) may, or may not, have been included in the miscellaneous 4.2 percent in 1937.

TABLE A 11

Population of the U.S.S.R.: By Social Class, 1937 and 1939
(Family Dependents Classified by Status of Principal Earner)

Class	1937[1] Percent	1939[2] Percent	1939[3] Number
Total	100.0	100.00	170,467,186
Subtotal A	34.7	49.73	84,773,000
Workers (Urban and Rural)	—	32.19	54,873,000
Employees (Urban and Rural)	—	17.54	29,900,000
Subtotal B + C	61.1[1]	49.50	84,381,000
Subtotal B	—	46.39	79,079,700
Collective Farmers	—	44.61	76,045,400
Individual Farmers	—	1.78	3,034,300
Subtotal C	—	3.11	5,301,500
Cooperative Handicraft Personnel	—	2.29	3,903,700
Non-cooperative Handicraft Personnel	—	0.82	1,397,800
Subtotal D (including in 1937: Pensioners and Military Personnel)	4.2	0.77	1,313,000
Nonworkers	—	0.04	68,200
Social Group not Indicated	—	0.73	1,244,400

[1] *Sotsialisticheskoye Stroitel'stvo, 1933-1938*, Title 410, p. 16. This classification does not give separate figures for agriculture and handicrafts. The collective and cooperative sector of this combined group was reported as 55.5 percent of the total population, i.e., 91 percent of this combined group (in contrast to 95 percent as reported in 1939).

[2] *Izvestiya*, April 29, 1942.

[3] Percentage distribution based on incomplete returns (169,519,127), applied to total population.

rived from a gross overestimate of total population) assigned to other classes, the resultant estimates of the agricultural and handicraft groups might have been greatly exaggerated. (2) The differences may have been due in whole or in part to ideological differences in the definition of social classes. Therefore it seems advisable to use other data, so far as possible, in studying the distribution of Soviet population by *occupational classes*, as distinct from ideologically defined *social classes*.

For this purpose, we use the employment statistics as a basis for estimating the total population dependent on workers and employees. In order to do so we must take account of various complicating factors.

(1) The average number of workers and employees reported in the employment statistics includes persons usually engaged in collective or private agriculture or handicraft enterprises but temporarily employed in other fields. It has been estimated that in 1937 members of collective farms contributed a total of 2,300,000 man-years of labor in other occupations.[5] On the other hand, the employment statistics do not include workers and employees during intervals between leaving one place of work and registering in another and, in view of the heavy turnover in Soviet industries, the total loss of employment during such shifts must represent a considerable aggregate amount. The average employment figure for 1926-1927 was 14 percent above the census figure for workers and employees in 1926. It is possible, however, that with greater specialization the two factors mentioned above, which affect the relation of expected census data to employment statistics, might have cancelled each

[5] Babynin, Title 16. This figure presumably includes labor by members of collective farms who worked full-time in industry and did not work on the farms at all or only during holidays and vacations.

other in 1939. The two interpolated employment figures obtained for January 17, 1939, differ from each other by less than 1 percent (see Table A 10). The lower of these two figures (28,539,000) is associated with an estimated distribution by major industrial categories. We shall proceed on the hypothesis that this figure corresponds to the total number of persons usually occupied as workers or employees at this time. If the amount of seasonal employment by members of farm families in the years 1937-1940 was greater than the amount of temporary unemployment among workers and employees (as was the case in 1926-1927), the actual number of workers and employees, classified by usual occupation, was presumably *lower* than the total volume of employed seasonal labor from other classes during this period. Conversely, if the total volume of temporary unemployment was greater, the actual number of workers and employees was somewhat higher.

(2) There was a decrease in child labor in the Soviet Union between 1926 and 1939. The legal age limit for entrance to employment was 16 years, prior to the emergency labor regulations announced in 1940. Presumably some children were employed in 1939 who were less than 16 years of age, but the number of older youth who were full-time students also increased. We shall proceed on the hypothesis that the net effect of these changes on the dependents-worker ratio was equivalent to the withdrawal of all children under 16 years of age from the labor force. Such an adjustment raises the ratio of dependents per worker in 1926 from 1.29 to 1.38 (see Table A 12).[6]

TABLE A 12

Worker-Employee Sector of the Soviet Population, 1926

Sex	Active	Non-Active	Ratio of Non-Active to Active
	(A)	(N)	(N)/(A)
I. Census			
Total	9,583,217	12,354,023	1.29
Males	6,637,190	4,057,058	0.61
Females	2,946,027	8,296,965	2.82
Percent Females	30.7	67.2	
II. Assuming Transfer of 187,825 Males and 179,681 Females under 16 Years from Active to Non-Active Status			
Total	9,215,711	12,721,529	1.38
Males	6,449,365	4,244,883	0.66
Females	2,766,346	8,476,646	3.06
Percent Females	30.0	66.6	

(3) The age structure of the urban proletariat as compared with that of the general population in 1926 was such as to give a relatively low ratio of dependents per worker. If the proportions of persons gainfully occupied in each age and sex class in the general population had been the same as those reported for the worker-employee population in the 1926 census, the ratio of dependents per worker in the general population at that time would have been 1.71 (assuming no employment of children under 16) instead of 1.38 (see Table A 13).

The estimated age and sex distribution of the *general* population in 1939, however, was such as to give a slightly lower ratio of dependents to workers than in 1926, that is, 1.62 as compared with

[6] We do not know how many of all children under 10 years of age in the Soviet Union in 1926 who were reported as gainful workers but not otherwise classified were members of the families of workers and employees. The assumption of proportional distribution among all classes, adding the resultant figure (169,000) to the "non-active" population in the worker-employee sector, would have raised this adjusted ratio from 1.38 to 1.40.

TABLE A 13

Proportion of Gainfully Occupied Persons in the Worker-Employee Population of the U.S.S.R., 1926, and Related Hypothetical Distributions: By Sex and Age
(Proportions at Early Ages Adjusted on Assumption of No Workers Under 16 Years)

Sex and Age	Proportion of Gainfully Occupied Persons in Each Age Class	Population, by Sex and Age, per 1,000 Total Population		Expected Number of Gainful Workers, by Sex and Age, per 1,000 Total Population		
		1926	1939	1926 (1)×(2)	1939 (1)×(3)	1939 Adjusted[1]
	(1)	(2)	(3)	(4)	(5)	(6)
Total		1,000.0	1,000.0	368.8	382.4	415.0
Males	—	483.1	479.0	255.1	264.8	264.8
0-4	0	76.4	64.7	0	0	—
5-9	0	52.1	51.3	0	0	—
10-14	0	58.8	61.3	0	0	—
15-19	.549	55.4	47.6	30.4	26.1	
20-24	.945	45.7	42.0	43.2	39.7	
25-29	.986	37.4	46.6	36.9	45.9	
30-34	.992	29.2	38.4	29.0	38.1	
35-39	.993	27.2	31.2	27.0	31.0	
40-44	.992	23.1	22.0	22.9	21.8	
45-49	.988	19.7	17.5	19.5	17.3	
50-54	.975	15.9	15.8	15.5	15.4	
55-59	.938	12.8	13.1	12.0	12.3	
60-64	.825	11.6	10.3	9.6	8.5	
65-69	.667	7.9	7.7	5.3	5.1	
70+	.379	9.9	9.5	3.8	3.6	
Females		516.9	521.0	113.7	117.6	150.2
0-4	0	75.4	63.2	0	0	
5-9	0	51.9	51.4	0	0	
10-14	0	57.4	61.7	0	0	
15-19	.369	60.2	48.8	22.2	18.0	
20-24	.454	48.3	42.3	21.9	19.2	
25-29	.380	44.5	50.0	16.9	19.0	
30-34	.367	32.4	42.2	11.9	15.5	
35-39	.382	30.4	37.6	11.6	14.4	
40-44	.372	24.2	28.0	9.0	10.4	
45-49	.350	20.6	22.4	7.2	7.8	
50-54	.282	18.4	19.3	5.2	5.4	
55-59	.216	15.8	16.0	3.4	3.5	
60-64	.153	14.5	13.4	2.2	2.1	
65-69	.113	9.6	10.4	1.1	1.2	
70+	.079	13.3	14.3	1.1	1.1	
Percent of Females in Total Worker-Employee Population	30.0	51.7	52.1	30.8	30.8	36.2
Dependents per Worker	1.38	—	—	1.71	1.62	1.41

[1] Expected number of female workers increased to give observed ratio of total female to total male workers and employees.

1.71 (see Table A 13). It is probable that the age structure of the urban proletariat differed less from that of the total population in 1939 than in 1926. Even so, this ratio of dependents per worker (1.62) would seem to be a maximum value for the worker-employee classes in 1939, *prior* to adjustments for change in the proportion of women among all workers and employees.

(4) There was a gradual increase in the employment of women during this period. The percentage of women among gainful workers shown by census statistics is usually higher than the corresponding proportion shown by employment statistics, owing to the greater frequency of unemployment among women. The proportion of women among workers and employees according to the 1926 census was 30.7 percent (see Table A 12). The proportion of women among workers and employees, according to employment statistics, rose from 27.2 percent in 1929 to 35.4 percent in 1937 and 37 percent in 1940.[7] Interpolating, we assume that the proportion was 36.2 percent at the time of the 1939 census, i.e., 56.74 women per 100 men. The transfer of women from a dependent status to that of workers and employees corresponding to this figure lowers the expected maximum ratio of dependents to workers, for 1939, from 1.62 to 1.41 (see Table A 13). The net effect of these observations is to suggest that the ratio of dependents per worker in the worker-employee sector of the Soviet population in 1939 must have been very similar to the figure for 1926 as adjusted to take account of the transfer of children from worker to dependent status (i.e., 1.38).

A different series of ratios, based on budget studies of the families of workers in heavy industry, covering the years 1930-1935, is reported in *Trud*.[8] In this series the number of dependents per worker is as follows: 1930, 2.05; 1931, 1.73; 1932, 1.73; 1933, 1.69; 1934, 1.66; 1935, 1.59. The average size of family (sometimes confused with the dependents-worker ratio) in this sample runs from 4.02 in 1930 to 3.80 in 1935—a decrease of only 5.5 percent, in contrast to the decrease of 22.4 percent in the dependents-worker ratio during the same period. Unfortunately, there is no exact information about the sampling procedure on which these statistics are based. Single persons are usually inadequately represented in budget studies. Where this is the case, the ratio of dependents to workers is, of course, higher than in the corresponding population. The dependents-worker ratio in this series declines sharply from 1930 to 1935, probably because of the increased employment of women, but one cannot safely assume that this indicates a general decline in the ratio of dependents to workers in the families of all workers and employees during the intercensus period, 1926-1939.

For our purposes it seems preferable to rely on the census data for 1926, with adjustments to take account of changing conditions during the intercensus period, rather than to use the data from an unspecified sample as reported in *Trud*. We will, therefore, proceed on the hypothesis that there were 141 family dependents per 100 workers and employees in the Soviet Union at the time of the 1939 census, applying this ratio uniformly to the major groups of employed personnel. It should be noted that this ratio of 141 is presumably a *maximum* value, since it is based on the application of age-specific ratios (from the 1926 census data for families of workers and employees) to the *general* population in 1939, with the specified adjustments, but with no adjustment for differences between the age distribution of the worker-employee sector and the total population.

The estimated population in the worker-employee sector indicated by these procedures is 68,779,000, or 40.3 percent of the total population of the Soviet Union (see Table A 14). This is considerably higher than the corresponding proportion reported for 1937 (34.7 percent), but it is much closer to the 1937 figure than that reported in the 1939 social class distribution (49.7 percent). In view of the arbitrary treatment of many of the factors affecting the determination of this estimate, it would certainly be unwise to treat it as having any high degree of validity. Consequently, we will experiment further with this result and test it against other data.

The miscellaneous group of pensioners, military personnel, and persons of unknown occupational status was reported as 4.2 percent of the population in 1937. This happens to be about the same proportion reported for these classes *plus* the unemployed and children under 10 years listed as gainfully occupied in 1926. The increase in institutional and military personnel had apparently offset the decrease in unemployment and in the labor of children under 10 years of age. Assuming the same proportion in 1939, the number of pensioners, military personnel, persons of unknown occupational status, and so on, was presumably about 7,160,000 at this time.

These estimates of worker-employee and miscellaneous sectors leave, as residual, a population of

[7] See American-Russian Institute, *Russia at War*, March 31, 1942.
[8] *Trud v SSSR, 1935*, Title 448, p. 342.

TABLE A 14

Estimated Population Dependent on Workers and Employees: U.S.S.R., 1939

Occupation	Estimated Number of Workers and Employees, 1/17/1939	Estimated Population in Each Group (2.41 x Figures in Previous Column)
Total	28,539	68,779,000
Agriculture and Related Occupations	3,935	9,483,000
Agriculture	2,535	6,109,000
Forestry	1,300	3,133,000
Fishing	100	241,000
Handicrafts and Shop Industry	400	964,000
Manufacturing, Mining, Construction, Transport, and Trade	16,955	40,862,000
Public Service (including Communication, Education, Art, Health, etc.)	6,932	16,706,000
Casual Labor, Domestic, etc.	317	764,000

94,528,000, or 55.5 percent of the total, to be distributed among groups dependent on collective and private enterprises in agriculture, handicrafts, and related fields.

Information about census procedures in 1939 affecting the social classification of the population would seem to indicate that the figure for the collective-private enterprise group is somewhat below, but not greatly below, the figure that would have been obtained by a repetition of the 1926 procedure of classifying occupation and dependence on the basis of reported "usual occupation." In 1939 members of collective farms and their families were assigned to this social class even though temporarily employed in industry, construction, and so on, except in the case of those "permanently engaged in industry, construction, and public service who do not work on the collective farms at all or work there partially during vacations or in spare time"; these were classified by social class according to usual occupation.[9] The definition of the collective farm group in 1939 was as inclusive as, or more inclusive than, the definition by usual occupation in 1926. On the other hand, individual farmers and their families who had any source of income other than private farming were assigned to the alternative social class corresponding to this other source of income, whether principal or secondary. This definition was therefore less inclusive than that used in 1926. We shall tentatively assume that the figure for the collective farm group as a "social class" in 1939 (76,045,000) describes an occupational group conforming to 1926 definition. We shall then apply the relative proportions reported elsewhere for private farm families and collective farm families in 1938 (6.5 and 93.5 percent, respectively, of all peasant households)[10] to give an estimated private farm population in 1939 of about 5,287,000 persons. This is 74 percent above the number assigned to this group as a "social class." If we arbitrarily assume that a proportional adjustment is warranted in the case of "handicraft workers not in cooperatives," the corresponding figure for this group becomes 2,432,000. The estimated number in the collective and private enterprise groups obtained on this basis is 87,668,000 persons, consisting of 81,332,000 dependent on agriculture and 6,336,000 dependent on handicrafts and shop industry (see Tables A 15 and A 16).

[9] Voblyy and Pustokhod, Title 346.
[10] See Table 39.

TABLE A 15

Estimated Population (Including Family Dependents) in Principal Occupational Classes in the Soviet Union, January 17, 1939[1]

Occupational Class	Total Population		Expected Urban Population
	Number	Percent	
Total	170,467,186	100	56,592,000[2]
Agriculture and Related Occupations	90,815,000	53.3	2,361,000[3]
Collective Farm Group	76,045,000	—	—
Private Farm Group	5,287,000	—	—
Worker-Employee Group in Agriculture	6,109,000	—	—
Worker-Employee Group in Forestry and Fishing	3,374,000	—	—
Handicrafts and Shop Industry	7,300,000	4.3	4,278,000[4]
Cooperative Group	3,904,000	—	—
Private Group	2,432,000	—	—
Worker-Employee Group	964,000	—	—
Industry, Trade, and Social Service	58,400,000	34.3	45,377,000[5]
Manufacturing, Mining, Construction, Transport, and Trade	40,862,000	—	—
Public Service	16,706,000	—	—
"Non-worker"	68,000	—	—
Casual Labor and Domestic Service	764,000	—	—
Miscellaneous	7,159,000	4.2	2,348,000[6]
"Social Group Not Indicated"	1,244,000	0.7	—
Pensioners, Military Personnel, etc.	5,915,000	3.5	—
Unaccounted (Total Population Minus Estimated Population in Specified Class)	6,793,000	4.0	2,228,000[6]

[1] Figures, unless otherwise indicated, are taken or derived from Tables A 11 and A 14.
[2] Urban population according to census of January 17, 1939, was 55,909,908.
[3] Applying proportion according to census, 1926 (.026).
[4] Applying proportion according to census, 1926 (.586).
[5] Applying proportion from *Trud, 1935*, pp. 26-27 (.777).
[6] Applying proportion of total population, 1939 (.328).

TABLE A 16

Estimated Population in Collective and Private Agriculture and Crafts, 1939

Collective and Private Sectors	87,668,000
Agriculture	81,332,000
Collective Farms	76,045,000[1]
Private Farms	5,287,000[2]
Handicraft and Shop Industries	6,336,000
Collective Handicraft and Shop Industries	3,904,000[1]
Private Handicraft and Shop Industries	2,432,000[3]
Estimated Farm Population	90,815,000
Total Collective and Private Farms	81,332,000
Workers and Employees in Agriculture, with Dependents	6,109,000[4]
Workers and Employees in Forestry and Fishing, with Dependents	3,374,000[4]

[1] From Table A 11.
[2] 6.5/93.5 x 76,045,000 (see text, p. 227).
[3] The 1,397,800 persons in non-cooperative handicrafts are increased 74 percent, similar to the increase estimated for private farmers (see Table A 11 and text, p. 227).
[4] From Table A 14.

As a check on this procedure, we refer to statistics on the change in the number of farm families in the Soviet Union during approximately the same period. According to official estimates, there were 24,800,000 farm families (individual peasant and collective farm households) in the Soviet Union in 1928 and 20,100,000 in 1938,[11] representing a decrease of 19 percent. The farm population (individual peasant and collective farm households), exclusive of employed personnel (workers and employees), numbered 111,928,000 at the time of the 1926 census. There was little change in farm population or the number of farm families between 1926 and 1928, as the drift to towns probably merely offset natural increase in rural areas in the years 1927-1928. If these two figures relate to approximately the same population, there were, on the average, about 4.5 persons per farm family in the years 1926-1928. It is probable that there was some decrease in the average size of farm families between 1928 and 1938, but there is no direct information on this point. It is not unreasonable, therefore, to estimate that there were around 81,332,000 persons in the farm population, exclusive of employed personnel, at the time of the 1939 census. This indicates an average of about 4.05 persons per farm family, if the official estimate of number of farm families in 1938 is correct.

We can now summarize the estimates developed above and check these estimates against one another. We can also check them against the distribution of the population by place of residence in 1939, applying the most appropriate earlier data on the proportion of urban residents in each of the major occupational classes except in the case of "miscellaneous" and "unaccounted," which are here distributed in proportion to the observed urban-rural distribution of the total population in 1939. This summary and accompanying check are shown in Table A 15.

The summation leaves a residual of 6,793,000 persons unaccounted for, in addition to an estimated

[11] *Sotsialisticheskoye Sel'skoye Khozyaystvo SSSR*, Title 454, p. 6.

5,915,000 persons in the class "pensioners, military, etc." We are unable to say how this residual should be distributed. We shall therefore present two alternatives:

(A) On the assumption that the estimates of the worker and employee sectors are valid, the residual is distributed proportionately and added to the figures shown in Table A 15 for the collective and private sectors of agriculture and handicrafts. This gives a total of 97,117,000 persons as the estimated farm population, including employed personnel in agriculture, forestry, and fishing and their dependents.

(B) On the assumption that the estimates of the collective and private sectors are valid, the residual is distributed proportionately and added to the various worker-employee sectors. This gives 91,751,000 persons as the estimated farm population, including employed personnel in agriculture, forestry, and fishing. The distributions obtained on assumptions (A) and (B) are shown in Chapter VIII, Table 40.

The change in the structure of Soviet economy during the period of the Five-Year Plans was so great that either procedure indicates a remarkable swing from agriculture and related occupations to industry, distribution, administration, and services, but the transition is sharper on Assumption B. These alternative assumptions are supported by various considerations, which we shall merely list without attempting to assay their relative weight.

In support of Assumption A:

(1) The higher estimate of the farm population, thus obtained, agrees closely with an estimate by Varga[12] that the farm population, including agricultural workers, included about 58 percent of the total population.

(2) This procedure is consistent with the estimated distribution of the Soviet population by social classes, 1937, which may have been based on unpublished census data with occupational categories more comparable to those used in 1926 than the categories and procedures used in the 1939 census.

(3) The reported distribution of the Soviet population in 1939 by urban and rural communities appears to be more consistent with this assumption than with its alternative (see Table A 15).

(4) The alternative procedure would indicate a ratio of 1.65 dependents per worker-or-employee relative to the 28,539,000 estimated number of workers and employees at this time—or a similar ratio of 1.63 dependents per worker-or-employee on the basis of another possible estimate of 28,747,000 workers and employees. These ratios seem highly improbable in the light of the data presented above. This difficulty could disappear *if* it were assumed that the usual number in industry, administration, services, and similar occupations was *greater* than that indicated by the statistics on employment. This seems unlikely in view of the large amount of part-time employment in industry by members of farm families. Moreover, the opposite relationship was observed in 1926; the number of workers and employees according to the 1926 census was 9,583,000 as compared with 10,944,000 according to the employment statistics for 1926-1927. It is doubtful that there was an excess in the number usually engaged as workers and employees over the number indicated by employment statistics around 1939.

In support of Assumption B:

(1) This assumption is most consistent with the published data on social classes, 1939, and the description of 1939 census procedures.

(2) It is possible that some types of employment, such as persons engaged in ordnance production under the Commissariat of Defense, are not covered in the employment estimates or the Gosplan figures.

Finally, it must be noted that in the Soviet Union, as in any other country, there is a marginal group partially dependent on industry and related occupations and partially dependent on subsistence agriculture. The classification of this group depends on varying definitions in the census procedures of different countries. Therefore, any rigid classification of population by occupational classes involves a certain amount of fiction. It is highly desirable that a consistent set of definitions be used in successive enumerations, or that the effects of changed definition be shown in a conversion table. However, this desideration is often neglected in census procedures. In any case, we may observe that the difference between the distributions indicated by our alternative assumptions is probably no greater than the margin of fiction that is inherent in any census classification.

[12] Published in the *Journal of the Academy of Sciences of the U.S.S.R.* in June, 1939.

APPENDIX VI

NOTES ON OBSERVED AND EXPECTED POPULATION, U.S.S.R., 1939, AND
ESTIMATED DISTRIBUTION OF POPULATION, 1939, BY AGE AND SEX

The account in this section is supplementary to that given in Chapter IX. Before a discussion of the procedures used in dealing with the 1939 population it should be pointed out that the various steps in several different procedures are mutually dependent, so that work on some of these logically requires revision of other procedures on which they are, in part, dependent. Where such revisions would materially affect the results, they have been carried through, leading in some cases to changes in other dependent values. Where such revisions would have had small effect on final estimates, no change has been made. This leaves minor inconsistencies in related estimates (whereof the most important are described here); these could have been eliminated only by many successive adjustments, representing a refinement that seemed unjustified in view of the merely approximate value of the final results.

1. The population of the U.S.S.R., distributed by sex and by single year of age, as reported for December 17, 1926, was adjusted by distribution of persons of each sex reported as "age unknown" and for apparent underenumeration of persons of each sex under 2 years of age. The basic 1926 census data are presented in Table A 17. The correction for underenumeration at ages under 2 years

TABLE A 17

Population of the U.S.S.R., by Age and Sex, according to
the Census of December 17, 1926

Age	Male	Female
Total Both Sexes	147,027,915	
Total	71,043,352	75,984,563
0-4	11,237,556	11,084,706
Under 1	2,632,094	2,550,517
1	2,285,192	2,241,931
2	2,216,659	2,197,650
3	2,279,212	2,264,274
4	1,824,399	1,830,334
5-9	7,649,869	7,619,732
5	1,794,614	1,748,385
6	1,531,029	1,526,669
7	1,486,618	1,525,534
8	1,673,862	1,660,645
9	1,163,746	1,158,499
10-14	8,643,293	8,447,561
10	1,462,768	1,438,257
11	1,346,591	1,321,881
12	2,177,160	2,059,978
13	1,854,539	1,811,428
14	1,802,235	1,816,017
15-19	8,132,822	8,843,709
15	1,808,249	1,832,067
16	1,788,268	1,946,944
17	1,563,576	1,745,066
18	1,614,633	1,814,724
19	1,358,096	1,504,908

TABLE A 17 (*Continued*)

Population of the U.S.S.R., by Age and Sex, according to
the Census of December 17, 1926

Age	Male	Female
20-24	6,712,200	7,101,200
20	1,638,895	1,955,537
21	1,223,774	1,023,498
22	1,412,639	1,488,232
23	1,322,589	1,399,624
24	1,114,303	1,234,309
25-29	5,490,375	6,547,207
25	1,299,529	1,810,845
26	1,200,759	1,332,612
27	1,030,210	1,235,799
28	1,131,315	1,350,412
29	828,562	817,539
30-34	4,297,238	4,767,933
30	1,373,719	1,860,318
31	595,042	529,657
32	890,663	928,673
33	796,958	803,547
34	640,856	645,738
35-39	3,994,175	4,458,329
35	1,038,357	1,344,735
36	768,909	796,869
37	694,567	786,425
38	868,868	947,721
39	623,474	582,579
40-44	3,392,966	3,561,975
40	1,121,764	1,506,785
41	459,880	380,377
42	739,718	677,924
43	592,981	545,049
44	478,623	451,840
45-49	2,892,782	3,014,541
45	892,100	1,077,181
46	578,761	515,074
47	479,530	471,849
48	554,481	592,830
49	387,910	357,607
50-54	2,343,373	2,697,742
50	892,685	1,281,665
51	297,886	269,702
52	464,911	454,087
53	380,091	370,379
54	307,800	321,909
55-59	1,886,779	2,318,208
55	650,405	897,504
56	423,248	467,078
57	302,973	356,495
58	311,938	386,539
59	198,215	210,592

TABLE A 17 (*Continued*)

Population of the U.S.S.R., by Age and Sex, according to the Census of December 17, 1926

Age	Male	Female
60-64	1,709,003	2,126,403
60	773,835	1,147,725
61	187,979	179,863
62	294,568	311,207
63	264,141	279,483
64	188,480	208,125
65-69	1,157,333	1,406,955
65	454,934	638,144
66	221,472	221,308
67	224,812	250,182
68	165,403	196,329
69	90,712	100,992
70-74	721,839	980,855
70	378,630	625,194
71	69,872	70,119
72	116,709	123,904
73	93,293	96,004
74	63,335	65,634
75-79	368,572	462,871
75	176,487	247,794
76	63,827	68,936
77	48,435	53,018
78	56,902	66,348
79	22,921	26,775
80-84	209,613	304,641
80	140,043	228,772
81	15,508	17,530
82	23,706	25,655
83	16,951	18,207
84	13,405	14,477
85-89	83,291	102,728
85	44,097	60,334
86	13,501	13,364
87	10,907	12,227
88	9,464	10,399
89	5,322	6,404
90-94	41,460	61,711
90	31,699	50,195
91	2,259	2,879
92	3,184	3,826
93	2,504	2,944
94	1,814	1,867
95-99	16,005	20,074
95	7,506	10,133
96	2,866	3,034
97	2,109	2,384
98	2,346	2,936
99	1,178	1,587
100+	12,369	17,193
Unknown	50,439	38,289

was made on the assumption of complete enumeration at age 2, by comparing the ratio of reported births in the European part of the R.S.F.S.R. in 1924 to persons reported as aged 2 years in the total U.S.S.R., December 17, 1926, with corresponding ratios for births in the same area in 1925 and 1926 to persons reported as aged 1 year or under 1 year, respectively, at the time of the census. The correction factors (which are conservative in view of experiments with census returns in other countries) are 1.082 for population reported as age 1 year and 1.042 for population reported as under 1 year. Persons of unknown age of each sex were distributed by multiplying the number of males reported at each age over 3 years by 1.00071 and the reported females in the same age classes by 1.00054.

2. The "expected" population, aged 12 and over, December 17, 1939, was obtained by applying twelve-year survival ratios to the 1926 population. These survival ratios were derived from the "adjusted" life tables for the European part of the U.S.S.R., 1926-1927, after adjustment by Coale. It is assumed that net migration across the Soviet borders during the period was negligible. The results show the number of persons "expected" in each age and sex class, December 17, 1938, if mortality by age and sex in the total U.S.S.R. during this twelve-year interval, in the case of the population already living in 1926, had been the same as that indicated by the adjusted life-table values for the European part of the U.S.S.R. The one-month interval to the date of the census is ignored, and these figures are taken as giving "expected" population, January 17, 1939 (see Table A 18).

3. The population of January 17, 1939, was reported in broad age classes (without sex) and by sex (without age). The age distribution was based on a tabulation of incomplete returns. The reported number in each broad age class was multiplied by 1.00559264 to give the total population. The number reported as "age unknown" was distributed in proportion to numbers reported at ages 15 years and over. The population under 12 years of age in 1939 was then distributed by sex in proportion to the sex distribution of the population under 12 years of age in 1926. The estimated sex distribution of the total population aged 12 years and over was obtained by subtracting the estimated number of males and females under 12 years from the total number of males and females. The distribution of the total population aged 12 years and over by broad age classes (12-14, 15-19, 20-29, 30-39, 40-49, 50-59, 60 and over) was accepted as given, except in the case of persons aged 12-19 years. Examination of the census data for 1926, as well as for 1897, shows heavy concentration at age 12, apparently due chiefly to the "drift" of 'teen age children into the lower age bracket in reports to census enumerators. The total group aged 12-19 is therefore treated as a unit, subject to later analysis, giving six broad classes: 12-19, 20-29, 30-39, 40-49, 50-59, 60 and over.

4. The "observed" population aged 12 years and over (as estimated from 1939 census data) *minus* the "expected" population of each sex gives negative values, interpreted as "excess" deaths of males and females, respectively, during the intercensus interval. Total excess deaths within each of the six broad age classes defined above were computed in the same fashion, and distributed by sex in proportion to the ratio of excess male deaths to excess deaths of both sexes at all ages, and subtracted from the expected population classified by sex and by broad age classes. By these means there is obtained an *estimated population* by sex and by broad age classes which gives results equal to the total number in each broad age class and, as regards the number of each sex at ages 12 and over, equal to the observed numbers presented in Table 56 and Appendix Table A 19.

5. The estimated population of each sex within each ten-year age class was then distributed by five-year classes in proportion to the corresponding distribution within each ten-year age class in the expected population, in the case of males under 50 years and in the case of females under 40 years. The same procedure was used to divide the population aged 60 and over into ten-year classes, and the population aged 12-19 years into the subclasses 12-14 and 15-19. Interpolation by formula was then used to give population by five-year age classes for males aged 50 and over and for females aged 40 and over. This was done to eliminate the effects of "bunching" at round decennial ages. The formula used here is:[1] $f_{na} = 1/2[f_n + 1/8(f_{n-1} - f_{n+1})]$.

6. In the case of the population under 12 years of age, estimates of births in the years 1927-1928 and 1935-1938 were used to estimate persons aged 10-11 years and those aged 0-3 years. In estimating expected survivors from birth at ages under 12 years, two sets of survival ratios were used. In the case of children born in 1927 and 1928, the survival ratios obtained from the 1926-1927 life

---

[1] Margaret J. Hagood, *Statistics for Sociologists* (New York: Reynal and Hitchcock, Inc., 1941), p. 760.

TABLE A 18

Estimate of Expected Population, Aged 12 Years and Over, December 17, 1938
(Numbers in Thousands)

Age 12/17/1926	Population, 1926		Life-Table Survival Values[2]	Expected Population, 1938	Age 12/17/1938
	As Reported in Census	Adjusted[1]			
Males					
Total	71,043[3]	71,336[3]	—	61,035[3]	
0-2	7,134	7,432	.84629	6,290	12-14
3-7	8,916	8,922	.94535	8,435	15-19
8-12	7,824	7,830	.95375	7,468	20-24
13-17	8,817	8,823	.93789	8,275	25-29
18-22	7,248	7,253	.92499	6,709	30-34
23-27	5,967	5,972	.91532	5,466	35-39
28-32	4,819	4,823	.90076	4,344	40-44
33-37	3,940	3,942	.87783	3,461	45-49
38-42	3,814	3,816	.84523	3,226	50-54
43-47	3,022	3,024	.79966	2,418	55-59
48-52	2,598	2,600	.73452	1,910	60-64
53-57	2,065	2,066	.64431	1,331	65-69
58-62	1,767	1,768	.52508	928	70-74
63-67	1,354	1,355	.37927	514	75-79
68-72	821	822	.22935	189	80-84
73+	888	889	.08170	73	85+
Age Unknown	50	—	—	—	
Females					
Total	75,985[3]	76,272[3]		66,188[3]	
0-2	6,990	7,281	.85685	6,239	12-14
3-7	8,895	8,900	.94820	8,439	15-19
8-12	7,639	7,643	.95717	7,316	20-24
13-17	9,152	9,156	.94350	8,639	25-29
18-22	7,787	7,791	.93094	7,253	30-34
23-27	7,013	7,017	.92223	6,471	35-39
28-32	5,487	5,489	.91464	5,021	40-44
33-37	4,377	4,380	.90532	3,965	45-49
38-42	4,095	4,097	.88917	3,643	50-54
43-47	3,061	3,063	.85780	2,627	55-59
48-52	2,956	2,957	.80303	2,375	60-64
53-57	2,413	2,415	.71775	1,733	65-69
58-62	2,236	2,237	.59581	1,333	70-74
63-67	1,597	1,598	.44149	706	75-79
68-72	1,117	1,117	.27839	311	80-84
73+	1,131	1,131	.10458	118	85+
Age Unknown	38	—	—	—	

[1] Assuming underenumeration equal to 4.2 percent of persons under 1 year and 8.2 percent of persons 1 year of age (with difference between these estimated values attributed to erroneous reporting of some children aged 1 year as "infants" under 1 year). Persons of unknown age distributed in equal proportion.

[2] From "Life Tables, European Part of the U.S.S.R., 1926-1927," as adjusted by Coale (no adjustment at ages under 25 years).

[3] Sums taken before smoothing to thousands.

TABLE A 19

Population of the U.S.S.R. Aged 12 Years and Over, as Expected (December 17, 1938) and as Observed (January 17, 1939)

Age	Expected[1]	Observed	Difference Absolute	As Percent of Expected Population
Total	127,222,281	122,378,409	—4,843,872	3.81
12-19	29,401,579	28,624,111	—777,468	2.64
20-29	31,697,250	30,819,743	—877,507	2.77
30-39	25,898,895	25,482,402	—416,493	1.61
40-49	16,790,568	15,325,722	—1,464,846	8.72
50-59	11,914,404	10,931,502	—982,902	8.25
60+	11,519,585	11,194,929	—324,656	2.82
Total by Sex				
Males	61,034,780	57,491,234[2]	—3,543,546	5.81
Females	66,187,501	64,887,175[2]	—1,300,326	1.96

[1] Consolidated, before smoothing to thousands, from figures given in Table A 18.
[2] Assuming a distribution by sex of the population under 12 years of age the same as that reported in 1926, and subtracting the estimated number of males and females under 12 from the total number of males and females.

tables for the European part of the U.S.S.R. were applied to give children aged 10-11 years in January, 1939. Since the hypothetical life tables for 1938-1940 could not be prepared until a detailed age distribution was available, the Polish life tables for 1931-1932 were used for a preliminary estimate (subject to later revision) of population aged 0-3 years in January, 1939. When an estimate of population 0-3 was obtained, the population 4-7 was obtained by subtraction—after adjustment to give "enumerated population" aged 0-3, using correction factors of 1926—and arbitrarily distributed in equal amounts among the four single year classes, to give estimated population by sex at ages 4, 5, 6, and 7 years. It is assumed again that the difference in the number of persons at each age between January 1 and January 17 is negligible. The observed population, aged 8-11 years, was used in the same way, after subtracting the estimated population aged 10-11 to give estimated population aged 8-9 years. (The 1938-1940 life-table population is given in Table A 20 and the revised values for ages under 12 are given in Table A 21.)

7. The procedures described above give a (preliminary) estimated distribution of population by age and sex, January 17, 1939. The midyear population in 1938, needed for the development of data relating to vital statistics, was derived from this estimate. The total population, July 1, 1938, was obtained by dividing the total population on January 17, 1939, by 1.0112 (one plus 54.66 percent of the rate of natural increase in 1938). A preliminary estimate of population under 3 years of age was derived from mean annual numbers of births 1935-1936, 1936-1937, and 1937-1938, and survival values from the Polish life table, mentioned above. This number was subtracted from the estimated total to give the population aged 3 years and over on July 1, 1938. Each age and sex group aged 3 and over in January, 1939, was then divided by the ratio of the estimated total population over 3 as of July, 1938, to that of January, 1939, (1.00776) to give an approximate distribution of population at 3 years and over by age and sex in 1938.

8. Two series of specific death rates $[m_x = d_x/L_x]$ were applied to the estimated population of the U.S.S.R., 1938, distributed by age and sex: (A) rates derived from the (adjusted) life tables for the European part of the U.S.S.R., 1926-1927, and (B) rates derived from life tables for Poland, 1931-1932. It was found that application (A) gave an expected number of deaths in excess of the observed number, and application (B) gave an expected number below the observed. The difference between the total deaths expected on application (B) and the observed number was 27 percent of the difference between (A) and (B). A hypothetical series of death rates

TABLE A 20

Life-Table Population, U.S.S.R., 1939-1940: Estimated L Values

Age	Male	Female
Total	466,924	502,073
0-5	40,135	41,493
0-1	8,627	8,843
1-2	8,124	8,402
2-3	7,893	8,181
3-4	7,781	8,070
4-5	7,710	7,997
5-9	37,995	39,465
10-14	37,341	38,830
15-19	36,740	38,185
20-24	35,869	37,326
25-29	34,843	36,296
30-34	33,815	35,171
35-39	32,709	33,986
40-44	31,410	32,752
45-49	29,796	31,445
50-54	27,695	29,857
55-59	24,955	27,707
60-64	21,503	24,753
65-69	17,295	20,817
70-74	12,431	15,889
75-79	7,553	10,420
80-84	3,568	5,406
85+	1,271	2,275

was then obtained by interpolation between the two experimental series, on the basis of the relation between aggregate expected and observed numbers of deaths $[B + .27(A—B)]$. This series (first approximation) was used to give revised survival values from birth to ages under 1 and 1 year and thus to give revised midyear population estimates at these ages, which are important in computations relating to mortality. The minor effect of comparable adjustments in the distribution of population aged 3-7 years was ignored. The application of the two series of death rates used in the first procedure was then repeated, using the revised estimate of midyear population. This yielded a new interpolation formula $[B + .21(A—B)]$. This was used to obtain a series of age-specific death rates, following a curve intermediate between the curves of the earlier U.S.S.R. and Polish life tables, which, when applied to the estimated midyear population in 1938, gives an aggregate number of deaths approximately equal to the observed number (see Table 53). Life-table values based on these rates were then used to give revised estimates of population under 8 years, by age and sex, on December 17, 1939.

9. In order to project this population to January 1, 1940, it was arbitrarily assumed that the ratio of births in 1939 to births in 1938 was equal to the corresponding ratio 1938/1937, and that the ratio of births to deaths remained as in 1938. Survival ratios derived from the estimated specific death rates in 1938 were applied to give estimated population at ages under 5 in 1940. The total population on January 1, 1940, was obtained by straight line interpolation between the population thus indicated for January 17, 1940, and that reported for January 17, 1939. The approximate number in each age class over 5 years was then obtained by applying the ratio between estimated total population aged 5 years and over at these dates.

10. A hypothetical age-specific schedule of fertility was obtained by averaging the age-specific

TABLE A 21

Estimated Distribution of Children Under 12 Years of Age: U.S.S.R., 1939
(Numbers in Thousands)

1. CHILDREN AGED 0-3 YEARS

Year of Birth	Births[1]	Males (1) x .514	Females (1)-(2)	Surviving Males[2] (2)x(Lx)	Surviving Females[2] (3)x(Lx)	Census Estimate[3] Males	Census Estimate[3] Females	Age 1/1/1939
	(1)	(2)	(3)	(4)	(5)	(6)	(7)	(8)
1938	6,457	3,319	3,138	2,863	2,775	2,694	2,605	Under 1
1937	6,542	3,362	3,180	2,731	2,672	2,553	2,493	1
1936	5,447	2,800	2,647	2,210	2,166	2,210	2,166	2
1935	4,829	2,482	2,347	1,931	1,894	1,931	1,894	3
Total				9,735	9,507	9,388	9,158	

[1] From Table 53.

[2] L_x values (radix = 1; x = age) from hypothetical life table, U.S.S.R., 1938-1940. (See Table A 20.)

[3] Adjusted for estimated underenumeration equal to 6.3 percent of expected population under 2 years of age. The figures shown in Columns (6) and (7) are actually derived from a preliminary computation. In effect, they correspond to an assumption that 6.3 percent of children under 2 years were not enumerated, and are used without revision in the final estimate. (See Table 58.)

2. CHILDREN AGED 4-7 YEARS

Observed Census Population Aged 0-7 Years (Table 56)	31,588
Estimated (Census) Population Aged 0-3 Years	18,546
Difference: Estimated Population Aged 4-7 Years	13,042
Average Number in Each of 8 Age-Sex Classes	1,630

3. CHILDREN AGED 10-11 YEARS

Year of Birth	Births[1] Males	Births[1] Females	Lx Values[2] Males	Lx Values[2] Females	Estimated Number Males	Estimated Number Females	Age 1/1/1939
1928	3,403	3,217	.6714	.7041	2,285	2,265	10
1927	3,460	3,271	.6695	.7023	2,316	2,297	11

[1] From Table 53, assuming 51.4 percent of births as males.

[2] From tables for European part of U.S.S.R., 1926-1927.

4. CHILDREN AGED 8-9 YEARS

Observed Census Population Aged 8-11 Years	16,501[1]
Estimated Population Aged 10-11 Years	9,163[2]
Difference: Estimated Population Aged 8-9 Years	7,338
Average in Each of 4 Age-Sex Classes	1,835

[1] From Table 56.

[2] The figure obtained in the preliminary computation (used in the final estimate of age distribution, Table 58), was 8,781 thousand. The preliminary figure was used without revision in the final estimates. The corresponding preliminary figure for the group aged 8-9 years (also used in the final estimate) was 7,720 thousand. Use of the revised figures would have the effect of *decreasing* the number in the age class 5-9 years by 2.2 percent and of *increasing* the number in the class aged 10-14 years by 1.8 percent (absolute change in either case would be 382 thousand).

5. SUMMARY: ESTIMATES BY TWO-YEAR AGE CLASSES

Year of Birth	Age 1/1/1939	Number (In thousands)
1937-1938	0-1	10,345[1]
1935-1936	2-3	8,201
1933-1934	4-5	6,521[2]
1931-1932	6-7	6,521[2]
1929-1930	8-9	7,338
1927-1928	10-11	9,163
Total According to Census		48,089

[1] Adjusted for hypothetical underenumeration. Estimated absolute figure for this class: 11,041 thousand. Adjustment for underenumeration relative to final estimates: 696 thousand. Corresponding adjustment according to computations used in Table 58: 678 thousand.

[2] One-half estimated total for group aged 4-7 years.

birth rates for (A) urban and (B) rural parts of the Ukraine, 1926-1927, weighted in proportion to the urban-rural distribution of the total population of the U.S.S.R. in 1939, and by "correcting" the values thus obtained to give the required total number of births in 1938.

11. The estimated number aged 4-9 years in 1939 is low in comparison with the estimated numbers aged 0-3 and 10-11 years (see Table A 21). This finding is consistent with the evidence of reduced fertility and possibly increased infant mortality during the years 1929-1934. These estimates represent *residuals* from reported numbers aged 0-7 and 8-11 after subtracting estimated numbers aged 0-3 and 10-11 years. Before making this subtraction, the estimated number aged 0-1 years (based on the hypothetical number of births in 1937 and 1938 and on life-table values) was adjusted on the assumption that children under 2 years of age would have been underenumerated in proportion to the estimated underenumeration in 1926. If this adjustment had not been made, the *residuals*, distributed among age classes 4-9 years, would have been 678,000 *smaller* than the figures obtained by our procedure. Our correction for supposed underenumeration of children under 2 years, therefore, makes the age distribution less irregular than it would otherwise have been. On the other hand, if our correction at this point was too conservative, and if the proportion of underenumeration of young children was also greater (in the same degree) in 1926, the difference between expected and observed populations aged 12 years or over in 1939 is greater than that shown above in Table A 19.

12. The discrepancies between expected and reported numbers by ten-year age classes, shown in Table A 19, do not form a consistent pattern. These detailed comparisons may be distorted by gross errors in reporting population by age. Such errors would presumably not have a large effect on comparison between expected and observed total populations aged 12 years and over.

13. The comparison between the expected and observed population may be affected by the unknown age distribution of the 948,059 persons whose census schedules were not available for classification in preparing data on age distribution in 1939. These persons were living in remote northern regions. It is likely that the population in these regions (other than the indigenous groups) included a disproportionate number of adults. We may, therefore, have erred in distributing this unknown population (948,059) in proportion to the age distribution of persons for whom ages were actually reported. This does not affect the sex distribution of the total population, which was completely reported. Our procedure assumed that 28.21 percent of the unknown groups were children under 12 years of age (i.e., 267,447 children). Conceivably, the actual number of children in this group was only half as large. If so, our figure for the observed population aged 12 years or over should be increased by 134 thousand, and the apparent discrepancy reduced by an equal amount. The age discrepancy of the population over 12 years of age may also be somewhat distorted by deviations of the unknown group from the population for whom ages were reported. This would not affect the size of the total discrepancy, but it would affect the distribution of this discrepancy among different age classes.

14. Finally, we should note that it is often difficult to get complete enumeration of adult males,

who shift residence in connection with their work. Any underenumeration of adult males in 1939, even though the absolute magnitude of such error was relatively small as regards the figures for the total population, would have appreciably exaggerated the discrepancies shown in Table A 19. In general, however, there seems no reason to suppose that there was less complete enumeration in 1939 than in 1926.

There are, of course, many other sources of possible error in all these computations. Consequently, the results should be accepted with many reservations.

APPENDIX VII

STUDY AREAS

Official data are available from the 1939 census releases on the population in each of the eleven Soviet Socialist Republics (1939 boundaries) for 1926 and 1939. Each of these units, except the R.S.F.S.R., is treated as a Study Area. The other Study Areas are formed by grouping autonomous republics, krays, or oblasts of the R.S.F.S.R. (1939 borders). These areas were outlined on a map of the U.S.S.R. with political divisions as of 1938, corrected for changes in boundaries to fit the 1939 census data. The same area outlines were then traced on a map of the same projection with 1926 political divisions. The maps used in these comparisons were enlargements from plates prepared by John Morrison[1] for maps originally published in *The American Quarterly on the Soviet Union*; the plates were supplied by courtesy of the author and the American Russian Institute, New York City. The minor divisions or parts of minor divisions as of December 17, 1926, within each area were then estimated by reference to maps published in the report on the First All-Union Census, with reference as regards the 1939 borders of various divisions to *Bol'shoy Sovetskiy Atlas Mira*.[2] The 1926 population in each area was then estimated by summing the population (total, urban, and rural, separately) of the component minor divisions or parts thereof.

A similar procedure was followed to obtain the estimated total population within the same, or groups of the same, Study Areas in 1897, with additional reference to Marks Atlas,[3] and maps and data in the report on the 1897 census of the Russian Empire.

The political divisions as of 1939 within each Study Area are shown in Table A 22, with population data from census releases and land areas from the sources indicated. The political divisions or parts thereof assumed to lie within specified Study Areas at each of the three census dates are shown in the three sections of Table A 23.

The estimates derived from this procedure are necessarily imperfect. An error in the estimate for any Study Area is offset by a compensating error in some adjacent area or areas. Therefore, the estimates for groups of Study Areas, or broad divisions of the U.S.S.R., have a higher validity than those for particular Study Areas.

[1] Morrison, Title 208.
[2] *Bol'shoy Sovetskiy Atlas Mira*, Title 469, Vol. II.
[3] *Bol'shoy Vsemirnyy Nastol'nyy Atlas Marksa*, Title 466.

TABLE A 22

Area and Population of Study Areas with Component Administrative Divisions, 1939

Area and Administrative Division	Area (Thousand Square Kilometers)[1]	Total Population (In thousands)	Urban Population (In thousands)	Percent Urban	Rural Persons per Sq. Km.[3]
U.S.S.R.	21,175.2	170,467	55,910	33	5.4
Belorussian S.S.R.	126.8[2]	5,568	1,373	25	33.1
Ukrainian S.S.R.	445.3[2]	30,960	11,196	36	44.4
Central Black Soil	246.7	12,112	1,918	16	41.3
Orël Obl.	64.4[2]	3,482	693	20	43.3
Kursk Obl.	55.7[2]	3,197	286	9	52.3
Voronezh Obl.	76.7[2]	3,551	658	19	37.7
Tambov Obl.	49.9[2]	1,882	281	15	32.1
Western	178.6	5,902	1,151	20	26.6
Kalinin Obl.	106.4	3,211	703	22	23.6
Smolensk Obl.	72.2	2,691	448	17	31.1

TABLE A 22 (*Continued*)

Area and Population of Study Areas with Component Administrative Divisions, 1939

Area and Adminis- trative Division	Area (Thousand Square Kilometers)[1]	Total Popu- lation (In thousands)	Urban Popu- lation (In thousands)	Percent Urban	Rural Persons per Sq. Km.[3]
Old Industrial Center	346.4	22,032	10,382	47	33.6
Moscow Obl.	49.4	8,918	6,268	70	53.6
Yaroslavl' Obl.	63.1	2,271	797	35	23.4
Ivanovo Obl.	63.4	2,650	1,168	44	23.4
Gor'kiy Obl.	89.2	3,876	1,219	31	29.8
Ryazan' Obl.	49.4[2]	2,266	219	10	41.4
Tula Obl.	31.9	2,050	711	35	42.0
Leningrad Oblast'	143.7	6,435	4,119	64	16.1
Karelia-Murmansk	275.3	760	396	52	1.3
Karelian A.S.S.R.	136.4[2]	469	150	32	2.3
Murmansk Obl.	138.9	291	245	84	0.3
Northeast	1,176.9	3,180	749	24	2.1
Vologda Obl.	150.0	1,662	285	17	9.2
Arkhangel'sk Obl.	652.0	1,199	435	36	1.2
Komi A.S.S.R.	374.9	319	29	9	0.8
Vyatka	185.6	5,103	858	17	22.9
Mari A.S.S.R.	23.3	579	76	13	21.6
Chuvash A.S.S.R.	17.9	1,078	132	12	52.8
Udmurt A.S.S.R.	38.9	1,220	321	26	23.1
Kirov Obl.	105.5	2,226	329	15	18.0
Tatar A.S.S.R.	67.1	2,919	622	21	34.2
Central Volga	284.0	8,069	1,936	24	21.6
Saratov Obl.	89.6[2]	1,799	666	37	12.6
Penza Obl.	44.5	1,709	283	17	32.0
Mordva A.S.S.R.	25.5	1,189	82	7	43.4
Kuybyshev Obl.	96.2[2]	2,768	773	28	20.7
Volga German A.S.S.R.	28.2	606	132	22	16.8
Lower Volga and Don	310.3	5,404	2,191	41	10.4
Kalmyk A.S.S.R.	74.2	221	35	16	2.5
Rostov Obl.	100.7	2,894	1,263	44	16.2
Stalingrad Obl.	135.4	2,289	893	39	10.3
Crimean A.S.S.R.	26.0	1,127	586	52	20.8
North Caucasus	217.2	6,508	1,597	25	22.6
Krasnodar Kray	81.5[2]	3,173	765	24	29.5
Ordzhonikidze Kray	101.5[2]	1,949	394	20	15.3
Kabardino-Balkar A.S.S.R.	12.3	359	85	24	22.3
North Osetin A.S.S.R.	6.2	329	155	47	28.1
Checheno-Ingush A.S.S.R.	15.7	697	199	29	31.7
Dagestan A.S.S.R.	35.0	931	196	21	21.0
Azerbaydzhan S.S.R.	85.5	3,210	1,161	36	24.0
Georgian S.S.R.	69.3	3,542	1,067	30	35.7

TABLE A 22 (*Continued*)

Area and Population of Study Areas with Component Administrative Divisions, 1939

Area and Adminis- trative Division	Area (Thousand Square Kilometers)[1]	Total Popu- lation (In thousands)	Urban Popu- lation (In thousands)	Percent Urban	Rural Persons per Sq. Km.[3]
Armenian S.S.R.	29.9	1,282	366	29	30.6
Ural	667.4	9,074	3,893	43	7.8
Perm' Obl.	190.2[2]	2,082	823	40	6.6
Sverdlovsk Obl.	189.9[2]	2,512	1,509	60	5.3
Chelyabinsk Obl.	163.5[2]	2,803	1,182	42	9.9
Chkalov Obl.	123.8	1,677	380	23	10.5
Bashkir A.S.S.R.	140.5	3,145	531	17	18.6
West Siberia	2,345.5	8,909	2,555	29	2.7
Omsk Obl.	1,440.5	2,367	495	21	1.3
Novosibirsk Obl.	611.0[2]	4,023	1,655	41	3.9
Altay Kray	294.0[2]	2,520	404	16	7.2
Central Siberia	3,043.4	3,227	1,113	34	0.7
Krasnoyarsk Kray	2,143.8	1,940	551	28	0.6
Irkutsk Obl.	899.6	1,287	562	44	0.8
East Siberia	4,082.3	2,102	753	36	0.3
Buryat-Mongolian A.S.S.R.	331.4	542	163	30	1.1
Yakutsk A.S.S.R.	3,030.9[2]	401	79	20	0.1
Chita Obl.	720.0	1,159	511	44	0.9
Soviet Far East	2,778.6	2,338	1,112	48	0.4
Khabarovsk Kray	2,572.0	1,431	648	45	0.3
Maritime Kray	206.6	907	465	51	2.1
Kazakh S.S.R.	2,734.7	6,146	1,706	28	1.6
Kirgiz S.S.R.	201.6	1,459	271	19	5.9
Uzbek S.S.R.	410.5	6,282	1,445	23	11.8
Tadzhik S.S.R.	142.3	1,485	252	17	8.7
Turkmen S.S.R.	484.7	1,254	416	33	1.7

[1] Area measurements, unless otherwise specified, are from *SSSR Administrativno-Territorial'noye Deleniye Soyuznykh Respublik na 1 Maya 1940 goda*, Title 481.

[2] Area measurements from *Ekonomicheskaya Geografiya*, Title 464, pp. 401-404, in cases where it appears that the figures from the later and more authoritative source used for other divisions in this table are not appropriate, owing to boundary changes between January 17, 1939, and May 1, 1940. In some cases the information from these sources is ambiguous with reference to the situation at the time of the 1939 census. The sum of the area measurements cited in Title 464 is 21,181 thousand square kilometers, i.e., 6 thousand in excess of the total area of the U.S.S.R. reported in Title 481.

[3] Rural population relative to total area.

TABLE A 23

Units Comprised in Population Study Areas

A. 1939 POLITICAL DIVISIONS

1. Belorussian S.S.R.
2. Ukrainian S.S.R.
3. Central Black Soil
   Orël Obl.
   Kursk Obl.
   Voronezh Obl.
   Tambov Obl.
4. Western
   Kalinin Obl.
   Smolensk Obl.
5. Old Industrial Center
   Moscow Obl.
   Yaroslavl' Obl.
   Ivanovo Obl.
   Gor'kiy Obl.
   Ryazan' Obl.
   Tula Obl.
6. Leningrad Oblast'
7. Karelia-Murmansk
   Karelian A.S.S.R.
   Murmansk Obl.
8. Northeast
   Vologda Obl.
   Arkhangel'sk Obl.
   Komi A.S.S.R.
9. Vyatka
   Mari A.S.S.R.
   Chuvash A.S.S.R.
   Udmurt A.S.S.R.
   Kirov Obl.
10. Tatar A.S.S.R.
11. Central Volga
    Saratov Obl.
    Penza Obl.
    Mordva A.S.S.R.
    Kuybyshev Obl.
    Volga German A.S.S.R.
12. Lower Volga and Don
    Kalmyk A.S.S.R.
    Rostov Obl.
    Stalingrad Obl.
13. Crimean A.S.S.R.
14. North Caucasus
    Krasnodar Kray
    Ordzhonikidze Kray
    Kabardino-Balkar A.S.S.R.
    North Osetin A.S.S.R.
    Checheno-Ingush A.S.S.R.
15. Dagestan A.S.S.R.
16. Azerbaydzhan S.S.R.
17. Georgian S.S.R.

18. Armenian S.S.R.
19. Ural
    Perm' Obl.
    Sverdlovsk Obl.
    Chelyabinsk Obl.
    Chkalov Obl.
20. Bashkir A.S.S.R.
21. West Siberia
    Omsk Obl.
    Novosibirsk Obl.
    Altay Kray
22. Central Siberia
    Krasnoyarsk Kray
    Irkutsk Obl.
23. East Siberia
    Buryat-Mongolian A.S.S.R.
    Yakutsk A.S.S.R.
    Chita Obl.
24. Soviet Far East
    Khabarovsk Kray
    Maritime Kray
25. Kazakh S.S.R.
26. Kirgiz S.S.R.
27. Uzbek S.S.R.
28. Tadzhik S.S.R.
29. Turkmen S.S.R.

Units Comprised in Population Study Areas

B. 1926 POLITICAL DIVISIONS[1]

1. Belorussia[2]
2. Ukraine[2]
3. Central Black Soil
    Kaluga Gub.: Kozel'sk uyezd
    Bryansk Gub.
    Orël Gub.
    Kursk Gub.
    Voronezh Gub.
    Tambov Gub., except parts in area 5
4. Western
    Pskov Gub., except parts in area 6
    Smolensk Gub.
    Kaluga Gub., except parts in areas 5 and 3
    Tver' Gub.
5. Old Industrial Center
    Moscow Gub.
    Kaluga Gub.: Kaluga, Tarussa, Likhvin, and Maloyaroslavets uyezds
    Tula Gub.
    Ryazan' Gub.
    Tambov Gub.: the uyezds of Kozlov (volosts 1,7,10,14), Morshansk (volosts 9,15,17), and
                Lipetsk (volosts 4,5,7,8,12,13)
    Yaroslavl' Gub.
    Kostroma Gub.
    Ivanovo-Voznesensk Gub.
    Vladimir Gub.
    Nizhniy Novgorod Gub.

6. Leningrad
   Pskov Gub.: the uyezds of Pskov, Porkhov, and Ostrov
   Cherepovets Gub.: Tikhvin uyezd
   Leningrad Gub.
   Novgorod Gub.
7. Karelia-Murmansk
   Karelian A.S.S.R.
   Murmansk Gub.
8. Northeast
   Cherepovets Gub., except Tikhvin uyezd
   Vologda Gub.
   Northern Dvina Gub.
   Arkhangel'sk Gub.
   Komi A. Obl., except Sissol'sk uyezd
9. Vyatka
   Vyatka Gub.
   Mari A. Obl.
   Chuvash A.S.S.R.
   Votyak A. Obl.
   Ural Obl.: Sarapul okrug; Sarapul City; Sarapul, Kiyasovsk, Karkulinsk, Kambersk, and
        Votkinsk rayons
10. Tatar
11. Central Volga
    Penza Gub.
    Saratov Gub., except part in area 12
    Samara Gub., except part in area 19
    Ul'yanovsk Gub.
    Volga German A.S.S.R.
12. Lower Volga and Don
    Saratov Gub.: Balashov uyezd (one-third of the rural population), and Kamyshin uyezd
    North Caucasus: Donets, Don Sal'sk, Taganrog, and Shakhtinsko-Donets okrugs
    Astrakhan' Gub.
    Stalingrad Gub.
    Kalmyk A. Obl.
13. Crimea
14. North Caucasus
    North Caucasian Kray, except parts in area 12
    Dagestan A.S.S.R.: Kizlyar and Achikulak rayons
15. Dagestan
    Dagestan A.S.S.R., except Kizlyar and Achikulak rayons
16. Azerbaydzhan[2]
17. Georgia[2]
18. Armenia[2]
19. Ural
    Orenburg Gub.
    Samara Gub.: Buzuluk uyezd (two-thirds of the total population), and Buguruslan uyezd
             (40 percent of the rural population)
    Ural Obl., except parts in areas 9 and 21
    Bashkir A.S.S.R.: Argayash canton
    Komi A. Obl.: Sissol'sk uyezd
    Kazakh A.S.S.R.: Aktyubinsk Gub. (volosts 1,4,5,11,24,26); Kustanay Gub. (volosts 1,11)
20. Bashkir
    Bashkir A.S.S.R., except Argayash canton

[246]

21. West Siberia
   Siberian Kray: Tara, Omsk, Barabinsk, Slavgorod, Tomsk, Novosibirsk, Kamen', Barnaul, Rubtsov, Achinsk (volosts 9, 10, 12), Kuznetsk, and Biysk okrugs, and Oyrot A. Obl.
   Ural Obl.: Tobol'sk, Ishim, and Tyumen' okrugs
   Kazakh A.S.S.R.: Akmolinsk Gub.: Petropavlovsk uyezd (volosts 2, 4, 16) rural population

22. Central Siberia
   Siberian Kray: Achinsk okrug (except volosts 9, 10, 12), Khakassk, Krasnoyarsk (including Turukhan Kray), Minusinsk, Kansk, Tulun, Irkutsk, and Kirensk (except Makarov volost') okrugs
   Buryat-Mongolian A.S.S.R.: Alarsk, Bokhan, and Ekhirit-Bulagat aymaks

23. East Siberia
   Buryat-Mongolian A.S.S.R., except parts in area 22
   Yakutsk A.S.S.R.
   Far Eastern Kray: Chita, Sretensk, and Zeya okrugs
   Siberian Kray: Kirensk okrug: Makarov volost'

24. Soviet Far East
   Far Eastern Kray, except parts in area 23

25. Kazakh[2]
26. Kirgiz[2]
27. Uzbek[2]
28. Tadzhik[2]
29. Turkmen[2]

Units Comprised in Population Study Areas

C. 1897 POLITICAL DIVISIONS[1]

1. Belorussia[3]
2. Ukraine[3]
3. Central Black Soil
   Kaluga Gub.: Kozel'sk uyezd
   Orël Gub.
   Chernigov Gub.: Novozybkiy, Starodub, Surash, and Mglin uyezds
   Kursk Gub., except Putivl uyezd
   Voronezh Gub.
   Tambov Gub., except parts in areas 5 and 11

4. Western
   Pskov Gub., except Pskov, Ostrov, and Porkhov uyezds
   Vitebsk Gub.: Sebezh, Nevel', and Velizh uyezds
   Smolensk Gub.
   Kaluga Gub., except parts in areas 3 and 5
   Tver' Gub.

5. Old Industrial Center
   Moscow Gub.
   Kaluga Gub.: Maloyaroslavets, Kaluga, Likhvin, Tarussa, and Peremyshl' uyezds
   Tula Gub.
   Ryazan' Gub.
   Tambov Gub.: the uyezds of Morshansk (13.5 percent of the rural population*), Kozlov (29.7 percent of the rural population*), Lipetsk (39.6 percent of the rural population*), Lebedyan', Shatsk, and Yelatma
   *Note: Percentage corresponding to adjustments made in 1926 census data for specified uyezds

6-8. Leningrad, Karelia-Murmansk, Northeast (Northern)
   Pskov Gub.: the uyezds of Pskov (except part ceded to Estonia), Ostrov (except part ceded to Latvia), and Porkhov

St. Petersburg Gub., except part, including Narva, ceded to Estonia
Novgorod Gub.
Vologda Gub.
Olonets Gub.
Arkhangel'sk Gub.[4]

9-10. Vyatka, Tatar (Upper Volga)
Vyatka Gub.
Kazan' Gub.
Simbirsk Gub.: Alatyr' and Buinsk uyezds
Samara Gub.: Bugul'ma uyezd
Ufa Gub.: Menzelinsk uyezd

11. Central Volga
Tambov Gub.: Spassk and Temnikov uyezds
Penza Gub.
Saratov Gub., except parts in area 12
Simbirsk Gub., except parts in area 9-10
Samara Gub., except parts in areas 9-10 and 19-20

12. Lower Volga and Don
Saratov Gub.: Kamyshin, Tsaritsyn, and Balashov (one-third of the rural population)
uyezds
Don Obl., except the uyezds of Taganrog (50 percent of the rural population), Donets (10
percent of the rural population), and Cherkassk (5 percent of the rural
population)
Astrakhan' Gub., except the Kirgiz orda

13. Crimea
Taurida Gub., except the uyezds of Berdyansk, Dneprovsk, Melitopol', and Perekop (one-
half of the rural population)

14-15. North Caucasus, Dagestan
Stavropol' Gub.
Kuban' Obl.
Black Sea Obl.
Terek Obl.
Dagestan Obl.

16-18. Azerbaydzhan, Georgia, Armenia (Transcaucasus)[3]

19-20. Ural, Bashkir
Perm' Gub.
Ufa Gub., except part in area 9-10
Samara Gub.: Buzuluk uyezd (two-thirds of the population); Buguruslan uyezd (one-
half of the population)
Orenburg Gub.

21. West Siberia
Tobol'sk Gub.
Tomsk Gub.

22. Central Siberia
Yenisey Gub.
Irkutsk Gub., except part in area 23

23. East Siberia
Yakutsk Obl.
Irkutsk Gub.: Irkutsk uyezd (10 percent of the rural population)
Transbaykal Obl.
Amur Obl. (12 percent of the total population)

24. Soviet Far East
Amur Obl. (88 percent of the total population)
Maritime Obl.
Ostrov and Sakhalin, except Korsakovskiy post

25. Kazakh
    Ural'sk Obl.
    Turgay Obl.
    Akmolinsk Obl.
    Semipalatinsk Obl.
    Syr Dar'ya Obl.: Aulieta, Kazalinsk, Perov, and Chimkent uyezds
    Semirechensk Obl., except parts in area 26-29
    Transcaspian Obl.: Mangyshlak uyezd
    Astrakhan' Gub.: Kirgiz orda

26-29. Kirgiz, Uzbek, Tadzhik, Turkmen (Central Asia)
    Syr Dar'ya Obl.: Tashkent uyezd and Amu-Darya otdel
    Samarkand Obl.
    Fergana Obl.
    Semirechensk Obl.: Pishpek and Przheval'sk uyezds
    Transcaspian Obl., except part in area 25
    Khiva Khanate[5]
    Bukhara Khanate[5]

[1] The transliterations of names of political divisions were first made before the scheme described in the Bibliography was adopted. In the case of minor political divisions in this list, these transliterations have not been completely revised.

[2] Population for 1926 from the 1939 census. The preliminary 1939 census report gives 1926 population in the 1939 area of each constituent republic. See Title 393.

[3] Population for 1897 from 1926 census. The 1926 census summary volume gives 1897 population for Belorussia, the Ukraine, Azerbaydzhan, Georgia, and Armenia, as of 1926. The population within the 1926 areas of these republics, as so reported, is assumed in Chapter X to correspond to these Study Areas as defined in 1939.

[4] Estimates of 1897 population in specified areas taken from Volkov, Title 352, p. 16.

[5] Population in Khiva and Bukhara estimated on arbitrary assumption that the ratio of population in the area included in these Khanates to other areas of Central Asia in 1897 was the same as corresponding ratio in 1926.

Bukhara Area, 1926:
    Uzbek S.S.R. (without Tadzhik A.S.S.R.), except Samarkand Obl. and the okrugs of Khodzhent, Tashkent, Isfane, Fergana, Khoresma, and Andizhan
    Tadzhik A.S.S.R.: Kurgan-Tyube, Garm, Gissar, Kulyab, and Gorno-Badakhshan (Iskashim, Roshan, and Shugnan) villayets

Khiva Area, 1926:
    Uzbek S.S.R.: Khoresma okrug
    Turkmen S.S.R.: Tashauz
    Kara-Kalpak A. Obl.: Khodzheyli and Chimbay okrugs

TABLE A 24

Population of Cities with Over 50,000 Inhabitants, January 17, 1939, and Comparison with Population in 1926[1]

City	Population		Ratio: Population, 1939, as Percent of Population, 1926
	Dec. 17, 1926	Jan. 17, 1939	
1. Moscow	2,029,425	4,137,018	203.9
2. Leningrad	1,690,065	3,191,304	188.8
3. Kiev	513,637	846,293	164.8
4. Khar'kov	417,342	833,432	199.7
5. Baku	453,333	809,347	178.5
6. Gor'kiy	222,356	644,116	289.7
7. Odessa	420,862	604,223	143.6
8. Tashkent	323,613	585,005	180.8
9. Tbilisi	294,044	519,175	176.6
10. Rostov-on-Don	308,103	510,253	165.6
11. Dnepropetrovsk	236,717	500,662	211.5
12. Stalino	174,230	462,395	265.4
13. Stalingrad	151,490	445,476	294.1
14. Sverdlovsk	140,300	425,544	303.3
15. Novosibirsk	120,128	405,589	337.6
16. Kazan'	179,023	401,665	224.4
17. Kuybyshev	175,636	390,267	222.2
18. Saratov	219,547	375,860	171.2
19. Voronezh	121,612	326,836	268.7
20. Yaroslavl'	114,277	298,065	260.8
21. Zaporozh'ye	55,744	289,188	518.8
22. Ivanovo	111,460	285,069	255.8
23. Arkhangel'sk	76,774	281,091	366.1
24. Omsk	161,684	280,716	173.6
25. Chelyabinsk	59,307	273,127	460.5
26. Tula	155,005	272,403	175.7
27. Molotov (Perm')	119,776	255,196	213.1
28. Astrakhan'	184,301	253,655	137.6
29. Ufa	98,537	245,863	249.5
30. Irkutsk	108,129	243,380	225.1
31. Makeyevka	79,421	240,145	302.4
32. Minsk	131,803	238,772	181.2
33. Alma Ata	45,395	230,528	507.8
34. Mariupol'	63,920	222,427	348.0
35. Kalinin	108,413	216,131	199.4
36. Voroshilovgrad	71,765	213,007	296.8
37. Vladivostok	107,980	206,432	191.2
38. Krasnodar	161,843	203,946	126.0
39. Erivan	64,613	200,031	309.6
40. Khabarovsk	52,045	199,364	383.1
41. Krivoy Rog	38,228	197,621	517.0
42. Krasnoyarsk	72,261	189,999	262.9
43. Taganrog	86,444	188,808	218.4
44. Izhevsk	63,211	175,740	278.0
45. Chkalov	123,283	172,925	140.3
46. Groznyy	97,087	172,468	177.6

TABLE A 24 (*Continued*)

Population of Cities with Over 50,000 Inhabitants, January 17, 1939, and Comparison with Population in 1926[1]

City	Population Dec. 17, 1926	Population Jan. 17, 1939	Ratio: Population, 1939, as Percent of Population, 1926
47. Stalinsk	3,894	169,538	4,353.8
48. Vitebsk	98,857	167,424	169.4
49. Nikolayev	104,909	167,108	159.3
50. Karaganda	—	165,937	—
51. Nizhniy Tagil	38,820	159,864	411.8
52. Penza	91,924	157,145	171.0
53. Smolensk	78,520	156,677	199.5
54. Shakhty	41,043	155,081	377.9
55. Barnaul	73,858	148,129	200.6
56. Dneprodzerzhinsk	34,150	147,829	432.9
57. Magnitogorsk	—	145,870	—
58. Gomel'	86,409	144,169	166.8
59. Kirov	62,097	143,181	230.6
60. Simferopol'	87,213	142,678	163.6
61. Tomsk	92,274	141,215	153.0
62. Rybinsk	55,546	139,011	250.3
63. Samarkand	105,206	134,346	127.7
64. Kemerovo	21,726	132,978	612.1
65. Poltava	91,984	130,305	141.7
66. Ulan-Ude	28,918	129,417	447.5
67. Ordzhonikidze: North Osetin A.S.S.R.	78,346	127,172	162.3
68. Ashkhabad	51,593	126,580	245.3
69. Tambov	72,256	121,285	167.9
70. Kostroma	73,732	121,205	164.4
71. Kursk	82,440	119,972	145.5
72. Murmansk	8,777	117,054	1,333.6
73. Sevastopol'	74,551	111,946	150.2
74. Orël	75,968	110,567	145.5
75. Semipalatinsk	56,871	109,779	193.0
76. Gorlovka	23,125	108,693	470.0
77. Prokop'evsk	10,717	107,227	1,000.5
78. Kerch'	35,690	104,471	292.7
79. Dzerzhinsk	8,910	103,415	1,160.7
80. Chita	61,526	102,555	166.7
81. Ul'yanovsk	70,130	102,106	145.6
82. Kirovograd: Ukrainian S.S.R.	66,467	100,331	150.9
83. Mogilev	50,222	99,440	198.0
84. Orekhovo-Zuyevo	62,841	99,329	158.1
85. Zlatoust	48,219	99,272	205.9
86. Kirovabad	57,393	98,743	172.1
87. Kherson	58,801	97,186	165.3
88. Ryazan'	50,919	95,358	187.3
89. Novorossiysk	67,941	95,280	140.2
90. Vologda	57,976	95,194	164.2
91. Zhitomir	76,678	95,090	124.0
92. Konstantinovka	25,303	95,087	375.8

TABLE A 24 (*Continued*)

Population of Cities with Over 50,000 Inhabitants, January 17, 1939, and Comparison with Population in 1926[1]

City	Population		Ratio: Population, 1939, as Percent of Population, 1926
	Dec. 17, 1926	Jan. 17, 1939	
93. Kramatorskaya	12,348	93,350	756.0
94. Vinnitsa	57,990	92,868	160.1
95. Frunze	36,610	92,659	253.1
96. Petropavlovsk	47,361	91,678	193.6
97. Serpukhov	55,891	90,766	162.4
98. Kremenchug	58,832	89,553	152.2
99. Kaluga	51,565	89,484	173.5
100. Ordzhonikidze: Ukrainian S.S.R.	24,329	88,246	362.7
101. Bryansk	45,962	87,473	190.3
102. Makhach-Kala	33,552	86,847	258.8
103. Voroshilovsk: Ordzhonikidze Terr.	58,640	85,100	145.1
104. Kokand	69,324	84,665	122.1
105. Bobruysk	51,296	84,107	164.0
106. Andizhan	73,465	83,691	113.9
107. Armavir	74,523	83,677	112.3
108. Stalinabad	5,607	82,540	1,472.1
109. Ordzhonikidzegrad	36,040	82,331	228.4
110. Leninsk-Kuznetskiy	19,645	81,980	417.3
111. Kutaisi	48,196	81,479	169.0
112. Novocherkassk	62,274	81,286	130.5
113. Noginsk	38,494	81,024	210.5
114. Biysk	45,561	80,190	176.0
115. Perovo	23,711	77,727	327.8
116. Syzran'	50,293	77,679	154.5
117. Namangan	73,640	77,351	105.0
118. Stalinogorsk	—	76,207	—
119. Melitopol'	25,289	75,735	299.5
120. Slavyansk	28,771	75,542	262.6
121. Tyumen'	50,340	75,537	150.1
122. Kineshma	34,110	75,378	221.0
123. Kolomna	30,767	75,139	244.2
124. Chimkent	21,018	74,185	353.0
125. Engel's	34,345	73,279	213.4
126. Podol'sk	19,793	72,422	365.9
127. Anzhero-Sudzhensk	30,199	71,079	235.4
128. Batumi	48,474	70,807	146.1
129. Komsomol'sk	—	70,746	—
130. Voroshilov	35,344	70,628	199.8
131. Losinoostrovsk	15,624	70,480	451.1
132. Michurinsk	49,853	70,202	140.8
133. Petrozavodsk	27,105	69,728	257.3
134. Sergo	17,224	68,360	396.9
135. Leninakan	42,313	67,707	160.0
136. Chernigov	35,234	67,356	191.2
137. Maykop	53,033	67,302	126.9
138. Kovrov	26,584	67,163	252.6

TABLE A 24 (*Continued*)

Population of Cities with Over 50,000 Inhabitants, January 17, 1939, and Comparison with Population in 1926[1]

City	Population Dec. 17, 1926	Population Jan. 17, 1939	Ratio: Population, 1939, as Percent of Population, 1926
139. Vladimir	39,654	66,761	168.4
140. Lipetsk	21,439	66,625	310.8
141. Berdichev	55,613	66,306	119.2
142. Ural'sk	36,352	66,201	182.1
143. Cheremkhovo	14,485	65,907	455.0
144. Orsk	13,581	65,799	484.5
145. Serov (Nadezhdinsk)	33,345	64,719	194.1
146. Lyublino	8,391	64,332	766.7
147. Sumy	44,213	63,883	144.5
148. Vyshniy-Volochek	32,022	63,642	198.7
149. Berezniki	16,138	63,575	393.9
150. Pyatigorsk	40,674	62,875	154.6
151. Dzhambul	24,761	62,723	253.3
152. Kuntsevo	9,978	60,963	611.0
153. Mytishchi	17,054	60,111	352.5
154. Pskov	43,226	59,898	138.6
155. Blagoveshchensk	—	58,761	—
156. Chapayevsk	13,529	57,995	428.7
157. Shuya	34,475	57,950	168.1
158. Nikopol'	14,214	57,841	406.9
159. Yegor'yevsk	29,674	56,340	189.9
160. Artemovsk	37,780	55,165	146.0
161. Vol'sk	35,272	55,053	156.1
162. Voroshilovsk: Ukrainian S.S.R.	16,040	54,794	341.6
163. Chardzhou	13,950	54,739	392.4
164. Rzhev	32,810	54,081	164.8
165. Kurgan	27,996	53,224	190.1
166. Borisoglebsk	39,788	52,055	130.8
167. Cherkassy	39,511	51,693	130.8
168. Osipenko (Berdyansk)	26,408	51,664	195.6
169. Kislovodsk	25,913	51,289	197.9
170. Lys'va	27,279	51,192	187.7
171. Kamensk Ural'skiy	5,367	50,897	948.3
172. Yelets	43,239	50,888	117.7
173. Krasnyy Luch	12,425	50,829	409.1
174. Bukhara	46,778	50,382	107.7

[1] Data from 1939 census, Title 393.

APPENDIX VIII

POPULATION PROJECTION DATA

TABLE A 25

Projected Population of the U.S.S.R., at Five-Year Intervals, 1940-1970: January-1939 Boundaries, without Adjustment for War Losses

A. TOTAL POPULATION

Age Group	Number (In thousands)						
	1940	1945	1950	1955	1960	1965	1970
Total	173,788	189,033	203,080	216,242	228,457	240,136	251,310
0-4	23,600	24,400	23,600	23,000	22,300	22,500	22,300
5-9	17,680	22,400	23,300	22,700	22,200	21,700	21,900
10-14	21,200	17,400	22,000	22,900	22,400	21,900	21,600
15-19	16,590	20,900	17,150	21,800	22,700	22,100	21,700
20-24	14,520	16,220	20,500	16,820	21,400	22,300	21,900
25-29	16,620	14,130	15,820	19,940	16,470	21,000	21,900
30-34	13,880	16,130	13,740	15,430	19,520	16,150	20,600
35-39	11,860	13,430	15,670	13,390	15,070	19,110	15,840
40-44	8,610	11,440	12,990	15,190	13,020	14,660	18,690
45-49	6,880	8,230	10,970	12,490	14,660	12,560	14,220
50-54	6,040	6,480	7,780	10,400	11,870	13,970	12,000
55-59	5,010	5,550	5,970	7,200	9,650	11,050	13,040
60-64	4,080	4,410	4,920	5,330	6,460	8,680	9,980
65-69	3,120	3,380	3,680	4,140	4,520	5,500	7,430
70-74	2,124	2,344	2,550	2,800	3,180	3,500	4,300
75-79	1,295	1,361	1,520	1,670	1,864	2,128	2,370
80-84	502	633	678	770	861	971	1,128
85+	177	195	242	272	312	357	412

B. MALE POPULATION

Age Group	Number (In thousands)						
	1940	1945	1950	1955	1960	1965	1970
Total	83,307	91,153	98,424	105,279	111,760	117,817	123,722
0-4	11,900	12,300	11,900	11,600	11,300	11,400	11,300
5-9	8,830	11,300	11,700	11,400	11,200	11,000	11,100
10-14	10,600	8,680	11,100	11,500	11,300	11,000	10,900
15-19	8,190	10,400	8,560	11,000	11,400	11,100	10,900
20-24	7,240	8,000	10,200	8,390	10,800	11,200	11,000

TABLE A 25 (*Continued*)

Projected Population of the U.S.S.R., at Five-Year Intervals, 1940-1970: January-1939
Boundaries, without Adjustment for War Losses

B. MALE POPULATION (*Continued*)

Age Group	Number (In thousands)						
	1940	1945	1950	1955	1960	1965	1970
25-29	8,020	7,040	7,800	9,940	8,210	10,600	11,000
30-34	6,610	7,790	6,850	7,610	9,730	8,050	10,400
35-39	5,380	6,400	7,570	6,680	7,440	9,530	7,900
40-44	3,790	5,180	6,180	7,330	6,490	7,210	9,310
45-49	3,020	3,600	4,940	5,910	7,040	6,220	6,970
50-54	2,720	2,810	3,360	4,640	5,570	6,660	5,900
55-59	2,260	2,460	2,550	3,070	4,250	5,130	6,160
60-64	1,780	1,950	2,140	2,240	2,710	3,760	4,570
65-69	1,330	1,440	1,590	1,760	1,850	2,250	3,150
70-74	874	964	1,050	1,170	1,300	1,380	1,700
75-79	512	536	599	660	744	838	900
80-84	194	235	252	287	321	369	422
85+	57	68	83	92	105	120	140

C. FEMALE POPULATION

Age Group	Number (In thousands)						
	1940	1945	1950	1955	1960	1965	1970
Total	90,481	97,880	104,656	110,963	116,697	122,319	127,588
0-4	11,700	12,100	11,700	11,400	11,000	11,100	11,000
5-9	8,850	11,100	11,600	11,300	11,000	10,700	10,800
10-14	10,600	8,720	10,900	11,400	11,100	10,900	10,700
15-19	8,400	10,500	8,590	10,800	11,300	11,000	10,800
20-24	7,280	8,220	10,300	8,430	10,600	11,100	10,900
25-29	8,600	7,090	8,020	10,000	8,260	10,400	10,900
30-34	7,270	8,340	6,890	7,820	9,790	8,100	10,200
35-39	6,480	7,030	8,100	6,710	7,630	9,580	7,940
40-44	4,820	6,260	6,810	7,860	6,530	7,450	9,380
45-49	3,860	4,630	6,030	6,580	7,620	6,340	7,250
50-54	3,320	3,670	4,420	5,760	6,300	7,310	6,100
55-59	2,750	3,090	3,420	4,130	5,400	5,920	6,880
60-64	2,300	2,460	2,780	3,090	3,750	4,920	5,410
65-69	1,790	1,940	2,090	2,380	2,670	3,250	4,280
70-74	1,250	1,380	1,500	1,630	1,880	2,120	2,600
75-79	783	825	921	1,010	1,120	1,290	1,470
80-84	308	398	426	483	540	602	706
85+	120	127	159	180	207	237	272

TABLE A 26

Projected Population of the U.S.S.R., at Five-Year Intervals, 1940-1970: January-1939
Boundaries, Adjusted for Hypothetical War Losses

A. TOTAL POPULATION

Age Group	Number (In thousands)						
	1940	1945	1950	1955	1960	1965	1970
Total	173,800	168,900	181,100	192,200	203,200	213,400	222,300
0-4	23,600	18,340	20,600	20,200	20,130	19,870	19,200
5-9	17,680	21,000	17,510	19,750	19,590	19,530	19,330
10-14	21,200	16,410	20,800	17,290	19,520	19,400	19,360
15-19	16,590	19,400	16,170	20,400	17,080	19,310	19,210
20-24	14,520	14,360	19,000	15,860	20,060	16,810	19,020
25-29	16,620	12,000	14,000	18,570	15,530	19,710	16,520
30-34	13,880	14,280	11,670	13,660	18,160	15,220	19,360
35-39	11,860	12,120	13,860	11,370	13,340	17,780	14,940
40-44	8,610	10,630	11,720	13,440	11,060	12,980	17,380
45-49	6,880	7,630	10,200	11,280	12,970	10,680	12,600
50-54	6,040	6,090	7,220	9,670	10,720	12,370	10,200
55-59	5,010	5,200	5,620	6,680	8,980	9,980	11,560
60-64	4,080	4,140	4,620	5,010	5,990	8,090	9,020
65-69	3,120	3,150	3,450	3,880	4,250	5,100	6,910
70-74	2,124	2,169	2,376	2,620	2,980	3,290	3,980
75-79	1,295	1,240	1,405	1,560	1,735	1,996	2,226
80-84	502	560	619	713	803	909	1,060
85+	177	157	213	247	288	333	386

B. MALE POPULATION

Age Group	Number (In thousands)						
	1940	1945	1950	1955	1960	1965	1970
Total	83,300	79,200	85,600	91,400	97,300	102,700	107,600
0-4	11,900	9,230	10,400	10,200	10,200	10,100	9,740
5-9	8,830	10,600	8,790	9,930	9,870	9,870	9,790
10-14	10,600	8,190	10,500	8,680	9,810	9,770	9,780
15-19	8,190	9,540	8,070	10,300	8,570	9,700	9,670
20-24	7,240	6,610	9,340	7,910	10,100	8,430	9,550
25-29	8,020	5,320	6,440	9,120	7,740	9,930	8,280
30-34	6,610	6,420	5,180	6,290	8,920	7,590	9,760

TABLE A 26 (*Continued*)

Projected Population of the U.S.S.R., at Five-Year Intervals, 1940-1970: January-1939 Boundaries, Adjusted for Hypothetical War Losses

B. MALE POPULATION (*Continued*)

Age Group	Number (In thousands)						
	1940	1945	1950	1955	1960	1965	1970
35-39	5,380	5,500	6,240	5,050	6,150	8,740	7,450
40-44	3,790	4,740	5,310	6,040	4,910	5,960	8,540
45-49	3,020	3,270	4,520	5,080	5,800	4,700	5,760
50-54	2,720	2,640	3,060	4,240	4,790	5,490	4,460
55-59	2,260	2,300	2,400	2,790	3,890	4,410	5,080
60-64	1,780	1,830	2,010	2,100	2,460	3,450	3,920
65-69	1,330	1,340	1,490	1,650	1,740	2,040	2,880
70-74	874	889	976	1,090	1,220	1,300	1,540
75-79	512	486	552	613	695	786	846
80-84	194	206	229	265	299	345	396
85+	57	54	72	83	97	112	131

C. FEMALE POPULATION

Age Group	Number (In thousands)						
	1940	1945	1950	1955	1960	1965	1970
Total	90,500	89,700	95,500	100,800	105,900	110,600	114,700
0-4	11,700	9,110	10,200	10,000	9,930	9,770	9,460
5-9	8,850	10,400	8,720	9,820	9,720	9,660	9,540
10-14	10,600	8,220	10,300	8,610	9,710	9,630	9,580
15-19	8,400	9,860	8,100	10,100	8,510	9,610	9,540
20-24	7,280	7,750	9,660	7,950	9,960	8,380	9,470
25-29	8,600	6,680	7,560	9,450	7,790	9,780	8,240
30-34	7,270	7,860	6,490	7,370	9,240	7,630	9,600
35-39	6,480	6,620	7,620	6,320	7,190	9,040	7,490
40-44	4,820	5,890	6,410	7,400	6,150	7,020	8,840
45-49	3,860	4,360	5,680	6,200	7,170	5,980	6,840
50-54	3,320	3,450	4,160	5,430	5,930	6,880	5,740
55-59	2,750	2,900	3,220	3,890	5,090	5,570	6,480
60-64	2,300	2,310	2,610	2,910	3,530	4,640	5,100
65-69	1,790	1,810	1,960	2,230	2,510	3,060	4,030
70-74	1,250	1,280	1,400	1,530	1,760	1,990	2,440
75-79	783	754	853	947	1,040	1,210	1,380
80-84	308	354	390	448	504	564	664
85+	120	103	141	164	191	221	255

TABLE A 27

Factors for Adjusting Fertility of Surviving Women to Hypothetical Effect of Depletion of Male Population in War[1]

Age of Women at Mid-Point of Each Period	1945-1949	1950-1954	1955-1959	1960-1964	1965-1969
15-19	.9708	.9957	1.0000	1.0000	1.0000
20-24	.9314	.9708	.9957	1.0000	1.0000
25-29	.8849	.9314	.9708	.9957	1.0000
30-34	.9083	.8849	.9314	.9708	.9957
35-39	.9531	.9083	.8849	.9314	.9708
40-44	.9839	.9531	.9083	.8849	.9314
45-49	1.0000	.9839	.9531	.9083	.8849

[1] On the assumption that fertility otherwise expected will be reduced by 75 percent of the *difference* between the number of women in each age class and the mean number of men in adjacent age classes (averaged to give mean number at ages 2.5 years older than women), with the difference expressed as a ratio to the number of surviving women.

BIBLIOGRAPHY

THE transliteration of Russian names used here in maps, tables, references, and bibliography follows the recommendations of the Permanent Committee on Geographical Names of the Royal Geographical Society, 1942, with minor modifications recommended by the United States Board on Geographical Names, 1944. The report embodying the original recommendations is cited below [see Title 239]. The modifications recommended by the United States Board on Geographical Names are as follows:

e, ye. The latter is used only at the beginning of a word, or following a vowel, soft sign, or hard sign.

The half-vowel or short *i* in Russian (used only in conjunction with and following another vowel) is always rendered as *y*, even when it follows the full vowel which is also rendered as *y*.

dzh, j. The latter is not used.

The soft sign (which modifies the preceding consonant) is rendered as an apostrophe, as in the original recommendations; the hard sign is rendered as a double apostrophe.

In the text proper, the soft sign and the hard sign in transliterated Russian names are generally omitted. The more exact rendition of these names is given in the accompanying maps, tables, and references.

NOTE: The soft vowels rendered here as *ya, ye,* and *yu* appear in some transliterations, notably that of the Library of Congress, as *ia, ie,* and *iu,* and in French texts as *ja, je,* and *ju*. The vowel rendered here as *ë* or *yë* is sometimes rendered as *io, yo,* or *jo*. The half-vowel rendered here as *y* is omitted in some transliterations and is rendered as *i* in others.

For further discussion of the transliteration of Russian geographical names, see Chapter IV, Footnote 2.

PART I: AUTHORS

1. American Russian Institute. "Information from the Central Administration of National-Economic Accounts of Gosplan, USSR, concerning data of the All-Union Census of Population, 1939," *The American Quarterly on the Soviet Union* 3(2-3):97-100. 1940.

2. ———. "Results of the Soviet Census," *The American Quarterly on the Soviet Union* 3(2-3):89-96. 1940.

3. Antsyferov, Alexei N. "Russian rural economy during the war," in: *Russian Agriculture during the War*. Carnegie Endowment for International Peace. Economic and Social History of the World War. Russian series. New Haven, Yale University Press, 1930. pp. 1-300.

4. Aristov, N. "Organizovannyy nabor rabochey sily" (Organized recruitment of labor force), *Planovoye Khozyaystvo* 1939:11:89-99.

5. Arsen'yev, Konstantin. *Statisticheskiye ocherki Rossii* (Essays on Statistics in Russia). St. Petersburg, Akademiya Nauk, 1898. 503 pp.

6. Avilov, B. "K voprosu ob agrarnom perenaselenii" (On the question of agricultural overpopulation), *Ekonomicheskoye Obozreniye* 7(2):81-93. February, 1929.

7. Babynin, B. "Demograficheskaya baza planov narodnogo prosveshcheniya" (Demographic basis of the planning on national education), *Byulleten' Gosplana RSFSR* 1929:5-6:99-109.

8. ———. "Demograficheskiye predposylki perspektivnogo planirovaniya" (Demographic prerequisites of the prospective planning), *Planovoye Khozyaystvo* 1928:8:315-332.

9. ———. "Naseleniye rayonov RSFSR v dovoennyy period" (Population of the regions of RSFSR during the prewar period), *Byulleten' Gosplana RSFSR* 1928:17-18:58-70.

10. ———. "Naseleniye rayonov RSFSR v 1926-1941 gg." (Population of the regions of the RSFSR, 1926-1941), *Byulleten' Gosplana RSFSR* 1927:5-6:46-58.

11. ———. "Naseleniye RSFSR v 1926-1941 gg." (Population of the RSFSR during the period 1926-1941), *Byulleten' Gosplana RSFSR* 1926:23-24:20-38.

12. ———. "Perspektivnaya dinamika kontingentov detey vozrasta 8-11 let po RSFSR" (Prospective movement of the class, children aged 8-11 years, in the RSFSR), *Statistika i Narodnoye Khozyaystvo*, No. 2, pp. 71-81. Moscow, 1928.

13. ———. "Perspektivy rosta naseleniya SSSR v 1927/28-1932/33 gg." (The outlook for in-

crease in population of the USSR during the five-year period of 1927/28-1932/33), *Planovoye Khozyaystvo* 1928:10:320-338.

14. ———. "Perspektivy yestestvennogo dvizheniya naseleniya RSFSR na blizhayshiye gody" (Prospects of natural movement of population in RSFSR in the near future), *Statisticheskoye Obozreniye* 1930:4-6:121-126.

15. ———. "Sila smertnosti v RSFSR i rost naseleniya" (The extent of mortality in RSFSR and the increase of population), *Statisticheskoye Obozreniye* 1929:1:98-104.

16. ———. "Trudovye resursy kolkhozov i ikh ispol'zovaniye" (Working resources of collective farms and their utilization), *Problemy Ekonomiki* 1940:2:66-74.

17. Bagaley, D. I. *Materialy dlya istorii kolonizatsii i byta stepnoy okrainy Moskovskago gosudarstva, Khar'kovskoy i otchasti Kurskoy i Voronezhskoy gub. v XVI-XVIII stoletiyakh* (Materials for the History of Colonization and Life Conditions in the Steppe Outskirts of the Moscow State, in the Kharkov and Parts of the Kursk and Voronezh Provinces in the XVI-XVIII Centuries). Khar'kov, Istoriko-Filologicheskoye Obshchestvo pri Khar'kovskom Universitete, 1886, 1890. 2 vols.

18. Baikov, Alexander. "The development of agricultural production in the U.S.S.R.," London and Cambridge Economic Service, *Bulletin* 19(1):26-29. 1941; also: Royal Economic Society, *Memoirs*, February, 1941, pp. 26-29.

19. Baranskiy, N. N. *Ekonomicheskaya geografiya SSSR* (Economic Geography of the USSR). Fourth edition. Moscow, 1938. 364 pp.

20. Barnes, Kathleen. "Eastward migration within the Soviet Union," *Pacific Affairs* 7(4):395-405. 1934.

21. Bekunova, S. "Yestestvennoye dvizheniye naseleniya Evropeyskoy chasti RSFSR v 1924, 1925 i 1926 gg." (Natural movement of the European part of the RSFSR in the course of 1924, 1925 and 1926), *Statisticheskoye Obozreniye* 1928:1:98-101.

22. Benediktov, I. A. "Sel'skoye khozyaystvo v 1940 godu" (Agricultural economy in 1940), *Sotsialisticheskoye Sel'skoye Khozyaystvo* 1941:1:23-33.

23. Benenson, S. D. *Okhrana materinstva i mladenchestva* (Protection of Mothers and Infants). Perel and Lyubimova, Editors. Moscow, Narkompros, 1932. 83 pp.

24. ———. *Sotsial'noye obespecheniye detey* (Social Security of Children). Perel and Lyubimova, Editors. Moscow, Narkompros, 1932. 51 pp.

25. Berg, L. S. *Priroda S.S.S.R.* (Natural Conditions in the U.S.S.R.). Second edition. Moscow, Narkompros RSFSR, 1938. 312 pp.

26. Bergson, Abram. *The Structure of Soviet Wages; a Study in Socialist Economy.* Cambridge, Mass., Harvard University Press, 1944. 255 pp.

27. Berman, Nathan. "The place of the child in present day Russia," *Social Forces* 21(4):446-456. 1943.

28. Bernstein-Kogan, S. *Chislennost', sostav i polozheniye Peterburgskikh rabochikh. Opyt statisticheskago issledovaniya* (Number, Structure, and Position of the Workmen of St. Petersburg. A Statistical Inquiry). St. Petersburg, Trudy Studentov Ekonomicheskago Otdeleniya St. Peterburgskago Politekhnicheskago Instituta Imperatora Petra Velikago, No. 4, 1910. 188 pp.

29. Besser, L., and K. Ballod. *Smertnost', vozrastnoy sostav i dolgovechnost' pravoslavnago narodonaseleniya oboego pola v Rossii za 1851-1890 gody* (Mortality, Age Composition and Longevity of the Orthodox Population of Both Sexes in Russia, 1851-1890). St. Petersburg, Zapiski Imperatorskoy Akademii Nauk po Istoriko-Filologicheskomu Otdeleniyu, 1897. Vol. 1, No. 5, pp. 1-124.

30. Bogdanov, P. "Sostoyaniye i problemy razvitiya rayonnoy promyshlennosti RSFSR" (The state and problems of the development of regional industry), *Planovoye Khozyaystvo* 1936:-12:42-60.

31. Bogolyubskiy, D. "Razmery sem'i krest'yanskogo khozyaystva i prirost chisla khozyaystv za 1916-1927 gg." (The size of a peasant family and the increase of households for the years 1916-1927), *Statisticheskoye Obozreniye* 1929:9:31-36.

32. Bogoslovskiy, S. "Fizicheskoye razvitiye promyshlennykh rabochikh i sluzhashchikh" (Physical development of industrial workmen and employees), *Statisticheskoye Obozreniye* 1927:8:88-93; 12:91-98.

33. Bortkiewicz (Bortkewitsch, Bortkevich), L. von. "Das Problem der russischen Sterblichkeit," *Allgemeines statistisches Archiv* 5:175-190. 1899.

34. ———. "Russische Sterbetafeln," *Allgemeines statistisches Archiv* 3:23-65. 1894.

35. ———. *Smertnost' i dolgovechnost' muzhskogo pravoslavnago naseleniya Evropeyskoy Rossii* (Mortality and Longevity of the Male Orthodox Population of European Russia). St. Petersburg, Zapiski Imperatorskoy Akademii Nauk. Vol. 63, Suppl. 8, 1890. 102 pp.

36. ———. *Smertnost' i dolgovechnost' zhenskago pravoslavnago naseleniya Evropeyskoy Rossii* (Mortality and Longevity of the Female Orthodox Population of European Russia). St. Petersburg, Zapiski Imperatorskoy Akademii Nauk. Vol. 66, Suppl. 3, 1891. 18 pp.

37. Bowman, Isaiah. "Imprisoned Siberia," in: *The Pioneer Fringe*. New York, American Geographical Society, 1931. pp. 241-266.

38. Brutskus, B. D. *Agrarnyy vopros i agrarnaya politika* (Agrarian Question and Agrarian Policy). St. Petersburg, Pravo, 1922. 235 pp.

39. Bukhman, N. "Golod 1921 goda i deyatel'nost' inostrannykh organizatsiy" (The famine of 1921 and the activity of the foreign organizations), *Vestnik Statistiki* 1923:4-6:87-113.

40. Buschen, A. B. von. *Aperçu statistique des forces productives de la Russie*. Paris, Imprimerie générale de Lahure, 1867. 268 pp.

41. ———. *Bevölkerung des russischen Kaiserreiches in den wichtigsten statistischen Verhältnissen dargestellt*. Gotha, Justus Peters, 1862. 61 pp.

42. Buzin, D. "Naseleniye strany sotsializma" (Population of the socialist country), *Problemy Ekonomiki* 1939:5:35-46.

43. ———, and I. Dubrovitskiy. "Pervyye itogi vsesoyuznoy perepisi naseleniya 1939 goda" (The first returns of the All-Union Census of Population, 1939), *Planovoye Khozyaystvo* 1939:6:-18-33.
Carnegie Endowment for International Peace. Economic and Social History of the World War. Russian series. (*See* Antsyferov, Golovine, Kohn, Meyendorff.)

44. Carr-Saunders, A. M. *World Population. Past Growth and Present Trends*. Oxford, The Clarendon Press, 1936. 336 pp.

45. Chaslavskiy, V. I. *Zemledel'cheskiye otkhozhiye promysly v svyazi s pereseleniyem krest'yan* (Agricultural Seasonal Work in Connection with Migration of Peasants). St. Petersburg, Sbornik Gosudarstvennykh Znaniy pod red. V. P. Bazarova, 1875. Vol. II, pp. 181-211.

46. Chechulin, N. D. *Nachalo v Rossii perepisey i khod ikh do kontsa XVI veka* (The Commencement and Procedure of Russian Census to the End of the 16th Century). St. Petersburg, Bibliograf, 1889. 23 pp.

47. Cherevanin, F. A. (*See* Libkind, A.) "Vliyaniye kolebaniy urozhayev na sel'skoye khozyaystvo v techenii 40 let 1883-1923 gg." (The influence of crop-fluctuation on the agricultural economy in the course of 40 years, 1883-1923), in: V. G. Groman, *Vliyaniye neurozhayev na narodnoye khozyaystvo Rossii*. Vol. I, pp. 160-301.

48. Chernyak, S., and G. Karanovich. *Sbornik deystvuyushchego zakonodatel'stva po zdravookhraneniyu* (Collection of the Laws on the Protection of Health). K. Konovalov, V. Berezin, and S. Makarenkov, Editors. Moscow, Gosud. Meditsinskoye Izd., 1929.

49. Chernyshev, I. V. *Sel'skoye khozyaystvo dovoennoy Rossii i SSSR* (Agricultural Economy in Prewar Russia and in the USSR). Moscow and Leningrad, Gos. Izd., 1926. 200 pp.

50. Chudnovskiy, N. "Narodnoye obrazovaniye v SSSR" (Public education in the USSR), *Planovoye Khozyaystvo* 1939:7:87-100.

51. Churayev, A. *Naseleniye Vostochnoy Sibiri* (Population of Eastern Siberia). Moscow, Irkutsk, 1933.

52. Clark, Colin. *A Critique of Russian Statistics*. London, Macmillan, 1939. 76 pp.

53. ———. *The Conditions of Economic Progress*. London, 1940. 504 pp.

54. Cleynow, Georg. *Neu-Sibirien. Eine Studie zum Aufmarsch der Sowjetmacht in Asien*. Berlin, Hobbing, 1928. 426 pp.

55. Conover, Helen F. *Soviet Russia: A Selected List of Recent References*. Washington, The Library of Congress. Division of Bibliography, 1943. 85 pp.

56. Conus, Esfir M. *Protection of Motherhood and Childhood in the Soviet Union*. Moscow-Leningrad, State Medical Editors, 1933. 117 pp.

57. Czaplička, Marie Antoinette. *Aboriginal Siberia*. Oxford, The Clarendon Press, 1914. 374 pp.
58. ———. *The Turks of Central Asia*. Oxford, The Clarendon Press, 1918. 242 pp.
Daniel'son, N. F. (*See* Nikolai-on.)
59. Davies, Raymond A., and Andrew J. Steiger. *Soviet Asia*. New York, The Dial Press, 1942. 384 pp.
60. Demidov, S. "Sotsialisticheskoye zemledeliye v 1941 godu" (Socialist agriculture in the year 1941), *Sotsialisticheskoye Sel'skoye Khozyaystvo* 1941:2:19-30.
61. Den, V. E. *Istochniki vazhneyshikh otrasley khozyaystvennoy statistiki SSSR* (Sources of the Most Important Branches of the Economic Statistics in the USSR). Leningrad, Priboy, 1929. 96 pp.
62. ———. *Kurs ekonomicheskoy geografii* (Textbook of Economic Geography). Leningrad, Gos. Izd. First edition, 1924, 625 pp.; Third edition, 1928, 595 pp.
63. ———. *Naseleniye Rossii po pyatoy revisii. Podushnaya podat' v XVIII veke i statistika naseleniya v kontse XVIII veka. Tom pervyy* (Population of Russia according to the Fifth Revision. Poll Tax during the 18th Century and Statistics of the Population at the End of the 18th Century). Moscow, 1902. Vol. I, 377 pp.
64. ———, and B. J. Karpenko. *Khozyaystvennaya statistika SSSR* (Economic Statistics of USSR). Leningrad, Priboy, 1930. 269 pp.
65. Dessonaz, George. "La famine en Russie (Ukraine)," *Revue internationale de la Croix-Rouge* 4(42):469-492. 1922.
66. Divnogortsev, D. "Migratsiya naseleniya cherez granitsy SSSR v 1926 godu" (Migration of the population through the frontiers of USSR in 1926), *Statisticheskoye Obozreniye* 1928:1:-101-104.
67. ———. "Yestestvennoye dvizheniye naseleniya v sel'skikh mestnostyakh na okrainakh SSSR v 1926 g." (Natural movement of the rural population of the borderlands of the USSR in the year 1926), *Statisticheskoye Obozreniye* 1928:4:99-101.
68. ———. "Yestestvennyy prirost naseleniya v sel'skikh mestnostyakh ZSFSR v 1926 godu" (Natural increase of the rural population in Transcaucasus in 1926), *Statisticheskoye Obozreniye* 1927:9:87-89.
69. Doerbeck, F. *Geschichte der Pestepidemien in Russland*. Breslau, Kern, 1906. 220 pp.
70. Dubnov, S. M. *History of the Jews in Russia and Poland*. Translated by I. Friedlaender. Philadelphia, The Jewish Publication Society of America, 1916. Vol. I, 413 pp.
71. Dubrovitskiy, L. "Narodonaseleniye Sovetskogo Soyuza" (Population of the Soviet Union), *Bol'shevik* 1939:15-16:109-123.
72. Dyubyuk, P. "Prishloye naseleniye Sredne-Aziatskoy chasti Soyuza po dannym perepisi 1926 g." (Immigrant population of the Central-Asiatic part of the USSR in the Census of 1926), *Statisticheskoye Obozreniye* 1929:6:100-106.
73. Ekk, Nikolay. *Opyt obrabotki statisticheskikh dannykh o smertnosti v Rossii* (An Attempt at Statistical Analysis of Mortality in Russia). St. Petersburg, 1888. 72 pp.
74. Eykhfeld, J. G. *Sel'sko-khozyaystvennoye osvoeniye Kraynego Severa* (Agricultural Cultivation of the Extreme North). Moscow, Selsko-iz, 1938. 148 pp.
75. Eykhvald, Eduard E. *K voprosu ob umen'shenii smertnosti v Rossii* (The Decline of Mortality in Russia). St. Petersburg, 1887. 64 pp.
76. Feld, S. "Balansovye svyazi mezhdu promyshlennost'yu i sel'skim khozyaystvom" (Balanced connection between industry and agriculture), *Planovoye Khozyaystvo* 1940:7:44-60.
77. Ferrière, Fréderic. "Situation épidémique de la Russie," *Revue internationale de la Croix-Rouge* 4(40):273-283. 1922.
78. Finn-Enotajewsky, A. "Die Grundlinien der wirtschaftlichen Entwicklung Russlands (1861-1917)," *Archiv für Sozialwissenschaft und Sozialpolitik* 64(3):547-594. 1930.
79. Gantt, W. Horsley. *History of Russian Medicine*. New York, Hoebar, 1937. 214 pp.
80. Gens, A. "Iskustvennyy abort kak sotsial'nobytovoye yavleniye" (Social-economic aspects of abortion), *Bol'shaya Meditsinskaya Entsiklopediya*. Vol. 1, Col. 40-47.
81. Gernet, M. "K statistike abortov" (On abortion statistics), *Statisticheskoye Obozreniye* 1927:3:66-69.

82. ———. "Povtornyye i mnogokratnyye aborty" (Repeated and reiterated abortions), *Statisticheskoye Obozreniye* 1928:12:110-114.

83. ———. "Statistika deto-ubiystv" (Statistics of infanticide), *Statisticheskoye Obozreniye* 1928:2:102-106.

84. Gibson, Etienne. "Enquête sur la situation actuelle des enfants en l'Ukraine et dans la région de la Volga," *Revue internationale de la Croix-Rouge* 4(46):883-897. 1922.

85. Golder, F. A. *Russian Expansion on the Pacific, 1641-1850.* Cleveland, Clark, 1914. 368 pp.

86. Golovine, Nicholas N. *The Russian Army in the World War.* Carnegie Endowment for International Peace. Economic and Social History of the World War. Russian series. New Haven, Yale University Press, 1931. 287 pp.

87. Goncharova, E. A. *Smertnost' i prodolzhitel'nost' zhizni naseleniya Karel'skoy A.S.S.R., 1926-27 gg.* (Mortality and Longevity of the Population of the Karelian Republic during the Years 1926-27). Leningrad, Akademiya Nauk SSSR. Trudy Demografîcheskogo Instituta, 1934. Vol. I, pp. 213-233.

88. Gozulov, A. I. *Morfologiya naseleniya* (The Morphology of Population). Rostov-na-Donu, Statisticheskoye Upravleniye Severn. Kavk. Kraya, 1929. 442 pp.

89. ———. *Perepisi naseleniya SSSR i kapitalisticheskikh stran* (The Census of the USSR and Capitalistic Countries). S. G. Strumilin, Editor. Moscow, TSUNKHU Gosplana i Soyuzouchet, 1936. 588 pp.

90. Great Britain. Foreign Office. *Eastern Siberia.* London, 1920.

91. Grierson, Philip. *Books on Soviet Russia, 1917-1942.* London, Methuen, 1943. 354 pp. (Annotated bibliography, complete for British publications only.)

92. Groman, V. G., Editor. *Vliyaniye neurozhayev na narodnoye khozyaystvo Rossii* (The Influence of Poor Crops on the National Economy of Russia). Moscow, Institut Ekonomiki, 1927. 2 vols. in 1.

93. Grunfeld, Judith. "Women's work in Russia's planned economy," *Social Research* 9(1):22-45. 1942.

94. Harper, Samuel Northrop, Editor. *The Soviet Union and World Problems.* Chicago, University of Chicago Press, 1935. xviii, 253 pp.

95. Hazard, John H. *Soviet Housing Law.* New Haven, Yale University Press, 1939. 178 pp.

96. Heyking, Baron A. Von. "The economic resources of Russia, with special reference to British opportunities," *Journal of the Royal Statistical Society* 80(2):187-221. 1917.

97. Hoffmann, Michael. *Die agrarische Übervölkerung Russlands.* Berlin-Mannheim, 1932. 143 pp.

98. Hopper, Bruce. "Population factors in Soviet Siberia," in: Isaiah Bowman, Editor, *Limits of Land Settlement.* New York, Council of Foreign Relations. 1937. pp. 89-118.

99. Hrdlička, Aleš. *The People of the Soviet Union.* Smithsonian Institution, War Background Studies, No. 3. Washington, 1942. 29 pp.

100. Hubbard, Leonard E. *Soviet Labor and Industry.* London, Macmillan, 1942. 315 pp.

101. ———. *The Economics of Soviet Agriculture.* London, Macmillan, 1939. 315 pp.

102. Hudson, Alfred E. *Kazak Social Structure.* Yale University Publications in Anthropology, No. 20. New Haven, 1938. 109 pp.

103. L'Institut international de statistique. *Aperçu de la démographie des divers pays du monde, 1929-1936.* La Haye, 1939. 433 pp.

104. International Labour Office. "The Five-Year Plan and the regulation of the labour market in the USSR," *International Labour Review* 27(3):349-377. 1933.

105. ———. *The Trade Union Movement in Soviet Russia.* Geneva, 1927. 289 pp.
    ———. (*See* also Kulischer, Eugene M.)

106. Ioffe, Ya. A. *SSSR i kapitalisticheskiye strany. Statisticheskiy sbornik tekhniko-ekonomicheskikh pokazateley narodnogo khozyaystva SSSR i kapitalisticheskikh stran za 1913-1937 gg.* (USSR and the Capitalistic Countries. Statistical Reference Book of Technical and Economic Indices of the National Economy of USSR and of Capitalistic Countries for the Years 1913-1937). L. Eventov, Editor. Moscow, Gos. Izd., 1939. 330 pp.

107. Isaev, A. A. *Pereseleniya v Russkom narodnom khozyaystve* (Migration in the Russian National Economy). St. Petersburg, Tsingerling, 1891. 192 pp.

108. Ivanov, M. "Rezervy sotsialisticheskogo sel'skogo khozyaystva" (Reserves of the socialist agricultural economy), *Planovoye Khozyaystvo* 1940:11:111-118.

109. Jochelson, Vladimir I. *Peoples of Asiatic Russia*. New York, American Museum of Natural History, 1928. 259 pp.

110. Just, Arthur W. *Die Soviet Union: Staat, Wirtschaft, Heer*. Berlin, Junker and Dünnhaupt, 1940. 140 pp.

111. Kablukov, N. A. *Statistika* (Statistics). Fifth edition. Moscow, Ts. S. U., 1922. xii, 319 pp.

112. Kaplun, M. "Brachnost' naseleniya RSFSR" (Marriages among the population of the RSFSR), *Statisticheskoye Obozreniye* 1929:7:90-97.

113. Kaufmann, Alexander. "Das russische Übersiedlungs- und Kolonisationsgesetz vom 6/19. Juni 1904 und die Aussichten der inneren Kolonisation in Russland," *Archiv für Sozialwissenschaft und Sozialpolitik* 22(2):371-423. 1906.

114. ———. "Die innere Kolonisation und die Kolonisationspolitik Russlands nach der Bauernbefreiung," *Jahrbücher für Nationalökonomie und Statistik*, Third series, 15(4):417-455. 1898.

115. ———. *Khozyaystvennoye polozheniye pereselentsev vodvorennykh na kazennykh zemlyakh Tomskoy gubernii po dannym proizvedennogo v 1894 godu po porucheniyu g. Tomskago gubernatora podvornago issledovaniya* (Economic Condition of Migrants Settled on State Estates of the Tomsk Gub. according to an Investigation assigned by the Governor of Tomsk in 1894). St. Petersburg, 1895-1896. 3 vols.

116. ———. *Pereseleniye i kolonizatsiya* (Migration and Colonization). St. Petersburg, Obshchestvennaya Pol'za, 1905. 349+ 81 pp.

117. ———. *Sbornik statey: obshchina, pereseleniye i statistika* (Collection of Essays on Community, Migration and Statistics). Moscow, Leman and Pletnev, 1915. 512 pp.

118. ———. "The history and development of the official Russian statistics," in: John Koren, Editor, *The History of Statistics*. New York, Macmillan, 1918. pp. 468-534.

119. ———. "Zemleustroystvo i zemel'naya politika" (Land settlement and agrarian policy), *Yezhegodnik gazety Rech'* 1912:189-216; 1913:90-115; 1914:84-116.

120. Kazantseva, M. N. "25 let Sovetskogo zdravookhraneniya v oblasti okhrany materinstva i detstva" (25 years of Soviet health protection in the care of mothers and children), *Pediatriya* 1942:6:11-26.

121. Keppen, P. I. *O narodnykh perepisyakh v Rossii* (On Census of Population in Russia). St. Petersburg, Zapiski Imper. Geograficheskago Obshchestva po Otdeleniyu Statistiki, 1889. Vol. 6, pp. 1-94.

122. Kerner, Robert J. *Northeastern Asia: A Selected Bibliography*. Berkeley, University of California Press, 1939. 2 vols.

123. ———. *The Urge to the Sea; the Course of Russian History. The Role of Rivers, Postages, Ostrogs, Monasteries and Furs*. Berkeley and Los Angeles, University of California Press, 1942. xvii, 212 pp.

124. Kheyman, S. "Materialy k kharakteristike zakona naseleniya" (Materials on the characteristics of the law of population), *Problemy Ekonomiki* 1935:6:88-103.

125. ———. "Tekuchest' rabochego sostava v promyshlennosti SSSR" (Labor turnover in Soviet industry), *Statisticheskoye Obozreniye* 1928:5:56-66.

126. Kholodny. "La situation sanitaire de l'Ukraine," *Revue internationale de la Croix-Rouge* 4(40):284-290. 1922.

127. Khryashcheva, A. J. *Gruppy i klassy v krest'yanstve* (Peasant Groups and Classes). Second edition. Moscow, 1926. 171 pp.

128. King, Beatrice. *Changing Man. The Education System of the USSR*. London, Gollancz, 1936. 319 pp.

129. Kingsbury, Susan M., and Mildred Fairchild. *Factory, Family and Woman in the Soviet Union*. New York, Putnam, 1935. 334 pp.

Klinger, G. K. (*See* Lozovskiy and Bibin.)

130. Klochkov, M. *Naseleniye Rossii pri Petre Velikom po perepisyam togo vremeni. Tom pervyy. Perepisi dvorov i naseleniya, 1678-1721* (Population of Russia at the Time of Peter the Great according to the Census of that Time. Vol. I. Census of Homesteads and Population, 1678-1721). St. Petersburg, Zapiski Istoriko-Filologicheskago Fakul'teta Imper. St. Peterburgskago Universiteta, 1911. 435 pp.

131. Kluchevsky (Klyuchevskiy), V. O. *A History of Russia*. Translated by C. I. Hogarth. London, Dent, 1931; New York, Dutton, 1931. 5 vols.

132. Kohn, Hans. *Nationalism in Soviet Russia*. London, Routledge, 1933. 164 pp.

133. Kohn, Stanislas. "The vital statistics of European Russia during the World War, 1914-1917," in: *The Cost of the War to Russia*. Carnegie Endowment for International Peace. Economic and Social History of the World War. Russian series. New Haven, Yale University Press, 1932. pp. 3-154.

134. Komarov, V. "Problemy razvitiya dal'nevostochnogo kraya" (Problems of the development of the Far Eastern region), *Planovoye Khozyaystvo* 1936:2:168-187.

Konstantinov, O. A. *See* Title 512.

135. Kopelyanskaya, S. E. *Sotsial'no-pravovaya pomoshch' materi i rebënku. Yuridicheskiy spravochnik i prakticheskoye posobiye* (Socio-juridical Assistance to Mother and Child. Juridical Reference and Textbook). Moscow, Gos. Izd., Sovetskoye Zakonodatel'stvo, 1934. 125 pp.

136. Korobkov, N. "Pereseleniye—krupnaya gosudarstvennaya problema" (Migration—the big state problem), *Planovoye Khozyaystvo* 1939:9:71-80.

137. Korobov, A. "Rayonnyy razrez narodno-khozyaystvennogo plana" (Regional division of the national economic plan), *Planovoye Khozyaystvo* 1939:1:58-68.

138. ———. "Sotsialisticheskoye razmeshcheniye proizvoditel'nykh sil" (Socialistic distribution of productive forces), *Planovoye Khozyaystvo* 1939:3:53-67.

139. Korsunovskiy, S. "Emigratsiya iz SSSR v zaokeanskiye strany" (The emigration from USSR to transoceanic countries), *Statisticheskoye Obozreniye* 1929:11:111-116.

140. ———. "Migratsiya naseleniya cherez granitsy SSSR v 1927 godu" (Population migration over the borders of the USSR in 1927), *Statisticheskoye Obozreniye* 1928:11:93-98.

141. ———. "Migratsiya naseleniya cherez granitsy SSSR v 1928 godu" (Population migration over the borders of the USSR in 1928), *Statisticheskoye Obozreniye* 1929:10:103-107.

142. Kraev, M. "Stalinskaya konstitutsiya i zemel'nyy stroy SSSR" (The Stalin Constitution and land settlement in USSR), *Planovoye Khozyaystvo* 1936:11:77-100.

143. Krasilnikian, Serge. *Russische Erfahrungen mit der Freigabe der Abtreibung*. Berlin, Ebermayer, 1930.

144. Krasil'nikov, M. "Agrarnoye pereseleniye v 1928/29 g." (Migration of agrarian population in 1928/29), *Statisticheskoye Obozreniye* 1930:5:84-92.

145. ———. "K voprosu ob ugasanii severnykh narodnostey" (On the extinction of the northern tribes), *Statisticheskoye Obozreniye* 1928:2:45-55.

146. ———. "Pereseleniye v 1925 i 1926 godakh" (Migration in the years 1925 and 1926), *Statisticheskoye Obozreniye* 1928:2:90-95.

147. ———. "Pereselentsy-obratniki" (Returning migrants), *Statisticheskoye Obozreniye* 1929:2:97-100.

148. ———. "Sostav pereselentsev" (The composition of migrants), *Statisticheskoye Obozreniye* 1928:12:107-110.

149. ———. "Svyaz' naseleniya goroda Moskvy s nadel'noy zemlëy" (Population of the city of Moscow and land allotments), *Statisticheskoye Obozreniye* 1928:6:103-107.

150. Kraval', I. A. "Itogi perepisi skota na 1. yanvarya 1936 goda" (Cattle census on January 1, 1936), *Planovoye Khozyaystvo* 1936:4:5-79.

151. ———. "Vsesoyuznaya perepis' naseleniya 1937 goda" (All-Soviet Census of Population of 1937), *Planovoye Khozyaystvo* 1936:12:17-35.

152. Krupskaya, N. K. *Novyy zakon o materi i detyakh* (The New Law on Mothers and Children). Moscow, Ogiz, 1936. 31 pp.

153. Kubiovich, Vladimir. *Die Verteilung der Bevölkerung in der Ukraine*. Berlin, Gesellschaft der Freunde des Ukrainischen wissenschaftlichen Instituts, 1934. 37 pp.

154. Kuczynski, Robert. *The Balance of Births and Deaths*. Vol. II. Eastern and Southern Europe. Washington, The Brookings Institution, 1931. 164 pp.

155. Kulischer, Alexandre. "La théorie des mouvements des peuples et la guerre civile en Russie," *Revue internationale de sociologie* 32:492-507. 1924.

156. ———, and Eugen M. Kulischer. *Kriegs- und Wanderzüge: Weltgeschichte als Völkerbewegung*. Berlin, W. de Gruyter, 1932. 230 pp.

157. Kulischer, Eugene M. *The Displacement of Population in Europe*. Montreal, International Labour Office, 1943. 171 pp.

158. Kulischer, I. *Istoriya Russkogo narodnogo khozyaystva* (History of Russian National Economy). Moscow, Kooperativnoye Izdatel'stvo "Mir," 1925. 2 vols.

159. ———. *Russische Wirtschaftsgeschichte*. Band I in: Handbuch der Wirtschaftsgeschichte, herausgeg. von G. Brodnitz. Jena, G. Fischer, 1925. 458 pp.

160. Kurkin, P. "Rost naseleniya v Soyuza SSR" (Growth of the population in USSR), *Nashi Dostizheniya* 1929:1:129-142.

161. Kuvshinnikov, P. A. "Yestestvennoye dvizheniye naseleniya RSFSR v 1920-1922 gg." (The natural movement of the population in the RSFSR in 1920-1922), *Vestnik Statistiki* 1925:4-6:99-135.

162. Kvitkin, O. A. "Naseleniye gorodov Evropeyskoy chasti RSFSR po perepisyam 1897, 1917, 1920 i 1923 godov" (Urban population of the European part of RSFSR according to the census of 1896, 1917, 1920, and 1923), *Byulleten' TSU RSFSR* 77:10-28. 1923.

163. Ladejinsky, W., and Alexander Gourvitch. "Some hints from foreign experience: Russia" (adapted by Theresa Richman), in: Carter Goodrich and Others, *Migration and Economic Opportunity*. Philadelphia, University of Pennsylvania Press, 1936. pp. 521-538.

164. Lagolim, B. "Rozhdaemost' po g. Moskve v svyazi s sotsial'nym sostavom naseleniya" (Differential fertility in the city of Moscow), *Statisticheskoye Obozreniye* 1928:10:85-88.

165. Laptev, I. D. *Razmeshcheniye sotsialisticheskogo zernovogo khozyaystva* (Distribution of the Socialist Grain-economy). Akademiya Nauk, Institut Ekonomiki (Academy of Science, Institute of Economics). Moscow, Sel'khogiz, 1940. 192 pp.

166. Latsis, M. I. *Agrarnoye perenaseleniye* (Agrarian Overpopulation). Moscow-Leningrad, Gos. Izd., 1929. 142 pp.

League of Nations. (*See* Notestein, Frank W.)

167. Lederer, Emil. "Das Problem der russischen Wirtschafts- und Sozialverfassung," *Archiv für Sozialwissenschaft und Sozialpolitik* 68(3):257-285. 1932.

168. Lenin, V. I. *Razvitiye kapitalizma v Rossii* (The Development of Capitalism in Russia). Works, Vol. III. Second edition. Moscow-Leningrad, Gos. Izd. 1930. 624 pp.

169. Levi, M. F. "Dvatsat' let deyatel'nosti organov okhrany materinstva i mladenchestva" (Twenty years of work by the organizations for protection of mothers and children), *Akusherstvo i Ginekologiya* 1937:11:5-18.

170. ———. "Rol' sanitarno-kulturnoy raboty v dele realizatsii zakona o zapreshchenii abortov" (Place of educational work in realization of the prohibition of abortion), *Voprosy Materinstva i Mladenchestva* 1937:9-10:1-8.

171. Libkind, A. (*See* Cherevanin.) "Kollektivizatsiya derevni i agrarnoye perenaseleniye" (Rural collectivization and agrarian overpopulation), *Na Agrarnom Fronte* 1930:40:74-87.

172. ———. "Mekhanizatsiya zemledeliya i prevrashcheniye sel'sko-khozyaystvennogo truda v raznovidnost' industrial'nogo truda" (Mechanization of agriculture and transformation of agricultural labor into industrial labor), *Planovoye Khozyaystvo* 1937:9-10:87-107.

173. ———. "Sdvigi v razmeshchenii sel'sko-khozyaystvennykh kul'tur" (Improvement in the distribution of agriculture), *Problemy Ekonomiki* 1938:3:62-83.

174. ———. "Sotsial'no-ekonomicheskaya geografiya krest'yanskogo khozyaystva" (Social-economic geography of peasant economy), *Na Agrarnom Fronte* 1929:2:43-68; 3:37-61.

175. Litvinov, I. I. *Ekonomicheskiye posledstviya Stolypinskogo agrarnogo zakonodatel'stva* (Economic Consequences of the Stolypin Agrarian Law). Moscow-Leningrad, Gos. Izd., 1929. 144 pp.

176. Litvinov-Falinskii, V. P. *Novyye zakony o strakhovanii rabochikh* (New Legislation on Workers' Insurance). St. Petersburg, Suvorin, 1912. 364 pp.

177. Lodygensky, Georges. "La famine en Russie soviétique," *Revue internationale de la Croix-Rouge* 3:794-802. 1921.

178. Lozovskiy, I., and T. Bibin. *Sovetskaya politika za 10 let po natsional'nomu voprosu v RSFSR. Sistematicheskiy sbornik deystvuyushchikh aktov pravitel'stv SSSR i RSFSR. Okt. 1917-Noyabr' 1927* (Soviet Policy on the Problem of Nationalities of the RSFSR during Ten Years. Systematic Collection of Acts Issued by the Governments of the USSR and the RSFSR). G. K. Klinger, Editor. Moscow, Gos. Izd., 1928. xxxvi, 499 pp.

179. Lubny-Gertsyk, L. I. *Chto takoye perenaseleniye* (What is Overpopulation)? Moscow, Vysshiy Sovet Narodnogo Khozyaystva, 1923. 101 pp.

180. ———. *Dvizheniye naseleniya na territorii SSSR za vremya mirovoy voyny i revolyutsii* (Population Movement on the Territory of the USSR during the World War and the Revolution). Moscow, Gosplan, 1926. 124 pp.

181. ———. "Yestestvennoye dvizheniye naseleniya SSSR za 1926 god" (Natural movement of the population of the USSR in 1926), *Statisticheskoye Obozreniye* 1928:8:85-90.

182. Lyashchenko, P. I. *Istoriya narodnogo khozyaystva SSSR* (History of National Economy in the USSR). Akademiya Nauk SSSR, Institut Ekonomiki. Moscow, Gosud. Sots.-Ekonom. Izd., 1939. Vol. I, 675 pp.

183. Lyubavskiy, M. K. *Obrazovaniye osnovnoy gosudarstvennoy territorii velikoy narodnosti; zaseleniye i ob'yedineniye tsentra* (Formation of the Basic Territory of the Great Russian Nationality; Colonization and Unification of the Center). Leningrad, Akademiya Nauk, 1929. 175 pp.

184. Magodovich, I. "Dinamika klassovogo sostava i dokhodov naseleniya SSSR za 1924-27 gg." (Changes in the social structure and the income of the population of the USSR during the period 1924-27), *Statisticheskoye Obozreniye* 1928:11:79-88.

185. Mandel, William. *The Soviet Far East and Central Asia.* New York, Institute of Pacific Relations, 1944. 158 pp.

186. Marbut, C. F. "Agriculture in the United States and Russia: A comparative study of natural conditions," *Geographical Review* 31(10):598-612. 1931.

187. Markus, B. "Sotsialisticheskoye vosproizvodstvo rabochey sily i yeyë ispol'zovaniye" (Socialist reconstruction of labor power and its utilization), *Problemy Ekonomiki* 1940:10:3-29.

188. Maslov, Pavel. *Perenaseleniye Russkoy derevni* (Overpopulation of Russian Villages). Moscow-Leningrad, Gos. Izd., 1930. 142 pp.

189. Maslov, Pëtr. *Agrarnyy vopros v Rossii* (Agrarian Question in Russia). Sixth edition. Moscow, Gos. Izd., 1926. 430 pp.

190. Mendeleev, D. *K poznaniyu Rossii* (Toward the Understanding of Russia). St. Petersburg, Suvorin, 1906. 157 pp.

191. Mertons, O. *Tridtsat' let (1882-1911) Russkoy zhelezno-dorozhnoy politiki i yeyë ekonomicheskoye znacheniye* (Thirty Years, 1882-1911, of the Russian Railway-transport Policy and its Economic Importance). Moscow, Nar. Kom. Putey Soob. [No date.] 280 pp.

192. Meyendorff, Alexander F. "Social cost of the war," in: *The Cost of the War to Russia.* Carnegie Endowment for International Peace. Economic and Social History of the World War. Russian series. New Haven, Yale University Press, 1932. pp. 154-215.

193. Michael, Louis G. "The Soviet Ukraine, its people and agriculture," *Foreign Agriculture* 3(7):281-306. July, 1939.

194. Mikhailov (Mikhaylov), Nicholas. *Land of the Soviets.* Translated by N. Rothstein. New York, Furman, 1939. 351 pp.

195. ———. *Soviet Geography. The New Industrial and Economic Distribution of the USSR.* Foreword by Sir Halford I. Mackinder. London, Methuen, 1937. 229 pp.

196. Mikhaylovsky, V. G., Editor. "Svodka dinamiki vsego naseleniya byvshey Tsarskoy Rossii za period 1.1.1800-1.1.1917" (Summary of the movement of the total population of former Tsarist Russia from January 1, 1800 to January 1, 1917), in: Ts.S.K., *Statisticheskiy Yezhegodnik Rossii*, 1916, Vyp. 1. [1918].

197. Miklashevskiy, I. N. *K istorii khozyaystvennago byta Moskovskago Gosudarstva. I. Zaseleniye i sel'skoye khozyaystvo yuzhnoy okrainy XVII veka* (On the History of Economic Conditions of the Moscow State. I. Colonization and Agriculture of Southern Outskirts during the 17th Century). Moscow, Inozemtsev, 1894. 310 pp.

198. Milyukov, Pavel N. (Milyoukov, Paul N.) *Gosudarstvennoye khozyaystvo Rossii v pervoy chetverti XVIII stoletiya i reforma Petra Velikago* (State Economy of Russia during the First Quarter of the 18th Century and the Reforms of Peter the Great). Second edition. St. Petersburg, Pirozhkov, 1905. 679 pp.

199. ———. *Ocherki po istorii Russkoy kul'tury. I. Naseleniye, ekonomicheskiy, gosudarstvennyy i soslovnyy stroy* (Outline of the History of Russian Culture. Part I. Population, Economic, Political and Class Structure). Sixth edition. St. Petersburg, Aleksandrov, 1909. 316 pp.

200. ———. *Russia and Its Crisis*. Chicago, University of Chicago Press, 1906. 589 pp.

201. Mints, L. E. *Agrarnoye perenaseleniye i rynok truda v SSSR* (Surplus of the Farm-rural Population and Labor-market in the USSR). Introduction by S. G. Strumilin. Moscow-Leningrad, Gos. Izd., 1929. 470 pp.

202. ———. "Otkhozhiye promysly v SSSR" (Peasants' work outside home areas in USSR), *Statisticheskoye Obozreniye* 1928:2:45-55; 9:55-62.

203. Mirsky, D. S. *Russia, a Social History*. C. G. Seligman, Editor. London, The Cresset Press, 1931. xix, 312, xxi pp.

204. Miterev, G. A. *Narodnoye zdravookhraneniye za 25 let Sovetskoy vlasti* (The Protection of the People's Health in 25 Years of Soviet Power). Moscow, Narkomzdrav SSSR Medgiz, 1942. 97 pp.

205. Mkrtumov, A. "Sel'skoye khozyaystvo v 1940 g." (Agricultural economy in 1940), *Planovoye Khozyaystvo* 1940:2:56-70.

206. Molotov, V. M. *The Plan and Our Tasks*. (Report at the second session of the Central Executive Committee of the USSR of the National Economy Plan for 1936.) Moscow, Cooperative Publishing Society of Foreign Workers, 1936. 71 pp.

207. ———. "Tretiy pyatiletniy plan razvitiya narodnogo khozyaystva SSSR" (Third Five-Year Plan of development of national economy of USSR), Report at the XVIII Conference of the Communist Party of USSR, *Problemy Ekonomiki* 1939:3:37-85.

208. Morrison, John A. "The evolution of the territorial-administrative system of the USSR," *The American Quarterly on the Soviet Union* 1(3):25-46. 1938.

209. Myakotin, V. A. *Ocherki sotsialnoy istorii Ukrainy v XVII-XVIII vekakh*. T. I, Vyp. 1-3 (Outline of the Social History of the Ukraine in the Seventeenth and Eighteenth Centuries. Vol. I, Books 1-3). Prague, Votaga and Plamya, 1924-26. 3 vols.
National Bureau of Economic Research. (*See* Willcox, Walter F.)

210. Newsholme, Sir Arthur, and John A. Kingsbury. *Red Medicine: Socialized Health in Soviet Russia*. New York, Doubleday, Doran, 1933. 324 pp.

211. Niedermayer, O. von, and J. Semjonow. *Die Sovjetunion: eine geopolitische Problemstellung*. Berlin, Vorwinckel, 1934. 151 pp.

212. Nikolai-on (Daniel'son, Nikolai F.). *Ocherki nashego po-reformennago obshchestvennago khozyaystva* (Outline of Our National Economy after the Reform). St. Petersburg, Beuke, 1893. 353 pp.

213. Notestein, Frank W., Irene B. Taeuber, Dudley Kirk, Ansley J. Coale, and Louise K. Kiser. *The Future Population of Europe and the Soviet Union: Population Projections, 1940-1970*. Geneva, League of Nations (Columbia University Press, Agent), 1944. 315 pp.

214. Novosel'skiy, S. A. "O prilozhenii metoda 'Standard Population' k izmereniyu rozhdayemosti" (On the application of the method "Standard Population" to the measurement of natality), in: *Materialy po statistike Petrograda*, No. 3, pp. 81-104. 1921.

215. ———. "Organisation und Hauptergebnisse der amtlichen Bevölkerungs und Medizinalstatistik in Russland," *Archiv für soziale Hygiene und Demographie* 10:1-76. 1915.

216. ———. *Smertnost' i prodolzhitel'nost' zhizni v Rossii* (Mortality and Expectation of Life in Russia). Petrograd, 1916. 144 pp.

217. ———. "Vozrastnoy sostav naseleniya Petrograda po perepisi 28 avgusta 1920 g." (Age distribution of the population of Petrograd according to the Census of August 28, 1920), in: *Materialy po statistike Petrograda*, No. 4, pp. 6-18. 1921.

218. ———. "Yestestvennoye dvizheniye naseleniya v Petrograde v 1919 godu" (Natural movement of population in Petrograd in 1919), in: *Materialy po statistike Petrograda*, No. 1, pp. 6-37. 1920.

219. ———, and V. V. Payevskiy. *O svodnykh kharakteristikakh vosproizvodstva i perspektivnykh ischisleniyakh naseleniya* (General Characteristics of the Reproduction and the Prospective Evaluation of Population). French résumé. Leningrad, Akademiya Nauk SSSR. Trudy Demograficheskogo Instituta, 1934. Vol. I, pp. 7-37.
———. *See* also Title 417, U.S.S.R., Ts. S. U. (Life Tables).
———. (*See* also Payevskiy and Novosel'skiy.)

220. Obolensky-Ossinsky (Obolenskiy-Ossinskiy), V. V. *Mezhdunarodnye i mezhdukontinental'nye*

migratsii v dovoennoy Rossii i SSSR (International and Intercontinental Migrations in Pre-war Russia and in USSR). Moscow, Ts. S. U. SSSR, 1928. 138 pp.

221. ———. *Idem.* Abridged translation: "Emigration from and immigration into Russia," in: Walter F. Willcox, Editor, *International Migrations.* National Bureau of Economic Research, 1931. Vol. II, Interpretations, pp. 521-580.

222. Obruchev, N. N., Editor. *Voenno-statisticheskiy sbornik* (Collective Volume on Military Statistics). Vol. 4, Russia. [1871] xxx, 922, 243 pp.

223. Obukhov, V. M. "Dvizheniye urozhayev zernovykh kul'tur v Evropeyskoy Rossii v period 1883-1915" (Crop movement in European Russia from 1883-1915), in: V. G. Groman, *Vliyaniye neurozhayev na narodnoye khozyaystvo Rossii.* Vol. I, pp. 1-159.

224. Oganowskiy, N. P. "Die Agrarfrage in Russland seit 1905," *Archiv für Sozialwissenschaft und Sozialpolitik* 37(3):701-757. 1913.

225. ———. "Ocherki po agrarnomu voprosu: I. Malozemel'ye, rost gorodov i sël. Pereselencheskoye dvizheniye" (Essays on agrarian questions: I. Shortage of arable land. Growth of urban and rural communities. Migration movement), *Vestnik Evropy* 48(9):274-310. 1913.

226. ———. *Ocherki po ekonomicheskoy geografii RSFSR. I. Sel'skoye khozyaystvo* (Outlines of Economic Geography of RSFSR. Part I. Agricultural Economy). Moscow, "Novaya Derevnya," 1923. 239 pp.

227. ———. "Rekonstruktsiya sel'skogo khozyaystva i generalnyy plan" (Reconstruction of agricultural economy and the general plan), *Sotsialisticheskoye Khozyaystvo* 1927:2:33-52.

228. ———, Editor. *Sel'skoye khozyaystvo v Rossii v XX veke. Sbornik statistiko-ekonomicheskikh svedeniy za 1901-1922 gg.* (Agricultural Economy in Russia in the Twentieth Century. Collection of Economic and Statistical Information for the Years 1901-1922). Moscow, "Novaya Derevnya," 1923. 340 pp.

229. Oppengeim (Oppenheim), K. A. *Rossiya v dorozhnom otnoshenii* (Russia in Relation to Her Transport Possibilities). Moscow, Vyshiy Sov. Nar. Khoz., 1920. 157 pp.

230. Orlikova, E. "Sovetskaya zhenshchina v obshchestvennom proizvodstve" (The Soviet woman in public production), *Problemy Ekonomiki* 1940:7:106-122.

231. Pavlovsky, George. *Agricultural Russia on the Eve of the Revolution.* London, Routledge, 1930. 340 pp.

232. Payevskiy, V. V. "O perspektivnykh ischisleniyakh naseleniya. Raboty Demograficheskogo Instituta Akademii Nauk" (On prospective estimation of population. Works of the Demographic Institute of the Academy of Sciences), *Vestnik Akademii Nauk* 1933:1:1-12.

233. ———. *Ob izmerenii smertnosti migriruyushchikh mass naseleniya* (Estimates of Mortality among Migrants). French résumé. Leningrad, Akademiya Nauk SSSR. Trudy Demograficheskogo Instituta, 1934. Vol. I, pp. 63-113.

234. ———, and S. A. Novosel'skiy. *K voprosu o vyravnivanii vozrastnykh gruppirovok* (On Adjustment of Age-groups). French résumé. Leningrad, Akademiya Nauk SSSR. Trudy Demograficheskogo Instituta, 1934. Vol. I, pp. 39-61.

235. Peller, Sigismund. "Abortus und Geburtenrückgang," *Medizinische Klinik* 27:847-849. 1931.

236. Pelzer, Karl J. "Population and land utilization," in: F. V. Field, Editor, *Economic Survey of the Pacific Area.* New York, Institute of Pacific Relations, 1941. pp. 16-23, 86-97.

237. Peretyakovich, G. *Povolzh'ye v XV i XVI vekakh. Ocherki iz istorii kraya i yego kolonizatsii* (The Volga Region in the 15th and 16th Centuries. Outline of the History of the Region and Its Colonization). Moscow, 1877. 329 pp.

238. ———. *Povolzh'ye v XVII i nachale XVIII veka. Ocherki iz istorii kolonizatsii kraya* (The Volga Region in the 17th and at the Beginning of the 18th Century. Outline of the History of the Region's Colonization). Odessa, 1882. 329 pp.

239. Permanent Committee on Geographical Names. *Glossaries: 2. Russian.* London, Royal Geographical Society, 1942. 55 pp.

240. Peshchanskiy, V. "Osnovnye pokazateli yestestvennogo dvizheniya naseleniya Evropeyskoy chasti RSFSR v 1927 godu" (Chief items of vital statistics of the European part of the RSFSR in 1927), *Statisticheskoye Obozreniye* 1928:11:89-98.

241. ———. "Prichiny smertnosti gorodskogo naseleniya RSFSR v 1925 godu" (Causes of deaths of the urban population of RSFSR in 1925), *Statisticheskoye Obozreniye* 1927:5:65-69.

242. ———. "Yestestvennoye dvizheniye gorodskogo naseleniya Evropeyskoy chasti RSFSR za

1924 i 1925 gody" (Natural movement of the urban population of the European part of RSFSR in 1924 and 1925), *Statisticheskoye Obozreniye* 1927:4:89-91.

243. ————. "Yestestvennoye dvizheniye naseleniya Evropeyskoy chasti RSFSR v 1926 godu" (Natural movement of the population of the European part of the RSFSR in 1926), *Statisticheskoye Obozreniye* 1927:7:82-85.

244. ————, and M. Kaplun. "Detskaya smertnost'" (Infant mortality), *Statisticheskoye Obozreniye* 1929:2:91-96.

245. Petrovskii, D. "Programma kul'turno-tekhnicheskogo pod'yema rabochego klassa" (Program for the cultural-technical advancement of the labor class), *Planovoye Khozyaystvo* 1936:5:107-119.

246. Pisarev, I. "K itogam perepisi naseleniya SSSR 1939 goda" (On results of the population census of the USSR in 1939), *Problemy Ekonomiki* 1940:7:82-90.

247. ————. "Naseleniye strany sotsializma. K itogam perepisi 1939 goda" (The population of the country of Socialism, according to the census returns of 1939), *Planovoye Khozyaystvo* 1940:5:12-21.

248. Plandovskiy, V. *Narodnaya perepis'* (Census of Population). St. Petersburg, 1898. 378 pp.

249. Plyushchevskiy-Plyushchik, Ya. *Suzhdeniya i tolki naroda ob odnodnevnoy perepisi 28 yanvarya 1897 goda. Materialy dlya istorii vseobshchey perepisi narodonaseleniya* (Reactions among the Russian Population to the Census of 1897). St. Petersburg, Suvorin, 1897. 94 pp.

250. Pokrovskiy, V. (also B. in French.) "Vliyaniye urozhayev i khlebnykh tsen na yestestvennoye dvizheniye naseleniya" (The influence of crops and corn prices upon the natural movement of population), in: A. D. Chuprov, Editor, *Vliyaniye urozhayev na nekotoryye storony Russkogo narodnogo khozyaystva*. St. Petersburg, 1897. pp. 171-370.

251. ————. *Idem*. Abridged French translation: "Influence des récoltes et des prix du blé sur le mouvement naturel de la population en Russie," *Bulletin de l'Institut international de statistique* 11(1, Part 2):176-219. 1899.

252. ————, and D. Rikhter. "Naseleniye" (Population), in: *Entsiklopedicheskiy Slovar'*. St. Petersburg, Brockhaus and Efron, 1890. Vol. XXVIIa, pp. 75-128.

253. Pokrovsky (Pokrovskiy), M. N. *History of Russia from the Earliest Times to the Rise of Commercial Capitalism*. Translated and edited by J. D. Clarkson and M. R. M. Griffith. New York, International Publishers, 1931. 383 pp.

254. Pollyak, G. "K voprosu o chislennosti ne-sel'sko-khozyaystvennogo proletariata SSSR" (Number of non-farm workers in the USSR), *Statisticheskoye Obozreniye* 1927:11:46-49.

255. Pomus, V. I. *Buriat Mongolia. A Brief Survey of Political, Economic and Social Progress*. Abridged and translated from the Russian work "Buriat-Mongol'skaya A.S.S.R." by Rose Maurer and Olga Lang. New York, Institute of Pacific Relations. 76 pp.

256. Postnikov, A. "Zemel'nyy nadel krest'yan. Pamyati 19 fevralya 1861 goda" (Peasant's land allotments. Anniversary of the emancipation of serfs, February 19, 1861), *Vestnik Evropy* 46(2):71-91. 1911.

257. Prasolov, L. I. "The climate and soils of Northern Eurasia as conditions of colonization," in: W. L. G. Joerg, Editor, *Pioneer Settlement*. New York, American Geographical Society, 1932. pp. 240-260.

258. Prawdin (Khorol), Michael. *The Mongol Empire. Its Rise and Legacy*. Translated by Eden and Cedar Paul. London, Allen and Unwin, 1940. 581 pp.

259. Prokopovich, S. N. "Changes in the location of population and industry in the USSR," *Quarterly Bulletin of Soviet Russian Economics* 1940:122-142.

260. ————. "Dinamika naseleniya SSSR" (Dynamics of the population of the USSR), *Byulleten' Ekonomicheskogo Kabineta Prof. S. N. Prokopovicha* 7(80):18-27. June-July, 1930.

261. ————. "Growth of population in the USSR," *Quarterly Bulletin of Soviet Russian Economics* 1940:4:101-121.

262. ————. "Results of the Census of 1939 in USSR," *Quarterly Bulletin of Soviet Russian Economics* 1940:5:29-55.

263. ————. "The national economy of Soviet Russia in 1939: standard of life of workers and peasants," *Quarterly Bulletin of Soviet Russian Economics* 1939:1-2:57-60.

264. ————. "The national income of the USSR," *Quarterly Bulletin of Soviet Russian Economics* 1941:7:101-124.

265. ———. *Über die Bedingungen der industriellen Entwicklung Russlands.* Archiv für Sozial-wissenschaft und Sozialpolitik, Erg. Heft 10, 1913. 87 pp.

266. Pryanishnikov, Dmitriy N. "Maltus i Rossiya" (Malthus and Russia), in: *Sobraniye statey i nauchnykh rabot.* Moscow, Rabotnik Prosveshcheniya, 1927. Vol. I, pp. 440-451.

267. Ptukha (Ptoukha), M. V. "Die Sterblichkeit in Russland," *Metron* 3:469-520. 1924.

268. ———. "La population de l'Ukraine jusqu'en 1960," *Bulletin de l'Institut international de statistique* 25(3):59-88. 1931.

269. ———, Editor. *Perepis'naseleniya* (Census of Population). Kiev, Akademiya Nauk Ukr. SSR. Pratsi Institutu Demografii, 1936. Vol. 10. 195 pp.

270. Pustokhod, P. J., and V. K. Voblyy. *Perepisi naseleniya* (Census of Population). M. V. Ptukha, Editor. Institut Demografii Akademii Nauk Ukr. SSR. Moscow, Gosud. Sots.-Ekon. Izd., 1936. 208 pp.

———. (*See* also Voblyy and Pustokhod.)

271. Rashin, A. G. *Formirovaniye promyshlennogo proletariata v Rossii* (Formation of the Industrial Proletariat in Russia). Moscow, 1940. 464 pp.

272. ———. *Sostav fabrichno-zavodskogo proletariata SSSR. Predvaritel'nye itogi perepisi metal-listov, gornorabochikh i tekstil'shchikov v 1929 g.* (Composition of Labor in the USSR. Preliminary Returns of the Census of Metalworkers, Miners and Textileweavers in 1929). N. Evreinov, Editor. Moscow, V.Ts.S.P.S., 1930. 171 pp.

273. Reznikov, B. *Demografiya Ukrainy za 1914-1928 gg.; bibliografichnyi pokazhchik, chastina persha* (Demography of Ukraine; Bibliographic Index, Part I). Kiev, Vseukrainska Akademiya Nauk, 1931. 275 pp.

274. Rimscha, Hans von. *Der russische Bürgerkrieg und die russische Emigration 1917-1921.* Jena, Frommann, 1924. 170 pp.

275. ———. *Russland jenseits der Grenzen 1921-1926.* Jena, Frommann, 1927. 238 pp.

276. Robinson, Geroid T. *Rural Russia under the Old Régime.* London, Longmans, Green, 1930. 342 pp.

277. Roesle, E. "Die Entwicklung der Bevölkerung in den Kulturstaaten in ersten Jahrzehnt dieses Jahrhunderts. Russisches Reich," *Archiv für soziale Hygiene und Demographie* 12:72-121. 1917.

278. Ropes, E. C. "The statistical publications of the U.S.S.R.," *The Russian Review* 1(1):122-125. November, 1941.

279. Roubakine, Alexandre N. *La protection de la santé publique dans l'U.R.S.S.: principes et résultats.* Paris, Bureau d'éditions, 1933. 91 pp.

280. ———. "Le mouvement de la population dans l'Union des Républiques Socialistes Soviétiques comparativement aux tendances démographiques des pays occidentaux," *Congrès international de la population,* Paris, 1937. Vol. 3, pp. 146-154.

281. Rumyantsev, V. "Proizvodstvo zerna v nechernozemnoy polose" (Grain production in the non-black soil zone), *Planovoye Khozyaystvo* 1936:4:141-151.

282. Russell, Sir E. John. "Collective farming in Russia and the Ukraine," *Science* 96:47-52, 74-78. July 17, 24, 1942.

283. ———. "The farming problem in Russia. How it is being met," *The Slavonic and East European Review* 16(47):320-340. 1938.

284. Russkoye Geograficheskoye Obshchestvo, Statisticheskiy Otdel. *Sbornik statisticheskikh svedeniy o Rossii* (Collection of Statistical Data on Russia). St. Petersburg, 1851, 1854. 2 vols.

Saucerman, Sophie. (*See* U.S. Department of State.)

285. Sautin, I. *Vsesoyuznaya perepis' naseleniya 1939 goda* (All-Union Census of Population of 1939). Moscow, Gos. Izd., 1938.

286. ———. *Idem. Planovoye Khozyaystvo* 1938:8:16-25.

287. ———, Editor. *Kolkhozy vo vtoroy stalinskoy pyatiletke. Statisticheskiy sbornik* (Collective Farms during the Second Five-Year Plan. Statistical Collection). Moscow, Gosplan, 1939. 142 pp.

Savitskiye, Z. M., and N. A. (*See* Title 446.)

288. Schnitzler, M. I. *L'Empire des tsars au point de vue actuel de la science. II. La population.* Paris-Strasbourg, Berger-Levrault, 1862. 748 pp.

289. Schultz, Arved. *Die natürlichen Landschaften von Russisch-Turkestan; Grundlagen einer Landeskunde.* Hamburger Universität, Abhandlungen auf dem Gebiet der Auslandskunde, Bd. 2, Reihe C. Hamburg, Friedrichsen, 1920. 165 pp.

290. ————. "Die Völker des russischen Reiches (SSSR)," *Petermanns Mitteilungen* 78(3-4) :72-77. 1932.

291. ————. *Sibirien, eine Landeskunde.* Breslau, Hirt, 1923. 246 pp.

292. Semashko, Nikolay A. *Health Protection in the USSR.* London, Gollancz, 1934; New York, Putnam, 1935. 176 pp.

293. Semenov-Tyan-Shanskiy, V. S. (Benjamin.) *Gorod i derevnya v Evropeyskoy Rossii* (Town and Village in European Russia). St. Petersburg, Zapiski Imper. Geograficheskago Obshchestva po Otdeleniyu Statistiki, 1910. Vol. 10, No. 2. 212 pp.

294. Shevelëv, A. "Sdvigi v zdorov'i trudyashchikhsya SSSR" (Health improvement of working people in the USSR), in: Kraval', Editor, *Zdorov'ye i zdravookhraneniye trudyashchikhsya SSSR.* Moscow, Ts.U.N.Kh. Gosplan, 1936. 224 pp.

295. Sigerist, Henry E. "Medical care through medical centers in the Soviet Union," *American Review of Soviet Medicine* 1(2) :176-190. 1943.

296. ————. "Rural health services in the Soviet Union," *American Review of Soviet Medicine* 1(3) :270-280. 1944.

297. ————. *Socialized Medicine in the Soviet Union.* New York, Norton, 1939. 378 pp.

298. ————. "Twenty-five years of health work in the Soviet Union," *American Review of Soviet Medicine* 1(1) :67-78. 1943.

299. Simpson, Sir John Hope. *The Refugee Problem. Report of a Survey.* London, Oxford University Press, 1939. 637 pp.

300. Smulevich, B. *Burzhuaznye teorii narodonaseleniya v svete Marksistsko-Leninskoy kritiki* (Bourgeois Population Theories. A Marxist-Leninist Critique). Moscow, Kommunisticheskaya Akademiya Nauk, 1936. 436 pp.

301. ————. "Fashistskiye teorii naseleniya i sotsialisticheskaya deystvitel'nost' " (Fascist theories on population and the socialist reality), *Problemy Ekonomiki* 1936:3 :93-106.

302. ————. *Materinstvo pri kapitalizme i sotsializme* (Maternity under Capitalism and under Socialism). Akademiya Nauk, Institut Ekonomiki. Moscow, Gosud. Sots.-Ekon. Izd., 1936. 152 pp.

303. Solov'yëv, A. V. *Kamchatskaya oblast'* (Kamchatka District). Khabarovsk, 1940.

304. Somerville, Rose M. "Counting noses in the Soviet Union," *The American Quarterly on the Soviet Union* 3(2-3) :51-73. 1940.

305. ————. "The problem of labor turnover. A review of Soviet legislation," *The American Review on the Soviet Union* 4(2) :11-32. 1941.

306. ————. "That Soviet standard of living," *The American Quarterly on the Soviet Union* 2(4) :3-27. April, 1940.

307. Sonin, M. "Voprosy pereseleniya v tret'yey pyatiletke" (Problems of migration during the Third Five-Year Plan), *Problemy Ekonomiki* 1940:3 :80-91.

308. ————. *Idem.* Abridged translation in: *The American Quarterly on the Soviet Union* 3(2-3) : 74-88. 1940; and U.S. Bureau of Foreign and Domestic Commerce, *Russian Economic Notes,* Vol. 2(N.S.), No. 4. February 29, 1940.

309. Soulas, Jean. "Le développement des grandes villes en URSS au cours du premier plan quinquennal," *Annales de géographie* 47(268) :400-405. July, 1938.

310. Spasokukotskiy, N. N. *Okhrana zdorov'ya detey* (Health Protection of Children). Perel, Editor. Moscow, Narkompros RSFSR, 1932. 233 pp.

311. Stalin, Iosif (Joseph) V. *Marxism and the National and Colonial Question. A Collection of Articles and Speeches. Nationalism and Nationality; Minorities.* Moscow, Foreign Languages Pub. House, 1940. 270 pp.

312. ————. "Otchetnyy doklad na XVIII s'ezde partii o rabote Ts.K. VKP" (Report at the 18th Conference of the Communist Party on activities of the Central Committee), *Problemy Ekonomiki* 1939:3 :3-36.

313. ————. *Problems of Leninism.* Moscow, Foreign Languages Pub. House, 1940. 667 pp.

314. Starodubsky, Leo. *Das Volkszählungswesen in der Union der sozialistischen Sowjetrepubliken;*

eine statistisch methodologische Untersuchung. Schriften des Instituts für Statistik der Minderheitsvölker, herausgeg. von Wilhelm Winkler. Vienna, Deuticke, 1938. 141 pp.

315. Strel'bitskiy, I. *Ischisleniye poverkhnosti Rossiyskoy Imperii v obshchem eya sostave* (Estimate on the Surface of the Russian Empire). St. Petersburg, 1874. 248 pp.

316. ———. *Ischisleniye poverkhnosti Rossiyskoy Imperii v obshchem eya sostave v tsarstvovaniye Imperatora Aleksandra III* (Estimates on the Surface of the Russian Empire in the Reign of Tsar Alexander III). St. Petersburg, 1889. 134 pp.

317. ———. *Superficie de l'Europe*. Publication du Comité Central Russe de Statistique. Traduit du russe par N. Masson. St. Pétersbourg, Trenké et Fusnot, 1882. xx, 227 pp.

318. Strong, Anna Louise. *The New Soviet Constitution*. New York, Holt, 1937. 169 pp.

319. Strumilin, S. G. "K perspektivnoy pyatiletke Gosplana" (On the prospective Five-Year Plan), *Planovoye Khozyaystvo* 1927:3:17-54.

320. ———. "Perspektivnaya orientirovka Gosplana" (Prospective orientation of the national plan), *Planovoye Khozyaystvo* 1926:5:30-58.

321. ———. *Problemy planirovaniya v SSR* (Problems of Planning in the USSR). Leningrad, Akademiya Nauk SSSR, 1932. 544 pp.

322. Sul'kevich, S. I. *Administrativno-politicheskoye stroyeniye Soyuza SSR; materialy o territorial'nykh preobrazovaniyakh s 1917 g. po 1 iyulya 1926 g.* (Administrative Political Structure of the USSR; Materials on Territorial Reorganization from 1917 to July 1, 1926). Leningrad, Gos. Izd., 1926. 300 pp.

323. ———. *Territoriya i naseleniye SSSR* (Territory and Population of the USSR). Moscow, Politizdat pei Ts.K. VKP, 1940. 72 pp.

324. Taracouzio, T. A. *Soviets in the Arctic; A Historical, Economic and Political Study of the Soviet Advance into the Arctic*. New York, Macmillan, 1938. 563 pp.

325. Tarassevitch, L. "Epidemics in Russia since 1914," in: League of Nations. *Epidemiological Intelligence*. Part I, No. 2, March, 1922. 48 pp. Part II, No. 5, October, 1922. 68 pp.

326. Terletskiy, P. E. *Naseleniye Kraynego Severa* (Population of the Extreme North). Leningrad, 1932.

327. Timasheff, N. S. "The population of Soviet Russia," *Rural Sociology* 5(3):303-313. September, 1940.

328. Timoshenko, Vladimir P. *Agricultural Russia and the Wheat Problem*. Stanford University, Food Research Institute and the Committee on Russian Research of the Hoover War Library. Grain Economic Series 1. 1932.

329. ———. "Soviet agricultural reorganization and the bread-grain situation," Stanford University, *Wheat Studies of the Food Research Institute* 13(7):309-376. 1937.

330. Tokarëv, S. A. *Ocherk istorii Yakutskogo naroda* (An Essay on the History of the Yakut People). Moscow, 1940.

331. Troynitskiy, A. A. *Krepostnoye naseleniye v Rossii po 10-oy narodnoy revizii* (Serf-population in Russia according to the 10th Revision Census). St. Petersburg, Ts.S.K., 1861. 92 pp.

332. Trubnikov, S. "Gosudarstvennye trudovyye rezervy SSSR" (State reserves of labor in USSR), *Planovoye Khozyaystvo* 1940:11:29-38.

333. ———. "Istochniki komplektovaniya rabochey sily v SSSR" (Sources of completion of working forces in USSR), *Problemy Ekonomiki* 1939:6:145-159.

334. Tugan-Baranovskiy, M. *Russkaya fabrika* (The Russian Factory). Sixth edition. Moscow-Leningrad, Gosud. Sots.-Ekon. Izd., 1934. 436 pp.

335. ———. "Sostoyaniye nashey promyshlennosti za posledneye desyatiletiye i vidy na budushcheye" (Russian industry in the course of the last decades and its future), *Sovremennyy Mir* 1910:12:27-53.

336. Turin, S. P. "Some observations on the population of Soviet Russia at the census of Jan. 17, 1939," *Journal of the Royal Statistical Society* 104(2):172-174. 1941.

337. Ukhanov, K. "K voprosu razvitiya mestnoy promyshlennosti" (Problem of the development of local industry), *Planovoye Khozyaystvo* 1936:5:55-74.

338. United States, Department of State. *International Transfers of Territory in Europe*. Prepared by Sophie Saucerman. Washington, 1937. 244 pp.

339. Unshlikht, I. *Gosudarstvennoye ustroystvo i natsional'naya politika Sovetskoy vlasti* (State Order and National Policy of the Soviet Régime). Leningrad, Ts.K. VKP(b), 1936. 39 pp.

340. Urlanis, B. Ts. *Rost naseleniya v Evrope. Opyt ischisleniya* (The Growth of Population in Europe. An Attempt at an Estimate). Moscow, Ogiz-Gospolitizdat, 1941. 435 pp.

341. Varga, E. S. (Eugene.) "Osnovnaya ekonomicheskaya zadacha SSSR" (Basic economic problem of the USSR), *Vestnik Akademii Nauk SSSR* 9(6) :1-15. 1939.

342. ———. *Two Systems.* New York, International Publishers, 1939. 268 pp.

343. Vernadskiy, G. *O dvizhenii Russkogo plemeni na vostok* (The Eastern Expansion of the Russian Race). Nauchnyy Istoricheskiy Zhurnal, 1914.

344. Veynberg, B. P. "Polozheniya tsentra naselennosti Rossii s 1613 po 1913 g." (Positions of the center of density of Russia's population from 1613 to 1913), *Izvestiya Imperat. Russkago Geograf. Obshchestva* 51(6) :385-408. 1915.

345. ———. "Polozheniya tsentra poverkhnosti Rossii ot nachala knyazhestva Moskovskago do nastoyashchago vremeni" (Positions of the center of Russia's area from the Muscovite Princes up to the present time), *Izvestiya Imperat. Russkago Geograf. Obshchestva* 51(6) :365-384. 1915.

346. Voblyy, V. K., and P. I. Pustokhod. *Perepisi naseleniya: ikh istoriya i organizatsiya* (Censuses of Population; Their History and Organization). Akademiya Nauk, Institut Ekonomiki. Moscow-Leningrad, Gosplanizdat, 1940. 160 pp.
———. (*See* also Pustokhod and Voblyy.)

347. Volin, Lazar. "Agrarian collectivism in the Soviet Union," *Journal of Political Economy* 45(5) :606-633; (6) :759-788. 1937.

348. ———. "Agrarian individualism in the Soviet Union; its rise and decline," *Agricultural History* 12(1) :11-31; (2) :118-141. 1938.

349. ———. "Effects of the drought and purge on the agriculture of the Soviet Union," *Foreign Agriculture* 3(5) :175-196. 1939.

350. ———. "The peasant house under the Mir and the Kolkhoz in modern Russian history," in: Caroline F. Ware, Editor, *The Cultural Approach to History.* New York, Columbia University Press, 1940. pp. 125-139.

351. ———. "The Russian peasant in serfdom," *Agricultural History* 17(1) :41-61. 1943.

352. Volkov, E. Z. *Dinamika naseleniya SSSR za vosem'desyat let* (Dynamics of the Population of the USSR during Eighty Years). Introduction by S. G. Strumilin. Moscow, Gos. Izd., 1930. 272 pp.

353. Voshchinin, V. P. "The bases of colonization in North European Russia; history, present policies and organization of internal colonization in the U.S.S.R.," in: W. L. G. Joerg, Editor, *Pioneer Settlement.* New York, American Geographical Society, 1932. pp. 236-239, 261-272.

354. Voznesenskiy, N. *Economic Results of the USSR in 1940 and the Plan of National Economic Development for 1941.* Report delivered at the 18th All-Union Conference of the C.P.S.U. (B), February 18, 1941. Moscow, Foreign Languages Pub. House, 1941. 39 pp.

355. Wachenheim, Hedwig. "Hitler's transfers of population in Eastern Europe," *Foreign Affairs* 20(4) :705-778. July, 1942.

356. Webb, Sidney and Beatrice. *Soviet Communism: A New Civilizadat?* New York, Scribners, 1936. 2 vols.

357. Weydemeyer, Alexandre de. *Tableaux historiques, chronologiques, géographiques et statistiques de l'Empire de la Russie avec une carte généalogique.* St. Pétersbourg, Bellizard, 1828. 17 pp.

358. Willcox, Walter F., Editor. *International Migrations.* Publications of National Bureau of Economic Research, Inc., No. 14 and No. 18. I. Statistics compiled on behalf of the International Labour Office by Imre Ferenczi. 1929. 1112 pp. II. Interpretation by a group of scholars in different countries. 1931. 715 pp.

359. Wilson, I. *Ob' yasneniya k khozyaystvenno-statisticheskomu atlasu Evropeyskoy Rossii* (Commentary to the Economic-Statistical Atlas of European Russia). Fourth edition. Department of Agriculture of St. Petersburg, 1869. 523 pp.

360. Winslow, Charles-Edward H. "Public health in the Soviet Union," *American Review of Soviet Medicine* 1(2) :163-165. 1943.

361. Woytinsky, W. S. *Die Welt in Zahlen.* Zweites Buch. Die Arbeit, Berlin, Mosse, 1926. xxi, 376 pp.

362. ———, and E. S. Woytinsky. "Progress of agricultural statistics in the world," *Journal of Farm Economics* 21(4):761-787. 1939.

363. Yakobson, Sergius. "The rise of Russian Nationalism," in: Royal Institute of International Affairs, *Nationalism*. London, Oxford University Press, 1939. pp. 57-80.

364. Yakovleva, E. N. *Bibliografiya Mongol'skoy Narodnoy Respubliki* (Bibliography on the Mongolian People's Republic). Moscow, 1935.

365. Yamzin, I. L. *Pereselencheskoye dvizheniye v Rossii* (Internal Migration in Russia). Kiev, 1912. 174 pp.

366. ———, and V. P. Voshchinin. *Ucheniye o kolonizatsiii i pereseleniyakh* (The Course of Colonization and Migration). Moscow, Gos. Izd., 1926. 328 pp.

367. Yanson, Yu. E. *Sravnitel'naya statistika naseleniya* (Comparative Population Statistics). Zhurnal Russkago Obshchestva Okhraneniya Narodnago Zdraviya, 1892. Supplement. 443 pp.

368. ———. *Sravnitel'nayà statistika Rossii i Zapadno-Evropeyskikh gosudarstv. I. Territoriya i naseleniye* (Comparative Statistics of Russia and Western European Countries. I. Territory and Population). St. Petersburg, Stasyulevich, 1878. 372 pp.

369. Yarmolinsky, A. "Biro-Bidzhan," in: *The Universal Jewish Encyclopedia*. New York, 1940. Vol. 2, pp. 372-378.

370. Yefremov, P. V. *Stolypinskaya agrarnaya politika* (Stolypin Agrarian Policy). Moscow, 1941.

371. Yugoff (Yugow), Aron. *Economic Trends in Soviet Russia*. Translated by Eden and Cedar Paul. New York, Richard R. Smith, 1930. 349 pp.

372. ———. *Russia's Economic Front for War and Peace*. Translated by N. I. and M. Stone. New York, Harper, 1942. 279 pp.

373. Zarubin, I. I. *Spisok narodnostey SSSR* (List of Nationalities of the USSR). Leningrad, Akademiya Nauk, Trudy Komissii po Izucheniyu Plemennogo Sostava Naseleniya SSSR i Sopredel'nykh Stran, No. 13, 1927. 50 pp.

374. Zaytsev, V. "K voprosu o chislennosti naseleniya Evropeyskoy Rossii" (On the number of population in European Russia), in: V. G. Groman, *Vliyaniye neurozhayev na narodnoye khozyaystvo Rossii*. Vol. II, pp. 60-93.

375. ———. "Vliyaniye kolebaniy urozhayev na yestestvennoye dvizheniye naseleniya" (Influence of crop-fluctuations on the natural movement of population), in: V. G. Groman, *Vliyaniye neurozhayev na narodnoye khozyaystvo Rossii*. Vol. II, pp. 1-59.

376. Zhemchuzhnikov, N. N. *Dvizheniye na vostok* (The Eastward Movement). Moscow, 1927.

PART II: OFFICIAL PUBLICATIONS
IMPERIAL RUSSIA AND U.S.S.R.

Official publications (except periodicals) are arranged by agency, within broad subject groups. The listings within each subject are divided as follows:

I.   Imperial Russia (Cf. Library of Congress: Russia—1917)

II A. Soviet republics before formation of the U.S.S.R. (Cf. Library of Congress: Russia 1917-1922—R.S.F.S.R.)

II B. U.S.S.R. (Cf. Library of Congress: Russia, 1923—U.S.S.R.)

The Tsentral'nyy Statisticheskiy Komitet (Central Statistical Committee) of Imperial Russia was superseded after the Revolution by Tsentral'noye Statisticheskoye Upravleniye (Central Statistical Board), as an organ of the R.S.F.S.R., 1918-1922, and as an organ of the U.S.S.R., 1923-1929. In 1930, its functions were transferred to Gosudarstvennaya Planovaya Komissiya (State Planning Commission)—Gosplan. Under Gosplan, these functions were located in Ekonomiko-statisticheskiy Sektor (Economic-Statistical Division) to December 17, 1931; thereafter, in Tsentral'noye Upravleniye Narodno-Khozyaystvennogo Uchëta (Central Administration of Economic and Social Statistics). These agencies are designated below, respectively, as follows:

Ts. S. K.

Ts. S. U.

Gosplan, E.-S. S.

Gosplan, Ts. U. N. Kh. U.

The place of publication is generally omitted in this list. Dates in brackets, or following place of publication, refer to year of publication. Otherwise dates refer to period described by subject matter.

I.

Ts. S. K.

377. Dépouillement des données sur la nationalité et classification des peuples de l'Empire de Russie d'après leur langue. [1899]

378. Goroda: poseleniya v uyezdakh, imeyushshiye 2000 i boleye zhiteley (Urban settlements of the Russian Empire of 2000 inhabitants and over). [1905]

379. Naselënnyya mesta Rossiyskoy Imperii v 500 i boleye zhiteley (Settlements of the Russian Empire of 500 inhabitants and over). [1905]

380. Obshchiy svod po Imperii resul'tatov razrabotki dannykh pervoy vseobshchey perepisi naseleniya (General summaries for the whole Empire of the analysis of data of the first general census of population). Headings in Russian and French. 2 vols. [1905]

381. Pervaya vseobshchaya perepis' naseleniya Rossiyskoy Imperii 1897 goda (First general census of population of the Russian Empire in 1897). 89 vols. [1899-1905]

382. Pervaya vseobshchaya perepis' naseleniya Rossiyskoy Imperii 1897 goda. Chislennost' i sostav rabochikh v Rossii na osnovanii dannykh pervoy vseobshchey perepisi naseleniya Rossiyskoy Imperii 1897 g. (The first census of the population of the Russian Empire in 1897. Number and class composition of workers according to the census of population of the Russian Empire, 1897). 2 vols. [1906]

383. Raspredeleniye naseleniya Imperii po glavnym veroispovedaniyam (Classification of the population of the Empire by principal religions). [1901]

384. Raspredeleniye naseleniya po vidam glavnykh zanyatiy i vozrastnym gruppam (Statistics of population by occupation and age). 4 vols. [1905]

385. Raspredeleniye naselennykh mest Rossiyskoy Imperii po chislennosti v nikh naseleniya. 1897 (Inhabited places of Russia classified by the size of their population, according to the census of 1897). [1902]

II A.

Ts. S. U.

386. Itogi perepisi naseleniya 1920 g. (Returns of the population census of 1920). [1928]

387. Itogi vserossiyskoy sel'sko-khozyaystvennoy perepisi:
   a. 1920 goda (Returns of All-Russian Census of Agriculture, 1920).
   b. Sel'sko-khozyaystvennoy i pozemel'noy perepisi 1917 g., 1-2, 1921-22 (Returns of agricultural and land census of 1917).
   c. Itogi razrabotki sel'sko-khozyaystvennoy perepisi po tipam i gruppam khozyaystv (Census of agriculture classified by groups and types of farms), 1 (1-1a), in: *Trudy* (Works). Vols. 2, 5, 14.

388. Vsesoyuznaya gorodskaya perepis' 1923 goda (All-Union Census of Cities, 1923), in: *Trudy* (Works). Vols. 17, 22, 27.

II B.

Ts. S. U.

389. Programmy po razrabotke materialov perepisi (Plan for the analysis of the census returns). 116 pp. [1926]

390. Sbornik proyektov program vsesoyuznoy perepisi 1926, vyp. 1-2. Formulyary dlya proizvodstva perepisi (Collections of schedules of the All-Union Census of Population, 1926. Issues 1-2. Questionnaires). [1926]

391. Vsesoyuznaya perepis' naseleniya 1926 g. (All-Union Census of Population, 1926). 56 vols. Headings in Russian and French. [1928-1933]

Sovet Narodnykh Komissarov (Council of People's Commissars)

392. "O vsesoyuznoy perepisi naseleniya 1939 g. Postanovleniye Soveta Narodnykh Komissarov" (On the All-Union Census of the Population of 1939. Decree of the Council of People's Commissars), *Planovoye Khozyaystvo* 1938:8:10-15.

Gosplan, Ts. U. N. Kh. U.

393. (Census, 1939. Release 1: Population, urban and rural, by constituent republics 1926, 1939, and by districts of the R.S.F.S.R., 1939: population of cities having, in 1939, 50,000 persons or more, 1926 and 1939), in: *Izvestiya*, June 2, 1939. Also: *Sotsialisticheskoye Stroitel'stvo Soyuza SSR*, 1933-1938 gg., pp. 8-15.

394. (Census, 1939. Release 2: Results of tabulation of 99.44 per cent of schedules. Ages, literacy, education, social classes, nationalities), in: *Izvestiya*, April 29, 1940. Also in: U.S. Bureau of Foreign and Domestic Commerce, *Russian Economic Notes* 2 (N.S.)(13) :7-10, July 1, 1940; and *The American Quarterly on the Soviet Union* 3(2-3) :97-100. November, 1940.

STATISTICAL COMPILATIONS

I.

Ts. S. K.

395. Sbornik svedeniy po Rossii (Collection of statistical data on Russia). 1882, 1883, 1884/85, 1890, 1896.
Note: 1883 as sub-series of Statisticheskiy vremennik Ross. Imperii s.3, v. 8; 1884/85, 1890, and 1896 as sub-series of Statistika Ross. Imperii Nos. 1, 10, and 40; 1882 has title: Sbornik svedeniy po Evropeyskoy Rossii (Collection of statistical data on European Russia). Continued by Statisticheskiy yezhegodnik.

396. Statisticheskiy vremennik Rossiyskoy Imperii (Statistical annals of the Russian Empire). Ser. 1, Vol. 1, 1866; Ser. 2, Vols. 1-25, 1871-84; Ser. 3, Vols. 1-25, 1884-90.
Note: Contains several sub-series. *See*: Dvizheniye naseleniya and also Sbornik svedeniy po Rossii. Continued by Statistika Rossiyskoy Imperii. *See* also: Vremennik Ts. S. K.

397. Statisticheskiy yezhegodnik Rossii za 1904 . . . 1916 gody (Statistical yearbook of Russia for the year 1904 . . . 1916). [1905-18]
Note: Continues Sbornik svedeniy po Rossii; Volumes 1904-1910 have title: Yezhegodnik Rossii. Volume 1916 published by Ts. S. K. Narodnogo Komissariata Vnutrennykh Del.

398. Statisticheskiya tablitsy Rossiyskoy Imperii za . . . god. (Statistical tables of the Russian Empire for the year 1849 [1852]; 1856 [1858]; 1858 [1863]).

399. Vremennik Tsentral'nago Statisticheskago Komiteta (Annals of the Central Statistical Committee). 52 vols. [1888-1903]
Note: This series has several sub-series. *See*: Glavnyye rezul'taty urozhaya. Most of the issues contain statistical monographs on various subjects. *See* also: Statisticheskiy vremennik Rossiyskoy Imperii, and Statistika Rossiyskoy Imperii.

II A.

Ts. S. U.

400. Petrogradskoye stolichnoye statisticheskoye byuro. Materialy po statistike Petrograda (Statistical material of Petrograd). Nos. 1-5. [1920-21]

401. Statisticheskiy sbornik (Statistical collection), 1913-1917; 1921-1922, in: *Trudy* (Works), Vol. 7. Preface and headings also in French.

402. Statisticheskiy yezhegodnik (Statistical yearbook), 1918-1924, in: *Trudy* (Works), Vol. 8. Preface and headings also in French.

II B.

Ts. S. U.

403. Itogi desyatiletiya Sovetskoy vlasti v tsifrakh, 1917-1927 (Statistics for the decade of the existence of the Soviet Government). [1927] 514 pp. English edition: Ten years of Soviet power in figures, 1917-1927. [1927] 516 pp.

404. Narodnoye khozyaystvo SSSR. Statisticheskiy spravochnik SSSR za . . . god. (National economy of the USSR statistics. Handbook for the year . . .: 1924, 1925, 1927).

405. Sbornik statisticheskikh svedeniy po SSSR, 1918-1923 (Collection of statistical data on USSR, 1918-1923), in: *Trudy* (Works), Vol. 18. [1924]

406. Statisticheskiy spravochnik SSSR za 1928 g. (Statistical information book for the year 1928).

Ts. U. N. Kh. U. Gosplana

407. Narodnoye khozyaystvo SSSR. Statisticheskiy spravochnik 1932 (National economics in USSR. Statistical collection, 1932). [1932]

408. Socialist reconstruction in the USSR; statistical abstract. Moscow, Soyuzorgouchet. xvi, 538 pp. (Based on Sotsialisticheskoye stroitel'stvo, 1935; *Ibid.*, 1936.) [1936]

409. Sotsialisticheskoye stroitel'stvo. Statisticheskiy yezhegodnik (Socialist construction. Statistical yearbook). [1934, 1935, 1936]

410. Sotsialisticheskoye stroitel'stvo Soyuza SSR. 1933-1938 gg. (Socialist construction of the USSR in the years 1933-1938). [1939]

411. S.S.S.R. v tsifrakh (U.S.S.R. in figures). [1934, 1935] Also, English editions: U.S.S.R. in figures. [1934, 1935]

DEMOGRAPHY, HEALTH, AND RELATED MATERIALS

Note: Vital statistics are also included in the preceding section, Statistical Compilations.

I.

Ts. S. K.

412. Dvizheniye naseleniya v Evropeyskoy Rossii (Movement of population in European Russia). 1867-1909. 1867-1884 as sub-series of Statisticheskiy vremennik Rossiyskoy Imperii (Ser. 2, Nos. 8, 12, 13, 14, 17, 18, 20-25; Ser. 3, Nos. 3, 7, 20, 21, 23, 24); 1885-1909 as sub-series of Statistika Rossiyskoy Imperii (11, 12, 18, 21, 24, 33, 34, 38, 41, 70, 74, 84, 85, 87, 88, 91).

413. Smertnost' mladentsev Evropeyskoy Rossii (Infant mortality in European Russia). Statistika Rossiyskoy Imperii, Vol. 82. [1914]

Ministerstvo Vnutrennykh Del (Ministry of Interior)

414. Tsifrovyy material dlya izucheniya pereseleniya v Sibir' (Figures for study of the colonization of Siberia). 6 vols. [1894-1897, 1899-1901]

Pereselencheskoye Upravleniye Glavnago Upravleniya Zemleustroystva i Zemledeliya (Colonization Division of Central Administration of Agriculture and Settlement)

415. Aziatskaya Rossiya (Asiatic Russia). 4 vols. [1914] I. Lyudi i poryadki za Uralom (Peoples and customs beyond the Urals); II. Zemlya i khozyaystvo (Soil and economy); III. Priolzheniya (Appendices); IV. Atlas.

II B.

Ts. S. U.

416. Samoubiystva v 1922-1925 gg. (Suicides in 1922-1925). Aborty v 1925 g. (Abortions in 1925), in: *Trudy* (Works), Vol. 35. Aborty v 1926 godu (Abortions during 1926). [1929]

417. Smertnost' i prodolzhitel'nost' zhizni naseleniya S.S.S.R., 1926-1927. Tablitsy smertnosti (Mortality and longevity of the population of the U.S.S.R. Life tables, 1926-1927). [1930] 139 pp.

418. Yestestvennoye dvizheniye naseleniya Soyuza S.S.R. v 1923-1925 gg. (Natural movement of the population of the U.S.S.R.). [1926]

419. Yestestvennoye dvizheniye naseleniya Soyuza S.S.R. v 1926 g. (Natural movement of the population of the U.S.S.R. in 1926). [1929]

Narodnyy Komissariat Zdravookhraneniya, R.S.F.S.R. (People's Commissariat of Health Protection, R.S.F.S.R.)

420. Statisticheskiy obzor sostoyaniya zdravookhraneniya i zabolevayemosti zaraznymi boleznyami v RSFSR v 1926, 1927 gg. (Statistical review on health conditions and on morbidity from infectious diseases in RSFSR in 1926, 1927).

421. Statisticheskiye materialy po sostoyaniyu narodnogo zdraviya i organisatsii meditsinskoy pomoshchi v SSSR za 1913-1923 gg. (Statistical material on health condition and medical care in the USSR in 1913-1923). Prefaces by N. Semashko. French foreword and table of contents. 1926. xiii, 378 pp.

422. Zakonodatel'stvo RSFSR po zdravookhraneniyu, 1930-1934 (Laws of RSFSR on public health, 1930-1934). [1935]

Ts. U. N. Kh. U., Otdel Naseleniya i Zdravookhraneniya (Division of Population and Health Protection)

423. Zdorov'ye i zdravookhraneniye trudyashchikhsya SSSR. Statistichskiy sbornik (Health and health protection of the working population of the USSR. Statistical collection). I. A. Kraval', Editor. [1936]

Akademiya Nauk S.S.S.R. Trudy Demograficheskogo Instituta (Academy of Sciences, U.S.S.R. Transactions of the Demographic Institute)

424. Trudy komissii po izucheniyu plemennogo sostava naseleniya i sopredel'nykh stran (Transactions of the Commission on the study on the ethnic composition of the population of the USSR and adjoining countries). Vols. 1-20. Leningrad, 1917-1930.

Ts. K. Vs. K. P. (B) (Central Committee of the All-Union Communist Party)

425. Postanovleniye Ts.I.K. i S.N.K. Soyuza SSR o zapreshchenii abortov uvelichenii material'noy pomoshchi rozhenitsam (Decree of the Central Executive Committee and the Council of People's Commissars on prohibition of abortions and on increase of allowances for women in childbirth). [1936]

Ukrainska S.S.R. Ts. S. U.

426. Statistika Ukrainy, Seriya I Demografiya, Vol. IV:
    No. 70, vyp. 1. Pryrodnyi rukh naselennya naivazhlyvyshchykh mist Ukrainy v 1923 r. (Natural population movement in the principal Ukrainian cities in 1923). Khar'kov, 1925. 37 pp.
    No. 80, vyp. 2. Pryrodnyi rukh naselennya naivazhlyvyshchykh mist Ukrainy v 1924 r. (Natural population movement in the principal Ukrainian cities in 1924). Khar'kov, 1925.
    No. 84, vyp. 4. Pomorshi v mistakh Ukrainy v 1923 i 1924 rr. za prychynamy smerti (Mortality in Ukrainian cities in 1923 and 1924 and causes of deaths). Khar'kov, 1926. 37 pp.
    No. 106, vyp. 3. Pryrodnyi rukh naselennya Ukrainy v 1924 r.Z oglyadom prirodnogo rukhu haselennya pered svitovoyu viinoyu (Population movement in Ukraine in 1924 with a review of the population movement before the World War). Khar'kov, 1927. lxxiii, 33 pp.
    No. 117, vyp. 5. Pryrodnyi rukh naselennya naivazhlyvyshchykh mist Ukrainy v 1925 r. (Natural population movement in the principal Ukrainian cities in 1925). Khar'kov, 1927. 162 pp.
    No. 120, vyp. 6. Pomorshi v mistakh Ukrainy v 1925 r. za prychynamy smerti (Mortality and causes of deaths in Ukrainian cities in 1925). Khar'kov, 1928. xxiv, 36 pp.
    No. 154, vyp. 7. Pryrodnyi rukh naselennya Ukrainy v 1926 r. (Natural population movement in Ukraine in 1926). Khar'kov, 1929. 178 pp.
    No. 169, vyp. 8. Pryrodnyi rukh naselennya Ukrainy v 1927 r. (Natural population movement in Ukraine in 1927). Khar'kov, 1929. 142 pp.

Ukrainska Akademiya Nauk, Pratsi Demograficheskogo Institutu (Publications of the Demographic Institute of the Ukrainian Academy of Sciences). M. Ptukha, Editor

427. Tom I. Materialy shcho do pryrodnogo rukhu naselennya Ukrainy 1867-1914 rr. (Data concerning the natural population movement of Ukraine, 1867-1914). Vol. I.

ECONOMICS

I.

Ts. S. K.

428. Glavnyye rezul'taty urozhaya (Principal figures on crop returns). Title also in French: Résultats généraux de la récolte en Russie. Vols. 1-33, 1883/87-1915. 1883-1887 in: Statistika

Rossiyskoy Imperii, Vol. IV; 1889-1892 as sub-series of Vremennik, Nos. 15, 19, 20, and 25; 1893-1915 as sub-series of Statistika Ross. Imperii.

Otdel Sel'skoy Ekonomii i Sel'sko-khozyaystvennoy Statistiki (Division of Rural Economics and Agricultural Statistics)

429. Sbornik statistiko-ekonomicheskikh svedeniy po sel'skomu khozyaystvu Rossii i nekotorykh inostrannykh gosudarstv (Collection of statistical and economic data on agriculture in Russia and in some foreign countries). Nos. 1-10. 1907-1917.
430. Sel'sko-khozyaystvennyya statisticheskiya svedeniya po materialam, poluchennym ot khozyaev (Agricultural statistical information obtained from the farmers). Nos. 1-12. 1884-1905.
431. Svod statisticheskikh svedeniy po sel'skomu khozyaystvu Rossii k kontsu 19 veka (Summary of statistical data on agriculture in Russia at the end of the 19th century). 3 vols. 1902-1903.

Departament Zemledeliya (Department of Agriculture)

432. Yezhegodnik ... (Yearbook ...), 1907 ... 1914.

Glavnoe Upraveniye Zemleustroystva i Zemledeliya (Central Board of Land Settlement and Agriculture)

433. Sel'sko-khozyaystvennyy promysel v Rossii (Agricultural trade in Russia). [1914]

Gornyy Departament (Mining Department)

434. Gornozavodskaya proizvoditel'nost' Rossii (Mining production in Russia). 1873-1885.
435. Sbornik statisticheskikh svedeniy o gorno-zavodskoy promyshlennosti Rossii (Statistical information on mining and metallurgical industry in Russia). 1882-1911.

Ministerstvo Finansov (Ministry of Finance)

436. Rossiya v kontse XIX veka (Russia at the end of the 19th century). V. I. Kovalevskiy, Editor. 1900.

Ministry of Finance, Department of Trade and Manufacture

437. The industries of Russia. Manufactures and trade with a general industrial map, for the World's Columbian Exposition at Chicago. 2 vols. in 1. St. Petersburg, 1898. 576 pp.

Otdel Promyshlennosti (Department of Manufacture)

Note: 1900-1905 in Ministry of Finance; 1905-1917 in Ministry of Trade and Manufacture
438. Dannyya o prodolzhitel'nosti i raspredelenii rabochago vremeni v promyshlennykh predpriyatiyakh, podchinennykh nadzoru fabrichnoy i gornoy inspektsii za 1913 god. (Data on duration and distribution of labor hours in industrial establishments under control of factory and mining inspection for 1913). [1914]
439. Svod otchëtov fabrichnykh inspektorov (Summary of reports by factory inspectors). 1900-1915.

II B.

Vysshiy Sovet Narodnogo Khozyaystva (Supreme Council of National Economics)

440. Statisticheskiy yezhegodnik (Statistical yearbook), 1923/24 ... 1926/27. Text in Russian and French.

Ts. S. U.

441. Fabrichno-zavodskaya promyshlennost' Soyuza SSR. Osnovnyye pokazateli eyë dinamiki za 1924-1927 gg. (Industry in USSR. Basic indices of its dynamics during the period of 1924-1927). [1929]
442. Fabrichno-zavodskaya promyshlennost' Soyuza SSR i ego ekonomicheskikh rayonov (Industry in the USSR and its economic regions). 3 vols. [1928-1930]
443. Materialy uchëta professional'nogo sostava personala fabrichno-zavodskoy promyshlennosti SSSR (Records for the census of industrial workers of the USSR according to their professional composition). [1925]
444. Mirovoye khozyaystvo. Sbornik materialov za 1913-27 (World economy. Collection of data for 1913-27), in: *Trudy* (Works), Vol. 9.

445. Soyuznaya promyshlennost' v tsyfrakh. Tempy rosta i faktory razvitiya. Materialy k part-konferentsii 1929 g. (Soviet industry in figures. Rates of its increase and factors of its development. Materials for the Party Conference of 1929). [1929]

446. Zemskiye podvornyye perepisi 1880-1913. Po-uyezdnyye itogi (Summary returns by counties of the selective surveys of households executed in the course of the time 1880 to 1913 by the zemstvos—local self-government). Compiled by Z. M. and N. A. Savitskiye. [1926]

Ts. S. U., Sektor Sel'sko-khozyaystvennoy Statistiki (Division of Agricultural Statistics)

447. Osnovnyye elementy sel'sko-khozyaystvennogo proizvodstva SSSR, 1916 i 1924-1927 gg. (Basic elements of agricultural production of USSR in 1916 and in 1924-1927). [1930] 170 pp.

Ts. S. U. and Ts. U. N. Kh. U. Gosplana, Otdel Uchëta Truda (Division of Labor Statistics)

448. Trud v SSSR. Statisticheskiy spravochnik (Labor in the USSR. Statistical reference book). 1924/25, 1931, 1934, 1935. [1926-36]

Tsentral'noye Byuro Statistiki Truda (Central Bureau of Labor Statistics)

449. Statistika truda (Labor statistics). 1922/23-1929. *See* also Ts. S. U., Trudy, Vols. 4 and 11.

Gosplan, E.-S. S.

450. Sdvigi v sel'skom khozyaystve SSSR mezhdu XV i XVI partiinymi s'yezdami. Statisticheskiye svedeniya o sel'skom khozyaystve za 1927-1930 gg. (Improvement in the agriculture of the USSR between the 15th and 16th Party conferences. Statistical information on agriculture for the time 1927-1930). [1930] 204 pp.

Narodnyy Komissariat Zemledeliya SSSR i Narodnyy Komissariat Sovkhozov (People's Commissariat of Agriculture and People's Commissariat of State Farms)

451. Sel'skoye khozyaystvo SSSR. Yezhegodnik 1935 (Agricultural economy of the USSR. Year-book 1935). [1936] 48, 1468 pp.

Ts. U. N. Kh. U. Gosplana

452. Kolkhozy vo vtoroy stalinskoy pyatiletke. Statisticheskiy sbornik (Collective farms during the Second Five-Year Plan). I. V. Sautin, Editor. [1939] 143 pp.

453. Posevnyye ploshchadi SSSR. Dinamika za 1928, 1932-1939 gg. v sopostavlenii s 1913 g. Statisticheskiy spravochnik (Sown land in the USSR. Dynamics for the years 1928, 1932-1939, in comparison with 1913. Statistical reference book). [1939] 331 pp.

454. Sotsialisticheskoye sel'skoye khozyaystvo SSSR. Statisticheskiy sbornik (Socialistic agricultural economy of the USSR. Statistical reference book). [1939]

455. Zhivotnovodstvo SSSR za 1916-1938 gody. Statisticheskiy sbornik (Livestock for the years 1916-1938. Statistical reference book of the USSR). [1940] 216 pp.

Gosplan

456. Kontrol'nyye tsifry narodnogo khozyaystva i sotsial'no-kul'turnogo stroitel'stva RSFSR na 1927/28, 1929/30 gg. (Control figures of the national economy and the social and cultural reconstruction of the RSFSR in 1927/28, 1929/30). 2 vols. [1928-30]

457. Kontrol'nyye tsifry pyatiletnego plana narodnogo khozyaystva i sotsial'no-kul'turnogo stroitel'stva RSFSR, 1928/29, 1932/33 (Control figures for the Five-Year Plan of the economic, cultural, and social reconstruction of the RSFSR). 2 vols. [1929]

458. Pyatiletniy plan sotsialisticheskogo stroitel'stva (The Five-Year Plan of socialistic reconstruction). Vols. 1-3 and App. 1, 1929; 2nd and 3rd ed., 1930. (The title of 1930 has "sotsialisticheskogo" changed to "narodno-khozyaystvennogo.")

459. Summary of the fulfillment of the First Five-Year Plan of the development of the national economy of the USSR. Second revised edition. [1935] 304 pp.

460. The Second Five-Year Plan for the development of the national economy of the USSR, 1933-1937. Foreword by V. I. Mezhlavn. New York, International Publishers. [1937] 671 pp.

461. Tretiy pyatiletniy plan razvitiya narodnogo khozyaystva Soyuza SSR, 1938-1942 (Third Five-Year Plan of the development of the national economy of the USSR). [1939]

Vsesoyuznaya Sel'sko-khozyaystvennaya Vystavka (All-Union Agricultural Exhibition)

462. Pobedy sotsialisticheskogo sel'skogo khozyaystva (Achievements in the socialist agricultural economy). 1939. 160 pp.

Narodnyy Komissariat Putey Soobshcheniya (People's Commissariat of Transport)

463. Trudy Nauchno-Tekhnicheskogo Komiteta, vyp. 20. Stoletiye zheleznykh dorog (Works of the Technical Research Committee, Issue 20. A hundred years of railway transportation). 1925. 261 pp.

Akademiya Nauk, Institut Ekonomiki (Academy of Sciences, Institute of Economics)

464. Ekonomicheskaya geografiya SSSR (Economic geography of the USSR). S. S. Bal'zak, V. F. Vasyutin, and Ya. G. Feygin, Editors. Vol. I. Moscow, 1940. 409 pp.

465. Ekonomika sotsialisticheskoy promyshlennosti (Economics of socialist industry). E. L. Granovskiy and B. L. Markus, Editors. [1940] 598 pp.

ENCYCLOPAEDIAS, ATLASES

I.

Marks, Publisher; E. Yu. Petri, and Yu. M. Shokal'skiy, Editors

466. Bol'shoy vsemirnyy nastol'nyy atlas Marksa (Great world atlas). St. Petersburg, 1905. European Russia, Nos. 14-30; Asiatic Russia, Nos. 45-47.

Brockhaus and Efron, Publishers

467. Entsiklopedicheskiy slovar' (Encyclopaedia). 84 + 4 suppl. vols. [1890-1907]
468. Novyy entsiklopedicheskiy slovar' (New encyclopaedia). Incomplete. [-1916]

II A, B.

469. Bol'shoy Sovetskiy atlas mira (Great Soviet world atlas). 2 vols. [1937, 1939]
470. Bol'shaya meditsinskaya entsiklopediya (Great medical encyclopaedia). N. A. Semashko, Editor. 35 vols. [1928-1936]
471. Bol'shaya Sovetskaya entsiklopediya (Great Soviet encyclopaedia). 65 vols. [1926-1931]
472. Krest'yanskaya sel'sko-khozyaystvennaya entsiklopediya (Encyclopaedia of peasants' economy). 7 vols. [1925-1928]

Vsesoyuznyi Institut Rasteniyevodstva Narodnogo Kommissariata Zemledeliya Soyuza SSR (All-Union Institute of Plant Cultivation)

473. Rasteniyevodstvo SSR (Plant cultivation). N. S. Pereverzev, Editor. [1933]

MISCELLANEOUS

II A, B.

Glavnauka

474. Trudy gosudarstvennogo nauchno-issledovatel'skogo instituta zemleustroystva i pereseleniya (Publications of the National Research Institute on land distribution and migration). 11 vols.

Gosplan, Ts. U. N. Kh. U.

475. Kul'turnoye stroitel'stvo SSSR (Cultural construction of the USSR). 1930/34-1935; 1935-1936; 1940.

476. Zhenshchina v SSSR. Statisticheskiy sbornik (The woman in the USSR. Statistical collection). I. A. Kraval', Editor. First edition, 1936; Second edition, 1937.

Narodnyy Kommissariat Yustitsii RSFSR (People's Commissariat of Justice)

477. Kodeks zakonov o brake, sem'ye i opeke (Code on marriage, family and guardianship). 1927-1929, Yurid. Izdat.; 1931, "Ogiz," Sov. Zakonodatel'stvo; 1932, Sov. Zakonodatel'stvo; 1932-1936, Gos. Izd., Sov. Zakonodatel'stvo; 1937-1938, Yurid. Izdat., N. K. Yustitsii SSSR.

Russian Soviet Government Bureau

478. The marriage laws of Soviet Russia; complete text of first code of laws of the RSFSR deal-

ing with civil status and domestic relations, marriage, the family and guardianship. New York, The Russian Soviet Government Bureau, 1921. 85 pp.

Tomskiy Gosudarstvennyy Universitet (State University of Tomsk)

479. Trudy nauchnoy konferentsii po uzucheniyu i osvoyeniyu proizvoditel'nykh sil Sibiri (Transactions of the scientific conference on the study and exploitation of the productive resources of Siberia). Tomsk, 1940.

Tsentral'nyy Ispolnitel'nyy Komitet SSSR (Central Executive Committee of the USSR)

480. Administrativnoye deleniye SSSR, 1924 (Administrative division of the USSR, 1924). 1 vol. Territorial'noye i administrativnoye deleniye SSSR, 1925, 1926, 1928. 3 vols. Administrativno-territorial'noye deleniye SSSR, 1929. 2 vols. Administrativno-territorial'noye deleniye SSSR, 1934. 1 vol. suppl. Administrativno-territorial'noye deleniye SSSR: kratkiy spravochnik na 1935 god. Administrativno-territorial'noye deleniye soyuznykh respublik, 1937, 1938/39. 2 vols.

Informatsionno-statisticheskiy Otdel pri Sekretariate Prezidiuma Verkhovnogo Soveta SSR (Information-statistical Section, Secretariat of the Presidium of the Supreme Soviet of the USSR)

481. SSSR administrativno-territorial'noye deleniye soyuznykh respublik na 1 maya 1940 goda (USSR administrative-territorial division of the constituent republics on May 1, 1940). [1940]

Ts. S. U.

482. Administrativno-territorial'nyy sostav SSSR na 1 iyulya 1925 g. i na 1 iyulya 1926 g. v sopostavlenii s do-voennym deleniyem Rossii (Administrative-territorial composition of the USSR from July 1, 1925 to July 1, 1926, compared with the prewar division of Russia). [1926]

Gosplan Ts. U. N. Kh. U.

483. Rayony i gorodskiye punkty Soyuza SSR po administrativnomu deleniyu. Alfavitnyye spiski (Regions and cities of the USSR, according to the administrative division. Alphabetical index). 1937. 176 pp.

Vedomosti Soveta RSFSR

484. Gosudarstvennoye ustroystvo SSSR; RSFSR (Political structure of the USSR and RSFSR). [1939] 56 pp.

PERIODICALS

485. Akusherstvo i ginekologiya (Obstetrics and Gynecology). 1936-   . Continuation of "Ginekologiya i akusherstvo."

486. Byulleten' Gosplana RSFSR (Bulletin of Gosplan of the RSFSR). 1925-1929.

487. Byulleten' Tsentral'nogo Statisticheskogo Upravleniya (Bulletin of the Central Statistical Board). Nos. 1-122, 1919-1926. Superseded by "Statisticheskoye obozreniye."

488. Gigiyena i epidemiologiya (Hygiene and Epidemiology). 1922-1931. Continued as "Gigiyena i sotsialisticheskoye zdravookhraneniye."

489. Gigiyena i sanitariya (Hygiene and Sanitation). 1933-   . Continuation of "Sotsial'naya gigiyena."

490. Gigiyena i sotsialisticheskoye zdravookhraneniye (Hygiene and Socialist Health Protection). 1932-   .

491. Gigiyena i zdorov'ye rabochey i krest'yanskoy sem'i (Hygiene and Health Condition of Workers' and Peasants' Families).

492. Ginekologiya i akusherstvo (Obstetrics and Gynecology). 1922-1932. Superseded by "Akusherstvo i ginekologiya."

493. Na agrarnom fronte (The Agrarian Front). Vols. 1-11 (No. 7), 1925-1935. (Suspended from December, 1931 to June, 1932.) Merged into "Sotsialisticheskaya rekonstruktsiya sel'skogo khozyaystva," later "Sotsialisticheskoye sel'skoye khozyaystvo."

494. Na fronte zdravookhraneniya (The Public Health Front). 1922-   . Title varies: 1922-1927, "Byulleten' Nar. Kom. zdravookhraneniya"; 1928-Feb. 1930, "Voprosy zdravookhraneniya."

495. Okhrana materinstva i mladenchestva (Protection of Maternity and Childhood). 1926-1931. *See* "Voprosy materinstva i mladenchestva."

496. Okhrana zdorov'ya detey i podrostkov (Health Protection of Children and Juveniles). 1931-1933. Supersedes "Pediatriya," Petrograd. United with "Zhurnal po rannemu detskomu vozrastu"; later "Pediatriya."

497. Pediatriya (Pediatrics). 1934- .

498. Planovoye khozyaystvo (Planned Economy). 1924 ff. Continues "Byulleten' Gosplana USSR"; also "Vestnik statistiki" and "Statisticheskoye obozreniye," and since April, 1930, "Ekonomicheskoye obozreniye."

499. Problemy ekonomiki (Problems of Economics). 1929- .

500. Sotsialisticheskaya rekonstruktsiya sel'skogo khozyaystva (Socialist Reconstruction of the Agrarian Economy). 1930-1938. Merged into "Sotsialisticheskoye sel'skoye khozyaystvo."

501. Sotsialisticheskoye khozyaystvo (Socialist Economy). Vols. 1-13. 1923-March, 1930.

502. Sotsialisticheskoye sel'skoye khozyaystvo (Socialist Agricultural Economy). 1925- . Title varies: 1925-February, 1930, as "Puti sel'skogo khozyaystva"; March, 1930-December, 1938, as "Sotsialisticheskaya rekonstruktsiya."

503. Sotsialisticheskoye zemleustroystvo (Socialist Land Distribution). 1930-1935. Supersedes "Vestnik zemleustroystva i pereseleniya."

504. Sotsial'naya gigiyena (Socialist Hygiene). 1922-1929.

505. Sovetskaya etnografiya (Soviet Ethnography). 1931- .

506. Statisticheskoye obozreniye Ts. S. U. (Statistical Review of the Ts. S. U.). French title. Vols. 1-4 (Nos. 1-5), 1927-March, 1930. June, 1930, merged into "Planovoye khozyaystvo."

507. Trudy Gosplana (Transactions of the Gosplan). 4 vols. 1922-1923.

508. Vestnik Akademii Nauk (Bulletin of the Academy of Sciences). 1931- .

509. Vestnik statistiki (Statistical Messenger). Published by Ts. S. U. 1919-1929. 1930 merged into "Planovoye khozyaystvo."

510. Vestnik zemleustroystva i pereseleniya (Bulletin on Land Distribution and Migration). 1927. 1929 superseded by "Sotsialisticheskoye zemleustroystvo."

511. Voprosy materinstva i mladenchestva (Problems of Maternity and Childhood). 1936 became official publication of Narkomzdrav (People's Commissariat of Health). Continuation of "Okhrana materinstva i mladenchestva."

ADDENDUM

512. Konstantinov, O. A. "Geograficheskiye razlichiya v dinamike gorodskogo naseleniya SSSR" (Geographical differences in the dynamics of urban population in the USSR), *Izvestiya Vsesoyuznogo, Geograficheskogo Obshchestva* 76(6):11-24. 1943.

INDEX

RECENT PUBLICATIONS OF THE ECONOMIC, FINANCIAL AND TRANSIT DEPARTMENT OF THE LEAGUE OF NATIONS

POST-WAR PROBLEMS

RECONSTRUCTION AND RELIEF

THE TRANSITION FROM WAR TO PEACE ECONOMY. Report of the Delegation on Economic Depressions, Part I (Third Impression)
(Ser. L.o.N.P. 1943.II.A.3) 118 pages ....cloth bound 6/– $1.50
paper bound 4/6 $1.00

ECONOMIC STABILITY IN THE POST-WAR WORLD. Report of the Delegation on Economic Depressions, Part II (Third Impression)
(Ser. L.o.N.P. 1945.II.A.2) 341 pages ....cloth bound 12/6 $3.00
paper bound 10/– $2.50

RELIEF DELIVERIES AND RELIEF LOANS, 1919-1923 (Second Impression)
(Ser. L.o.N.P. 1943.II.A.1) 62 pages ....paper bound 3/6 $1.00

EUROPE'S OVERSEAS NEEDS, 1919-1920, AND HOW THEY WERE MET
(Ser. L.o.N.P. 1943.II.A.6) 52 pages ....paper bound 2/6 $0.50

AGRICULTURAL PRODUCTION IN CONTINENTAL EUROPE DURING THE 1914-18 WAR AND THE RECONSTRUCTION PERIOD
(Ser. L.o.N.P. 1943.II.A.7) 122 pages ....cloth bound 10/– $2.25
paper bound 7/6 $1.75

INTERNATIONAL CURRENCY EXPERIENCE (Second Impression)
(Ser. L.o.N.P. 1944.II.A.4) 249 pages ....cloth bound 15/– $3.25
paper bound 12/6 $2.75

URBAN AND RURAL HOUSING (Third Impression)
(Ser. L.o.N.P. 1939.II.A.2) xxxvi + 159 pages ....paper bound 3/6 $0.80

TRADE AND COMMERCIAL POLICY

THE NETWORK OF WORLD TRADE (Second Impression)
(Ser. L.o.N.P. 1942.II.A.3) 172 pages ....cloth bound 12/6 $2.75
paper bound 10/– $2.00

EUROPE'S TRADE (Second Impression)
(Ser. L.o.N.P. 1941.II.A.1) 116 pages ....cloth bound 7/6 $2.00
paper bound 5/– $1.25

COMMERCIAL POLICY IN THE INTERWAR PERIOD: INTERNATIONAL PROPOSALS AND NATIONAL POLICIES (Third Impression)
(Ser. L.o.N.P. 1942.II.A.6) 164 pages ....paper bound 7/6 $1.75

COMMERCIAL POLICY IN THE POST-WAR WORLD
(Ser. L.o.N.P. 1945.II.A.7) 124 pages ....paper bound 5/– $1.25

QUANTITATIVE TRADE CONTROLS: THEIR CAUSES AND NATURE. By Prof. G. Haberler and W. M. Hill
(Ser. L.o.N.P. 1943.II.A.5) 45 pages ....paper bound 2/6 $0.50

TRADE RELATIONS BETWEEN FREE-MARKET AND CONTROLLED ECONOMIES. By Prof. J. Viner (Second Impression)
(Ser. L.o.N.P. 1943.II.A.4) 92 pages ....paper bound 4/6 $1.00

INDUSTRIALIZATION AND FOREIGN TRADE
(Ser. L.o.N.P. 1945.II.A.10) 167 pages ....cloth bound 8/6 $2.15
paper bound 7/6 $1.75

CONDITIONS OF PRIVATE FOREIGN INVESTMENT
(Ser. L.o.N.P. 1946.II.A.1) 45 pages ....paper bound 2/- $0.50

RAW-MATERIAL PROBLEMS AND POLICIES
(Ser. L.o.N.P. 1946.II.A.2) 110 pages ....paper bound 4/- $1.00

ECONOMIC SECURITY

ECONOMIC FLUCTUATIONS IN THE UNITED STATES AND THE UNITED KINGDOM, 1918-22 (Second Impression)
(Ser. L.o.N.P. 1942.II.A.7) 93 pages ....paper bound 6/- $1.50

PROSPERITY AND DEPRESSION. A THEORETICAL ANALYSIS OF CYCLICAL MOVEMENTS. By Prof. G. Haberler. (Third Edition—Revised and Enlarged—1941) (Fourth Impression)
(Ser. L.o.N.P. 1943.II.A.2) xxiv + 532 pages ....cloth bound 12/6 $2.50

DEMOGRAPHIC QUESTIONS

THE FUTURE POPULATION OF EUROPE AND THE SOVIET UNION: POPULATION PROJECTIONS, 1940-70. By Dr. Frank W. Notestein and others of the Office of Population Research, Princeton University
(Ser. L.o.N.P. 1944.II.A.2) 315 pages ....cloth bound 15/- $3.50
paper bound 12/6 $2.75

ECONOMIC DEMOGRAPHY OF EASTERN AND SOUTHERN EUROPE. By Dr. Wilbert E. Moore, Office of Population Research, Princeton University.
(Ser. L.o.N.P. 1945.II.A.9) 299 pages ....cloth bound 12/6 $3.00
paper bound 10/- $2.50

In the Press:

EUROPE'S POPULATION IN THE INTERWAR PERIOD. By Dr. Dudley Kirk, Office of Population Research, Princeton University

TAXATION

MODEL BILATERAL CONVENTIONS FOR THE PREVENTION OF INTERNATIONAL DOUBLE TAXATION AND FISCAL EVASION: SECOND REGIONAL TAX CONFERENCE, MEXICO, D.F., July 1943
(Ser. L.o.N.P. 1945.II.A.3) 85 pages ....paper bound 3/6 $1.00

CURRENT EVENTS

WORLD ECONOMIC SURVEY, 1939/41
(Ser. L.o.N.P. 1941.II.A.2) 275 pages ....cloth bound 10/- $2.50
paper bound 7/6 $2.00

WORLD ECONOMIC SURVEY, 1941/42 (Tenth Year) (Second Impression)
(Ser. L.o.N.P. 1942.II.A.5) 198 pages ....cloth bound 12/6 $3.00
paper bound 10/- $2.50

WORLD ECONOMIC SURVEY, 1942/44 (Thirteenth Year)
(Ser. L.o.N.P. 1945.II.A.4) 299 pages ....cloth bound 12/6 $3.00
paper bound 10/- $2.50

WARTIME RATIONING AND CONSUMPTION (Second Impression)
(Ser. L.o.N.P. 1942.II.A.2) 87 pages ....paper bound 3/6 $1.00

FOOD RATIONING AND SUPPLY, 1943/44
  (Ser. L.o.N.P. 1944.II.A.3) 101 pages ....paper bound 4/6 $1.00

STATISTICS

RAW MATERIALS AND FOODSTUFFS: PRODUCTION BY COUNTRIES, 1935 AND 1938 (Second Impression)
  (Ser. L.o.N.P. 1939.II.A.24) 75 pages ....paper bound 2/6 $0.60

MONEY AND BANKING, 1940/42
  (Ser. L.o.N.P. 1942.II.A.1) 202 pages ....cloth bound 15/– $3.00
                                                                                          paper bound 12/6 $2.50

MONEY AND BANKING, 1942/44
  (Ser. L.o.N.P. 1945.II.A.1) 221 pages ....cloth bound 15/– $3.00
                                                                                          paper bound 12/6 $2.50

STATISTICAL YEAR-BOOK OF THE LEAGUE OF NATIONS, 1940/41
  (Ser. L.o.N.P. 1941.II.A.3) 271 pages ....cloth bound 12/6 $3.50
                                                                                          paper bound 10/– $2.50

STATISTICAL YEAR-BOOK OF THE LEAGUE OF NATIONS, 1941/42. Including Addendum 1942/43
  (Ser. L.o.N.P. 1942.II.A.8) 279 pages, plus 80 pages of Addendum ....cloth bound 12/6 $3.50
                                                                                          paper bound 10/– $2.50

STATISTICAL YEAR-BOOK OF THE LEAGUE OF NATIONS, 1942/44 (Seventeenth Year)
  (Ser. L.o.N.P. 1945.II.A.5) 315 pages ....cloth bound 12/6 $3.50
                                                                                          paper bound 10/– $2.50

MONTHLY BULLETIN OF STATISTICS
  Annual subscription .... (12 numbers) £1.0.0 $5.00
                                                                                     single number   1/9 $0.45

COMMITTEE REPORTS

DELEGATION ON ECONOMIC DEPRESSIONS:
  The Transition from War to Peace Economy (above)
  Economic Stability in the Post-War World (above)

ECONOMIC AND FINANCIAL COMMITTEES: REPORT TO THE COUNCIL ON THE WORK OF THE JOINT SESSION. London, April-May 1942; Princeton, N.J., U.S.A., August, 1942 (Second Impression)
  (Ser. L.o.N.P. 1942.II.A.4) 23 pages ....paper bound 1/– $0.25

ECONOMIC AND FINANCIAL COMMITTEES: REPORT TO THE COUNCIL ON THE WORK OF THE JOINT SESSION. Princeton, N.J., December, 1943
  (Ser. L.o.N.P. 1944.II.A.1) 81 pages ....paper bound 2/6 $0.50

ECONOMIC AND FINANCIAL COMMITTEES: REPORT TO THE COUNCIL ON THE WORK OF THE 1945 JOINT SESSION. Princeton, N.J., April, 1945
  (Ser. L.o.N.P. 1945.II.A.6) 5 pages ....paper 6d. $0.15

CATALOGUE OF SELECTED PUBLICATIONS ON ECONOMIC
AND FINANCIAL SUBJECTS

A Guide to League of Nations Documents of Value in Connection with the Formulation of Postwar Economic Policies.
  69 pages .... Sent free on application to the Authorized Agents

AUTHORIZED AGENTS FOR THE PUBLICATIONS OF THE LEAGUE OF NATIONS

SOUTH AFRICA (Union of)—Maskew Miller, Ltd., 29, Adderley Street, Cape Town.

ARGENTINE—Librería "El Ateneo," M. Pedro Garcia, 340-344, Calle Florida, Buenos Aires.

AUSTRALIA (Commonwealth of)—H. A. Goddard Pty., Ltd., 255a George Street, Sydney.

BELGIUM—Agence et Messageries de la Presse, S.A., 14-22, rue du Persil, Brussels.

BOLIVIA—"La Universitaria," Gisbert y Cia., Comercio 125-133, Casilla 195, La Paz.

BRAZIL—F. Briguiet & Cia., Rua do Ouvidor 109, Rio de Janeiro.

CANADA—United Nations Society in Canada, 124, Wellington Street, Ottawa.

CHILE—Librería y Editorial Nascimento, Calle San Antonio 240, Santiago.

CHINA—Commercial Press, Ltd., Sales Office, 211, Honan Road, Shanghai.

COLOMBIA—Librería Voluntad S.A., Calle 12, No. 7-39, Apartado Postal, No. 2555, Bogotá.

CUBA—La Casa Belga, René de Smedt, O'Reilly, 455, Havana.

CZECHOSLOVAKIA — Librairie F. Topic, 9, Narodni Trida, Prague 1.

DENMARK — Librairie internationale Einar Munksgaard, Nörregade 6, Copenhagen.

ECUADOR—Victor Janer, Guayaquil.

EGYPT—G.M.'s Book Shop, 116, Mohamed Bey Farid Street, Cairo.

FINLAND—Akateeminen Kirjakauppa, Keskuskatu 2, Helsinki.

FRANCE—Editions A. Pedone, 13, rue Soufflot, Paris (V).

GREAT BRITAIN, NORTHERN IRELAND AND THE CROWN COLONIES—George Allen & Unwin, Ltd., 40, Museum Street, London, W.C. 1.

GREECE—Librairie Internationale, Eleftheroudakis, Place de la Constitution, Athens.

GUATEMALA—Goubaud & Cia., Ltda., Sucesor, Guatemala.

ICELAND—Peter Halldorsson, Reykjavik.

INDIA—The Book Company, Ltd., College Square, 4/4 A, Calcutta. League of Nations, New Delhi Office, 8, Curzon Road, New Delhi 1.

IRELAND—Eason & Son, Ltd., 40-41, Lower O'Connell Street, Dublin.

LUXEMBURG—Librairie J. Schummer, place Guillaume, Luxemburg.

NETHERLANDS—N. V. Martinus Nijhoff's Boekhandel en Uitgevers-Mij., Lange Voorhout 9, The Hague.

NORWAY—Olaf Norli, Universitetsgaten, 24, Oslo.

PALESTINE—Leo Blumstein Book and Art Shop, 35, Allenby Road, Tel-Aviv.

The Palestine Educational Co., Messrs. B. Y. & W. A. Said, Jaffa Road, 98 & 100, P.O.B. 84, Jerusalem.

PANAMA—Isidro A. Beluche, Apartado 755, Avenida Norte No. 49, Panama.

SPAIN—Librería Bosch, Ronda Universidad, 11, Barcelona.

SWEDEN—Aktiebolaget C. E. Fritzes Kgl. Hofbokhandel, Fredsgatan, 2, Stockholm.

SWITZERLAND—Librairie Payot & Cie., Genève, Lausanne, Vevey, Montreux, Neuchatel, Berne, Bâle. Hans Raunhardt, Buchhandlung, Kirchgasse 17, Zurich 1.

TURKEY—Librairie Hachette, succursale de Turquie, 469, av. de l'Indépendance, Boîte postale, 2219, Istamboul.

UNITED STATES OF AMERICA—Columbia University Press, International Documents Service, 2960 Broadway, New York 27, N.Y.

URUGUAY—"Casa A. Barreiro y Ramos" S.A., 25 de Mayo, Esq. J. C. Gomez, Montevideo.

For other Countries, apply:

PUBLICATIONS DEPARTMENT OF THE LEAGUE OF NATIONS

GENEVA (Switzerland)